Margaret OLLEY
FAR FROM A STILL LIFE

Also by Meg Stewart

Non-fiction
Autobiography of My Mother
Margaret Coen: a Passion for Painting
Norman Lindsay, Artful Cats

Fiction
Modern Men Don't Shift Fridges
The Dream Life of Harry Moon

Editor
The Woman I Am, Poems by Nancy Keesing

MEG STEWART

Margaret OLLEY

FAR FROM A STILL LIFE

RANDOM HOUSE AUSTRALIA

Random House Australia Pty Ltd
20 Alfred Street, Milsons Point, NSW 2061
http://www.randomhouse.com.au

Sydney   New York   Toronto
London   Auckland   Johannesburg

First published by Random House Australia 2005

Copyright © Meg Stewart and Margaret Olley 2005
Foreword © Barry Pearce 2005
Map on p.xiii © Caroline Bowie 2005

All rights reserved. No part of this publication may be reproduced,
stored in a retrieval system, or transmitted in any form or by any means,
electronic, mechanical, photocopying, recording or otherwise, without
the prior written permission of the publisher.

National Library of Australia
Cataloguing-in-Publication Entry

Stewart, Meg, 1948–.
Margaret Olley: far from a still life.

ISBN 1 74051 314 2

1. Olley, Margaret, 1923–. 2. Painters – Australia –
Biography. I. Title.

759.994

Front cover photograph: Margaret Olley by Alice Pagliano, 2003
Back cover photograph: Margaret Olley painting in Newcastle, New South Wales, 1965
Endpapers painting: detail from *Pears and Wildflowers* by Margaret Olley
Drawing on p.xvii: Margaret Olley by Donald Friend
Cover design by Christabella Designs
Typeset in 12/16 pt Fairfield LH Light by Midland Typesetters, Australia
Printed and bound by Griffin Press, Netley, South Australia

10 9 8 7 6 5 4 3 2

Contents

List of Principal Figures	vii
Map	xiii
Foreword by Barry Pearce	xv

Part I: 1923–49

1. Green, Green, Green	3
2. Living on a River	34
3. Forever on the Move	53
4. Life Begins	80
5. Doors Open	110
6. Keeping the Rent Paid	147
7. 1948	170

Part II: 1949–59

8. Culture Shock	207
9. In and Out of Paris	231
10. Back in Brisbane	271
11. Blame it on the Peacock Feathers	310

Part III: 1960–2005

12. The Flood Tide	333
13. In Search of the Sex House	386
14. Living in a Basket	414
15. Once More, Then No More	447
16. Celebrating Life	487

Selected Solo Exhibitions	507
List of Illustrations	511
Acknowledgements	519
Notes	523
Bibliography	545
Index	553

List of Principal Figures

Philip Bacon (1947). Art dealer, patron and Margaret's agent. He established the Philip Bacon Galleries in Brisbane in 1974. In 1990 he was made a consultant to the Margaret Hannah Olley Art Trust, and he remains a close friend and adviser of hers today.

Pam Bell (1928–95). Writer, poet and horsewoman, and the subject of a prize-winning portrait by Margaret. Their friendship began in the 1950s when Margaret had come back from overseas and was living in Brisbane.

Jean Bellette (1908–91). Painter. She was one of Margaret's teachers at East Sydney Technical College and one of her earliest influences. Married to art critic Paul Haefliger, she moved with him to Europe in 1957 and from 1960 lived primarily in Majorca.

Wolfgang Cardamatis (1917). Painter and designer with whom Margaret became friends in Sydney in 1945. He designed the sets and costumes for the Kirsova Ballet Company in 1942, as well as dancing in the company. He moved to Europe after the Second World War and has lived there to this day, currently in France.

Margaret Cilento (1923). Attended Somerville House in Brisbane with Margaret during their high school years, where they were both taught art by Caroline Barker. Later the two were at East Sydney Technical College together and became flatmates and close friends. Cilento lived, apart from brief periods back in Australia, in New York, France and London until the late 1960s. Still painting and exhibiting today.

Far from a Still Life

William Dobell (1899–1970). Painter and key figure in the Sydney art world in the 1940s. Awarded the 1943 Archibald Prize for his portrait of artist Joshua Smith, to great controversy. In 1948 he painted Margaret's portrait, for which he also won the Archibald, causing almost as much of a furore.

Russell Drysdale (1912–81). Major Australian painter, married to Elizabeth (Bonny), with whom he had children Lynne and Tim. Well known for his depictions of inland Australia and its inhabitants. The family became close to Margaret in the mid 1940s and it was at their house in Rose Bay, Sydney, that she first met Donald Friend. Drysdale also painted a highly regarded portrait of Margaret in 1948.

Moya Dyring (1908–67). Painter with whom Margaret became friends in Paris in 1949. Married to artist Sam Atyeo. After separating from Atyeo in 1948, Dyring lived permanently in Paris, where she was known for her generous hospitality and encouragement of visiting Australian artists.

Ian Fairweather (1891–1974). Reclusive influential painter whose major works verge on abstraction. Studied at the Slade School of Art in London before travelling extensively throughout the world and eventually settling on Bribie Island off the north coast of Australia. He became a friend of Margaret's in the 1960s when she visited him there.

Donald Friend (1915–89). Painter, writer and diarist. His friendship with Margaret began in the mid 1940s and lasted until his death. After serving as an official war artist Friend lived briefly at the artists' commune Merioola. In 1947 he bought a cottage at Hill End, which he shared with English-born Donald Murray (1908–88). He met up with Margaret in London on her first trip overseas; subsequently, back in Australia, they travelled to north Queensland together. Between 1957 and 1962 Friend lived in Sri

List of Principal Figures

Lanka and for most of the years between 1968 and 1979 in Bali. His last years were spent in Bondi Junction, Paddington and Woollahra in Sydney.

Attilio Guarracino (1931). Italian friend of Donald Friend, whom Margaret first met in London in 1950. He subsequently returned to Australia with Friend and moved to Melbourne, where he worked in various professions, including as Friend's agent whilst the painter lived in Bali. Remains a friend of Margaret's to this day.

Paul Haefliger (1914–82). Painter and art critic for the *Sydney Morning Herald* from 1942 to '57; married to artist Jean Bellette.

Elaine Haxton (1909). Artist and designer, whose decorative paintings were well known in Sydney in the 1940s when she lived in Elizabeth Bay. She was a close friend of Margaret's, the Drysdales and Donald Friend, and was also painted by Dobell.

Van Hodgkinson (1919–2001). Friend and travelling companion of Margaret's; married to artist Frank Hodgkinson. Loved by all her friends for her zest for life and the arts.

Sam Hughes (b. unknown–1982). Gallery manager, theatre director and interior decorator. From 1935 to 1939 Hughes managed the Zwemmer Gallery in London, and then resided in Sydney in the 1940s and '50s, before returning to Europe, where he lived between London, Sydney and Mykonos in Greece for years. He and Margaret lived together in Paddington from around 1973–74 until his death.

Frederick Jessup (1920). Awarded the New South Wales Travelling Scholarship for landscape painting in 1945, which he delayed taking up until 1948 because of the war. Margaret first met him at East Sydney Technical College. He travelled with Margaret and Mitty Lee-Brown to Paris early in 1949. There began a love affair for Jessup with France, where he has lived since.

Brian Johnstone (1920–88). Gallery owner; he founded in Brisbane with his wife Marjorie (née Mant) first the Marodian Art Gallery, then the Johnstone Gallery, which he ran with Marjorie in the Brisbane Arcade and later at their residence at Bowen Hills. Showed major artists such as Ray Crooke, Donald Friend and Jon Molvig, as well as Margaret throughout the 1950s and '60s, significantly enriching the Brisbane art scene.

Mitty Lee-Brown (1922). Artist who lived at Merioola and studied in the same year as Margaret at East Sydney Technical College, where they became close friends. Lee-Brown spent years as an expatriate in Europe and now lives in Sri Lanka.

Frank Mitchell (1920–99). Model at East Sydney Technical College with whom Margaret became friends. He went on to become a sought-after dressmaker in Sydney and was loved by his friends for his great wit. Took up painting late in life.

Justin O'Brien (1917–96). Painter and teacher, who moved to Merioola in 1945, when he became part of Margaret's close circle of friends. Taught at Cranbrook School in Sydney's eastern suburbs from 1946 to 1967, when he moved to Rome where he lived until his death.

Jocelyn Rickards (1924–2005). Painter and costume designer. Rickards studied at East Sydney Technical College in the same year as Margaret, where they became lifelong friends. In late 1948 she moved to London where she worked as a costume designer on film and stage productions such as *Sunday, Bloody Sunday* and *Ryan's Daughter*.

Loudon Sainthill (1919–69). Stage designer and artist. He lived with Harry Tatlock Miller at Merioola after the Second World War, where he came to know Margaret, before returning with Tatlock Miller to England in late 1949 where he became a well-known theatre designer and lived until his death.

List of Principal Figures

David Strachan (1919–70). Painter renowned for his lyrical still lifes, nudes and landscapes. In 1945 he attended classes at East Sydney Technical College with Margaret and in 1948 went to Paris to study at the famous art school Académie de la Grande Chaumière. He was close to Margaret from the 1940s and, following his death, she painted a number of works in his Paddington house, including a series of interiors that some claim are among her best work.

Harry Tatlock Miller (1913–88). Art gallery director, writer, publisher and critic. Lived at Merioola in the 1940s, when he became friends with Margaret. In 1949 he moved to London with his lifelong companion Loudon Sainthill and became director of the Redfern Gallery, which exhibited contemporary Australian artists such as Sidney Nolan and Donald Friend.

Anne von Bertouch (1915–2003). Gallery owner, arts patron, writer and friend of Margaret's, who exhibited in her Newcastle galleries in the 1960s.

Anne Wienholt (1920). Painter and sculptor who studied at East Sydney Technical College just before Margaret and lived at Merioola. They met when Wienholt was working at the painting studio at tech and it was through her that Margaret first visited Merioola. Wienholt also introduced her to Sam Hughes. Wienholt went on to study in New York and now lives in San Francisco.

Jocelyn Zander (1921). Studied at East Sydney Technical College before Margaret. Margaret was close to both her and her mother, Clarice. Jocelyn's early childhood was spent in Melbourne and London, before returning to Australia in 1940. She was married to artist Carl Plate.

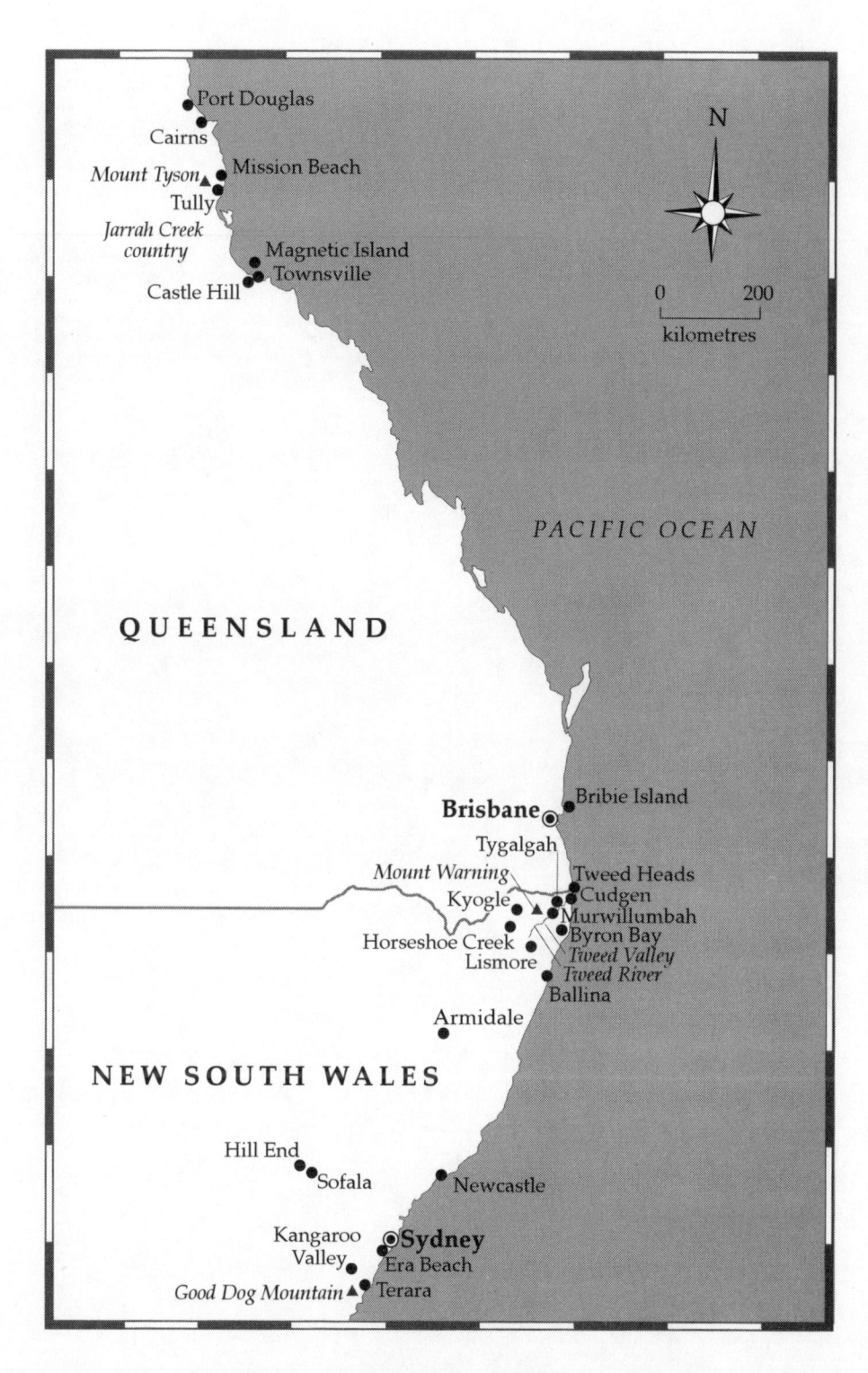

Map of the east of Queensland and New South Wales

Foreword

During the 1960s when I was learning about art in Adelaide, and occasionally in Melbourne, I never saw a painting by Margaret Olley. Yet her name had become etched in my mind as much as any of her illustrious contemporaries.

The reason was that one of my art history lecturers had fixated us with the idea that Dobell's 1948 Archibald-winning portrait of Margaret represented nothing less than an emergence from crisis. Whilst we young things were being conditioned at frenetic pace to banish content from painting, it was refreshing to look at an image redolent with biographical importance. Four years before that portrait was made, Dobell's timid personality had been subjected to the hellish glare of an infamous trial, and his encounter with Margaret signified a brave re-entry into the spotlight of public notoriety. Clad with flower-bedecked sun hat, white shimmering dress embellished in parachute silk, black ribbon hovering like a butterfly on her bosom, she was living proof of his recovery. Who, mesmerised by this wondrous, larger than life being on the slide screen, would have imagined that she too would come to wrestle with demons spawned by shyness?

I met Margaret Olley soon after starting work at the Art Gallery of New South Wales in 1978. Immediately, the flamboyant Dobell creation was subverted. In the flesh, she appeared far more modest. As I got to know her better, seeing how unrestrained she was with her opinions, I wondered how I could have got her so wrong. Maybe she had just been cautious, observing my take on the scene before declaring her hand.

Far from a Still Life

Wrong again, right in the first place. But it may be impossible for anyone who has been bruised by Margaret's honesty to see that she has always been shy, and still is. Her views – verging on bullish, sometimes cruel – and a passionate, indefatigable public benefaction that parallels her momentum with the brush, really constitute another kind of obsession behind which she can retreat; just as she did with alcohol until forty-six years ago, when she decided to straighten herself out. Henry James once said that artists are made not so much by talent as sheer force of character to break through and keep going. In this regard, Margaret Olley is one of our great survivors.

I am fortunate to have been invited along on several of her trips abroad, and in more recent years have witnessed her journeys with pigment across endless sheets of hardboard sprinkled throughout her living space. From looking at the work of others in museums and galleries to the struggle pulling one of her own compositions together, everything she does is an act of determination. It is quite something to experience. She has taught me to notice things I would have passed over; about painting, and about the human condition, too. I cannot say I agree with everything she says, especially her politics of self-sufficiency. But on the whole it is hard to imagine life without her exuberant belief there is a blessing to be had from each moment, no matter how ordinary, and her luck in being alive to witness it.

Artists' biographies don't *have* to be published. Their works should speak for themselves. But curiosity is insatiable. And in Margaret's case, she has touched so many lives with her personality the telling of her story is mandatory, before the paraphernalia and settings that fill her world recede into the wings of imperfect memory.

Barry Pearce
August 2005

'God gave Olley an extra battery.'
JUSTIN O'BRIEN

Margaret Olley by Donald Friend

Part I
1923–49

I

Green, Green, Green

*I'm always so busy living that I don't think back. My mother
was the historian in the family. I used to ask her, please, to
write things down, but she never did. When she died,
I realised there were all these things I'd meant to ask her,
and hadn't. It's only just recently that I've been made
to think back myself...*

'GREEN, GREEN, GREEN' WAS THE COLOUR OF MARGARET Olley's early childhood.

In the mid 1920s, the Olleys had a farm at Tully, in far north Queensland, about a mile and a half out of the raw, new sugar town, sandwiched between the single railway line and Banyan Creek.

Green cane grew in rows, higher than the tallest adult, with stalks that rustled when you came up close and sharp cutting leaves. At the slightest breeze, it rippled like a green sea touched with silver. Green tangles overhung the creek; rainforest tendrils spiralled from verdant heights along the road, more sand than dirt, which ran out to the real ocean, warm as bathwater, and every way you looked there was a brooding green mountain. Mount Tyson, the biggest, loomed right at the end of the main street of town.

Tully was wet. It was reputedly the wettest place in Australia. Tropical rain bucketed down on the single-roomed timber house that Joe Olley, a skilled bush carpenter, had built for his new wife Grace and their young daughter Margaret. Everything smelt, half of green growth, half of rotting vegetation. Drops cascaded off the cane's bladey greenness, made muddy rivulets between the stalks and swelled the creek so it ran a banker and everything went swirling past at a high rate of knots.

To Margaret the rain had an added mystery:

You could hear it coming. I can still remember that sound of the approaching rain roaring down the broad-leafed foliage in the forest on Mount Tyson. My mother would hear the roar and just have time to run out to the clothes line – a wire strung from one bush post to another with a prop – and bring in the washing before the rain arrived.

The rainfall meant Tully had a very unhealthy climate. We had to sleep under mosquito nets because mosquitos were in plague proportions and people caught dengue fever. Everything you touched turned to mildew overnight and the mosquito nets got very frowsty – musty and dusty was how they smelt. I used to feel as if I was suffocating under them. We would visit friends of my parents who lived near a waterfall, which seemed very magical to a child, but inside their house even the chairs were damp.

Years later, I was reminded of it when I went to stay with Donald Friend, the artist, in Bali. Donald and I had been close friends since my early days painting in Sydney. I'd been allocated his little guest cottage in the garden and I thought, Why is he giving me these dirty, old, smelly towels? Sanur was so close to the sea, the air was always moist and the towels never dried. That's why Donald got TB there. I used to think it was raining all night, but it was just the moisture in the air and the wind in the palm trees.

Tully's unhealthy climate also gave Margaret chest trouble. Grace Olley would heat up dark grey antiphlogistine, which looked like putty or chewing gum, and it was put on her chest under her nightie at night. Dampness aside, Tully held other vivid unpleasantnesses for the dark-haired small girl so fond of wandering off on her own. Chillies that grew by the bottom veranda step stung her flecked eyes painfully. The hornets' nest that she – 'always curious and picking at things' – once put in her mouth hurt, too.

But Tully did provide entertaining oddities. Two pet cassowaries followed the three Olley children round like dogs and swallowed bananas whole. Margaret's cousin, Douglas Temperley, also saw the cassowaries ingesting, gruesomely, whole little chickens. It wasn't long before the Olley parents, frightened the pets might peck their offsprings' eyes out, decided the cassowaries were too dangerous to keep. But before they were dispatched, the pets were taught a new trick. Some workmen gave them what must have been half-cigarettes and the children watched transfixed as the cassowaries smoked them down and then spat out the butts.

Tully, fortuitously for an artist who'd later paint so much still life, also provided an introduction to a superabundance of exotic edibles that was distinctly intriguing to a constantly curious child like Margaret. The neighbours next door grew giant grapefruit called pomelos. And the Italian migrants who'd come out to work on the cane fields and ended up buying farms grew, ate and eventually sold strange vegetables like eggplants, zucchini and garlic.

For Margaret, though, the most entrancing aspect of Tully life was close to home:

There was a lavatory built so it looked out onto the creek. The water was crystal clear, but the logs left in it from floods used to get very slimy because of what the mill tipped in. It was the best lavatory. I'd just sit there gazing out at a sort of bottlebrush with pom-pom flowers. Probably people said, Hurry up, but I never heard them. I was too busy dreaming away at the bottlebrushes and the enormous blue butterflies that were all around. Right from the start I could lose myself in the visual.

Years later, when Margaret was in her last year at school and the Second World War had begun, William Dobell (the artist who would later so famously paint her portrait) wrote an article for *Art in Australia*.[1] Dobell believed an Australian artist should seek in painting 'integrity in imagination' – Michelangelo's idea of 'Truth' – rather than 'literal fidelity'.

Dreaming of butterflies in Tully, it could be said, began this path for Margaret.

◆

The Olleys were in Tully because of Margaret's maternal grandfather, Thomas Temperley, or 'Grandpa Temperley', as the family knew him.

When Grace and Joe Olley were first married they lived at Horseshoe Creek, near Kyogle, in northern New South Wales. As Margaret has always understood it, Joe Olley, being of a practical bent, and Erasmus, the second of Grandpa Temperley's sons, were then delegated by the Temperley family to go up to Tully and take up 'a parcel of land' acquired there by Grandpa Temperley. Margaret's father and Erasmus duly took themselves up to Tully but Grandpa Temperley's parcel of land was 'really jungly' – in Margaret's words – and her father acquired a property closer to the town. At which point Grace Olley, with her and Joe's young daughter, followed the men north. The young daughter was, of course, Margaret.

Grandpa Temperley's parcel of land not only instigated a move to wetter and greener scenery for the Olleys (Horseshoe Creek would have been green enough, anyway, except in drought time); more importantly it began a pattern that involved 'relatives' and 'moving'. 'Always moving' would become the theme of Margaret's childhood as the family upped sticks again and again. 'We were almost like nomads – except that we always had a purpose,' she sums up.

To understand the move to Tully more fully one has to delve into Margaret's family history on both sides. Although Grandpa Temperley died before she was born Margaret grew up listening to her mother's stories of him. There was quite a bit to tell. Dubbed 'the stormy petrel of the North Coast', and a staunch churchgoer, Grandpa Temperley was a man of many parts. His obituaries mostly credit him with doing an apprenticeship as an engineer. He was also a teacher, a newspaper proprietor, an author (his article *The Autobiography of an Echidna* was issued to schools in reading-book form) and devoted to communication. In this last role he founded and was the chairman of the Independent Cable Association. The Association was formed in 1909, primarily by proprietors of New South Wales country papers, with a view to getting a special cable service for overseas news apart from the monopoly controlled by the large daily newspapers in Australian cities.[2]

He was an advocate for the north coast sugar and dairy industries and associated with the introduction of fast-growing, hardy South American paspalum grass to farms around Lismore, which proved a godsend in providing abundant fresh forage for dairy cattle.[3] Between 1905 and 1907 he unsuccessfully stood for election to the Legislative Assembly of New South Wales five times (the first three occasions contesting the seat of Ballina, then when this disappeared in 1904, Richmond) and once missed out to the sitting member, John Perry, by only forty votes.

Grandpa Temperley's parents and older siblings arrived from England on the ship *Nabob* in 1842, and Grandpa Temperley was born at Parramatta three years later, in 1845. His father, also a Thomas Temperley, was given a certificate declaring him to be a 'Free Emigrant' and set up business as a tailor in Clarence Street, Sydney. Thomas Temperley senior was listed as a tailor in Ford's *Sydney Commercial Directory* for 1851, but after that he disappears from the story without trace. There was a suggestion by Margaret's Aunt Madge of a drinking problem, which may have caused a fall from grace in the eyes of the family that would explain the lack of information.[4] It may also explain why for most of his life Grandpa Temperley was a total abstainer who didn't even smoke.

In his early twenties, presumably after completing his engineering apprenticeship, Grandpa Temperley worked as a teacher in an Anglican school in Richmond, west of Sydney. He lived with his mother and a sister on the ground floor of the two-storey building that had earlier served Richmond as a church, as well as a school, and classes were conducted upstairs. In 1869, Grandpa Temperley's mother died and round this time he took a teaching position in Picton, south of Sydney.

Temperley's next move was to the north coast of New South Wales. Here, in 1883 at Lansdowne, between Taree and Port Macquarie, he married Margaret Louisa Cross, daughter of the Reverend John Cross who, when he first arrived in Australia, was one of only five clergymen serving in New South Wales. According to the birth date entered in her father's Bible, Margaret was thirteen years younger than her husband.

Following his marriage to Margaret Louisa, Grandpa Temperley became Inspector of Northern Fisheries in New South Wales. His duties included looking after the oyster trade of the

Richmond River and its tributaries, which an enthusiast of the day described as 'a perfect paradise' for 'succulent bivalves'. Perhaps oysters gave Grandpa Temperley a taste for the Richmond River, or his official journeying had allowed him to explore other opportunities in the area, for in the mid 1880s he decided to embark on a new career – he acquired the *Richmond River Times*. By 1889, the whole Temperley family had moved to a house called 'The Pines', in Ballina.

Grandpa Temperley and Margaret Louisa Cross had eight children. Three (two boys and a girl) were born before the move to Ballina and five were born at Ballina, four of whom were girls. The first of those born in Ballina died as a baby. The next was Grace Sarah Temperley, Margaret's mother, born on 6 November 1890.

Ballina, a low-lying town at the mouth of the Richmond River, had come into existence with the arrival of cedar cutters in the mid 1800s and had soon expanded into a port for inland settlements and farms. As the cedar was felled and supplies dwindled, sugar cane became a favoured crop and mills sprang up along the river. But by the time the Temperleys arrived in the area, local sugar growers were struggling and their numbers had fallen, owing to a slump in world sugar market prices in 1884 and the effects of competition from countries such as Fiji and Java, which could grow sugar more cheaply, as well as from Queensland, where growers persisted in cutting costs by using indentured Pacific Islander labour on plantations.

By the time the Temperleys arrived local sugar growers were fewer in number and struggling. Ballina itself, however, was bustling. It boasted a lighthouse, at least three good hotels, several stores, Church of England and Catholic churches, and an ornate courthouse. Grandpa Temperley's *Richmond River Times* operated out of premises in River Street. Buildings on one side of the street backed onto the river, some even having their own wharves. A wooden walkway made a pleasant spot for dogs to sit while men, if so inclined, threw out a line for fish. As well as the congregations of oysters and pelicans drawn to its waters, the river was crowded with craft of all sorts, from passenger steamers that went upstream as far Lismore, to tugs and little sail boats.

The *Richmond River Times* was a chirpy journal. Priced at twopence, published twice a week, its circulation reached four figures every issue. News from Australia and overseas was run in columns with extremely small print while the print of the plentiful advertisements was larger and more readable. There were ads for everything, from dentists to local pig and calf sales, plus a remarkable cure for biliousness called Bile Beans (at nine pence halfpenny a box) and an amazingly wide selection of boots.

The Temperley children, except for Madge, the baby of the family, were all involved in the paper's production from a young age. Margaret's Aunt Mary, the oldest of the girls, who later went to Sydney University and was one of the first physiotherapists in Queensland, read for correction and Grace typed for it. Margaret remembers her mother liked to boast to the Olley children about her typing skills.

Grandpa Temperley used the newspaper to champion many causes. Although, during his time in Ballina, his political inclinations changed from Independent Labor to Unattached Protectionist to Liberal to Independent Liberal, chief among his abiding causes was sugar. In his obituary in the *Sydney Morning Herald* on 6 June 1918, and in other newspapers' farewell tributes, he was credited with being 'the first to promulgate the introduction of an excise duty on black-grown sugar with an exemption or bonus in favour of the white-grown product', using the unfortunately racist terms of the day. When the principle he promulgated was adopted after Federation (of which he was also a vocal supporter) Grandpa Temperley was feted by the sugar growers of the Richmond River at a public banquet.

Green, Green, Green

Clearly, sugar was dear to his heart. This might explain why he came to acquire his 'parcel of land' near Tully, which was a location with as yet unrealised sugar potential. According to his grandson Douglas Temperley, 'He was interested in everything. He was a newspaper proprietor, interested in anything that made news and looked like he could make some money out of. He took up land in all sorts of odd places. Unfortunately none of them really came to fruition.'

Unfortunately, also, Grandpa Temperley's propensity for taking up causes landed the *Richmond River Times* in hot water as far as libels went. His frank reporting of events resulted in at least one court case, which left him financially depleted and, possibly because of this, Temperley eventually handed over the editorship to his son John Erasmus, who was always known by his second name, Erasmus.

In 1909, Grandpa Temperley was chosen to represent the country press at the Imperial Press Conference in London. In England, not only did he meet King Edward VII, Queen Alexandra and the Prince and Princess of Wales (as Grace Olley would frequently remind her children), he also won applause for his no-frills oratory when he argued in favour of smashing the existing monopoly of cable communication.[5] Like many at the conference he believed a shilling a word was a ridiculously high rate for cablegrams to Australia. He also declared that people in Australia wanted their overseas news faster. The remedy put forward was the establishment of an 'all-red' route to the most distant part of the Empire, whereby wires would touch nothing but British soil on their way to destinations.

Around 1912, Grandpa Temperley sold up the *Richmond River Times* and moved with his family to Marrickville, Sydney, where he continued to work for the Independent Cable Association that he had helped set up. Another of his interests was the Country Press Association. It was in their Sydney chambers in Castlereagh

Far from a Still Life

Street that he died in 1918. At the time of his death, Grandpa Temperley was seventy-three and busily at work on a press directory of Australia. In Margaret's mother's version – an oft-repeated story much loved by her children – Grandpa Temperley died while laughing at a visitor's joke. While the obituaries were glowing and many, like his death certificate, however, they soberly attributed his death to heart failure. His wife, Margaret Louisa Cross, caught a cold at his funeral which turned to pneumonia, then meningitis, and she died just seven days after Grandpa Temperley.

◈

It was not surprising that Margaret's father, Joseph Olley, should have found himself farming in the green of Tully; generations of Olleys had been farmers in the green countryside of England.

Joseph's grandfather, William Olley, the first male of the family to come to Australia, was certainly a man fond of moving. William was born in 1819. His parents, Jacob Olley and Mary Hillder, were tenant farmers at 'Rymer Farm' near the village of Barnham in Suffolk. A photograph of Jacob, taken in his middle years, shows him wearing a three-piece suit, with a coat that reaches to his knees; a stiff, high-collared shirt; wide neck-bow and watch chain. At his feet is a mottled dog with its paws crossed. Jacob looks short but strong, a hard-working man who may have been a tad uncomfortable in formal attire.

In 1846 William Olley, Jacob's ninth child, married Sophia Brown. The couple had seven children, four of whom were born in England, including their second son, Alfred, Margaret's grandfather. The family left Liverpool for Australia on 10 March 1858, on board the steamship *The Herald of the Morning*, and arrived in Sydney three months later.

Little is known about the Olleys' decision to emigrate,

although the fact that William's older sister, Mary Mulley, was already in Australia with her husband, Robert, must have helped to make up their minds. On their arrival, the Olleys joined the Mulleys at Good Dog Mountain (now Cambewarra) in the Shoalhaven, south of Sydney. Good Dog Mountain's peak and extraordinary rainforest slopes dominate the spread of flat farming land around the Shoalhaven River on one side and on the other Kangaroo Valley.

William Olley didn't stay long at Good Dog Mountain. In a few years' time he was on leased farm land at Terara, a relatively large settlement on the Shoalhaven River itself. Here he grew vegetables, including potatoes, for Sydney. But the district suffered terrible floods. In 1867, fed up with having his crops washed away, William packed his sixteen-year-old son, Alfred, off on the new schooner *Euroka*, which sailed direct to the Richmond River, to investigate alternative farming opportunities.

Alfred was another restless Olley. After arriving on the New South Wales north coast, he soon selected two hundred acres at Rosehill, north of Lismore. Life here was more primitive and pioneering than it had been in the Shoalhaven area, and involved a lot of hard labour. But undoubtedly it would also have been lush, green and extraordinarily beautiful, particularly where the forest was untouched. Alfred quickly secured a block of about fifty acres for his father, on which he built a slab timber dwelling typical of the time, with two windows on either side of the front door and a front veranda held up by sturdy poles.

In 1869, Alfred's father, mother, a brother and three sisters followed him up north and moved into the cottage he had built, calling their property 'Mayfield'. The family was soon grazing stock and growing grass seeds. More land was selected until the Olleys' holdings totalled more than seven hundred acres. William extended their dwelling into a more comfortable home, which survived until around 1920.

Far from a Still Life

In 1873, Alfred Olley married Hannah Sophia Simes, whose father, John Simes, another early selector in the Lismore area, was a locksmith, blacksmith, cabinet maker and composer. Marriage didn't stop Alfred Olley's moving. While he continued to haul timber at Rosehill and his farming interests there expanded to include dairying, he also selected more land further to the north-west of Lismore, at Hanging Rock Creek. It was here that Hannah first began tutoring her children (she eventually had eleven) at home and soon the neighbouring children attended as well.

In 1888, the third youngest of their children, Margaret's father, Joseph Daniel Olley, was born. Around this time Alfred moved the family to Hanging Rock Creek, where he took up still more land and Hannah established another school. It was easier, she felt, to teach their children at home, rather than have them tired out from travelling miles to school elsewhere, so Margaret remembers her father telling her. The Olleys' final move was to a two-storey house called 'Tower Villa', which Alfred built at Georgica, a few miles closer to Lismore. A photo of Alfred taken later in life shows him to be remarkably similar in stance and physical build to his farming English grandfather, Jacob Olley. Alfred died in 1915 and his wife, Hannah, died a decade later, in 1926. Both are buried in the Methodist section of Lismore Cemetery.

Joseph 'Joe' Olley, their fifth son, was a good-looking and down-to-earth young man with blue eyes and brown hair. His early adult years were eventful, if not downright harrowing. In his early twenties he married a Muriel Carr, who died in childbirth a year or so later. Then in March 1916 at the age of twenty-seven he enlisted in the Australian Imperial Force (AIF) to serve abroad in the First World War. When he joined the army his height was five feet seven and a quarter inches, his weight eleven stone two and his chest measured 35½–38 inches. So he had inherited the Olley males' compact build with some added stockiness. In answer to the question 'What is your Trade or Calling' on his Attestation Paper he wrote 'farmer'.

Joe Olley embarked for the Western Front from Melbourne in June 1917. By August he was with the troops in France; by December he had been wounded in action. After a brief hospitalisation he was back fighting again and was wounded for a second time in France in late August 1918. This time he was twenty-four days in hospital. During his recovery period he worked a piece of embroidery, which he brought back to Australia and, according to Margaret, it always hung in a frame near the bathroom wherever the Olleys were living in her childhood. Although the war was soon over, Joe did not leave for home until late 1919. On 5 January 1920, he was discharged from the army. It's not recorded in his military record what his weight or chest measurement were then.

After his discharge Joe resumed farming on land he had previously selected at Horseshoe Creek, near Kyogle and Nimbin. At Horseshoe Creek itself there was very little except the creek, prettily overgrown with green vegetation, and a timber hall, which was shared with the neighbouring farming community of Green Pigeon. The calm of Horseshoe Creek must have been a welcome balm to the horrors of the trenches in Europe.

Despite the relative isolation there, or perhaps because of it, Joe managed straight away to meet and fall in love with Grandpa Temperley's third daughter, Grace. Grace, one imagines, may well have helped restore Joe's equilibrium as much as, or even more than Horseshoe Creek's placidity. As well as having helped out with the typing on the *Richmond River Times*, Grace Temperley was a qualified nurse. She had done her training in an inner Sydney hospital, and at some stage she'd looked after what were probably the first of victims of the great influenza epidemic that began in 1917. In later life Grace would recall how she and others had had to cut the clothes off patients who had worn layer upon layer of garments, each one greyer than the next.

Far from a Still Life

In 1917, Grace – or 'Nurse Temperley', as she was formally referred to – and a Doctor A.M. Aspinall opened a small hospital in northern New South Wales, at Nimbin, to care for returning soldiers. The hospital was set up in a house that had belonged to one of the town's earliest inhabitants. Nimbin had come into existence round the turn of the century as struggling settlers cleared the nearby rainforest hills and sold the timber to support themselves until dairy herds could be brought in. Grace arrived in Nimbin the same year as the town's first resident policeman. Buggies frequently pulled up in the main street and patiently waiting horses hitched to the outside of shops were a common sight. But compared to Horseshoe Creek, Nimbin was a hive of sociability. It even had Mrs Allsopp's tea rooms where romance might blossom amidst the refreshment served.

By 1921, Grace Temperley and Joe Olley were married and Grace, now in her early thirties, was installed at Horseshoe Creek. A wedding photo shows her in a restrained white dress rather than an elaborate bridal creation, and the beginnings of Joe's early baldness are also evident. While the war was obviously a cause of Grace marrying relatively late, her marriage at an older age might also indicate a certain independence of spirit that her artist daughter would inherit. By the spring of 1922, Grace was pregnant.

On 24 June 1923, a mild Sunday with light rain forecast, Grace and Joe's first child, Margaret Hannah Olley, was born at Nurse Elliott's hospital, 'Alkoomie', in Conway Street, Lismore. An announcement appeared the following day on the front page of the *Northern Star*; the details inconspicuously positioned between the Auctioneers' Notices and a poignant Roll of Honour in memory of soldier Clarence Deeves who had died of wounds in France six years earlier.

Green, Green, Green

The art world of Australia was of course oblivious to the birth of a new star. The quarterly magazine *Art in Australia* of 1 May 1923 featured an article by Sydney Ure Smith on the revival of the woodcut. Ure Smith wrote that the works of Mrs Margaret Preston added a 'modern note' to the established mastery of male artists, such as Lionel Lindsay, whose brother Norman was already famous for his voluptuous nudes.

Art in Australia was also enthusiastic about an exhibition of Australian art, organised by the traditional Society of Artists, about to make its way to London to be shown at the Royal Academy of Arts. The two hundred and fifty works had been chosen by a committee that included Hans Heysen, Norman Lindsay and George Bell. The selection had caused trouble in Victoria because so many of the works were by artists from New South Wales; affronted individuals had also lobbied for the exclusion of Lindsay's own work on moral grounds.

The Society of Artists' Travelling Scholarship of two hundred and fifty pounds per annum for two years had just been won by Mr Roy de Maistre. De Maistre a few years before had painted what is now celebrated as Australia's first abstract – *Rhythmic Composition in Yellow Green Minor* – and together with Roland Wakelin, another modernist, had held an exhibition in Sydney demonstrating his theory of the relationship between colour and music.

Australia was not entirely isolated from overseas art at this time. In the following month, July, an exhibition of modern European pictures opened at the Sydney Town Hall. The works were selected by the youngish Australian artist Penleigh Boyd, who had been acclaimed for his lyrical landscape paintings before the First World War. Most of the pictures were, in fact, British and Ure Smith declared much of the exhibition dull. However the renowned sculptor George Lambert gave it a favourable review in *Art in Australia*. Lambert hoped that the parochialism which a young country like Australia still clung to would not frighten viewers off the more modern works and that such an exhibition would become an annual event 'relentlessly dispelling by its aesthetic influence the apathy of the man in the street'.[6]

Among the paintings Lambert singled out for mention was *The Barn* by English artist Ivon Hitchens, with its cunning use of rhythmic and discordant lines, modelling suggestive of bent tin and broken crockery, simple colour gradations and rejection of realistic representations of detail. Strangely enough twenty-odd years on, when Margaret Hannah Olley was an eager young art student in Sydney, another painting by Ivon Hitchens would play a significant part in her life.

All in all, it was not such a bad time for an Australian artist to be born.

Four days before Margaret's birth a portentous event outside the art world had occurred. The Queensland Labor Government of Edward 'Red Ted' Theodore made the long-awaited announcement that a sugar mill would be built on the bank of Banyan Creek, in far north Queensland. A sugar rush was about to ensue and Joe Olley's ear would soon be cocked to the stories on everybody's tongues of big money to be made from sugar farming up north.

Although the pervasive greenness of Tully was a long way from Lismore and Kyogle, where the Olleys' baby daughter's birth was registered, and further still from Horseshoe Creek, with its overgrown little creek and wooden hall shared with the people of Green Pigeon, in only a short while Joe Olley was on the move.

Margaret's earliest memory is of her father going up ahead of Erasmus Temperley to see if it would be possible to take advantage of Grandpa Temperley's parcel of land in Tully in the sugar rush. Margaret and Grace Olley, who may well have been pregnant with Elaine, stayed with Grace's sister Mary in Brisbane. Mary Temperley – Aunt Mary as she would soon be known by Margaret – was by this time working as a hospital physiotherapist and lived in a boarding house in Wickham Terrace, which overlooked Roma Street railway station. To Margaret the whole house seemed to be covered in white lattice. Much stronger is her memory of the park's fig trees – even at that young age she claims to have been aware of their 'winey, hot summery smell' that is still so much a part of Brisbane to her.

Grandpa Temperley's parcel of land, on which there was a tree marked with his initials and those of his oldest son Will, turned out not to be at Tully but in the hinterland behind Tully, known as Jarrah Creek country. Joe Olley, having rejected Grandpa Temperley's Jarrah Creek holding as unsuitable for sugar cane, took up another piece of scrubland at Euramo, a bit south of Tully. When Erasmus Temperley joined him the two men worked together on this new land, using mattocks to plant sugar cane between the logs they'd felled. At this time Joe also bought land on Banyan Creek that had originally belonged to a member of the Dean family, very early settlers in the area, and was already well cleared.

It's possible that Joe purchased the Banyan Creek land with Temperley money that Grace had inherited and that the farm was in her name. Erasmus's son, Douglas, has certainly always believed this to be the case. Since Margaret herself was so little at the time, and never discussed it afterwards with her mother, she is uncertain about such details. But if this was so, then not only was it the beginning of Grace playing a saving role in the Olley family finances but also of the acumen she'd later display in property buying – a trait that would eventually be handed on to Margaret.

Joe and Erasmus were in Tully about a year before the opening of the new mill, the largest and most modern in Australia. It was a boom period generally for Australian sugar. During the First World War production had dwindled and sugar had to be imported, a costly exercise. After the war, the Commonwealth Government under Billy Hughes granted Australian growers a stabilised price and by 1925 Australia was a sugar exporter. Although Joe and Erasmus did not send cane to the first crushing at the Tully mill in November 1925, by 1927 the names Olley and Temperley were listed among its cane-growing assignees.[7]

Grace and Margaret, who would have been a toddler, made the steamer trip up the coast from Brisbane before the end of 1924 or early 1925. Margaret's only recollection of the voyage is of looking over the side of the boat and seeing 'lots and lots of huge jellyfish in the water'.

Steamer passengers often disembarked at Mackay, rather than going on north to Townsville, and were swung off ships in a basket attached to a derrick. Erasmus Temperley was deposited ashore this way when he'd come up from Ballina, and Margaret and Grace may have similarly begun their new life. The railway line only reached Tully in December 1924, so the final part of their journey may have been completed by road.

Even though Grace, as far as is known, took Tully in her stride, one imagines she must have wondered what she had come to at times, especially when she first arrived. There's an oppressiveness about Tully that is not just to do with its climate – you could easily feel trapped in its greenness. And in the 1920s Tully was a very wild young town.

The prospect of the new sugar mill in Banyan, as the early settlement there was named, had swiftly increased a population that until then had been declining. Droves of hopeful, in some cases often downright desperate, men came looking for land and employment. Not only was labour needed on the new cane farms, there was also work to be had on the railway line, which had been constructed in stages, north from Townsville and south from

Green, Green, Green

Cairns, with the last section running through Tully. A shantytown soon sprang up along the creek, with lawlessness and liquor – 'Banyan Rum' particularly – being the order of the day and night.

Along with the mill, a new town called Tully was founded, and by end of 1925 most of Banyan's dwellers had shifted into these hastily erected buildings. But the recklessness that had held sway in Banyan continued unabated as an influx of canecutters swelled Tully's numbers. There was gambling, murder and mayhem. It is said the pub had counters five feet wide to protect the barmaids from lustful customers, and about a mile out of town a row of brothels eased the pent-up sexual urges of the canecutters.

In keeping with Banyan's past shantytown habits, sly grog and home-brewed rum lubricated Tully's more disorderly inhabitants. Two women, known as Black Sadie and Hot Pie Annie, were chief among its sellers. Neat's-foot oil, boot polish and Flytox were rumoured to be ingredients of Black Sadie's overproof mixture. But there were also more ordinary activities in the new town. Shops had opened, even if prices were sometimes overly high. There was a drapery, a bakery, a fruit and vegetable store, a butchery (owned by Alwyn Collins, a man who will briefly reappear in the story), as well as a barber and bootmaker.

The waywardness of Tully seems not to have impinged on the Olleys: they did not live right in town; Joe was working; and Grace, after any initial gulp of trepidation or surprise, must have had her hands full at home. Margaret and her younger sister and brother, Elaine and Ken, were undoubtedly kept safely out of its way. And there was a dog to bark if any unwanted stranger came onto the farm. Except for the odd sighting of people who refused to abandon the old Banyan and lived by the railway in hammered-out kerosene tins, the town's colourful past and present might not have existed for the Olleys.

Despite the wet and sweltering summer, the niceties of life were not forgotten. On social occasions, the women, like Grace and Erasmus's wife, Gertrude Temperley, wore cloche hats and loose, long-waisted dresses, and the men put on dark suits with shirts and ties. Gloves were dispensed with, stockings were only occasionally worn, and a little girl like Margaret could easily get away with no socks and sturdy, open-toed sandals. The Olleys and Temperleys were not at the top of the social pecking order of the town: those positions were reserved for bank managers, the mill manager and solicitors. The Olleys and the Temperleys would have been in the middle of the social order, neither overly rich nor pressed for funds.

Margaret's own impressions of Tully life as it unfolded by Banyan Creek are naturally very much centred around home:

We were probably the first farm away from the town. My father, who was a great improviser – as people had to be then – built what was essentially one big room. There was a kitchen that ran right down one side, with a veranda and steps going down to where the chillies were. The kitchen had tin windows that you propped open and when it rained you just shut them down.

There were bedrooms down the other side of the main room. My sister and I slept in one. I think Ken might have slept with our parents. We always had people to stay, so there would have been another bedroom for them. You never went into other people's rooms. Elaine and I had our room, and that was that. Being children, we were outside most of the time, anyway. There was also another veranda running across the end of the big room. My father was always handy with building. If my mother wanted stairs changed, he'd say, All right, I'll do it. He never consulted a carpenter.

Our furniture was mostly makeshift. Cupboards were made out of packing boxes covered with cretonne. We did have some proper large, black dining-room furniture made of mission oak, which was probably silky oak stained dark. But not much else. When we first went up there were no shops to buy furniture. You would have had to go up to Cairns for anything like that. A man called Mr Shakespeare used to come round on horseback. I don't know if that was his real name or whether he just called himself Mr Shakespeare, but he was a lending library, with a saddlebag of books you could borrow.

We had our baths in a round tub in front of the kitchen stove. For refrigeration, we used homemade drip-safes covered in damp hessian. Ice was delivered by the iceman, or sometimes my father picked it up. There was no electricity. We carried round kerosene lamps at night. Because the insects were so bad, quite often we pushed the lamp away and sat in the dark. We'd put a bowl of water under the lamp, so the insects would congregate round the light and then fall into the water.

The Temperley family lived on the same property as the Olleys. Their two-storeyed house was closer to the railway line and built of tin, by which was meant corrugated iron. Despite big windows, which were thrown open to let the breeze through, the tin made the house terribly hot in summer, accordingly to Douglas Temperley. Douglas and his mother, Gertrude, who had been living in Ballina, probably came up to Tully not so very long after Margaret and Grace. Douglas remembers he turned six, which would have happened in May 1925, shortly after he and Gertrude arrived.

Margaret recalls of her Uncle Rassy and Aunty Gertie, as the adult Temperleys were known, that Erasmus had 'frizzy hair' and Gertrude 'was a sweet woman with a very relaxed attitude to life'.

In Margaret's own family Elaine was born in March 1925 and Ken, her brother, at the end of 1927. Elaine's arrival was made significant to Margaret by the fact that soon after the birth their mother dramatically choked on a fishbone. As a consequence Margaret, while a great painter of fish, has been very wary of eating it ever since. Otherwise, the presence of her sister and brother impinged very little on the imaginative world Margaret had created for herself:

'Laine used to say, Why won't Margie play with me? Make Margie play with me. But I was always a loner. You have your own secret world and you get carried way with it. Even now I can look outside and just watch a bird, become completely engrossed. It's like meditating. I did join in with the others sometimes. Once when we were playing, Ken fell into a well in the cane field and I had to hold on to him while Elaine ran back to the house to get help.

By far the most exciting aspect of growing sugar cane and living on a cane farm for all the Olley children was the burning of the cane at night:

They'd light it after dark. Very pyromaniacal, balls of fire lighting up the night. You'd hear it crackle and crisp with all the dry leaves burning. And smell it, the whole air was filled with an acrid mixture of sugar and smoke. When the trash was burnt all that was left was black ash and black stalks, with maybe a few bits of green. Then the canecutters would quickly come in, bringing with them a meccano-like set of train tracks and great big iron carriages on wheels. The cane was cut and bundled onto those.

A good time was when the cane was just shooting. You'd walk through it then, and so would the chooks or anything else. I remember going over with one of my relatives, or a friend, to visit neighbours. Walking through the paddocks, we came across what I thought was a curled-up snake. As we approached, the snake put all the eggs in its mouth and swallowed them. I thought it must have been swallowing the eggs to protect them. Of course, it was probably just a large lizard eating stolen hen's eggs.

Tully was clearly where Margaret's love of flowers began. Besides the entrancing pom-pom bottlebrushes by the creek, she encountered other seductive blooms in her daily ramblings about the farm. Some, such as allamandas and the Eucharist lilies, especially, would in future years become recurring subjects of much-cherished Olley paintings. But back then it was simply their intoxicating smells and colour that captivated her:

All the flowers in Tully had a fragrance. There was allamanda, a climbing plant with very shiny leaves and strong yellow flowers which sort of spin open; also funny little purple and white flowers; and lovely white-cupped Eucharist lilies, which grew around the creek and around the outside toilet that I spent so much time in. My mother must have planted the lilies because they're not native to Tully. People also kept lots of staghorn round their houses.

In these early years Margaret remembers Grace Olley, above all, as the parent who was always 'just there'. Grace was the one who cared for the family and neatly organised the household. But even her chores were sometimes a source of intrigue to the ever-curious Margaret:

My mother had an iron that you put methylated spirits in. You pumped it to make it work and it had a wonderful smell. Then one day the iron suddenly burst into terrifying flames and she had to hurl it out the kitchen window, so it was lucky the windows had no glass in them.

I have no clear image of what either of my parents looked like. It's of no concern to you when you're a child. I certainly never thought of my mother as being particularly small. She was about five foot five, I think. My parents didn't ever talk about how they met or their courting days. Any snippets of personal information about the adults was gleaned by listening at the keyhole.

Joe Olley, it seemed to Margaret, was always working; away from the house and the family. On one never-to-be-forgotten afternoon, he arrived back in the rain after inspecting the cattle that were kept on Grandpa Temperley's first property and almost fell from his horse unconscious. Out at the property the horse had slipped and a stump had gone into Joe's leg. He ended up with a streptococcal infection in the wound and, without penicillin, it was unclear for some time whether he'd pull through. He did. But he was left with a scar on his leg for life. Like him, Margaret is susceptible to streptococcal infections, and has twice had to endure a bout of cellulitis.

Another image of her father in the Tully days has remained in Margaret's mind over the years. It's not only a disarming picture of a very young girl observing a parent but also gives an indication of Joe Olley's readiness to improvise:

We had a banana passionfruit growing in the garden and my father had also trained a granadilla vine over the water tank. The granadillas had huge passionfruit flowers; the fruit were like giant pawpaws, but when you opened them up they looked like passionfruit. My father, who had quite big fingers but was not at all clumsy, used to climb up a ladder and go from one flower to another, pollinating them with a chook feather, which I found fascinating to watch.

Joe Olley at this time may also have instilled in Margaret the beginnings of a passion for collecting the eclectic objects that are now so permanently a part of her personality, not to mention her present notoriously cluttered abode in Sydney:

One of our great treasures was an Aboriginal shield, which my father had found on that first property of Grandpa Temperley's. It was always kept in the house. My father used to point to where a spear or something had been thrown at it. You could see a dint and a slight look of blood. It might have been used in some sort of pay-back law ceremony. My father used to say that once somebody was injured in these ceremonies, the Aboriginal men threw down their shields and the fighting stopped. That was the end of the matter. The shield was beautiful, quite light to hold and it went with us wherever we moved. We were also brought up with those bicornual, crescent-shaped baskets that the Aboriginal women put over their foreheads and carry on their backs, with yams or other food, and even babies, in them. We used them in a domestic way, pegs went in the biggest and so on. Now they fetch vast sums of money.

The shield and the baskets were about the only contact the Olley children had with the local indigenous people, except for a story that was told and retold by the adults at their get-togethers:

A travelling pastor had called in to visit some household in Tully and brought with him an Aboriginal boy. The boy wouldn't have a cup of tea with the family, but when he was left on his own he was seen to lift up the teapot and drink from the spout, which seems to have scandalised some of the grown-ups as a terrible breach of manners. We children just thought how sensible the boy was. What else are spouts for?

◆

It wasn't long before Joe Olley, who would have been well aware of the potential in dairying, realised there was no milk-run in Tully. He and Erasmus Temperley then started a dairy, called 'Olley and Temperley', on the farm at Banyan Creek. They also may have run cattle on leased land where the Tully high school now is.

Joe Olley soon organised for his nephew, Lionel Crawford, to come up from Kyogle to work for him and Erasmus in the dairy. In a family as large as the Olleys', it was always easy to find a relative to help out. When Crawford arrived he became friends with the Townsville railway clerk and sometime canecutter Mick Leahy, whose sister Molly was married to Collins, the butcher in Tully. In 1926 Leahy suddenly set off on a steamer bound for New Guinea, in the hope of finding gold. He and his three brothers, Paddy, Jim and Dan, were all subsequently involved with prospecting and pioneering in New Guinea, and in 1933 Mick and Dan, together with administration officer James Taylor, achieved fame for being the first Europeans to explore the Western Highlands and reach Mt Hagen.

Throughout Margaret's childhood the exploits of Mick and the other Leahy brothers (as well as of Lionel Crawford, who also soon went prospecting in New Guinea) were talked about with awe by the Olleys. The romantic tales of New Guinea fed Margaret's reveries and from then on she harboured a desire to experience the country herself. Later, in a chain of coincidences that Margaret still finds amazing, Mick Leahy would marry Jeanette Best (the daughter of the Tully mill manager, Stanley Best), whom Margaret then met and became friends with when she finally began her painting expeditions to New Guinea in the 1960s.

Margaret has few real memories of Tully itself. However, there were some town-dwelling friends of her parents who impressed her. They were a childless couple called the Dingles. Percy Dingle was an auctioneer and real estate agent, whom the Olley children thought was a bit arrogant. Elsie, his wife, was like an aunt to them. Both the Dingles were decidedly 'exotic' in Margaret's eyes. They spoke differently and their food was different to the Olleys': to everyone's astonishment Elsie would have delicacies such as peas sent up from Melbourne. Long after Margaret had left Tully, she met Elsie again. Elsie, in her role as aunt, gave her a present of a glamorously impractical camisole and pants all in one.

Green, Green, Green

Margaret in her inimitable way promptly cut the garment in two and used the bottom half as knickers for years afterwards.

If Margaret's recollections of the Tully township are scant, the family's excursions out of Tully have very much stayed with her. Despite being the domestic mainstay who was always there, Grace Olley loved going on 'rides'. When she and Joe were first married and living at Horseshoe Creek, they would often escape in a sulky for swimming parties with friends to a pool in the creek. In Tully, Erasmus Temperley had bought an old second-hand ambulance that proved ideal for transporting the Olleys and Temperleys to picnics at Mission Beach, just east of Tully. They'd sit on the side seats and bounce along a rough single-lane track out to the long strip of sand looking over to Dunk Island. On one such excursion Elaine was stung by a jellyfish. As there was no chemist or shop of any sort nearby, all her parents could do was rub sand on the reddened skin and tell her the pain would eventually go. On another occasion the ambulance, a Dodge, became bogged in sand at Mission Beach and broke an axle. When the tide came in it had to be abandoned and everyone had to find lifts home. Eventually the ambulance was dragged out. After fresh water was thrown over it and the axle repaired, the vehicle was as good as new.

Around 1927, Joe Olley bought his first 'perambulator car', as Margaret always thought of them – a dark Chevrolet open tourer. The 'Chev' had a roof that folded down and celluloid side curtains that snapped on and off and were stashed under the back seat when not in use. More exciting outings took place in the Chev. Clump Point, at the north end of Mission Beach, was a popular spot for the Olleys' days out, or Bingal Bay, further up the coast, where there were about half a dozen houses.

Picnics aside, other events were taking place in Margaret's life. It was time for her to join her cousin Douglas at the local school. At first, Margaret doubled up behind Douglas and they rode to school on one pony. But one day, taking the corner where the road doglegged round their pigsty, Douglas went too fast and Margaret ended up on the ground. After that she was given her own pony. Joe Olley had already broken in a foal, intending that she would ride it to school. But the pony was wall-eyed and Joe decided it might be too fractious for her, so she and Douglas swapped – Douglas was given the frisky pony and Margaret rode his.

Her main memory of the Tully school is of playground activities that did not entirely impress her:

There was a fence between the school and the Catholic church, which was higher up on the hill, closer to Mount Tyson – the Catholics always liked the really high positions – and the Catholic children used to have their lessons in the church. So we all used to hang onto the fence, pull it backwards and forwards, and sing 'Catholic dogs, sitting on logs, eating frogs', or something similar. I didn't know what the words meant. I just did it because the others were doing it.

Margaret hadn't been at the Tully school very long when there was another riding accident:

We used to cross the creek, then take a short cut across the paddocks. We had to almost swim the horses across the creek. I was never a horse person and when the creek flooded the horse really did have to swim across and I came off. After that I was sent to boarding school. My uncle Erasmus's daughter Dorothy, who was the oldest of us children and in high school, was already boarding at Townsville. When the rest of the family came up to Tully, Dorothy boarded in Ballina for a while, but then she came up to St Anne's in Townsville, which was a Church of England convent. Since Dorothy was already at St Anne's, it was logical that I should go there, too.

Grace Olley may also have decided to send her daughter to boarding school because she had worries about a rough element in the local school. Or perhaps keeping an eye on three small children with a creek nearby was too much for her, particularly with Margaret, who was so inclined to dreamy exploring by herself.

The landscape of Margaret's childhood was broadening. Townsville was not hemmed-in like Tully. The town was well established and spread out. Its colonnaded government and commercial buildings, often two-storeyed and decorated with cast iron, must have seemed very grand compared to the simpler shopfronts of Tully's main street; and the Edwardian Gothic railway station (where Margaret would have alighted, unless Joe drove her down) was more like a palace than a train stop.

Again a mountain dominated Margaret's view – the molar-like Castle Hill, which jutted up at the back of the town. Denuded of any greenery, its bare top was an inescapable presence in Townsville. But now also the Coral Sea was within walking distance and the mouth of Ross Creek, wide as a river despite its name, was home to maritime vessels galore. Canopied launches that served as ferries scooted busily from one side to another. Close to the bank, fishing boats and coastal traders were moored. Long, low hulls lay mysteriously on the water's surface with no visible support that Margaret could see.

Margaret would have been about six when she was enrolled at St Anne's. The school's old attendance ledger has an entry for Olley in September of 1929. Recorded next to it in neat pen are the sums of ten pounds eight shillings for board, one pound one shilling for tuition, and one pound eleven and six for laundry – St Anne's certainly kept its new little pupil clean.

St Anne's had been founded by the Sisters of the Society of the Sacred Advent in Townsville in 1917. By the time Margaret donned its uniform – blue skirt and blue blouse with lacing at the neck and sides and a white collar – the school occupied four houses bounded by Willis, Walker and Stokes Streets, right in the centre of town. Sister Alice, who was in charge, and the other nun, Sister Vernon, wore long, dark habits and veils, complete with stiff white guimpes, ignoring the tropical climate, and around their necks hung very large crosses. As well as the nuns, there was also a number of lay teachers. Altogether, it must have been a formidable array of unfamiliar faces for a small girl away from parents and home for the first time:

It sure did cut the umbilical chord. Being away from my sister and brother, I drifted more into that world of my own. But I definitely wasn't homesick. Children adapt. I've never been desperately homesick; where I am is where I am. The school was surrounded by mango trees. They used to serve us stewed mangos for desert. Stewed mangos! And they were turpentine mangos. They tasted like turpentine to begin with and stewing made it even worse. Revolting! I wouldn't touch a mango for years afterwards because of those stewed turpentine mangos.

But I enjoyed St Anne's. Quisqualis, Rangoon creeper, grew all round the veranda where our dormitory was. It had the most wonderful smell, like the earth. The flowers come out a greeny white, which changes to pale pink and then turns dark. I remember putting my hand through the railing and picking the flowers to make daisy chains. The little flowers had such long stems it was easy to thread them through the holes and make miles and miles of chain.

We also had to march along to church in the heat, but I just accepted it as part and parcel of life. Once I was sick, which wasn't much fun. I had to go along to the Sisters at night to be put in the hospital bay, and I was very disturbed by the sight of Sister Alice, whom I didn't recognise without her veil. She was wearing a little white cap and underneath her hair was shaved. What a shock it was! Things like that are obscene to a child.

St Anne's – naturally, being run by nuns, usually with their veils firmly in place – put great emphasis on religion. Divinity was the first lesson of every day, there were regular prayers and ringing of bells for the Angelus, as well as a children's Eucharist on Fridays. The school also valued education highly and was especially keen on art and music. Every child had art lessons and by the early 1930s the school even had its own orchestra. Sister Vernon, who taught both art and drama, was also responsible for the school's much-loved outdoor theatrical performances. At these events the audience would sit on the lower tennis court and the girls would emerge from tropical garden shrubbery to perform plays, which included the works of Shakespeare. But it was the art lessons at St Anne's that were important to Margaret:

I was given a brown paper book and pieces of coloured paper to cut up. You made pictures – like Matisse – out of the cut-up paper, using the coloured squares and triangles. That was the first art I did.

In the brown paper book, which Margaret's mother Grace carefully kept, the collages included a still-life arrangement on a table and chair. There was also a drawing of 'the lady's garden' and another of 'God's sun and sky'.[8] 'So even at this early age', as friend, curator and art historian Christine France would write much later on, '[Margaret] was attracted to the idea of her immediate surroundings as subject matter for her art.'[9]

2

Living on a River

*Living by the Tweed River I first experienced the
intoxicating smell of grass after rain. At Tully it rained all
the time, so you didn't notice the sweet smell that comes
with rain. I still wait for that sweetness, but in the city
after rain all you get is the smell of asphalt. Smell plays a
very important part in one's life. It can bring back
such memories.*

AROUND 1931 OR 1932, ERASMUS TEMPERLEY BOUGHT THE Banyan Creek dairy – apparently running smoothly – and the Olleys were on the move again. Margaret was collected from St Anne's and the whole family drove down to the Tweed River, on the far north coast of New South Wales. In some ways the Tweed Valley was another Tully, only the greenness was not so claustrophobic; nor was it as persistently wet, or hot, and a river's placid spread replaced the slime of Banyan Creek.

The colour, however, was still overwhelmingly green. Sugar cane waved just as seductively in the breeze and once more the outline of a rainforest mountain presided – there was no getting away from a mountain for the Olleys. Mount Warning was once a volcano and the Tweed Valley is part of its caldera. Perhaps this gives the valley its particular richness, for there's an intense attractiveness about its bright cane, blue sky and dancing water sparkle.

The circuitous car journey down to their new home was memorable for Margaret, Elaine and Ken. The flies were atrocious and they spent the trip squinting at the scenery through thick fly veils. As they circled out west from Townsville, staying overnight at various isolated properties, they were surprised at how warmly the women on the stations greeted them. It was because they were so deprived of female company, Grace explained; they were simply pleased to see another woman.

When they finally arrived in Brisbane there was another surprising turn of events. Joe Olley went into a police station to get a driver's licence. When he was asked where he'd come from, he answered north Queensland. According to Margaret, no one turned a hair at the fact that her father had driven unlicensed all the way from Tully. A licence was simply handed over, she says. In those days that's how it was done.

At the Tweed, Joe Olley bought another sugar cane farm, on the northern side of the river at a place called Tygalgah. The Tweed Valley had long been established as a sugar-growing district and cane farms proliferated on both sides of the river. Cane, in fact, was pretty much all there was to Tygalgah. Paddocks filled with cane stretched as far as a line of blue-green hazy hills, and to the south-west Mount Warning's distinctive peak was clearly visible.

The Olleys' single-storey house was within easy cooee of the river. In front of their house there was a narrow road, a grassy strip with a few trees, and then the river. On the other side of the river was the Condong C.S.R sugar mill, which had opened back in

1860. Around the mill the air was thick with a choking sugary odour. When the Olleys arrived at Tygalgah, Margaret's uncle Tom Temperley was working for the mill as an inspector of cane farms, which may have been a reason for their choosing to buy land there. It was also a lot closer to where both Grace and Joe had grown up.

At Tygalgah Margaret resumed exploring the secret realm of daydreaming she'd first discovered at Tully. Now even an ant in the grass could be endlessly distracting to her. Despite this propensity of Margaret's for being abstracted, Elaine recalls that she was easy to get on with and that they never fought.[1]

However, the Tweed Valley and surrounds, where 'everything was taken in by observing' – in Margaret's words – were more than just an unfailing source of stimuli for Margaret's interior world; living at Tygalgah also provided lessons in real life far more valuable and enjoyable than any school classroom learning. In all, although the family was only there for three or four short years, for Margaret this period was clearly paradise:

The Tweed is really where my childhood began. What a place for children to grow up – living by a river! My father loved fishing in it and catching mud crabs in crab pots, which you could get because the river was tidal and partly salty. We were always fishing. We'd go to the tip, find big bottles and tie a long piece of string around them. At the bottom of the bottle went a bit of bread. We'd lower it slowly into the water – the trick was to keep the bread in the bottle – and wait for a big fish to swim in. Once a fish was in the bottle, it couldn't turn around and get out. All we had to do was drag the bottle up quickly.

I learnt to swim there. I was just thrown into the river and started dog paddling. There was a tiny island between us and Condong. To us children it was a magical place. We would row up to it in a boat with my father and net fish. He'd tan the big net every year in a huge vat so it wouldn't rot. When cousins from Sydney came to stay, we'd go over and play there, be pirates or anything we liked to imagine.

Living on a River

The Tweed Valley itself was a very strange area. There were volcanic rocks everywhere, big outcrops of boulders that looked rather like a Chinese painting. We had a whole lot of these rocks in our back paddock. They were almost like glass and used to glisten. We always regarded them as sinister and we never climbed up on them. The spare allotment that belonged to the people next door was full of trees and quite swampy. That's where the death adders are, we were told. The death adders will jump out of trees and get you, was the further warning. So, of course, we would enlarge on this to frighten ourselves.

Once, Margaret climbed Mount Warning on a Sunday School excursion. About halfway up the steep trek, she scooped up some fresh, cool creek water into her mouth. She remembers thinking how beautiful the water tasted as she gulped it down, but later she wondered what the lump inside her mouth was, and realised it was a leech. Though the adults extracted it, she could taste blood for ages afterwards. However the panoramic views from the top of Mount Warning were worth it, she says.

At home on the farm, the Olley children mostly amused themselves quite independently: being brought up in the country they were sensible and didn't fall into any trouble. Toys were never bought; Margaret and Elaine saved the knuckle bones from stews and used them to play a game where the bones were tossed in the air or swept off the ground with one hand. Marbles from their Christmas stockings were another source of amusement. Margaret remembers Ken had a galvanised iron canoe that he paddled, more on the grass than the river's edge, and Joe made them stilts, long timber sticks with little platforms to put their feet on. 'I don't think I was ever very good at using the stilts,' she recalls ruefully.

The Olley house had a veranda that went round on two sides. A third was closed in with louvres and turned into a bedroom, where Margaret and Elaine slept, which was especially cosy in winter:

The roof of our house was tin. I loved snuggling up in bed, hearing the rain on the tin roof overhead. It's marvellous, that sense of being sheltered in the rain. When I had full balance I used to recreate that sensation in the shower. I'd start drying myself while the shower was still on my back. It's the same feeling. I love it.

You could really hear the rain, especially when it flooded. One year I thought the end of the world had come, the sound was so loud. It was not just rain. Ice was pelting down on the roof. The neighbours were building a new house that was propped up high on poles. Suddenly there was an enormous crash and the whole thing slid over. The weight of the hail had made it collapse. A week later, the whole of the Tweed Valley was brown with bruising. A man who worked for us was out ploughing with two draught horses and was caught in the storm. He had to stand out in the paddock holding onto the horses and ended up with great lumps all over himself from the hail. It rained and rained for weeks afterwards. We used to sit on the front veranda and watch the passing parade in the flood waters; logs would go past, blown-up cows with their legs in the air and birds sitting on them, even people's furniture.

As for the Depression, which would have been at its worst, the Olleys were virtually self-sufficient on their farm and seem to have emerged from it unscathed. The chooks laid plenty of eggs and a couple of house cows provided fresh milk. The cows were milked by hand and the children all had a go at squirting the thin streams of warm liquid, which steamed in the air on chilly mornings, into tin buckets. The milk was taken to a room beside the hay barn where it was separated for making butter. One of the tasks the children were given was to clean the separator – a complicated and tedious process, according to Margaret. Another of their chores was cleaning the chooks' pen. 'Having these jobs, as well as all our playing, meant the days were very full and we always went to bed tired,' she says.

Joe Olley grew all their vegetables. His patch beside the house produced everything from beans and cauliflower to beetroot and onions and the children were also given their own plots to tend. 'We had far more vegetables than we needed and what we couldn't use was given away,' Margaret says. Her father, who was a Methodist but not much of a churchgoer, believed in helping others, she explains. So did her mother, whose religion was Church of England. And although religion was not unduly stressed in the Olley household, grace was said at all meals, except breakfast. 'I still say grace,' Margaret comments. 'We should be grateful for what we receive.'

Not only did Joe Olley keep all and sundry supplied with vegetables, his ingenious horticultural methods were often a source of wonder to Margaret, Elaine and Ken:

I remember he planted some peas which he intended ploughing in to put nitrogen back into the soil. As it happened they were edible and we ended up with a very large crop. So he employed great numbers of people who, I think, were unemployed because of the Depression, to pick peas. Consequently we had whole meals of peas. I have to say, they tasted much better in those days than they do now.

He was always improvising and inventing things. When he grew too many carrots, he'd pull them out as soon as they were ready and bury them in sand, which kept them fresh. Then he came up with an idea for improving the rhubarb output. He cut the bottom and the top out of a kerosene tin and put it round the plants. For the green leaves to come out the top, the rhubarb stalks had to grow very long. Fortunately we all liked rhubarb. I still cook it now as my mother did then, with lemon rind to make it sharp.

For one of his inventions he got hold of a long cable from the sugar mill. He anchored the cable to posts on both sides and ran it across the bottom of the river. Then he secured traces with hooks to the cable, on which he caught sharks and stingrays. These were dug into the garden as fertiliser. Although, when I think about it, they would have only been baby ones and would have been delicious to eat. Another of my father's intriguing skills was tapping watermelons to see if they were ripe. He'd knock on the melon before cutting us out a sample with a knife. If we didn't like that slice, he'd knock on another melon.

The Olley children's favourite haunt inside the Tygalgah house was the kitchen. They loved watching Grace cooking, especially when she was making cakes and jams, or bottling fruit from the trees. Inspecting jellies as they set was another kitchen activity and the children also took turns in churning the butter. The butter had to be kept under the house on tank stands because that was where it was coolest, while meat safes were placed in breezeways or on the veranda.

The only food items Margaret remembers being bought were flour, sugar and ice, which was collected once a week in a sugar bag; although a travelling salesman also came round with extras like vanilla essence, junket tablets and nutmeg. Grace made all the children's clothes on a treadle sewing machine, which had been in her possession since she was married. 'We were very fortunate,' Margaret says of the family's situation.

However there was one sign of the Depression she saw:

In front of our house, on the grass by the river, people would walk along and strip the seeds off the paspalum. The seeds went in chaff bags, which they dragged behind them. When I asked my mother what they were doing she said they were collecting the seeds to sell to the IXL factory. For making raspberry jam, she'd add darkly. That was to turn you off tins of jam. Despite our parents thumbing their noses at it, we, of course, regarded it as a treat if we went out anywhere and had tinned jam or bought butter.

School may not have had a great deal of appeal for Margaret, but at least getting there was an adventure at the Tweed. Every morning the spruced-up Margaret, Elaine and Ken had to be rowed across the river's usually sun-lit, glittering expanse – to catch the school bus that went along the main road into Murwillumbah. Then, in the afternoons, they were picked up again. Occasionally Grace Olley rowed them over herself, but mostly it was done by a farm handyman. On Sundays they were similarly transported to Sunday School.

For Margaret the school week went round from one art class to another. Art was the only lesson she really liked. She was put off other lessons even further when an appalling insult was delivered to her. As a result of inattention and failures in spelling she was sent down to sit with the babies to learn to spell.

During these school days, Elaine and Margaret both had short hair with fringes. Margaret's was dark, with a little tinge of red. Elaine was fair; she was the pretty one who was always chosen to sing in the choir or given parts like Bo-Peep in concerts, according to Margaret. Margaret recalls that once, when visiting relatives or friends, the children overheard the adults talking about their father's first wife. Afterwards Elaine and Ken ganged up on her. You belong to the first wife, they teased. For quite a long time Margaret believed it was the truth. 'You remember these things because they cut in like acid,' she says.

Although the Olley children were sometimes banished to the 'sulk room' – the spare room, also known as the 'box room', where chores such as ironing were done – on the whole not much punishment was meted out at home:

Our parents were not overly strict. I do remember my father hitting my brother. He never hit me. He would give you 'serious talks', which hurt far more. I used to wish he'd hit me, instead of delivering these talks. On one occasion, I was put in the clothes basket, because I wouldn't say I was sorry for something or other. The clothes basket was an enormous cane basket that came with us wherever we travelled. It carried the china during the move.

We rebelled once. I was the leader of the pack who decided that we should all leave home. Elaine went down the road. Ken and I went and sat in the boat. I think it was because we didn't like the castor oil we'd been given, or were about to be given, or the Epsom salts. Castor oil was always threatened if you were ill. You only had to take that a few times and you'd think twice about whether you were sick. When we were visiting relatives once at Kyogle, we had methylated spirits and sugar, or some similarly obnoxious concoction, foisted on us. My mother also administered Epsom salts to us once a week on Saturdays. The smell was vile and, to make matters worse, it was hot. The Epsom salts were dissolved in hot water and you drank them down warm – talk about punishment – with a boiled lolly afterwards.

Everybody used home remedies. No one ever thought of going to the chemist. If you had a boil, bread poultices were used to draw the pus out. The bread was mashed up and went on a bandage, which was a torn bit of cotton sheet (old sheets were always used for bandages) that was put into a bowl; then boiling water was poured on to sterilise it and it was lifted up and twisted, not only to squeeze out the water but also to let off the steam, because steam burns. Even so, it always felt awfully hot.

◈

One startling event soon interrupted the mostly tranquil flow of Tygalgah life. Grace Olley suddenly vanished without a word of explanation. A cousin, Thora Crawford, arrived to look after the children in Grace's absence. Their mother seemed to be gone for months, though in reality it was probably only about six weeks. Margaret always assumed that she must have gone to Lismore for some medical procedure. But recently Thora revealed to Elaine that, in fact, Grace had been in Sydney on a holiday.

Whether Grace was seriously considering leaving farm life or just wanted a brief break remains a mystery – she may have been attending a wedding or social gathering in Sydney – but the children felt they had been abandoned. Six weeks was an unheard-of amount of time for a mother to be absent, Margaret says. In those days only 'bolters' took off. But the young Olleys didn't brood for too long. Being practical children, they adopted the next-door neighbours as a substitute family. They also sensibly took advantage of their mother's absence to build an elaborate cubbyhouse with rooms made out of old butter boxes and planks, with bits of lino and carpet for flooring. When their mother finally reappeared, again without explanation, the cubbyhouse had to be dismantled. It never occurred to any of the children to ask where their mother had been. As Margaret observes, 'You simply never questioned what your parents told you to do or queried their behaviour.'

A big wind-up gramophone and records of opera singers such as Enrico Caruso and Nellie Melba provided indoor diversion for the Olleys, young and old, at Tygalgah. The children were all taught the piano, but the lessons were not very successful, to the disappointment of Joe Olley, who'd been hoping for some musical accompaniment to family singalongs. As far as art went, there were no books on painting in the house, nor prints hanging on the walls that made an impression on Margaret. Nor was anyone much of a reader (which must have had Grandpa Temperley, with his fondness for the written word, turning in his grave).

Despite the attraction of art classes at school, Margaret had not the slightest inkling of what an artist was. She was far too busy being a child ever to think what she might want to be when she grew up, although a visit from her city cousin Tom Temperley proved an eye-opener:

Tom was much older and worked in the advertising department of David Jones, which was like an art department. He did sketches for their catalogues. Tom was the first person I met who was actually interested in art, not that I had any idea what that meant, but I was fascinated to see what he did. He had an easel, canvasses, oil paints and brushes, and used to go off to the back paddock by himself. Then he'd come back with landscape paintings. It was like a miracle. Tom gave me a little start.

Another inspiring person also came into Margaret's life at this time – her mother's sister, Aunt Mary. Aunt Mary, by her mere presence, provided hints of an undreamt-of way of living:

Aunt Mary, the physiotherapist, would appear out of the blue. She brought the outside in, an outside world that was wonderful and exotic. Her suitcase always smelt different. She'd have pieces of cotton Tobralco material for us. I remember I was given one with butterflies and there was another piece that had buttercups on it.

Aunt Mary was my first role model. She was single, she was a working woman and she treated everybody as a person, no matter how young or old. So although you don't think about it at the time, patterns are set for you. Hearing about the things Aunt Mary was doing was fascinating. She was one of the first people who went to Heron Island when it was covered with nesting birds. Later on, she took me bush walking with groups of wildlife enthusiasts she knew. Aunt Mary seemed to have the freedom to do what she wanted. My mother loved getting out, but she always seemed to be so centred around home. Actually, I think she would have liked to have been more like Aunt Mary. Maybe that's why she went off for the six weeks' holiday: put her foot down. I know I would have.

Living on a River

While Aunt Mary's wider world beckoned enticingly, there were still enriching experiences to be had close to Tygalgah. These experiences were connected with the Olleys' frequent excursions; never again in her childhood would Margaret and her family have quite such pleasant times as on their day trips out along the Tweed River and camping holidays at the coast nearby.

Every Sunday, while the children were at Sunday School, Grace Olley would cook up a roast fowl, roast vegetables and peas. These were packed up in Nally Ware bakelite containers and put in a wicker picnic hamper which was stowed in the car, then the family set off for Tweed Heads or some unpopulated beach. If they were going to Tweed Heads they had to travel on four punts – the first of which was a hand punt – which greatly enlivened the journey in the children's eyes. Although once when their mother was learning to drive their father said, 'Go on, Grace, you take the car onto the punt,' and she, Elaine and Ken promptly jumped out, according to Margaret. 'We had no confidence in my mother's driving abilities, at all,' she says.

There were also other diversions for the children along the way:

If you were crossing into Queensland you had to go through exciting border gates. Sometimes we would travel as far north as Coolangatta and relatives or friends from Brisbane would come down and join us. My father had also bought, or leased, a banana plantation on the way to Tweed Heads so we'd call in there, too. Relatives of some sort used to manage it for us. They had flying foxes to take the bananas up and down to the packing sheds, which immediately captured our attention.

At the mouth of the Tweed River on the Queensland side there was the most exciting headland where we used to play amongst dark volcanic boulders. We'd find caves which seemed very large to us at the time, but when we went back as older children they turned out to be so much smaller. On the New South Wales side, near where the Tweed River runs into the sea at Fingal, there was a big Aboriginal area. Fingal had an atmosphere of its own. People were always getting washed off the rocks there while fishing, which was a disturbing thought. In the river itself was a huge island full of palm trees. We never crossed over to it because the vegetation was so dense and we thought it might harbour all sorts of secrets. My father used to tell us the whole of the Tweed Valley was like that before it was all chopped down for a bit of sugar cane or a dairy farm.

The picnic lunch was followed by swims and afternoon tea. Finally, tired out, we'd start making our way home. If we were coming back from Tweed Heads and there was a big queue waiting for the punt, we'd have an early supper by the river. The riverside was built up with the same big volcanic boulders as the headlands at the mouth of the river. Sometimes the men went fishing while the women got the food ready. The children's job was to stab the oysters off the rocks. We used to murder the oysters. First of all it was hard to get them off, they were so firmly clamped on; then we didn't know how to open them properly and when they were finally open you had to wash out the grit. I hate oysters now because of it.

As in Tully, it was their mother Grace who engineered the family's outings to places like Byron Bay, where there was only a wharf and the butter factory, or Bangalow, where a friend of hers lived. She was constantly hatching plans for more expeditions. At Easter or the school holidays she would blithely announce: 'Well, let's go down to Lismore for a week.' Then, when the rest of the family were packed up, eager to set off, she'd still be fussing around. 'Grace, not another thing in the car,' Joe Olley would command. Grace would covertly hand the children another cushion. 'Sneak it in,' she'd whisper. 'Your father will never notice.'

Once they finally took off, Margaret's eyes would be peeled. 'Stop the car!' she would suddenly call out as they were driving

Thomas Temperley, 1908

Joseph Daniel Olley and his wife Grace Sarah Temperley on their wedding day, 1921

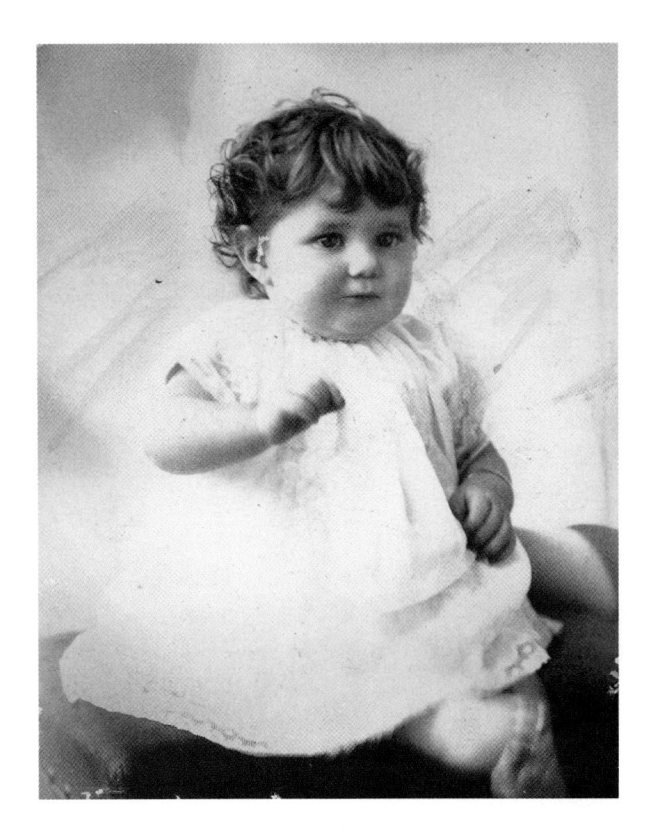

Margaret as a baby, *c.* 1924

Joe Olley with Margaret, Elaine and Ken in Tully, 1920s

Margaret (centre), Ken and Elaine in Murwillumbah, *c.* 1931

Grace Olley rowing Margaret (far left), Elaine and Ken to catch the bus to school in Murwillumbah, *c.* 1932

Margaret on the beach at Magnetic Island

Margaret Cilento and Margaret Olley in their McMahons Point days, Sydney, 1940s

Margaret Cilento in Marseilles, 1949

Donald Friend and Russell Drysdale in Drysdale's studio, Albury, 1942

William Dobell in his studio, 1944

Merioola Group, 1946. Left to right: Arthur Fleischman, Alison Lee, Justin O'Brien, Donald Friend, Loudon Sainthill, Peter Kaiser, Edgar Ritchard, Harry Tatlock Miller, Jocelyn Miller, Chica Lowe, Alec Murray, Roland Strasser

Sir Francis Rose by Cecil Beaton, 1939

Frankie Mitchell working on a ball-gown on a dressmaker's mannequin at his Dowling St, Woolloomooloo studio, *c.* 1950

A painting trip *en plein air* with Moya Dyring in France, in the early 1950s

Fred Jessup, David Strachan and Moya Dyring in Moya's apartment on the Ile St Louis, Paris, in the early 1950s

along. Their father would pull up instantly, thinking an accident had occurred, the children would jerk forward off their seat and Margaret would be out in a flash. It would be because she had spotted 'a find', such as a flower, that she had to have. 'I'm still the same,' she remarks, 'whether it's an old chair, a second-hand straw hat or a lamp from a throw-out. A gatherer.'

These car trips are also associated with a favourite story of Margaret's about Joe Olley:

The roads from Murwillumbah to Lismore were very rough and when we asked my father why he was so bald he said, Oh, I went over a bump and the top of my head stuck to the car. I remember too he was never one for talking about the war, but every Anzac Day he went off marching with his mates, and on our trips through the countryside if we came across the little figure of a soldier on a war memorial near a school or a church, as we passed by we always did a salute to the Anzac.

At Lismore on Fridays all the country people came into town. Many of them, it seemed, were Olleys. As the children made their way in tow with their parents around the big square block of shops, their eyes darting to shop windows displaying unlikely items such as elegant ladies' overcoats with Coney fur collars, striped men's pyjamas or boys' smart, fancy-coloured bowties, they kept running into strangers. Strangers their parents greeted enthusiastically and familiarly. It was both puzzling and embarrassing. Margaret, as a consequence, retains a residual distrust of relatives. Too many of them, she says bluntly.

A visit to the Lismore relatives entailed staying with Uncle Alf and Aunt Rose:

Uncle Alf was my father's eldest brother. He used to sit on their wide veranda, which went all round the house, and smoke a pipe. It was a big house and we all had to help with the chores. No sooner had you finished sweeping the veranda than Uncle Alf would knock his pipe out and say, You missed that. Out the back of the house, oleanders were growing and nearby Aunt Rose kept her chooks. She was a bit rough, Aunt Rose, but she had a heart of gold and wrote the most wonderful letters.

Uncle Alf and Aunt Rose also had a pianola in their parlour. We used to reach down with our small feet – they'd barely reach the pedals – and pedal away. The keys coming up and down were mesmerising. The parlour was filled with souvenirs from Cairo that Uncle Alf had bought when he was away with the war: dreadful tourist memorabilia like the Pyramids painted on velvet, which we children thought were very exotic. The parlour had a funny musty smell, as well, because no one ever really went in there. When visitors came everybody sat on the veranda. Probably they kept the parlour for funerals. We only ventured in ourselves if it was raining. But we did like playing the pianola.

My sister and I slept in a great big bed when we stayed with them. You had to get up on a step to climb into it and the mattress was filled with chicken feathers. It was so soft, you just seemed to sink into it. On the dressing table of the room we slept in was a lock of blonde hair tied up with ribbon, which my mother told us had belonged to Aunt Rose's only daughter, who had died as a baby. The rest of her children were sons. The idea of the dead baby and the lock of hair struck my sister and me as very solemn and sad.

In the Tygalgah days, the Olleys would also motor down to Armidale, in northern New South Wales, to stay with the Wright family at their big property 'Wallamumbi'. Grace Olley's sister Dora was the second wife of Philip Wright, father of the poet Judith Wright. Thanks to Aunt Dora, Margaret has had a long association with Armidale, which continues to this day.

Dora and Philip Wright's own two children, Margaret's cousins

Pollyanne and David, were considerably younger than the Olley children, so in those days they did not have a great deal to do with them. Judith Wright was older than them all and, according to Margaret, seemed 'alienated' and was not fond of her stepmother. Much later on, when Margaret was living in Brisbane, she and Judith did become friendly and Margaret began a portrait of her. Unfortunately, the painting was interrupted and was somehow never resumed.

When the Olleys were at Wallamumbi, it was Aunt Dora who was the centre of attention as far as the children were concerned:

Dora had been a teacher and was rather theatrical. We loved watching her antics. I can still picture her making scones at Wallamumbi. She'd get into a corner of the kitchen and throw the flour high into the air to aerate it and, of course, most of it ended up outside the bowl. She was full of fun and nonsense, but also had very definite ideas. She used to give us boxes of glazed fruit that we'd never eaten or even seen before, and was adamant about drinking dandelion coffee. She was into herbs and always put alfalfa (which is lucerne) on everything she ate. When I was grown up and living in Paris, Dora came over and insisted on covering the lovely French food with her dried-up, grass-like alfalfa. I'm a bit like her now, with the amino acid bag I carry everywhere.

Every Christmas, or just afterwards, the Olleys went camping for a month or six weeks at the beach, usually at Cudgen Headland, where there were wide stretches of sand and a vast expanse of ocean with white foam-capped breakers rolling in. The Olley camp site was on the northern side of an outlet (a little creek that flowed down from the lake), where there were a few houses, including one belonging to the Condong mill, which was often lent to their Uncle Tom Temperley for the holidays. Margaret remembers that when the two families met up at

Christmas, the children would perform plays on the veranda of this house. And there was an Indian greengrocer who would come round selling what he'd grown in the red soil on the hill behind Cudgen Headland, which was ideal for market gardening. He'd bring pineapples, pumpkins and pawpaws that were priced at a penny apiece. 'You cry, you getting; you cry, you getting,' he'd sing out to the children, who would cluster around looking on from a slight distance.

The Olleys were not the only ones camping at Cudgen. Margaret recalls it was like a little tent town, but Joe Olley would always go on ahead of the family and pick out a site where they could be on their own, away from the rest of the campers. Despite this, at night when they sat outside or wandered about, they could see the comforting lights of other tents dotting the darkness and smell their acetylene gas lights, something the Olleys never had.

The Olley camp was very neatly laid out. There was one big tent for sleeping and a kitchen tent, with a fly between them. Hessian was used for floor covering and trenches were dug around the tents to protect against the rain. Camp beds and a dining table were set up. Grace Olley had an early gas cooker with gas cylinders, which she insisted on taking, as well as the primus stoves. The Olleys ate very well. Their festive fare consisted of Christmas cake and puddings in cloth wrapping, which would have been cooked by Grace about a month beforehand, and roast chooks and ducks.

The Christmas pudding was Margaret's favourite. It was tastier than Christmas cake, but there was also the excitement of finding the silver coins her mother had deftly pushed deep into the hot puddings; no family member or visitor ever missed out. The pudding was served with a plain sauce made with a little sugar, butter and flour, which Margaret still prefers to brandy butter. The sauce was beaten up and then boiling water was poured into it, after which it was just slightly cooked on the stove. It did have the appearance of glue, but it was a perfect foil for the rich pudding.

Before the family left for Cudgen, there would be a huge Christmas celebration filled with people, half of whom would be relatives. Presents were homemade – Margaret and Elaine would painstakingly hem bits of torn sheet to transform them into handkerchiefs, then embroider grub roses on the corners. Santa Claus, with a sackful of presents, would be rowed across the river, to the delight of all the children present. But one day, playing around in the box room, the young Olleys discovered the Santa costume. Margaret, being the oldest, thought quickly. 'Let's pretend we've never seen it,' she instructed Elaine and Ken. So Santa's presents continued for another few years, until Grace Olley finally said: 'Now, you two girls are old enough to know about Santa Claus.'

Once Christmas was over, Margaret, Elaine and Ken spent days exploring the beach at Cudgen with their cousins, collecting shells, poking at the ocean's flotsam and jetsam, popping seaweed beads, draping smelly green lengths of seaweed around themselves, marvelling at misshapen sponge hands and fish bones. Every curiosity and treasure the beach yielded fired Margaret's imagination. On their wandering, the children would sometimes cross to the other side of the outlet – on which they found only miles of sandy nothingness. At low tide, there would be people walking along trailing an old dead fish head to catch beach worms for bait; others would collect funny, squirting cunjevoi by a rocky outbreak. It was all fascinating to Margaret.

But the days were scorchingly hot, and they all got very sunburnt. The burning was even worse on overcast days when they least expected it. Ken once had such huge blisters on his shoulder blades that he had to be treated at the 'ambulance tent', which was always set up by one of the other campers. Margaret herself now regularly has skin cancers 'lopped out', as a result of her early sunning.

When it rained at Cudgen, all the tea-trees growing along the little creek turned the water the colour of tea and the dark water would spill out, staining the ocean. Margaret, Elaine, Ken and their cousins loved swimming in the rain at this spot. Once they even came across a platypus that had been washed out in the surf because the creek had filled up. Joe Olley, while being very wary of the mammal's spurs, managed to put it in a kerosene tin full of water. He then drove all the way to Burleigh Heads to hand it over to a man who ran a sanctuary for platypuses.

Of all Margaret's childhood times, the idyllic days spent camping at Cudgen were the happiest and most fun:

Cudgen was such a romantic place, with the creek and the long, beautiful beach. Children now haven't got the freedom to move about like we did at Cudgen and Tygalgah. It was such a busy life. You were completely absorbed in whatever you were doing. It was really like Zen Buddhism. No one ever said they were bored or didn't have anything to do. They were golden days.

3

Forever on the Move

Always moving, things changing all the time – that was our life. Moving was very disruptive and it certainly didn't help my schoolwork – the only thing that glued it together for me were the art classes. I think I'm part gypsy because of all those moves. And we were always discarding. I suppose that's why now I don't want to throw a thing out. So those two different aspects of my early life have governed me.

BACK AT TULLY, THE DAYS WERE FAR FROM GOLDEN. UNCLE Erasmus Temperley was in trouble with the farm, due to the endless Tully rains.[1] The Banyan Creek property had suffered substantial flood damage in the wet season of 1933–34, in which crops and topsoil were lost. Erasmus then mortgaged the property to buy farm implements and fertiliser to work the land up again. But the next wet season brought another inundation, which left Erasmus facing bankruptcy, although the dairy kept going.

In response, in 1936 Joe Olley sold the property at Tygalgah and arrived up in Tully in a big, heavy Chrysler to rescue the cane farm. The rest of the Olley family was also on the move. Grace went to Brisbane, presumably to find a place for them to live, and the children found themselves on their own in Cudgen:

We were left in care with somebody in a boarding house above a shop in Cudgen Headland. Cudgen was where the school bus to Murwillumbah started, so we kept going to school. Of course, as usual we didn't know what our parents were doing. We might have been in Cudgen a week or a fortnight, but it seemed like ages. We felt abandoned, as when my mother had made her trip to Sydney. I know I must have been deeply disturbed or disorientated, because I wet the bed.

The children then joined Grace in Brisbane; whether Joe Olley was back from Tully is uncertain. It was at this time that Margaret's lifelong affection for Brisbane began. Although Sydney has long been her 'spiritual home', she still hankers to be living in Brisbane on visits back there. In 1936, she remembers Brisbane was like 'a sleepy, large town':

The houses had green louvres, white lattice and ironwork and were built on stilts to keep them cool, with roofs going right out over the verandas. It was all very tropical. Frangipani and poincianas grew everywhere. Every house had bananas growing, a mango tree and pawpaws in the garden. You'd hear flying foxes squeaking at night as they flew over looking for fruit to eat. My father had a very good trick for picking pawpaws. He used to get a pole and hammer a tin the size of a pawpaw onto it. Then the tin was put up under the pawpaw you wanted to pick and twisted around so the stalk snapped. The pole was slowly brought down and there was your pawpaw.
  The streets were lined with fig trees. The birds and the flying foxes loved them. Fallen fig berries littered the roads. They lay on the ground, all ripe and rotting, which made their fruity smell even

more pungent. You were more conscious of smells then because there were fewer motor cars. People took trams to get about and used the little ferries when they had to cross the river. We settled into a big house at Annerley and were sent to the Annerley school. Annerley was where I went to the pictures for the first time. The local picture theatre was built out of tin. It had an asphalt floor and canvas chairs. A 'Flash Gordon' serial was running and we were totally taken in by his outer-space adventures.

Another of Brisbane's attractions was Aunt Mary, who now lived nearby. She was the aunt who used to arrive in Tygalgah with suitcases full of gifts and stories of her adventures that kept the children, Margaret especially, wide-eyed with wonder. Her house had a wonderful view over Brisbane and was supported by large tree trunks. The entrance was at street level but because the land dropped away so steeply the house had to be propped up. Inside the house there were more surprises:

Aunt Mary had the first wireless that I ever came in contact with. It had a big horn speaker and a wire called a cat's whisker. It was magical to hear the sound coming out of it. I can always smell nasturtiums when I think of Aunt Mary: she always had a bunch of them in a little blue vase on the table. She was a very keen gardener. When she was visiting people, she'd arrive with a bunch of cuttings to give them. Then, after she'd admired their garden and was about to leave, she'd ask for a few more cuttings to hand on to the next person she dropped in on. She was like a bee spreading the gardens about.

From Annerley we moved to Hendra, where there was a big block of land round the house. I remember the winter was very cold at Hendra. My father used to spend a lot of time sitting on the step thinking. Of course, he never said what was on his mind.

We attended the Hendra school for a little while but I don't think *we liked it, because we changed to the Ascot school. Then there was another upheaval: we moved in with Aunt Mary at Highgate Hill and had to go all the way over to the Ascot school from her place. As a child, you just fit in with whatever's happening and, in our case, it meant an awful lot of shifting about. There was never any time to make friends. I used to envy people who stayed in the same house.*

While Margaret was blessed with loving parents, they did absent themselves for chunks of her childhood. Soon, her mother packed up yet again and the whole family moved back to Tully, except for Margaret, whom Grace Olley decided to send to boarding school.

Her new school was Somerville House, one of Brisbane's best schools, if not *the* best school, for girls. The fees were twenty-two pounds one shilling per quarter, with extras of one pound three and six for drawing, one pound five shillings for dancing and a changeable amount for incidentals, which suggests that the Olley finances were in reasonable shape. (The Commonwealth of Australia basic wage rose to three pounds fifteen shillings per week in 1937; the Queensland state basic wage was a few shillings higher.) But, financial considerations aside, in Brisbane at that time, many middle-class families considered a private secondary school obligatory, following primary state school. And the Olley children certainly never thought of themselves as rich. Nor did Tully have a high school, anyway; if Margaret had returned there she would have had to board at her old school, St Anne's in Townsville.

Margaret was, it seemed, a feisty thirteen-and-a-half-year-old when she arrived in her navy blue Tobralco school uniform at Somerville House in February 1937. She was placed in Form 4B with girls considerably younger than her, which indicates that she had slipped behind with her school work. Artist Margaret Cilento, now a close friend of Margaret's, was a day pupil at Somerville

House when Margaret started there as a boarder. Cilento describes Margaret in her school days as: 'Always rushing around, quite rebellious, doing her own thing. She wasn't particularly academic, so she wasn't interested in any of that.'[2]

Somerville House, on Vulture Street (a name that has been a source of amusement for generations of Brisbane children), is situated on the ridge of a hill in South Brisbane, overlooking the Brisbane River. 'Cumbooquepa', the main house, was built in 1890 by William Stephens, the son of Sir Thomas Blackett Stephens, for his widowed mother, Mrs Anne Stephens. When the house passed out of the Stephens family in 1906, it became a boarding house. Then, in 1919, it was acquired by the Presbyterian and Methodist Schools Association to house the Brisbane High School for Girls, as Somerville House was then known.

Cumbooquepa was, and still is, a surprising school building. The architecture, an adaptation of Victorian Italianate, is highly decorative. The house is built of red brick and the façade has light-coloured rendered ornamentation, which looks a bit like icing on a cake. Nothing could have been further, visually, from the cane fields of Tully or the Tweed Valley than its arches, colonnades and parapets, not to mention the small tower atop it all, although two tall palm trees in the front garden did maintain a tropical touch.

The dim vestibule of the main house has stained-glass windows, depicting six characters from Shakespeare's plays, above a black and white chequered marble floor. It's an impressive entrance. According to school mythology, girls who had been naughty were sometimes banished to the vestibule and would count the tiles as they stood out their punishment. Through a breezeway is the wainscoted dining room with more stained-glass windows and two massive sideboards (in Margaret's era there may have been even more intimidating furniture), which take up almost the whole of one wall. This is where boarders like Margaret ate off thick white china embellished with the royal blue school badge. Although they attended the same classes, the boarders inhabited a world that felt quite separate from that of the day girls, which must have added to the underlying sense of displacement Margaret was experiencing at the time.

The school itself was started by an independent-minded English woman called Miss Eliza Fewings in 1899. After ten years, Miss Fewings sold the school to the acting principal, Miss Constance Harker, and her friend Miss Marjorie Jarrett. These two academically qualified and formidably sized women then became co-principals. In 1918 'the ladies', as the two women were known, sold the school to the Presbyterian and Methodist Schools Association. 'The ladies', however, along with their cat, Peter, and a parrot called Archie, continued to reign over the school until 1931, when Miss Harker retired. After her retirement, Miss Harker continued to live at Somerville House, while Miss Jarrett, at whose ample waist a large bunch of keys always jangled, was in sole charge:

Miss Jarrett had a huge bosom. Her hair was done up in a bun and she wore pince-nez glasses. At meal times, she would put on an apron, pull herself up straight and stand at the table sharpening her knife. The school girls would be looking up at her expectantly and she'd look back imperiously over the top of her pince-nez glasses. Miss Jarrett excelled at carving. She could carve a huge chunk of meat into paper-thin slices. Broiled beef, I think the meat was, and it tasted like shoe leather.

As for the school itself, Margaret loved the old building where her dormitory was:

We slept on the veranda of the original house. The veranda wasn't closed in, it had louvres installed. I don't think they were ever opened, but the draught came through, anyway. Miss Jarrett, who slept in the dormitory to keep an eye on us, had a pet parrot. She would walk past us boarders to the bathroom, taking the parrot with her. Of course, we'd all be peeping out at this big-breasted apparition in a dressing gown with a parrot on her shoulder. Miss Jarrett and the parrot used to kiss, and it could speak French.

Miss Jarrett's regimen outside the dormitories soon proved difficult for Margaret:

I was constantly getting into trouble for what seemed to me trivial offences and as punishment my hatband was removed, so I had to walk in the crocodile down the hill to church in my white church dress and a Panama hat that had no band. But I regarded it as a badge of honour.

Margaret's tendency to rebel and be proud of doing so may well have been a cover-up for an adolescent shyness that was beginning to assail her, as well as an assertion of independence. But although she may have masked any interior diffidence this way, she also began to suffer from an external malady that could not be so easily disguised:

While I was at boarding school I developed hay fever. It was so bad I used to feel like getting a knife and chopping my nose off. I was sent along to have a series of injections, which showed I was allergic to grass seeds, pollen, old clothes, house dust, carpets, virtually every kind of dust. This meant I had to endure the stigma of joining 'the bed-wetters'. The bed-wetters had waterproof sheeting over their mattresses. Since I was allergic to dust, my mattress and also my pillow had to have the same waterproof covering. Children are very cruel and I copped quite a bit of taunting because of my hay fever.

Not only did I join the bed-wetters, but the matron, Miss Nutting, whom I detested and who detested me, because I was the naughtiest boarder, put me in the worst bed in the school, right next to where Miss Jarrett slept, with only a heavy, dark green felt curtain separating us. So then I really had to behave myself. In another attempt to cure my hay fever, I was told to go along and have my nose cauterised. I can still smell the flesh burning. But the worst thing was Miss Nutting watching the procedure. I felt sure it was giving her pleasure, so I willed the pain to go to her. After that I always willed any pain I might be having, at the dentist or wherever, to go to her. It was how I coped.

Apart from such disadvantages, Somerville House did have its compensations:

Every morning, we assembled before school in a big room; about halfway down the walls of either side there were two easels. On these were put some Medici prints that the school owned. It was the first time I'd ever seen really good prints. There were two in particular I remember: a Degas of a group of dancers with their ballet teacher, which has a marvellous sense of design,[3] and another of the Gauguin painting of a white horse standing in a pool with big white lilies.[4] I didn't care what was being said at assembly. I used to lose myself in those prints, the same way I used to get carried away in the beautiful lavatory at Tully overlooking Banyan Creek, watching the various bottlebrushes and the big blue butterflies. I just daydreamed away.

But Medici prints were not all Somerville House had to offer. At the school Margaret encountered Caroline Barker. Barker was her art teacher and the person who would change Margaret's life:

Caroline Barker was a tiny woman. She wore glasses and her hair was plaited at the back and came up round her head like a coronet. She was prim and quaint, like a little bird, but so enthusiastic. She could go into peals of laughter at the drop of a hat; she was a free spirit who really stood out from all the serious people at school. Her skill was to get you interested in things. She wasn't a great painter herself, although she had exhibited in the Salon in Paris, but she had a twinkling spark, and that spark really inspired you. Later on, at Somerville House, she taught the artist Ann Thomson, and Betty Churcher, who had so much to do with Australian art. Even Philip Bacon, my agent, had lessons with Caroline Barker.

We were taught French by a Miss George. Miss George was a house mistress, which meant she used to take us for preparation after dinner at night. Looking back on it, I think she must have been a frustrated artist, because she most generously gave a lot of art books to the library at Somerville House. But, strangely, she also had it in for any girl who showed a leaning towards the arts. She used to pick on me – I don't know why, but she did – and on Margaret Cilento.

Because Miss George was picking on me, I went to see Miss Jarrett, the headmistress, in her parlour and said I'd had a letter from my mother, who had agreed I should drop French and take an extra art lesson with Caroline Barker. Miss Jarrett never even asked to see the letter, which, needless to say, didn't exist. But as a consequence I took an extra art lesson, dropped French and Caroline Barker became my mentor. So, in a way, I preordained my destiny. You could say I was manipulative even then, in that I knew what I wanted to do – which was to participate more in the art classes. I was not, however, at all filled with a great aspiration to be an artist. I just liked drawing and painting.

Born in 1894 to a businessman father and artist mother, Caroline Barker grew up in Melbourne. Not only did her mother paint, there was a family lineage of artists going back to the famous eighteenth-century English enameller and miniature painter Henry Bone. In 1912 Barker enrolled at the National Gallery of Victoria Art School, where her tutors included Frederick McCubbin, who taught drawing. Among her fellow students were Adelaide Perry, Marion Jones and McCubbin's own daughter Sheila, who all went on to be recognised artists. When the Barker family moved to Brisbane in 1920 Barker took the position of art mistress at Ipswich Girls' Grammar School. Having left Australia in 1923 she became a pupil at London's famous Byam Shaw School of Art. Before she returned to Australia in 1926, her painting *Delphiniums* was accepted by the Paris Salon.

When Barker was back in Brisbane, her sister, Agnes Richardson, remembers that their mother used to call Caroline 'a bed and breakfast boarder', referring to her customary habit of leaving home as soon as she'd finished breakfast to paint in her studio and only returning on the last tram at night.[5] In 1935 she began teaching art at Somerville House, where artist Vida Lahey had also earlier taught and where, by Margaret's last year at school, a special art studio would have been built for pupils.

By the late 1930s, as well as teaching at Somerville House and other schools, Barker gave lessons in a studio she'd acquired in George Street, in the centre of Brisbane. The studio was a huge room that had been a dance studio and for many years to come it would be an artistic hub. It had tall windows down one side and was set up with antique furniture, including a chaise longue, cedar chiffonier and miscellaneous chairs. Potted ferns contributed to the look of a salon and numerous paintings were in evidence, both hanging on the walls and stacked against them. Spiritualism was another of Barker's interests and sometimes in the George Street studio, according to Margaret Cilento, there would be special music playing, which Barker implied brought the spirits around.

The studio was a meeting place for both Brisbane locals and artists from interstate, especially during the war years when servicemen and women from overseas flocked there. Later, when she gave up the studio in town, Barker still gave lessons underneath her own old Queensland house in Coorparoo, which she had turned into a studio. Barker never married; art, her own paintings and those of her students, more than filled her life, Agnes Richardson says.

Margaret believes that, though the seeds of her love of painting were sown earlier on, it was Barker who nurtured her talent. With Barker's encouragement she began painting in oils, which, as she says, 'was a big breakthrough'. She remembers in particular two of her early efforts under Barker's tutelage: a painting of some blue flowers with yellow berries and one of the exterior of the school library. But there was more to it than that. Barker was the first truly artistic person Margaret had ever known, and although she never had lessons with Barker outside school, she did visit the George Street studio, where she was struck by its unusual atmosphere:

She used to have soirées and there were always mysterious people in attendance. I remember her telling me about one of her friends, who had great empathy with people with illnesses. The friend would sit in the tram opposite someone and he would actually feel whatever illness the person had. Those sorts of stories make a big impression on you when you're young.

It was through Barker's classes at Somerville House school, too, that Margaret's friendship with Margaret Cilento really began:

Margaret, whose little sister grew up to be the actress Diane Cilento, was a year ahead of me at Somerville House, even though we're virtually the same age, because I was so behind with school work. The school magazine was always full of her drawing and I'd watch her when we had sport. Margaret was a great hurdler. I didn't really have much to do with sport – apart from throwing basketball goals – so Caroline Barker's art classes became a link between us.

Margaret Cilento, the daughter of the well-known Brisbane doctors Lady Phyllis and Sir Raphael Cilento, had started at Somerville House in 1935 as a day pupil (which was probably another reason for the initial lack of contact between the two Margarets). Cilento, who, by her own account, was already fully determined at that age to be an artist, remembers with gratitude Barker's 'championing' of them in art classes.

According to Agnes Richardson, Barker was impressed by both Margarets' artistic abilities. Richardson recalls her coming home from teaching at Somerville House and saying: 'I've got two clever girls in the class. I can't get over it, two wonderful girls, and they're going to be marvellous artists. One's Margaret Olley and the other's Margaret Cilento. It's not often you have two that are so good.' Richardson also remembers Barker saying that the Olley family had no idea how clever their daughter really was. So it's possible that Caroline Barker had her eye on Margaret's talent much more intently in the Somerville House days than Margaret herself ever realised.

Although Margaret was now a teenager she was not, as yet, interested in the opposite sex; not that there would have been much opportunity for dallying with boys in her present situation:

As a school girl, I would occasionally get crushes. It's a way of admiring people and has nothing to do with the sexual urge. My first sexual experience with a boy took place playing a game like doctors and nurses with other children at the Tweed. It was very innocent – I suppose you could call it a bit of experimenting. At Somerville House, we were all too busy with school work to be thinking about boys. There were some girls who were referred to as 'very fast' but I don't know what they got up to. They were just 'very fast'.

Caroline Barker and her art classes at Somerville House were increasingly Margaret's sole – and soul – sanctuary. Although

Aunt Mary used to visit Margaret at school, there was not much other family contact. Some holidays she spent with a girl from her class on her parents' property out of Bundaberg; only once or twice a year she made the two-and-a-half-day-long train haul home to Tully:

They were very creaky, comfortable old trains, all made of wood with leather seats. Right at the end of the carriages was the observation car with swivel chairs for watching the miles of landscape. You'd buy a ticket for either the dining car or a restaurant at one of the stations. We'd stop at every station along the line; some were famous for their lunches, one, in particular, was renowned for its fish. It was a big industry for the little towns. As the train drew into the station, the waitresses were waiting in their starched caps and aprons, with folded laundered napkins and iced water ready.

At night a bunk was pulled down in the carriage and that's where you slept. The train would arrive at Townsville at breakfast time on the third day. It stayed long enough for you to either walk down to the town or have a shower. I always chose a shower. After you left Townsville, the landscape became really tropical and I couldn't wait for us to pull in at Tully's little station.

Once, when I was due to come back down to Brisbane, my father, a great one for observing nature, said, Ah, Grace, I think she'd better leave a week earlier, the ants are trying to get into the sugar bins. In other words, rain was on the way. When ants start coming into your house, you know there is long rain ahead, and once the Burdekin River on the other side of Townsville overflowed its banks the trains couldn't get through. So I was packed off back to school early, much to my annoyance.

Joe Olley himself did not stay much longer in Tully either. Once he had worked up the cane farm sufficiently, it was sold and the dairy was shifted to leased land. Joe then returned to

Brisbane, leaving Grace, Elaine and Ken in Tully living in a rented house right in town, at Grace's insistence. A buyer was then found for the dairy, and Erasmus and Gertrude moved south to Brisbane. But the buyer defaulted and Erasmus returned once again to run the dairy, until a riding accident, in which he broke a leg, put an end to any active role he could take in it.

By 1939 all Olleys and Temperleys had returned to Brisbane. Coincidentally, as the Olleys were settling back, an extraordinarily large collection of contemporary French and British art was making its way across the ocean to Australia. The exhibition was chosen by the art critic Basil Burdett, who worked for Melbourne's *Herald*, and was funded by Sir Keith Murdoch. Burdett's selection of over two hundred paintings and sculptures, many of which were for sale, included paintings by artists who would later have enormous impact on Margaret's own work: Matisse, Vuillard, Bonnard and Cézanne. There were also eight original Gauguins, which one imagines would have been thrilling for her to see. Works by Picasso and Salvador Dali added a more avant-garde note. The exhibition first went on show at the National Art Gallery of South Australia on 21 August 1939.

The *Herald* exhibition, which arrived at the Melbourne Town Hall in mid October 1939, was for many years celebrated as Australia's introduction to modern art. Although it has recently been revealed that this view was more myth than reality, nevertheless for many Australians, artists and otherwise, the exhibition did offer a unique chance to experience modern European art at first hand. It caused an enormous ruckus among conservative art devotees. The director of the National Gallery of Victoria, John Stuart MacDonald, who coined the phrase 'degenerates and perverts' to describe the exhibiting artists, was an especially vocal detractor.

The exhibition came to Sydney in late November 1939. Charles Lloyd Jones, who was the board chairman of David

Jones, a keen art supporter and a National Art Gallery of New South Wales trustee, organised for it to be displayed on the sixth floor of the David Jones George Street store – a space not normally used as a gallery – for a reduced rental. But another trustee, the sixty-five-year-old traditional painter Lionel Lindsay, was so incensed by the show that he wrote a book attacking modern art, entitled *Addled Art*.

On the other side of the world, a far more ominous conflict had begun. On 1 September Germany had invaded Poland. Three days later Britain and France were at war with Germany, and Australia had soon joined them. The escalation of the war in Europe made it difficult for the *Herald* exhibition to be shipped home in 1940, so many of the works remained in Australia until 1945. Fifty-two of the works finally reached Brisbane and were shown at the Queensland Art Gallery in 1945. However strangely Margaret seems never to have seen them and regrettably the state galleries did not avail themselves of the opportunity to purchase the more major works by artists such as Bonnard and Picasso during this period.

Back in 1939, the hostilities in Europe seemed very distant to sixteen-year-old Margaret:

I knew the war was on. It was a dreadful thought, but it didn't affect our lives at school, where Elaine had now joined me as a day pupil. I continued to board because my mother wisely decided that it would be too unsettling for me to change to being a day girl. The war, however, did have one rather unexpected consequence for our family. My father had started buying property – houses, I think – round Brisbane. But then my Aunt Mary said, Get out of property, the war's coming. Go on the land. My father listened to her, unfortunately, and bought a cane farm outside Brisbane, which turned out to be a bad mistake.

Round about this time, my mother with her money bought a big house up on stilts in Westbourne Street, Highgate Hill, which became our new home. It had a beautiful view of the city and was very close to Aunt Mary's house. My mother also made another real estate purchase – 'Farndon'. Farndon was an old schoolhouse (a private school, I think) on Morry Street that had been turned into flats. It was built on a large block bounded by three streets, just a street back from the Brisbane River and the old Hill End ferry wharf. Underneath Farndon was where I would have my Brisbane studio, more than a decade later. But back then, as soon as mother bought it, Uncle Erasmus, Aunt Gertrude and my Aunt Mary moved in. They were all installed in a flat upstairs about the size of half the house.

At the beginning of 1940 about forty works from the original *Herald* exhibition were hung at the National Art Gallery of New South Wales. Six months later, as this smaller exhibition selection was being taken down from the gallery's walls, Margaret, then in Form 5B, was also packing up her belongings at school. By July 1940, just after her seventeenth birthday, she had left Somerville House for good, without having sat for her Junior Exam.

What to do next was not immediately obvious to Margaret. Although her artistic talent was so clearly apparent to Caroline Barker, Margaret is adamant that it had not entered her own head to be an artist. Nor, it would seem, had it entered the head of anyone else in the family. Grace Olley was certainly aware that Margaret loved drawing – she'd known that since Margaret first started school. But she had not envisaged her elder daughter making a career out of art. Studying art was not the most predictable or desirable path for a middle-class young woman at the best of times, let alone in the midst of a war that seemed to be getting closer to home all the time.

But then Caroline Barker took a hand in settling Margaret's future:

My mother was hell-bent on making me a nurse as she had been. I would have killed people if I had been a nurse. Mercifully it didn't happen. The matron at St Martin's Hospital said, Oh, take her away and bring her back in a year's time. That's when fate stepped in. Since I'd been rejected as a nurse, my mother went along to Caroline Barker and asked her what she thought I should do.

Send her to the tech, Caroline Barker said.

And so Grace Olley did just that. Whether Barker in any way orchestrated the meeting with Grace will never be known. But Barker, once consulted, certainly tipped the balance in favour of art as far as Margaret's immediate future was concerned. Margaret was pleased with this turn of events because it meant she'd be blissfully drawing and painting full-time. Or so she thought.

The Brisbane Central Technical College where Margaret enrolled was right at the bottom of George Street, past the solid grandeur of Queensland Parliament House and the white wrought-iron veranda tiers of the Bellevue Hotel opposite. The college was also close to the Botanic Gardens, where there were inviting clumps of tropical foliage and cages filled with monkeys and birds. Because of the war, most able-bodied people were beginning to disappear into the army, so there was a smaller than usual number of pupils, and possibly of teachers, at the college, which also provided courses in subjects such as building and chemistry.

At the art school itself, Margaret's expectations were to meet a rude awakening:

The art school was dreadful. I hated it. Before I went it had been run by Martyn Roberts. Then a man called Cyril Gibbs took over. Gibbs had gained his numerous diplomas mainly by doing night courses. His real forte was airbrush and advertising. I just wasn't interested in the way they taught. It was all a bit constipated. We were made to use very sharp pencils and do tight little drawing on Watmans paper. There were only models about once a week, if at all, as far as I remember. Occasionally we used to go and sketch the boats moored out at Breakfast Creek. That was one of the very few things I enjoyed – I've always loved the sculptural shape of boats.

As an act of rebellion, I took myself off to Ball's, a large paper wholesaler, and bought reams of butcher's paper. I also purchased a big bag of burnt sienna or raw umber. I used to pin the paper up, dip my hand into the bag of colour and do big loose drawings, with my hand. This was the only way I could buck the system. In their eyes I was being absolutely rebellious and they hated it.

The only teacher who inspired me was Maria Corrie, who taught us modelling. Maria Corrie was probably the only real art teacher there. She was a sculptor herself, and had a small studio in the same building as Caroline Barker in George Street. I think I had a bit of a student crush on her because she was young and energetic, especially compared to the rest of them, who were so stuffy.

Maria Corrie, a serene-looking young woman said to have had a strong sense humour, was born in Melbourne but grew up in Brisbane.[6] As a schoolgirl at St Margaret's she was known for her talent in drawing and for carving the tops of pencils – often in the form of miniature devils – during French lessons.[7] A scholarship win enabled her to study art in Melbourne; after which she returned to Brisbane and began teaching. Corrie was, in fact, only three years older than Margaret, so it's easy to see how she might have become a heroine for Margaret, longing as she was for any sign of life in a stultified regime.

Outside the Brisbane Central Technical College, two other women had been tirelessly campaigning for art in a very public way for some years in Brisbane. They were painter and educator Vida Lahey and sculptor Daphne Mayo. Lahey, as an artist, was mostly known for her watercolours of flowers, while the younger

Mayo's commissioned works included friezes in the new City Hall, the Queensland Women's War Memorial, Anzac Square and the Stations of the Cross for the Church of the Holy Spirit in New Farm.

Prior to 1930, when it moved to new premises in the Exhibition Building, the Queensland Art Gallery in Brisbane had been at a standstill. The collection, as Mayo later described it, was 'housed in a long tunnel-like room in the Executive Buildings, the walls of which bristled with large and mostly gloomy pictures, which hung one above the other almost to the ceiling, the monotony of which had not been disturbed by the acquisition of a new work for many years'.[8]

In 1929 Lahey and Mayo, who'd both returned from studying abroad, started the Queensland Art Fund in an attempt to lift the art gallery out of the doldrums by purchasing overseas art works. The following year, through the Fund, they organised for an exhibition of Australian artists' works from the southern states to be shown in Brisbane, and held a carnival on the roof of Brisbane's new City Hall to help finance it. Then, with money raised from the exhibition, the Queensland Art Fund bought works by four contemporary Australian artists – Elioth Gruner, Nora Heysen, Arthur Murch and Robert Johnson – for the Queensland Art Gallery.

In October 1936, with Lahey's and Mayo's keen support, the Queensland Art Library was opened. For the first time ever, Brisbane had a proper art reference library. It was situated in the Old Railways Building in Police Court Lane, off George Street. As well as two hundred books and thirty-four large reproductions of famous paintings, the collection had two thousand photographs of art works, and immediately became the favourite haunt of art students like Francis Lymburner, whose world would interconnect with Margaret's in a few years.

Margaret had no real contact with Lahey and Mayo in her

student days, except for distant sightings of Lahey at openings of the Royal Queensland Art Society, but they were shaping the Brisbane art world in which Margaret, two decades on, would have such personal artistic triumph. Certainly, Margaret's later role as a benefactor can be seen as continuing the spirit of Lahey and Mayo.

Margaret's name was mentioned twice in the Technical College examination results for 1940, with passes in freehand drawing and modelling.[9] By the start of 1941, her first full year as an art student, Japan and Australia were officially at war. This was to become a tumultuous year all round for the Olleys. Not only was Margaret struggling to come to terms with classes at the Central Technical College, as the Second World War continued the Olley family finances, or at least her father's share of them, were thrown into disarray:

My father had lent somebody money to buy into a restaurant called Craigmore in the centre of Lismore. The man must have been a con artist and seen my father coming, because he proceeded to run up vast debts in my father's name. I think the money was spent equipping another restaurant. So then both my parents had to go down to Lismore and take over Craigmore. It was more of a café than a restaurant really. It sold fish and chips, milkshakes, the usual run of old-fashioned food. Neither of my parents had ever done anything like that before. It must have been quite a challenge, especially for my mother, who, I think, probably bore the brunt of it.

I was left to look after my brother and sister in Brisbane. Elaine was still at Somerville House and my brother was going to a school in South Brisbane. So as well as being at art school, I was running the domestics, cooking and cleaning for the family. Elaine helped, but it was a big four-bedroom house.

Round about this time, too, something had gone wrong with the cane farm my father had bought outside Brisbane. He decided to sell the farm and ended up having a court case over it. My father lost the court case and everything that he had ever made and worked for. He was left with nothing. Fortunately, our home and Farndon, the block of flats in which my Uncle Erasmus and Aunt Gertrude and Aunt Mary were still living, were in my mother's name.

It was not a good time for Margaret, either. 'I really hated that Brisbane Tech,' she recalls with passion. One exam time she was given such low marks that a number of the students, herself included, decided that the results must have been rigged. According to Margaret they indignantly marched up to the Education Department offices in the old Treasury Building and demanded a recount. But their protests were given very short shrift. 'This is war time,' an Education Department employee said to them. 'If I hear another word out of you I'll close the art school.'

Despite this Margaret managed to score a credit in modelling, stage two, and passes in geometric drawing two and painting one, in the exams at the end of 1941.[10] The war had assumed a worrying seriousness for all Australians by then. Rationing of food and clothing was in place. Silk stockings, previously taken for granted as a female accessory, became an almost unattainable luxury. Even women's make-up was affected: lipstick shades with patriotic names like Victory Red appeared at cosmetic counters and customers were urged to buy refills rather than new compacts, so the metal could be saved for cartridge cases.

Brisbane women turned their hands to making brooches out of bread. They'd mix up a dough and mould it into flowers, usually poinsettias. These were then painted and, with safety pins inserted at the back, sold as jewellery. Since imported costume jewellery was unavailable during the war, there was quite a demand for the bread-flower brooches. Poker work was another popular home industry. Everywhere you went in Brisbane during the war, according to Margaret, you'd see bread boards with poinsettias burnt into them.

More dramatically, Brisbane soon filled up with American servicemen, many of them black Americans. Even Margaret's Somerville House would soon be emptied of schoolgirls and American military personnel installed in their place. Then in January 1942, ten days or so before her exam results were published in the *Courier Mail*, Margaret's own father enlisted in the Citizens Military Force, or CMF.

The CMF, also known as the Militia, was essentially concerned with Australia's home defence and could not fight overseas. However, during the Second World War, several of its units did distinguish themselves away from Australia, in New Guinea, which was then an Australian territory. Joe Olley, who was now in his mid fifties, seems to have spent a great deal of the twenty-odd months he served in and out of hospital at the 101 Convalescent Depot, Coorparoo, not far from his own home, according to Defence Service Records. He was officially discharged as medically unfit, myocardial degeneration being given as the cause, in September 1943.

Joe would have worn an army uniform and, normally, would have slept with his unit. But since most of the time, when not sick, he appears to have been stationed in Brisbane, he may have been able to spend nights at home. Certainly no one regarded him as being in any danger, according to Margaret. The younger Olleys, or Margaret at least, were now conditioned to their father's absences and went on with life as best they could:

The rest of us left Westbourne Street and went to live in one of the flats that Mother owned in Farndon. Westbourne Street was rented out to American officers and, because I knew the house, I was offered a job as cleaner, which earned me a bit of money. I also did some voluntary work in the American canteen. I couldn't believe the size of the meals they ate before going off to work. I felt such huge meals were a wicked waste of food.

I hadn't really paid that much attention to the war before. But you couldn't avoid it once the Americans came. There were so many of them in Brisbane. They were so neat and starched in their uniforms and they got all the girls. Once you left Queen Street and went over the Victoria Bridge into South Brisbane, where we were living at Farndon, you were in the Negro area, where all the black American servicemen were. I remember it as being very lively.

We went over to Coolangatta one holidays. The family had rented a house at Kirra Beach. Coolangatta was also packed with American soldiers. They all drank Coca-Cola and apparently used to put an aspirin in it to get high. Wherever the Americans went they had their music and the first time I ever heard big band music like Artie Shaw's was at Coolangatta. I'll never forget it — it was the most exciting music. Listening to that on a hot summer's day was quite an experience.

Kirra Beach was also where Margaret wrecked her knees roller skating. A rough wooden skating ramp had been built out on the sand. The Americans were there, music was playing and Margaret was skating away enthusiastically when she fell and hurt one knee. But instead of stopping, she kept skating with her good leg straight and the injured knee bent. Then she had another fall and hurt the good leg. Consequently she had to be carried home by two American soldiers — a circumstance she seems to have rather enjoyed. However, that was the end of skating and her knees, as Margaret says, with a touch of regret.

Grace Olley, it would appear, was in her element during these war years, as she threw herself into helping others. Margaret remembers that relatives always seemed to be coming to stay, and friends passing through Brisbane frequently arrived on the Olley doorstep. There were beds all over the house and her mother seemed to be constantly cooking. Grace no doubt saw this hospitality as part of her very minor contribution to the war effort, but Margaret says her mother also loved having the people around.

Margaret herself was reluctantly coerced into more organised support for the troops:

Every Saturday I was seconded into the Trocadero dance hall near the South Brisbane railway station to make camouflage nets. We were given great rolls of chicken wire into which we had to weave long strips of hessian soaked in khaki-coloured brown or green paint with a bit of oil in them so they wouldn't rot. The paint on the hessian was still moist and it had an awful smell. We wove yards and yards of any sort of pattern that would do for camouflage. As soon as we finished one roll it was wound up and we started on another.

Aunt Mary, who felt I should be participating more, also had me knitting socks for the soldiers, but I could never turn the heels.

On the whole, life just meant existing in wartime. Umbrellas were one of the many things you couldn't get hold of. I used to borrow everyone else's umbrellas. Then I'd forget to bring them home. When we were down to the last umbrella in the house, I asked my mother if I could borrow it. Yes, but please don't lose it, she pleaded. Of course, I left it on the tram again.

⋄

Maria Corrie's classes were still the only high point at the Brisbane Central Technical College as far as Margaret was concerned. Following Corrie's example, Margaret and another girl decided they would take up sculpture in earnest. They rented a studio in the city and diligently laboured away, modelling a dog – a golden retriever – out of clay. The appeal of modelling to Margaret was simply that she liked the look and feel of things 'in the round', as she puts it. But what Corrie was instilling, or encouraging, in her was a sense of form. That sense of form, when later translated into her painting, would be one of Margaret's great strengths as an artist.

There's a shocking addendum involving Maria Corrie tucked away in artist Donald Friend's diaries.[11] Friend met Corrie a few years after Margaret's time at college, when he visited Caroline Barker's sketch club in Brisbane, after Corrie had been working as a war artist. According to Friend, who was himself in the army at that time, 'a vandalising mole' had broken into Corrie's studio, smashed statues and taken away her nude drawings. The drawings were then pasted to the walls of army latrines and 'filthy' remarks scrawled across them. Rather than the culprit being punished, as Friend reports it, Maria was confined to what he calls a 'mental ward' in an army hospital before being discharged with the threat that her Austrian fiancé would be interned if she went to the press about any of this.

The incident, even if exaggerated in Friend's retelling, is a reminder of how appallingly artistic pursuits can be denigrated or misunderstood, not only in Brisbane then but at any time.

In proof of Margaret's early attraction to sculpture, at the end of 1942 two of her modelling works were accepted for the junior section of the Royal Queensland Art Society's 54th Annual Exhibition: *Man Power* and *Public Servant*. (Perhaps the latter exorcised some of the feelings she harboured about her teachers at college.) An entry by Margaret Cilento, entitled *Diane*, presumably of her sister, was also included in the same junior section.

This exhibition would seem to be the first time Margaret's work was shown in public. It should have been an exciting, memorable occasion, but Margaret's dislike of her time at the Brisbane Central Technical College – a 'disturbed period', as she sums it up – was such that over the years she's managed to blot out the memory even of seemingly significant events like this. The exhibition was a big show: over two hundred works were displayed, and the adult section included paintings by established artists like Vida Lahey, who had three watercolours hanging. There were also six sculptures by Maria Corrie on view. Grace Olley must have been proud to see her daughter's efforts among such a collection.

In her exams at the end of 1942 Margaret gained another credit in modelling, stage three, and also in perspective drawing two.[12] She had now endured two and a half years of the Brisbane Central Technical College and must have been chafing at the bit to pursue her studies in a more fulfilling manner. It may also have been a convenient moment at which to move on, as she'd completed a sufficient number of preliminary courses to begin the Advanced Diploma Course at the East Sydney Technical College. Grace Olley must have fully realised by this time that Margaret was never going to follow in her nursing footsteps. Given all of the above, it seems Grace did not need any prompting to seek out Caroline Barker's opinion again about Margaret's future art studies:

Send her down to the Sydney Tech, Caroline Barker said.

My mother must have seen how unhappy I was at art school. Looking back at it now, I realise she was very advanced in her thinking. A lot of people wouldn't have wanted their daughter to leave home at such a young age. I know my other relatives used to think I was a bit wild. Looking at nude models was considered a bit risqué, to say the least. In those days, being an artist was something nice people didn't do. But my mother was always supportive of me.

Going down to Sydney did mean I was away from my family

again, but there was nothing new about that. Elaine went her way, too. She became a nurse. After that she went overseas; she married while she was away and then had a family back here. My brother, when he finally finished school, went into the bee business and made his life in Brisbane. We all took different paths. But it was like heaven on a stick when I came down to Sydney and I will always be eternally grateful to Caroline Barker and my mother – especially my mother – for their encouragement of this.

4
Life Begins

East Sydney Tech was where my life began. I was like a flower that had suddenly been fertilised or pollinated. This was what I had been waiting for my whole life. It was where friendships started that lasted lifetimes. I just loved the environment at tech. In Brisbane I had had all those allergies. When I came down to Sydney they completely disappeared. They do say that hay fever and similar ailments are partly psychosomatic.

FIVE FOOT FOUR, WITH SHOULDER-LENGTH DARK HAIR THAT LIT up red in the sun and beautifully shaped eyes that gazed quizzically out – perhaps her best feature – Margaret arrived in Sydney in February 1943 to begin her studies at the art school of East Sydney Technical College, where the classes were held behind the sandstone walls of the convict-built, former Darlinghurst Gaol.[1] Although in her own mind she was 'plain and plump', the artistic circles in which she quickly blossomed (and soon the press as well) described Margaret's particular beauty as Renoir-like. She was nineteen and a half. Unsophisticated and unused to

Life Begins

the ways of artists and bohemians, except for the smatterings of unconventionality she'd picked up at art school in Brisbane, Margaret was nevertheless very eager to begin the biggest adventure of her life.

In wartime Sydney, blackout cloth had gone up on bare windows; barbed wire had been unwound across Bondi Beach to repel invaders and the populace had cowered under tables – a recommended safety measure – when Japanese submarines complete with torpedoes dared to enter Sydney Harbour the preceding May.

In the art world, too, there were hostilities. First, there was disagreement between those who upheld traditional practices and those who espoused a more modern approach to art. Second, there were distinct and conflicting art movements in Sydney and Melbourne – they being the only two cities to which much real attention was paid in Australia at the time.

Although individual artists had been painting in a modernist style since the 1920s, the art establishment, particularly the trustees and directors of both state galleries – like the reactionary James Stuart MacDonald, who'd served terms as director at both – tended to be older, blinkered conservatives. In Sydney, many of the early modernists were women, such as Grace Crowley, Dorrit Black and Grace Cossington Smith, all of whom had travelled or studied overseas. The more senior Margaret Preston was another Sydney artist who forthrightly championed modernism, not only in her own graphic works, but also in support of others. Men who painted in a modernist manner in Sydney included Roland Wakelin, Roy de Maistre and Rah Fizelle. Cubist influences, such as geometric forms and bright colour, were characteristic of the group as a whole. Sunny modernists, you might call them. Despite the objections to modern art raised by those in high places, Sydney modernists and more traditional landscape and portrait artists usually painted alongside one another without too much spatting.

Then, in the late 1930s and early 1940s, young Melbourne artists, chiefly Sidney Nolan, Albert Tucker, Arthur Boyd, John Perceval, the Jewish Josl Bergner and the older, Russian-born Danila Vassilieff, began producing paintings that were more confronting in subject matter and style than their Sydney counterparts. Prettiness in art, particularly the pastoral paintings of Australia's past, was not their objective. They were modernists with attitude and the art critic Robert Hughes would later dub their era – the years 1937 to 1947 – the 'angry decade'.[2] Tucker's series of thirty-five paintings, *Images of Modern Evil* (later renamed *Night Images*), painted between 1943 and 1946, with its lurid combination of bizarre surrealism and familiar scenes of Melbourne at night such as the promenade and tramline at St Kilda, and Nolan's Ned Kelly paintings, especially of 1947, are famous examples of the edginess of the Melbourne painters.

With a few exceptions, notably Sam Atyeo, pure abstraction in art had not yet taken hold. The newer Melbourne artists were supported in their endeavours by the art collectors John and Sunday Reed, who drew artists, especially Nolan, into a close circle of friendship.

In contrast, Sydney artists of the early 1940s like Douglas Dundas, Elaine Haxton, Jean Bellette, Paul Haefliger and Arthur Murch, who were promoted in the publications of painter, etcher, editor and publisher Sydney Ure Smith, might generally be described as less socially concerned and stylistically more romantic. The difference between Melbourne and Sydney art continued throughout the 1940s. Emerging Sydney-based artists, such as David Strachan (originally from Victoria, anyway), Justin O'Brien and even Margaret herself would produce works that were seen as softer, or perhaps subtler, than the gutsy Melbourne painters. This in turn led Hughes to tag them 'the Charm School', a title now regarded as unfair.[3]

Out on a limb by himself in Sydney was William Dobell.

Although in many ways Dobell confounded all the divisions, ironically he would end up becoming the artist probably most viciously attacked by upholders of the conservative view. Newly returned to Australia after an absence abroad of almost ten years, Dobell had studied at the Slade School in London for a term and had travelled in France, Belgium and Holland. Despite the traditional techniques he employed, his works were uncompromising in their observation of human behaviour and personalities, and his sensibility was therefore acclaimed by modernists.

Russell Drysdale also occupied a unique place among artists in Sydney at this time. After leaving school in Victoria, Drysdale had worked for several months at his uncle's sugar plantation in north Queensland, which began his lifelong attachment to the far north – one that may well have later contributed to his bond with Margaret.

It was not until 1935 that Drysdale began formal art studies with the famous progressive Melbourne teacher George Bell. In early 1938, with his wife, Elizabeth 'Bonny' Stephen, and their young daughter, Lynne, Drysdale went to live in London and also briefly visited Paris. After returning to Melbourne in 1939 and some chopping and changing between Sydney and Albury, the Drysdale family, which by then included son Tim, finally settled in Sydney at the end of 1942. In late 1944 Drysdale, a *Sydney Morning Herald* reporter, Keith Newman, and a driver called Tim undertook a tour of drought-stricken far north-western New South Wales. The journey led to series of devastating drawings by Drysdale of the conditions there. The drawings developed into the emotive paintings of inland Australia and its often despairing inhabitants, for which he is now so acclaimed.

In Sydney in the 1940s, one other artist stood out as defying categorisation. And that was Donald Friend, whose art combined some of the attractiveness of the Charm School with a wryness of eye that matched Dobell's and an often wildly satirical frame of mind. Friend was particularly close to Drysdale during this time and was also destined to become one of the most enduring of Margaret's new friends.

The war itself had several repercussions for Australian art. Initially the onset, or imminent onset, of fighting in Europe brought artists rushing back from abroad to the security of home shores. This in turn meant they brought with them whatever they'd absorbed of overseas art in their time away and so in this roundabout way the war was actually enriching to Australia. Many artists enlisted in the armed forces immediately; more joined up as the war worsened, or they were forced to participate once conscription became compulsory for males over twenty in 1943. So the conflict temporarily deprived Australia of artists. But a number of them, including Donald Friend, ended up as official war artists and as such provided valuable and moving records of its progress. Others, like Dobell, who was an unofficial war artist, and Drysdale, who was not able to serve because of problems with an eye, were also stirred to produce permanently memorable images of soldiering within Australia.

Donald Friend was not one of those who were immediately eager to join up. It was only after he witnessed the Japanese submarine invasion of Sydney Harbour from his run-down bed-sit amid the faded grandeur of Elizabeth Bay House that he became convinced of the war's seriousness and the following month finally enlisted. Although Friend did not enjoy military life, his creative capacities were not stifled and, as well as being a war artist, he wrote a very personal account of army life in his diaries, which were later published in the volume *Gunner's Diary*.

⸢◆⸣

When Margaret enrolled at East Sydney Technical College, she was as unaffected by divisions on the art front as she was resilient to the war's depressing domestic restrictions:

Life Begins

For me it was an age of innocence and excitement. You'd hear references to the painting feuds between Melbourne and Sydney at tech, but I thought nothing about it. I was more concerned with surviving and getting on with what I was doing.

Margaret did not come to Sydney filled with burning ambition and determination to be an artist, she insists. What possessed her was a keen appreciation that this was a rare opportunity in her life to immerse herself in art. She was not, therefore, going to waste a minute of it:

To be an art student in wartime you had to have a real belief that this was what you wanted to do. I didn't feel guilty that I wasn't involved with the war. I'd done my bit making camouflage nets in Brisbane and knitting socks for soldiers. That was my war effort. I knew I was really privileged to be an art student and I just focussed on that. I never felt arrogant at that age – there was always so much to be learnt from others. I listened and absorbed. This was my opportunity to do what I wanted to full-time and I relished it. I even stayed back at night. I hated the place where I was living, anyway, so I was glad of a good excuse to be absent.

To begin with she boarded with a nursing friend of her mother's, whom she called Aunt Linda even though she was not a blood relative, at Mosman.[4] Despite the suburb's well-established neatly prolific gardens, with hydrangeas, roses and even frangipani, which should have lifted her spirits, and the plentiful harbour views on three sides, which had long made it an attractive place to painters, Margaret did not feel at home with Aunt Linda and her family:

I had nothing in common with any of them. Aunt Linda was a widow and she was always pinching and punching you for no apparent reason. She used to make horrible soap out of dripping – a leftover habit from the Depression – and give me Weet-Bix spread with a bit of butter and jam to take to tech for lunch. I've never liked breakfast cereal, so you can imagine what a penance it was munching away on Aunt Linda's cardboard sandwiches.

The children weren't much better. She had two boys and a girl who was rough and tumble. We'd go down to Balmoral Beach on the weekend and swim. Once we even got hold of a boat and rowed under the Harbour Bridge right up the Lane Cove River. I didn't enjoy these outings. The boys were older and had one thing on their mind as far as girls were concerned. They'd have knocked you up if you'd given them half a chance. I wanted nothing to do with them.

Every morning to get to tech Margaret took a bus from Mosman across the Harbour Bridge to Wynyard Station, then she would catch the tram to Taylor's Square, Darlinghurst. At the end of the day the journey was repeated in reverse, often in the dark:

Blackout made the city a bit grim coming back from night classes. It seemed to rain a lot through that first winter and walking down to Wynyard was unpleasantly dark and wet. I used to get holes in my shoes, so I'd be squelching along with wet feet, which made it even more miserable. But then suddenly you'd get a whiff of brown boronia. In the doorway of a building there'd be a little crouched figure, hoping for a passing American, selling brown boronia. It was such an unusual sight to come across in the dark, and I'd never smelt boronia before. Sometimes they'd sell daphne as well. Both boronia and daphne have the most wonderful permeating perfumes and the rain made their smell even more poignant.

If there was half an hour between trams to tech or I missed a bus home, I'd go into the newsreel beside Wynyard. I never bought newspapers, so it was a cheap way of catching up with the news. At Mosman I'd get off the bus at a stop in Military Road, walk down

Life Begins

from there for a block, then turn off another couple of streets. One night, outside a butcher's shop on a corner I had to walk round, there was a man on a bike who turned out to be a flasher – the first time I'd ever encountered a flasher. I didn't scream or call out. I just pretended I didn't see. Flashers really only want to shock.

⋙⋘

There seems to have been some confusion as to what study year to put Margaret in when she began tech in Sydney. The usual procedure of study at East Sydney Technical College at that time, which was not prescriptively adhered to, was that students did a one-year Introductory Course, followed by an Intermediate Course; they then did a three- or four-year Diploma Course in one of four departments: Drawing, Painting, Sculpture or Design. It was quite common for students to do various other day or night classes even after they had finished their Diploma Courses. Passing an entrance exam was normally required to gain admission to the art school, but as Margaret does not remember sitting for this exam it's possible her Brisbane courses counted instead, which may account for the difficulty in deciding where she should be placed.

On top of that, Margaret says that she didn't know at this stage whether she wanted to be a painter, or a sculptor like Maria Corrie. Modelling appears to have been her strongest subject, both by inclination and as indicated by her exam results, and she had not done much painting (again, as far one can judge by exam results). So she tried out both courses.

It wasn't long before Margaret found her true metier. After being relegated early on to a class where students only drew from the antique – replicas of famous statues – which she'd already experienced in Brisbane and, like most art students, was dying to escape, she went into the painting studio. To Margaret, the painting studio, where they had live models to work with, was simply 'divine'. Now her appreciation of 'things in the round' was about to be translated into drawings and forms on canvas, rather than being moulded by her hands in clay.

The painting studio was run by Douglas Dundas, who sported an artistic-looking beard and moustache. Dundas's own art at this stage was going through a transition, according to an article written by Kenneth Wilkinson in *Present Day Art in Australia* in 1945.[5] His earlier, lyrical Impressionist-influenced landscapes were now touched with an unrest and becoming more modern. Also, since he'd started teaching at East Sydney Tech in 1930, Dundas had been giving more attention to figure drawing and composition, which Wilkinson attributed to his prior study of Florentine masters, with their emphasis on form. One of Dundas's most famous figure paintings is a portrait of his wife, artist Dorothy Thornhill (who taught drawing at tech), wearing a snappy black hat with a camellia in her buttonhole, a cigarette in her hand and an empty wine glass on the table in front of her.

The painting studio itself had been added onto the original gaol building in the 1920s and was positioned between the stone wall surrounding the gaol and one of the stone cellblocks. Its other two walls were wooden. The main entrance was through a narrow doorway in one of the wooden walls and a row of high windows above let in light. Opposite the entrance was a heavy sliding door that opened onto a garden. The model's platform, a moveable structure about a foot off the ground, was positioned as required, with students' easels usually arranged in circular fashion around it. At the sliding door there were two steps down into the garden, where students would sit with cups of tea in their breaks, eat their lunch or pass the time chatting, smoking and reading.[6]

A number of teachers made an impression on Margaret in her first year. Among them was the head of East Sydney Tech himself, London-born painter and teacher Frank Medworth. It was not just Medworth's teaching methods that were distinctive, his appearance was also startling:

Medworth was very dapper. He had a long pointed nose, a moustache that turned up at the ends and a little goatee beard between his lip and chin. During classes he would stand and rock up on his toes as he talked, which may have been a form of shyness. But the most unforgettable aspect of his appearance was the hole in his head and the plate in it that used to pulsate. You couldn't keep your eyes off it.

Medworth's class for tonal painting used to drive me insane. We would first do a design. Then we'd mix up three tones of grey oil paint on a piece of glass. At the end of a class the piece of glass with the paint on it had to be submerged in water until the next week's class. By doing that the paint stayed fresh and didn't grow a skin. But it also became very smelly, putrid, in fact, and I loathed working with it.

His drawing classes, however, were fantastic. We never knew when we came in what he'd ask us to do. Some days it would be a figure in motion where the model would hold one pose for five minutes, so it was quick drawing; at other times the model would do half-hour poses; or it could be a two-day drawing. Sometimes you'd have to draw the point closest to you, or the darkest point. In other words, he made you think. Sometimes he'd get you to draw around the volume of the figure. It could also be shut-eye drawing. Shut-eye is where you put your pencil down and just look at the model, then draw without looking at the paper again, which teaches coordination between eye and hand. Everything in his class made you use your mind in different ways.

Painter and etcher John Barclay Godson, also originally from England, was another teacher Margaret remembers. He taught lettering, which was not a subject she enjoyed, or was good at, and she frequently wondered why on earth she was made to do it. Nevertheless, a dictum of Godson's has stayed with her:

Just remember, it's not the letter you're making, it's the spaces in between, Mr Godson would say. Now that, of course, seared into my brain. The spatial qualities between objects are what count in painting. I'm conscious of Mr Godson even now when I'm working. There was also Mr Badham. He taught perspective and told us, *You learn it and then you throw it away*.

Sculpture was taught by Lyndon Dadswell, who was in his mid thirties and had already had a distinguished career as a sculptor by 1943. Having studied at the Julian Ashton School in Sydney in the 1920s and then under the famed English-born sculptor Raynor Hoff at East Sydney Tech, Dadswell won the Wynne Prize for sculpture in 1933 and then studied in London at the Royal Academy. During the Second World War, after being injured in battle, Dadswell was commissioned as an official war artist. He resumed teaching at East Sydney Tech in July 1943, so presumably it was then that Margaret may have attended or observed some of his classes.

However, although Margaret loved modelling in clay (to this day she confesses a hankering to take up sculpture again), the sculpture classes did not suit her:

Being wartime, there was no pouring metal and I found the process of casting plaster most unsatisfactory. You made an initial clay model, then you put plaster of Paris around it to make an impression, or mould, in sections. Next you separated the mould, cleaned out the clay, shellacked it, put the mould together again and poured in a slightly stronger plaster. After that, you had to chip the plaster mould off, which was very messy. And in the end all you had was a little plaster cast. It was very unfulfilling. If they had been pouring bronzes, or teaching any other processes, like Degas's modelling with wax, I might have stayed with it and become a sculptor.

Life Begins

The war affected Margaret's early time at East Sydney Tech in several ways. Not only was there no metal for sculpture classes, according to her, the etching press was also shut up and only made available as she was leaving. She did use it a few times and would have liked to have explored the process further. The most obvious difference in the tech caused by the war was the drop in student numbers, as in Brisbane. There were far fewer students than ordinarily attended and men, especially, were few and far between.

Of the women in her year Margaret remembers most clearly Jocelyn 'Yossie' Rickards, Mitty Lee-Brown, Yvonne Francart and Ena Joyce. She would become lifelong friends with Rickards and Lee-Brown, in particular, but when she arrived at tech Lee-Brown definitely made the biggest impression on her. Margaret had never encountered anyone with quite such pizzazz:

When I first saw Mitty, she was wearing a very expensive black dress of heavy crepe, with tassels coming down and bare feet. She often wafted round tech in bare feet. She was in black because her mother had just died in an accident. Mitty was also always very tanned, which showed up her pale eyes to advantage. And she never seemed to carry any money. I was always having to lend her tuppence, or whatever it took, to make a phone call to one of her beaux to get them to take her to Prince's or Romano's. I thought she and Yossie Rickards – who was very beautiful and who had come to tech very young, straight from Ascham School in the eastern suburbs – had very elegant lifestyles quite different from mine. I was fascinated to observe them.

Margaret also made friends with another female student, who was much older than her and whose name she no longer recalls. Not only did this student live with an older man in a mansion at Mosman, she also frequented the Arabian Coffee Shop in Kings

Cross. The Arabian was situated up a flight of stairs in Darlinghurst Road. There were plane trees growing on the footpath outside and a medley of intriguing little shops with striped awnings nearby.[7] At the Arabian, 'endless conversations and encounters' took place.[8] For Margaret, it was a glimpse of yet another way of life:

The fact that she lived with an even older man gave her a certain cachet, and she used to go to the Arabian, a coffee house in Kings Cross, which was very daring. She was working on a painting of the Arabian's interior. I'd trail along after her, playing follow-the-leader, and have a coffee there, too. That was all I could afford. But just being there seemed adventurous and bohemian. Kings Cross was like a little European village then.

As far as male students went, Margaret has memories of only three. There was a boy called Tony, who had terrible acne and hardly ever said anything. His face had very simple lines like a Picasso drawing and if a model didn't turn up the class would draw him instead.

Then there was the perennial student, Irish Warren Stewart, who had frizzy hair like a pot cleaner and limped. Stewart used to thump Margaret on the back in a friendly, if slightly annoying greeting. He was also a great believer in folk medicine: if you were sick, he'd put a clove of garlic in your sock. Stewart also had something else to offer:

Warren had been at tech when Bill Dobell was teaching there at the start of the war and Bill had painted him. So during a lunch break in my first year, Warren took me off to the Cross and introduced me to Bill. I suppose because I was naïve, I just said hello and stood back. Bill was living above a bank and his room had a little balcony that overlooked the street. It suited Bill, because he was a very shy person who loved observing. You can recognise Warren in Bill's portrait by his frizzy hair. He's wearing a maroon jumper and has his arms crossed.[9]

Finally there was Ronald Millen, who had already finished his Diploma Course when Margaret arrived, but would have been doing extra classes. Millen would become Margaret's first real male friend at tech:

Ron was gay, but in those days I didn't even know what gay was. He had a very different way of painting – very textural, rather murky colour, almost abstract. Ron introduced me to music. We used to go together to symphony concerts in the Sydney Town Hall where we sat on uncomfortable bentwood chairs. Despite the chairs, I loved the symphonies. They inspired me to buy a little second-hand radio in a pawn shop, on which I listened to music on the ABC. So my painting to music, always the ABC, started way back then.

After a while Ron went off to work in a munitions factory for the war. I think they had access to some sort of pure alcohol, because he used to come back from the factory with the most dreadful homemade liquor. Gin, I suppose you'd call it. Lethal! Our birthdays were round about the same time and we decided to celebrate with this poisonous concoction at his parents' house at Mosman. The parents were sent off to the pictures while we had our party. We downed the gin and then ate the birthday cake, which unfortunately was a cream cake. When his parents arrived back home, I remember his mother saying to me, Oh, Margaret, are you all right? You look green. At which I disappeared into the bathroom, took one look at my face in the mirror, and was violently ill.

The models Margaret encountered in the painting studio were a varied lot. Perhaps the most conventionally pretty was the petite

Miss Morgan, who wore a velvet ribbon with a cameo round her neck and looked to Margaret like a woman from a Manet painting. Frank Medworth referred to her as 'exquisite'. Miss Hobson[10] was another model. She had a figure like a marrow, with thighs that folded over the chairs, according to Margaret, of which the sculpture class was very appreciative. Miss Hobson would put white powder all over her feet and leave a trail of white footprints across the floor whenever she was posing, to the amusement of students. Then there was Eileen Cramer, whom Margaret preferred drawing of all of them. Cramer was very strong and looked like a lion tamer, hence the class christened her 'the Lion Tamer'.

But the most extraordinary of all the female models, the one who would have easily confirmed Margaret's relatives' worst fears, was the bohemian artist Rosaleen 'Roie' Norton, who herself had studied drawing and sculpture at East Sydney Tech. 'Roie' had flaming red hair, eyebrows plucked in high arches, and was involved with the occult and black magic:

Roie was unusual, but I did not know anything about her other activities then. She was terrific as a model, because she could hold a pose perfectly for such a long time, which was especially good in the painting class. It was as if she was in a trance. When we had a break, Mr Dundas would have to go over and tap her on the shoulder, because she'd still be holding the pose. Miss Norton, he'd say, time for a rest.

In the break she wouldn't bother to put on a kimono like the other models, she'd just open up an old tin and begin rolling up one of her cigarettes. We all smoked in those days. I started the moment I left school. But cigarettes were hard to get in wartime. People used to pick up butts, anything for a smoke. When Roie had smoked her cigarette down, she would open up the tin again, get out a long pin and stick it through her cigarette so she could smoke it to the very end. It was very intriguing.

Life Begins

Although it was a vastly different world from Tully, Tygalgah or Somerville House, Margaret seems to have taken life at East Sydney Tech very much in her stride. It did not seem at all strange to her to be drawing from nude models. She'd already had some experience of life classes in Brisbane and, as she says, everybody was doing it, so it seemed quite natural. Male models were very few and far between so the fact that the models were mostly women also probably helped eliminate any initial awkwardness. Margaret remembers only one old professional male. His name was Frank, but he was known as 'Droopy Drawers' because of the knitted codpiece he wore. Then the much younger Roland Robinson came along. 'Rollo' was good-looking with wavy hair and he turned out to be a far better model than Droopy Drawers, Margaret says.

Robinson, an ardent nature lover and a fine poet, was introduced to modelling by Eileen Cramer, 'the Lion Tamer'. Robinson was an 'Essential Industry' escapee – if you weren't in the armed services, you were supposed to have an identity card that showed that you were working in 'Essential Industry'. The lack of a card made employment dicey. But modelling was an occupation in which questions weren't asked, so Cramer explained to Robinson.

When a student at tech asked Robinson what he thought about while posing, Robinson replied that he was 'away in the bush composing'.[11] Despite his appropriation of the enforced stillness required by modelling for poetic composition, Robinson took his modelling duties seriously. By his own account, he spent the breaks studying the stance of famous sculptures such as Michelangelo's *David*.[12] In his autobiography, Robinson also points out that he always stood for his poses, whereas most of the other models suffered from 'slipped discs or varicose veins and had to sit or lie down'.[13] It's easy to see why Rollo might have been a preferable subject to Droopy Drawers.

Although he had a few rather scathing remarks about 'snooty' girl students from well-to-do families, 'socialites' in his eyes (of whom Margaret would not have been one), Robinson enjoyed East Sydney Tech. He and Margaret did not become close friends. His social interaction was mostly with her teachers: Dundas, Dorothy Thornhill and Dadswell. But the mention of Robinson's name still brings a spark to Margaret's eye.

The male model Margaret was closest to was Frank 'Frankie' Mitchell:

Darling Frankie Mitchell. Frankie must have been a little older than me, but I always liked people who were slightly older. They were far more interesting than people my own age. (Now, of course, I've reached an age where the more interesting people are the younger ones.) Frankie's life and mine were interwoven from the moment we met at tech. We were the greatest of friends and it was a terrible loss when I came back from Europe a few years ago and found he'd died.

Frankie grew up in Newcastle. His mother had a pub at Swansea. When he first arrived in Sydney, which was before the war, he studied art and that's when he started working as a model, to help with his finances. Before I met him, he'd also been in Cairns with Donald Friend and he had a lot of stories about the goings-on up there. He'd volunteered when war broke out, but when I knew him he'd been discharged and, as well as occasionally modelling at tech, had opened a flower shop in Taylor's Square.[14] In those days you just paid a minimal rent, went out to the flower markets, set out some buckets and said you were in business. We all had to troop off to his shop, but none of us had any money to buy flowers in those days. I don't think he made any money at all from it.

Like Ron Millen, Frankie had a birthday round the same time as me, so we often had parties together – he was a real party person. Everybody would bring along a bottle. Nobody had any money so you just brought whatever you could afford. That was what our social life was like in those days. Frankie was always very amusing. He was sharing a place with a man whom he didn't like. I remember the man was shaving once and Frankie, who was very quick to come out with his little toss-away lines, had had a few drinks. Oh, why doesn't the razor slip and cut your bloody throat? Frankie joked.

Mitchell and Margaret would soon converge beyond tech. In 1945, Mitchell joined a troupe of performers – which included the 'Sensational Fan Dancer, Champagne Ravini'; 'Udinus, the Lady Escapologist'; and the 'St Louis Lovelies' – in a show called 'The St Louis Vanities', which travelled round the countryside with a canvas tent:

Frankie, who had a good voice and could play the piano, was billed as a cabaret vocalist. 'The Golden Voice', he was called. The St Louis Vanities got about as far as Casino before going bust. Those who could afford it went back to Sydney on the train, the others came up to Brisbane. Frankie only had enough for the fare to Brisbane. In Brisbane, he decided to open a coffee shop called the Pink Elephant Café in Queen Street.

People flocked to it, myself included. There was nothing else like it in Brisbane. In those days, if you wanted to have a cup of coffee after a movie in Brisbane, there was only Haddon Hall and the Shingle Inn (which had lots of flowers everywhere and waitresses wearing little Dutch hats and long dresses with big aprons), or Rowe's Café, which was more up-market. The Pink Elephant had candles on the tables and prints on the wall that Frankie had somehow borrowed from the Carnegie Library. His business partner was a woman with blonde hair, who was very voluptuous, had an even wickeder tongue than him and could drink anybody under the table.

Frankie also dragged in a piano and well-known musicians

would play there. Donald Friend's friend, the Torres Strait Islander singer Dulcie Pitt, was among them.

Whenever I returned home to Brisbane from Sydney, I would drop in on the Pink Elephant. *Use the spoon, darls, give it a stir*, Frankie would say when your cup of coffee arrived. If you were a friend, there'd always be sherry in your coffee, that's why you had to give it a stir.

Unfortunately the Pink Elephant didn't last very long. The Brisbane police apparently couldn't understand such a strange dive with candles on the tables and jazz playing. According to Margaret, two drunken detectives came in one night and started haranguing a couple at a table. The detectives, who were in plain clothes and hadn't revealed their identity, were demanding to know where the grog was and were using bad language, which the young man at the table objected to. Then they suggested the young man step outside:

The police punched him to the ground and arrested him for using obscene language and resisting arrest. The victim was initially found guilty, but his father was influential and a huge fuss ensued. It was called 'the Pink Elephant Case' and went on for ages. There were all sorts of protests. I think the university students had a parade with a giant float of a pink elephant, until finally the verdict was overturned. Brisbane was like a country town back then.

Frankie came back down to Sydney soon afterwards and started a dressmaking business. He'd always liked sewing. In fact, when he first came to Sydney from Swansea, he brought a little sewing machine with him. He ended up with his own frock shop in Queen Street, Woollahra, called 'My Husband and I', which was very fashionable and successful. I don't think I was up to its standards. I always remember Frankie used to tease me, saying I had no waist *when he was measuring me up for something. But I loved him dearly.*

―◆―

In 1943, as Margaret was becoming increasingly swept up with her classes at East Sydney Tech, her father, now out of military uniform, had set about a new enterprise in Brisbane, the news of which must have enlivened the letters Grace Olley dutifully dispatched to her daughter:

Bee-keeping had long been an interest of his. So he rented a spare block of land not far from Farndon, where he raised queen bees and also had a few hives. He used to collect the bees out in the countryside. He'd get permission from property owners then go and extract the bees from a tree. After the queens were reared, he sent them through the post to customers. He used to make two little open-topped boxes out of thin board with a hole between them. The queen bee went in one compartment and some worker bees in the other. The hole was so the workers could go through and feed the queen bee with royal jelly, because the queen never feeds herself. He'd put some gauze over the top, address the parcel and send it off. There'd be a strike if you did that today.

Although her studies were absorbing, Margaret was finding Aunt Linda and her Weet-Bix sandwiches increasingly intolerable. But towards the end of the year her pleas home for alternative accommodation were finally addressed:

Aunt Mary arranged for me to board with another woman who had umpteen children. It turned out to be even worse than the first place I'd stayed. One of the children was a cretin. The woman spent all her time looking after this child and so the others felt they had to be naughty to get any attention. I just had to leave. I couldn't bear it. So then Margaret Cilento, who had also come down to tech in Sydney, and I decided to rent a funny little flat together.

The Cilento family was the only continuation from school in my life. I had known both Margaret and her younger sister Ruth, who was in the same class as me at Somerville House. But it was only afterwards that our paths really crossed. Margaret left Somerville House the year before me. She came down to Sydney and went to tech when Bill Dobell and Eric Wilson were there. Then she came back up to Brisbane and took a job in a drafting office. We used to go to sketch clubs together, that's how we really became friendly. Margaret's mother, Lady Cilento, became a role model for me during that time. As well as having a family, practising medicine and delivering children, Lady Cilento wrote books and articles and also found time to do craftwork, such as burning designs onto leather. I was enormously impressed and inspired by how active she was.

Margaret's and my flat was in McMahons Point, in East Crescent Street. We didn't choose McMahons Point because of the other artists who had lived round there. It was just a cheap flat – a cheap flat that had wonderful views. The rent was about thirty shillings a week for the two of us, I think, so that was fifteen shillings each. My mother gave me a little stipend, which paid the rent and also helped with my living expenses.

The fact that Margaret Cilento's mother, Lady Phyllis Cilento, had wanted to be an artist in her own youth made her particularly supportive of both her own red-headed daughter and her new friend with the same name, who joined them for holidays at their shack at Caloundra, north of Brisbane. It's difficult to pinpoint exactly when the two Margarets became flatmates. Margaret Cilento has a firm memory of them hatching a plot to flat together on long walks over a Christmas break at Caloundra. Cilento also recalls how on the same holiday the two of them were drawing each other nude one day when a baker doing his round in a horse and cart spied them from afar and immediately headed their way. By the time he appeared at the door they'd managed to grab some clothes but she and Margaret both thought the incident very funny.

So perhaps the scheme of flatting was dreamt up in Margaret's first long holiday back home in 1943. Cilento remembers them knocking on doors in several Sydney suburbs in an effort to find accommodation, and also that they considered renting a boathouse before they stumbled on the flat in East Crescent Street.

In January of that holiday break, Margaret would also have learnt that she had received a grade A mark in painting at tech. The exciting news of her success may well have helped persuade her parents that she was responsible enough to flat with Cilento. As for Margaret herself, it must have been a relief to know her future in the painting studio was assured and a joy to know that her choice of painting rather than sculpture was indeed the right one. Even though the war was still on, it did not encroach on them too greatly at tech, and the prospects for the year ahead were looking rosy for both the Margarets.

Not only do they have the same first name, the two Margarets are remarkably similar in height and build. 'Compactly buxom' best describes it. With a similar sense of humour and fun, they seem to have thrived at McMahons Point. The sight of them setting off at the gallop in the mornings along narrow East Crescent Street clutching canvasses and parcels galore must have amused onlookers and added considerably to the neighbourhood's charms.

East Crescent Street runs along a ridge of land above the harbour and the Margarets' flat was on the upper street side. Although the house at the top of which their flat perched has now been pulled down, some of the street and surrounds remain the same. There are still Moreton Bay fig trees giving shade and in early summer the bright mauve of jacaranda flowers flaring against blue sky can be savoured. Near the flat are the steps the two young art students rushed down to reach the ferry. Boats are still moored in Lavender Bay; the harbour laps gently and the salty breeze coming off it could blow away anyone's troubles.

Their flat itself was eccentric, not only by way of its various other inhabitants, animal and human, but also because of its dodgy architecture:

There was a front parapet and a roof, which actually had quite a slope to it, where people who lived in the house used to hang out their washing. Our flat had been added onto the roof. The walls were fibro and the sloping floor was malthoid. The balcony in front, which the people from downstairs still used to dry their clothes, looked over towards Lavender Bay and Luna Park. You could also see the bridge very well. Margaret had that view from her big front room. My quaint little back room, which I painted a pale blue, had views over Balls Head and Berry's Bay parkland.

The fibro walls used to leak in the rain and I was always having to bale out my room, because it was at the back where the water collected from the sloping floor. I just used to throw the water out my window. Then there were the possums. If we didn't shut the kitchen door, when we came in at night a possum would be eating our tomatoes. Or, after we'd gone to sleep, we'd be woken up by a sneezing sound – atishoo-atishoo – and there would be a possum right beside the bed, so close you could feel its warmth.

It wasn't just possums. The two Margarets also shared their flat with a brother and sister called Ken and Kathleen.[15] Kathleen had the room opposite Margaret Cilento and Ken's bedroom was across the hall from Margaret's. They had their own kitchen, but the nasty dingy bathroom and the central hallway were communal. Margaret remembers that it was like a comic stage play: everyone used to open the door of their room quickly, come out, shut the door equally quickly behind them and then go across the passage to another door, which was opened and shut speedily, too. And Ken and Kathleen had other peculiar practices:

They were devout Catholics. You could hear them praying through the fibro walls of the flat. I could hear him turning in bed, the walls were so thin. Being so religious, it must have been awful for them having to live next to artists who'd been drawing naked people. But not only were they into prayer, they were also into flagellation. We heard that, too, so we thought. They used to beat each other, we imagined. The sounds coming from their rooms were really quite extraordinary. Out the front on the balcony there would be the squeals of everyone going round on the Big Dipper across the water at Luna Park; inside we had Kathleen and Ken.

One of the joys of living at McMahons Point for both Margarets was the calming effect of the ferry rides to and from Circular Quay, which they particularly appreciated in the morning since their departures from the flat were usually hectic. From their big front veranda they had a view of the wharf at Lavender Bay where the ferry stopped before coming across the water to them. They'd wait until they could see the ferry at Lavender Bay before making a dash down the steps of the house out into the street:

Everything was rationed, but you could buy wooden shoes, like clogs, without coupons. Running along Crescent Street, clickety-click in those clogs, and hurling ourselves down the long flight of stairs, two at a time, to the wharf was perilous. It's a wonder we didn't kill ourselves. Of course, because we were always carrying so much for tech, it was even more touch and go. Once Margaret dropped her handbag in the water, which caused a dreadful commotion. I'm still 'the Paddington Bag Lady' as far as parcels go. I'm not happy unless I'm carrying something. If I find myself empty-handed I start looking around, thinking I've left something behind.

Often on the way to the ferry, I'd grab a few flowers out of a garden, hydrangeas or something, and pin them in my hair instead of a hat. There was a particular vine growing that had furry sort of green pods. I don't know what the flower was like, but it had pods which were like cape gooseberries, only larger and furrier, and they came out in bunches. I was always putting a few of those in my hair as I ran to catch the ferry. We also used to make excursions into June Millinery, which was in Pitt Street. I don't think I ever bought anything, but I used to like looking at the accessories. They had every sort of frippery – particularly after the war was over – for decorating hats.

For some special occasion, both the Margarets had an outfit made by the same dressmaker. Having clothes made was a rare occurrence; Margaret was more likely to run up a frock for herself out of cheap mattress ticking, a material not rationed. The corduroy velvet the two Margarets chose came from Mark Foys city store, which was conveniently located near a tram stop on their route to tech. No doubt their parents helped out with the cost of the fabric and the dressmaker, whose premises were not so handily situated at Redfern. To Margaret Cilento it seemed they had to travel miles every time they went for fitting. However, the outfits were a great success and Margaret, who has a marked fondness for hanging on to clothes that are years old, even wore the winey-red dress she had made to an opening a couple of years ago.

In those days Margaret was also addicted to fossicking for household goods in the second-hand shops round Crown Street, Surry Hills. The shops always had a terrible stale smell about them, but they were treasure troves as far she was concerned. She

Life Begins

also loved the pawn shops in Castlereagh Street in the city and once, when her mother sent her some money for a birthday, she bought herself a silver necklace she'd been eyeing as a treat.

For day-to-day groceries, the two Margarets did their shopping in Oxford Street, which was full of cheap butchers and greengrocers, pubs and, again, pawn shops:

The pawn shops used to sell false teeth. They were lined up on trays in the windows and the gums were an awful Nally-Ware red. I remember seeing an old man go in and as I stood gawking outside he took set after set out of the window to see which one fitted.

The Margarets were always inviting people back to the flat at East Crescent Street. As there was no sitting room, their guests usually sat around in Margaret's back bedroom. An aluminium bread bin bought in one of the Crown Street second-hand shops served as their main cooking pot. The standard meal for large numbers was spaghetti with a bit of meat sauce and cheese. Occasionally, they would substitute the meat with pickled walnuts, which, according to Margaret, tasted very similar and came in big jarfuls from an Oxford Street greengrocer. Surrealist artist James Gleeson, who a couple of decades later would be one of Margaret's most favourable reviewers, and his artist friend Errol Peisley are two of the people Margaret remembers coming to McMahons Point for a meal.

Margaret did not do a great deal of painting in the flat:

I do have one painting looking out over the North Sydney rooftops that I did from my room. We mostly used to stretch our canvasses and prepare them ourselves. There were also second-hand shops up in North Sydney that sold frames with old paintings still in them. We'd buy them in the frames and then paint over the paintings, or take the painting out and put our own canvas over the stretcher. A shop at tech had a supply of paint for us. I can't remember there ever being any shortage of paint because of the war.

Margaret and I did used to draw each other in the flat, but it would get very cold while we worked. Eventually I bought a little kerosene heater from a second-hand shop. Kerosene heaters are very unhealthy. You're meant to put a pot of water on top of them to get rid of the fumes, but instead of having just water we used to make soup on ours, so when it was very cold we'd put pea soup on the heater while we worked. There was a little gas stove in the kitchen that we used for our normal cooking.

Grace Olley was still keeping a watchful maternal eye on her daughter despite the distance between them. The two Margarets' enthusiasm for their new living arrangement did not stop Grace harbouring reservations about their future matrimonial prospects, it seems. Accordingly, she decided that both the Margarets should lose weight so they'd become prettier and more acceptable as potential wives. At least, that was Margaret Cilento's impression; Margaret herself claims she had no idea this was the reason her mother organised for them to go to the Bjelke Petersen School of Physical Culture on the corner of Castlereagh and Market Streets in the city. At the school the two Margarets used to get into what they describe as 'sweat boxes': boxes lined with mirrors and electric lights to create the heat. 'We were shut in them up to our necks and stayed there until we were practically red in the face,' Margaret says. 'I lasted a little longer than Margaret Cilento who, because of her red hair, used to go red very easily!'

On the weekends when they weren't at tech, the Margarets found various diversions to get them out of the flat, which didn't involve spending money:

On Sunday mornings we often went to the Speakers' Corner in the Domain. There were always crowds of people because it was about the only free entertainment available. Anyone with anything to say stood on a soapbox. Some read poetry, others shouted politics, Mrs Green with her portable organ sang hymns. Afterwards, we'd walk back through the Botanic Gardens to the ferry.

Margaret and I also used to walk along the railway line to Berry's Point. We'd take the Sunday paper to read and some chops or sausages to grill, we even had our own little griller to cook them on. There were fireplaces there that you could use, so all we had to do was grab a bit of wood from the bushes. Often we would come across two men and a small group of people painting. The men were the famous artists Lloyd Rees and Roland Wakelin, but we never stopped to talk – we were too shy. What a missed opportunity!

Although the two had admirers, such as the art student who climbed up onto the front balcony of the flat in pursuit of Margaret Cilento, it was definitely art, not men, that the two Margarets were pursuing.

'One of the good things about our friendship,' Margaret Cilento recalls, 'was that we were both one-eyed about being dedicated to painting. Nothing much else impinged. There were other people in the painting studio who were out every night at parties, which we couldn't possibly have afforded. Margaret always had, and still has, the gift of being able to cut herself off. Of course, she does have favourite people – favourite males that she likes and has affairs with – but in those days neither of us could possibly have dreamt of indulging in love affairs. Maybe we dreamt about it, but that was all. You just wanted to get on with the job. Marriage didn't seem to be a very happy prospect for anybody who wanted to keep on painting.

'Margaret had an enormous amount of energy. Much more than me. Ebullient is a word I'd use to describe her, but that doesn't quite convey that she was also a very feminine person. Very good with her clothes. Every day she would have a wonderful new way of doing her hair, which was long in those days, and she'd make strange little hats to wear. I suppose you could say she liked to have a bohemian image. We both did, probably.'[16]

Flat-sharing did, however, result in the meeting of one man for Margaret Olley. Through Margaret Cilento's grandmother, Alice Lane McGlew, 'Nanny McGlew', she was introduced to Cilento's godfather, art collector Howard Hinton. This contact with Hinton – while not romantic – would have a lasting effect on Margaret's life.

The bond between Alice McGlew and Howard Hinton went back a long way. Hinton, who was born in England in 1867, first came to Australia in 1892. He started working for a shipping firm and, in the tradition of artists like Tom Roberts and Arthur Streeton with their harbour camps, lived under canvas with some friends at Balmoral Beach in Sydney. At Balmoral, Hinton met Charles 'Charley' McGlew, with whom he became best friends. McGlew married Alice, then, when he deserted her as a result of trauma he'd suffered in the First World War, Hinton took her under his wing, as Cilento puts it. He would ring Nanny McGlew every morning at nine o'clock and send her sentimental postcards from around the world whenever he travelled.

'I would say that only a chaste kiss was ever shared between them,' Cilento concludes in summation of the relationship, 'but they were great friends.'[17]

When Cilento left Somerville House and came down to Sydney for the first time in 1940, she lived with Nanny McGlew in a liver-coloured brick block of flats at Spit Road, Mosman. Although Hinton, a very conservative old gentleman, was horrified by his goddaughter's inclination towards abstraction in art, they remained on formally cordial terms over the years because of Nanny McGlew, and whenever the two visited her on Sunday evenings Hinton would be present. Both the Margarets were deeply in awe of Hinton, but there was an unexpected aspect to the evenings:

Life Begins

We asked him over to McMahons Point once. He sent us a polite little note of acceptance and managed to make it up all the stairs to our flat, so he could see what we were doing. Nanny McGlew always had boiled eggs for supper. Howard Hinton's hands used to shake. Margaret and I would sit there watching him trying to tap the top of the egg off. I realise now that he must have had Parkinson's disease. But back then, being young, we couldn't help looking. However, it didn't stop us admiring him and we thought it was such a wonderful honour to have him there.

Hinton was the very first person I knew who bought art and then gave it away. He lived very simply in a room in a boarding house at Cremorne and used to donate paintings to the Armidale Teachers' College. You could link my own donating back to his example. There were others, like Lucy Swanton of the Macquarie Galleries, but he was the first. And, of course, because of the Wrights in Armidale, I've always had a strong connection not only with Armidale, but also with the New England Regional Art Museum, which inherited Hinton's collection from the Teachers' College.

But Margaret's own role as benefactor was a long way ahead. Meanwhile, many doors were about to open in her life.

5

Doors Open

To have friends who are all interested in the same things as you is very liberating. Alcohol hadn't really been in my life before my first night at Sam's. Drinking didn't play a role in our family life when I was growing up. As children we were never really aware of what the adults were having. But that entire evening was just so gorgeous. The alcohol seemed to have overcome my shyness and I remember thinking that if this was drinking then it was going to be part of my life from then on.

AT THE BEGINNING OF 1944 THERE WAS AN UNPRECEDENTED uproar in Sydney's art world when it was announced that William Dobell's portrait of painter Joshua Smith had been awarded the 1943 Archibald Prize. Dobell had known the doleful-looking Smith since his early days as an artist and had more recently worked with him in an army camouflage unit. He could hardly have envisaged that his inoffensive portrait of his friend would create such a fracas.

Doors Open

Dobell was born in Newcastle in 1899. While working as a draftsman for Wunderlich (famous suppliers of decorative metal ceiling panels) in 1925, he began night classes at Sydney's Julian Ashton Art School, where he was influenced by the famous painter and sculptor George Lambert. In 1929 he was awarded a Society of Artists' Travelling Scholarship, which enabled him to leave Australia and live in London. During his time away Dobell's skill at observing the foibles of human behaviour and character was sharpened. He returned to Australia in 1938 and the next year began teaching at the East Sydney Technical College. In 1941 he was drafted into the Civil Construction Corps of the Allied Works Council where he ended up as a camouflage artist, which was why Margaret missed out on being his pupil.

The camouflage work required artists, including Dobell, to transform airfields close to the city, at Bankstown and Menangle, into market gardens — Chinese, in the case of Menangle — so they would not be bombed by the Japanese. According to Dobell, a woman was even required to make huge white chooks out of papier mâché to authenticate the rural look.[1] However ridiculous the work, it did mean Dobell could come home on weekends and work in his studio at Kings Cross.

At the time of his Archibald Prize win, Dobell's talents both as a portraitist and a painter of scenes from ordinary life were beginning to be hailed, not just by modernists in Sydney but by the art world generally. Nevertheless, the announcement of his Archibald win infuriated arch-conservatives. They denounced the painting as a caricature rather than a portrait, which as such contravened the terms set out in Archibald's will. Derogatory remarks flew thick and fast in the press. The portrait was featured in a newsreel and lines of cars were parked outside the National Art Gallery as the public turned up in droves to check out the offending work for themselves. Disgruntled viewers complained that the portrait — in which Smith does look a bit bug-eyed — turned its subject into a praying mantis. Smith's parents were called in, asked whether the portrait resembled their son, and then misquoted in the sensationalist daily newspaper *Truth*. More upsets with the Smiths followed when Mr Smith and his son Joshua visited Dobell and begged for the portrait to be destroyed. Donald Friend reported in his diary that the Smiths wept during their visit and Dobell had to lend them a paint-splattered handkerchief.[2]

Dobell's supporters were varied. The usually conservative Sir Lionel Lindsay, having purged himself of his contempt for modernists with his book *Addled Art*, spoke passionately in the portrait's favour at the initial judging. As the squabble escalated, Douglas Dundas also defended the work, as did Elaine Haxton and Donald Friend, who had seen the painting before it was entered and regarded the portrait as 'a superb piece of work'.[3] When the press put a photograph of Smith next to the portrait, Friend wryly commented in his diary: 'I thought they looked very alike except that one was a work of art.'[4] It's a comment that neatly sums up the absurdity of the reaction against the portrait.

Artists and fellow entrants in the prize Joseph Wolinksi and Mary Edwards continued to attack the judges' decision. Edwards' litigious nature was well known in Sydney at the time, after her successful lawsuit against a truck driver (or taxi driver, in some accounts) for injuries sustained when her cat escaped from her lap and caused an accident while they were travelling in his vehicle. (Donald Friend, who at one time lived opposite Edwards in Edgecliff, later murdered – while nude – the troublesome cat with a silver dagger. Or so he claims in his diary.[5]) The subsequent proceedings dragged on for almost a year, and although the award was finally upheld in November 1944, the case was enormously harrowing for both Smith and Dobell.

Most of the fuss passed completely over Margaret's head. Although her sympathies lay with Dobell, she was too preoccupied with being an art student to become involved and didn't dream of attending the court proceedings. But 1944 was significant for her. Not only were she and Margaret Cilento now established with possums and flagellators in McMahons Point; during this, her second year at tech, Margaret would make still more friends who would win a permanent place in her heart. The first of these was Anne Wienholt, later a sculptor as well as a painter, who says of her long connection with Margaret: 'It's more than a friendship: it's like an entanglement of lives and memories and communication.'[6]

For Margaret each new friendship was exciting in itself, as well as soon leading to other encounters:

I met Anne, who was another Queenslander, in the painting studio. She'd been to East Sydney Tech before I started, when Dobell was there and, although she had now finished her course, she wanted to do her two entries for the New South Wales Travelling Scholarship in the studio. She used to work on them at night: one was a nude of Miss Cramer, the Lion Tamer, the other was a landscape of a little house with a gate, which must have been part of her family's Queensland property. Recently Anne told me that she also submitted a drawing of Margaret Cilento's hands for the scholarship.

I was intrigued by the way Anne set about the landscape. She had worked out exactly what she wanted to do. Having drawn it in from a sketch, she started in one corner and methodically painted her way across the canvas. I'd never seen anybody work like that. It was obviously a technique she'd been taught.

Anne was living at 'Merioola'. Her two rooms were at the back of the house overlooking Chica Lowe's cottage. She used one as a bedroom and the other as her work room. It was because of Anne that I first started visiting the house. It's become a cult thing now, but Merioola was really only a boarding house that a lot of interesting people gravitated to. It just happened at the right time, when the boys were coming back from the war, with the right landlady – Chica. Of course, there were lots of stories about it.

Merioola was a grand two-storeyed Victorian house with a maze of passageways and unexpected courtyards in Rosemont Avenue, Woollahra. It had wrought-iron lace round its verandas, a vast formal ballroom and impressive stone pillars at the front entrance. 'Calm and mellow, surrounded by its running-to-seed ruin of a garden, shaggy lawn and old trees' was how Donald Friend once described the house.[7]

Friend moved into Merioola to battle its ancient gas bath heaters when he was finally free of the army, in March 1946, a little later than many of the other boarders. In a less romantic mood, before he took up residence in the house he referred to its inhabitants as a 'community of arty-minded snobs and hermaphrodites'.[8] Tantalisingly, just whom he had in mind for the latter he does not reveal. However, when established in his own room, Friend quickly became much more gracious about Merioola's 'butterfly people',[9] who busily painted away while the house resounded with gramophones playing with music that ranged from Scarlatti to Bach, Prokofiev and boogie.[10]

Until 1941, Merioola had been the home of property developer and patron of the arts Arthur Wigram Allen, solicitor and partner in the vastly respectable law firm Allen Allen & Hemsley, and had seen many lavish parties, including a ball thrown for the Prince of Wales in 1920.

Originally from Melbourne, its bohemian landlady was born Chica Edgeworth Somers. Following the breakup of her first marriage in 1935, she went to London. Here, in 1939, she let rooms of her house to two Australians who would later feature in Margaret's life: art critic and writer Harry Tatlock Miller and nineteen-year-old artist and theatre designer Loudon Sainthill, who were in London for an exhibition of Sainthill's works inspired by Colonel Wassily de Basil's Russian ballet company at the influential Redfern Gallery. When war broke out, Edgeworth Somers returned to Australia and, following the death of Arthur Wigram

Doors Open

Allen in 1941, leased Merioola from his family. She is usually referred to as Chica Lowe, in deference to her second husband, an American called Bernard Lowe whom she married in 1946 and who died just before their first anniversary.

Amply bosomed and suntanned, Chica Lowe wore her hair in a silver chignon from which pink ribbons cheerfully fluttered, and ran Merioola from a pink weatherboard office in the back garden called 'Lolly Lodge'. From 1941 on the house was filled with a mêlée of artistic tenants. As well as painters and art students, there were musicians, a writer, an architect, and even an astronomer. Many of the tenants, like art enthusiast Clarice Zander or Tatlock Miller and Sainthill, who took up residence there in 1945, had lived in or visited Europe before the war, so the house had the additional fillip of being linked to a cultural world outside Australia.

Anne Wienholt not only introduced Margaret to Merioola, she also took her to meet a decidedly out-of-the-ordinary friend of hers. This was the man whom many, many years later Margaret would call 'the one' for her: worldly gallery manager, theatre director and interior decorator, reader of Gertrude Stein, connoisseur of cravats, excellent ice-skater – his only athletic prowess – bisexual and man of mystery, Sam Hughes.

Margaret had not met anyone like the older Hughes before. Her contact with teachers at art school had been mostly essentially formal. With Hughes, who treated her like an equal, it was immediately personal. 'Sam opened doors,' she now simply says of his impact. He proved that there were lively cultural worlds beyond the painting studio at East Sydney Technical College that were waiting to be enjoyed. Also, that the way you live life – even the food you eat – can be rich, stimulating, stylish. Not that there was anything wrong with the food Margaret had eaten growing up – to the contrary. But it was not sophisticated.

Whether Margaret had a physical crush on Hughes from the start but kept it under wraps, she's not revealing. She may well have, however it would be wrong to infer that she was pining for a physical relationship with him – or anyone else, for that matter – at this point. But she certainly craved Hughes's intellect and insights.

Wienholt knew Hughes through his production of Ferenc Molnár's play *Liliom*.

The choice of play indicates how Hughes was in tune with the Zeitgeist. Molnár was a Hungarian playwright who reached the height of his fame in Europe in the 1920s and '30s, when he was part of a circle of artists and musicians in Budapest known as 'the Elastics' because of the innovative shoes without laces they sported.

Hughes's version was staged in the basement of St Peter's Church in Forbes Street, Darlinghurst, in 1941 and involved a number of students from East Sydney Tech. The sets were designed by Wienholt, and Jocelyn Zander, who had the lead acting role, helped with their painting.[11] Hughes's links to the wider art world extended all the way to London, where from 1935 to 1939 he had managed the Zwemmer Gallery, known for its exhibitions of innovative modern artists, including, through the 1930s, Picasso, de Chirico, Modigliani and Henry Moore. Hughes's intimate knowledge of these artists must have added considerably to his appeal to Margaret:

Sam was . . . the only way I can describe it is exotic. He was shortish, slight and very well dressed. He must have been about fifteen or twenty years older than me, but I never thought about people's ages. Sam was an innovator. He designed the most marvellous catalogues for artists like Picasso when he was at Zwemmer's. He had very definite ideas and was very modern in his thinking. He opened doors for people. He opened doors for me. He encouraged, would be another way of putting it.

Hughes had a flat at 15 Billyard Avenue, Elizabeth Bay, in a five-storeyed, inconspicuously tasteful building (which is still there today), not far from the Spanish-looking residence 'Del Rio', near a flight of steps that came down from the relatively cosmopolitan atmosphere of Macleay Street, Potts Point. The address was probably another attraction in Margaret's eyes. Elizabeth Bay had long been a haven for those in the arts, as well as the clusters of glossy-feathered pigeons that gathered in its streets hoping for crumbs scattered by kindly flat-dwellers.

Sharing Hughes's living quarters was painter and actor John Richards:

John was a theatre actor and full of confidence. He had a great voice and striking, pale eyes with long lashes. Unfortunately, he'd had rheumatic fever as a child, which had affected his heart and eventually killed him, but he always lived life to the hilt. He couldn't have made old bones, anyway, he was so attractive.

I'll always remember John saying, If you're not meeting a new person every three months, there's something the matter with your lifestyle. It struck a chord with me. What he meant was that if you don't, you are living a very closed life. It's very true if you think about it. It doesn't have to be striking up a whole new friendship, it could just be making an acquaintance or coming into contact with someone even quite briefly. It's the contact that counts. Every now and again, I've thought about it, too, when I've realised I'm getting too close to a certain group of people. You feel yourself being sucked into their orbit and it becomes confining. I like having contact with all sorts of different people.

Sam was bisexual, so he might have had a little fling with John.

But I never saw any sign of it. Sam always wanted John to marry Anne. He thought it would be a perfect union. Then Anne won the Travelling Scholarship and before the war was even over she set off for New York, where she fell in love with her future husband, Japanese-Hawaiian Masato Takashige, who was an art student there.

Just up the road from Hughes and Richards' flat was Elizabeth Bay House, another property that briefly belonged to Arthur Wigram Allen, which had had artists living in it since Allen had allowed the Melbourne-based academic portrait painter Sir John Longstaff to have a studio there in the late 1920s. When Allen sold the house in the early 1930s, artists Wallace Thornton and Wolfgang Cardamatis (and after them Donald Friend) moved in and its run-down splendour became the setting for many bohemian revels. In 1944 artist Elaine Haxton was decidedly domiciled in Elizabeth Bay. Haxton was very much part of wartime Kings Cross bohemian life. In 1942, she had painted a mural at the Claremont Restaurant in Darlinghurst Road, Sydney's first truly European dining place, which served such novel cuisine as garnished lobster, spatchcock with garlic, goulash and Vienna schnitzel, and whose owner, dentist Walter Magnus, was the subject of a Dobell portrait.

While Margaret did not encounter these people on her visits to Billyard Avenue, later Haxton, Cardamatis and Friend would become dear to her, and the artistic flavour of Elizabeth Bay would have rubbed off on her to some extent. Once inside Hughes and Richards' flat, Margaret was stunned by its interior, which provided an extraordinary contrast to the fibro walls and sloping malthoid floor of the McMahons Point digs she and Cilento shared. There was nothing bohemian about this living space. The colours and furnishings were put together by Hughes with impeccable flair:

There was the white room, which Sam used to call his mother's sitting room, even though she never sat in it that I saw. The white room was where the Ivon Hitchens painting hung. I think Sam acquired it when he was working at Zwemmer's. The Hitchens was a flower piece of poppies and other field flowers, and I loved it straight away. The flowers looked as if they were dancing. In the white room, Sam had built glass shelves into a dividing wall to display his glass collection. He'd placed white glass on one shelf and old blue Bristol glass on another. The glass shelves showed them off perfectly. Then he had a most beautiful settee, rather French, upholstered in white damask. It was all just so elegant.

The dining room where we ate the first night I went to Sam's was red. Bright, bright red. He and John had candles on the table and the talk really woke your mind up. I was completely swept away. I loved the whole night. Looking back on it, I've realised that was the very first time I had alcohol with a meal. We had a little glass of sherry before and then wine with the meal – at least, that's my memory of it.

I have been over it again and again in my mind through the years and it is always that particular night I pinpoint as the beginning of my liking to drink. What happened gradually after that was I'd have a bottle of sherry at home in the flat in case anybody came round or we were doing any entertaining, and I'd have a few nips from it before I went out. That's how the drinking started. A few nips to overcome shyness. I was always so shy and drinking makes you feel better. The drinking probably gave the Gemini half of me free rein. I think that's why so many young ones take drugs now – so they feel accepted. Eventually, of course, it got out of control.

There were no bedrooms as such in the flat. Hughes and Richards slept in the green-painted front room on divans that were like settees with big cushions at the back – another unique and modern aspect of the furnishing. A second room held bookcases, a desk and a settee for anybody who wanted to stay over, which people frequently did, especially once the war had ended. There were parties in the flat then that ended with all the guests staying the night, Margaret included. Mostly not because of any high jinks or sexual frolicking, she says, but simply because public transport, such as trams, stopped so early it was impossible to get home after a certain hour. Margaret remembers dragging her clog-clad feet on the mornings after up the flight of steps at McMahons Point, and identifying with Hans Christian Andersen's mermaid who swapped her fish's tail for feet that felt as if they'd been cut by knives.

These dinners and parties were part of the attraction Hughes held for Margaret. Through him she met other articulate and energised people to whom she could relate, and more and more doors opened. Very early on, Hughes introduced her to Clarice Zander. Zander, who had earlier been one of Merioola's first tenants, was by this stage living next door to the main Merioola house. Margaret already knew Zander's daughter Jocelyn, who'd finished at East Sydney Tech just as Margaret was about to begin, but had not previously met Clarice herself. Zander was a woman devoted to art. Originally a commercial artist, journalist and short story writer, when her marriage to Charles Zander collapsed, she was forced to look for work in Melbourne, which resulted in her managing Melbourne's New Gallery (which had been started by James Stuart MacDonald in his early conservative but perhaps not quite so irascible days). Here Zander met numerous Melbourne art identities, including a youthful John Reed (who credited her with 'leading him to art'[12]) and the brilliant cartoonist, later to become her lover, Will Dyson, who had recently returned from a successful career in London. When Dyson returned to London in 1930, Zander followed and found work in London's Redfern Gallery, and in 1933 organised to bring an important exhibition of contemporary British art to Sydney and Melbourne that included works by Walter Sickert, Augustus John and sculptor Jacob Epstein.[13] Dyson died in 1938 and then at the outbreak of war Zander and Jocelyn returned to Australia.

Margaret immediately found in Zander, 'so full of energy and information' and with a predilection for extravagant hats, another female role model – only this time a role model, unlike Aunt Mary or even Lady Cilento, whose life was centred round art.

Hughes was also friendly with the artist Margaret Preston and, following his visits to the Mosman hotel where she lived, would report back to an intrigued Margaret with stories of how Preston and her husband preferred to live in a hotel so Preston would not be hampered with domestic chores, such as cooking, that might interfere with her painting. To Margaret's regret, she herself was never included in Hughes's visits to Mosman and, though she was always hoping to, never actually came face-to-face with Preston.

Although Hughes opened up Margaret's life so greatly, he was strangely reticent about his own history:

I never really knew whether Sam was Australian or English. He was in England at the start of the war, because that's when he was working for Zwemmer's. There was a story about his passport being lost in the bombing, but he was always very secretive about it. Even later on he would never let me see his passport. I think he must have been Australian. He once told me that his great-grandfather owned a lot of property in Sydney in the inner city, round the Town Hall. Apparently he left the lot to his housekeeper, whom he had married late in life and who looked after him in his old age. There was another tale about one of his relatives being the illegitimate offspring of George IV, so it was very hard to know what had gone on.

I gathered Sam's father was an eye doctor who worked in Macquarie Street, in one of those buildings almost opposite the Mitchell Library. His father married twice. Sam was the child of the first marriage and he had a stepsister called Olga from the second marriage. He also had a brother who died in an accident. His mother must have gone to live in England when she and Sam's father separated and – again, I think – that's where Sam was brought up. Then she and Sam came back here at the start of the war. These are bits and pieces I picked up over the years. Sam himself lived very much in the day. He never talked about his past.

I never met Sam's mother. But a very ancient retainer of his mother's called 'Old Mary' would appear to lend a hand when Sam had dinner parties. Old Mary would help with the cooking, do the washing up, then quietly leave by the back way. I thought her helping out like this was terrible because she was so old. Sam always served wonderful food. The first time I ever had zabaglione was at a dinner at his flat. John Richards used to make it.

About the same time that Margaret met Sam Hughes, her life beyond tech started to open out in another and very different way that was a perfect foil for, and rest from, the urbane and urban unconventionality of Elizabeth Bay:

My cousins, the Temperleys, had a little tin shack at South Era, a beach in what's now the Royal National Park, just south of Sydney. It was amongst a collection of shacks that I was told had mostly been built by coal miners during the Depression. I know it was a life-saver for my cousins, because there were five boys in their family. Uncle Will worked with the cable company. He was very bright but he'd had a nervous breakdown at one stage, and he and his wife, Ann, who was like a saint, and all the boys lived in a very small house in Canterbury. Because none of us had any money and bushwalking didn't cost anything, often our recreation was going down to Era.

Gil, the second oldest of them, first went to Era when he was nine. He and his brother Tom, who was two years younger, took a mystery hike to Era that was advertised on the radio and cost two bob.[14] *Gil and Tom used to camp a lot at Era when they were only boys. They'd take a tent and then hide their pots and pans and things* for the next time they went. Then Gil and his friends built the hut from scratch in Easter of 1938. A Mr Gray used to come round on his horse collecting the rent of two and six a week, or thereabouts, for the lease of the land. The first time I visited was during the war, after a big storm had hit the hut, and my cousin Colin, who was much younger than the other boys, and his father, Uncle Will, had to make some repairs on the roof. After that they gave me the key to the door and I made regular expeditions to Era with friends.

All that was required was your train fare down and back. I'd meet up with people at Central Station and we'd catch the 'midnight horror' – the last train for the night. If you went on a Friday you could have the full weekend away. We had to carry our food with us in rucksacks because there was no shop at Era (as is still the case). I would be carting canvas and oil paints as well, so I had quite a load. We used to get off the train at Lilyvale and walk for miles through the bush. Usually we tried to pick a full-moon night. It was very romantic, staggering along through the gum trees and down the steep winding track to Era in the bright moonlight.

Anne Wienholt came down several times, as did Margaret Cilento, Sam and John, John Duffecy, the furniture designer, and his wife, Lyndsay, who were friends of Sam. Also Paul Jones, the artist, whom I met at a party that John and Lyndsay gave. Paul was very handsome – I did love handsome men – but, like most of the others, he was gay. Lots of artistic people have fallen for Era. Tom, my cousin, who was in the army, even took a Russian ballerina to the shack in one of his breaks, I believe. Roland Robinson, the model from tech, used to camp at Era, and later, in the 1950s, Hal Missingham, who was the director of the Art Gallery of New South Wales, had a place there.

Era was like the paradise of Margaret's childhood when she camped on the north coast beaches near the Tweed River. Roland Robinson, with his poet's love of nature, was enraptured by Era's unspoilt crescent of beach and nearby valleys of gums, banksias and cabbage tree palms. Although Robinson preferred to sleep out in a cave or with only a thin calico tent separating him from the stars, he also relished the company of Era's regular shack dwellers of the mid 1940s. In his autobiography, he details their varied lot with enthusiasm. In particular, he enjoyed the company of some who 'were not interested in girls', as he delicately puts it, and 'used to surf in the nude and lie among the flowering tea-trees on the sides of the valley sunbathing'.[15]

Margaret did not become friends with Era's more unconventional inhabitants as Robinson did, but there is a story that still persists round Era of how Margaret – described as 'curvaceous' – and some other women artists were spotted cavorting nude at the shack after a swim, much to the delight of some male beholders. One of Margaret's own favourite Era anecdotes that she heard from her cousins was about a piano being carried down the hill to the lifesaving club. As she recalls it, the men got themselves good and drunk and then just lifted the piano up and took off down the hill with it.

The Temperleys' shack was in the row furthest from the sea, nicely distanced from the surf's night thud. The bush, with rainforest shining greenly through it, was right behind. In front there was a grassy apron with a view straight across what was known as 'bug flat', because of the insects that bred there, to the ocean. The whole of the Era valley was cleared in those days because of the horses and cattle grazed by Bob Gray. Dotted round the shacks were pink oleanders, the only shade trees cattle wouldn't eat. Bird life abounded. Whip birds sent out sharp cracking calls from the bush; currawongs, kookaburras and tiny blue wrens ventured up close to the shacks; while down on the beach seagulls congregated and the odd shag sailed right out to sea.

When Margaret visited, the shack, which is still there now but has been extended, consisted of a single room:

Doors Open

The shack was just a tin shed with a fireplace. It had about six simple bunks, a kitchen table and a few chairs. Outside there was a tank to collect water off the roof. At the back of the shack there was a little stream with running water where we used to clean our teeth. After you had undone the padlock and gone inside, the first thing you did was open up the windows, which were sheets of corrugated iron on a hinge, to let in the light. There were lots of quite friendly horses around and often, as soon as you'd propped the windows open, a horse would come and put its head in. A few stupid people even encouraged the horses inside, which was very dangerous because a horse needs room to turn to get out. If a horse can't manoeuvre itself around, it can go a bit mad with panic.

There was no electricity, but I was brought up with no electricity and what you don't have you don't miss. Besides, we were so tired from swimming or walking that we never wanted to stay up late. Down on the beach at North Era, there was a huge midden full of shells left by the Aborigines. It was easy to imagine how the miners might have lived off what they caught there, too, as the fishing was so good.

Margaret and company would sketch and paint. Margaret remembers, particularly, a painting that she did looking down from the hut to the beach and another of the little valley of palms to the south of Era called Burning Palms. In between working they often swam. 'I can't remember taking a swimming costume,' Margaret says, 'so maybe we did just take our clothes off and go in.' As well as painting and sketching a fair bit of collecting went on:

You'd find big cuttlefish on the sand that were lovely to carve into. There were wonderful stones, too. When we had to come home, all our supplies having been eaten, we'd fill our rucksacks up with these stones. It was great if you were the last person coming up the cliff, because as the stones got heavier no one saw if you threw a few out to lighten the load.

Once on the way back to Sydney, I think Margaret Cilento was there, too, and another new artist friend, Cedric Flower, we missed the train from Lilyvale. There's a short cut, I said, being a know-all. If you go through a disused tunnel, you can pick up the train somewhere else. My cousins had told me about this short cut, but I'd never actually done it. So we bravely went into the tunnel and were feeling our way along the wall in the pitch darkness, when all of a sudden we heard a train approaching! We ran towards the little circle of light at the end of the tunnel but the train came rushing through before we could make it. We had to flatten ourselves like flies against the wall.

The painter and designer Cedric Flower, in return for participating in the mixed delights of Era, introduced Margaret to yet another part of free-spirited Sydney. Flower, who possessed a thick head of hair and a large moustache, lived in a boarding house of sorts called 'Buggery Barn', or the Ship and Mermaid Inn, to give it its formal title, in Gloucester Street, high up above George Street near the Rocks.

The Barn was a three-storeyed, typically Georgian building with thick sandstone walls and windows that became slightly smaller as the storeys went up.[16] In Flower's days, there were still traces of the original name written on the stonework below the second floor. Supposedly, the building had first been the quarters for Governor Macquarie's officers, after which it became the Ship and Mermaid Inn. The origin of its other, less salubrious name may have related to the sailors who stayed there and their possible nocturnal activities with a cabin boy; or perhaps was simply a reference to the bed bugs that infested its rooms and mattresses, to the constant annoyance of boarders.

The Barn had a tradition of bohemian inhabitants. The American adventurer and novelist Jack London reputedly stayed there at the beginning of the last century; 'Roie' Norton was a resident in the late 1930s, until she was evicted, as legend has it, for keeping too many cats in her room; and, during Flower's time, the musicians Jimmy Somerville and Ray Price lived there.

Although the Barn wasn't central to Margaret's life, she did have a couple of connections to it:

Buggery Barn wasn't a big part of my life. It was somewhere I visited because of Cedric. Opposite there was a terrace house where a couple, not artists themselves but interested in the arts, called Mavis and Robert Mace lived, with the artist Francis Lymburner, who was also a Queenslander. Robert and Mavis were there first, and then Francis moved in with them. Margaret Cilento knew Lymburner from her Brisbane days, she used to run into him at the Carnegie Art Library. So she and I would go over and visit him at the Maces'. Francis, of course, seemed to be much older than us. 'Been there, done that' was the feeling he gave you. We were shy students and he was always so self-confident. But he had a great talent. He was an excellent draftsman and did rather European-style paintings. I've always admired a simple painting he did of an artist's paintbrushes and pots on a table, which is now in the Art Gallery of New South Wales.

Cedric's room at the top of the building had a wonderful view of Circular Quay. All you were conscious of, looking out at Sydney then, were the little copper domes and spires. There was no high rise. That's why now I always think Sydney looks so romantic in a mist. The mist brings the city down to its original size.

Circular Quay itself was marvellous. Going backwards and forwards in the ferry to McMahons Point past all the old buildings at night was magical. Some of those buildings, like the Seaman's Mission on the western side, are still preserved. On the other side, there was the tram terminus and a series of warehouses that might have been woolsheds. One of them had a night club in it called Carl Thomas's. I never went to it – I was far too serious about going to art school for night clubs. But I'd hear the music floating over the water as I was going home at night, which was very romantic.

The musician Jimmy Somerville, who lived at the Barn from 1943 to 1948 (shortly after which the building was pulled down), has many memories of both the bugs and its boarders. 'Cedric had an easel in his room, a little wind-up gramophone like all of us – Sibelius was mostly what was played – and a wonderful antique armchair which he'd picked up for a song somewhere,' Somerville recalls. Fellow musician Ray Price's room at the Barn looked straight across into the room of the terrace house where Francis Lymburner painted, and Price, Flower and Somerville would often watch him playing *his* little gramophone before getting to work at the easel in the morning. 'Lymburner wasn't your characteristic matinee idol or anything like that, but I thought he had fine features,' Somerville says. 'He did a painting of the Barn with vague mists swirling round which made it look rather magical. When the landlady went along to see the painting in an exhibition, Cedric asked her what she thought of it. Oh, she answered, it's a house in a dream. Well, it was. She was right.'

◆

Round about 1944, an American war artist called Arthur Deshaies came into Margaret's life. Deshaies organised Margaret and others, including Anne Wienholt, Margaret Cilento and Jocelyn Zander, into forming what was called 'the Under 30 Group'. The initial meeting, according to Zander, was held in the house where she and her mother lived, at 17 Rosemont Avenue, next door to Merioola, and the group was open to anyone under thirty years of age who was interested in the arts. 'Members took themselves very seriously,' Margaret recalls.

As well as trooping off to listen to some 'very Bauhaus' music, as Margaret remembers it, played by a young Charles Mackerras (later to become the famous conductor), more excitingly in June 1944 the group had an art exhibition where Margaret had her first picture sale.

The Under 30 Group was Margaret's first chance to exhibit with more established artists in Sydney. Her only previous showing had been at the annual exhibition of final year tech students for 1943 (in which she was included although not in her final diploma year). The Under 30 Group exhibition was held at a real gallery, the Education Department Gallery in Loftus Street, and Margaret exhibited five works: *Little Middle Street*, *The Pink House*, *St Paul's Terrace*, *Boys in a Grandstand* and *Honey Boy*, which were all priced between five and ten guineas. Among the other young painters showing were Anne Wienholt, Cedric Flower, Jocelyn Zander, Ronald Millen, John Richards, Justin O'Brien and Francis Lymburner (the last two being non-members), as well as fellow students Margaret Cilento, Jocelyn Rickards and Yvonne Francart.

The *Sydney Morning Herald*'s art critic (who, though uncredited, must have been Paul Haefliger) reviewed the exhibition. While not fully enamoured of the works, the reviewer found the exhibition 'stimulating' and used the words 'talented and enthusiastic' to describe its exhibitors.[17] Their efforts, he noted, had a 'similarity of feeling, not untouched by the work of Dobell and Drysdale' and also 'a strong poetic strain'. However Margaret's painting *Boys in a Grandstand* was criticised for employing conventions beyond her range of experience. What exactly that meant, the reviewer did not explain. The show therefore also initiated Margaret to the reality of the life of an exhibiting artist, which is never entirely plain sailing. The brickbats will come as surely as the praise.

Margaret herself claims that she has never, not even right back then, taken any notice of what critics write. But you can't help wondering, especially given her shyness, if the words didn't cause her puzzlement or any embarrassment.

The day after the Under 30 Group exhibition closed, she had her twenty-first birthday, in Sydney, not at home in Brisbane. To celebrate, the Temperleys took her to the theatre to see Gladys Moncrieff in *Maid of the Mountain*. Margaret remembers that they had seats close to the front and at one point Gladys Moncrieff, who was a largish woman, had to drop to the floor. As she did so, she lifted up her skirt and Margaret was shattered to see that she had large cushions strapped to her knees to soften the jarring. All the illusion of the theatre disappeared instantly.

Towards the end of 1944, Margaret also had an oil painting, *Sister and Brother* (for sale at fourteen guineas), hung in the annual Royal Queensland Art Society's exhibition in Brisbane. As usual, this large event (over two hundred works were selected) took place in the Banquet Hall of Brisbane's Hotel Canberra. Both Margaret and Margaret Cilento had exhibited paintings in the junior section the previous year. But now Margaret was in the exhibition proper, alongside paintings by Caroline Barker and two sculptures by her heroine, Maria Corrie. This time, too, she received praise from an unnamed reviewer,[18] who called her painting the only adventurous work in the show and applauded her for 'trying to make some significant social commentary'. The brother and sister in Margaret's painting *Sister and Brother* were not portraits of her own family. Maybe they were children who had lost a parent in the war, or perhaps they were slum children. It's not hard to imagine a couple of figures in front of some of Margaret's early images of decaying houses.

The reviewer also observed that it was unfortunate that three other paintings by Margaret were rejected from the show as being 'too ugly', which presumably referred to their subjects. Unfortunately no one, not even Margaret, now seems to know what these paintings were of. This is a pity, given it's the only time her work has been described in terms of 'social commentary'.

Nineteen forty-five was Margaret's last full-time year at East Sydney Technical College. It, too, was a year of doors opening that brought increased exposure as more of her paintings were hung in shows. There was also change in the wider Sydney art world. Hal Missingham became the director of the National Art Gallery of New South Wales, an appointment that would lead to the gallery acquiring a far wider range of Australian art and also to its presenting international art exhibitions that would keep it up-to-date with what was happening overseas.

In 1945 Margaret also encountered the teacher who would have the most significant impact on her work – Jean Bellette. Bellette gave her first night life class at the tech on 1 May 1945, which most likely Margaret attended, because soon, like everyone else at tech, she was enthralled by the new teacher's weekly classes.[19]

Apart from her teaching skills, the fact that Bellette was a stylish woman whose own neo-classicist paintings had an undeniably European sensibility must have contributed to the appeal of her classes. In a photograph taken by Merioola resident Alec Murray in the 1940s,[20] Bellette is wearing a sleeveless black jumper and slim, draped skirt. Lying propped on her side on a couch, with an intensity about her expression, she looks both lithe and elegant. A length of printed cloth behind her hints at the exotic, and a row of books, a framed painting and a folding screen of maps indicate her intellectual preoccupations. Only the clouds of cigarette smoke that usually surrounded her – and perhaps a glass of spirits – are missing.

Bellette was born in Hobart in 1908. After studying in Hobart and then at the Julian Ashton school in Sydney, she married fellow art student German-Swiss Paul Haefliger in 1935. The following year they travelled to London. There Bellette attended the London Central School of Arts and Crafts and the Westminster Art School. At both she studied with the Ukraine-born Jewish artist Bernard Meninsky. According to writer and art historian Christine France, Meninsky taught that drawing was to painting what the bony structure is to the living organism and saw the essence of art running from fifth-century BC Greek sculpture through to Italian Renaissance artists.[21]

So during her time in London, Bellette both encountered modernism at first hand and was made keenly aware of European traditions, including those of classical sculpture. This contributed to her own particular painting style, which was often a blend of old and new. In many of Bellette's paintings, figures are grouped as if in a classical frieze, even if they are bathers on an Australian beach with a life-saver's flag.

Bellette and Haefliger returned to Sydney just before the war began, where Haefliger was asked to be a guide for the famous 1939 *Herald* exhibition of modern art. Then in 1941 he was appointed art critic for the *Sydney Morning Herald*, in which role he championed painters such as Dobell, Drysdale and Friend, and attacked what he perceived as the reactionary and academic in Australian art. (When the poet Roland Robinson became friendly with Bellette and Haefliger through his posing at tech, he passed on a few writing tips to Haefliger: namely, to avoid the use of complex sentences and to study Tolstoy rather than the Proust he was always referring to. Given the sometimes incomprehensibly intellectual tone of Haefliger's prose, he perhaps should have heeded Robinson's advice.[22]) Haefliger also contributed articles to *Art in Australia,* as did Bellette, and appeared as a witness for the defence in the court case about Dobell's portrait of Joshua Smith.

As far as their own art went, it was exhibitions of Bellette's and Haefliger's paintings at the Macquarie Galleries in 1939 that prompted William Dobell's praise and remarks in *Art in Australia* that 'integrity in imagination' rather than 'literal fidelity' was what an Australian artist should seek in painting.[23] It might be said that, under Bellette's tutorage Margaret's inner imaginative world, which first came to life dwelling on the butterflies of Tully, now began to guide her eyes and drawing hand.

As Margaret has said to Christine France, Bellette taught her to 'look'.[24]

She taught you the classic construction: to draw around the forms, to draw the simplicity of forms. Her classes were always packed, the sculpture students loved coming to them as well. But it wasn't only that, her classes really lifted you. She was always very positive; if there was something wrong in your drawing she'd just get you to look at it again. Of course, we all admired her painting and drawing. But she was also so encouraging – in a critical way. If I had to sum her up, I'd say above all she was inspirational.

I was a bit in awe of both her and Paul Haefliger. I used to have dinner with the Dundases, but never with Jean and Paul. They weren't part of the circle of friends I made in the 1940s. Later on I knew them better. Jean had a great personality, she was very sophisticated and funny. She was always pulling people's legs, almost going too far with her joshing. She was a little older than Paul and she was very aware of it. Paul had to come first. 'Paulie' had to have his coffee. Paulie had to have this and that. She devoted herself to him and really I think she was a far better painter than Paul. And she was a great teacher.

Among those who went out of their way to attend Bellette's classes was David Strachan. Strachan, renowned for his lyrical still lifes, nudes and landscapes, as well as portraits of his friends, is talked about with reverence by those who knew him, as a man with a real aura or grace. The same is true of his paintings, which have an elusive poetic quality one might easily call an aura. In photographs, Strachan nearly always appears to be gazing unflinchingly ahead, as if more concerned with a reality beyond his immediate surrounds.

Although she was already friendly with Ronald Millen, Strachan was really the first of the coterie of homosexual male artists to whom Margaret would become remarkably close:

I used to see a lot of David. He was living in a house that Jean and Paul Haefliger had in Double Bay in Ocean Avenue. 'Sophisticated primitive painter' is how I'd describe him. David was a very gentle and sweet man. He was older, quite handsome and sophisticated, and had a caustic sense of humour.

I must say, looking back, I think my preference has always been for men who are gay. I don't know why — maybe because they were always gentle, or more sensitive. I just liked the company of gay people. Not that I ever thought of them as gay, nor were they ever referred to as such. I always found them more sympathetic and more interesting. And they were doing things. I could never stand people who were idle.

I don't think I've ever liked that sort of one hundred per cent male. You need the yin and yang in people. There's nothing worse than a one hundred per cent woman either. Silly females are pains in the neck. We're all different. I'm just more interested in individuals than a label for their sexuality.

Strachan's father, who would oppose his son being an artist, was an Australian army doctor and his mother was English.

Strachan was born in England in 1919 and came with his parents to Adelaide, Australia, the following year; then in 1921 they moved to the old gold-mining town of Creswick, Victoria.

In 1936 Strachan returned to England and studied full-time at the Slade School of Art in London. In the summer of 1937, he attended the famous Académie de la Grande Chaumière in Paris and then spent time painting at Cassis near Marseilles, a haunt much beloved by the Bloomsbury group and an area in which Margaret would later live. On his return to Australia in 1938, Strachan shared rooms with the irrepressible artist Wolfgang Cardamatis in Melbourne and attended the George Bell School.

During this period, Strachan was interested in, and was perhaps influenced by, the work of the highly regarded English artist Christopher Wood, a lyrical painter whose career was cut short in his twenties (and with whom Margaret's life would also be interconnected in not so many years' time). Wood was pre-occupied with darkness and once wrote in a letter: 'No black is black enough.'[25] Strachan's paintings, too, as critic and writer John McDonald has noted, are often pitched into a blackness from which partially submerged colours shine through with startling intensity.[26]

In 1941, Strachan moved to Sydney where he worked in the same camouflage unit at Bankstown as William Dobell and shared a flat with Wolfgang Cardamatis in McDonald Street, Potts Point. Next door lived ballerina Hélène Kirsova and Peter Bellew, who was at that stage the editor of *Art in Australia*. In 1939 Bellew had instigated the formation of the New South Wales branch of the Contemporary Art Society, the 'express purpose' of which was to provide 'a meeting ground for all artists and laymen interested in the fostering of purely creative art'.[27] Margaret would soon become a regular exhibitor with the Society. Its first president was the abstract artist Rah Fizelle and for the next few years its annual exhibitions provided 'a much-needed stamping ground for young artists' and were 'guaranteed to cause a hubbub of battle-cry and caterwauling, argument and comment'.²⁸

After being deployed around New South Wales, Queensland and the Northern Territory with the Civil Construction Corps, in 1944 Strachan had his first solo exhibition at the Macquarie Galleries. Margaret remembers him attending Jean Bellette's classes at tech in 1945 and it's most likely this was when their friendship took off:

Often at tech at the end of the day I would go and have a drink in the pub with David and the others before we went on to Jean Bellette's night classes. The boys would go in and order us girls a shandy, which we'd have in the Ladies' Parlour while they went back to the bar. It was six o'clock closing so we never stayed very long. On a couple of occasions I saw a rather foul-mouthed woman drinking there. It turned out to be Tilly Devine, who ran a house down the road.²⁹ That part of Darlinghurst was all a 'working' area in those days.

After we'd been for a drink in the pub, David and I and the others would go off to the Rose Café, which was opposite the court house in Oxford Street. David had a little allowance so he could afford a slightly more expensive meal, like steak, that cost perhaps two and sixpence, while the rest of us could only have a cheap dish which cost about one and six. Soup and scrapings, I think it mainly was. But at least it stalled our hunger. Then we'd all go off to Jean Bellette's life class. As I recall he was working in the painting studio on a nude and a composition, which I think, he wanted to enter in the Travelling Scholarship.

I used to go over to Ocean Avenue and have little dinners with him in his attic room, which also served as his studio. He was painting all his 'Sick Girls', as he called them, at the time. We used to laugh about the titles. Probably it was just an excuse to do pensive-

looking studies of females – he must have seen it as a bit romantic. I think one of the Sick Girls was me, in fact. I didn't actually pose for him, it was more like an image of me that he had in his mind. David and I were companions. I was so committed to painting, companionship was all I wanted.

It was from David Strachan that Margaret first heard of Wolfgang Cardamatis, whose life seems to have furnished many stories. Cardamatis was born in Berlin in 1917 and, according to Margaret's friend Robin Dalton, his German mother died in childbirth and he was bought up by his Greek grandmother until the age of fifteen, when his father, Dr Raoul Cardamatis, a conductor, arranged for his son to join him in Australia.[30] Cardamatis was so unhappy about the move, apparently, that he locked himself in a lavatory in Port Said and was left behind when his ship sailed off. Dalton goes on to add that when Cardamatis finally arrived in Australia he did a flourishing business at his Sydney public school selling hand-painted copies of the dirty postcards he'd bought waiting for the next ship in Port Said. After later being expelled from school, Cardamatis studied art with Antonio Dattilo-Rubbo in Sydney before moving to Melbourne in the late 1930s where he joined George Bell's school and met Strachan.

Strachan often regaled Margaret with stories of the time he and Cardamatis had had bit parts in Hélène Kirsova's ballet *The Revolution of the Umbrellas*, for which Cardamatis also designed the set and costumes. The ballet was performed for two short seasons at the Sydney Conservatorium in 1943. Apparently, on one occasion Cardamatis, running late for a performance, had borrowed a bicycle to get himself there on time – but the ballet had already started when Cardamatis, still astride the bike, finally sailed across the stage.

When Strachan finally introduced Margaret to Cardamatis in

person, she found him 'charming'. Subsequently she kept running into him at parties and another lifelong friendship was established. Cardamatis was also a crony of Donald Friend's. Although in 1945 Margaret hadn't actually met Friend because he'd mostly been out of Sydney with the army, their lives were starting to converge more and more:

I used to hear about Donald when I went back to Brisbane, through my friend Annie Ross. I can't exactly remember how I first met Annie, probably through Margaret Cilento. Annie was also older than me. She was very voluptuous and had black hair that turned out at her neck and a little fringe. She'd been to art school in London, where she had met the artist and illustrator Blair Hughes-Stanton, with whom she had fallen madly in love but who already had a wife. So, again, Annie was worldly, which appealed to me.

Annie's mother was a Russian Jewess whose father had had an antique shop in London. So when Mrs Ross, having fallen in love with an Aussie in England during the First World War, came out to Australia as a bride, she brought the most wonderful furniture with her and the Rosses' wooden house in Brisbane was filled with it.

Annie was one of the first people who bought my work in Brisbane. Eventually, after the war, she went back to England and married Hughes-Stanton, but during the war she was involved with all the war artists stationed in Brisbane, including the American art historian and patron Edgar Kaufman. She would have met Donald, who was great fun at parties, with them. I was never part of that scene because I was studying down in Sydney.

Donald Friend's diary for the years 1944 and 1945 has a number of mentions of Anne Penelope Ross, whom he describes affectionately as 'amusingly exagérée'.[31] That she bought his work was another boost to their friendship, but he was also genuinely fond of her. After he had been flown back from Borneo by the

Doors Open

army, he wrote with heartfelt gratitude in his diary of a crazy, glorious day he'd spent at the Ross home where civilised food was eaten, he could listen to good talk, and Purcell and boogie were played on the gramophone.[32]

◆

By far the biggest event of 1945 for most Australians occurred on 6 August when America dropped an atomic bomb on Hiroshima; three days later Nagasaki, too, was bombed. The tidal waves some Sydneysiders feared as an aftermath of the bombing never happened; and on 15 August Japan surrendered. The war was officially over for Australia. Streamers crisscrossed Martin Place and the civilian population kicked up their heels, kissing uniformed soldiers and sailors with happy abandon in the street. But, as she remembers, Margaret didn't join in any of the celebrations in town. 'I just kept on working. Work was all that mattered to me,' she says.

Margaret may have stayed clear of the partying but the end of the war would affect her. Outside East Sydney Tech, more established artistic figures arrived on the Sydney scene, who contributed an added feeling of creative energy to her world.

At Merioola, Harry Tatlock Miller and Loudon Sainthill had moved in. The war had initially separated Tatlock Miller and Sainthill, who'd been a couple since they met in the 1930s in Melbourne. But eventually they both became army medical orderlies on the same hospital ship and so served out the remainder of their military duty together.[33] Tatlock Miller and Sainthill brought a new touch of chicness to Merioola. As well as a love of theatre, art and ballet the two shared a penchant for gossip and wandering the garden dressed in sarongs. Inside their large quarters Tatlock Miller, who before the war had produced the avant-garde literary and arts magazine *Manuscripts* in Geelong, clacked away on a small portable typewriter writing art reviews for the *Sun* newspaper; while Sainthill, clad in a modish dressing gown, stood at his easel deliberating brushstrokes.

Among Merioola's other new tenants was the artist Justin O'Brien, who had joined the army almost by accident when he was attracted to the sound of a band playing in Martin Place, which turned out to be part of a recruitment drive. O'Brien's father was Australian-born, but his mother was from Kilkenny in Ireland and O'Brien grew up in Hurstville, Sydney, surrounded by an extended, fun-loving, if highly religious Catholic family. O'Brien, whose own sense of humour, warmth and humanity were treasured by his friends, would also become close to Margaret over the years:[34]

At Merioola, not only did I get to know Harry Tatlock Miller and Loudon Sainthill, but also Justin O'Brien. Justin had been taken prisoner in Greece and ended up in a prisoner-of-war camp in Poland. When he finally arrived back in Sydney, he rented a front room upstairs at Merioola. Justin was a very serious worker. In those days he did paintings with very Byzantine-looking elongated figures. Merioola must have been heaven for him after the prisoner-of-war camp. Despite his seriousness, Justin could also be very funny. All these people were opening up my life in a way that I'd never dreamed possible before I came to Sydney.

The infusion of new faces also occasionally made even Margaret's dedicated-to-art heart skip a beat:

Peter Kaiser, who lived at Merioola a bit later on, was another person I became friends with. He arrived in Melbourne at the start of the war after having been interned in Britain for being a German National, and came to Sydney in about 1945. Peter was so handsome. I used to go to films with him. I remember once being in seventh heaven when we went to see The Sheik *together. Peter looked like the Sheik himself. After the film had finished and the lights came on, the theatre was full of sobbing women. I felt great being there with such a handsome man.*

Through the Commonwealth Reconstruction Training Scheme, which was established in 1944 to offer vocational or academic training for ex-servicemen and women, the end of the war also brought an influx of mostly male students to East Sydney Technical College. This would provide Margaret with yet more lasting friendships as well as giving an added vitality to classes:

The men started coming back to tech in dribs and drabs even before the war was over. The artist Lindsay Churchland was one of the first of these to join us in the painting studio. Lindsay was always quoting James Joyce and had a very black sense of humour. We used to call him 'the Black Devil'. I used to think he should have been a writer. As well as tech, he used to go to Jos Holloway's sketch club at night. I never went to Jos Holloway's myself, but he had models posing and apparently people traipsed along just to perv at the breasts. They did details of breasts for their drawings.

Bob Klippel came out of the navy and went into Dadswell's sculpture class. I remember him chipping away at a big stone figure, his one and only stone sculpture before he took up assemblage work. Tommy Bass was also in the sculpture class. Tony Tuckson, a shy, pale, redhead, appeared in the painting studio from the air force. Fred Jessup, who's still a dear, dear friend, left the army and also joined us in the painting studio.

Fred Jessup then introduced Margaret to three people with whom she straight away clicked. Although she finds it difficult to put an exact date on when the meetings occurred, they all happened shortly after the war ended and pretty much simultaneously.

The first two of these simpatico people were Russell 'Tas' Drysdale and his wife, Bonny. ('Tas' was Drysdale's childhood family nickname that came when his younger sister was unable to say 'Russell' and so called him 'Tussell', which developed into Tass or Tas).[35] The Drysdales were living with their children, Lynne and Tim, at 3 Bayview Hill Road, Rose Bay, in a house halfway up a steep hill beside the imposing Rose Bay Sacred Heart Convent that looks out over the harbour. Either the first time Jessup took her to the Drysdale house, or very soon afterwards, Margaret at long last met Donald Friend, who had just come back from serving as a war artist in Borneo. The Drysdales and Friend were all older than Margaret, but over the next few years, as she says, she would 'naturally be drawn to them'.

Donald Friend's father, Lesley Friend (who changed his surname, Moses, to his mother's maiden name, Friend), was a grazier and Friend's early childhood was spent on various properties around New South Wales. As a small boy, he boarded first at Tudor House in Bowral and then at Cranbrook in Sydney's eastern suburbs, after his mother Gwendolyn moved to nearby Double Bay. It was Gwendolyn – 'L'Adorable', as Friend then called her – who introduced her son to the arts at an early age.[36] When his mother relocated to the Double Bay flat, Friend became a day boy at Cranbrook and took art lessons outside of school with painter Sydney Long. After changing schools to Sydney Grammar, he became fixated with Norman Lindsay's romantic watercolours and drawings, which he emulated in pen and ink. When, because of the Depression, his mother gave up her flat, Friend, aged sixteen, left school to work out west on a family property called 'Glendon', near Moree. Around this time, his parents divorced.

Soon afterwards, Friend ran away to wander blissfully around north Queensland with a swag and for a while worked on a pearling lugger in Torres Strait. The trip resulted in an abiding fixation with the far north, its landscape and people, especially a Torres Strait Islander family called the Sailors, with whom he struck up a friendship in Malaytown, Cairns. Thereafter, he would repeatedly seek out the Sailor family when he wearied of the guiles, or even just the company, of the rest of the world, and frequently would retreat to tropical climates with their less hectic lifestyle, more conducive to being an artist.

After his adventure up north, Friend returned to Sydney in 1934 and enrolled in Antonio Dattilo-Rubbo's art classes. The dashing, handsome Italian artist had started teaching art in Sydney at the end of the nineteenth century and, in its heyday, attendance at his 'Atelier' rivalled that of the other great private Sydney art school, Julian Ashton's. Among his earlier pupils were modernists Grace Cossington Smith, Roland Wakelin and Roy de Maistre.

In 1936, Friend took off for London, where, like Jean Bellette, he studied with Bernard Meninsky at the Westminster School, met other Australian artists, including Dobell, and had his first one-person show, in 1938. He also frequented African night clubs like the Shim-sham in Soho and fell, temporarily, in love with a Nigerian male model, which led to his lasting fascination with African art, African dancing and African men. He returned to Australia in 1940 and had his first Sydney one-person show at the Macquarie Galleries in 1942, the year he finally enlisted. In February 1945 he was appointed an official war artist and was posted first to Labuan and then to Borneo. When he returned to Sydney from Borneo (although not yet formally discharged from the army), he stayed with the Drysdales and before long he and Drysdale were 'dabbing' away together.[37] Margaret recalls of their close relationship:

The friendship between Tas and Donald really began when Donald joined the army and was stationed at Hume, near Albury. Tas and Bonny, with the children, Lynne and Tim, were living in Albury, because after the submarine attack on the harbour they wanted to be out of Sydney. Albury was where Tas did his great painting of soldiers asleep on the railway platform at night. Donald used to visit Tas and the family in their house at Albury and he and Tas would work together in Tas's studio, which was in a stable. Painting together sets up a real rhythm, you bounce off one another. Then, when the Drysdales came back to Sydney, Donald was always visiting them when he was on leave. He not only adopted Tas like a brother or a father, he also embraced the whole family. I think in a way they replaced his mother, whom he later abandoned.

Lynne Clarke, the Drysdales' daughter and herself an artist, who was about eight or nine at the time, remembers of the wartime period: 'A lot of servicemen came to the house. There were parties all the time for people who were on leave and a lot of artists were there, too. My father felt dreadful about being rejected from the army – Donald loathed the army, and there was my father wishing he was in the war – so my parents had this open house for people who were in the forces. It was like a war effort. There were divan beds in the sitting room for people who stayed on after the parties. That's where Donald slept when he stayed. My mother used to talk about the men, like the young ones who were on the midget submarines, how they would drink, then fall asleep – pass out, I suppose, from the drinking – and have nightmares. She said it must have been horrific for them. My parents were just trying to give them a little bit of R & R.'

Now with the war over, thanks to Fred Jessup Margaret was also experiencing the Drysdale household's unique hospitality and personalities:

Tas and Bonny were both larger than life, although Bonny physically was a small, wiry person. She was very short, fair and full of fun, very direct, and always taking the mickey out of people. She had great wit, even if she had drunk too much, which she sometimes did. Tas, of course, was very tall and very entertaining. He could drink and drink, yet never get drunk. As darling David [Strachan] used to say, he was like a sandpit with water – no matter how much water you put in (only in his case it was alcohol), it never fills up.

If Tas started talking about the studio he was going to build one day, Bonny would come out with, The best studios are in the bedroom. Meaning you don't have to have a special studio to paint well. Bonny was never interested in housekeeping. She used to say, What you want is a big concrete floor and then hose it all out. But she made great stews, so there was always food in the house, plus a lot to drink. And lots of music. Early jazz, real early black American jazz. Boogie-woogie. They had a wonderful record collection. Music was going all the time at Rose Bay. Donald Friend loved boogie, too. He and Bonny were great at dancing to it together. Donald was very good-looking. I only ever saw the amusing party side of him in those days.

Although it seems Margaret's socialising was beginning to increase towards the end of 1945, her dedication to studies didn't slacken. She had ten paintings hung in the Under 30 Group's second show in March. Then her drawing *The Red House*, priced at three guineas, was included in a special Society of Artists exhibition of small drawings and sculpture at the David Jones Art Gallery in April. In November, four of her paintings were hung in the Contemporary Art Society's seventh annual show, which was a big first for her, and she was favourably mentioned in the *Sydney Morning Herald*'s review. (David Strachan's *The Sick Girl* was also singled out, for its display of 'the rarest charm and understanding' of a young girl; while Wolf Cardamatis's *Portrait of Nicolas d'Ivangine* was described as his finest work yet.[38])

One month later, in December 1945, there was an exhibition by East Sydney Technical College Diploma students, of whom Margaret was one. The *Sydney Morning Herald*'s art critic (although not named, presumably Paul Haefliger again) wrote that their Diploma works were 'the brightest seen to date', and pronounced the new artists 'alive and ready for the fray'.[39] The *Daily Telegraph*'s critic lavishly praised the work of the female students but found the male students' offerings lacking in talent.[40] He went on to say that Margaret Olley's *Circus* painting had 'precision and vigour' and 'seems to indicate the road she is searching'. When the results of East Sydney Technical College were published in the *Sydney Morning Herald* a little later, Margaret, along with Margaret Cilento and Ena Joyce, received a Grade A in the final stage (and her friend Jocelyn Rickards a Grade B).

Margaret was now twenty-two years old, remarkably young to be entering the fray of Sydney's art world. Unencumbered emotionally – in that she was happily free of lovers or even a wishfully courting boyfriend who might distract her from the fray (although she had met a number of men who would remain important to her) – Margaret was raring to get on with the real love affair of her life, which was painting. There was only one hitch, now that she'd found a nip or two held her niggling shyness at bay, and that was the small matter of paying the rent.

6

Keeping the Rent Paid

I was determined to go on painting and living in Sydney. I was mainly doing still lifes and landscapes in oils. There was a boat-building place on the water at Lavender Bay opposite the flat and I loved drawing the ribs of the boats there. Buying flowers to paint from a florist shop was unheard of. Any flowers I incorporated into my paintings were mainly what I'd found over a fence. 'Doing a bit of pruning', it's called. Brisbane was still home, but the flat was my Sydney base. I used to go backwards and forwards between the two like a yo-yo.

THE SHARED WORLD OF THE TWO MARGARETS NOW ENDED. After they graduated Margaret Cilento went back to Brisbane, where she was awarded the 1946 Wattle League Scholarship, which amounted to one hundred and fifty pounds. With that in hand, the following year she set off for New York, where her father was working with the United Nations and her mother was researching nutrition. But Cilento was nevertheless determined to tough it out on her own in New York. Her first studio was 'an empty bathroom behind a butcher shop in the tough Bowery', which was followed by a basement in Greenwich Village. In the Village she also studied at Stanley William Hayter's Atelier 17, which specialised in experimental print workshops.[1] In 1949, Cilento won a French government scholarship and went to Paris to study at Hayter's Paris Atelier 17.

In Sydney, Margaret stayed on alone at the McMahons Point flat. Although she had officially graduated at the end of 1945, she continued to do additional classes at East Sydney Tech for the next two years, which was a common practice. This first year she did Art Modelling II with Lyndon Dadswell, which was perhaps indicative of a lingering attachment to sculpture, and an advanced evening class in life painting in oils. However, these extra classes aside, 1946 was Margaret's first real year as an artist on the loose:

I took whatever jobs I could to earn enough money to pay the rent. At Christmas time in Brisbane, I'd go off picking grapes at Samford. In Sydney, Sam organised some work for me decorating drinking glasses. I painted figures in oil paint on them, which mustn't have been very hygienic. But at any rate, the paint would have been dry by the time anyone drank out of them.

During this period, set-painting also became a small but staple income-earner for Margaret. Her work in the theatre, as well as supporting her as an artist, may also have helped to develop her sense of the placement of objects within a three-dimensional framework, which she would incorporate in her own painting, especially her later interiors. Her first set-painting had come about in 1945 through Cedric Flower:

Cedric was asked to design a set for Tartuffe *at the New Theatre and I was his assistant. The New Theatre was a communist-oriented theatre with premises, in those days, in Castlereagh Street in the city. They usually put on propaganda shows, but for comic relief or to show the buffoonery of the other side, they did a season of Molière's plays. We had to paint the sets on the stage, so when they were rehearsing we had to stop work and sit up the back waiting until they had finished.*

People used to say that there was nothing going on in theatre in those days, but there was probably more happening than there is now. People did it because they loved it. At rehearsals, even the electricians used to come along and be there until 12.30 a.m. if they were wanted, just because they loved the theatre. Often they did it for no pay at all. Working on theatre sets, you learn to be adaptable; we had to paint sets in all sorts of odd places. Once you're given a date in the theatre, you just have to get the work done in that time. It was good training for me because the same principle applies to exhibitions. So now if I'm given a date for a show, I just work towards it.

Margaret's next venture into the world of the theatre came when she worked for theatre director Sydney John Kay. The life story of Sydney John Kay, whose original surname was Kaiser, is a drama in itself. Born in Germany around 1900, of Jewish and Peruvian extraction, in the 1920s and '30s Kay played in Weintraub's Syncopators, a German jazz group that was famous across Europe for its mix of music and comic entertainment. The group also featured in the famous 1930 Marlene Dietrich film *The Blue Angel*. By 1933, with Nazism on the rise, Weintraub's Syncopators, who were mostly Jewish, had left Germany on a world tour that ended in Australia in 1937. In 1941 they were interned in Australia as enemy aliens.

When Kay was released in 1942, and having changed his name by deed poll, he became the musical arranger of the Colgate-Palmolive radio unit in Sydney. In 1946, in an effort to improve the state of Australian theatre, Kay, along with several others including Peter Finch and drama critic Allan Ashbolt, founded the Mercury Theatre Company. The Company's first performance, of three classic European one-act plays, was staged at the Conservatorium of Music in July 1946, and was greeted with acclaim. The plays chosen were Spanish playwright Lope de Vega's *The Pastry-baker*, directed by Finch; German dramatic poet Heinrich von Kleist's *The Broken Pitcher*, directed by John Wiltshire; and Russian Anton Chekhov's *Diamond Cut Diamond*, which Kay himself directed and in which Finch acted:

Sydney John Kay had a bald head and enormous energy, he had his finger in a lot of pies to do with theatre. The costumes and set for Diamond Cut Diamond *were designed by William Constable. Yvonne Francart and I were chosen to help him. Yvonne, who had swept-up hair and a long neck, was at art school with me. I had to collect the designs for the set from Constable at his paint workshop, which was a cream corrugated building in Glenmore Road, Paddington, about a block or so along from Oxford Street. He handed me some scrawny little drawings – a series of little squiggles best describes them – which I was then supposed to enlarge.*

Diamond Cut Diamond was also where I first met Peter Finch, who was very handsome. You could see why Vivien Leigh, when she came here a bit later on a tour of Australia with Laurence Olivier, would be so mad about him. When I was working with him, he was still married to the ballerina Tamara Tchinarova. Even before I did the play I used to hear Donald Friend talking about Peter Finch, because in the Depression he and Finch had jumped on the rattler and gone up together to Cairns.

Friend, in fact, had had a brief love affair with Finch in the early 1930s.[2] He and Finch had lived together in Sydney before taking off for north Queensland and occasionally hung out at an underworld club in William Street called the Mirrors, where they would perform on stage in return for a meal. Friend kept tabs on Finch's theatrical career, somewhat critically, thereafter. An entry in his diary for June 1946, when *Diamond Cut Diamond* would have been in rehearsal, or close to it, describes a chance meeting between the two.[3] Friend, by now well established in Merioola and inexplicably down in the dumps after pleasant Sunday morning drinks with friends, was on his way to lunch when he ran into Finch who: 'Looked and spoke very actorishly – a voluminous stagey greatcoat, large gestures, rolling voice and eyes, and hair curling down his neck and over his collar like a Drury Lane ham.'

According to Margaret, *Diamond Cut Diamond* was a nightmare to work on. As she remembers it, after giving her his vague squiggles, William Constable went away and she just had to interpret them as best she could:

I hate to think what the set ended up looking like – especially since I might have been having a few nips to help me along. Two and six an hour we were paid. Kay rented the basement of an office block in the city for us to work in, which was where the workers came down and made their cups of tea. So we'd be painting away and boiling up all our stinking size, while the poor workers were trying to have their morning or afternoon tea-breaks. You mix the size (which is like glue) in with the paint to make the paint stick on the canvas backdrops. Size was made out of horse hooves and the smell was foul.

Another time, Kay rented a space for us at the back of a house in Darling Point. This time there was a shed where we could mix up the paints. But before we could do any painting, I had to stretch out the big canvas flats on the cement in the backyard. Then people would come and hang out their washing, and the washing would drip on the canvas flats. It was not easy. I think that's why I began painting my own work on masonite. I just found it more practical and easy. I still do.

The following year, in 1947, Kay founded the Mercury Mobile Players, which took theatre to the people, with a folding stage and proscenium that fitted onto the back of truck. The Mobile Players' productions of classic comedy, usually in abridged versions, visited factories, hospitals, schools and public halls. It was in a Mobile Players' production of Molière's *The Imaginary Invalid* at O'Brien's Glass Factory in 1948 that Laurence Olivier and Vivien Leigh first saw Peter Finch acting. Olivier consequently persuaded Finch to try his luck in London and by the end of that year Finch had left Australia for England.

―◆―

At this stage, Margaret was still far too busy for any love interest. As she says, she was just 'smitten' with painting. Perhaps, too, her covert crush on Sam Hughes allowed her to keep other admirers at arm's length – although she did very occasionally let her guard down:

One year, when I was going home to Brisbane for the Christmas holidays, I decided to sublet the flat for the six weeks I was away, and ended up renting it out to an architecture student who was living in a boatshed along the bay. I remember having a bit of a fumble and scrum with him. Nothing ever came of it. Once, too, at Era, someone made a pass at me. I really wasn't looking for a relationship or sex. But men, or youths, just automatically think it's their right, or they did then.

Painting was far more rewarding to me than dining out and having a good time at night clubs in the way Jocelyn Rickards or Mitty Lee-Brown did. That's why I was so pleased I never lived at Merioola. Jocelyn, who was very young then, rented a little room down the hall and Mitty also had a room there. Alec Murray, the photographer – Jocelyn's especial friend – was living in the stable of the house and using the ballroom as a photographic studio. Donald's room was at the front on the ground floor. I used to go over to see Harry Tatlock Miller and Loudon Sainthill, and I'd run into Jocelyn or Mitty in the hallway. But I never went out socially the way they did. I was never one for sitting round having cups of coffee, as people do. I liked McMahons Point because I was on my own. Mitty did invite me up to Palm Beach once. During the week she stayed at Merioola, then had weekend parties at her family home in Palm Beach. Roland 'Roly' Pullen (who was a journalist and a very funny man) and I were asked along more as court jesters than anything else, I think.

As I said before, most of the men I really liked best were gay. Harry and Loudon were another example. Loudon, who stuttered really badly, was a darling, the sweetest person and so talented. Harry and Loudon were like a happily married couple who kept their relationship alive by having little affairs, I realised later. But in those days I never ever thought that there was a sexual thing between them. They were just friends. Two people living together. Companions.

Tatlock Miller and Sainthill, as one might expect, threw wonderful parties in their room at Merioola, which Margaret, despite her frequent shunning of other social occasions, did attend. The writer and artist's huge room had a rounded bay window opposite the fireplace and was very elegantly decorated. The fireplace itself was draped with cheesecloth, which had been dipped in plaster of Paris and then allowed to dry in folds. The walls of the room, except for a white border, and ceiling were painted a rich brown and there was a lime green carpet that matched the colour of the panels in the white doors, while the furniture was what Donald Friend described as 'Vogue Regency'.[4] According to Margaret, the room's theatrical lighting added even more of an atmosphere to parties held there.

Apart from their entertaining, Margaret has another favourite memory of Tatlock Miller and Sainthill's Merioola days, which is to do their with dachshund, who was called Emily:

Colin Brown (who was in the sculpture studio at tech and used to pose for Donald in his front room) and another student had made a rubbery penis, quite a large penis, and brought it to the house. The penis became a toy for the dog. Harry and Loudon used to throw it outside and then the dog would get the exercise of running down the stairs and out into the garden to retrieve it. One day Mary Edwards (who brought the case against Dobell's portrait of Joshua Smith and was living out the back of Merioola) accidentally discovered the penis in the grass. She rang up the police in a great state, saying that she had found a 'mutilated member'. A terrible commotion ensued. The story of this episode subsequently did the rounds of the town, much to everyone's amusement. It was even in the press.[5]

◈

Sam Hughes organised another means of making money for Margaret by arranging for her to paint the flat next to his in Billyard Avenue. The flat belonged to a friend of Hughes called Dorothy Buchanan. Buchanan, who wanted every wall a different colour, which made the painting less of a chore, was interested in art and attended classes with Desiderius Orban at his art school in Circular Quay. Orban, who was born in Hungary, had studied art in Paris, where he had also sat in on the famous Saturday evening gatherings of writer Gertrude Stein and met artists such as Duchamp, Picasso and Matisse. He had arrived in Sydney in 1936 and established his art school in 1941. Orban, whose own paintings were not dissimilar to the neo-romantic work of other artists in Sydney at this time, would remain an important figure in the emergence of modern art in Australia.

However, in Margaret's opinion, at the time she was painting Buchanan's walls, Orban's students were 'dilettantes' who did not take art nearly as seriously as she herself and the other students at East Sydney Technical College did. Nevertheless, she and Buchanan became firm friends:

Dorothy had the use of a place called 'Careel House' at Whale Beach. This was a strange old stone house built right up on a sandstone ridge of the headland. It was great for drawing. The house belonged, I think, to a milliner in Melbourne who seldom came up to Sydney. Dorothy and her boyfriend, Greg, had been asked if they would caretake the house and they had the full use of it. Their only duty seemed to be looking after the occasional boxes of plants that were sent up from Melbourne for the garden.

There was one big room inside and a bathroom with a sunken bath. Once I found a big koala bear trapped in the bath. I don't know who was more surprised, me or the bear. We all benefited by being able to go there. Sam, John Richards and I would go up and take a picnic with us. Sometimes we'd stay for a week. Paul Jones was another person who came to Careel House. We did plenty of work there, both drawing and painting. The others often drew the bush nearby. I was mostly busy doing big gouaches of the garden. Whenever I went away painting anywhere I'd usually take gouache (opaque paint) because it was easier to manage. Although I did lug canvas and paints down to Era.

Margaret also has fond recollections of an Easter she spent camping with Hughes, Richards, John and Lyndsay Duffecy and the artist Paul Jones at the Nepean River near Castlereagh, where they all slept under she-oaks or pine trees in a row. As Margaret remembers, the others set off a little ahead of her for their outdoor adventure:

Apparently, John and Lyndsay arrived at Central Railway in their proper walking boots with rucksacks, expecting a real hike, while Sam, John and Paul turned up with their things in brown paper shopping bags. Then, when they got off the train at Penrith, much to John and Lyndsay's surprise, Sam and his lot hailed a taxi to take them to the river bank. According to John [Duffecy], when they came to meet me at the station I was rigged up with what I called my 'night walking hat', which was a white American sailor's hat with the little brim turned down all the way round. I ended up wearing some willow wands like a crown in my hair and spent most of the weekend floating up and down the river with nothing on, while Sam sat on a rock watching me. Some old fisherman started perving on me, too, which was a bit annoying.

'Looking so Renoir, it was unbelievable' is how John Duffecy affectionately describes Margaret in her willow wands.[6] It's a vision that has stayed indelibly with Duffecy, who at that stage was working behind a counter at Gowing's men's store, selling ties, but would soon begin his career as a furniture designer by making coffee tables in a workshop at an old iceworks in Rockdale.

Dorothy Buchanan and John Richards also eventually went into business together, painting fabrics. They worked in a room of a house at 151 Dowling Street, Woolloomooloo, which Margaret and her friends referred to as 'the poor man's Merioola'. This three-storey white terrace house, originally named 'Roseville', was bought in a virtually derelict state around 1947 by Bob Howland. Howland set about restoring it, ripping off flowery Victorian wallpaper with gusto, and by 1949 was renting out studio spaces in it. He himself continued to live in the house, sharing a room with clerk and part-time ballet dancer Alan Hopwood, and found a more conventional day job while studying pottery at night at East Sydney Tech.[7] The rest of the house was filled with a gaggle of artistic boarders who both lived and worked there:

Keeping the Rent Paid

Paul Jones, who was painting delicate flower studies, rented a room that was full of shells he'd collected. Ina Morriss made corsets during the week and painted in her time off in what used to be the maid's quarters.[8] The artist Alannah Coleman, with her noisy Siamese cats, was in another room, and Frankie Mitchell had his very first dressmaking business in the stone basement.

Alannah Coleman was very blonde. She used to wear a red cloak to openings and swish it over her shoulder. Later she went to London, where she had a gallery in Qantas House and kept hairless Rex cats instead of the Siamese. She used to judge Rexes at cat shows, in fact. Whenever I was in London, Alannah would take me to dinner at the Arts Club. She was very knowledgeable about London and was keen to take you on walks, insisting you go to various places and so on.

It must have been very early in the 1950s when Dorothy and John set up in Dowling Street. Sam rented a room for them and brought in a big trestle table. They used to get special paint for fabric and with the utmost confidence do great swirling patterns on very expensive materials, like satin. Even though the war had been over for a while, there were still hardly any interior decorating shops and imported fabrics were scarce, so John and Dorothy's swirls really had an impact. By then Sam and John had also started an interior decorating business in a shop on New South Head Road, Edgecliff, which was where Dorothy and John sold their material. The shop was already special because of Sam's taste, then Paul Jones did a mural on the wall of life-size or over life-size eighteenth-century ladies, which added to its uniqueness.

Art galleries were also a bit of a rarity in Sydney of the 1940s. Apart from the Education Department Gallery in Loftus Street, there were the Macquarie Galleries at 19 Bligh Street, the

Grosvenor Gallery at 219 George Street, the gallery in Farmers department store (now Myer) and the new David Jones Gallery, which had opened in 1944. And that was about it.

The Macquarie Galleries had the most kudos, as far as both artists and collectors were concerned. It had been started by John Young in 1925. Its first exhibition was of Roland Wakelin's avant-garde, Cubist-inspired, light and softly coloured paintings. The Macquarie continued to show modernist painters, including such artists as Grace Cossington Smith and Grace Crowley, throughout the 1920s and '30s, and was the only commercial gallery in Sydney to survive the Depression years. In 1938, Lucy Swanton and Treania Smith became the gallery's directors. According to Margaret, the Macquarie Galleries were smallish but just the right size. Swanton and Smith always had a few nice pieces of furniture on display, including the set of drawers in which they kept the drawings, a small table and a couple of little red lacquered chairs with a chinoiserie-look and hand-painted decoration, which Margaret found especially appealing:

I love the look of furniture in a gallery. It's nothing to do with making a gallery domestic. The furniture breaks up the line that goes round a gallery or a room – that awful line you're so conscious of in contemporary galleries – where the light strikes the end of the wall as it meets the floor. I loathe that hard line. If you break up the space your eyes go up to the paintings. The French, in particular, often do this in interiors. It's called a chair rail. The wallpaper goes from there up to the ceiling – and so do your eyes.

I liked Lucy Swanton, who ran the Macquarie Galleries, along with Treania Smith, in the 1940s. Lucy was a Quaker and must have had independent means, because she used to buy up paintings very wisely and discreetly. Then, when the regional galleries such as Newcastle and Wollongong started opening up, she gave paintings to them, just quietly. So she's another person, like Howard Hinton, who early on inspired me for the Trust I've now set up.

The Contemporary Art Society shows, state and interstate, and the Society of Artists, which I also exhibited with, were all held at the Education Department Gallery. The Contemporary Art Society was a great opportunity for everyone to show their work – for some people it was the only place they could – and their exhibitions were always really big occasions. In those days there were little circles of friends: Tas had his friends; Bill Dobell had his; Grace Cossington Smith and Grace Crowley had theirs; and they all linked up at art openings. The Contemporary Art Society was also important because it was the only place where Sydney artists hung side-by-side with artists from other states.

Sam Hughes's experience at the Zwemmer Gallery in London led to his being asked to hang the Contemporary Art Society Eighth Annual Interstate Exhibition in 1946. In it were works by the big three Melbourne painters, Arthur Boyd, Sidney Nolan and Albert Tucker. But it was Nolan's work, which included his painting of a *Hare in Trap* with its wide-open, terrified blue eye, that hit home with Margaret:

It was really in-your-face. So different. Very alive. He had a very definite view. Everybody said, Wow, what a shot in the arm. There was a sort of urgency with which he painted. It created an energy. Of course, there were those people who said it shouldn't be hung, that it was like children's art and so on. To me that was his strength. It had the impact of child art. But, of course, children's art is not consistent whereas Nolan's was.

There were also three of Margaret's paintings in the show: *Late Afternoon, Berrie's Bay* (spelling as per the catalogue), *Venus and Cupid Reclining* and *Quay Building*. Hughes also hung the

Contemporary Art Society's second state exhibition earlier in 1946, as well the Society of Artists' annual show in August of the same year. Margaret had four works in the Contemporary Art Society's state exhibition: *Breakfast Creek, Brisbane*; *Brisbane Church, St Paul's Terrace* and *Evening Betrothal*. Margaret was part of Hughes's special hanging committee for the Society of Artists, and three of her own paintings – *Era Landscape*; *Early Morning, Lavender Bay*; and *Afternoon* – were included. The Society of Artists' Medal for 1946 was awarded to Thea Proctor, for her valuable work 'developing taste in New South Wales'.[9] Margaret was keeping prestigious company this year. What's interesting about the paintings she submitted to these shows in 1946 is that none of them was a still life. They were nearly all landscapes, water scenes and Brisbane streetscapes. Obviously Margaret wasn't spending much time 'pruning' flowers for subjects.

The Contemporary Art Society show, with the Nolans that so impressed Margaret, opened on 12 November 1946 to a mixed reception. The problems, according to Donald Friend, began with the official opening speech: 'a very long, tediously worded and dully delivered sermon delivered by Hal Missingham, most of which was drowned out by the greater volume of Paul Haefliger's irrepressibly exuberant conversation at the other end of the gallery.'[10]

But this wasn't the only fly in the ointment. According to Friend, there was a severe dearth of the usual art-show-opening crowd in attendance. 'Sensation-seeking old ladies' and 'society dames in window hats' (whatever they might be) were noticeably absent. Worst of all, there were no sales! Not one.

The introduction Sam Hughes had written for the show also came in for some mild flack. His romantic prose stressed the importance of the 'precious element of imagination' to art and likened the Society to a 'tolerant gardener waiting or wandering with a watering can' in a wilderness to bring unimaginable flowers to blossom. It concluded with the enigmatic statement: 'I hear the camel bells.'[11] This last reference caused Harry Tatlock Miller, writing in the *Sun*, to confess himself completely mystified as to its meaning.[12] The whole piece seems decidedly akin to the tone of James Elroy Flecker's poetic drama *Hassan*, which Hughes would produce the following year. Perhaps he was rehearsing.

Although Tatlock Miller thought the show in general lacked the exotic blooms promised by Hughes, he noted that Margaret's 'sombre landscape', presumably *Late Afternoon, Berrie's Bay*, showed 'much promise'. In the *Sydney Morning Herald*, however, Margaret received a slight slap on the wrist for her 'rather ponderous composition, *Venus and Cupid Reclining*'.[13] So her artist's progress was still a bit 'one foot forward, one foot back', as far as the critics went. But she did have their attention.

―◆―

In 1947 Margaret's additional courses at tech were Painting and Drawing Stage III and Life Drawing Advanced. Outside these classes, the year presented a new source of painting inspiration. Margaret's friend Jocelyn Zander was by this time married to the innovative artist Carl Plate and had moved to the Woronora River on the outskirts of southern Sydney:

I first met Carl Plate at his Notanda Gallery in Rowe Street, Sydney. Rowe Street was very narrow, not much wider than a lane really. It ran beside the Australia Hotel, between Castlereagh and Pitt Streets, and was full of intriguing little shops. The Notanda Gallery was a Mecca for art students and artists. It was the only place in Sydney where you could buy art books, postcards or prints. Carl also had exhibitions and on the walls there were always modern paintings that he'd bought overseas before the war, which was an eye-opener to us students, because we were so deprived of that kind of art due to the war.

Before Carl married Jocelyn, he lived in one of a row of cream terrace houses with big French windows near Phillip Street, where the tram ran down to Circular Quay. The tram passed another lot of old-fashioned terraces at Chifley Square that I remember painting. I loved buying postcards of paintings at the Notanda. A painting postcard establishes your home. Some of these postcards ended up in my own paintings, but I didn't arrange them into paintings. They weren't posed, I would have had them there to begin with. I still buy postcards of paintings. When I'm travelling I always have a few postcards with me. Prop a postcard of a painting in any hotel room and you're perfectly at home.

After I'd left tech I came to know Carl better, through his involvement with the Contemporary Art Society, and when Jocelyn was having their first daughter, I looked after the house at Woronora for them. Then I house-sat for them again a bit later on, it might even have been the next year.

Margaret used to drive down to Woronora with her friend Dorothy Buchanan and the pair of them would paint the whole time. Margaret not only painted the nearby landscape, including the river, but, perhaps encouraged by the artistic atmosphere and a more spacious interior than her McMahons Point flat, also did a number of still lifes. Although what she regards as the best of these, 'a still life with a draped white cloth – rather influenced by Cézanne', unfortunately no longer exists, another, *Still Life in Green*, is now part of the Art Gallery of New South Wales' collection. In this painting fruit and eggs are spread out beside a couple of bottles on a dark green cloth with what appear to be cushions behind. It looks simple, almost empty, compared to Margaret's later work, but it does show how even then the background domestic environment was of interest to her.

Keeping the Rent Paid

The house at Woronora was right out in the bush and quite isolated. Carl Plate, as Margaret remembers it, had a collection of Granada gypsy music. She and Buchanan, taking advantage of the lack of neighbours, would wind up the gramophone and have the gypsies going full blast as they worked away. Suddenly one night in the midst of all this there was a tap on the glass window. Much to their amazement, it was Godfrey Miller.

Godfrey Miller, a painter and teacher with strong philosophical leanings and an obsessive interest in biology, is one of those artists whom other artists regard with reverence. His abstract paintings were complexly structured and sprang from an intensely private intellectual core. It's been said of Miller that he believed the cellular secrets of the universe are contained in a drop of water and that his art was a reflection of this.[14] He was born in 1893 in Wellington, New Zealand, where he grew up and studied architecture. He then travelled to London to continue his studies, which were interrupted by the First World War and only completed after he'd served in Egypt and at Gallipoli with the New Zealand army. It was not until he was nearly thirty that he changed to a career in painting, and not until the outbreak of the Second World War that he settled into a studio near Circular Quay, Sydney.

While Margaret knew of Miller by reputation, because of his reclusive nature she had not encountered him before his appearance at the windowpane at Woronora. A number of surprises were to follow:

Godfrey, who was much older than us and very, very shy and quiet, said he'd come down to stay.
Oh, I said, can I make you up a bed?
No, he replied, I'll sleep under the stars.
There was a deck on their roof and that's where he slept. I never went up. I don't know if he had a mattress or any bedding. All I can

tell you is that he was having a love affair with a couple of angophoras on the track at the back of the house. He would disappear up the track to study the angophoras, then he'd come back and I'd see him, hunched in concentration, scratching away, very slowly, at a few lines on a piece of paper. One of the conditions of staying at the house was that I had to water the garden. So I'd get the hose out, do the watering, come back and Godfrey would still be in exactly the same position, still doing the two trees. One was slightly at an angle against the other. I can see them now. He just kept slowly scratching at them for days. Such a sweet, gentle, reclusive fellow. I was very fond of him.

The major excitement of 1947, which took place mid-year, was the most perfect melding of art, theatre and friends that Margaret would ever experience. It was Sam Hughes's extraordinary theatrical production of *Hassan*.

Hassan, by James Elroy Flecker, was first published in 1922. During the course of the play's five acts Hassan, the humble Baghdad confectioner, attempts to seduce Yasmin, his love, with magic. But through a series of remarkable accidents involving the Caliph Haroun Ar Raschid, Hassan ends up taking 'the Golden Road to Samarkand', a much chastened, possibly wiser man. Flecker's language, even his elaborate stage directions, is as richly image-steeped as Persian poetry and the play must have seemed a wildly exotic choice for Sydney in the 1940s; small wonder that Margaret found working on it such a captivating experience:

Hassan was really like a big paint-off, or a happening with a purpose. Jimmy Cook, who was a teacher at tech, organised the set-painting. The sets were blown-up copies of sixteenth-century Persian miniatures and we rented part of the old Sydney Showground to work on them. Loudon Sainthill did the front curtain. I did a backdrop for the prison scene, with rabbits and flowers in a garden outside, David Strachan did another and so did Fred Jessup.[15] We had gold and silver powders, which were used to add to the richness of the sets. I ended up keeping a jar of gold as a souvenir when we'd finished. Hassan, the confectioner, was acted by a Russian friend of Sam's called Dmitri Makaroff; John Richards played Ishak, the minstrel; and my friend Nigel Hawkins was Rafi, the King of the Beggars. Sam organised the people in the Music Department of Sydney University to do the music, which was composed by John Antill.

At the opening, Sam had so much incense burning, it was incredible. In fact, there were a lot of protests from the university people who were sitting in the front row and were incensed out. Afterwards the production went up to Brisbane. I was down in Sydney, but my mother went along. Sam recognised her and ran down, jumping over the seats to greet her, which was a thrill for her.

Hassan was where Margaret first met Nigel Hawkins, who (along with his wife, Norma, later on) has been in and out of her life ever since. At the time of *Hassan* Hawkins was a medical student. He was walking across a quadrangle at Sydney University when Sam Hughes spotted him and asked him to read for a part in the production, which subsequently took up so much of his time that he had to do an extra year of medicine. Hawkins's parents were Weaver Hawkins, the painter, and Irene Villiers, a wood carver, whom Margaret had seen and admired at the Contemporary Art Society shows even before she knew Nigel:

Weaver was friends with people like Rah Fizelle, Arthur Murch and later on Elaine Haxton. He and Rene [as Irene was known] were a most distinguished couple, quite different from everybody else. Beautiful Rene, with her long hair almost down to her waist, had the most unusual clothes, long dresses or pants. She and Weaver wore sandals, summer or winter, which Weaver probably made. He had a paralysed right hand, the result of an injury in the First World War, and had to learn to paint with his left. They lived at Mona Vale, which was very much a rural area, where people had market gardens and kept chooks and horses. I remember going up with a group of Contemporary Art Society people to visit Rene and Weaver at their house, which was right at the end of a long road out in the bush.

Hassan was designed, staged and presented by Hughes for the Sydney University Dramatic Society (SUDS) at the Conservatorium of Music and ran for five nights in August 1947. It was SUDS's first major production since 1941. Any profit from the performance was to be devoted to finding a well-equipped theatre for the Dramatic Society to perform in, because the new lease of its regular clubrooms at 700 George Street forbade any public performance on the premises.

Apart from the artists involved, *Hassan* had an impressive list of production credits. First, there was Antill's contribution, described in the program as 'atmospheric sounds incidental to the play'. Antill was the composer of the moment. The year before, he had won applause for his work *Corroboree*, the first attempt by an Australian composer to combine Aboriginal and Western musical influences. For *Hassan*, he created a slightly Westernised version of Persian music and when a particular ancient instrument required for this could not be found, it was replaced by noted soprano Elsie Findlay's singing.[16] The costumes were made by Dorothy Buchanan and the turbans were provided by Miss C. Crowley and the Stella Fraenkel Studio. Stella Fraenkel was a Viennese milliner with a flair for the unusual, who had sought refuge in Sydney after Hitler annexed Austria and whose former clients included Marlene Dietrich.[17] Photographer Max Dupain did the lighting; John Richards was responsible for the program, which was enhanced by romantic snippets from the play; and its advertisements were the work of the acclaimed designer and artist Douglas Annand.

As well as acting in *Hassan*, Nigel Hawkins also helped with painting the scenery, which was where he first encountered Margaret.

'Sam and John Richards were always talking about Olley,' he recalls. 'She was renowned for her marvellous hats and French postcards of ladies with various accoutrements, like butterfly wings. I had heard about her hats and the postcards before we ever met. When we were working at the showground, we used to send Margaret to get anything we wanted because she was the most adept person at getting things from people. She used to be deputised to go and ask if we could have a pail of water or whatever was needed from the cleaners.'

As Margaret explains, it's a trait that has become a lifelong habit:

Only because it doesn't cost anything to ask, providing you don't mind being refused. Once you've grasped this, you become fearless. I learnt that lesson very early, perhaps from my mother. My mother was never afraid to ask for a favour.

The French postcards Hawkins refers to came from the second-hand shops in Crown Street that Margaret habitually combed for treasures. She would thumb through piles of these cards looking for one she liked. They usually featured women with wasp waists attired in tutus and not much else:

I suppose they were from the 1890s. No one was really naked in them. The women, and the men, all wore body stockings. They just appealed to me. Sam must have been over for lunch at McMahons Point and seen them and then told the others about them. I know he used one in another production of his. He blew it up and later I took the blown-up picture, rolled up, with me to England. I loved it because it was life-size. I probably left it at Harry Tatlock Miller and Loudon Sainthill's house in London. It would have fitted in with their sort of decoration.

The next highlight of 1947 for Margaret was winning the Mosman Art Prize at the beginning of October. Although this was not the most prestigious prize, it did mean fifty guineas in prize money and some write-ups in the paper (which Margaret couldn't have cared less about, so she says). What was exciting to her was that Lloyd Rees, who already had considerable standing as an artist, had judged it. Margaret's entries, *New England Landscape* and *New England Country,* had been done while staying with her Aunt Dora and Wright cousins at Wallamumbi. *New England Landscape* turned out to be the winner.

Paul Haefliger, for the *Sydney Morning Herald,* was rather sniffy about the quality of artists the competition had attracted, which he saw as typical of small art competitions generally, but conceded that Margaret's two paintings 'raised the exhibition from oblivion'.

'The first painting [*New England Landscape*] has more unity,' he expounded, 'but the second is more vivacious and comparatively more colourful and embraces in its nervous shapes an individual conception of the Australian countryside. The colours are a little thin,' he continued, 'and there is a pronounced fear of commitment, but it is much richer than all the others in subtle changes. Here are the ingredients for an unusually fine development.'[18]

Harry Tatlock Miller was much more enthusiastic about the competition, and actually praised the Mosman Council for initiating it and for stimulating interest in art. However, he agreed with Haefliger's assessment that Margaret's were the only two paintings in the show that warranted serious attention. He described both landscapes as 'sombre equations of rolling hills

Keeping the Rent Paid

and lowering skies'. Tatlock Miller concluded his remarks about Margaret's works by saying: 'Among their neighbours they immediately stand forward with their imprint of individuality and personal mode of expression.'[19]

Nineteen forty-seven finished up with a somewhat fishy flourish. No sooner had the Mosman Prize been announced than it was time for the Ninth Annual Interstate Exhibition of the Contemporary Art Society, in November. Two hundred and thirty-two paintings were hung. Although the critics weren't too fired up about the show, which was opened by conductor Eugene Goossens, the press was quick to pick up on a prevalent fishy theme among the work.[20] One commentator suggested that it was probably because of the higher cost of human models that fish were so well represented that year.

Margaret was chief among the perpetrators of the theme with her painting titled *Pink Paper and Kippers*, which had a bunch of yellow roses on one side and three rust-coloured smoked kippers laid out on a blue and white plate, amid assorted still-life objects, including eggs and apples displayed on muted pink paper. Douglas Annand contributed *Four Fish* and Elsa Russell's *Trawling Folk* was another fish-flavoured offering. Mr B. Butcher's (a rather inappropriate coincidence of name) *Still Life with Fish*, at forty-five guineas, was the most expensive dish presented, while Gordon Chapman's linear *Fish in Stream* was a bargain at one guinea. Buyers seemed to relish the piscine turn of events. The National Art Gallery of New South Wales snapped up Cesare Vagarini's *Still Life* for twenty guineas, despite some complaints about the lifelessness of its subject. Margaret's *Kippers*, which the *Sydney Morning Herald*'s art critic declared 'ridiculously underpriced', were bought by a private buyer for eighteen guineas.

So, as the year ended, Margaret was well and truly in the swim of things.

7

1948

20 Coast Crescent
McMahons Pt
Friday

Dear Donald

Murray came out for dinner the other night and asked if I would like to go up to Hill End. Would I what! Would next Friday be too soon??

If I can come what must I take besides a hot water bottle and new boots.

Love Olley[1]

(Letter received by Donald Friend, 24 April 1948)

NINETEEN FORTY-EIGHT WAS AN EVENTFUL YEAR FOR MARGARET. Most importantly, her friendship with Donald Friend developed into a rapport that extended far beyond party witticisms. To understand how this came about, we must backtrack almost a year.

Towards the middle of 1947, Donald Friend, unsettled after a trip of almost five months to his beloved Malaytown and the

1948

Torres Strait Islands, became fed up with Sydney and life at Merioola. Donald Murray, the charming Englishman on whom he seemed to rely heavily for companionship after his infatuation with the art student Colin Brown had come to nothing, was away in Melbourne. Murray, a onetime artist's model, had been a friend of Friend since they'd shared a house in Sydney (in the Rocks) in the early 1930s. To top off Friend's current exasperation, his mother was now also living at Merioola. Communal sharing was not her style. She insisted on keeping her own and Friend's food and milk behind a padlocked grille in the fridge to ensure no pilfering went on.[2] Even making a cup of tea had become a logistical nightmare.

Murray's return to Sydney did not improve Friend's mood. Murray had failed to land the job of running an art gallery that he had wanted in Melbourne and now also missed out on the position of director of the David Jones Gallery (which went instead to interior designer Marion Hall Best). Merioola continued to get on Friend's nerves, so, with Murray, he began hatching a plot to retreat to Tasmania. But the proposed destination of their retreat altered in August, when Friend chanced upon an article about deserted gold rush towns in western New South Wales and realised there might be an escape closer to home – in the hills behind Bathurst. He inveigled Russell Drysdale into exploring the possibilities with him in the Drysdales' new car, a swish dark-green Riley Tourer. Their first stop north-west of the Blue Mountains was Sofala, with which both men were immediately taken. From Sofala they drove on to spend the night at Hill End, where they found a handful of people eking out an existence by fossicking and rabbiting.[3]

On their return to Sydney, Friend and Drysdale both started work on paintings with identical subjects – Sofala's main street – and Friend dispatched Murray to investigate the possibilities of renting or buying a house, preferably in Sofala. After some

Far from a Still Life

characteristic procrastination by Murray, Friend made his way by train and bus to Hill End where they finally discovered a habitable cottage they both liked. It had four rooms with wattle and daub walls, a well, a couple of acres of land for Murray, who was a keen gardener, and the owner Mr Lister was willing to sell to Friend for seventy pounds.

On 18 September 1947, despite a rambling digression by Lister and Murray about the growing of delphiniums that threatened to delay the proceedings, the papers were signed. By early October they were installed in the cottage and enthusiastically buying extra furnishings, such as a lovely old mirror and a cedar sofa, and digging up iris bulbs for the garden after a shopping excursion to Bathurst. Later that same month, Friend's father died.

Sofala is a snug little hamlet beside the Turon River. It's so close to the river that you can hear the water gurgling away as you walk down the main street. Hill End is entirely different. There are kilometres of steep road, interspersed with views of folding hills that look more like paintings than actual landscape, before you drive down an avenue of interlocking English trees. Suddenly you're on a high plateau of cleared ground rimmed by bush and mullock heaps. Only a few old houses and giant pines break up the space. Hill End feels like a destination. Once you're there, you're there. You can see why Friend might have felt safely removed from the rest of the world at Hill End.

◆

In April 1948 Friend was busily engaged at Hill End on his vast and complex work *Apocalypse of St John the Divine*, which he envisaged would take a couple of years to complete. Most of the ink and gouache drawing was pinned up in the cottage, almost covering an entire wall. Although the thought of his upcoming

1948

show at the Macquarie Galleries, for which he should have been painting small landscapes, nagged at the back of his mind, now that the detailed drawing of *Apocalypse* was finished, he was about to start working over it 'boldly'.[4]

But despite the idyllic lifestyle Friend and Murray were enjoying and the fact that their garden, thanks mainly to Murray, was now one of the finest in Hill End, Murray suddenly announced to Friend that he was leaving.

Discontent had been brooding in Murray for a while, Friend realised. The role of artist's companion apparently made him feel inadequate. Still, his decision to quit the cottage rocked Friend, who promptly panicked at the prospect of spending a Hill End winter alone and sent off a spate of letters to friends in Sydney, including Lindsay Churchland, Fred Jessup and Tas Drysdale, to see if they could find a replacement tenant. A few days later Murray was gone.

Friend, however, was not on his own for long. A 'glorious' visit from his adored friend Dulcie Pitt, the Torres Strait Islander singer, whom he knew from his connections in Malaytown, soon cheered him up.[5] No doubt it set the locals' tongues wagging at a furious rate, as well. Friend now also put aside *Apocalypse* and dutifully turned to painting landscapes – but without much success unfortunately, as he noted in his diary.[6] Then Murray, back in Sydney and already pining for Hill End, reported in a letter to Friend on a dinner he'd had with Fred Jessup and Margaret Olley. Margaret was keen to go to Hill End, Murray wrote, because she needed to get on with work for her first one-person show. Margaret's 'fantastic note' (as Friend described the letter that heads this chapter) came in the same mail.[7]

There'd been a bit of a bumpy start to April, as far as Margaret was concerned. She was not, unlike Jocelyn Rickards, 'silently screaming with claustrophobia' from being in Australia.[8] Nevertheless it seemed obvious to her that the next step in her life was to go overseas. But how to achieve that was not so straightforward:

Everybody had gone overseas or was talking about going away. Anne Wienholt first, and then Margaret Cilento, had taken off for America. David Strachan was leaving for England. Clarice Zander had gone back to London. Justin O'Brien had set off on a two-year study tour of Europe. Fred [Jessup] was about to set off on the New South Wales Travelling Scholarship he'd won in 1945, but postponed taking up. It was the automatic thing to do. So I, too, early in the year went in for the Travelling Scholarship. There was no other way I could afford to go. I entered [under the pseudonym Mynine because odd numbers were lucky for her] a small version of my Ophelia *painting, which had a figure floating in a river. It was based partly on the weekend I had away with Sam and the others on the Nepean River, and partly on my stays at Woronora. I also entered a nude of my friend Annie Ross. But I didn't win. I came second. The scholarship was awarded to the sculptor Oliffe Richmond, who went on to study with Henry Moore.*

The 1948 scholarship results were made public on 8 April 1948. Not winning was a disappointing blow for Margaret, especially since the quality of her work, like Richmond's, towered over the rest of the entrants, Tatlock Miller pointed out in the *Sun* (while heartily congratulating the winning Richmond).[9] But there was no time to brood about missing out on an overseas trip with her solo show coming up. The sudden opportunity of staying with Friend, coming shortly afterwards, must also have helped make up for it.

At the end of April, for the first time Margaret had two paintings, *Still Life with Post Cards* and *Grey Day*, hung in an exhibition of the elite Sydney Group, which had been founded in 1945 by artists, including Jean Bellette, David Strachan, Wallace

Sam Hughes skating at St Moritz, 1930s

Margaret at Elaine's wedding in London, 1952

Brian and Marjorie Johnstone with Margaret at the Johnstone Gallery, 1950s

Geoff Elworthy on his plantation at Merani

Margaret with Elaine Haxton and her spaniel on Pittwater, Sydney, 1960s

Laurie Thomas, Sir Herbert Read and Margaret Olley with her painting *Susan with Flowers*, 1962. The painting won the 1963 Finney's Centenary Art Prize

Grace Olley in her eighties, *c*. 1970

Margaret and Justin O'Brien

Margaret with Philip Bacon, receiving her Honorary Doctorate of Letters from the University of Queensland, 1999

Margaret and Barry Humphries at Margaret's Paddington home – the Hat Factory – Sydney, 1996

Margaret and Edmund Capon at Margaret's retrospective at the Art Gallery of New South Wales, 1996. Behind her hang *The Chinese Screen* (1994–5) and *Homage to Manet* (1987)

Margaret Whitlam, Sir Roden Cutler, Peter Sculthorpe, Margaret, Thomas Keneally and Barry Humphries, 1997

Neil McGregor (then director of the National Gallery, London), Margaret and Edmund Capon at the Hat Factory, Sydney, 1998

'Perseverance': Margaret at the Pyramids, 2000

1948

Thornton, Justin O'Brien and Francis Lymburner, to counter what they felt were the declining standards of the NSW Society of Artists. In 1948 the group was still small, but, as well as Margaret, Sidney Nolan and Desiderius Orban were among the thirteen artists exhibiting, so it was an honour to be included.

Almost straight after the opening, at the start of May, Margaret arrived at Hill End, where the spreading trees along the avenue approaching the cottage were 'startlingly gold and scarlet'.[10] Friend was now thoroughly anxious about the lack of work for his show and desperate for the company of another artist to spur him into painting. So, disregarding the almost constant rain, the two plunged into work:

It was bitterly cold. We used to go out painting and drawing in the paddocks. Donald mostly sketched and then painted when he was back at the cottage. But he did do some work out in the open when I was there. I did drawings on site but I also quite often painted while we were out. We'd roam around the countryside until we'd found a subject like an old sulky and then we'd settle down to it. There's nothing like being with somebody compatible when you're working. You spark off each other.

The last day was so freezing I wore a hot-water bottle strapped to my stomach to keep me warm when I went out into the paddocks. I've always been an improviser – I'm my father's daughter. I would find a stump or a tree to prop up my big canvas (my father being a bush carpenter came in handy) and sit on the ground to paint, which made it even colder. I have no idea what happened to all the paintings I did there. Some were exhibited, others were probably never finished or painted over in some drunken moment.

Friend was immediately invigorated by Margaret's presence. Soon after she arrived, he wrote in his diary: 'Olley and I haven't let up on painting. She seems to love the place as much as I do.

These days with their stormy skies, the trees raining a golden snow of leaves seem to me more beautiful even than before, which is surprising, for in the past I have always disliked wind and wetness – the intimacy of the cottage provides, whenever we re-enter it from one of our expeditions into the brisk cold, a delicious contrast of warm, white walls, shelves and books and *objets d'art* and mellow fire glow, usually with a large black pot of soup bubbling on the hob.'[11]

Friend was not so very much older than Margaret, only eight years, but his experiences as an artist – and in life – may have made him seem older to her. He was also very handsome (a fact to which she was not oblivious) and seemed to her to be particularly at home in Hill End:

Donald wore a big army belt and had naughty twinkles in his eye. Hill End suited him. He did some of his best work there, I think. Later on he loved being in Bali. But after the war and all those parties at Merioola, he just wanted to get away and work. He was earthed at Hill End. Chopping the firewood, going up the butcher's, all those ordinary domestic chores were relished by him.

But that wasn't all. In those days you could feel the presence of ghosts at Hill End. You felt you were in the shadow of all those thousands of people who had lived there when Hill End was a thriving big town and the Holtermann nugget, the biggest nugget ever mined, came to light nearby.[12] *When we went off on expeditions, to see the Chinese cemetery, for instance, it was like walking over history. Donald also loved the mad stories of the fossickers who were still around. There was one old bloke, in particular, who amused him and he used to point out his house to me. According to Donald, this old fossicker used to support himself by going down to the Salvation Army Hotel in Sydney and then conning a few people into investing their savings in looking for gold. He'd even bring them up and show them the mine shaft.*

1948

Friend had a very definite morning routine in the cottage. He would get up, light the fire, then go off and collect the milk and the paper, which was dropped off by bus from Bathurst. Margaret has vivid memories of the next ritual:

I learnt very early on not to talk to Donald in the morning until he'd finished 'the Proust part' of the paper. 'The Proust part' of the paper was the stock exchange report, that's how he always referred to it. I haven't a clue if he had any shares or not. It was gobbledegook to me. But he was deadly serious. He became very angry if he was interrupted and I can tend to be a chatterbox. (Sam used to say, You've got a head like a tin of worms. When I'm talking, one thing leads to another.)

Often after breakfast he'd do a careful draft of the diary before he wrote it up properly and added a nice little drawing on the page. Donald revelled in being accepted by the locals. You'd think we'd been invited to Buckingham Palace, it was such a delight for him when Mrs Lister, who lived across the way, or anyone asked us over for afternoon tea or supper. Mrs Lister was a naïve painter who used to do watercolours, so she was very admiring of Donald. He even ended up giving Mrs Lister a lesson in oils. Of course, all these events would be written up afterwards in the diary.

The cottage was on a corner of a little lane and the main road into Hill End, set well back from prying eyes. It was low to the ground and tiny. As Margaret remembers it, when you came into the cottage the room with the fireplace where they often cooked was on the right-hand side. This was also the main living room. Off to the other side was the little room in which Margaret slept. Then you went through to a kitchen area and another room. In the living room a hook and chain were suspended over the fire on which kettles and the big iron soup pot were hung. According to Margaret, there were also some trivets on which stood the smaller pots, used to boil potatoes and such.

One of the pleasures of Hill End was picking mushrooms. Whenever Margaret and Friend went out for a walk they would take gunny sacks and fill them with the big brown-sided mushrooms that grew everywhere and made a tasty addition to meals. Collecting pine cones from tall trees that had been planted during the gold rush and watching them glow in the cottage fireplace at night afforded another simple enjoyment.

In the evening, while their soup or stew was cooking, Friend would fill another pot with water from the well outside and heat it on the fire. Then he'd pour the warm water into a tub for Margaret to have a bath. While this sounds romantic and the cottage would have been warm from the fires and wood stove, such bathing might well have been a bit nippy on evenings in May. When Margaret had finished, Friend would use the same water for his own ablutions (which suggests that Margaret mustn't have lingered very long in the tub). They'd have a glass of sherry before dinner and perhaps a glass of wine with their meal. Margaret has no memory of ever drinking at the Hill End pub with Friend on this visit, nor of any alcoholic excesses at night with him.

Margaret was not at all put off by the primitive conditions of the cottage:

It wasn't rough for me. It was simple and basic, but so rich. You had a bed to sleep in and the fire to cook on, which was really all you needed. In a way, it was like domestic bliss, the two of us being there. Donald had a small wind-up gramophone and lots of records, jazz, but also wonderful classical music. Some of the records were so old and had been played so many times that he had to put a bit of gin on them to make the needle go round. I remember once walking down the main street with the pine trees on one side, everybody going about their ordinary day-to-day business, when suddenly out of Donald's tiny house came belting Vivaldi's Four Seasons. *It was quite extraordinary. I just stood under a pine tree and tried to imagine what on earth the locals were making of all of this. God knows what wild goings-on they imagined took place when Donald's boogie-woogie was playing.*

Although she only stayed at Hill End for just under three weeks, for Margaret, who does not like normally to be watched by anyone while she is painting (or even for anyone to be around), the painting camaraderie it afforded was rare and special. Friend himself had thrived with Margaret at the cottage. Her presence suited him creatively and he managed to complete enough landscapes for his now imminent show. He was delighted with his efforts at *en plein air* oils, which he hoped were infused with a new 'calm and lyrical quality' and admitted he wouldn't haven't dreamed of painting in the open without the example of Margaret lugging huge canvasses for miles through the bush.[13]

On 18 May, Margaret scrubbed out the cottage while Friend packed up his barely dry oil paintings to take down to Sydney to be framed. The following day they left together for the city. And so the interlude ended, although its resonances would long stay with them both.

It was almost two years since Donald Friend had had a solo exhibition and it would be his first solo show in which paintings from Hill End were included. Two days before his opening on 2 June 1948, a jittery Friend met up with Loudon Sainthill in the city. The pair spent most of the daylight hours drinking brandies before Friend paid a brief visit to his family. This having passed off without strain, he took himself off to dinner with Margaret, where amongst the 'bric-a-brac' of her McMahons Point flat he was finally able to relax.[14] Also at Margaret's flat on this 'amusing evening', as Friend described it, was Bonny Drysdale's brother John Stephen, whom Bonny was trying, without much success, to matchmake with Margaret.[15]

Before the opening of Friend's exhibition there was a luncheon at Romano's arranged by Tas Drysdale's mother. Romano's in Castlereagh Street, which boasted good food, lots of mirrors and a tiny dance floor, was one of the two fashionable and expensive eating places of the day (the other being Prince's in Martin Place). After lunch Friend made his way to the opening. By the end of the afternoon he was happy and exhausted from being polite to people.

Among the guests at the opening was Elaine Haxton. Haxton had had a remarkable career for a woman artist at this time. Born in 1909, she had enrolled at East Sydney Technical College while still in her teens and first showed with the conservative Society of Artists when she was seventeen. By 1933 she was on her way to England, where she studied and worked as a freelance commercial artist for magazines like *Vogue* and *Harper's Bazaar*. Like so many others, she was brought back to Australia by the threat of war and also the desire to see her family; but only after visiting New York and a trip through Mexico, where she succumbed immediately to the country's vibrant colours, especially as reflected in the murals of Mexican artists. She was also briefly arrested in Cuernavaca for allegedly sketching the poverty of local people for subversive purposes.

In 1945, Haxton travelled to New Guinea as a theatre designer and show manager for the Dutch dancer Darya Collin, which began her career in ballet and theatre design. As soon as the war was over she headed back to New York, where she studied theatre design before moving on to England. Here she met her future husband, Brigadier Richard Foot, with whom she returned to Australia, via America, in 1948.

It was probably at Friend's opening that Margaret first caught up with a rather colourful-looking Haxton:

1948

Elaine was wearing a red coat like Mother Christmas and had hydrangea-blue hair. It was because she went white very early, she dyed her hair that amazing blue, I realised later on. She was a delightful, talkative woman, quite small (only about five foot) and she lived with Englishman Brigadier Richard Foot, whom we all called Dickie. Elaine had been a friend of Tas for years and had stayed with him and Bonny down at Albury. She also knew Donald and had painted him lying asleep on a red sofa at the Drysdales'. Cedric Flower was another friend of hers. It was such a small community of artists in those days. Everybody seemed to know one another.

Elaine and Dickie had a flat in a row of terrace houses opposite Hyde Park, in College Street, just before Oxford Street. I remember going to their flat and driving up to Pittwater with them, where they had a boathouse at Stokes Point near Avalon. You had to scramble down a hillside but once you were there it was absolutely idyllic. The front door opened onto a view across Pittwater and you could hear the water lapping underneath the whole time. Eventually they built a house higher up the hill. It was split-level and very open, with lots of light. There was bush all around and a tropical garden Elaine had planted coming right up to the house. Over the years I often used to stay with Elaine and Dickie at Pittwater. Lucy Swanton also had a place nearby. She bought a double block with a fisherman's cottage right on the water and, with a few adjustments, she just kept it pretty much as it was. In the 1950s Lucy used to stay with me in Brisbane and it was then, also, that Elaine became particularly important in my life.

◈

Margaret's friendship with the Drysdales continued to deepen during the course of 1948. This was in part due to her strong connection to Donald Friend, who was so fond of the whole family, but there was also her own affection for Tas and Bonny and her admiration of Tas as an artist. And, wrapping around it all, drinking:

If the first night I had dinner with Sam was where I decided that drinking overcame my shyness and was going to be part of my life from then on, it was with Tas Drysdale that I learnt to drink all night. Tas and Bonny had parties at the house at Rose Bay that went on right through the night to daybreak. We would drink away, solving the problems of the world, everybody talking and nobody listening. Bon used to make home-brew during the war, and even after the war was over we sometimes drank beer she'd concocted. Half the time we were drunk with tiredness, I think, more than alcohol. We'd go down to Vaucluse House to watch the sun rise and then come back to Rose Bay for breakfast, where Tas would eat bacon and eggs.

Bonny was a great guardian. Later, when she and Tas were living in Challis Avenue in Potts Point, other artists would come round about lunchtime to see if Tas had finished painting for the day and wanted to go out for a beer. Bonny would sit at the door, holding a glass of gin. When the interlopers arrived she'd answer the door with the glass in her hand and say, Piss off, he's working. His best paintings came when Tas was living with Bon. Absolutely, there's no doubt about it.

We all drank a lot in the Rose Bay days. I thought it was normal. I felt I could drink anybody under the table. But it does take a toll on you. After breakfast at Rose Bay, I'd walk up the hill to New South Head Road, get the tram back to Circular Quay and then the ferry over to McMahons Point, where I'd stagger up all the steps to Crescent Street, then up more to the flat at the top of the building, and flake out for the rest of the day. Tas would just go on working. He did great work at Rose Bay. I remember going back to his house after some social occasion and posing while both Tas and Donald did

1948

a drawing of me. Tas then slowly turned his drawing into a portrait of me, but I never sat formally for it again.

The Drysdale house at Rose Bay was small but always full of people. Margaret recalls how Lynne Drysdale, who was a young school girl of about ten, would be trying to do her homework while the parties were going on. When the imbibing artists became too noisy for Lynne, she would hover behind her bedroom door, plucking up the courage to object. Eventually she'd fling the door open and shout, Will you all shut up! Then she'd quickly retreat.

From those rackety Rose Bay days, Lynne (now Clarke) and Margaret have gone on to become firm friends. Lynne remembers her family's time at Rose Bay and the house itself with great affection:

'It was a brick bungalow. You had to walk down a steep hill to reach the house and then you had to go up some stairs to the front door. The hall seemed very wide in comparison to the rest of the rooms (it's probably wider in my memory than it was in reality) and the bedrooms were off to one side. The kitchen was at the back; next came the dining room, where people sat around for the parties. Then there was a sort of double living room with a beach mural – two figures with a boat – by Elaine Haxton on the wall. It had an enclosed veranda with big floor-to-ceiling windows and divans that people slept on when they stayed. If he wasn't painting in the bedroom, that was where my father worked. And Donald, too, most of the time he was in Sydney. My father would be at the easel and Donald at the drawing board.

'Margaret was always plump. Even now you get a sense of what she was like when she was young, from the shape of her face. She was lovely. I suppose you could say cuddly. The first night we met she talked about going to a party all dressed up. There was another afternoon when she and Fred Jessup came round. Fred had made her a dress out of an old green wartime mosquito net and she had a hat with real grapes on it. I remember the excitement of Margaret and the dress and the hat. As a little girl I thought it was wonderful.

'When you're that age and someone's twelve or fourteen years older than you, and an adult, they seem much older. I feel Margaret, Donald and David Strachan influenced me a lot with the way I now live my life. They influenced me with the objects that they had around them, like Donald's African carvings, and even the food they cooked. My parents loved very modern things. My mother loved Frank Lloyd Wright. The designer Gordon Andrews was their friend. They had Gordon Andrews furniture and everything in the house was as modern as it could be. The others were wonderful because they weren't my parents; they were of their generation but they were friends to me as well, and they loved exotic things that were completely different to those my parents had. And when I got older, Margaret was always just a good woman to have in my life.'

―◆―

Margaret's very first one-person exhibition, of twenty-one paintings and three drawings, opened at 1.30 p.m. at the Macquarie Galleries on Wednesday 30 June. The day before the momentous occasion, Donald Friend spent the afternoon with Margaret at her flat in McMahons Point, which was now so chock-a-block with paintings it was hard for them to move around while they were fixing up frames for her work.[16]

Margaret's parents did not travel to Sydney for the show's opening, at which Drysdale was doing the honours. As Margaret puts it matter-of-factly, her parents were busy with their own world and expected her to come home to them, rather than the other way round. Before the opening Friend took Margaret and a group of friends, including Fred Jessup, the Drysdales and John Stephen (again), to lunch at Romano's. Friend claimed to have been almost as nervous playing host in such a swanky restaurant as Margaret was later to be at her opening.[17] But the afternoon at the Macquarie Galleries proved not such a terrible ordeal for Margaret, mainly because of the way her friends rallied round:

It was a huge event in my life. Of course, I was scared, nervous. But I had the support of Tas and Donald and my other friends, and that made a big difference. I'd been exhibiting in group shows for a couple of years, so it wasn't a totally new experience. I did fully consider myself an artist by now – not a female artist, just an artist. I was an artist and artists have exhibitions. You never really see a painting until it is taken out of your environment and put on someone else's walls. Whether they sell or not is secondary, it just allows you to see your own work. Also, artists mostly work in isolation and paintings are meant to be seen in the way that books are written to be read. So exhibiting is part of the process of being a painter. But with that first show it was the support of my friends that really got me through it.

A number of red spots, indicating sales, went up. Also, a real thrill, two state galleries made purchases. The National Art Gallery of New South Wales bought *Still Life with Pink Fish* for thirty guineas, while the Victorian National Gallery chose *Hill End Ruin* – thirty-five guineas – and a drawing, *Kilmorey Terrace*. The most expensive work in the exhibition was a large version of the painting Margaret had entered for the Travelling Scholarship – *Ophelia*, priced at fifty guineas. *Pink Paper and Kippers* was included, marked 'Not for sale', as was *Era Landscape*. Again landscapes, many with old buildings as subjects (two being of Hill End), dominated. There were only five straight still lifes (*Still Life in Green* among them, and another enticingly called *Plums and*

Prawns), as well as the self-portrait entitled *Portrait in the Mirror*, which has a strong still-life component.

Portrait in a Mirror was painted at McMahons Point. In front of Margaret's reflection, with its faintly troubled expression, is spread a selection of flowers, fruit, vegetables, postcard reproductions of art (from Carl Plate's Notanda Gallery, perhaps) and shells collected at Era. On the left-hand side there's a mask-like white face, which is a cuttlefish carving, another souvenir of Era.

Art historian Christine France in her book *Margaret Olley* writes that two paintings in Margaret's first show were indicative of her future direction.[18] These were *Pink Paper and Kippers* and the self-portrait, *Portrait in a Mirror*. Of the self-portrait, France points out that the still-life arrangement in the foreground is 'structured to send the eye back and forth between the objects and the reflected image'. Of *Kippers*, she writes: 'Here fruit, roses, small bowls, jug and kippers are viewed from a plunging perspective. Radiating from the centre they are, like much of Cézanne's work, arranged against a hugely structured cloth which flattens out the picture plane and creates a degree of spatial ambiguity.'[19]

These early paintings of Margaret's all seem remarkably serious. There's not much flippancy or effervescence of youth about them. The colour is subdued compared to her later work. There's plenty of variation, but the tones are far from riotous. One can't help wondering if some of David Strachan's love of darkness in painting had rubbed off on her. It's a little as if part of her personality has been suppressed. Over the next couple of years, an overseas sojourn that included living in close proximity to a vineyard would release more of her personality. But ironically, further down the track, it would also wreak havoc on her ability to paint.

As regards her first solo exhibition, the critics of the day were mostly impressed. Harry Tatlock Miller commented that she'd

1948

broken the prevailing local convention for small canvasses and that 'with nothing cabinned, cramped or confined in her paintings' their scale almost dwarfed the gallery they were hung in.[20] He concluded his review with the prophetic words: 'her work holds those rare qualities which can make of a painter the true artist'. Like France, he noted the Cézanne-like accessories of cloth and apples in her still lifes, but found the composition of *Pink Paper and Kippers* too scattered, despite 'the gentle aureole of light' playing on the flowers. Paul Haefliger also singled out *Kippers*: 'Nothing could be more charming and unexpected than the roses with their aroma of fragile mystery in prosaic surroundings . . .'[21] He also wrote that Margaret was, without doubt, an artist who would shun conventional routes in favour of the excitement of exploring 'uncharted and tempestuous seas'.

So, with her first show, Margaret, who had just turned twenty-five, was established as an artist in the eyes of the critics, buyers and the official art hierarchy. That night there was a party at the Drysdales' to celebrate. To prepare for it, Drysdale and Friend ducked off early from the opening to buy supplies and fortify themselves with a few drinks. Besides the relieved artist herself, among those loyally kicking up their heels and undoubtedly downing copious drinks at the shindig were Jocelyn Rickards, Fred Jessup, John Stephen, Peter Kaiser (handsome as ever), Dulcie Pitt, Harry Tatlock Miller, Loudon Sainthill and, of course, Friend.

The day before Margaret's opening, Laurence Olivier and Vivien Leigh had begun their Sydney season at the Tivoli with Richard Sheridan's *The School for Scandal*. The following day the *Sun* ran a review of their show in the column next to the review of Margaret's exhibition. (Needless to say, the Oliviers were given more space.) Everyone in town seemed to be a-twitter – or in a 'ferment', as Donald Friend put it – over the famous thespian pair, who were seen dining at the Claremont, among other places.[22]

Alec Murray postponed his trip overseas to be their official photographer; Tatlock Miller somehow acquired the job of being their escort; while Jocelyn Rickards had a fabulous slim-fitting sheath of grey satin made for the opening night of the duo's season. Rickards' sheath turned out to be so tight that she was unable to walk and had to be carried to her seat in the theatre.[23] Friend himself, together with the Drysdales, stayed up until four in the morning drinking and talking with the Oliviers (but he refused to borrow Drysdale's tails when he went to see the Oliviers perform at the theatre).[24] Friend found both the Oliviers 'absolutely charming'.

Margaret was also swept up in the Olivier excitement, though not quite as literally as Jocelyn Rickards:

It was about the first overseas piece of theatre to come to Australia after the war and they were brilliant. I went with the Drysdales. Bonny was always pairing me up with her brother, John Stephen, whom we called 'Steve'. I think she thought we would be a good match. Steve was a dear fellow and had been a prisoner of war in Changi. He used to talk about how the men there would take the rags off their wounds so they'd get flyblown and then the maggots would clean up the pus. He also drank a lot. But he was a regular at the Drysdales' parties and I enjoyed going to dinner with him.

Anyway, I was partnered off with Steve when we went to see the Oliviers. I had made myself a long wine-red taffeta dress, which I was planning to wear, but it was the middle of winter and very cold. I'd also bought from Barry Stern's father's army disposal shop in George Street a bright red, pure wool, very warm pair of men's prisoner-of-war long underwear, which I used to sleep in. So I wore the prisoner-of-war red long johns under my taffeta skirt to the theatre and kept myself nicely warm.

1948

A month after Margaret's show, Loudon Sainthill held his second exhibition of drawings and paintings, at the Macquarie Galleries. The usual landscape, nudes and still lifes of Australian artists were not for him. Sainthill's private world was peopled with spangled and tinselled 'ballerinas, clowns, circus ladies and trapezists', his lover Harry Tatlock Miller once observed, and whether framed by proscenium arch or picture frame, was always 'at its best in an artificial light'.[25]

One of Sainthill's earliest memories was seeing his mother dressed up in a Paul Poiret lavender-coloured dress, carrying a parasol, going off to the Melbourne Cup. The vision, which stayed with him always, was indicative of his artistic future. (Poiret was a French dress designer much influenced by the Oriental costumes of the Ballet Russe in Paris in the early twentieth century.)

The arrival in Sainthill's home town, Melbourne, of the Colonel de Basil's Ballet Russe de Monte Carlo in 1936 became a turning-point in his life. As Tatlock Miller would later write, to Sainthill the ballet became 'an exotic oasis in what seemed an antipodean desert' and he became intoxicated by the colour of the costumes and sets, as well as the performances of the dancers.[26]

In Sainthill's show of July 1948 there were twenty-eight richly intricate works, with titles such as *The Masquerade*, *Harlequin with Dog*, *Ornamental Costume for a Dancer* and *Jewelled Costume*. Not surprisingly, given his last exhibition had been crowded with women in outlandish attire, according to Donald Friend, fancy dress was de rigueur at the opening. But what no one could have suspected was that it would result in what is now perhaps Australia's most familiar portrait of a female subject:

Loudon sent me an invitation to the opening of his show on which he'd written: 'Darling Oll, come as a duchess.' Many of my friends had started calling me Oll or Olley by then. I thought I'd rent an outfit from one of those firms that supply theatrical costumes. But then Freddy Jessup decided to help me make a dress out of parachute silk with a bit of netting under it (we chose parachute silk because you could buy as much as you wanted without coupons). Fred found his grandmother's wedding dress, or what was left of it, which were the leg-of-mutton sleeves, some pink ribbons and a little bit of lace at the neck, and so we put together a dress that I wore to Loudon's opening.

Naturally the paintings were all very theatrical. After the opening we all went back to a party at the Drysdales' at Rose Bay. Bill Dobell and I left the party at the same time and both caught what was probably the last tram for the night, back to King Cross for him and Circular Quay for me. As we rattled along in the tram Bill said, I'd like to paint you. So an arrangement was made that I'd come along and sit for him. It was nothing to do with flattery. I was just helping out a fellow artist. It didn't seem unusual. I was used to drawing my friends and being drawn by them. If somebody wanted you to sit, you sat for them. I'm a bit cagey now, because it takes up a lot of time. But then, if someone was around you used them as a model and if there was nobody about, you popped yourself in – nothing to do with I-love-myself vanity, just for an image.

Some time in August, on a warm pre-spring day judging by the outfit she wore, Margaret took herself off to Dobell's studio in the Union Bank Chambers at the Cross:

I didn't go to the sitting in the duchess dress. I wore a plain cotton dress in a similar beige colour and I took a hat in a bag with me, just in case he needed a prop. The hat is the one you see in the portrait, a leghorn. It was the first hat I had when I left Somerville House and it was so worn I'd turned it inside out to freshen it up. When I was out painting at my cousin's property at Armidale, I'd collected a lot of tiny everlasting daisies, and I made a decoration for the hat out of those before I went.

1948

We chatted away. Bill did one little sketch of me, then a detailed drawing, nothing more. That was how he worked, he always painted from drawings. For the portrait, he painted the dress I'd worn to the party from memory. He also did a number of nudes of me from those first drawings, which I only saw years later. There is one of me sitting nude in the hat, which Lucy Swanton gave to Sydney University. But I didn't sit for those. I was a bit embarrassed by them, really. He just did them, the same way I can look at a person and undress them. You see the form underneath the clothes, you know the shape it is instinctively.

❖

Not only were Melbourne artists angrier than Sydney painters, they also had very complicated love lives. Though Margaret herself would never have much contact with the art patrons John and Sunday Reed, she would now (and again in the future) become involved with members of their almost incestuously connected circles of artist friends.

In 1938, the twenty-one-year-old Sidney Nolan, who came from a working-class St Kilda background, was invited to visit the intellectual, art-loving Reeds' house 'Heide' on their property just outside Melbourne. For the next ten years he would be intensely involved with both Reeds in what was essentially a ménage à trois, but most especially he bonded with Sunday, who would become his muse. At this young age Nolan was torn between wishing to paint and wanting to write poetry. According to Janine Burke (in her book *The Heart Garden*), to settle the matter Sunday would set Nolan at the dining table with painting and writing materials, start reading the phantasmagorical poetry of Rimbaud – of which Nolan was a passionate fan – aloud in the original French and tell Nolan to write or paint his response. Although both drawings and verse flew from his hand, after a week it seemed clear that painting would be Nolan's vocation.[27]

Nolan was already seeing fellow art student Elizabeth Paterson when he began visiting Heide in 1938, and married her that same year. But in 1941, shortly after the birth of their daughter, they separated and Nolan began living with the Reeds. The following year he was drafted into the army and shortly afterwards was sent to Dimboola, north-west of Melbourne. Due to the not very onerous nature of his military duties he was also able to paint his acclaimed Wimera landscapes during this period.

In 1944, faced with the possibility of being sent to serve with the army in New Guinea, Nolan went absent without leave and hid out, mostly at Heide, with false identification papers arranged by John Reed. In 1945 and 1946 he worked on his famous Ned Kelly paintings there, with Sunday acting very much as his muse. However, in January 1948 Nolan defected permanently from Heide when he arrived on the Sydney doorstep of John Reed's novelist sister Cynthia, whom he'd met briefly in Melbourne in 1941. Cynthia was now estranged from the Reeds, having just published a novel (*Daddy Sowed a Wind!*) in which thinly disguised portraits of her family, including John and Sunday, appeared. Despite this, in *The Heart Garden* Janine Burke comments on the similarity between Sunday and Cynthia. According to Burke, both women were fragile, highly strung and tempestuous, as well as witty, seductive and loyal.[28]

In March 1948, Cynthia, who was living with her small daughter Jinx in a tiny cottage at Woniora Avenue, Wahroonga, and Nolan married.[29] Not long afterwards, as Margaret remembers it, Clarice Zander organised Sam Hughes into having a dinner party for the Nolans. Zander had known Cynthia Reed (now Nolan) since her New Gallery days in Melbourne in the 1920s, and Cynthia had helped her with the presentation of the exhibition of modern British art she later brought out. Hughes's dinner party was Margaret's first meeting with Sidney and Cynthia Nolan. Following the dinner, she called on the Nolans several times at Wahroonga, where she was rather surprised by how small their bedroom was – the bed seemed to fill the entire room. However, she also noticed that Nolan had an impressively large studio running the length of the back fence.

In the second half of 1948, which was also the year Nolan took advantage of a government amnesty to obtain a dishonourable discharge from the army, Margaret found herself wielding a paintbrush alongside him:

I worked with Sid on Sam's next production for SUDS. There were two plays on the same bill this time, Cocteau's Orphée *and Shakespeare's* Pericles. *Sid did the front curtain and the backdrop for* Orphée. *Jean Bellette had done the design notes for* Pericles, *but she didn't have the time to paint the sets, so I painted them from her design.*[30] *Sam had arranged for Sid and me to work in the Tivoli workshop, which was high up in the theatre above the stage. We used to start in the morning. Sid would be busy with* Orphée *on one side of the workshop, I'd be on the other side painting* Pericles. *Then at about midday we'd go out for a Chinese meal in Campbell Street. To get to the paintroom you had go across the stage, so when we came back after lunch we had to wait until the dancing girls, or whatever, had ended, and then while the curtain was down we'd run across the stage and climb up the ladder to where we were working.*

You couldn't quite hear what was happening on stage, but we could tell if it was a successful house by the laughter at the jokes and the applause. The curtains we were painting were lowered down on big winches for us to work on them. If we were working on the top of the backdrop, we obviously had to let the whole curtain down, and sometimes it would block the entrance to the stage, which was particularly a problem for those scenes where they had trick bikes with people riding on top of one another, or some such. We'd be happily working away when the stagehand would suddenly shout, Roll 'er up! We can't get the bikes in. So we'd have to get on the winch and wind up what we were working on.

Orphée and *Pericles* played from 11 to 17 September. The best seats cost seven shillings and could be booked through Paling's. This was only Nolan's second effort at theatre design. His first had been nine years earlier, when he did the sets and costumes for the ballet *Icarus*. Initially with *Orphée*, Nolan attempted to follow Cocteau's stage directions literally, but these included countless mirrors made of silver paper, which unfortunately blinded the audience at rehearsals and so had to be abandoned. Nolan finally settled for a much simpler version of his original drop curtain.

As with *Hassan*, the list of production acknowledgements reads like a mini *Who's Who* of the arts. Stella Fraenkel was once again responsible for hats, although Sid Braceford of the Tivoli Theatre provided Orphée's and the Horse's heads (the Horse was played by Wally Johnstone). Alannah Coleman designed the gown for Madam Death (played by Diana Burton). Paul Haefliger made the woodcut, to a Nolan design, which was used for the handbills to advertise performances. Nolan's artwork also stylishly transformed the program, as Margaret particularly remembers:

Sid did the drawings for the advertisements in the program. There was one for Stella Fraenkel's hats; another for the airline ANA, with a figure in a primitive flying machine; and others for David Jones, Paling's, Penguin Books, Searls flowers. All wonderful drawings.

❦

Almost as soon as the *Orphée* season was over, at the end of September 1948 Margaret arrived at Hill End for another stay with Donald Friend. Friend and Donald Murray, who was now back in residence at the cottage, had already had a few beers at the Hill End pub before Margaret arrived. They were then sharing a bottle of sweet wine with 'an amiable peasant' at the cottage when the bus deposited Margaret at their door.[31] Murray, by this stage 'quite tipsy and very whimsical', according to Friend, proceeded to cook them up 'an appalling meal of greasy fried chops'.[32] The evening further declined when the two men quarrelled over Friend's inability to take criticism. Margaret was amused by their bickering but Friend was offended.

However, as before, he was quickly inspired by Margaret's visit. Two days later he suddenly decided to get back to work on an unfinished panel of *Apocalypse*, while also drawing with her the landscape, which was everywhere bursting into spring blossom, the flowering pear being especially lovely. The garden round the cottage was looking good, too, with anemones, daffodils, pansies and soon iris, too, in flower. Margaret's reappearance at the cottage also fuelled local gossip. Father Stewart, the rector, reported to Friend one old local's remark: 'I see Donald Friend's lady love is in town again!'

On a memorable occasion, Murray accompanied Friend and Margaret on a painting excursion:

I remember catching the bus to Sofala with Murray and Donald to do some drawing. Sofala was a much better subject than Hill End. Murray was English and he could be very amusing. He was always extremely gracious. How do you do? he used to say, in a very English way. However, on this particular day he was not so charming. It was very cold and we were all wrapped up in coats. When we arrived at Sofala, Donald and I immediately sat down in the gutter with our sketchbooks and started drawing. Murray was ashamed of us sitting in the gutter and proceeded to pace up and down the ghost town, pursing his lips, pretending he didn't know us.

Friend was so irritated by Murray's sulking while he and Margaret were trying to draw that he did a caricature of Murray as Death walking up Sofala's main street.

At the same time, a small boy with mumps kept pestering Friend and Margaret about what they were doing. Finally Friend snapped and told the child that he was drawing Death, and that Death was a friend of his and was coming to have lunch with them. Margaret couldn't stop laughing and the mumpy child fled. Murray's bad humour and Friend's crossness about it finally abated, and the excursion ended with the three of them picnicking under the willows by the river.[33] They eventually returned home, with Friend and Margaret exhausted from sketching.

Margaret remained at Hill End until the beginning of October. The time passed pleasantly with no more eruptions between Friend and Murray. Friend's diary for 5 October begins with the simple entry: 'Olley left. We both miss her.'[34]

Margaret was certainly on a roll. Her second one-person exhibition opened two weeks later at the Moreton Galleries in Brisbane. Though a little more than half the works for the Brisbane show had already appeared in her Sydney exhibition, it was still quite an achievement An even bigger percentage this time – fifteen of the twenty-one works – were landscapes, again mostly of old buildings in Hill End, Sofala or Brisbane. There were only two purely still life paintings: *Bowl of Fruit and Flowers* and *Still Life*, the former having already been shown in Sydney. *Portrait in the Mirror* and *Ophelia* made another appearance, while *Venus with Rose* was a romantic newcomer.

The review in the *Courier Mail* on 19 October, by a critic with the initials T.F.M., was lukewarm. 'Her work, with a fair trace of Drysdale influence, seems to be essentially that of an "in-between" school whose followers fear classification with the extremists, yet will not paint on orthodox lines,' T.F.M. wrote, after he'd commented on how different her world was from that of the previous artist exhibiting – Sir Lionel Lindsay. T.F.M. went on to describe the top-priced *Ophelia* as 'a mural-like study, with a semi-ultra-modern slant', before adding that it was Margaret's scenes of Hill End and Sofala and their 'attractive modern quality' that had the most appeal.

About a month after Margaret had stayed with him, Donald Friend began working on a portrait of her in oils at Hill End. Jean Bellette and Paul Haefliger, accompanied by Peter Kaiser, had just made their first visit there and been 'entranced' by the cottage and spring-filled ghost town – although privately Friend thought Kaiser was the only one who saw the point to it all. Haefliger was also 'bowled over' by Friend's *Apocalypse*.[35] These visitors had scarcely departed when Margaret, in synchronicity with his starting the portrait of her, wrote to ask if she and Annie Ross could stay with him. The letter, however, came late – it arrived on the same day they did – so there was no chance for Friend to say no should he have wanted to, which seems unlikely.

Margaret and Ross arrived drunk. It's an occasion that has been much written about, despite Margaret's protestations – probably quite true – that Ross was the ringleader and the more inebriated of the two. Friend's diary entry regarding this episode offers a fascinating glimpse of the non-serious, endearing, misbehaving side of Margaret. And also one of the few accounts of her drinking:

'When the bus came, Anne Ross and Margaret practically tumbled out of it, madly giggling and very drunk. The whole bus craned to watch them. Bruce the driver seemed scandalised. Anne sat in the gutter and refused to budge. Margaret luckily had a little sense left and I finally lugged Anne into the cottage where they regaled us with a hysterical tale of how they had bought a bottle of sherry at Sofala and drank it all because the journey was so terribly long. I could cheerfully have strangled them, but they were very funny and of course penitent.'[36]

By the time his two remorseful visitors departed two days later, Friend had nearly finished his oil painting of Margaret, which he thought looked good, although he did not dispatch it to Lucy Swanton at the Macquarie Galleries until the end of the first week in December. It's fascinating to think that in the last few months of 1948, three such redoubtable Australian artists as Friend, Dobell and Drysdale were all living with Margaret's image in their painting spaces, and perhaps daily considering the nuances of her face, even if they were not actually at work on the portraits. They would have been pondering the tilt of her nose; wondering if they'd quite captured her expression; worrying if the wry twist of her lips needed just a little touch more; perhaps also, once in a while, turning her face to the wall in exasperation; and even – well, probably only Friend – occasionally allowing themselves a little pat on the back.

⋞◈⋟

Margaret may well have been more distressed about missing out on the Travelling Scholarship than she let slip. Or maybe Sam Hughes was more appreciative of her talent than he let on, and knew from his time at the Zwemmer Gallery in London how exciting it could be to experience the work of overseas artists in Europe. Probably Hughes saw that Margaret had taken as many classes as she needed in Australia and that it was time for her to explore a wider world. Margaret would argue now that the opposite was true of her work. Nevertheless, her travelling may have seemed imperative to Hughes at the time:

When I didn't win the Travelling Scholarship, Sam must have written to Anne and said what a pity Olley missed out. Because then, completely unexpectedly, Anne, whose family was quite wealthy, sent me some money to go overseas. I forget how much it was. My memory is that it was three thousand pounds. But I'm not very good at remembering sums of money and that does seem a rather large amount.

Now, looking back at it, I think it's a pity I went. I was getting along well with painting. I was developing my own style. Going away interrupted that. I don't think I was ready for it. However, that's the wisdom of hindsight. At the time it was like a dream come true. Anne showed me a great kindness and I have tried to repay it ever since by helping other people.

Before I left I gave up the flat at McMahons Point and went back up to Brisbane for a bit. This explains why I didn't ever see Bill's portrait of me while he was painting it. In fact, I never really knew that he was painting it. I'd sat for him, he'd done the drawing and that was it as far as I was concerned. I certainly never thought about him putting it in for the Archibald Prize. I was really far too busy getting ready to go away to be wondering about what Bill was doing.

Something else may have been occupying Margaret's mind, too:

Just before I went away, Sam took me to Stanwell Park down on the coast for a bit of 'nookie'. It was a farewell sort of thing. I think he was probably claiming me before I left. It worked, because if men made advances that weren't welcome or appropriate for some reason or other, I could always have at the back of my mind, Well, I'm saving myself for Sam.

The 'bit of nookie' is a subject about which it's hard to get more out of Margaret. It seems to be the one thing she'd like to keep private and precious. She and Hughes did not start up a sexual relationship as a consequence. There would be other men in her life but, in a way, as she says, her heart was given to Hughes from then on. However it would be another couple of decades before a real romance took place.

Meanwhile, there were the more mundane matters to do with leaving the country to be attended to:

My mother insisted that if I was going overseas I had to have proper luggage — as if it matters. So I bought myself an old travelling trunk in a second-hand shop at Woolloongabba [in Brisbane]. One side was like a wardrobe, the other side had drawers with little silver handles on them, and it weighed a ton. How that travelling trunk dogged me! I came to rue the day I ever set eyes on it. My mother also tricked me into getting a corset. I always kept my stockings up with suspenders. I hated the idea of being strapped into a corset.

I think we'll go shopping, my mother said innocently one day. I'll meet you in the underwear department at Allan & Stark. In Brisbane, everybody had their favourite shops and Allan & Stark was my mother's. When I turned up, she had already picked out this awful corset I could hardly breathe in. I gave in to her, but I had no intention of ever wearing it.

Margaret's departure from Australia turned out to be chaotic. It started out calmly enough. She had booked a passage on a ship that was due to leave Sydney early in 1949. So, in about the third week of January, having finished packing in Brisbane and loaded up with the travelling trunk, she caught the train to Sydney:

I said my goodbyes to the family in Brisbane. 'I'm not going down to Sydney to see you off,' my father said. 'I'll meet you when you come back.'

This was not upsetting. It was my father's way of making my

1948

eventual return something to look forward to. But I was in a state getting away. It was only when I was finally settled on the train that I realised I hadn't organised any traveller's cheques for myself.

When she arrived in Sydney, Margaret booked the trunk into storage at Central Station and went off to stay with friends. Suddenly there were several dramatic turns of events. Mitty Lee-Brown, who had been at tech with Margaret (but was now living in Paris and about to return there via London), persuaded her to change her plans and travel with her to London on the *Moreton Bay*. 'Oh, Oll, don't go on that boat, join my boat,' Margaret recalls Lee-Brown insisting. So, at the last minute, Margaret booked herself on the *Moreton Bay*. To complicate things further, although the *Moreton Bay* had actually begun its journey in Brisbane, the impromptu nature of Margaret's new travel arrangements meant she had to embark in Melbourne, where she'd never been before.

Then, on Friday, 21 January 1949, it was announced that Dobell's portrait of Margaret had been awarded the 1948 Archibald Prize. Dobell's win was splashed across the afternoon papers and was again big news the next morning.

Confusion reigned on the Saturday. First thing in the morning, Margaret remembers, she went to Central Station to send the trunk on ahead of her to Melbourne. In the midst of doing this, she remembered she still hadn't arranged any travelling money. Feeling quite desperate, she shoved the trunk into an out-of-the-way corner of the station and dashed back into the city to find a bank. Mercifully, in those days banks opened on Saturdays. At the bank, much to Margaret's surprise, all the tellers recognised her as the subject of the winning portrait of the Archibald Prize and wanted her autograph. While this was embarrassing, it did speed up the processing of her cheques. That done, Margaret had to return to Central and have the trunk sent down to Melbourne.

Far from a Still Life

At some stage on this Saturday, Margaret also saw Dobell's portrait for the first time, which turned out to be yet another ordeal. According to Brian Adams's biography of Dobell, Margaret was asked by the Education Department in Sydney to pose for a couple of shots in the hat she'd worn for the portrait, and was afterwards driven by a film crew to the National Art Gallery of New South Wales, where she was reluctantly coerced into posing beside the portrait.[37] Margaret was so flummoxed by the hullabaloo at the gallery that she does not remember this, but certainly photos of her in the hat did appear in the paper on Sunday. To Margaret, the whole visit to the gallery was nothing but distressing:

There was just nothing but photographs and press. Press, press, press. It was quite frightening. I was so shy and upset that I couldn't even look at Bill's portrait. I was embarrassed by all the publicity. It took me years to get over the fuss. It was years, too, before I was able to look at the portrait. I was too terrified. I used to sneak up, peek round the corner to see if anyone else was looking at it, take a brief look myself and then run away. I've actually always liked the little Drysdale one. It's more intimate.

Drysdale, according to Donald Friend, was putting the finishing touches to his portrait of Margaret, which Friend believed to be one of his best works to date, at the time the Archibald announcement was made.[38]

Dobell had not only won the five hundred pound portraiture prize that year, but also the Wynne Prize for landscape with his work *Storm Approaching, Wangi*. He, too, received a fair share of attention. The *Sydney Morning Herald* and the *Telegraph* featured articles relating the story of how Dobell had been so disappointed by the work in its early stages that he was about to scrape it off until fellow artist Sali Herman (who won the Sulman Prize) intervened, declared it a masterpiece and suggested Dobell just paint over what he didn't like.[39]

The *Sun* ran with an account of how the two entries were rushed to the art gallery for the judging with quarter of an hour to spare and the paint still wet.[40] The paintings were too big to fit in an ordinary taxi, the *Sun* continued, and it was raining cats and dogs as Dobell and a friend from the Minerva Theatre tried to organise transport. In the end, the driver of a taxi truck, an admirer of Dobell's work, had taken pity on them and loaded up the paintings. Dobell, now fifty-one, also admitted to the *Sun* that he had been so down in the dumps and nervous in the afternoon before the announcement was made, that to distract himself he had gone into town and, rather fortuitously, bought a new suit and a dressing gown. The dressing gown, one presumes, was the striped one in which he was photographed the next day receiving congratulatory phone calls.

Harry Tatlock Miller, in the same edition of the *Sun*, wrote that compared to the many other 'dead and lifeless' entries, Margaret in the portrait breathed 'with a life superbly manufactured for her by Dobell's incisive brush'. The trustees of the gallery were divided about the work, in particular the artist Sydney Long, who declared the result 'a farce'. However, except for one attack by the *Truth*'s unnamed art critic, who called Dobell 'a distortionist', the critics generally were warmly in favour of the painting's win.[41]

Most of the controversy in the press centred around whether the portrait actually looked like Margaret; and if her expression – with the enigmatic little smile that everyone noticed – resembled the Mona Lisa's. Dobell, as quoted in various papers, fuelled matters when he said her expression, as he'd painted it, was like that of da Vinci's famous subject.[42] Desiderius Orban promptly contradicted him. Tatlock Miller declared the expression of both portraits 'sphinx-like'. Drysdale applauded the work for its own merits: 'I know Margaret and the likeness is there, but Dobell has done more than get a likeness, he has painted a portrait which is also a picture.'

One doctor, who had seen the portrait, was quoted in the *Telegraph* as saying the portrait reminded him of a woman who had kidney trouble. So it went on. The *Telegraph* also claimed that only two out of fifty onlookers recognised Margaret from the portrait when she herself visited the art gallery:[43]

I think Bill painted what people become. I've probably become more like the portrait now than I was when it was first painted. I used to get really offended when people said to me, Oh, you're the sitter for the Dobell painting. I used to reply, I also paint.

There were all sorts of parties before I left Sydney. I had to say goodbye to Sam, who was one of the few people who weren't going overseas at that time. The Drysdales threw a going-away gathering for me. Donald was up at Hill End, so he wasn't present. Bill was there and wanted to give me a little sketch as a farewell present. But Bonny said, No, no, no. She'll need money, she doesn't need that. Give her money. So Bill gave me some money, Tas gave me some money, and away I went. I was poured onto the train, I think. Then it was off into the unknown.

Part II
1949–59

8

Culture Shock

I should never have gone away. Seeing all those paintings was like a culture shock. A huge culture shock. I'd been used to looking at reproductions and when I came face to face with the painting themselves, it was altogether too much.

JUST THREE DAYS AFTER DOBELL'S ARCHIBALD PRIZE WIN WAS announced, Margaret posed resignedly for a newsreel cameraman on the deck of the *Moreton Bay* in Melbourne. It was 24 January 1949. She wore a navy and white spotted dress with a full tiered skirt, demure neckline and three-quarter sleeves, and a small, subdued hat; not quite the outfit for a Melbourne summer, nor seafaring. Her expression as she sat on the deck in front of the camera definitely resembled Mona Lisa's – albeit a slightly downcast Mona Lisa. Next up, it was a snap for the Melbourne *Herald*. The media of the day were not going to let Dobell's subject – and a young, pretty artist to boot – escape Australia or their lenses easily.

Far from a Still Life

But the Woolloongabba travelling trunk was safely on board. Her mother's gift corset from Allan & Stark was stowed away in the depths of the trunk's silver-handled drawers, together with the big sheepskin coat – all the rage – a friend had made her, and a bundle of sketchbooks, which was within handier reach. That afternoon Margaret at last set off overseas. The famous galleries of England, France, Italy and Spain would soon be hers to explore. She was twenty-five-and-a-half to the day.

As the *Moreton Bay* steamed out of Port Phillip Bay, debate over the Archibald winner didn't ease off. Margaret's enigmatic gaze continued to fill up newsprint and domestic conversation. As the ship heaved across the Great Australian Bight, forty thousand visitors packed the National Art Gallery of New South Wales to see for themselves what all the fuss was about.[1]

In the Hill End pub locals lifted their glasses in approval. Dobell's picture did 'great honour' to Hill End, they felt, since its subject was Donald Friend's guest, who'd already impressed them with her eccentric clothes and arrival on the bus more than a tad tipsy.[2] At Kyogle, in northern New South Wales, a local paper was quick to point out in genteel terms Margaret's family connections to the area.

However, despite the press hounding her even as far as Colombo, shipboard life did offer distractions:

Somebody had told me, when you travel just take a few clothes and then add different scarves to change the look of your outfits, which seemed very practical advice. I was amazed how many women spent their entire sea voyage ironing all the clothes they'd brought. Another person said to me, Well, what you should do is wear all your old underwear and throw it out the porthole as you go! That was one piece of advice I did not adopt.

At Fremantle, when Margaret and Lee-Brown disembarked for some sightseeing, there were photographers waiting for her there, too:

Culture Shock

All that terrible press just kept on. When my mother came down to see the portrait in Sydney the press attacked her, wanting to know her reaction to the portrait. They were hoping that she'd be like Joshua Smith's parents, who said, That's not my son. But she wouldn't.

At Fremantle also two female friends of Mitty joined the Moreton Bay *as passengers, which perked things up. The captain wanted to put us four women at his table, but Mitty made sure that we had a table on our own. I think she thought we could keep an eye on the available males better that way. Mitty had already been married to Peter Russo, a journalist, and gone off to Hong Kong with him. There was a story that when she left Sydney, the bar of the Australia Hotel was filled with her admirers commiserating with each other. Then she'd been living in Paris, so she'd fitted in quite a lot since leaving tech.*

The next port of call was Colombo. Here Margaret first experienced the allure of foreign parts:

You could smell Ceylon before we even arrived. I've always had a great nose for smells, and approaching Colombo the aromas of the spices and curries really hit you. I loved breathing in the heady exoticness of it. We were berthed at Colombo for a few days because the Moreton Bay *carried cargo as well as passengers, and had to unload and load its goods. But I liked Colombo that first time. I could have quite happily got off the ship and stayed there.*

Mitty organised us ashore and into a big room at the Galle Face, a grand old colonial hotel, right on the beachfront. It also overlooked a square where people strolled up and down, taking the evening air. Mitty wanted to stay at the Galle Face so she could have a couple of her Dior dresses, or some such, copied overnight by the hotel tailors.

Why don't you get one done, too? she said. Which I did. God only knows what's happened to it.

Years later a strange coincidence happened at the Galle Face. I had gone back there with Sam and Paul Jones. We had been to the

Maldives because Paul was a shell collector and we were staying at the Galle Face before visiting Mitty, who by then was living at her present home in Trincomalee. I looked out of the hotel window and realised that it was exactly the same room that I had stayed in with Mitty, so many years earlier.

After Colombo, Archibald hoo-ha subsided into sea and white foam as the *Moreton Bay* covered more and more nautical miles. Aden, Suez, Malta, Gibraltar: to Margaret it felt like they were at sea for months. In fact, the journey took about five weeks. She and Mitty Lee-Brown passed some of the time making collages to send home instead of letters.[3] Margaret also did renditions of the song 'See What the Boys in the Backroom Will Have' from the Marlene Dietrich Western *Destry Rides Again*, in which Dietrich plays a sultry saloon trouper called Frenchy. Margaret's version of Frenchy's drinking refrain – an entertainment with a touch of prophecy about it – proved a hit with fellow passengers, Lee-Brown remembers.[4]

Margaret, in an attempt at more serious diversion, had armed herself with textbooks to learn Italian on the way over. Not having had much luck earlier with French, she thought she might do better with Italian. But it was Lee-Brown, according to Margaret, who, as well as collecting her fair share of admirers in the weeks at sea, was speaking fluent Italian by the journey's end, having borrowed the books from Margaret.

Coincidentally, on 3 March, as the *Moreton Bay* would have been docking in London, back in Australia a piece by Harry Tatlock Miller appeared in Sydney in the *Sun*, enthusiastically praising Donald Friend's newly completed *Apocalypse* mural, on which he'd been working when Margaret stayed at Hill End. When the *Moreton Bay* finally berthed, there was an oddly assorted welcoming party waiting for Margaret and Lee-Brown:

Culture Shock

Mitty was met by a male friend of hers. I was greeted by my two aunts, my Aunt Mary, and Aunt Madge, who was the baby of my mother's family. Aunt Madge had married an Englishman, Uncle Stanley, who worked laying cables for overseas telephones, and she had been living in England for some time. Aunt Mary was just on holidays, travelling around. Also on the station – we had to catch the train into London – were Jocelyn Rickards and Alec Murray, my friends from Merioola, who just took over.[5] You're staying with us, they said, and swept me up.

I don't know where I thought I was going to stay. I hadn't thought about it. Talk about an innocent abroad. I remember we went by Hyde Park and it was the first time I'd seen snow. The crocuses were just peeping up, white, yellow-orange and purpley-mauve. It looked absolutely marvellous. I thought all snow would be as beautiful and white as it was in the park, but I was soon disenchanted. The snow beside the road and in the gutters was just grey and dirty slush, as they call it.

Jocelyn Rickards, who had arrived in London at the beginning of January 1949 – six months after Alec Murray – and Murray himself, were at this time living at Cranley Gardens in South Kensington in a large Victorian house owned by a Czechoslovakian refugee known as Dimi, where presumably Margaret now joined them.[6]

Shortly after Margaret's own arrival in London there was yet another to-do about Dobell's portrait, which had been bought for the National Art Gallery of New South Wales for six hundred pounds by the gallery's director, Hal Missingham. The purchase provoked a particularly mean-spirited attack by the cranky James Stuart MacDonald. 'What sort of a public,' he fumed in the pages of the *Daily Mirror*, 'wants to look forever at a fat, dress-bursting woman – unhealthily obese from eating wrong[ly] or over-feeding, fat, fatuous and falling over.'[7]

It was not Margaret he was castigating. In MacDonald's opinion, the painting was unlike her in every way, including bodily. It was the gallery trustees and Dobell he was annoyed with, and the painting itself. But, needless to say, it was not the painting that might have been stung by his insulting words. MacDonald's diatribe could hardly fail to be anything but hurtful to both artist and sitter. It was lucky that Margaret was on the other side of the world – and that there were a multitude of quite different paintings to concern herself with:

The Wallace Collection was the first gallery I went to in London – to see the beautiful Rembrandts and wonderful Velasquezes. Then I went to the National Gallery and saw the El Grecos and Titians. This was before they were over-cleaned, too, when they were a beautiful honey colour. You'd hardly recognise Titian's Ariadne *for the same painting today. I prefer it the way it was. They look a little bit raw now. A lot of things go wrong in the restoration of paintings.*

On my first trip away, some paintings I'd always admired in reproduction didn't live up to expectations; others that didn't reproduce well were wildly exciting. But I wasn't ready for it. I'm a firm believer that knowledge and application should go hand in hand. If your knowledge of paintings upsets that balance, it's a setback. You become intimidated. I had a direction in my painting before I went away, but overseas I became so overwhelmed by the paintings, I couldn't paint myself.

I stopped painting almost completely. I went around looking and drawing. I just drew and drew. I used to do pen and wash mainly. I'd put down a wash of watercolour and then I'd draw over that with a pen. I also drew with chalks. It's a lot easier to go around with a sketchbook than a heavy paintbox. If you've got a sketchbook, you're free to roam around at will by bus or the metro. One day on a bus in London, coming up to Hyde Park, I saw the Coldstream Guards marching in their bearskins. I jumped off the bus and followed them with my sketchbook. I drew the Changing of the Guards, too. I found the pageantry very exciting and colourful.

Culture Shock

Despite the pomp, pageantry and a plethora of art, which, though inhibiting, she loved seeing, London had its downsides, Margaret soon found:

It was cold and miserable. I'd just come from summer in Australia. The air was always damp. The fires didn't dry it out. There was so much moisture in the air it was almost impossible even to dry a handkerchief in front of the coal fire. Then the fogs would descend – you could hardly see the end of your fingers. Fog might look very romantic in photographs, but in London then it was the colour of phlegm and had an awful sulphurous smell from the burning coal. How anybody survived, I don't know.

Now that the coal fires have been abolished you can actually see the sun in winter. They've cleaned up the buildings and it looks quite different. But London was really very depressing when I was first there.

As an escape, I visited my Aunt Madge who was living out of London in the country. That was where I abandoned the corset my mother had given me. I gave it to Aunt Madge, who was short of everything because of the war and very pleased to get it. From Aunt Madge's I went on to the Cotswolds, where I did a little watercolour (when I said I wasn't painting, I meant large oils) that now hangs in my sitting room. I must have been very influenced by Cézanne at the time because it has a very Cézanne-like look. I gave it to Aunt Madge as a present and she then left it to me in her will.

Back in Sydney, Russell Drysdale's first show in four years, since 1945, opened at the Macquarie Galleries on 23 March. Though only small, the exhibition was a triumph for Drysdale. Harry Tatlock Miller described it as 'rich with his development, intensity and power' and added that the show was 'the most important to be seen for many years'.[8] Among the twelve works hanging was Drysdale's portrait of Margaret that had been completed at the same time Dobell's portrait of her was attracting so much attention. Tatlock Miller was glowing in his praise of Drysdale's rendering of Margaret. 'Eloquent, sensuously passaged in paint, *Margaret Olley* shows him to be a sensitive, sympathetic portrait painter of the first order.' Two days later in the *Sydney Morning Herald*'s Column 8, 'Granny' gleefully pointed out, as a follow-up to the Archibald commotion, that though Drysdale's treatment was entirely different from Dobell's, the face was almost identical in both portraits. 'Can they both be wrong?' Granny innocently asked in conclusion.

After Drysdale's sherry opening there was a champagne and sandwiches celebration at Rose Bay. The following night Tas and Bonny threw yet another party. This time it was a going-away party for Donald Friend, who was about to leave with Peter Kaiser by the ship *Toscana* for Italy. Friend, who seems to have been showered with fond farewells and cocktail dos, was once again fed up with socialising. He was feeling sick from inoculations and was longing, as he wrote in his diary, 'to go gently to sleep and wake up far away at sea'.[9]

On the other side of the world, Margaret, too, was soon travelling again:

After I'd been about a month in London, Mitty announced that we were going to Paris. Paris seemed a good idea to me. Mitty, Fred Jessup (who had been in England for a while already on his Travelling Scholarship) and I went over. Fred was carrying Mitty's silver and the various bits and pieces she'd brought over from Australia to set up home in Paris, as well as food supplies for her. We had to go out to Southampton, walk – with Fred laden up – along the wharf and then get onto one of those ships that crossed the English Channel.

David Strachan had been in Paris since July the year before, staying in various hotels while attending the famous art school

Culture Shock

Académie de la Grande Chaumière. The Paris spring of 1949 was the most beautiful he had ever seen, he enthused in a letter home to his parents.[10] In another letter to his parents, dated 25 April, Strachan wrote that Margaret Olley was now in Paris. He told them that when she'd disembarked after crossing the English Channel, she found the landscape at Dieppe so beautiful she couldn't believe it and burst into tears.[11] Looking through the catalogues of Margaret's shows during her time overseas, there certainly are a remarkable number of drawings of Dieppe. It was the harbour at Dieppe that, above all, attracted her:

I loved the sailing boats. On subsequent trips from London I used to get off the ship, stay in Dieppe drawing the boats, then catch a later train to Paris. It was fascinating because of the way the tide changed so drastically and suddenly. I'd be working away on a drawing and by the time I'd finished, I'd only be able see the masts. The boats would have dropped so much because of the tide.

Paris also instantly struck a chord with Margaret. The city was still flavoured by the École de Paris, which had nurtured the world's modern art movements for the first four decades of the twentieth century. It was where every artist hankered to hang out, wearing the proverbial beret, with their own atelier, drinking vin ordinaire and breathing the same air as that which had filled the lungs of Manet, Cézanne, Picasso and so many other painters. Unlike Sunday Reed who, having arrived with John Reed and the little boy Sweeney a month or so after Strachan, found Paris dirty and worried about the rationing of dairy products while longing for a decent cup of tea, Margaret was unequivocally besotted with the art-redolent city:[12]

Paris is like a spiritual home to me. I love it because it's always the same. I walked and walked the first month I was there. Walking is the only way to experience Paris properly. Mitty and I had an apartment in the Trocadéro area above an ice-skating rink. We'd hear muffled waltz music wafting up from it at all hours. The apartment was furnished and had dreadful heavy, padded duvets that felt as if they were made of old carpet. Not that it mattered. Being in Paris was all I cared about.

Fred, who never left France from then on, moved straight away into a hotel on the Left Bank and immediately went out drawing. The first thing I did was to go to galleries. That's what I felt I was there for – to see. The Marmottan Museum wasn't far away from us, though the Monets weren't there then.[13] Of course, I went to the Louvre. I'd been brought up believing that the Mona Lisa was the most important painting in the world, but when I finally stood in front of it I was disappointed, let down. I was more interested in the people who had set their easels up all around and were busily copying it. But then I discovered the Chardins and lovely Corots that I adore. My favourite gallery, far and away, was the Jeu de Paume, with its Manets, Monets, Cézannes, Degas and Rousseaus, its vibrant Matisses and Bonnards. I drank all those in.

The ice-skating apartment lasted a week or so. Then Mitty found another apartment in quite a posh suburb near the Arc de Triomphe, where Sunday and John Reed had been staying. I knew of the Reeds, but I didn't really know them because they were from Melbourne. The apartment was full of Tibetan Buddhas, wall-hangings and gilt sculptures, probably from Thailand, which was all very novel and exotic to us.

During this time in Paris, Margaret teamed up with another friend from Sydney, the 'charming' Wolfgang Cardamatis. Cardamatis had come over to Paris sometime earlier in the company of a male Russian ballet dancer called Nicolas 'Nicki' d'Ivangine. D'Ivangine had originally come to Australia with the de Basil Russian ballet company and had had to be left behind when the company departed because he had broken his leg. Then, although only young, he had become ill with an incurable disease and wanted to see his parents, who were living in Paris, before he died.[14] Despite the sadness Cardamatis felt at his friend's eventual death, he had stayed on in Paris afterwards. For Margaret, he was the most 'entertaining' guide:

Wolf is a person who could pick up a leaf and give it to you as if it was the most precious thing in the world. A great ability. Having him show me around was definitely a bonus. I remember especially a Chinese gallery near Parc de Monceau he took me to where there were replicas of famous antiquities, which has always struck me as a sensible idea for an exhibition. Sometimes after we'd been to the galleries together I'd go up to his little room and he'd cook us a meal. He had devised an ingenious system whereby he'd partly cook a casserole or something on the small gas ring in his room, then he'd transfer it to a box with a lid that he lined with cushions of hay. The hay kept the heat in and the meal would go on slowly cooking.

Margaret wasn't at all lacking for Australian company. On one occasion she ran into sculptor Bob Klippel, whom she'd known briefly at East Sydney Technical College, and the two spent a memorable day together:

Have you ever been up the Eiffel Tower? I asked him. He hadn't and neither had I. So that's what we did. Suddenly the whole of Paris made total sense. In those days Paris stopped at the ring road. After that you were in the country, where people had summer holiday houses and grew fruit and vegetables.

But it was David Strachan who introduced Margaret to the woman would become her closest friend at this time – artist Moya Dyring. Dyring was another artist whose love life was intermeshed with John and Sunday Reed. Dyring had studied art in both Melbourne and Sydney, but was primarily connected to the Melbourne art scene of the 1930s. While still an art student, she became romantically involved with Sam Atyeo, who became Melbourne's most adventurous modernist, championed by Clarice Zander, among others.

Atyeo and Dyring's lives soon became caught up with the Reeds. The quietly handsome John and the chic, sexily sophisticated Sunday had met in 1930, just after Sunday's brief first marriage had ended disastrously. Both the Reeds came from privileged backgrounds and they had started buying modern art together even before they married in January 1932. After their marriage they lived in fashionable South Yarra. Here they began what Janine Burke describes as a 'culturally committed, communally oriented life, shared with artists and those interested in modern art'.[15] According to Burke, this time not only marked for Sunday the start of her devotion to modernism, but also signalled a growing self-confidence in herself as 'an aspiring artist, a patron and a collector, and as a sexually independent woman embarking on her first affair'.[16]

Sunday's new lover was Atyeo, who seems to have been an inveterate womaniser and was also close to John Reed. This would be the Reeds' first ménage à trois (the second, involving Sidney Nolan, has already been mentioned). In 1933, to further complicate matters, John Reed had an affair with Dyring. The following year John and Sunday bought a property in the Yarra Valley near Heidelberg and over the next year remodelled the existing weatherboard dwelling, which they called 'Heide', to look like a French farmhouse.

In 1936, the complexities of the Reeds' sexual relationships lessened. Atyeo departed for France. Sunday, the affair with Atyeo over, took off on a world trip the following year, and John and Dyring's affair petered out as well. Despite the twists and turns of her love life, Dyring continued busily painting. In 1937, not only did she look after Heide and its garden in Sunday's absence, she also had a successful one-person exhibition at Riddell's Gallery in Melbourne. The exhibition, in which Dyring's works reflected the Cubist influences of both Cézanne and Picasso, made her the first woman in Melbourne to have a solo show of modernist paintings. There was additional excitement when the first floor of the gallery started to buckle under the weight of the crowd packed in for the opening and it was feared the ceiling might fall in.[17]

Despite their various affairs, Atyeo and Dyring remained a couple and in 1939 they retreated together to a farm in Vence, France. In 1941 they finally married in Barbados.[18] After the war Atyeo, accompanied by Dyring, started working in Paris for his friend Herbert Vere 'Doc' Evatt. Evatt, Australia's deputy Labor prime minister between 1946 and 1949, was also very much involved with the setting up of the United Nations and, in the late 1940s, he and his wife, Mary Alice, visited Paris several times in connection with this. Mary Alice, another keen modernist, had been friends with Dyring in Melbourne in the 1930s, and she and Dyring often painted together during the Evatts' Paris stays.

In 1948, the Dyring–Atyeo marriage fell apart irreparably. Following their separation, Dyring supported herself by taking tourists round Paris in her car when she wasn't painting. According to David Strachan, she 'sparked' off life and just to be in her presence made others happy.[19] For Margaret, Dyring made Paris come to life:

Moya had a great heart; she was a very generous, loveable person. She was like a soul-mate. I loved the way she lived. I always thought if people didn't like Moya, there was something wrong with them. But some people didn't, because she never conformed. She had dark hair cut short. After she'd washed it she used to put a stocking over it to make it dry flat. She was older than me and had studied with

Far from a Still Life

George Bell in Melbourne. As well as running an open house for all the Australian painters in Paris, her studio on Ile St Louis was filled with divans so she could put people up. She was also friends with French artists like Eugene Baboulene, and used to stay with him and his wife in the south of France. Years later, at an auction, I bought a portrait Baboulene did of Moya. I couldn't resist it.

Moya would take me out painting in her car. I used to pick huge bunches of flowers and bits of grass by the roadside to bring back to the apartment. Clarice Zander came over from London at one stage and we all drove off in Moya's car to the outskirts of Paris, where Vincent van Gogh and his brother were buried in a church. Their tombs were covered in simple ivy and on the other side of the road were fields with poppies and crows flying about. How much more van Gogh can you get? It was an incredible experience – especially when I'd just been looking at his paintings in museums – suddenly to see his landscape in reality. To me, van Gogh is the closest thing to music in painting. Each brushstroke is like a note of music, adding up to the whole score.

Moya and Sam Atyeo had parted not that long before I arrived in Paris. I met him once in Paris, then he disappeared off to Vence. Moya had been trying for years to have a baby and she was in quite a bad state when Atyeo first left. But then Mitty, who was looking out for a place to buy in Paris, heard of the apartment on the Quai d'Anjou. It had been completely gutted during the war – the walls of three small flats on the second floor had been knocked down – because the family didn't want it to be occupied by the Germans. Mitty decided against the apartment, due to its run-down state, so Moya took it over and did it up. The apartment brought Moya a whole new life and on subsequent trips to Paris I often stayed with her there.

Moya Dyring's studio at the Quay d'Anjou on Ile St Louis, an island in the Seine in the heart of Paris, would become legendary.

Ile St Louis, with its seventeenth-century houses, wrought-iron balconies, quaint courtyards, tree-lined embankments and views of Notre Dame, had long been the haunt of musicians, writers and artists. Dyring was given her sixteen-year lease of the flat on the condition that she made the place habitable within six months. From about mid 1950, 'Chez Moya' would be the scene of countless parties and endless conviviality for Margaret, Strachan and Jessup.[20]

After Margaret had been in Paris for about a month, Mitty Lee-Brown made another suggestion:

I think Mitty's love life was becoming a bit hectic, so she thought I might like to take over a farmhouse she knew about in Cassis. I was put on the train with instructions about where to get off and away I went. But Paris to Marseilles is a long, long trip. It was hot on the train and I was also terrified that I wouldn't get off at the right stop. When I finally clambered out at Marseilles, it seemed even hotter. It must have been late spring but it felt like mid-summer. I caught a taxi to my new home. I was too exhausted for anything else.

Cassis is the first little town over the hills from Marseilles. When I arrived there, the cicadas were deafening and the air was full of the smell of pine trees, which grew everywhere, and instead of grass the hillsides were covered with different sorts of thyme. Rosemary also grew wild and where the water collected in the little gullies between the hills there was mint – the French hate mint, so perhaps the English community who adopted Cassis brought it in. The whole countryside was like a garden. In summer it was especially magical because the colour of the landscape lingered long into the night. No wonder Rupert Bunny [a Melbourne painter] and other artists lived there for years.

Far from a Still Life

Cassis, about halfway between Marseilles and Toulon, has long been beloved by both artists and writers. French painters, including Matisse and Dufy, spent summers there in the early 1900s; the Bloomsbury set, including Virginia Woolf and her sister Vanessa Bell, adored it in the 1920s. David Strachan painted its terraced hillsides on his first trip to Europe in 1937. It's hard to imagine a more picturesque and artistically appropriate spot for Margaret to have ended up in France.

Virginia Woolf, who first visited Cassis in 1925, was intoxicated by its heat and light and colour.[21] When Margaret arrived, Cassis was essentially unchanged since Woolf's day – it was an unspoilt fishing port, complete with sixteenth-century buildings, narrow cobbled streets and a fourteenth-century castle fort. Vineyards surround the town, while along the coast steep white limestone cliffs run down to the sea. The stretch of coast between Marseilles and Cassis is famous for its calanques, the narrow inlets of dark blue water that cut into the limestone cliffs. Apart from wine, the gastronomic specialty of Cassis is sea urchins.

In a letter to the painter Roger Fry in 1925, Woolf described artists Vanessa Bell and Duncan Grant, two frequent visitors to Cassis, as 'humming with heat and happiness like sunflowers on a hot day'.[22] The same was no doubt true of Margaret, for most of her time in Cassis, at any rate:

The farmhouse I rented must have originally been workers' quarters. It belonged to a woman who lived in a little château nearby and grew grapes for making wine. My bedroom was on top of a wine cellar, in fact. When they were pressing the grapes, my landlady, whom I'll call Madame S., would say, Keep the windows open. That was so I wouldn't pass out from the potent fumes coming up from the cellar. Next door to the cellar Madame S. kept a mule. I could hear the poor animal kicking against the wall at night.

It was very primitive. There was a tap with running water and a charcoal burner and a gas ring to cook on. No bathroom. You learnt to use clothes in a different way. It was mainly hot, so I'd just go down at night to the pump in the yard and throw a bucket of water over myself. The toilet was very much an outside one. All the waste went down into a big tile-lined pit to the side of it, like an open compost heap, over which they used to throw hay.

If you wanted to buy any food, you had to walk down to Cassis. It was only a few kilometres, even less if I made a short cut through the vineyards. I did an enormous amount of drawing at Cassis. If I had friends like Margaret Cilento or Fred Jessup staying, we'd often take sketchbooks and swimmers – there was a very nice white sandy beach near the port – and go out for the day. We used to watch the locals diving off the cliffs into the calanques for sea urchins. The urchins, which were black and prickly, were easy to spot because the water was so clear. Fred used to dive for them, too. The first time he went in feet-first and landed right on an urchin, so then we had to pick all the spikes out. You ate the urchins raw, like oysters. I never liked them for that reason. The Cassis fishermen also used to trawl for sardines. We'd buy sardines, take them home and cook them, scales and all, with salt, pepper and a bit of flour, in olive oil, then eat the scales. Those I did enjoy.

Margaret's first shopping expedition to Cassis turned out rather oddly. Madame S. could only speak broken English and Margaret's French was not that up to scratch either. But as she was about to set off, Madame S. managed to convey that she wanted a parcel picked up at the chemist's. Margaret had no idea what she was supposed to be collecting until she was in the shop:

I was more than a bit taken aback when the chemist handed me a little black worm in a bottle. A leech! I never discovered what purpose she put it to, but when the leech was full of blood I was asked to return it to the chemist and get the deposit I'd left back. She was certainly a very frugal woman. If I needed any firewood, she would carefully weigh it up and sell it to me. If I wanted any grapes, they had to be bought from her; no idly wandering along putting grapes in your mouth.

She also kept goats. One day there was a great to-do because the buck goat, which you could smell from afar, had arrived. The female goats were hustled together and then everyone stood around while the buck goat serviced them. Being very practical, as the French are, there was also a great deal of inspecting to see whether the females were ready and if the job had been done properly.

Margaret soon encountered the remnants of the Bloomsbury group still resident in Cassis. Again, it was Mitty Lee-Brown who was responsible. Before Margaret had left Paris, Lee-Brown had said casually, 'If you're bored you might like to see these people who were part of the Bloomsbury set and live in the next valley each summer.' Accordingly, Margaret walked over the thyme-covered hills and introduced herself to Bertha Wright:

Bertha was much older than me but we hit it off straight away. Earlier on she'd been married to Alec Penrose, the oldest brother of Roland Penrose, the English surrealist who himself lived and painted at Cassis between the wars.[23] She and her present husband lived in a house that had once been a piggery. They had done it up and grown grapevines and fig trees in the garden.

Even though Bertha was older, she was still an attractive woman, very animated. She had long salt-and-pepper hair, which she wore in a bun at the back, and she was a Quaker. It was fascinating hearing her tales of the Bloomsbury set. Duncan Grant and Vanessa Bell had actually lived in a house that was halfway between Bertha's place and the Château [de] Fontcreuse that belonged to Colonel Teed.[24]

Colonel Arthur Seymour Holland Teed, the owner of Château

Culture Shock

de Fontcreuse, supposedly fell in love with Cassis while holidaying on the French Riviera in 1922, when he was an officer with the British army in India, and promptly decided to settle there. From the 1920s on, Teed was as much a part of Cassis as its limestone cliffs or vineyards; at least, for the visiting bohemians whose company he enthusiastically cultivated. The Colonel did not live alone at the Château de Fontcreuse. Since the 1920s, his mistress, Jean Campbell, had been with him:

I used to see Jean Campbell drifting past the bars on the waterfront. She was never without a hat and seemed rather fey and frail. Probably her hair had once been blonde, but by then it was mousy grey. She and the Colonel lived at the Château Fontcreuse and made a very good drop of rosé, which they exported to America.

Virginia Woolf, whose first mention of Fontcreuse was in a letter to her close friend, writer Vita Sackville-West, in April 1927, described the château as a divine seventeenth-century manor house set amid cypresses, complete with tanks of frogs and Roman aqueducts.[25] On Woolf's visit that night, Peter (as everyone called Colonel Teed) gave her tastings of various wines and bunches of wild tulips, which particularly appealed to Woolf.[26]

According to Woolf, who actually staying at the château in 1928 and 1929, as well as tending the chickens she bred, Jean Campbell was also known to sit in the dusk listening to the croaking of the vociferous, amorous and never-satisfied Fontcreuse frogs.[27]

The first of what would prove to be a steady stream of friends who visited Margaret at Cassis seems to have been Fred Jessup. Next on the scene was Margaret Cilento, who had arrived from New

York to take up her French government scholarship and study art in Paris. After, one imagines, much catching up, gossiping, laughter and rosé, the two Margarets intrepidly decided to hitch-hike to Florence:

We took a billycan to boil water and cook spaghetti in, and not much else. Hitchhiking was not as easy as we thought it would be. We stood and stood by the roadside. No cars came. At last a truck gave us a lift to La Ciotat, the next town on. Then we managed to score a lift to Nice, where we thought we should have a swim since it was such a famous seaside.

Down we went to the beach full of cobblestones. Because the French seemed to like changing on the beach, Fred had made me a bathing costume of mattress ticking designed to be discreetly put on under my clothes. It had a halter neck and was made out of one piece of material with strings attached, which I tied round my waist before taking anything off. After I'd secured Fred's costume and Margaret had changed into hers, we went into the water. The first thing that happened was Margaret Cilento copped a big turd. I was disgusted. All my life I'd been hearing about the beautiful beach at Nice and now we discovered they were using it as a lavatory.

After that we dressed ourselves up to the nines and walked round Antibes hoping that Mr Picasso, who was meant to be living there at the time, would appear and want to draw us. But we never saw him. Our next lift deposited us at the Italian border just on evening. We thought we'd walk over and sleep under the olive trees on the Italian side, but as we were going through the check-point the border police took a liking to Margaret's red hair. I hightailed it up the hill, leaving Margaret, who was armed with a hatpin, to sort out the police. She finally managed to escape without using the hatpin, and we crept into a farm on the Italian side and spent the night under its olive trees as planned. The next morning we had to set off early because the dogs started barking at us.

Culture Shock

After their night under the olive trees, the two Margarets scored a variety of lifts. On several occasions they ended up in carts added to the back of motorbikes, squashed in with shopping or other goods and chattels. By time they approached Florence, the two were beginning to feel like seasoned locals. But the driver of the last car to pick them was not fooled into thinking they were other than foreigners and considerately dropped them and their billycan outside an expensive hotel in Florence that was far beyond their budget.

The two Margarets stayed one night, nervously doing their sums about what it was costing them, then set off the next morning in search of cheaper accommodation. As luck would have it, they straight away ran into Australian artist Justin O'Brien, who'd lived at Merioola, and two other well-known art identities in Sydney: interior designer Marion Hall Best and her sister Dora Sweetapple, a designer and silversmith. O'Brien and the women had been staying in the well-known and atmospheric Pensione Morandi in the Piazza SS Annunziata. Although they themselves were moving to another hotel, they recommended the Pensione Morandi to the two Margarets as being very cheap.

Their new accommodation, which had been built in the sixteenth century and had been home for three hundred odd years to the religious order Servi di Maria, was well located. It was just around the corner from the Museo di San Marco, a former monastery the cells of which are painted with frescos by Fra Angelico. Another of the Pensione Morandi's attractions was that meals were included in the tariff, which suited the two Margarets down to the ground. Margaret Olley remembers in particular eating there for the first time baked fennel and lamb, which she found delicious. The Margarets also met up again with Justin O'Brien:

Justin took us along to the church near the railway station, Basilica di Santa Maria Novella. It was a Sunday and Mass was on. Nevertheless, Justin was adamant about wanting to see some frescos behind the main altar. I thought this would have been a sacrilege, but Justin insisted it was all right.

Trust me, I'm a Catholic, he said.

So we sneaked round the back of the altar and looked at the frescos (which apparently Michelangelo might have helped to paint when he was a young artist) while the service was on. No one took the slightest notice.

What struck me on this first trip to Florence was how art, life and religion were interwoven in Italy. Worshipping God wasn't just something you put on your best dress to do on Sundays; it was part of daily life. After they'd been to the markets, people would drop into a church full of wonderful paintings by famous artists and light a candle as if it was the most natural thing in the world.

The two Margarets were ensconced at the Pensione Morandi for about a week and the rest of their visit to Florence was unforgettable for several reasons:

There weren't very many tourists in those days. When we went to the Uffizi it was marvellously empty. We could stand and look at the Botticellis with the greatest of ease. We didn't have to contend with the stifling security and the crowds that block your view now. We also saw one of those football matches where the players wear heraldic costumes. It was fabulous being transported back through the ages like that. But after the week was up, we came down to earth with a crash. It turned out we'd done our sums wrong and we didn't have enough money to pay the Pensione Morandi's bill. I think we'd mistaken the daily rate for the weekly rate. A great fuss erupted with the owners, one of whom might have been Scottish and not the least sympathetic to our situation. The wrangling went on and on. I had to promise to send money the moment we got back to Cassis. Finally they let us go.

Margaret Cilento stayed on with Margaret when they returned to Cassis and then Fred Jessup joined them for the grape picking:

It must have been very late summer or early autumn when Madame S. asked us if we would help with the vendange. We assumed we were going to be paid, but all we were given was our midday meal – pasta, because they had an Italian cook, and a glass of wine. We did a few days, but it was backbreaking work and Madame S. was quite picky: only some grapes were to be used for the wine-making, others had to be saved for the table.

'They had a special ritual in which they took around a big carafe of wine to everyone picking grapes,' Margaret Cilento recalls. 'Of course the locals picked faster and faster the more they drank. Margaret and I just got slower and slower.'

Cilento also remembers that while Margaret had only learnt a bit of French, she never had a problem making herself understood. 'For instance, we'd go to a market in Marseilles. While I would probably be able to ask for things in French, Margaret would just put a pumpkin on her head. Everybody would laugh and know what she wanted to buy. Margaret's sense of fun has always been one of her most attractive traits. In France she was called an *"originale"*. She's an original in the sense that her view of the world and her sense of fun are particularly hers.'

❖

Around this time Margaret had another female visitor at Cassis, who was not nearly so compatible:

Far from a Still Life

A friend of a friend in Australia arrived. I'll call her Edna. She was hoping she could live cheaply by staying with me at Madame S.'s. Edna was not very interested in art. God only knows what she was actually interested in. Anyway, she turned up in Cassis and we were stuck with each other. We were not at all on the same wavelength. 'When you're finished doing that muck, I'll give you a game of cards,' Edna would say. 'Muck' referred to my drawings.

Before long Edna became bored. She was forever wandering down on her own to Cassis in search of amusement. On one occasion she inveigled me into going along with her to a bar on the waterfront known as the Cabin Cubanna. It was run by a very fat woman named Yvette. Edna and I spent the evening drinking cocktails called sidecars. I didn't have any money so someone must have been buying them for us. When we'd finished with the sidecars I was dragged off into the night by some woman. I had no idea who she was, but she turned out to be a lesbian. I eventually made my escape. That's been my one and only lesbian experience. I like men too much. I know people have speculated otherwise, not that I'm ever worried by what people think, but it's not the case. As for Edna, she finally found a man to live with, which took her off my hands.

9

In and Out of Paris

*I used to take a room overlooking the Pont Neuf with
a view straight across to Albert Marquet's studio. Marquet
was always a hero of mine – I love his watercolours
of the Paris bridges and quays. They're so simple, yet
they capture everything.*

*In Paris, Moya gave the parties. At the end of the day
everyone would congregate at her studio for drinks – we all
loved socialising there.*

BY THE BEGINNING OF NOVEMBER 1949, MARGARET HAD WRITTEN Bonny and Tas Drysdale a long letter enthusiastically describing her adventures in Italy and France.[1] In a letter of Drysdale's own to Donald Friend, he wrote that it filled him with a 'hell of a nostalgia' for his own first experience of Europe and that he envied Margaret and Fred Jessup's youthful energy.[2] Margaret's energy does seem to have been boundless. Although Cassis would be her base for the next two years, she was often on the move, as in the days when her family had tripped around Queensland. But now she had friends new and old to keep her company, along with her sketchbooks, and she savoured every new experience:

In France at that time you were only given a limited stay with your carte d'identité. Every few months or so I had to leave Cassis and go up to Paris to have mine renewed. The other option, which I also adopted because I was travelling so much anyway, was to go out of the country and have it freshly stamped as I came back in. On my carte d'identité excursions to Paris, I often stayed at a little hotel on the Ile de la Cité where Notre Dame is. The hotel was above a ground-floor bar that opened onto the triangular Place Dauphine, where the tall spindly trees would lose their leaves in winter and look like ghostly sentinels.

I felt I was really in the centre of Paris there. Later I found out that it actually was the centre of Paris in Roman times, and earlier, the site of the first settlement. My room at the hotel was wonderful to draw from. In between going to galleries, I used to just draw, draw, draw. If I became too cold sitting still inside, I'd make a sortie out and have a cup of coffee with a little brandy chaser in a bar.

When Margaret wasn't painting, Paris was still full of friends to have fun with. She and Fred Jessup, who was now living in rue Dauphine, and sometimes Wolfgang Cardamatis would go to the flea market in nearby rue Mouffetard, which Margaret, with her love of bric-a-brac, always relished:

People would spread out a sheet of newspaper on the pavement from which they'd sell virtually anything: old photographs, bits of jewellery, furniture, just an odd collection of old stuff, but it was fun checking it all out. None of us had any money, but we could usually afford to buy a few mementos. I bought a little snuff box there once.

In and Out of Paris

Margaret and Cardamatis also undertook an exciting and somewhat hazardous journey to Spain, third class on the train:[3]

There were troops on the move everywhere in Spain and the trains were packed full with people, so travelling around was a bit unnerving. But Wolf opened my eyes to paintings like nobody else. I was particularly impressed with the [Francisco de] Zurbaráns he showed me down the south at Málaga near Seville; they were very rich still lifes, like his famous painting of the lemons.

At Seville we must have eaten at the wrong cheap restaurant, because on the train up to Madrid we were both on the brink of terrible diarrhoea, but it was impossible to fight our way to the toilets. The train was completely chock-a-block with soldiers, families with crying children, chickens in cages – not to mention the water-sellers, who barged through the people crammed in the corridors regardless. Wolf and I just had to exercise all of the self-control we could muster.

This trip was the first time I'd ever seen all the Velázquezes in Madrid. God, what a painter he is! Those equestrians of his are monumental; they're like sculptures. We also saw Goya's dark paintings – including the head of a dog baying to the moon, Perro semihundido – black and morbid but so powerful, almost the exact opposite of the delightful works he painted for the court. Many of these paintings are not reproduced in books; they're either too long or too wide. It was quite extraordinary to be suddenly surrounded by them. Then we went to the Hieronymous Bosch room and saw works like The Garden of Earthly Delights. *Wolf was in his element, inventing stories about them, full of amazing little details. He was the most delightful travelling companion.*

Back in Paris, in January 1950 David Strachan rented an apartment at 4 rue de Chatillon in Montparnasse, which would also serve as his studio for the next five years. Often when Margaret visited Paris, Strachan would join her and Moya Dyring on painting expeditions:

We'd go outside Paris in Moya's old Citroen car, which she called 'a studio', and settle up by the roadside. They'd paint and I'd mainly draw. David did his best paintings during this time away. We all had folding easels and I did occasionally make use of a paintbox like the others. Moya and I also used to go for picnics on a plot of land a friend of hers had near Monet's house and garden, so we'd go and look at those while we were there. In those days, you had to cross the railway line to get to the lily pond. At one stage, too, I attended some life classes at the Académie de la Grande Chaumière, but I didn't find the classes nearly as rewarding as the ones at East Sydney Tech had been. In Paris, I was over-stimulated and therefore less able to focus intensely on studying. It's better to study when you're living in a boring environment. There were a lot of distractions in Paris.

Donald Friend, who was wintering in the warmth of Ischia, an island off Naples, was able to catch up with Margaret's 'mad doings at Cassis' in February of 1950, when Margaret Cilento arrived to stay with fellow Australian painter Jeffrey Smart.[4] The next bulletin about Margaret was delivered to Friend by Wolfgang Cardamatis, who visited him in March. Friend had now moved on to Florence and, over flagons of wine, Cardamatis had him laughing until he almost cried with tales of Cassis.[5]

Cardamatis had come to Cassis alone, as Margaret remembers, and then her friend from Brisbane, Annie Ross, had arrived:

On one occasion we set off on a trip to Arles. We spent quite a bit of time dallying in Marseilles; we must have been getting quite drunk because we kept having our photographs taken behind those funny boards that you put your head through and then you're turned into a sailor or a fat lady. The results were hilarious, or so we thought. After this we piled onto the bus for Arles.

I don't remember what happened but I suddenly became very offended with Annie and Wolf and when we arrived in Arles I decided to leave them. I stalked off in high dudgeon to make my way from Arles all the way back to Cassis. I got a lift to Marseilles and then walked from Marseilles to Cassis. I now know what it's like to be a long-distance walker – you just get into a rhythm of walking and become like a zombie. However I had to go to bed for two days afterwards to recover. Wolf and Annie eventually turned up back at Cassis, cheery as ever, with a present for me of a lace-maker's lamp from Arles, which I still have.

In April 1950, Friend finally received a note from Margaret herself, whom he confessed in his diary he was 'longing' to see.[6] The note announced that she and Annie Ross were going to Venice and would drop in to see him in Florence on the way back.

Friend's life, or at least his love life, was presently a mess. In Ischia, as well as being at the tail-end of a romance with Omar Ali, a Pakistani prince, he had fallen in love with – or become besotted by, to put it more accurately – a handsome eighteen-year-old local, Attilio Guarracino, to whom he was introduced by Jeffrey Smart. Friend was so infatuated with Attilio he proposed that once he had the proper documents for travelling, Attilio should return with him to Australia and Hill End.

When Margaret and Ross arrived in Florence, Friend was very much preoccupied with his emotional entanglement with Attilio and it was his artist friend, Aberdeen Goodwin, in whose studio the two women stayed, who made the greatest impression on Margaret:

Aberdeen was the only black person I can remember seeing in

Florence at that time. Annie and I used to peek into his room every time we passed by. We were fascinated by the richly coloured sheets on his bed. The coloured body on the coloured sheets must be tantalisingly exotic and erotic to whomever he invited in, we thought. Being young and insatiably curious, sneaking a quick look wasn't enough for us. One day we went right into his bedroom, and then we started thumbing through the magazines he had lying about. They turned out to be magazines full of ads for how to de-crinkle your hair and bleach your skin. It seemed so sad.

Friend had planned that he and Attilio would go from Florence to London, where Friend would sort out the necessary formalities for Attilio to enter Australia. However in Florence there were repeated 'calms and storms' while they stayed at Goodwin's studio until Attilio finally made it clear to Friend that he loved him only as a father.[7] Nevertheless Attilio still wished to join Friend in London, as soon as he was able, and come to Australia with him.

Accordingly, Friend went off to London at the beginning of May and Attilio eventually followed him there at the end of June. Friend's despair over his late arrival lifted almost immediately when the Redfern Gallery Summer Exhibition opened with three of his drawings on show. Although the drawings were inconspicuously hung, he was pleased to find one in a corner next to a Picasso.

A few days later he and Attilio both attended a cocktail party that Friend described as 'a scramble of well-dressed nymphomaniacs and gigolos and nephews of peers, and Australians'.[8] With them was Mitty Lee-Brown, who was over from Paris for a short visit. As well as providing news of David Strachan and other friends, Lee-Brown delivered a rather alarming, perhaps alarmist, update on Margaret. Margaret's amusing 'mad doings' of Friend's earlier diary entries changes dramatically to 'gone off the rails very much'.[9] Friend does not provide any details but drinking is mentioned.

Like the sound of a cork being pulled from a bottle briefly heard above jollities, the few sentences are the first indication of Margaret's drinking problem. No one appears to have taken it very seriously. It was France, they were artists and everyone drank like fishes, anyway.[10]

Margaret's own point of view now is that she was merely following the lead of her friends. 'We would all go out together, perhaps to a bar, and then end up having soup at Les Halles,' she says. 'I was never an instigator in any of this, it all seemed quite normal.' In her defence, Margaret was experiencing the stress of a show about to open, or just opening, at the Moreton Galleries back in Brisbane. Perhaps she was downing a few extra glasses of wine or going out on the town in nervous anticipation of the event.

Her Brisbane exhibition of twenty works opened on 4 July 1950. There were Paris scenes, such as the Pont Neuf and the Place Dauphine, probably done while she was staying at her favourite hotel on the Ile de la Cité; and various landscapes of Cassis, Nice and Cannes. Also included was a painting titled *The Pink Church, Choiselle*, the frequently reproduced work of that name using the spelling 'Cloiselle'. (There are no geographic references to Cloiselle today; on the other hand, Choiselle is about a thirty-minute drive from the centre of Paris and still looks prettily rural, so it seems safe to assume that the original catalogue spelling was correct and that *The Pink Church* was possibly painted on an excursion with Moya Dyring and David Strachan.)

The *Courier Mail*'s reviewer, poet Paul Grano, wrote that the show had three striking features: 'The first is the impressive advance [Olley] has made in technique since leaving Australia to study abroad. The second how sure, freer and fresher is her work in pen and wash than it is in oils. The third is her sensitivity to immediate influences. Practically all indications of the impact of certain Australian artists apparent in her earlier work are gone. She has been studying in France and French influences now dominate her brush.'[11] Such sensitivity to outside forces could be a great advantage, Grano continued, as long as the artist was strong enough to use them to express their own vision. He then added that he thought this would probably prove to be the case with Margaret. Although he was not impressed by most of the oils, Grano concluded his review by urging readers not to miss the show.

Margaret was not alone in kicking up her heels in Paris; the whole city was soon partying with wild abandon. July the fourteenth 1950 was celebrated with street parades and a giant statue of Adam and Eve, which had red wine spurting out of a serpent's head that looked like an enormous penis, according to Moya Dyring.[12] Dyring and friends, Margaret quite likely among them, danced around the serpent, filling and refilling their glasses. The revelry continued until dawn for three days, after which Dyring had to go to bed for four days. One can see what Jessup meant by 'drinking like fishes'.

By now Dyring, who herself had had a successful one-person show in London at the end of 1949, had transformed the gutted shell of her apartment into an open studio space with large windows overlooking the Seine. In one corner of 'Chez Moya' there was a built-in circular bar, designed to look like the counter of a Paris café. The bar had cupboards, a fridge and a stove underneath; on shelves behind were Dyring's Breton Quimper dinner set. The bar also ensured Dyring, who was an excellent cook – curries and pasta being her specialties – was not banished to a kitchenette while entertaining. Friends were encouraged to help out with the cooking, sometimes even barbecuing meat on her open fireplace, then everyone ate perched on high stools at the counter.[13]

Like Strachan and Jessup, Margaret was a regular attendee if she was in Paris. She remembers some of Dyring's celebrated entertaining with particular affection:

Moya would save the leftover red wine and use it to concoct her famous 'Algerian Aperitif' – mulled leftovers with cloves. She used to call it 'a period' instead of 'aperitif' as a joke. She'd do the same with 'hors d'oeuvres', which she turned into 'whore's ovaries'. It was her private little joke.

Besides painting and studio merriment, there was also a bond of another sort between Margaret and Dyring:

Moya and I were both close friends with Theo Schlicht. I'd first met Theo back in Sydney after the war. On his way home to Melbourne after having been stationed in Japan with the air force, Theo came to one of those parties of Sam's where everyone stayed the night on the floor. He and I had a bit of a fling then – nothing serious. By the time I arrived in Paris Theo was living and working as a psychiatrist in London. He was married, but his wife and young family were still in Australia.

He used to come over to France and ride around on a motorbike making little 'passion stops' everywhere. He'd call in on me at Cassis; then he'd get on his bike and visit Moya, who would be so excited she'd drive out to the Bois de Boulogne to meet him and they'd have a little roll in the park. Moya was absolutely dotty about Theo, so I never said anything to her about my time with him. I don't know exactly when Moya and Theo became involved, she may have known him in Melbourne.[14] *But their romantic involvement was only ever in passing. Theo wasn't a part of the regular scene in Paris.*

By the end of July 1950, Margaret had arrived in London. She and Friend immediately went on a pub crawl – several pub crawls, in fact.[15] On the second occasion, by Friend's account,

Margaret became 'maddeningly wildly drunk' and 'kept dancing in the middle of the street, singing bawdy songs and pretending to jump in front of cars'.[16] This last bit of behaviour attracted the attention of a policeman, who warned Friend to keep his friend (Margaret) off the streets.

Attilio Guarracino has a flattering memory of this occasion: 'I thought Margaret was the most beautiful woman. Perhaps I'm exaggerating if I say "the most beautiful woman I had ever met", because my mother was also extremely beautiful, but Margaret was very attractive.'[17] The night was, in fact, Margaret's introduction to Attilio, with whom she's stayed friends ever since:

To begin with, Attilio was Jeffrey Smart's friend. Then the wicked Donald came along and next thing Attilio was Donald's friend. I didn't know Jeffrey at that stage and I never went to Ischia, but over the years I kept hearing the three sides of the story. What was the real truth, I don't know. Islands seem to me to be full of desperate people who are trapped with all their intrigues. They're not good places to be, which is ironic when you think about it, because Australia is really only a large island. Donald, I suppose, was in love with Attilio initially. But Attilio wasn't at all interested in that sort of relationship. So then Attilio became like a son to him.

I can only remember one pub crawl. Annie Ross was there, too. It was a terrible night: we went from one pub to another. Donald was trying to work out which was the most lethal – beer on cider, or cider on beer. We ended up sitting in the gutter, with Annie and me – probably Annie more than me, because she was always more sophisticated – calling for brandies. I think those pub crawls in London turned me right off beer. After I left England I didn't really drink it again.

It may well have also been during this visit to London that Margaret became familiar with the famous 'House of the Sons of

God'. Harry Tatlock Miller and Loudon Sainthill had finally made it to London at the end of the English summer of 1949.[18] They lived briefly with their friends from Merioola, Jocelyn Rickards and Alec Murray, at Cranley Gardens. Then the four of them moved to nearby eccentric rented accommodation named the 'House of the Sons of God' at 666 Clareville Grove, near Gloucester Road. Here, Tatlock Miller and Sainthill's room was soon filled with a collection of broken columns, stuffed birds in Victorian glass cases and gilded female figurines, which, no doubt, Margaret encountered, along with the rest of the house's peculiarities.

The name of the house was written on a brass plaque outside the front gate. Its owner was an Englishwoman who wore trailing chiffon and whose piled-up hair was topped with broad-brimmed or feathered hats to rival Margaret's own millinery creations. The house had been war-damaged, but it was in the process of reconstruction when the Merioola contingent moved in, which meant a cheap rent of five pounds a week. The house itself was fitted out with a conglomeration of oddities, including concealed light switches, which, if accidentally touched, projected onto the ceiling a larger than life-sized silver paper collage portrait of the owner's son, who had been killed in the war.[19]

It was Loudon Sainthill's stuttering that inadvertently helped to secure the Merioola group rooms at Clareville Grove. When he and Tatlock Miller first answered the 'to let' sign on the house, they were so taken aback by their prospective landlady's appearance that Sainthill's stuttering increased. He became stuck on the 'Saint' part of his name and could only get out, 'I'm Saint…'

'A saint, a real saint,' the landlady responded. 'It is heaven that sent you to this house, it's yours.'[20]

By the middle of August, Margaret was still in London, as were Friend and Attilio. Friend was now trying to organise passages for himself and Attilio on a ship to Australia. From his diary entries of early August, it would seem that he was enormously stressed at the time and beset with doubts as to what was best for Attilio and himself.

He was therefore extremely grateful when Margaret whisked him away in the middle of August for a weekend at a farm in Hampshire belonging to Sydney Cooper. Margaret had been introduced by Clarice Zander to the then extremely wealthy, gay Cooper, who was a gentleman of leisure, and the two became friends. Cooper was descended from Sir Daniel Cooper, the first Speaker of the Legislative Assembly in New South Wales. (Sir Daniel's son William bought and then demolished 'Henrietta Villa', the grand and gracious house built by Captain John Piper at his Point Piper estate in the 1800s. After building an even more splendid residence, 'Woollahra House', William Cooper promptly departed Point Piper to live in England.) During their weekend at Cooper's farm, Margaret and Friend went for restorative 'long sunny walks in the woods gathering wildflowers'.[21] Once again, being with Margaret revived Friend's creativity and he did five 'rustic' drawings, which pleased him as much as calming him down.

At the end of August, Margaret took part in a final London pub crawl with Friend and a group that included Wolf Cardamatis (also back in London by now), Peter Kaiser and Kaiser's girlfriend Pat Jones. After this Margaret returned to France and a little later Friend and Attilio flew off to Australia.

Back in Cassis, Margaret soon had her hands full with visitors. Moya Dyring, David Strachan and his sister Veronica 'Ronnie' Rowan (who had been staying with Dyring in Paris since late August) were next to arrive. Margaret decided to lay down the law vis-a-vis entertaining:

Cassis was very well situated. People were constantly dropping in on their way somewhere or coming back from somewhere. Either they stayed with me, or, if there were too many, those who weren't broke booked into a hotel in Cassis. When one particular crowd descended, I had the brainwave of making a rule that everybody had to be responsible for a meal. They had to buy and cook the food for that meal. Those who didn't have any money rustled up a simple dish with tomatoes, onions or garlic, and perhaps a few herbs. Those who had money could buy a bit of steak. Not only did we eat well, everyone learnt to be very inventive with their cooking.

Rowan would later recall being struck by how much faster Margaret and Dyring painted than Strachan, who liked to consider his subject more. Margaret, it seems, worked especially quickly. According to Rowan, she completed three paintings to Strachan's one.[22] However, Margaret was probably working in pen and wash or watercolour, which is not a medium you can deliberate or dawdle over.

Towards the end of 1950, Margaret sent ten watercolours back to a Christmas exhibition of paintings in Brisbane. This was the first show in the new Marodian Gallery, which was set up by Captain Brian Johnstone, then aide-de-camp to the governor of Queensland, Sir John Lavarack, and Hugh Hale, the furniture specialist. Brian Johnstone was determined to bring contemporary artists from both Sydney and Melbourne to Brisbane. The objective of the gallery, as expressed by Johnstone at the opening and dutifully reported in the press, 'was to put an original painting in every home in Queensland'. Over the next couple of decades, Brian Johnstone would, indeed, be responsible for a great many of the paintings hanging on Brisbane walls – many of them Olleys.

The opening of the Marodian was quite an event. Cocktails were served, speeches made and Grace Olley attended in a grey and tangerine frock in lieu of Margaret. Among Margaret's ten works on show were drawings of Buckingham Palace, Trafalgar Square and Notting Hill Gate, as well as one of Bourton-on-the-Water in the Cotswolds, and various French scenes.

'Margaret Olley Steals the Show' was the headline of the review in the *Courier Mail* by Elizabeth Young.[23] 'Her ten watercolour drawings have dash and vigour, and though contemporary French influences are obvious in many of them, they are the work of a most promising young painter,' Young went on to say in the review itself. '*Bourton on the Water*, No. 18, and *Tourettes-Sur-Louys* [although this is how the work was titled in the original catalogue it was probably meant to be Tourettes-sur-Loup, a town close to Nice], No. 16, though reminiscent of Cézanne, are charming, competent, and direct. Similarly the influence of Dufy is discernible in the cleanly drawn *Dieppe*, No. 20,' she concluded.

In the *Brisbane Telegraph* the following day, Melville Haysom was more picky. He felt that while Margaret's work dominated the show numerically, it was not without flaws. To him *Dieppe* was 'interesting', but the reason for its sloping waterline was not apparent. He noted that *Nottinghill Gate* (spelling as per catalogue) would have been a better work if the phantom figure to the left of centre had been left out, and that in *Trafalgar Square* there was something amiss with the drawing of the base of Nelson's Column.

Looking back, Margaret was lucky to have received a review as good as the one in the *Courier Mail*, not because her watercolour drawings weren't 'charming, competent, and direct', but because they were, effectively, done on the run; they were travel notes rather than major works. For her own development, on the other hand, it is arguable that working on these quicker drawings was freeing up her hand for when she would return to more serious painting.

◆

In November 1950, Colonel Teed of the Château de Fontcreuse was diagnosed with cancer in both lungs.[24] An operation was out of the question and Teed was given four months to live. Instead, he lasted for ten.[25] In a letter written to Vanessa Bell in February 1951, Teed's handwriting had altered considerably from the robust hand of his earlier letters, but the tone was still perky. The Colonel remained cheerful throughout most of his illness.[26] He refused to admit he was going to die and continued driving the car and lunching out in his usual manner. Nevertheless, Jean Campbell apparently found caring for him taxing. So, by early in 1951, Margaret had found herself a new role in Cassis:

Jean Campbell turned up at Madame S.'s one day and asked if any of my friends would be interested in living in at the Château de Fontcreuse because the Colonel was ill.

What about me? I asked.

I was decidedly short of money by then and I was over at the château like a shot. As I understood it, the Colonel had been about to set off to America on wine business when he had a check-up and discovered he had cancer. Although I knew he was sick, it wasn't too depressing being there, to begin with, at least. The frogs were extremely loud, but I had a room to myself and the change of location provided me with new subjects to draw. I sent out another show from the château, in fact.[27]

In March 1951, Margaret was the first artist to have a solo exhibition at the Marodian Gallery in Brisbane. The show of twenty-eight paintings – watercolours, a few oils and two pastels – nearly didn't make it back to Australia in time because of an airline strike in France. However, the gallery had framers standing by to begin work the moment the paintings arrived in Brisbane, and the show opened on 6 March.

It was a bit of a triumph the works arrived at all. Somebody at an art gallery in Marseilles told me the best way to send art works out of the country was just to roll them up, put them in cylinders and send them back as family photos. I remember posting the cylinder – or cylinders – off and thinking, God, there goes the whole show, will it ever get there?

Not all the works were inspired by the château. A number of Paris paintings were included in the exhibition, as well. 'In some of the sketches there is a new and vivid use of colour, in some a leaning to lavender – this is evident also in some of the oils, which needs to be held in check,' Elizabeth Young wrote in the *Courier Mail*.[28] Interestingly, not so many years on Brian Johnstone would blame Margaret's love of lavender-like hues for landing her in trouble with the Brisbane art-buying public. But what's more significant about Young's remarks is that they are the first mention of Margaret's pursuit of colour that would so preoccupy her painting when she eventually returned to Australia.

Young continued her review by praising Margaret's watercolours: 'The best of the watercolours – among these we would place numbers 8 [*Chateau Fontcreuse, Cassis*], 10 [*Palais de Justice – Place Dauphine, Paris*], 11 [*Pont Neuf, Paris*], 18 [*L'Arc de Triomphe du Carrousel*] and 20 [*Pont des Arts, Paris*] show a firmer grasp of essentials and restrained and subtle colour.' The oils, Young thought, had a dryness in the painting and a lack of feeling for the actual medium, as well as a paucity of the vitality that was one of the most charming qualities of the watercolours. But Young's final summation was flattering: 'Altogether this is a live and interesting exhibition by a young artist who is already producing work that is a definite contribution to the art of Queensland.'

This same year Margaret had a small number of works in group shows back home and participated in the 'Exhibition of Australian Art from the Queensland National Art Gallery Jubilee Art Train', which toured the state for several months to give Queenslanders living outside Brisbane the chance to experience the gallery's collection. Margaret's pen and wash *Jardin du Luxembourg* was hung in Car 2, alongside works by such famous names as Tom Roberts and Rupert Bunny, and the indigenous artist Albert Namatjira, whose watercolours had become popular in the 1930s.

In addition to these shows, in 1951 Margaret also had an exhibition of seventeen watercolour drawings – again with one of the Château de Fontcreuse – at the Macquarie Galleries in Sydney. This was a joint exhibition with lithographs by English artists, including, by a strange coincidence, Vanessa Bell and Duncan Grant, who were so fond of Cassis. Paul Haefliger, writing in the *Sydney Morning Herald*, was impressed with Margaret's efforts.[29] He felt that the typically Australian 'happy-go-lucky attitude' of her street scenes had been 'lent piquancy by a certain French élan'. 'This has added tremendously to her development as an artist, and while she has not yet gained a particularly profound reason to paint, one sees a charming flowering of her imaginative faculties,' Haefliger concluded his review.

It would appear that living in France was suiting Margaret down to the ground. But there were a few minor hiccups in her new routine at the Château de Fontcreuse:

The worst aspect of living with the Colonel was his appallingly racist attitude, which stemmed from his time in India with the army. The way he talked about people on the streets in India was awful. I remember Cedric Flower and his wife Pat turned up to visit me and were totally taken aback by the way he carried on.

I had to go into Marseilles to do the shopping which was a lovely break. My shopping duties included buying little birds, like quail, on skewers, which the Colonel liked eating, and lung for the château's household of cats. The lung had to be boiled and then chopped up with scissors, which was disgusting! Luckily I didn't have to cook the little birds I bought – a maid came in and prepared the main meal in the middle of the day if the Colonel wasn't going out and did the cleaning. I was responsible for the evening supper, which was usually just a boiled egg or something equally light. Apart from that I had all the time in the day to more or less do what I liked.

Virginia Woolf once said of Cassis when she was staying at the Château de Fontcreuse that characters of the strangest sort abounded there and that the eccentricities of the Bloomsbury group seemed to flower in the south of France.[30] Small wonder, then, that even Margaret's leisure time at the château provided glimpses of these:

Jean had lots of stories about Vanessa Bell and Duncan Grant, whom she'd known quite well – one of the aspects of the château that appealed to me was the connection to when Cassis was in its heyday with the Bloomsbury artists. At night after supper, when I was diligently working on one last drawing in the kitchen, where the light was very good, most likely perhaps with a glass of rosé beside me, Jean would shuffle down from upstairs and put her head around the corner to see if I'd gone to bed. I never understood what she wanted. But afterwards I decided that perhaps it was to do with a place in the pantry where there were preserved peaches and cherries in alcohol!

Margaret must have stayed at the château for most of Colonel Teed's last ten months.[31] She remained a short time after he died but had left before the end of 1951. At the start of 1952 Jean Campbell, in a letter to Vanessa Bell, writes of being alone at Fontcreuse, of having no money because of death duties, and of converting the first floor of the château to accommodate paying tenants.[32] She also mentions the possibility of returning to her family in New Zealand. However, it would seem Campbell's plans for the château came to naught, because by 1953 a new owner had taken over.

In and Out of Paris

For Margaret, the act of extricating herself from the château and Jean Campbell was not entirely easy, as she remembers:

As I stayed on with Jean, I started to become a bit fey, like her. Fortunately, then Moya and David, who had been down painting near Toulon, called in to see me. They sized up the situation straight away.

We're leaving for Paris tomorrow, Oll, they announced. I think they must have made a pact between themselves to rescue me. You're coming with us, they continued together. You're not staying here any longer.

So Moya and David swept me off with them. Thank heavens, otherwise who knows how long I would have stayed there, drifting and drinking. I felt I was depended on, but anybody could have done the work. It was as if I had become marooned on an island but couldn't see it. I went back once more to Cassis, to pay Madame S. some rent I owed her and to collect what possessions I'd left behind there. But I've never forgotten how Moya and David helped me out of the château.

The complex chronology of Margaret's life at this point is for a biographer like looking into a kaleidoscope. Memories and anecdotes come sharply into focus, then are replaced by more stories and conflicting tidbits of information. But it's fairly clear that it was now that Margaret became involved with Sir Francis Rose. Although Rose may have visited her earlier at Cassis, the major part of their relationship, including their travelling together, took place after she had left the château, in late 1951 and early 1952:

I met Francis through Moya. I was staying with Moya at her apartment on Ile St Louis and she introduced me to her neighbour down along Quai d'Anjou. The neighbour turned out to be Sir Francis Rose. Francis was charming, quite a bit older than me, and Picasso and Dalí were among the artists he'd known. I must say I adored him. He was like an incarnation from another century. He took snuff – just like tobacco only it makes you sneeze – all the time. The snuff was specially made for him in England and he made a real ceremony of sniffng it from the hollow between his thumb and forefinger.

Francis had had a lot of money, but by that stage it was all gone. Much earlier he had been the boyfriend of Christopher Wood, who was such a lovely painter. Francis told me that the figure in a painting of Wood's, of a male nude in a room in Brittany, was him.[33] *He was also very friendly with Gertrude Stein, who'd admired his painting when he first came to Paris. Unfortunately, he didn't have the staying power as far as being an artist went. He'd also lived in China, where he'd done a lot of his later work. All this made him quite fascinating to me.*

Sir Francis Rose, a baronet, was born into a family of landed Scottish gentry in 1909. A portion of his teenage years – from sixteen onwards – was spent in Villefranche, on the Riviera between Nice and Monte Carlo. Here he and his mother lived at the rackety, bohemian Welcome Hôtel. It was at the Welcome Hôtel that Rose first encountered the scintillating Jean Cocteau, who was also a resident of the hotel at the time and would have been about to write his play *Orphée*. Cocteau's balcony room, in which Rose spent many hours, was pungent with the smell of opium and filled with the products of Cocteau's fertile imagination. Little skeleton figures of twisted pipe-cleaners were suspended from a naked electric light bulb and strewn about were innumerable objects made of matchboxes, lumps of sugar, sealing-wax and torn pieces of corrugated cardboard, which apparently represented scenes from Greek tragedies.[34]

The Welcome was a haven for many eccentric and artistic figures. As well as Cocteau, among those whom Rose claimed to have met there were Picasso; Scott Fitzgerald; Faulkner; Stravinsky; Kiki of Montparnasse, the famous and enchanting model (Eton crop, scanty frock and a long cigarette holder) who lived with the photographer Man Ray; an unknown Christian Dior; a short-skirted Coco Chanel; and Christopher 'Kit' Wood (although they did not become intimate then).

Cocteau initially insisted the teenage Rose should not dabble with opium. But, by his own account, Rose was soon smoking the relaxing narcotic. He indulged regularly from 1928 until 1939, and his memoirs contain a loving and detailed account of the paraphernalia involved in smoking it. In those early years at Villefranche, Rose was also close to Isadora Duncan. The once famous dancer still exuded a bewitching presence, although by then she was fat with falling flesh and untidy magenta hair.[35] Rose became a visitor to her studio in Nice and painted several portraits of her.

Before he turned twenty-one, Rose had moved from Villefranche to a studio in Paris. In Paris he re-met 'Kit' Wood and the two later travelled together in Brittany. But then as Rose was planning his lavish twenty-first birthday party, he received the news that Wood had died – possibly suicided – under a train at Salisbury Station. Though it was 'marred' by Wood's death, Rose nevertheless went ahead with his party, which was held at the villa where his mother was then living.[36] In one room, with the help of the famous Jansen of Paris furniture makers, an American bar made of mirrors was installed, with tall stools covered in lemon-yellow leather to match the carpet on which a leopard skin had been placed. There were also easy chairs covered in silk leopard-skin-patterned velvet and yellow folding beach mattresses. Outside, carpets and cushions were laid out under trees and drinks were served by a family of midgets.[37]

Rose's introduction in Paris to Gertrude Stein and Alice B. Toklas came about some time later. Stein once wrote of Rose (also referring to the artist Francis Picabia to whom Rose had introduced her): 'anybody called Francis is elegant, unbalanced and intelligent'.[38] It's also often said that Rose inspired Stein's famous 'A rose is a rose is a rose' remark, though this is probably a literary myth.

At the time Margaret met him, Rose was married to his second wife, Lady Frederica Rose, who wrote travel books under the name Dorothy Carrington and lived in Corsica. Although he and Frederica did not divorce until 1966, Rose was effectively living a bachelor's life in Paris in 1951:

Francis's apartment on Ile St Louis looked out on a courtyard rather than over the Seine, but it was very grand and he gave wonderful parties. I'd go off to them dressed in whatever I could throw together and that was where I met Alice B. Toklas. All I can remember of Toklas is that she wore the most extraordinary clothes and was always the centre of attention with the men. She was small and bird-like, quite old, or so I thought then, and had plumes in her hair. On her feet she wore open, workmanlike leather sandals that were designed by Raymond Duncan, the brother of Isadora.

After that first party, Alice B. Toklas asked me to afternoon tea. I can't really remember much of her, but I was overwhelmed by the art that was hanging in the apartment. In the room I saw there seemed to be wall-to-wall Braques and Picassos of the Cubist period.

Francis was full of stories about people he'd known. Beside tales of his artist friends like Cocteau, Picasso and Matisse, he had all sorts of gossip about other identities. He used to tell a story of how the Duke of Windsor visited him in his flat. The Duke, who was dead drunk, had to wait for Francis in a room in which there was a bottle of Pernod. When Francis arrived back he noticed the water level in a vase of flowers had dropped. The Duke had been drinking the flower water with his Pernod.

As to the exact nature of her relationship with Rose, Margaret would prefer 'to do a little tease':

Let's just say that he came down to stay with me in Cassis and I stayed with him in Paris. We'll let people infer what they want from that. But there definitely was an unusual bond between us. After I'd been in his apartment for a while, he suggested I take over a maid's flat he had, which was halfway between his place and Moya's. To be honest, it's so long ago that exactly when and where I moved is a bit hard to remember.

Some time in October 1951, Margaret and Moya Dyring set off in Dyring's old Citroen on a six-week trip to Italy:[39]

On the way we collected Francis, who had been staying with some wealthy friends around Nice. We had decided to camp out, sleeping on li-los, blow-up rubber mattresses. But it was quite different from camping in Australia, where you could pick up wood anywhere to make a camp fire and boil a billy of water. The French were very protective of their firewood. And it seemed that during the war they had walked up into the hills and scoured them for every burnable scrap, pine cones included. There was absolutely nothing lying about that you could light a fire with. We had to make do with two little methylated-spirit burners, which the French called 'brûleur'. We managed to cook on them, but it was time-consuming. We'd call in at every market we saw and buy up fresh food supplies, so in the end we ate very well. In Italy, that meant pasta, perhaps with a few truffles – ambrosia.

But it wasn't all heavenly. At one place in Italy where they camped, stones were thrown at them – apparently the locals had thought they were gypsies because they were sleeping out.[40] In Venice, camping was abandoned:

When we arrived in Venice it was raining. We wanted to stay as long as we could but none of us had any money for a hotel. So we persuaded a little pensione on the mainland to hire us a shed where they kept their potatoes, and we put our li-los down there. Francis insisted on leaving his shaving gear and belongings, including a pair of yellow diamond cufflinks Gertrude Stein had given him, out in Moya's car. Then the cufflinks went missing. I don't know whether he sold them or if they were stolen by a boy he was interested in (despite being married, he was definitely inclined that way). I think he was probably rolled by a dalliance.

We used to walk into Venice and spend the day wandering around drawing. I had the most wonderful pen with a bristle nib which you can't get anymore. The whole time it was just spitting with rain, which was very good for my pen and wash. It's much easier to draw and do a wash of watercolour on a day with a slight misting rain. The rain keeps the paper moist and allows the pen to be more fluid. On a hot dry day everything dries too quickly. Donald loved working this way. He'd actually take a sheet of paper into the bathroom – go into the shower with it because it was easier to manipulate the colour about there – and push the paper around until he'd got a good background. Then he'd pour the water off and superimpose his drawing. Watercolours are always controlled accidents. Donald didn't like the medium of oils. It was too slow for him. He loved the fluid line, the accident of the watercolour.

Francis Rose, as well as having introduced Margaret to Toklas, also took her to meet the artist Marc Chagall:

We'd been staying with an artist friend of Moya's in Vence and had been to see the chapel Matisse had been decorating there. Afterwards in a bar we ran into Sam Atyeo, who lived not far away. Chagall was home when we called in on him. His English was quite good and he talked for most of our visit about how he was all set to do a synagogue the way Matisse had done his chapel.

Rose also showed Margaret a new artistic medium, which turned out to be far more relevant to her career than his other famous contacts:

It was Francis who introduced me to monotypes. A monotype is where you take just one print. You can do it from anything, but I used a piece of glass. I'd put some oil paint on the glass and position a clean sheet of paper in between that and a drawing I'd already done – say, of Venice. I'd go over the drawing, which was face up, to get the impression. Then I'd pull the middle sheet of paper off and end up with a print. Fred Jessup often incorporated this technique in his paintings. He'd do a monotype and use that as the point of departure for the rest of the work. I was very taken with the medium and my own next few shows, which included works of Venice, were also made up of monotypes.

―◆―

Halfway through 1951, David Strachan had installed a printing press in his apartment at rue de Chatillon and set up a printing business, Stramur-Presse, with the Dutchman Jacques Murray. As well as printing coloured lithographs for the Redfern Gallery, they were busy with the publication of a book of poems called *Accent and Hazard* by Alister Kershaw, a Melbourne avant-garde poet of the 1930s and '40s who had moved to Paris in 1947. The book was designed by Murray and illustrated with twenty-two etchings by Strachan. The etchings are exquisite and all highly poetic, not the least of which is a compelling image of a naked woman's body floating lightly in space which Strachan titled *The Muse*.

After such an intensely creative period, by late spring of 1952 Strachan must have been more than ready for some relaxation, which, as is usually the case with an artist, meant a new painting expedition:

I had been staying with David in Paris. In May he and I went to Portugal to meet Francis, who was currently the house guest of yet more rich friends in Lisbon. We made our way through France and Spain by train and bus. The poverty we saw coming into Spain from France was shocking enough, but Portugal was even poorer. Alongside that were the extravagant lifestyles of the rich, of which Francis relayed accounts. I found it hard to come to terms with the gap between the two.

In Lisbon, much to my surprise, I bumped into Rex Wood, the brother of an artist called Noel Wood, who had settled on Bedarra Island out from South Mission Beach in the 1930s, when my family went back to Tully. Rex had moved to Lisbon and was teaching painting to the un-poverty-stricken upper circles. He showed us around the night life of Lisbon, which meant listening in bars to Fado singers – those strange, emotional, Moorish-sounding Portuguese folk musicians – long into the night. We also made expeditions out to the Estoril coast where there was a palace in a town called Oeiras that had wonderful tiles. It was a very productive period for me and I did lots of drawings everywhere we went.

Margaret, Strachan and Rose then decided to continue their journeying north along the coast from Lisbon. When they visited the local tourist bureau there was only the vaguest information available about transport and destinations. Eventually the trio boarded a bus and after several long hours were deposited in the strange little village of Nazare, which Margaret immediately recognised from photos she'd seen in *National Geographic* magazines at school at Somerville House:

We fell in love with Nazare. We had a night in a hotel, then the next day went round the village to see if we could find a flat to rent. The villagers were so poor they would have turfed out their old granny if it meant they could make some money by letting her room to us. The *only problem was, they thought we had more money than we did. But in the end we found a flat we could afford and stayed there for what seemed like ages but was probably only a couple of weeks. It was another world.*

Life there revolved around the wide beach. Even the bullocks were kept on the beach and used to haul the fishing boats out of the water. The men cleaned the sardines they'd caught on the beach and women sat around mending the fishing nets. None of them could swim but their whole livelihood – such as it was – depended on the sea. They were also very superstitious; they didn't like foreigners watching them when they were launching the boats.

At the village itself there were no greengrocers. You'd go along to the markets and all they had to offer were what looked like the outside leaves of cabbages. At the butcher's – when it was open – you bought whatever piece of the carcass they were cutting at that moment. And not very much of that, either. It was as if all food was severely rationed.

Margaret's fascination with Nazare was evident in a letter she wrote to her mother. She describes in detail how the men wore 'funny little black caps' with their tartan shirts and trousers; and pictures the women's 'coloured blouses' they wore with their tartan skirts, under which there were 'no less than 16 petticoats'. In Nazare, she concludes to her mother, 'Everything is carried on the head and no one wears shoes.'[41]

※

In June 1952 Margaret had a solo show of monotypes in Brisbane at a new gallery Brian Johnstone had opened in February 1952 in the basement of the Brisbane Arcade. Johnstone's first gallery, the Marodian, had not only shown such artists as David Strachan, Elaine Haxton, Moya Dyring and Donald Friend, as well as Margaret herself, but had also scored a real coup with an exhibition of paintings by Melbourne's Arthur Boyd. This was a decidedly radical event for 1950s Brisbane, but the exhibition had also caused the breakdown of the partnership between Johnstone and the Marodian's co-owner, Hugh Hale, who thought Boyd's work was 'rubbish'.[42]

What had initially inspired Johnstone, an army man, to go into the art business and a partnership with Hale is not known, but, once there, he threw himself into selling pictures with verve. Johnstone's wife, Marjorie Mant, who had studied acting in London before the war, gave up her career as an actress in Brisbane to devote herself to the galleries, bringing a touch of theatrical style to openings and events. The site of their new venture, the Brisbane Arcade, was a three-storeyed 1920s baroque building and popular haunt of Brisbane matrons bent on clothes shopping. The Johnstones soon transformed the basement into a relaxed and inviting gallery for exhibiting contemporary art, with floor-to-ceiling bamboo poles and cane chairs with calico cushions providing a tropical atmosphere, while red-and-white striped curtains added a touch of French chic.

There were seventeen monotypes in Margaret's new show, more than half of which were of Venice, including one appropriately titled *Rainy Day, Venice*. In the *Courier Mail* Ernest Briggs (who called the pictures line-and-wash impressions) wrote: 'the works reveal a uniformly strict economy of treatment that at times is strongly atmospheric, and particularly so in *Venetian Houses*, and *Gondolas, Venice*, where there is a fine sense of distance.'[43] *Dieppe Harbour* and *Crucifix, Dieppe*, he noted, displayed 'a pleasing unity', but, unfortunately, in his opinion this quality was not sustained throughout the show. Instability of architectural line and a wash that appeared to be applied 'more at random than with reason' were the faults he found in several works.

Meanwhile, in France Margaret's finances were at a drastic

low. The seventeen works on show in Brisbane were priced at fifteen guineas each, so if the whole show had sold – not a likely occurrence – Margaret would have received her percentage of two hundred and fifty-five guineas, excluding framing costs. In the meantime, day-to-day living money was needed:

My money had almost run out by this stage. But luckily, through Francis, who had designed materials for the fashion house in Paris, I was able to earn some money doing design work of another sort. I started doing wallpaper designs for an American firm based in Glen Falls, New York, which had a line called Imperial Washable Wallpapers. They paid a hundred and fifty dollars per design. Good money. But it was flukey. Sometimes you'd work away on designs, then they wouldn't buy any of them. The designs had to be very much the next fashion and if you weren't up on that it was hit and miss. Sometimes your design would be good, but too advanced for them. This happened with some designs – a lot of them based on ancient Portuguese palaces – that Francis and I did in Portugal.

Obviously, Margaret and Rose were close. Equally obviously, although Margaret was moving with a decidedly bohemian set, a degree of practicality still ruled her heart:

Francis and I were keen on each other – we did work well together – but it never quite happened as far as an intimate relationship. It was just as well really. Francis thought he was going to marry me. He often said, We must get married. What a disaster that would have been. I think he looked a bit like my father and that was partly what attracted me to him. That and the fact that he conjured up a bygone artistic Paris. I knew he was still married to his second wife, but that wasn't an issue. He was of an era when people married and then went their separate ways. I met her – Frederica, the writer – several times and got on well with her.

There were some odd sides to him. I must have been putting two and two together even then. I think he might have been using drugs: he was always smiling. Nothing worried him. Everything was very calm. I used to think of what on earth people would think of him if he came out to Australia. We corresponded for while after I returned home but then it petered out.

Sir Francis Rose had three wives in all, as well as numerous homosexual encounters. Despite his charming and intriguing artistic persona, there *were* unsavoury sides to him – for one, his relationship with Ernst Roehm, the influential Nazi whom Hitler had murdered as part of the 1934 'Night of the Long Knives' purge of his own party. Despite Rose's fierce defence of this relationship in his memoirs, *Saying Life*, as strictly Platonic, it's even been alleged that Rose was in Roehm's bed when Hitler rounded up the dissidents.[44] This was no doubt an unpopular sort of anecdote for early 1950s Paris, and it is not one that Rose ever recounted to Margaret, one imagines.

Another of Rose's old friends was Cecil Beaton, who found Rose's frequent impecuniousness increasingly burdensome as the years wore on, especially as he was continually being asked to assist Rose in rectifying it. There's a much repeated story about how, after Beaton had donated an old suit to him, Rose was soon swanning around in it, announcing that he and Beaton shared the same tailor. Rose's last public appearance was in the Kenneth Anger cult film *Lucifer Rising* (along with others such as Marianne Faithfull), in which he played Chaos, aptly enough. He died in Charing Cross, London, in 1979.

Margaret's relationships with other men at this time, and the nature of her connection with men like Fred Jessup, Wolfgang Cardamatis, Donald Friend and David Strachan, with his tender, naked female *Muse*, could perhaps be summed up by Jessup's comment on his own relationship with Margaret: 'We were close,

close friends. She was between my sister and my lover. I mean in the sense of the closeness of our contact. She was like part of me. I knew everything that she was interested in and she was interested in the same things as I was.'[45]

'Between a sister and lover' probably best describes the affection these men felt for Margaret. She was, after all, the oldest of the Olley children. Even though she may claim to have dodged, by and large, any responsibility for her siblings, nevertheless the role of the oldest child is often one of caring for others. Perhaps Margaret took her role of caring older sister and her nurturing Cancer personality into her circle of close male friends – as well, of course, as entertaining them with her outgoing Gemini side. (Margaret likes to believe that since she was born virtually on the cusp of these two astrological signs both influence her behaviour.) And we might also assume, from the passing hint about Theo Schlicht's 'passion stops', that at this time, too, she was exploring what Donald Friend would later describe as her 'lively and sensual' nature.[46]

In July 1952 Margaret was on the move again with David Strachan and Moya Dyring, this time travelling in Brittany. The three stayed mainly at Pont-Aven, where Gauguin and his followers painted towards the end of the last century. Margaret found the wild countryside, with its rolling hills that went down to the sea, a delight. She was also enchanted by the sight of Breton women in the white hats, the *coiffes*, that she recognised from Gauguin's paintings. 'You actually felt as if you had stepped into one of his paintings,' Margaret recalls. She was in the company of two of her dearest friends and the whole of the Brittany trip was an harmonious interlude:

Far from a Still Life

The people in Brittany were particularly friendly and kind. We rented a couple of rooms on the quai at Pont-Aven from a woman called Georgette. Although the kitchen was tiny, she was a marvellous cook, and most of the food preparation was done on the floor. Perhaps she had a table somewhere, but I never saw it. There was no running water. We had to pump any water we wanted into a bucket on the quai and bring it back.

Just out of Pont-Aven there was a wonderful old church, which we all drew both inside and out. But most of my time was spent drawing the Breton trawlers in the Pont-Aven harbour and at the nearby fishing port of Concarneau. I've always loved boats. At Brisbane Tech, as I said before, we used to go out to Breakfast Creek and sketch the moored boats. Then there was the boat-building place at Lavender Bay that I painted. It probably goes back to my childhood on the Tweed River – being rowed across to school. There's something beautiful about the shape of a boat and magical about being on water: watching the reflections, running your hand in the water and feeling it pass through your fingers, seeing the fish swimming past.

Then we went on a trip round the 'calvaires' – the carved crosses the Celts made when they came to Brittany – and I drew those as well. Some were quite primitive, others really elaborate. There were also amazing stone walls that were built way back. Long afterwards, when I'd come back to Australia, I saw documentaries shot from the air in which you could make out the lines of the walls running through people's backyards and properties. But we weren't aware of that on the ground.

◈

The next big event in Margaret's life was the marriage of her sister Elaine in London. Elaine, having completed her nursing training in Sydney, went to Melbourne to study obstetrics. It was there she first started going out with Richard Wilkinson, a Merchant Navy engineer:

After a while Elaine and Richard became engaged, but the engagement lapsed because Richard was away on ships so much and Elaine came over to London on a working holiday on her own. Richard arrived, I think, to get his engineer's certificate, and they met up again and decided to get married then and there.

A friend of Moya's had already helped me make a bridesmaid dress. So I volunteered, with Moya's assistance, to provide a wedding cake, because there was still a lot of food rationing in England. It was rather a rash offer. There I was in Brittany, suddenly faced with trying to make an Australian fruit cake. No packets of sultanas or dried fruit were to be had, for love or money. In the end I used glace fruit instead and liberal amounts of rum. I made up the recipe as I went along. It doesn't matter what you put into a fruit cake, really. So long as you have the basic ingredients of butter, eggs, a bit of flour and fruit, it's bound to turn out all right.

Once the cake was mixed up ready to go, I took it round to be cooked in the local baker's oven, after which Moya and David drove me to the nearest port where I could catch a boat to England. Off I went, cake in tow. I have to say, it was very heavy to carry round, being full of prunes and glacé fruit.

Whether it was due to happiness earlier in the year with Sir Francis Rose, or just because it was summer, Margaret was looking 'wonderful – much slimmer, and very nicely dressed', Donald Friend reported after they met up in August 1952.[47]

Friend himself had won the Flotta Laura Travelling Art Prize in September 1951 in Australia, which included a free return trip from Australia to Italy plus living expenses. In January 1952 he sailed for Italy, where he revisited both Ischia (picking up a new love interest, Rosario) and Florence and travelled through Greece and Corfu, before settling down to work in Florence on his first one-person exhibition at the Redfern Gallery, to be held later that year.

He had arrived in London at the beginning of August and promptly presented himself at the doorstep of the elegant new bachelor flat in South Audley Street, Mayfair, where Loudon Sainthill and Harry Tatlock Miller were living with Sainthill's corgi, Edith. Tatlock Miller and Sainthill had both well and truly found their feet in London by now.

Tatlock Miller was at the helm of the Redfern Gallery, which was just around the corner from their new flat and increasingly showcasing Australian artists. Sainthill had already met with outstanding success for his work in the theatre when in 1951 he designed *The Tempest* for director Michael Benthall at the Shakespeare Memorial Theatre at Stratford-on-Avon, a production that had Michael Redgrave as Prospero and a young Richard Burton playing Ferdinand. *The Tempest* convincingly launched Sainthill's career as a costume and set designer and he then proceeded to go from triumph to triumph in theatre and ballet.

Sainthill and Tatlock Miller's West End flat had watermelon-pink wallpaper in the entrance hall, black-and-white monkey-fur rugs in the living areas and baroque, black-browed Spanish saints standing guard on fluted marble columns in the bedroom.[48] No sooner was Friend installed in this luxury, than he and Sainthill rang Margaret and Jocelyn Rickards, who immediately came round. The newly slim Margaret then proceeded to briskly cook a meal while recounting the adventures of all their friends in Europe.[49]

In London, Margaret had found a little relief for her straitened finances. Michael Benthall wanted his acclaimed production of *The Tempest* at Stratford-on-Avon preserved in film and Robert Helpman, who was also part of the Shakespeare Memorial Theatre company, was raising money for the project. Sainthill was asked to 'Mickey Mouse' it, which meant producing a drawing for every shot in the film.[50] After two days a desperate Sainthill beseeched Rickards and Margaret to help out with the endless postcard drawings needed:

We did little drawings, working from the script, that people could flick through and get an idea of the film, for which chore we were paid a pittance. Unfortunately the film was never made. The finances couldn't be raised. Maybe they never found the money because of our drawings!

But in her biography, Jocelyn Rickards claims that in the drawings they churned out for *The Tempest* Margaret's fairies were much 'ballsier' than hers and that she had to redraw Margaret's sprites on that account! [51]

At the beginning of September, after a Friday night dinner at Clarice Zander's in Chelsea and front row seats at the musical *South Pacific* – courtesy of Sydney Cooper – Margaret and Donald headed off to spend a weekend at Cooper's Hampshire farm. Friend's description of their time away is rhapsodic: 'The weather was lovely. Olley and I sketched. We used to eat blackberries and great bowls of cream under an apple tree, and squash wasps, and walk through the green tunnels of lanes, the green banks on either side of the narrow ways and tapestry of leaves in articulated detail, like Pre-Raphaelite painting.'[52]

After this idyll Margaret returned to France for an exciting event. An exhibition of her monotypes was about to open at the gallery-bookstore opened by Cocteau's friend, publisher Paul Morihien, in the Jardins du Palais Royal, Paris. Fred Jessup had now landed the job of managing the gallery and he had organised her exhibition there.

David Strachan and his Stramur-Presse made a poster for it on the back of a rejected Mondrian print originally intended for the Redfern Gallery. The highbrow French newspaper *Le Monde* described her monotypes as pretty pictures – *'bien jolie images'* – and noted the young Australian artist's love of Venice, with its winged lions, decorated gondolas and balconies fit for an Othello. And five of her works sold. In all, not bad for her first and only exhibition in Paris.

Then, little more than a month later, at the beginning of November 1952, a sudden, unforeseen happening threw Margaret's life into utter disarray:

I was staying with David [Strachan] in Paris when I received the news that my father had died. He was out attending to his queen bees, which he still raised and sent through the post to customers. My mother said he fell asleep under a tree. Then he died. I was never really sure of the causes, but I suppose it was either a stroke or a heart attack – he did eat an awful lot of red meat, like everyone else then.

My father's death was my first experience of grief. Since then grief has recurred again and again in my life. In many ways, his dying was unreal to me. I didn't leave Australia thinking I wouldn't see him again – I was expecting he'd be there to meet me when I came home. But I'd always been much closer to my mother – as I said before, she was always there, my father was always elsewhere. So his death didn't seem to affect me too deeply, or that's what I thought.

Joseph Olley died on 3 November 1952. He was sixty-three years old. A funeral notice appeared in the *Courier Mail* on 5 November. At 10.15 a.m. that day he was cremated at the Mt Thompson Crematorium, with members of the Brisbane Branch of the Queensland Bee Keepers' Association in attendance. Although Margaret's brother Ken was there, Elaine was on a ship en route from Hong Kong to Australia, so Grace Olley was left to deal with the loss of her husband without the support of either of her daughters. According to Elaine now, Grace was particularly upset at seeing her husband in an open coffin during the service.

In and Out of Paris

That Margaret – presumably on a high after her Paris exhibition – was naturally completely unprepared for her father's death is borne out by an entry in Donald Friend's diary. On 4 November 1952, Friend casually remarks that he has just received a letter from Margaret, 'dear soul', asking him to go on a painting tour of France with her.[53] However the painting trip, like any other plans Margaret might have been harbouring, was destined to become a pipe dream and Margaret left Paris, if not for good, at least for almost two decades, not long afterwards:

I must have been in a bit of a daze. I don't remember organising to go over to London or buying my ticket back to Australia. I had to go to London, of course, to get the trunk, which I was storing in Mitty's friend's basement. I do know my visa for staying in France had expired and I had trouble leaving, but I pretended I was drunk and didn't understand what they were saying. I probably was drunk. I was being farewelled by David and Fred Jessup and a whole crowd of people. Once again I was poured on my way.

Donald Friend would later recall in his diary that Margaret in January of 1953, just before she was due to board a ship for home, was 'very unhappy over an emotional mix-up with Sir Francis Rose and also over the prospect of returning to Australia'.[54] Whether the mix-up was a product of Friend's imagination; or occasioned by the parting with Rose; or brought about by Rose's confused sexuality; or even a rejection by Rose, remains speculative. But also Moya Dyring had leased the Île St-Louis apartment, sold her trusty painting car and set off on a protected sea voyage via Indonesia back to Australia for a year's visit. Margaret Cilento had already come back to Brisbane in 1951. So, although she had Clarice Zander in London, Margaret would have been very much deprived of a female support network had she stayed on in Paris.

Margaret now sees her return to Australia following her father's death more as a spiritual and physical necessity than a cause for any distress:

It was because of my father's death that I came back. It was just as well – a little problem to do with drinking was rearing its head. After all, I had been living above a cellar at Madame S.'s. Then there was the Château Fontcreuse. It would be much better to be out of France and away from temptation, I thought. Also, although I'd been having those shows back in Australia, I had run out of money. And I was unhappy about my father's death, even though I didn't admit it to myself.

So, after a final afternoon of chatting with Friend, followed by a drink with him at two or three pubs and supper at Clarice Zander's, Margaret boarded the liner *Strathmore* and set off home to Australia. But immediately a hold-up occurred – as the ship was about to depart, its engines failed. Passengers, including Margaret, were put up in London for six days at P&O's expense. The journey home, once the *Strathmore* was up to speed, was plagued with inconveniences, according to an exasperated letter Margaret wrote to Friend, posted from Aden.[55]

No sooner had Margaret finally managed to secure a quiet working space in the 'hell-hole' of second class, than the purser gave 'an old Duck permission to practise Spanish dancing' in the same area, much distracting clicking of castanets and stamping of feet being involved. Worse followed. The woman hired a musician with a fiddle from the ship's band to accompany her and the pair's activities took up even more room. The noise as she hopped away to the fiddler's scratchy rendition of *Carmen* was terrible, according to Margaret's frustration-filled letter. She then discovered the 'old Duck' was none other than Helen of Helen's Happiness Club – a well-known, respectable introduction agency, with rooms in the Piccadilly Arcade near Sydney's David Jones department store. What's more, Helen was eager to have Margaret visit her when they arrived in Sydney.

'Will have to get out of that one,' the letter concludes.

On her return, Margaret settled back into life in Australia. Donald Friend, still in London, brooded about himself. And about Margaret. In August 1953, he and Clarice Zander spent a day picnicking and sketching in a garden on the edge of the Thames. Swans floated on the river below and clouds scudded overhead, which changed the light from bright to dark, forcing Zander's brush to scurry across her work. Friend then confided what he'd been turning over in his mind for the past months. Should he marry Margaret Olley?

Friend's desire to marry was not as unusual as one might think. He had already fathered a daughter as a result of one of his 'London indiscretions' and he had also once proposed to Peter Kaiser's girlfriend – admittedly when she was about to tell her parents that she was marrying Kaiser, so there was not much chance of an acceptance.[56] It seems that the notion of a heterosexual future sometimes presented Friend with an appealing solution to the depression that periodically assailed him, brought about by a loneliness stemming from his homosexuality. 'I must marry or burn,' he wrote in his diary after the confession to Zander.[57] 'Burn up either with solitude or with excesses of promiscuity that rises from loneliness.'

Friend recognised that such a marriage would be fraught with danger for Margaret because it would hinge on his being able to give up 'the private actions and dreams' from which had flowed all his 'inspiration and understanding'.[58] Not a very likely, or desirable occurrence, one would imagine. But, as he reminded himself in his diary, his aging homosexual lot would not necessarily be a happy one and young men did not want 'their sport spoilt by the leering presence of an aging Satyr'.[59]

Friend then concluded the soul-baring in his diary with a touching and quaintly nineteenth-century outpouring as to why Margaret would make him a good wife: 'There are few people a selfish man dare trust with his body, mind and soul. Olley is only one of whom, my fondness apart, I feel sure, for she is both sensible and sensitive and tender, stubborn and intelligent, proud, simple and complicated. She is not a wasting frippery woman, she work and enjoys, she is gay and serious and independent.'

None of the above, needless to say, had ever crossed Margaret's mind. Not yet, anyway.

⊰ 10 ⊱

Back in Brisbane

As far as putting colour into my own work, I was particularly influenced by the Bonnards and Matisses that I'd seen while I was away. Sunlight is what Bonnard is about. He paints light and life. Matisse and Bonnard instinctively put colours together so they sing – pink with a bit of red, or just a surprising black dot placed somewhere. It's magic.

MARGARET WAS JUST OVER TWENTY-NINE-AND-A-HALF WHEN SHE ARRIVED back in Australia. She disembarked from the *Strathmore* in Sydney on a Friday morning at the end of February 1953. Almost the moment she stepped off the ship, she and Sam Hughes attended the opening of 'French Painting Today' at the National Art Gallery of New South Wales. This was a touring exhibition organised by Hal Missingham, comprised of one hundred and twenty-three works, including paintings by Braque, Picasso, Chagall, Matisse and Miró. The show caused a degree of controversy, though not as much as Burdett's 1939 exhibition. 'If the collection of French (modern) pictures represent the best in French art today, God help France!' Howard Ashton began his review in the *Sun*.[1]

In Sydney, newsreels and a feature in the *Sunday Herald* showed shots of the public looking bewilderedly at the exhibition's more abstract works. Margaret and Hughes were photographed in front of German-born French painter Hans Hartung's dark *T.50-50*. The caption underneath their photograph said Margaret was listening to Hughes 'expand his theory on Hans Hartung's series of angry paint strokes'.[2]

Margaret remained a few days in Sydney. She did not stay with Hughes. Apart from the initial excitement of their reunion, nothing else happened to further her relationship with him. Then, having finally sold off the travelling trunk – what a relief it was to get rid of its cumbersome bulk – and regaled the press with selected snatches of her travels away, she went home to Grace Olley's willow-patterned china and the familiar winey smell of Brisbane's fig trees in summer.

At Farndon a great welcome went on. Grace Olley fussed; Aunt Mary, too. Both looked older. There were endless cups of tea; cake was produced to go with them. Needless to say, wine was not flowing. Stories of Margaret's time in Cassis and Paris had to be told and retold. All was slightly imbued with the unsaid idea that, 'Now you can put that behind you and get on with the proper business of living in Brisbane.' It was enough to make Margaret consider – briefly – that maybe it might be better to escape back to Europe.

The Brisbane she returned to was still just a large country town, sleepy as ever. Spreading poincianas shaded pedestrians from the heat, fruit bats squeaked at night, gardens were scented with creamy frangipani and fallen figs littered footpaths. If you were running late an obliging tram driver might wait at a stop or even drop you off at your house coming back at night. The same

Back in Brisbane

small ferries took people to and fro across the Brisbane River. Women wore hats and gloves to bond with one another over afternoon tea in houses up on stilts with iron-trimmed verandas and lattice underneath. Rowe's Café, with its starched white tablecloths and peaked white napkins, dark wood wall panelling, chandeliers and waitresses in black skirts, white pinafores and little white caps, remained the pinnacle of classy eating out. The Shingle Inn in full Tudor swing could be relied upon for less formal gentility, while at the Bellevue Hotel out-of-town parliamentarians and overseas dignitaries dined in quiet opulence.

At home at Farndon the paperbark trees Joe Olley had planted when Margaret was at school were going strong. The camphor laurels seemed even huger and the garden more of a jungle. Orange-red gloriosa lilies and massed white Eucharist lilies grew wild in the front yard. Cuttings Grace Olley had struck competed for light in the profusion of tropical greenness, much like Margaret's own garden in Sydney now. The tribes of possums in the trees were no less clumsy and the branches they inhabited still pressed so close to the house they almost came in the windows:

Possums used to jump from the trees onto the roof at night and land so heavily you'd think they had hobnailed boots on. Then you'd see branches swinging as they took off back into another tree. Once I must have forgotten to shut the window next to my bed and I woke up with one sniffing my face; luckily I managed to reach out my arm and push it back out again. If we didn't make sure the windows and front door were closed at night they'd come in and make havoc.

I'd liked Brisbane ever since I was a child, so really I was quite happy to be back there. Farndon was just a street back from the river. From my bedroom I could see little bits of its greeny-coloured water. At night the river cruise would come past. It used to go about as far up the river as Lone Pine and there was dancing on board. You'd hear faint chugging; the music would be slowly swelling as the boat came closer then fade away. Then just as we were about to fall asleep, the faint sound of music would drift off the water again as it came back down.

As Margaret remembers it, when Elaine, her sister, first arrived back in Australia she stayed with their mother in Brisbane for a while to help her recover from their father's death. Then Elaine and her husband Richard Wilkinson rented a flat at Kirribilli in Sydney, with a view over rooftops of the harbour (which Margaret often drew if she was visiting Sydney). However there was still quite a collection of Margaret's family resident at Farndon:

Aunt Mary ended up with us when her private physiotherapy practice at Maryborough closed up. She was trying to decide what to do next and just never moved. But Fardon was quite capacious. In its former life as a school house there would have been verandas on three sides, but these were long gone by the time my mother bought it. In our days there was a little porch at the entrance and then a long hall going down to the dining room and the kitchen. My mother and I had one side of the house with a little nick into the other side, which was the kitchen. There were two flats on that side and then a fourth flat downstairs where Ken, who was busy with his honey business, lived. Like Elaine, he too was now married and had started a family.

My studio, which was never locked, was also downstairs, at the front under the house. Apart from McMahons Point, it was my first proper studio. It had a strong wooden floor, windows at one end and typical Brisbane lattice, painted black with some sort of tar across the front. I covered some of the lattice with blinds and hessian so the wind and rain wouldn't come in and to control the light. But I also quite often used the lattice as a background in my paintings. In those days I didn't really notice the heat. On very hot days in

January, I'd go off and see a film. But mostly I just painted on regardless, with a radio tuned to the ABC.

In winter, it might be added, the studio was not so ideal. Although the lattice offered some protection from the elements, it was still rather like painting out on the lawn with just a radiator to keep you warm.[3]

Margaret's return to Brisbane had dropped her into the bosom of her family, or, at least, it had brought her closer to Grace Olley's bosom, in a way she'd not really experienced before, given the years she spent at boarding school and in Sydney. This new family intimacy, whether she admitted it or not, must have added to the jarring sense, not only of geographical isolation, but also of emotional amputation, which most Australians experience when returning home after a prolonged absence overseas. Not only were Paris and her friends a long way away, she was removed from her Sydney milieu and, as well, she had to acclimatise to the closeness of a family whose values might be somewhat different from her own. Underlying all this was grief. Her father's death was never talked about, but every so often she felt a pang at his absence – like when she passed by the Aboriginal shield that Joe Olley had found at Tully, which was still hanging in the house. As for Grace, it seemed losing Joe only made her gather in Margaret closer:

I coloured my mother's life from this time on. My mother was the one who'd encouraged me to go to art school in my early days. She always had that belief in me and now she just loved participating in my openings and meeting my friends. It almost reached the point of embarrassment. She'd go along early to Brian Johnstone's openings and stand there announcing to everybody, It's the best work she's ever done. Her best work. I used to think, Oh, dear. But I must say she was a great champion. I'll always be grateful to my mother for all the encouragement she gave me.

I still couldn't escape the notoriety attached to having been painted by Dobell. The papers always mentioned it. Every interview, the portrait had to be included. When I first came back I often went to the theatre and film festivals in Brisbane. I was in the foyer of the theatre one night when a woman came up and started gushing over me.

Oh, Miss Olley, she said, I must congratulate you on winning the Nobel Prize.

No, I don't think so, I replied. But she kept on insisting that I had. The more I said no, the more adamant she became. Finally she said, Well, maybe you don't know yet, but you are getting it. In the interval she came up to me very embarrassed because she'd mixed up my sitting for the Dobell portrait with the Nobel Prize.

Brisbane might not have changed much but Margaret had – and not just in her fondness for alcohol, which was beginning to assert itself. After four years of observing the art of others, she had formed a new resolve about her own painting. 'Paris made me realise that people in Australia just do not use colour,' she told the *Sunday Herald* when she first landed back in Sydney. 'I shall have to absorb that feeling for colour into my work by degrees. One cannot just switch to a whole new set of ideas all at once.'[4]

Although, in fact, she may have actually begun the pursuit of colour in France, it seemed to take Margaret most of 1953 to get this process underway in Brisbane. But by 1954 her paintings did look decidedly different from the low-toned work she'd done in Australia in the 1940s:

The last exhibition I saw before leaving Paris was of Bonnard's painting of his wife Martha in the bath. Despite all the upset of my father's death I can remember that clearly. They were an inspiration to me. It's also about learning to see. Once my mother asked me why I'd painted the asphalt purple in a street scene. So I sent her outside to look at the asphalt with the sun on it and she had to admit it did have a purple tinge.

Not only are Bonnard's bath scenes sometimes flooded with the strong gold of sunlight and stippled with incandescent mauves, but they are also intensely intimate studies of domestic life. So while, on the one hand, Margaret's return to the family nest in Brisbane might have seemed constricting after her time away, this family environment would also ultimately provide a perfect backdrop against which she would begin her Bonnard-inspired intimist interiors that would eventually become so much a part of her oeuvre. As always, Margaret's life was filled with paradoxes.

And now she not only had a new painting style, but also a new gallery in which to exhibit – the second Brian Johnstone gallery in the Brisbane Arcade. Johnstone's first exhibiting space, the Marodian Gallery, had opened the year after Margaret went to Europe. Before then, the only real commercial gallery in Brisbane had been the more conservative Moreton Galleries. In the six years that followed the 1952 opening of his new gallery in the Brisbane Arcade, Brian Johnstone would present Brisbanites with contemporary paintings by a wide range of Australian artists, some of whom were new talents, others more established, and many of them from Melbourne. Among the exhibiting artists were Sidney Nolan, Arthur Boyd, Donald Friend, John Brack, John Molvig, Clifton Pugh, Lawrence Daws and Margaret Olley.

But the Johnstone Gallery was to bring more to Margaret's life than providing an exciting exhibiting space:

My mother had started going to openings at the Johnstones' while I was overseas. She'd made friends there who naturally now became my friends as well. (Before this I hadn't really had friends in Brisbane apart from the Cilento family.) That was how I met Ron

Sabien, the interior designer, who has been dear to me ever since. Ron had worked for Hugh Hale, which was how he became involved with the Johnstones. Ron was a great supporter of the arts; he used to recommend that his clients go along and look at the paintings in Brian's shows. He also gave me wonderful lengths of exotic material that I put in my paintings and used to help me at night in the studio with my framing. People like Ron, who get others to appreciate paintings, are really as important to the art world as artists.

'When you knew Margaret, she was bubbly and chatty,' Sabien recalls, 'but she was always very reserved when new people were around. She was interested in everything that was going on in the world, politics included. Of course, she loved music as well and always listened to that in the studio. She spent so much time alone there then.'[5]

Next door to the Johnstone Gallery was the Old Vienna Coffee Inn, which was run by Magda and Igor Wollner. The Old Vienna was the first eating place in Brisbane to offer European food such as schnitzels and it attracted an artistic crowd of diners longing for a touch of sophistication in a town where roast beef reigned supreme. The Old Vienna and the Johnstone Gallery complemented each other perfectly. When the café needed repainting and Magda Wollner was running low on funds, Brian Johnstone organised Donald Friend and Margaret into doing the job for her.

Farndon also became the setting for many a dinner party of Johnstone Gallery patrons and artists. Grace Olley, affectionately known as 'Mother Olley' or 'Mrs Oll', was soon fabled for effortlessly producing home-cooked feasts at the gatherings. 'Brian's shows always finished up with either a luncheon at Margaret's or a dinner at my place,' Sabien remembers. 'Mrs Oll was a tiny, grey-haired woman with wonderful conversation. She was also very interested in things. She always did a lovely baked dinner. It all just seemed to come out of nowhere. There'd be tureens of vegetables on the table and various dishes. Mrs Oll would sit at the head of the table and serve. Margaret would be passing it all around. They were great days, great days.'[6]

Life at Farndon was obviously far from dull. It seemed, as far as anyone could tell, that Grace Olley and Margaret had both knitted up the gap left by Joe Olley's death without a hitch.

In some ways 1953 was the calm before the storm of the next few years. But the year was still hectic enough. Its activity began in Sydney even before Margaret was back in Australia; as she contended with shipboard life on the *Strathmore*, her work was being fought over at the Macquarie Galleries for what was the event of the year for the budget-minded collector: the 'Show of Sixes', held early in February.

At these Sydney 'Show of Sixes' exhibitions, which started in 1951, all paintings for sale were priced at six guineas. Margaret had previously sent back work from Europe for the first two shows and in this year her watercolour *Notre Dame* was included. According to the *Sydney Morning Herald*, art devotees streamed in by taxi and hire car at six in the morning to join the 'Dawn Patrol' and queue on the pavement outside the gallery in search of a bargain.[7] In 1953, such early birds were pipped at the post by two far keener fans, one of whom was none other than arts student Roddy Meagher, who'd gone straight from a party at university to take up his position on the bottom step of the building at 4.30 a.m.[8] When the gallery opened at ten o'clock some thirty men, women and a few very uninterested children (to judge by the photo in the *Sydney Morning Herald*) were lined up in the sweltering Sydney sunshine waiting to stake their claim on the forty-four exhibits.

Meagher (now a friend of Margaret's and part of the Olley inner lunching sanctum at her house in Paddington) went straight for Jean Bellette's *Trojan Theme*. Margaret's *Notre Dame* was snapped up by number four in the queue, Mrs John Spencer, who'd thoughtfully provided a thermos of hot tea for the early starters.[9] Artists participated almost as enthusiastically as buyers in the Show of Sixes, which later prompted the Macquarie Galleries to initiate their 'Show of Eights' and 'Fifteen-Guineas Pictures' exhibitions. All three shows were to be a regular part of Margaret's exhibiting life over the coming years.

The new Johnstone Gallery was not the only change in the Brisbane art world to which Margaret returned. In 1951, Robert Haines had taken up the position of director of the Queensland Art Gallery and in 1953 Gertrude Langer became the *Courier Mail*'s art critic. The Jewish Langer – whose considerable academic knowledge of art was gained at the University of Vienna and the Sorbonne – moved to Australia after Austria was annexed by Germany in 1938. In Brisbane, she was not only influential as a critic but also became passionately involved with all aspects of contemporary art. Her husband, architect Karl Langer, is credited with introducing the concept of modernism to building design in Brisbane.

Margaret's success was certainly not dependent on Langer, but Langer did consistently review her work favourably over the coming years and undoubtedly contributed to her rise an artist. One senses Margaret's own view of Langer was a bit ambivalent (although this could simply be an artist's natural antipathy to the role of critic). And Donald Friend lets slip in his diary how Margaret had dubbed her 'the power-drunk Gertie Langer'.[10] Today, though Margaret is polite about Langer, she admits her perceptive eye created a few problems for the Johnstone Gallery:

Gertrude and Karl regarded themselves as the art experts. They were cultured European people who loved Japanese art and had bonsai

Back in Brisbane

trees at their house. She was a good art critic, but Brian Johnstone had to stop her coming to the openings to write her reviews. He had to suggest she come beforehand, because as she went by people would be saying to each other, I'm thinking of buying that one, what do you think? No, no, Gertrude would reply and put them off.

The new director of the Queensland Art Gallery, Robert Haines, lived with his mother (a great friend of Grace Olley) almost directly opposite Farndon, on the other side of the Brisbane River at St Lucia. Shortly after Margaret arrived back in Brisbane, Haines commissioned her to paint a mural of a Parisian scene in the foyer of the Queensland Art Gallery for the opening in April 1953 of the touring 'French Painting Today' she'd seen in Sydney. The mural, measuring ten by seven feet, was designed to give visitors a taste of Paris on their way into the gallery and featured a large fountain in the foreground backed by the buildings that surround the Place de la Concorde. Margaret painted it over two days, mostly from memory, with only one small painting as an aid.

Of Haines's contribution to the Queensland Art Gallery, Margaret recalls:

I used to see a lot of Robert in those days. The director before him, Robert Campbell, had already initiated some improvements. The Queensland Art Gallery was in a big exhibition building back then. Campbell broke up the space by lowering the ceilings and creating rooms out of hessian. But it was Robert Haines who had the great art of display, he really made it a beautiful space. So things were happening in the art world in Brisbane when I returned – although Sydney never thought so. It was also through Robert Haines that the Queensland Art Gallery acquired [in 1959] the magnificent collection belonging to Major H. de Vahl Rubin of modern French painting, with works by Degas, Renoir, Picasso and others that we all benefited so much from.

Far from a Still Life

The French Painting Today exhibition of 1953 reportedly baffled the Brisbane crowds that poured into gallery, as much as it had Sydney viewers. To coincide with the opening, the lowbrow magazine *Pix* voted Picasso's distorted cubist portrait, *The Orange Bodice,* the most-discussed painting of the exhibition and ran a spread that included photos of well-dressed young women looking wide-eyed at nudes, while older women in neat hats and gloves, of course, appraised the works more circumspectly and school children bashfully pointed.[11]

One imagines their reactions might have seemed rather curious to Margaret, herself so recently arrived from France. But she was probably far too busy to overly concern herself with their gawking. As well as executing the mural, in April she also designed and painted sets for the flourishing and lively Twelfth Night Theatre, which had been started as an amateur dramatic society in 1936 by Rhoda Felgate. Felgate, a large woman who 'never let up', according to Margaret, was a great friend of Marjorie Johnstone from her acting days. This connection may help to explain how Margaret came to be working at the theatre so soon after coming home. 'Everyone knew everyone,' Margaret recalls of the cosy arts interaction at the time. 'Rhoda used to come to openings at the Johnstone Gallery. I always went to see all the Twelfth Night productions, as well as working on the sets.'

By 1953, the Twelfth Night Theatre, though still maintaining its amateur status, was staging increasingly more adventurous drama and after working on their production of Shakespeare's *Twelfth Night* in April, Margaret then designed Christopher Fry's *The Firstborn* for the company in June.

Another exciting event in April 1953 was the hanging of one of Margaret's paintings, *Crucifixion*, in the Blake Prize for religious art, which was displayed in the art gallery of Mark Foys Sydney department store. (*Crucifixion*'s price tag of ninety-five guineas was unusually large for one of Margaret's paintings, especially when you consider that in her upcoming solo show all works would be priced at fifteen guineas.) The Blake Prize, first awarded in 1951, was worth two hundred guineas and seemed to tempt a surprising number of normally secular artists to a sudden piety in painting. The winner for 1953 was the Ukrainian-born Michael Kmit with *The Evangelist John Mark*. Kmit was among the few entrants whose paintings, which usually drew on Byzantine icons, did regularly deal with religious themes.

Margaret's one-person show opened in June, at the Macquarie Galleries in Sydney. It consisted entirely of works done overseas, mainly monotypes from her Brittany and Portugal trips. This was no doubt largely due to the fact that she had been so busy with earning money since her return that she'd hardly had time to paint many new works. Obviously, too, there were no new explosions of colour evident in her palette here, but the exhibition was probably valuable in helping Margaret reconnect with the feel of showing in Sydney. The Macquarie Galleries had by this time also implemented an innovative scheme that would prove a small financial godsend for Margaret over the next few years:

The Macquarie Galleries were ahead of their time. As an artist you agreed that the gallery could have a few paintings they could rent out to people for so much per week. It provided a nice little bit of pocket money for us artists. Sometimes the paintings would be returned after a while; but a lot of the time the people who had rented a painting fell in love with it and eventually bought it. It really was a marvellous scheme.

In August there was a bittersweet reminder of Margaret's life in Paris when Moya Dyring came up to Brisbane for an exhibition of her work at the Johnstone Gallery. Dyring, who had left Paris just before Margaret, had been back in Australia since the end of 1952. She'd had Christmas with her family, seen the New Year in

Far from a Still Life

with John and Sunday Reed in Melbourne, and was not planning to return to France until the year was over. In Brisbane, as well as, catching up and exchanging news of friends, she and Margaret once more went off on painting trips:

Moya came out several times over the next ten years or so. One time we went up to Childers [a Queensland country town]; another time we stayed at Noosa, which was like a fishing village in those days. We'd rent a place and then paint or draw away. I remember Moya made me drive when we went to Noosa – one of the few times in my life I've been forced to take the wheel of a car. I did actually have my licence. Since I'd been back, I'd had umpteen lessons in a little truck belonging to Ken, my brother. I was more than a bit drunk when I sat for my test. Afterwards I stayed in the car outside the police station, thinking, Thank God, I've failed. But then the driving examiner said, What are you waiting for? Go over and get your licence. I'd had so many driving lessons they just caved in and passed me. They probably decided, Oh, she's a bit nervous, but she can drive. I thought you'd suggest I go out to the country and learn to drive properly, I replied to the examiner. It wouldn't be a bad idea, he answered.

    Next I resolved to drive over to visit Margaret Cilento in her studio at Kangaroo Point, where she was teaching. Ken's wife Laurel came out with their daughter Helen Rose, who was a small child then, and said, Why don't you take Helen Rose? It was the first time I'd driven since getting my licence – probably I'd had a few nips – and the responsibility of having Helen Rose was terrifying. I kept wishing the traffic lights would turn green before I reached them, so I wouldn't have to stop and start. The worst of it was I assumed everybody else on the road must be as bad a driver as me. Somehow I made it to the studio, had a few drinks to recover, then had to face the drive home. There seemed to be no alternative. I did do a U-turn in front of the traffic and hoped nobody would hit me.

Back in Brisbane

Mercifully, I arrived back at Farndon without an accident. Never again, I thought.

As well as explaining her reluctance to drive, that Margaret, who'd happily hitchhiked across Europe, was so unnerved by a drive across Brisbane is another small clue to her demons. Like the shyness that had plagued her early years, there was a great deal of underlying nervousness within her now. And, unfortunately, the same remedy from a bottle could all too easily dispatch it.

In October 1953, Donald Friend arrived back in Sydney on board the Flotta Lauro's SS *Surriento*. Tas Drysdale and the Drysdale children went out in a little motorised dinghy to greet the *Surriento* as it came into the harbour. Attilio Guarracino was on the wharf when it berthed to whisk Friend's heavy suitcase off his shoulders, which was just as well as there were no porters about.[12] By this stage Attilio had a job in Sydney caring for a man who was paralysed. A couple of days later Friend flew up to Hill End, where his dog Butch gave him an enthusiastic welcome, as did Donald Murray.[13]

Friend was soon back at work on an entry for the following year's Blake Prize, a big oil titled *Deposition*, which included Mary Magdalene and Christ's body. He was also busily planning renovations, which included replacing floorboards eaten away by white ants. But there was absolutely no attempt by him, at this point, to act on the resolution he had blurted out to Clarice Zander only a couple of months earlier about marrying Margaret Olley, either by way of a confession in his diary or in real life.

As 1953 came to its close, Margaret and Grace Olley scoured out the copper under Farndon with sandsoap, in preparation for boiling the Christmas puddings they'd wrapped in calico cloths.

To Margaret, the prospect of her mother's Christmas puddings, which she had loved all her childhood, was an indisputably good thing about being back in Australia. Light shone through the lattice for hours into the night as the copper was stoked until the puddings were cooked. Finally they were fished out on a poker and deposited in enamel bowls.

Margaret had also been asked to paint a four-hundred-square-foot mural in the saloon bar of the Grosvenor Hotel, George Street, for which she was paid two hundred and fifty pounds. Clad in shorts and a shirt, she worked through hot December nights after the bar had closed, transforming the yellow plaster above head-high wood panelling into a panorama of Brisbane a century before.[14] The mural, which she finished a week or so before Christmas, included such scenes as a team of horses ploughing up the original wood-block surface of Queen Street; whiskered street sweepers and an old-fashioned drapery shop; a young lair in a blazer and flat-topped hat riding a penny-farthing bicycle; a school girl in frilly pantaloons; and a street photographer on the job. It remained above drinkers' heads until the mid 1980s, when the building changed hands and the familiar vista was demolished to accommodate a McDonald's restaurant:

Those things disappear. The French-themed mural in the Brisbane Art Gallery I did for Robert Haines went, too. I think it must have been around this time that Sid, Cynthia and Jinx Nolan arrived on their way to England on a ship. Cynthia had rung me up and I'd gone in to see them or they'd come out to see me. I must have just been paid for the mural and I remembered how Dobell had given me money when I was going away. So before the boat sailed I handed Sid some money as a present. He rushed off into his cabin and did a little drawing which he presented me with just as the ship was leaving. He almost had to throw it over the side.

A couple of years later [in 1957] I did another mural – Circular

Quay in the 1900s this time – on a curved wall of the Leagues' Club in Phillip Street. That doesn't exist anymore, either. I didn't regard these murals as paintings; they were more like the stage sets I did. So I'm not upset that they aren't there anymore. If people would only realise you're really interested in what you're doing at the moment. I wasn't painting away on the murals, or the sets, thinking, How wonderful, this is going to be preserved for all eternity.

At Hill End, Attilio Guarracino (having given up his latest job as a carer) had arrived back at the beginning of December. A couple of days later Donald Murray went off to have Christmas with the Drysdales (and possibly stay on in Sydney). The Drysdale family was by now living in larger quarters at 29 Sutherland Street, Darling Point, where the acrid smell of Drysdale boiling up the medium of black oil often stank out the house, much to Bonny's annoyance. By Christmas the Hill End weather had turned baking hot and Friend, Attilio and a lone local male enjoyed a quiet Christmas, with a baked goose to celebrate. Still not a skerrick of a declaration to Margaret.

However, by early in 1954, Friend had written to Margaret, hatching a plot to spend the winter with her in his much loved territory of old – north Queensland.[15] In March there was a barely readable, bulky reply, complete with wacky spelling, from Margaret, suggesting that he accompany her on a trip to New Guinea in September to visit a new friend she'd made – Geoff Elworthy.[16] 'Of course, it means getting there and back but he could easily keep us for a month or 2 without even feeling the strain,' she wrote enthusiastically. 'He really is a darling and a madly happy sort of cove,' she went on, before adding in enticement that he seemed 'to live a wonderful life up there but I'm sure the main enjoyments are for men only. Anyway think about it.'

The letter, which went on to say that she hoped he'd win the Blake Prize, also contained a significant update on her own painting: 'My painting has changed quite a bit, I wonder if you would like it or not. I suppose not. All the old brown scrubby paint is disappearing, and for the first time I'm trying to tackle the problem of colour which is quite something of an ideal but I'm enjoying it, which is the main point and it's also becoming more personal and I'm afraid to say more feminine, which I suppose is only natural.'[17]

In early March 1954, the winner of the Blake Prize was announced. Friend, whose entry, *Nativity* (he'd scrapped *Deposition*), included three prominently positioned, naked, sheep-less shepherds (who could as easily have been angels) missed out to a severe-looking and decently robed *Judas Iscariot* by the Adelaide artist Charles Bannon. A degree of controversy erupted over Friend's painting, between those offended by the shepherds and those, mainly Friend, who took offence to this response.

Later in the month, Friend made a weekend trip to Sydney. After attending a party where other artists were as mad as bulldog ants over the Blake judging, he sat up drinking with Drysdale until 5.30 in the morning. During this session, Drysdale persuaded Friend to abandon going to New Guinea with Margaret, and instead to go to Cairns with him, in an exploration further north. Although in the small hours of the morning Friend agreed to Drysdale's proposal, back at Hill End he confessed to his diary that his preference was really to go to New Guinea with Margaret. Several weeks later, Friend regretfully wrote off to Margaret saying that it seemed likely he wouldn't be able to afford even the trip to Cairns with her, unless the Redfern Gallery unexpectedly came up with some money they owed him. But he nevertheless expressed his longing to escape the southern winter and experience once again the warm friendly north.[18]

Shortly afterwards, Margaret and Grace Olley visited Sydney for the opening of David Strachan's paintings at the Macquarie Galleries and to catch up with Strachan himself. Strachan, though his heart was still given to a life overseas, was back in Australia to see his family in Victoria and for exhibitions in Sydney and Brisbane. It's worth remembering that while Strachan had not yet really begun to paint the Australian landscape (which he would do with great, if somewhat melancholic, feeling in the 1960s), his attitude to the Australian countryside – especially once there was some evidence of human contact in it – was not at all hostile. So his trip home may also have allowed him to renew a little his appreciation of this aspect of Australia.

While Margaret socialised with Strachan in Sydney, Friend sat by his fire at Hill End drinking coffee laced with rum and savouring a moment of solitude, Attilio having gone off to experience the wonders of the Bathurst agricultural show.

A couple of days later a cheque from the Redfern Gallery arrived and Friend's trip with Margaret was on again – at least, he could now afford the first stage of their planned trip. A quarrel with Attilio, which meant a complete severing of ties between the two – for the time being – left Friend alone at Hill End, both relishing the freedom of being without responsibilities but also battling a degree of pessimism. 'I am middle-aged. I am beset with doubts' was the refrain in his diary.[19] Round about this time, also, a not entirely unexpected turn of events occurred:[20]

Donald must have been planning his proposal since he talked to Clarice Zander about it in England. Of course, I'd had all that time with him at the cottage before I went overseas, when there were just the two of us, and he used to draw the water from the well and heat it up so I could have a bath in his studio. Perhaps he peeked round the corner when I was in the bath. I haven't the faintest idea. But it certainly never crossed my mind that he was interested in me that way. I was just enjoying being there; painting, going about daily life with him.

I came up to stay at Hill End, just briefly, for a few days. We'd had a nice meal one night, drunk some wine, but then we always did that. Usually afterwards we'd listen to music, read or even sketch, but on this particular night he decided to read Michelangelo's love poems out aloud in front of the fire. Then I went off to bed. Suddenly Donald was in the bed with me. It came as a terrible shock. I'd always regarded Donald as a great friend, not a lover. I think he'd been setting it up, with the nice dinner and love poems. But there was nothing leading up to it. No declaration of his feelings or any show of emotion. No courting.

A great deal of fumbling went on. Poor fellow, he'd chosen a night when I was having a period, of all nights for a gay person. Thank God, is all I can say now. If I'd had a tussle with him, God knows where that would have ended. We couldn't have settled into cosy domesticity. I couldn't have lived with Donald. Donald was homosexual. But also, I wouldn't have been a free agent. All my life – even though you aren't conscious of it at the time – I'd had role models like Aunt Mary, who'd never married and used to do exotic things. Patterns are set for you almost without you knowing. In my case it meant I had no desire whatsoever to be beholden to a husband.

Neither Margaret nor Friend allowed this attempted pounce in the night to interrupt their friendship; nor did it cause them to postpone their trip north, and so, for the time being, their rapport remained much as before:

It's so long ago now. I clearly remember the event, but I can't recall what – if anything – happened the next day. There was no unpleasantness between us because of it. But it was a shock. I was very fond of Donald. But whom you really want to sleep with – I don't mean just sharing a bed with, I mean whom you really want to be intimate with, have sex with – is another thing. I was so innocent. I had no idea it was going to happen until he suddenly appeared in my bedroom.

Back in Brisbane

The other thing was, shock and fumbling aside, Donald was not very well endowed!

◆

At the end of May, Friend drove up to Brisbane in his jeep, accompanied by David Strachan, whose second show since his return home was about to open – at the Johnstone Gallery, naturally. By 14 June, Friend was in Brisbane and comfortably ensconced 'chez Olley', where he promptly took advantage of Margaret's studio to do a bit of work. Before Strachan had to head south again, he, Margaret and Friend made several sketching expeditions out of Brisbane.

One of their excursions was to the historic cattle station 'Coochin Coochin', south-west of Brisbane near Boonah, where the famous nineteenth-century landscapist Conrad Marten had painted several watercolours almost exactly a century before. Three elderly Bell sisters now presided over the old family homestead, which was set amongst extensive gardens filled with trees named after the distinguished, preferably titled visitors who'd planted them, including the Prince of Wales.[21] More importantly, on this day Margaret met for the first time the writer, poet and horsewoman Pam Bell. In not so many years to come, Bell would become a close friend of Margaret's, provide her with landscape-painting opportunities at her nearby property 'Aroo', and would herself become the subject of a prize-winning portrait by Margaret.

The reason for Margaret and Friend's delay in setting off on their adventure north was that Robert Haines had tentatively secured a commission for Friend to paint a mural at the original Lennons Hotel in George Street, Brisbane. Friend was tempted by the project. Although the mural might interrupt their time up north, in that they would have to come back after a month to do the job (Friend seems to have intended from the start that Margaret would work with him on the mural), the four hundred pound fee might mean that he could go on with her to New Guinea. So their holiday departure was postponed until Friend had sketched some designs to leave with the hotel for their consideration.

A few days later, finally Margaret and Friend were 'bowling along' in his battered jeep:[22]

No sooner had we left Brisbane when Donald said, Do you mind if I put down the windshield? The windshield, at least, protects you a bit from the wind. With the windshield off, it almost felt as if we were running along the road, so much wind was coming in. There was no way you could smoke a cigarette. In the back of the jeep we'd packed a water bag, a hamper of food and some li-los to sleep on. The plan was to stop wherever we wanted to draw and just camp out at night. We used to make a fire, boil the billy, cook a simple meal and then bed down under bridges or whatever. There was always some sort of shelter to be found in those days. We often went off the beaten track along the coast and I remember Donald saying, Anybody could land here and no one would ever know.

A few days into their journey, Margaret and Friend camped at Gin Gin Creek, out from Bundaberg. They woke the next morning drenched with dew. As they were breakfasting, a squatter and two stockmen rode past. 'I see mum's got some toast on,' the squatter called out in greeting.[23] A couple of nights later, after grinding over the worst road imaginable – chosen by Margaret – and failing to reach their destination, the pair stayed the night at a wildly beautiful, jungle-like spot surrounded by riotous foliage next to a stream, which was undoubtedly infested with crocodiles, in Friend's hyperactive imagination. But any defects Margaret showed as a navigator, he conceded, were more than made up for by her speedy efficiency in setting up camp and getting the evening meal going.[24]

Their next overnight stop was at Proserpine, a town set amongst cane fields and purple mountains, where nearly every house had its own whirring windmill. Friend was ecstatic, and probably Margaret too, to be reaching the real far north. But instead of camping out, because of the frequent rain squalls that interrupted the sunlight, Margaret organised them both into a hotel for the night:[25]

I had to be the one to go in and get the rooms. Donald could never be bothered with that. He never liked going into shops either. It wasn't exactly that he felt it was beneath him, it just wasn't his role. Once we were in the hotel, he loved telling stories of how he'd found a spy-hole in the bedroom wall – perhaps where white ants had eaten away the wood – and elaborating about what he'd seen in the room next door. Whether the spy-holes were there or not I have no idea. I never saw any. But his tales were certainly amusing.

Next it was on to Townsville. Here they planned to take a break from travelling and indulge in some tropical living:

Tas had a contact in Townsville who was to hand over the key to a house on Magnetic Island. We reached Townsville early in the morning and went to the address in the main street that Tas had given us. Oh, come down to the basement, the man said hospitably, it's cooler there. In the basement he insisted we have an OP rum. This was about nine in the morning. One rum followed another rum. It was a couple of hours before Donald managed at last to extricate us by saying, I think we'd better go and have some lunch. We staggered up into the midday heat and fierce light. After we'd located the jeep, Donald, decidedly the worse for OP rum, drove off very quietly, very slowly, down the main street. But then in search of something to eat he turned into a side street where there was a famous old-fashioned hotel called the Queen's Hotel and promptly hit a car. Unfortunately it was a one-way street and we were going down it the wrong way!

The car belonged to a man with a limp or a built-up shoe, and an enormous palaver ensued. Donald kept suggesting they go into the hotel and sort it out over a drink. That was so no one would smell the alcohol on his breath. I thought the only thing to do was to stay out of it, so I took out my sketchbook and went on drawing as if nothing had happened. The police turned up. More discussion. In the end we were let off with a caution for driving the wrong way down a one-way street and allowed to go on our way.

We caught the ferry over to Magnetic Island and stayed in the house Tas had arranged for us. I first became aware of bougainvillea there, the whole place was filled with branches of the most brilliantly coloured flowers. I also did a lot of painting. As always, being with another painter like Donald was very conducive to work. I was thoroughly enjoying what I was doing and he was thoroughly involved with whatever he was doing. It was a mutual thing.

The house at Magnetic Island was located, appropriately, at Arcadia Bay, an isolated beach edged with a riot of palms, pines, frangipani, mangos and bougainvillea, all flamboyantly and wildly mingled, according to Friend.[26] His description of the tin-walled house, which had a concrete floor and hinged windows propped open with sticks, is reminiscent of the Temperley shack at Era. It must also have brought back memories for Margaret of her Tully childhood and she bloomed in Arcadia's tropical lushness. For Friend, too, it was a place imbued with a special character, because he had lived in a cave on the island on his very first bout of adolescent wandering.

Margaret took huge canvasses to the beach each day and worked in the open from nature.[27] Friend, who couldn't face painting in oils in such an exposed manner, presumably worked more inside. The initial joys of Arcadian life, however, were soon interrupted by a telegram from Haines telling Friend that his design for the Lennons mural had been accepted. The nagging thought of having to return to Brisbane then began to inhibit Friend's work progress.

His admiration for Margaret remained undiminished. He describes in his diary the 'jovial indefatigable determination' with which she set about painting, 'splendidly ignoring the weather, the ants, the mosquitoes and the boisterous wind that blusters her canvas as though it were a sail'.[28] Almost exactly two weeks after they'd arrived – by now both of them a bit weary of Magnetic Island, but not of each other – the inevitable had to be faced. It was departure time. Friend locked up the jeep with their belongings inside, which he left in the yard of the man who'd plied them with rum in Townsville, then he and Margaret flew back to Brisbane:

It was Donald's mural, not mine. I was only the helper. Donald paid me to assist him with the painting. But we worked well together, as always he was great company. The mural went right round the bar and was made up of scenes of north Queensland: pubs, people sitting on chairs on verandas gazing out to sea, houses up on poles, women knitting. As with my other pub mural, we had to wait for the bar to close before we could begin. They'd leave us sandwiches, drinks and the radio, then we worked until we'd had enough; often we were up all night painting away.

Working on this mural was when I discovered that Donald could paint with his left and right hand. His left hand was the delicate one which he used most of the time. The detailed work was always done with this hand. But when we were up on a trestle or a ladder, rather than getting down, he would swap over and paint with the other hand. Much later, after he'd had the stroke, people used to say, Isn't it marvellous, he's learnt to paint with his right hand. I used to reply, He always could. The painting he did then looked different though, because it was much broader. It didn't have the finesse of the previous work done with his left hand.

Margaret's physical and nervous stamina, which Friend found to be much greater than his own, astounded him as they worked on the mural. That first weekend they painted furiously from 10 p.m. on Saturday night until 2 a.m. the following Monday. Apart from one breakfast, endless cigarettes and black coffee kept them going on, plus rum supplied by an amiable drunk in the small hours of the Sunday morning.[29] One wall of the mural measured forty by six feet, so it was obviously a mammoth job. While they were busy with it, Drysdale arrived in Brisbane on business of his own and stayed a night at Lennons. After he'd inspected the mural's progress, the three retired to his room for drinks. 'Alcohol has an unfortunate effect on Margaret, who becomes madly wayward and peculiar,' Friend commented later.[30] According to his diary, she spent the remainder of this night 'wildly slopping and daubing, making an unholy mess', as she 'tottered and reeled perilously on the scaffolding', to Friend's mixed irritation and fears for her safety.[31]

The passing references in Friend's diary are about the only real documentation of Margaret's drinking at this time. While Friend's exuberant way with words may not give an entirely accurate slant to her drinking, the entries nevertheless show that her problem was not to be solved as simply as moving away from France.

In July 1954, while the mural was being painted, Grace Olley was in hospital with gallstones. Her return home stalled any chance of Margaret going back to Townsville with Friend. To complicate things further, David Strachan also arrived to stay at Farndon around the same time. Friend immediately departed the overcrowded household and flew north, leaving Margaret intending to join him in a few days. But Grace Olley was then hospitalised again, which meant Margaret was delayed even longer. Having received a telegram from her to this effect, Friend left Townsville and drove on alone to Cairns to stay with his old Torres Straits Islander friends, the Sailors.

A few days later, Friend received a second wry telegram from Margaret. 'Mother's gallstones are a Millstone,' she wrote, before announcing that she would be in Cairns the following Sunday.[32] Friend, meanwhile, prowled about Cairns, discovering to his dismay that nothing of Malaytown's shanties and the vivid, noisy life of their inhabitants that he had so loved now remained. Even Alligator Creek, once so crowded with little boats and ramshackle jetties, had vanished.

Nearly a week later, Margaret was still in Brisbane. Yet another telegram from her arrived in Cairns. Grace Olley's gallstones were again the problem: they had to decide whether to operate or not. However, Margaret said she was now definitely coming in three days' time. At this time Friend concluded that due to the state of his financial affairs, a trip to New Guinea was out of the question as far as he was concerned. He was both disappointed and a bit relieved about this realisation. As he admitted to his diary, while he was looking forward to Margaret's company stimulating his painting, he felt that, like an old fox, he might be quite glad to get home to his Hill End lair by September.[33]

When Margaret finally did arrive in Cairns towards the end of August, there was no room for her at the Sailors'. After trying about twenty hotels and boarding houses, some temporary shared accommodation was found for her on a portioned-off veranda. They soon found that the accord they'd had in Arcadia was not immediately resumed. It was raining, which was no good for painting oils or expeditions in the jeep, and Friend was tetchy. As a consequence, Margaret soon headed off on her own:

I went off with a friend, Julia Famula, whose husband had a cane farm a bit south of Cairns at Edmonton. That was where I painted Cane Farmer's House *– the painting that was stolen from the University of New South Wales a couple of years ago and then turned up again. When Gavin Wilson was doing his north Queensland painters book* [Escape Artists: Modernists in the Tropics], *he advertised for its return and the painting was left on a church doorstep. At Edmonton, an Italian canecutter also fell in love with me and wanted to marry me. No good at all that would have been!*

There is a curious mention of Margaret's drinking in Friend's diary at this point, which seems to imply that sometimes her apparently drunken behaviour was in fact caused by nothing more than natural high spirits. He describes his exasperation when he'd tried to elicit an account from her of an expedition to the Yarrabah Mission south of Cairns. Instead of answering, Margaret kept dissolving into giggles and waving her hand in front of her face. Friend adds here that he often thinks she's quite drunk – only to discover that she hasn't had a drink all day.[34]

The tropical rain that had turned everything to mildew now finally eased, and Margaret and Friend were at last able to undertake some of the sightseeing he'd promised her:

Donald and I went up to Port Douglas and camped out on that long beach that runs south from Port Douglas, which I remembered from my childhood in Tully, when my father used to drive along it in his old perambulator motor car with the side boards. Donald and I slept under a tin awning where the fishermen kept their nets and watched for passing shoals. I've never been back up there since then, I think we had the best of it on that trip before all the development happened.

Back in Brisbane

The Nautilus Restaurant was already there in those days. It was run by a woman called Diana Bowden and her husband, Max. Diana collected shells; she used to slice through sections of them and make necklaces. It was long before anyone else thought of doing that and her necklaces were like really little pieces of sculpture. After Port Douglas we went up to the Daintree River, where Donald regaled us with gory crocodile stories.

As a final treat, Friend took Margaret out with the Sailor family for a picnic at Pine Creek, which was about the only place he found unchanged from when he first fell in love with Cairns. Harmony between the two of them was restored, and he was reminded of how much he valued a life like this, as they frolicked in a pool high up in a rainforest gorge and looked for native orchids with Lulu, one of the Sailor grandchildren. Friend's diary entry describing the day evokes the magic of the surroundings and the delight he and Margaret shared on this outing:

'Olley was enchanted with the wild ravine of Pine Creek, where the huge boulders are crowned, as though by over-ornamented hats of the nineties, by tiaras of strange ferns and exotics, and by trees and palms. Every tree there assumes a conglomerate of several trees embracing and wrestling, their writhing roots assume shapes as fantastic and interesting as the upper branches with their festoons of lianas and creepers, and the hanging gardens of ferns that 60 feet up extend feathery silhouettes against the sky.

'Olley scrambled and slid with us down mad rocky slopes into the black and green caverns where the waters rushed into remote subterranean streams.'[35]

Back at the Sailors' sugar farm, Margaret and Friend, exhausted but content, drank tea under the moonflower tree. It had been 'a perfect day', Friend reflected.[36] A week or so later, in the middle of September 1954, Margaret flew off to New Guinea alone. There she was to stay with her friend Geoff Elworthy, who had initiated the trip:

I met Geoff at an opening at Brian Johnstone's gallery. He'd had a property at Emerald in Queensland, which he then sold in order to buy his rubber plantation in New Guinea. Geoff was gay but I didn't know that then, I don't know if anyone did. He was quite a character. Donald used to say, The trouble with Geoff Elworthy is that he takes a breath in the middle of a sentence — you could never get a word in edgeways with Geoffrey because he was so talkative, and Donald had analysed it was because he took a breath in the middle of a sentence. Trust Donald.

Geoff also had an amazing quacking laugh. He would come along to openings with a big chequebook — one with multiple cheques on the page — under his arm, which tantalised gallery owners. He hardly ever bought anything, but he flashed his chequebook about. However, he was very entertaining, and insistent that I should come up and paint New Guinea. He talked about the wonderful colour and it was just too tempting. He paid my fare up this first time and on several other occasions, as well. I couldn't have gone otherwise, and in return I gave him a painting of Hill End. Geoff and I weren't involved romantically or sexually. He might have liked to imagine that people in New Guinea thought we were a couple, but we definitely weren't.

When I landed at Port Moresby on that first trip, the women had bare breasts and were wearing grass skirts, which I hadn't quite expected. To fill in time before going on to Geoff's plantation, I went to the Port Moresby Museum. It was a horrible little museum and at the entrance they had a hairy bird-eating spider — the size of a dinner plate — alive in a glass box. It was enough to scare the life out of anyone.

From Port Moresby Margaret took a cargo boat that was transporting copra and passengers up the coast to Elworthy's plantation, which was at Baramata Point, halfway between Port Moresby and the island of Samarai. According to Margaret, the drinks she was given that night at sea must have been laced with additional liquor:

I woke up a bit hungover in my cabin the next morning, to put it mildly. The boat was close in to shore, and when I went on deck in the early morning light I could see a native woman with a child on one breast and a pig on the other. That was my introduction to rural life in New Guinea.

I was put ashore in a lugger and next thing I was at 'Merani', as Geoff's plantation was called. He was living in style there, like an English gentleman, with his polished silver, nice crystal, gramophone for playing music and his Dobell paintings, in a two-storeyed house, surrounded by several acres of green grass on which he could beam out searchlights if he felt threatened in any way. But what amazed me was that he didn't have any artefacts except for a few beautiful carvings from the Trobriand Islands, which were not so far from there.

Margaret had come well prepared for work. She was equipped with oil paints and canvasses – canvasses being easier to carry than the board she usually preferred to paint on. Just to be on the safe side, she also had a folding saw stowed away her luggage, in case she needed to cut up a piece of board. Despite this planning, a painting complication occurred at Elworthy's that she hadn't foreseen:

While I was staying with Geoff I was bitten by a mosquito, which developed into a tropical ulcer. The pain was throbbing and it made working impossibly awkward. I was trying to keep the ulcer up, so I had to stand on one leg as I painted. Luckily a district nurse turned up and gave me what I suppose must have been penicillin to take, otherwise it would have just gone on boring in. As it is, I still get trouble in the same spot now. The nurse also warned me, Whatever you do, don't go in swimming. The sea there is milky green and full of the little pieces of coral that turn it that colour and get in your wounds.

I did lots of portraits and figure studies of the local New Guinean people at Geoff's plantation. But then I think I more or less exhausted the painting possibilities. I'd also run out of tobacco and started smoking black twist like the locals did. You had to be strong to stomach that. It was almost enough to make me give up smoking. Geoff was very keen then that I go on to Kwato Island – a most beautiful island – off Samarai, where there was a famous mission station. So off I went by boat again to Kwato.

Kwato was far from an average mission. It was started in 1891 by Charles Abel of the London Missionary Society, with initial help from fellow missionary Frederick William Walker. Abel, usually attired in tropical whites and a neat bow tie, was a man equally at home on a cricket pitch as in a church. Having left school at the age of sixteen, he signed up in London for a farming cadetship in New Zealand. The long sea voyage out instilled a lasting love of ships in him, but Abel did not enjoy farm labouring and soon ran off to live on his own in the bush near a Maori settlement. The sympathy he felt for the Maori people he encountered there inspired his return to London in order to become a missionary.

However, rather than going back to New Zealand as he'd intended, in the course of his studies he became attracted to the possibilities of missionary work in New Guinea. Right from the moment he arrived at Kwato, Abel was determined that the mission would be a place where Papuans would not only receive religious instruction but also be taught trade skills, such as ship building, and receive an education that would set them up for the

William Dobell's portrait *Margaret Olley*, which won the Archibald Prize amidst great controversy in 1948

Russell Drysdale's *Portrait of Margaret Olley*, 1948

Era Landscape, c. 1946

New England Landscape, 1947

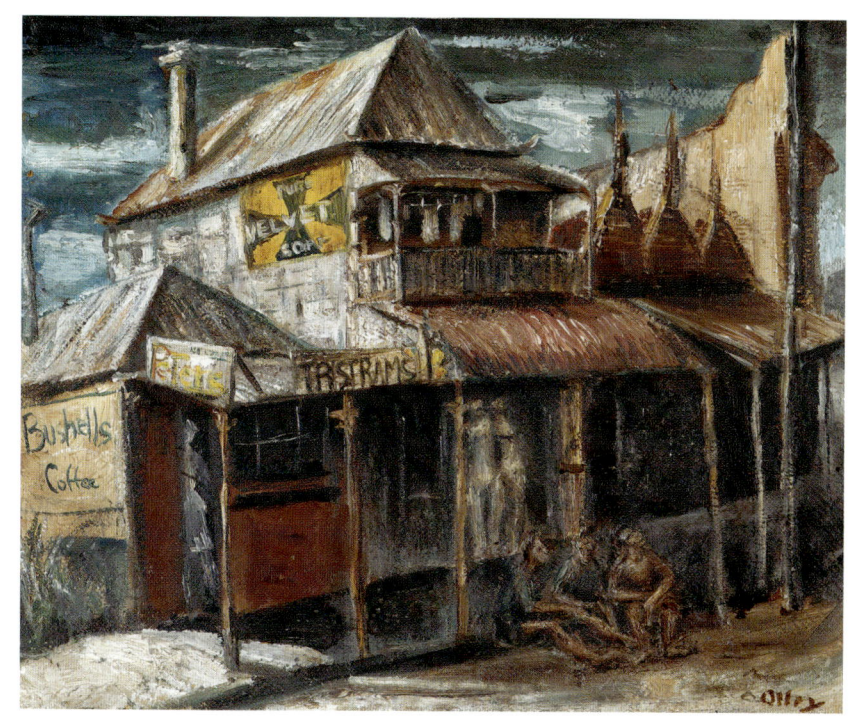

St Paul's Terrace, Brisbane, 1946

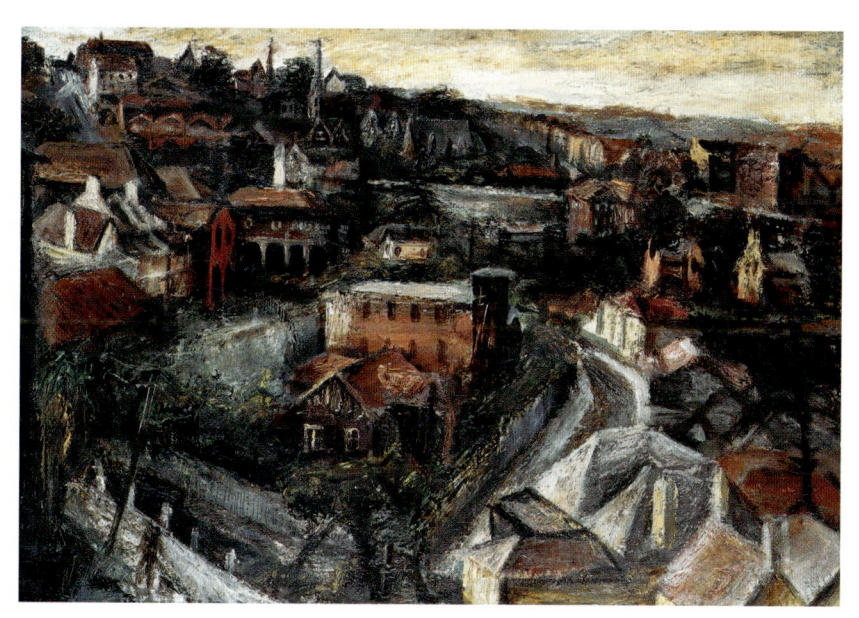

North Sydney, 1947

Pink Paper and Kippers, 1947

Still Life in Green, 1947

Hill End Ruins, 1948

The Cotswolds, c. 1950

Chateau Fontcreuais, Cassis, 1951

Gondolas, Venice, 1951

Concarneau, Britanny, 1952

Still Life with Kettle, 1955

Susan with Flowers, 1962, which won the 1963 Finney's Centenary Art Prize

changes occurring in their world, once they left the island. Abel and Walker as well filled in a malodorous black swamp on Kwato, ostensibly to put a stop to the malaria-spreading mosquitos that bred in it, but also to ensure that there would soon be an excellent cricket pitch on the island.

In 1892 Abel married Elizabeth Beatrice (usually referred to as Beatrice) Moxon, whom he had met aboard the ship that brought him from London as he made his way to New Guinea. Though Abel's unconventional missionary style became increasing frowned upon by the London Missionary Society, the 'Kwato way' flourished and Charles Abel continued to guide Kwato in an enlightened manner until 1930, when he was killed in a motor accident on a visit back to England. In the early 1930s, the second generation of Abels kept the mission active until it finally went out of existence in 1972. It's interesting to note that in the 1970s, several Kwato-educated Papuan New Guineans (as well as Charles Abel's son, Sir Cecil) were prominent in the Pangu Pati that dominated the winning coalition in the elections of 1972.

Margaret was not the only artist to sojourn at Kwato. The intrepid and meticulous flower painter Marian Ellis Rowan had visited at the beginning of the twentieth century and more recently William Dobell had called in. When Margaret arrived, she was given 'the big bedroom' in the middle of the house that had originally been Charles and Beatrice Abel's. At the time, their son Russell, his wife Sheila and two of their three children, Liz and Murray, were in residence in the big, open, wooden mission house set on a rise, with seductive views on all sides of sea and other China Strait islands.

'Geoff Elworthy, who was a planter friend of ours, just wrote and said, I want to bring Margaret Olley along to Kwato to meet you all,' Sheila Abel, now in her nineties, remembers.[37] 'I was scared stiff. We knew who she was because of the portrait that Dobell did of her. Margaret Olley, I thought, this famous person, how am I going to look after her? What sort of meals does she like? Which bedroom can I give her to sleep in – the house was very old and rather rickety by then. I remember my husband, whenever important visitors were coming, would paste large bits of white paper on the ceiling to hide the holes made by the termites.'

To Margaret, it must have been like landing in the middle of a gently unfolding tropical comedy of manners. The trappings may have been a bit worn, but life in the mission house proceeded at a genteel pace. Soup came from a silver tureen on the table. The main course, usually tinned meat, often sausages, was correctly served from the left-hand side by the girls who were studying there. A dessert of fruit and coconut cream or banana custard would follow.

'We had our main meal at night,' Sheila Abel describes their evening ritual. 'The girls who came in from the outlying villages to do a course of housekeeping and cooking shined the silver and brass, and decorated the big table in the dining room beautifully, with hibiscus flowers and sometimes orange African tulip tree flowers. Everyone dressed nicely for dinner, my husband would have worn a tie. There was always a lot of noise at dinner; the conversation was amusing and quick-witted.

'Margaret was lovely round the house. So bright and appreciative of everything, she cheered us all up. The only clear picture I have of her working is when, quite late one morning, she suddenly decided to set herself up below the veranda where there was a little garden area with a clothes line and, I think, some washing hung out on it. We were rather amused that she would bother painting it. The kindergarten children must have been having their lunch break because they immediately came running round her. Oh, you mustn't bother *Sine bada*, I said – "*Sine bada*" is the polite name in the Suau language for "the important lady". Don't worry, Margaret answered, I don't mind them being there. So they all crowded round and watched her painting.'

Murray Abel, who was a small boy when Margaret stayed, has a clear recollection of Margaret, a bit red-cheeked, also painting his mother's willowy figure bending over the veranda. Perhaps these were even the same work. Murray particularly recalls being fascinated by the way Margaret highlighted in her painting the orange mildew or mould on an old fibro wall.[38] Sheila Abel remembers, too, being startled and almost envious when Margaret, at the end of her visit, gave a painting of a Kwato scene to one of the senior mission girls, with whom she'd become friendly, as a farewell present.

Margaret remembers being impressed with both the mission's achievements and the quaintness of life there:

I was absolutely fascinated with Kwato. They had their own hospital; a boat-building place; a furniture workshop; they printed out a newspaper; there was a wonderful church high up on a hill; and the singing was out of this world. However, it seemed to me that the mission was, at this stage, also very taken up with the Moral Rearmament movement, which I was less keen on. I thought they sat about and prayed that something would happen quite a bit.

I was given the best bedroom in the house. I used to hear a scratching sound at night and wonder what it was. Then one day someone came into the room to look for some china or linen in a cupboard, and found it was about to collapse, it was so eaten away with white ants. That was the noise I'd been hearing.

The mission was teetotal, of course. They didn't know that I was drinking. Any imbibing had to be done very secretly. When I ran out of grog I'd catch the little boat to Samarai and do my own shopping – not letting them know what was going on. I mostly painted landscapes when I was there.

After leaving Kwato, Margaret further briefly explored the Milne Bay Province. At Milne Bay itself she stayed on the beach about half a kilometre from the village of Waga Waga, where Cecil Abel was living with his family. Here her experiences were richly mixed:

I was put up in a house made of native materials, which usually accommodated visiting administration officers. You'd walk along a jungle road and wonder why the trees were in such strange shapes. The reason was they were growing over military installations, old guns and the like, left behind from when the Australians and Americans fought the Japanese there in the Second World War.

One night when the moon was right, we went off with little lamps in a boat to catch fish. When we were holding our lights up high and looking down into the deep coral reefs, it was like flying over mountains in a plane. We went out for what seemed like miles, and then they said, Everybody out of the boat. Next I was standing in the sea with an enamel bowl with which I was meant to catch ... I had no idea what. For someone who had a few drinks under their belt, this was unnerving enough. Then one of the men caught an octopus and showed me how to turn it inside out. I still have an a image of the octopus crawling up his arm. Worse was to come. Suddenly the boat I'd come in took off at a great rate because they'd seen a turtle. I was left stranded in the dark in the middle of the ocean. Terrifying.

❖

By the beginning of December, Margaret was back in Brisbane with a great pile of New Guinea canvasses, enthusiastically reporting by letter to Friend in Hill End her plans for new work. In Kwato, Sheila Abel was reading a letter from a friend describing how Margaret had finally departed from Port Moresby laden with artefacts, many of them from Kwato, including a clay pot – and all of them hung round her neck for ease of carrying. Friend responded to Margaret's letter by praising in his diary her especial attributes of 'warm heartedness, energy, affection and uncertainty of herself in relation to other people'.[39]

Margaret's optimism on returning home, however, went temporarily sour a few months later. At the beginning of March 1955, Friend arrived back in Hill End after two weeks in Sydney to find a very different communication from her.[40] This letter was tender, sweet, painfully heartfelt – and also stunningly out of the blue. Simply put, in it Margaret asked Friend if he would consider marrying her. Margaret was not quite thirty-two. To build a life and exist by oneself can be terribly unsatisfactory, she wrote. Now is the time, she feels, that she must face reality, settle down and – if possible– have a family, even though she has previously pooh-poohed such ideas.

The letter goes on to say that Friend has said to her on several occasions how very fond of her he is, and that he thought that if he ever married anyone, it would be her. Did you mean this, Donald? she asks. Or were these just idle words spoken in the heat of the moment? The plea concludes with her saying that she is terribly serious and it has taken a lot of courage for her to write this way. She also adds that she sometimes wonders if others see the side of him that she adores so much – his principles, intelligence, calmness and drive for work – that is, coupled with his role as a teller of tales, which he does so well and so amusingly.

Friend, faced with the reality of his romantic daydreaming about marriage and Margaret, did a complete backflip. He sat down to answer straight away, probably out of shock. This time there were no flowery embellishments; but his refusal does make sense:

'I now know only too surely about myself, that as a husband I simply couldn't function, and that if Olley and I were of an age when passion is spent, we would be happy together, but as we both now are lively and sensual natures, such a marriage (in view of my own peculiarities) would be a pretence and result in mutual infidelities of a sort that could only result in self-disgust and disgust of one another. I only wish that this were not so.'[41]

Why had Margaret so suddenly, meekly and uncharacteristically (except, perhaps, for a faint hint of softening in her letter to Friend when she first came back to Australia, in which she wrote that she was afraid to say her painting was becoming more feminine) now suggested marriage as her chosen path?

I'd had a drunken night with a man and ended up pregnant. The most hateful thing about the whole episode was he gave me crabs. That was worse than discovering I was pregnant. It was quite disgusting, I think that really made me wildest. I could not have entered into a relationship with the father. That was not feasible. Donald thought Geoff Elworthy was responsible for the pregnancy. He always disliked Geoff, I think partly perhaps because of this assumption. I never said who the father was, but it certainly was not Geoff Elworthy.

In my drunken, muddled mind, when I first found out I was pregnant, I weakly and momentarily thought that asking Donald to marry me was a solution. If he hadn't got into bed with me at Hill End that night, I would never have suggested it. We had had a sort of domestic bliss when I'd stayed before I went away. We did get on very well. You can see from his diaries what he was thinking about me at this time and we'd just had that trip up north to Magnetic Island together. All that tempted me briefly to make such a proposal.

But despite what I said in the letter, which was probably blotted with tears, it was not what I wanted. I went to a woman friend and she arranged for an abortion. I've never doubted that I did the right thing. It was not upsetting to me. I've never wanted to have children. I've never had a mothering urge. It's just not an instinct that's in me. As for marrying Donald, for all the reasons I said before, that also would have been absolutely impossible.

There's no actual mention of her pregnancy in the letter to Friend, but it sounds exactly like a letter one would write in such a situation. The abortion appears to have left no residual emotional scars for Margaret, only relief that she did not have the child and a faint embarrassment about the proposal to Friend. Their friendship had teetered towards something else and, remarkably, continued, despite the perils entailed in overstepping boundaries, as Friend had done earlier and Margaret on this occasion. Reading Friend's diaries, one is struck again and again by his enormous affection for Margaret. If he hadn't been homosexual, it seems likely that they would have had an intimate relationship; what would have happened then is a more vexed and ultimately pointless question. And, of course, as Friend had pointed out in his diary back in London, if he hadn't been homosexual, he would not have been the person he was, to whom Margaret was so drawn.

11

Blame it on the Peacock Feathers

I used to lie in bed and look at a bunch of peacock feathers I had in a vase on the wardrobe. The French regard peacock feathers as very unlucky and won't have anything to do with them. I used to lie there blaming everything that was wrong in my life – by this time I was enjoying a little nip of brandy fairly regularly – on the peacock feathers. I'd promise myself to put more water in my drinks, anything to slow the drinking down. But then the next morning I'd just forget about it.

DESPITE THE DISTANCE BETWEEN MARGARET'S LIFE BACK IN AUSTRALIA and the vineyards of France, despite her new friendships and the bright colour that now suffused her paintings, the peacock feathers were hovering closer and closer to her. The image of her father, Joe Olley, who'd promised to meet her on her return home but had died instead, was also haunting her. And the secret tipple that had always chased both these phantoms away was becoming a habit on which she relied more and more.

Blame it on the Peacock Feathers

Towards the end of April 1955, Margaret arrived in Sydney for the opening of a new exhibition of her work at the Macquarie Galleries, primarily of Queensland and New Guinea still lifes and landscapes (although landscapes still predominated, the number of still lifes was edging up in this show). She herself made the wooden crates for transporting the paintings by road. The crates filled with paintings arrived a cat's whisker before Margaret did, as she chirpily told the *Mirror* the day before the show opened.[1] The reporter then asked her about Dobell's portrait of her, but, once again, she refused to comment. There were two Kwato landscapes in the exhibition and one of Wagawaga[2] from Milne Bay Province, some from Magnetic Island, and *Cane Farmer's House* was included. Among the portraits on show were several from New Guinea, as well as a painting of her cousin Pollyanne Wright at Wallamumbi; while of the still lifes, *Moreton Bay Lobsters* enhanced her depiction of fishy subjects.

Donald Friend came down for Margaret's April opening. Shortly after having replied to her letter proposing marriage the previous month, Friend had at last – much to his delight and that of the locals in the Hill End pub – won the Blake Prize, with *St John the Divine and Scenes from the Apocalypse*. He now bought a work of Margaret's called *Still Life with Kettle*. It's a painting that abounds with colour. The kettle and other objects, including a blue-and-white willow-patterned Farndon tea cup and a plate of fruit with plump, purple grapes, are spread out on a cheerful blue, orange, yellow and green chequered cloth. The *Bulletin*'s art critic quickly picked out the painting for comment. The prosaic title was a mask, he wrote, for objects that 'burgeon and flare in the most vivid yet admirably controlled profusion'.[3] The critic began his review by announcing that the show was the brightest, gayest and most vigorous Sydney had seen for many a day.

Friend himself thought the show was uneven. To him, several of the paintings were downright bad and others slapdash. The good ones, he felt, made it apparent that Margaret lacked a critical faculty to judge her own work and needed someone to help her choose what she exhibited.[4] Though Margaret was deeply appreciative that he had bought one of her paintings, she thought his criticism about her judgement may well have been unfair:

It was very touching that he actually bought a painting at an exhibition like that. I think he first saw it in my studio and decided he wanted it. Often what you intend, or aspire to, and what you achieve, are vastly different. But the Kettle is, I think, a painting where I did achieve a combination of colours that sing. Donald used to say that most work should be destroyed, but he never seemed to do it himself. It's all very well to say that, but it's not what most people do. If you destroyed everything you'd never have anything to show.

How do you judge your own works? That is a very difficult question to answer. It's like, When do you think a painting is finished? A while ago I said to someone that the answer to that is, When it's first begun – the first sketch could be the best. But then you go on teasing it like an old dog with a bone. I'm very guilty of that; at times I lose spontaneity. Sometimes, too, there might be a part of a painting you like, but ultimately you have to lose it. You do have to make sacrifices.

Misfortune seemed to dog Margaret in 1955. No sooner had her show opened on 20 April than a misadventure occurred. At the time she was staying with her old painting friend, Dorothy Buchanan (who had lived next door to Sam Hughes in Elizabeth Bay), and Dorothy's mother. Margaret had gone off from their Darling Point flat to a party thrown by her even more longstanding and dear friend, Frankie Mitchell. She was dolled up for the occasion in a black dress, which Moya Dyring had given her in Paris. The frock had originally belonged to Dyring's friend, Mary

Alice Evatt, and was adorned with a rose and a few sequins. The party went off well, as always with Mitchell as host. It was on the way home that disaster struck:

Drunk and disorderly again – that was the problem. I'd had too much OP rum, or whatever it was we were downing at the party. Coming back to Dorothy's flat afterwards, I got out of the taxi and tripped on the steps going up to the entrance. I fell down the stairs, landed on my nose and knocked myself out. Somebody must have heard the dull thud as I hit the ground and rung the police. The next thing I knew, I came to in a police car, in between two officers, and immediately threw up, probably over them. I was then driven to the Rose Bay police station. Every time I go by it now, I think of that occasion.

The sequence of events is a bit furry in my mind. I think I would have ended up spending the night at the police station, but I complained so bitterly they took me along to St Vincent's Hospital. At St Vincent's I kept saying that my friends would be worrying about me and I had to get home. Eventually I managed to convince them to let me make my way back to the flat. My nose might have been set at the hospital that night. But then I had to go back and see a doctor the next day. The doctor asked me if there was anything troubling me that I wanted to talk about. I said no, not really; knowing full well what he was getting at. He wanted to discuss the drinking. But you're very clued-up to that when you're drinking too much and quite defensive. I just felt like telling him to mind his own business. I had no intention of admitting I had a problem.

At the police station money went missing from my purse. It's called 'a little perk' – She'll never remember, they think, too drunk. But a drunk always knows how much money they have in their handbag because of what it means – that is, how many bottles it'll buy.

There was also another more permanent and rather sad consequence of the incident:

Before the fall I had a little retroussé nose. Sam used to say it was a wombat's nose. It turned up just slightly at the end like a wombat's. So now I can tell when portraits of me have been painted. People are always claiming that they have a portrait of me from the early days, but if it hasn't got that little retroussé nose it's not me then.

I suppose underneath I sort of knew what was going on with my drinking at this point, but even breaking my nose wasn't going to make me look for help from anyone.

While this mishap was taking place in Sydney, Donald Friend and Bonny Drysdale's brother John Stephen were house guests at Farndon. Grace Olley was 'in great kindly garrulous form', Friend reported in his diary. Aunt Mary on this occasion he found an irritating busybody, but nevertheless was amused by her goings-on.[5] Friend was in Brisbane to gild a door at Robert Haines' house. He then shot off to Cairns before Margaret returned for the opening of her exhibition at the Johnstone Gallery on 20 July 1955. The show received good reviews. Seven drawings sold but sadly no paintings. Notably, the Queensland Gallery did not purchase any works. Brian Johnstone had his own slant on why: 'I have often noticed before, and remarked on it, the Brisbane public's hostility to mauve and violet, and these New Guinea and Queensland landscapes of Olley's were full of it.'[6]

How ironic. The very thing Margaret had been struggling to instil in her work was now her undoing, as far as sales went – and in her home town, to boot, where tropical colour would not look at all out of place. At the end of August, Margaret's portrait of her niece Helen Rose with her mother, Laurel (Ken Olley's wife), was hung in the inaugural *Australian Women's Weekly* Portrait Prize at the National Art Gallery of New South Wales. This was a major new art contest (which unfortunately only stayed in existence for five years), which offered a one thousand five hundred pound prize and a special five hundred pound award for the best portrait by a woman artist. The entries went on show at the National Art Gallery of New South Wales in Sydney and then toured interstate.

In September, Donald Friend, having camped out, in more ways than one, with a wandering stockman he'd picked up on route down from Cairns, was once more resident 'chez Olley'. His exhibition 'North Queensland, 1955' was due to open at the Johnstone Gallery and he was about to paint more 'fantastic, rich, absurd, detailed decoration' on every inch of the door he'd already gilded for Robert Haines:[7]

Donald used to have breakfast at Farndon and then catch the ferry across to St Lucia and stay all day working at Robert's, so it was very convenient for him being at our place. My mother used to cook him chocolate cakes for breakfast and spoil him rotten. Then, whenever the opportunity arose, she'd invite all her friends over to meet him. My mother would say, Oh, Donald, tell us that story again. Donald never minded, so long as he had an audience, because he loved hearing himself talk. He'd re-tell his stories in another way to amuse himself.

(In his diary, Friend remarked that he was beginning to feel like a goose being got ready for pâté de foie gras, such was the culinary attention he received from Grace Olley.[8])

Towards the end of his stay, there was an exasperating incident with Margaret, similar to the one that had taken place the night they drank with Drysdale while working on the Lennons mural. It occurred at a suburban party thrown by a rich female art collector and her amiable husband, who was in manufacturing. Already that afternoon Margaret had been acting in a manner that led Friend to comment, as before, that he couldn't tell if she had been drinking or not. Then they were an hour late for 'the buffet supper and a lot of extraordinarily nasty drinks – liqueurs', as Friend described the refreshment provided.[9] The liqueurs were Margaret's undoing. She proceeded to get seriously – and comically – drunk, until she finally passed out, to Friend's vast relief. That, at least, is his version of the night.

Two days later Margaret had been forgiven by Friend, who reports on a perfectly pleasant and much more congenial evening at the Olley house. On this happier occasion, Margaret cooked a magnificent meal and her other guests included the Johnstones. A couple of nights later, after Friend had made a rather welcome (as far as he was concerned) escape southwards, Margaret dashed off a letter of apology for her behaviour, which ended up in the Farndon fireplace. More than a month later, in response to a letter from Friend, she finally sent off a long and repentant letter to Hill End. 'I'm afraid I wasn't a very good hostess,' she begins, 'and know that many times I must have embarrassed you, and have been kicking myself ever since, as I'd hate to lose your friendship, you know, darling, how fond of you I am, and always will be.'[10]

Margaret's letter contains a number of revelations. Although drawing like mad, she confessed to Friend that she'd gone 'completely dead' as far as painting was concerned. Nevertheless, she was still compulsively planning work. Seeing her paintings on display, such as the recent entry in the *Australian Women's Weekly* Prize, had convinced her of the need to adopt new strategies: 'I've decided I must A – unify my Blues, Purples and that green I use, and B – work with one of those beastly fluorescent electric lights, as they simply kick up those 3 colours, and all the galleries seem to use them.'

She mentions having won a second prize for a drawing, which had done nothing to help her bank balance, however. She also refers to her new model, a shop girl called Marg, whom she had been getting to pose for her. The letter also contains a very amusing account of a run-in with artist Sali Herman, who was in Brisbane for a show at the Moreton Galleries. (It was Herman, incidentally, who persuaded William Dobell not to scrap his initial attempt at painting Margaret's portrait back in the 1940s.) Herman had rung Margaret and asked if he could visit her, saying he'd bring a crab and a bottle of white wine. During their conversation, Margaret had suggested to Herman that he might like to draw Marg with her – and that they save the wine for dinner, because they wouldn't get much work done if they drank it at lunchtime.

Herman duly arrived with crab and wine – and promptly upset Marg, a Seventh Day Adventist, whom Margaret had been gradually coaching to accept posing in the nude, to such an extent that Margaret had not been able to entice her back afterwards. In return for his embarrassing and, one gathers, suggestive behaviour, Margaret set him to chasing thirty chickens that had escaped from their pen in the heat. To top off his errors, Herman's white wine turned out to be sweet. When Margaret pointed out to him that wine should be dry for crab, Herman replied that he thought all girls liked sweet wine, which annoyed her even further.

There are other snippets of news in Margaret's letter. Geoff Elworthy had paid her a fleeting call; Ken Olley's honey business was the best it had been in seven years; Elaine Haxton's husband, Dickie Foot, had been to dinner; Grace Olley was in Armidale with the Wrights, making Christmas puddings and cakes for relatives. Margaret finishes up her letter with a startling bombshell. A month earlier, her beautiful titian-lit hair had been shaved off: 'It's only an inch to an inch-and-a-half long all over. I feel awful, it's like wearing a fur cap, as it sticks up all over. But still, everyone says it suits me and makes me look 10 years younger. God only knows what I looked like before. With love Olley.'

Far from a Still Life

Which seems a good point to leave 1955.

❦

'Marvellous!!' Friend responded in February 1956 to a letter from Margaret announcing that she would be visiting him in a few weeks at Hill End, travelling from Sydney, where she was staying with Elaine Haxton and Dickie Foot at Pittwater.[11] (Although inwardly Friend groaned slightly at the thought of having to give up his bedroom for her and subsequently not knowing where to put his hands on shirts and socks.) Hill End was about to be inundated with artistic visitors, in fact. Jean Bellette and Paul Haefliger, who in 1954 had acquired their own cottage there, were the first on the scene, bringing Lynne Drysdale and another friend with them.

Margaret then came up earlier than anticipated. At the same time, repairs and renovations to Friend's cottage, including the installation of a stove in the new fireplace, were also happening at a furious pace. Next Tas and Tim Drysdale arrived. Drysdale had just bought a painting in Sydney from local Hill End resident, Mrs Lister, who had entered it in the 1956 Blake Prize. (Mrs Lister was the neighbour to whom Friend had given an oil-painting lesson back in the late 1940s.) After a goose dinner for seven accompanied by a tremendous amount of wine, dancing, shouting and hilarity – the rowdiest party Friend had ever thrown at the cottage – the Drysdales, Bellette and Haefliger finally departed, leaving Friend and Margaret alone. Margaret then stayed on at the cottage for about a fortnight:[12]

Jean [Bellette] and Paul [Haefliger] had given Donald some boxes of wall tiles. He and I laid them out into a patchwork quilt on the floor. Then Donald started to plaster them up onto the fireplace around the new stove. No, not that one, I'd say, move it a little bit to the left.

To the right? he'd ask. *When the plastering was finished it was really a thing of beauty and wonder. Straight away we both took out our sketchbooks and made drawings of it. I did a pen and wash; Donald finally ended up painting it oils.*

Though bad weather kept them cooped up most of the time, Friend was still 'most sorry' to see Margaret go, because he so enjoyed her 'wisdom, simplicity, sensitiveness and sweetness' – something he would not say of any other woman in the world, he added in his diary.[13]

In June 1956, Margaret had a show of drawings at the Johnstone Gallery, which included several works from her European trip. Gertrude Langer's review, which appeared in the *Courier Mail* the day of the opening, was unreservedly enthusiastic. 'She is at her best ever,' Langer wrote, echoing Grace Olley. 'They must not be considered as anything less "substantial" than paintings in oils,' Langer added. 'Miss Olley's line is open and firm, seemingly effortless and full of vitality and strength.'[14]

Yet the following month Margaret sent Friend a long letter in which he felt she sounded despondent. The letter ended with a new proposal of marriage from Margaret, or so Friend's diary implies: 'I wish, and quite often, that Olley didn't write such *enormous* letters (they are all six pages and more) and further, that when she is depressed, she had not the habit of ending up with a proposal of marriage.'[15] In October, there was another letter from Margaret, who had been about to come and stay with Friend, announcing that she had broken her ankle, which meant she would be in plaster for eight weeks, so the visit was cancelled.[16]

After this Margaret is not mentioned in Friend's diary for over three years. Clearly the phase – during which they had both in their own ways wanted to push their relationship to a more intimate level – now ended. Margaret was too innately wise and ultimately too protective of her calling as an artist to pursue it;

and Friend was too self-aware. (Also Friend's life soon went off geographically in a new direction when at the start of 1957 he moved to Sri Lanka.)

In light of Margaret's increasing reliance on alcohol, it seems likely that her proposals to Friend – other than her first desperate appeal – came from the bottom of a bottle. And his absence from her life now must surely have given her additional reason to seek consolation in drinking. For Margaret, the disappearance of not only a close friend but also the person whom she had viewed as a potential solution to her moments of despair (no matter how fantastical this vision may have been) could only have exacerbated the feelings of isolation that sometimes beset her.

The broken ankle happening at the same time only added to her woes:

I was down in my studio, probably a little bit drunk, and either getting into the chair or getting up, when I twisted myself and the ankle went. To make it worse, I was getting ready to have a show at the Macquarie Galleries in Sydney. On top of that, with the ankle in plaster, I couldn't get the tram to the local bottle shop. So I had to resort to inveigling a friend to keep me stocked up. Everybody knew about my drinking but I thought – or pretended to myself – that they didn't. So I was driven to measures like asking this acquaintance to secretly bring me bottles.

❖

In August 1956 Moya Dyring was in Brisbane for a show at the Johnstone Galleries, which must have had a cheering effect on Margaret. But despite this and her own upcoming show, Margaret was still painting very little. In August, another of her portraits, *Ann*, was hung in the *Australian Women's Weekly* Prize (though there is no indication of when it was actually painted). Then, in

October (while her ankle was in plaster), her Macquarie Galleries exhibition opened, which included a drawing she'd made after the tiling session on her last visit to Hill End, *Tiled Stove*, and two she'd done at Childers with Dyring, *Childers Garden* and *Childers Blood House*. There were also a number of works from her previous Brisbane show, all of which were drawings, mostly pen and wash.

The *Sydney Morning Herald*'s art critic was not impressed. Although unnamed, it was presumably as usual Paul Haefliger, which must have made the comments all the more stinging. The critic thought Margaret's brush moved ponderously over the paper and asked where the precocious talent displayed in her early paintings had vanished to.[17] It was a double buffeting, because only a couple of months before, Langer had described some of the very same work as 'effortless'.

The *Sun*'s review by Dora Sweetapple was kinder. 'Interesting and decorative,' Sweetapple began, then went on to say that she preferred the plain black-and-white works. 'Her handling of the medium is clever, although the breadth of line is uniform, there is no monotony,' she went on. 'Short strokes make a break in the line which gives it quality, and a close texture of lines in some cases gives a variety of tone.'[18] James Cook, in the *Daily Telegraph*, commented that Margaret's strong sense of form in her early works had been overtaken, perhaps in compensation, by her skills as a pattern designer in the manner of van Gogh.[19] The *Herald*'s critic, too, had noted the van Gogh quality but then dismissed it. In all, not exactly a confidence-bolstering round of reviews.

In the studio under Farndon, Margaret's tubes of oil paint remained largely unsqueezed. Dust collected on blobs of colour dried solid on palettes. Light flickered through lattice on unprimed boards. Although Margaret herself now says she never entirely gave up painting during this period, as far as anyone could tell back then, her talent was languishing.

Far from a Still Life

But she was still wielding a brush. In 1957 she painted the large mural at the New South Wales Leagues' Club in Phillip Street in Sydney. Towards the end of 1958 there appeared to be a resurgence of a more personal creativity when she won the sixth Lismore Art Prize of a hundred guineas for her oil painting *Lilies and Grapes*. However, it seems, this was not new work.[20] At the time her Lismore win was announced, Margaret was also busy putting last-minute touches to backdrops she'd designed for the Twelfth Night Theatre's production *Shadow of Doubt*.[21] The following year, 1959, as well as doing the sets for the Twelfth Night's *Le Bourgeois Gentilhomme* by Molière (which was directed by Rhoda Felgate), Margaret had two drawing shows as part of group exhibitions, one in Melbourne and one in Perth, both of which consisted entirely of European drawings. But, despite all this activity, there had been not been a solo exhibition of Margaret's oil paintings since 1955. And by 1959, not even much new drawing was evident.

Round this time Sam Hughes took himself off to London, and with him went Margaret's vague thought of eventually rekindling a more intimate relationship. Doors were closing now rather than opening. Any hurt – or simply surprise – at Hughes's sudden departure was numbed with another drink. There was no chance even to say goodbye to him:

Sam suddenly went off overseas. He stayed there for years. I used to get the odd card from him but that was all. John Richards had died. The rheumatic fever he'd had when young weakened his heart, I think. I remember visiting him in St Vincent's Hospital and then waving from the street to him up on one of the verandas where they used to put patients.

Blame it on the Peacock Feathers

I wasn't in Sydney when Sam left, but I heard about it from friends. They gave him a farewell party at the ship and apparently he was carrying on board everything under the sun from the flat: gas heaters wrapped up in bathmats, lights, a vacuum cleaner. The dancing Ivon Hitchens painting went off to London and he also took the blue-and-white Bristol glass that had been on display in the open glass shelves and slowly sold it in England. A lot of his possessions, such as the glassware, he stored at Theo and Katie Schlichts' place over there. I don't know what happened to the rest of the furniture, like the lovely settee in the white room. The Russian actor Dmitri Makaroff, who had played in Hassan, *took over the flat.*

⋄

The peacock feathers in her bedroom were now a smothering presence, as Margaret's drinking increased still more:

When I was out, I'd pretend I didn't want a drink. But I'd be thinking to myself, If they only realised how much I want a drink. Acting as if I wasn't drinking only made it worse. Oh, the madness that went on in one's brain. Insanity. Thinking that no one knew. I was very clever, so I thought, at hiding it.

I was a 'soak' drinker. I'd just have a little bit here and there. Brandy, mostly. Gin makes you depressed so I didn't drink that and I never liked the taste of whisky or beer. I didn't go on binges. It was as if I was drinking coffee – a little something here, a little something there; knowing the places where you could duck round the corner and have a nip. It becomes a way of life. I knew what it was doing to me. But at the same time, I just thought I was different from other people and it wasn't affecting me. Luckily, it wasn't for all that long. As for my painting, let's just say it had slowed down.

What caused the drinking to accelerate I don't really know. I don't think my father's death helped. He wasn't there when I came

Far from a Still Life

back, so I just carried on. It helped, the drinking. But I'm not going to blame it on that. It was always connected to shyness. I still am shy.

I'd never met anybody who had recovered from alcoholism. I didn't even know what it was until Theo Schlicht explained it to me in a letter back when I was still in France. I didn't know there was something that could be done about it, so there was no point in stopping. I felt I was doomed.

It got so bad that people were saying, She'll never paint again. I heard them saying it — not to be trusted; can't be relied upon; don't leave your child with her — which, of course, was very hurtful and a cause for another drink. I did still go through the motions of painting, occasionally. I couldn't say now if there was any oil painting at all or if they were just drawings. I'd pretend what I was working on was all right as I was doing it, but I knew it wasn't. I'd lost my ability.

According to Margaret, her family was convinced she'd never paint again. Or, at least, it seemed that way to her at the time. So, in an effort to help the situation, the family organised an alternative occupation for her:

They decided I needed something to keep me busy; something to get me out of the studio, where they didn't know what I was up to. It turned out to be a blessing in disguise, because it brought my problem into the public eye. Ken rented a shop. As far as I can remember Aunt Mary put a little money into it and I think Ken might also have helped financially. Then he and I went out and bought a truck-load of antiques and we started an antique business. I suppose they thought it would suit me because I'd always been such a collector of bits and pieces. The shop was called 'Olley's Antiques' and it was at Stones Corner, Buranda, just near the bridge over the railway lines. Ken was hardly ever there because he was busy with his honey. But Aunt Mary used to come over and help me look after it. I did a bit of pottery at home, that was it as far as work was concerned.

My mother came over one day to mind the shop while I attended an auction. When I came back she was so pleased with herself. I sold the table and six chairs, she announced proudly. The trouble was, she'd sold the lot for the price of the table. A doctor's wife had snapped them up. She couldn't have fitted the table and the chairs in a car, but somehow she managed to whisk them away immediately. It was dreadful — another round of explaining to do. My mother never gave a hand in the shop after that. But I have to say, she was never critical of my drinking. She stood by me through it all.

I remember getting a bit sloshed at the shop and coming home late. I might have passed out or had a little nap; probably I'd just had a little nap, then woken up and pretended I'd been busy doing something. But coming home, I had to change trams at South Brisbane, which was very run-down in those days, full of depressed-looking hotels, real bloodhouses. I leant up against a pole at the tram stop and thought, How can I go on living until I'm old enough to die? How will I ever live to be old enough to die? Wasn't that a terrible thought? Pathetic. Some moments in your life you never forget. I can still conjure up the feeling as I stood there thinking, How will I ever live to be old enough to die? If that's not a death wish ...

Round about now, artist Elaine Haxton intervened. Haxton, who was another Johnstone Gallery exhibitor, and her husband, Dickie Foot, would always catch up with Margaret when they visited Brisbane. 'They had the most interesting contacts from overseas,' Margaret recalls. 'Dickie, for instance, introduced me to Elspeth Huxley, the Englishwoman who wrote *The Flame Trees of Thika*, about growing up in Kenya.' This time, however (presumably when Haxton's 1959 Johnstone Gallery show opened at the beginning of August), Haxton was taken aback by Margaret's state:

Elaine and Dickie noticed the change in me. After they went back to Sydney this time, she wrote me a letter about her brother, who was an alcoholic. Only true friends will put friendship on the line by speaking out like that. A lot of people won't say anything because they think if they do, they'll lose a friend. Elaine's letter did help. I put it away in a drawer. Then I kept going to the drawer and reading it when I really felt the urge to have a drink.

But the person to play an even more critical role in Margaret's redemption from alcohol was Fred Jessup:

Fred, who'd arrived back from France earlier in the year, came up to stay with us while I was in the throes of all this. He helped decorate the shop. We bought a whole lot of old cane chairs, which Fred painted white and hung over the iron roof. He also painted a big mural of antique furniture on the outside wall of the shop and did the signs for it. When we'd finished working for the day and were going home, as we were strap-hanging in the tram, every now and then he'd point to an AA sign – ring this number for help – and nudge me. I used to wish he'd mind his own business. It's nobody's business but mine, I'd think. But, of course, it's so obvious to everybody. It does impact on them. Slowly you lose friends.

To Jessup, who had not seen her for six years, the change in Margaret was glaringly obvious. He had probably stayed with the Olleys twice during his trip to Australia in 1959. First, he was in Brisbane for his solo exhibition at the Johnstone Gallery in May 1959, then he came back again in October, just before he was due to return to France, when he was part of a group show at the gallery.

'She'd fallen into a trap with the grog,' Jessup says simply.[22] 'It catches up with you and then you can't control it. You didn't see her drinking. She did it secretly. But when I was designing the outside of the antique shop, I suddenly realised she was high as a kite. You're either born a painter or a copyist. Margaret was born a painter. She was painting beautifully those summers we spent at Cassis. Her paintings were good in Australia, but they were not as fantastic.'

So, rather than see Margaret ruin her life and squander her talent, on his second trip to Brisbane, Jessup was impelled to act:

It was Fred who finally brought it to a head. He said, You must go and talk to Lady Cilento about it. So I agreed to go over and see her, which was a cause for a celebration in itself – meaning, an excuse for another drink. It was all set up, of course. I've been waiting for you to come for so long, Lady Cilento greeted me. I really know nothing about your particular illness, she went on, but would you mind if I referred you on to a doctor who's a specialist? I thought that was marvellous. For the first time, somebody had identified it as an illness. It was all handled so professionally.

An appointment was made. That was also cause for a celebration. More drinks. Then I saw the specialist doctor and agreed to go into a clinic. As I was coming out of his rooms in Wickham Terrace, I caught sight of Peter Bennie, the minister, standing outside All Saints, the church opposite. Peter was a friend of Brian Johnstone, and he and his family often had meals with us. So I crossed the road and told him about going into the clinic. In admitting my problem to him, I'd automatically done the first step of AA. Oh, come over to the rectory and we'll have a little talk, he said. But even in the state I was in (probably I'd had a drink to give me courage to see the doctor), when he started going on about how we are all conceived in sin, it was too much for me. I don't believe in burdening people with guilt like that. But, at least, I had the chat.

Agreeing to the clinic was yet another cause for a celebration. That weekend before going in I really made whoopee. I knew they'd search me, so I devised an extremely clever hiding place I thought they'd never spot. When I arrived, out went the bottle I'd secreted. At the clinic they just filled me up with vitamin B and sleeping pills. Then the AA people came round and spoke to us very nicely. But I couldn't grasp the point of the meetings they kept talking about. What exactly do you do at the meetings, I asked the woman running the clinic, who was also a member of AA. Do you have a lending library, a restaurant, play records? She pulled herself up, gave me a funny look and then explained.

Her first week back home sober was particularly hard. Margaret tells a story about this time that is both funny and extremely moving. It's also very indicative of her personality. While she'd been drying out her family had cleared out her stash of alcohol, but, as she recalls, she'd cunningly planted a bottle where she knew no one would look:

As soon as I came back from the clinic, I thought, Well, everybody's done their best, now I have to live up to it. After which I took out the hidden bottle. Then I started mowing the lawn. It was Brisbane and approaching summer. I was hot and red in the face. I'd mow for a bit, then I'd stop, go inside the studio and pick up the bottle. I'd look at it and say, It's either you or me. It's either you or me. I'd go back to mowing the lawn. I'd sweat away in the blazing heat. After a little while, I'd go back inside and pick up the bottle. It's either you or me, I'd say again. It was my own personal battle. When I felt strong enough, I poured the contents of the bottle down the sink.

Margaret's powerful act of will in refusing to drink was crucial, not just for her painting, but also for the longevity she's now enjoying. It was a far wiser decision, even, than not marrying Sir Francis Rose. To stick by it, while still moving in the party-loving circles she did, must have required yet more stamina. Occasionally, these days, you'll see Margaret pass a cork from a bottle, opened for friends, under her nose in fleeting appreciation. But she's never lapsed since her first sobriety:

For quite a while afterwards I'd have nightmares that I started drinking again. I'd wake up crying because of it. But apparently that's part of the process. AA really helped to begin with. Because the AA people had been kind enough to come and see me in the clinic, I felt obliged to go along to a meeting. It was the least I could do. It had also occurred to me that perhaps listening to other people who'd drunk a lot might just be the cure I needed. So I went to a meeting. You had to walk down a side path to the back of what had once been a fine old Queensland building in the city, but by then was badly deteriorated.

I just sat there and listened. I kept going back for years after that. Twice a week; always the same group. I'd look round each time to see if the same faces were there – usually they were, which was comforting in itself. I never spoke. I thought if I spoke I might go back to the drink. The group I went to, no one was asked to speak, anyway, until they'd attended meetings for about six months. Finally I was asked to speak – the most embarrassing thing that's ever been asked of me – and I refused. I just couldn't. But it's a marvellous philosophy. Anybody could apply it to their life. I don't go to meetings anymore, but AA is still like breathing in and breathing out to me. I'm very comfortable with it.

Part III
1960–2005

12

The Flood Tide

*I regard stopping drinking as very much starting another
life; in other words, like coming back from the grave and
celebrating life – which is what I still do every day.
Everything was fresh again. People used to say I'd
become a workaholic, but I felt I had to work to
make up for the time I'd lost.*

THE 1960S WERE, INDEED, CAUSE FOR A CELEBRATION – OF A STRICTLY non-alcoholic variety. For this was the decade when the butterfly dreaming of nearly forty years earlier in Tully would pay off dazzlingly.

'I feel so much better and have Freddie to thank, from the bottom of my heart, for the first push in the right direction,' Margaret wrote to Donald Friend, a week before the Christmas of 1959, in her first letter to him since she had emerged from her 'cellar', as she put it.[1] 'The rest is up to me to maintain my sobriety and paint again,' she continued humbly.

Far from a Still Life

One could date Margaret's period in her 'cellar' from her first drink on that wondrous night at Sam Hughes's flat in the mid 1940s. But that seems unfair – alcohol certainly didn't interfere with her life at that time. In France, both in Paris and at Cassis, drinking wine was so taken for granted that it hid, for the most part, any intimations of a susceptibility. But Margaret herself, or at least in retrospect, was aware that she might have been having more glasses 'socially' than she should by the time she left London at the beginning of 1953, and as the 1950s progressed in Australia, close friends did notice her drinking, even if they didn't say anything. Nevertheless, it seems safe to assume that only in the years from 1955 to '59 did it really become a problem for her, especially the last two years of that period.

Having said all this, one must remember that Margaret's drinking never brought her any real public disgrace. Hers was not a descent into the gutter witnessed by the wide world; rather it was a private slide that transformed her haven under Farndon from studio to cellar. As Margaret says simply now: 'I have an intolerance to alcohol, so I mustn't touch it.'

Margaret's stay in the clinic was only brief – about ten days, by her reckoning. Not only did she soon resume painting again; in a very short space of time, having vanquished the vineyards of France and the peacock feathers for ever, she produced works so joyous and ravishing in colour that they caused her friend Ron Sabien to burst into tears when he attended an opening of them at the Johnstone Gallery; and made critics unanimously chorus with Grace Olley and Gertrude Langer: it's her best work ever. Her paintings broke gallery sales records and she collected a swag of prizes.

Farndon resounded even more than before with artistic and happy repartee as Grace Olley served up three shoulders of lamb at a sitting, with Margaret providing the mint (picked through a neighbour's front fence) for the sauce. On such occasions, Mrs

The Flood Tide

Oll issued invitations that read: 'Sherry at seven; carriages at eleven' so guests knew exactly the evening's timetable.

The Olleys' antique shop drew in Johnstone Gallery regulars with its eclectic bric-a-brac and in 1962 even a stylish Barry Humphries turned up, in tow with Brian Johnstone. Humphries, on the look-out for French glass, was eager to meet the artist he'd admired since, as a boy, he saw Dobell's portrait of her reproduced on the pages of his mother's *Women's Weekly*, or some such reading matter. Humphries himself had been drawing and painting all his life, and suffered frequent punishment at junior school in Melbourne for 'sketching scurrilous caricatures of school masters under the desk'.[2] He owned his first set of Winsor & Newton student oil paints and a small easel at about the age of twelve, with which he attempted to emulate the landscapes of van Gogh and Cézanne. Later, in his teens, he was a pupil of George Bell and attended a Saturday morning life-drawing class at Bell's studio in Melbourne. So Humphries may well have had several reasons for wanting an introduction to Margaret Olley, his boyhood art idol. Margaret insists that he was also gathering local material for his show *A Nice Night's Entertainment*, which was playing at Her Majesty's Theatre in Brisbane in 1962. But Humphries himself swears it was more Margaret and French glass that attracted him to Olley's Antiques and the 'denseness and richness' of its interior.[3]

This was as well a time during which Margaret spread her wings geographically. She partially escaped from the family nest at Farndon and established a base of her own in Sydney – and became besotted with a city that was neither Brisbane nor Sydney. These years also brought several affairs of the heart, and very much of the body, with heterosexual men, and saw her intrepidly embark on a number of painting excursions, quite often entirely on her own, to exotic locations outside Australia.

Though tinged with the sadness of her first experience of the deaths of friends, the 1960s would be the most remarkable decade of Margaret's life so far – perhaps of her entire life. The 1940s had been dedicated to studying. The '50s had been about travelling, and the shock of discovering art and life outside Australia. This was followed by the almost inevitable crash, as she entered her thirties, of coming back not just to Australia, but to an even more parochial Brisbane. In the 1960s, Margaret revealed her true strength as an artist. By not allowing her work to be stymied by drink, she proved that hers is a talent that transcends negativity. She is a painter whose creative impulse is essentially life-affirming and celebratory.

❖

Donald Friend was still in Sri Lanka when he first heard of Margaret's recovery from alcoholism, in a first-hand report from Fred Jessup. Friend had rowed out into the harbour at Colombo and plucked Jessup (on his return to France) off his liner, so he could catch up with the news of Australia. Margaret had rung Jessup when his ship stopped in Fremantle to assure him of her having undertaken a cure. On his arrival in Colombo, Jessup then filled in Friend. Wise after the event, Friend claimed that he, like everybody else, had long known about Margaret's 'secret drunkenness', but could do nothing about it.[4] He also, quite unfairly, lumped the bulk of the blame on Geoff Elworthy for having allegedly dumped Margaret when she was pregnant.[5]

Friend did, however, also write a letter of encouragement to Margaret, which prompted her Christmas 1959 epistle to him.[6] After the almost formal acknowledgement of her new-found sobriety that begins Margaret's letter, the rest of it is chatty, funny and packed full of day-to-day family gossip and local happenings.

Aunt Mary, who'd acquired the title of 'the Scrabble queen', was now a permanent resident at Farndon. Although Margaret found the frequent polite differences of opinion between her and

The Flood Tide

Mrs Oll 'nerve-racking, in their unspoken words', Aunt Mary and her mother were also her main family support during her crucial first period of alcoholic abstinence.[7] Margaret remembers, in particular, how Aunt Mary suggested she put some paintings up for sale in the antique shop. Not long afterwards some people from out of Brisbane, who were on their way to buy a tank stand, stopped at the shop and ended up buying a painting instead. 'It was very uplifting for me at that time,' Margaret says.

Though she made very little of it in her letter to Friend (as one might expect), attending church was also important to Margaret's recovery:

Peter Bennie had visited me in the clinic and I did appreciate that. Although I loathed the dogma, I loved the ceremonial aspect of the High Church: the incense and the music. I looked forward to going each week; it put an order in my life and helped nurture the spiritual. Alcoholism affects you three ways: mentally, physically and spiritually. That's why it's such a difficult illness to treat. Mentally, you become almost a schizophrenic; physically, anyone can see what happens; and spiritually, I think you sort of die. In the end I found church interrupted painting too much and I stopped going. I realised I could tune into a service on the radio while I was working and still get as much from that. But it was a great help in the beginning.

Now that she was attempting to paint seriously again, Margaret's efforts to divide her time between the Farndon studio and the antique shop were not without problems:

Aunt Mary used to say, You go on painting, dear. I'll go over and open up the shop for you. Then often I'd get a phone call: Oh, Miss Olley, I hope you don't mind me ringing, a strange voice would say, but I'm in the shop. Your aunt's here sound asleep and we don't like to wake her. Aunt Mary used to nod off after meals – instead of taking

NoDoz, it was a case of Doz-off. Anybody could have walked in and made off with what they liked. God only knows what went missing.

Aunt Mary and my mother did grind on each other. Didn't you hear me, Mary? my mother would call out. It's all very well for you, Grace, Aunt Mary, who left it too late to get a hearing aid, would answer back. Wait until you're deaf. The big camphor laurels round the house used to drop their leaves in winter and the pair of them would rake away furiously at the leaves. They loved lighting bonfires once they'd swept them up. I think it got the angst out of their systems. Eventually, my mother and Aunt Mary realised they needed a little bit of distance. Aunt Mary took over the flat down below, which Ken had by now vacated, but still came up and had the evening meal with us.

The problem of Aunt Mary's snoozing was temporarily alleviated when Margaret converted the back room of the shop into a studio.

There were some changes in the streets of Brisbane during the 1960s. A new crop of shops selling television sets suddenly appeared and a profusion of modern veneer was added to city buildings. There was also an addition directly connected to the Olley family, which was becoming a familiar sight. A truck with an intriguing advertisement destined to be much loved by Brisbanites was frequently spotted driving in and out of town on the road from Ipswich:

That was where Ken had his hives. The first time he pulled up outside Farndon with the honey truck, he ran up the stairs excitedly saying, Come outside. My mother went out, took one look at 'By Golly it's Olley's' on the side, and was immediately offended. Take that thing and park it round the side, she ordered. I'm not having it in front of the house.

◆

The Flood Tide

Of all Margaret's Johnstone Gallery friends, Pam Bell, the physically strong and raw-boned horsewoman who later wrote enthusiastically about art and penned poetry, was particularly helpful at this time. Bell not only dropped into the shop to see how Margaret was going – the odd encouragement like this from friends really helped – but also provided her with new inspiration for painting. There were probably reciprocal benefits for Bell, given her increasing interest in art, but even so, Margaret was deeply grateful when Bell invited her out to Aroo, at Boonah, west of Ipswich, near the historic Coochin Coochin she'd earlier visited with Donald Friend:

Pam and her mother, whom everyone called Kieser, both lived at Aroo. Kieser, who had been married to Bert Bell [dead by then], was an extraordinary pioneering woman, real salt of the earth. I adored her and her presence really added to my visits to Aroo.

I went to stay with them several times. I painted landscapes and did drawings outside and inside the kitchen. Apart from the painting, it was nice just to be able to get out of Brisbane. In return for going to Aroo, Pam often stayed with us at Farndon, in the little guest bedroom, if she wanted to go to an opening. She'd arrive with a basket filled with fruit from the property and bunches of grasses and interesting seed pods she thought I might like to draw. Scratchy Aunt Mary would be sitting in the dining room reading the paper. She'd look over the top of her glasses and see Pam with her basket in the hallway. Hmm, she'd snort, then go back to reading the paper. Why don't you like Pam? I'd ask. Very self-opinionated, she'd reply.

When I first met Pam her main interest was gymkhanas and going to the Brisbane Club. Then she took up writing. She had a column in Vogue *and books of poetry published. But she also started falling in love with artists, which I don't think made her terribly happy. Although eventually we became less close, I'll never forget her great kindness in asking me out to Aroo.*

It was about this same time that Laurie Thomas came into Margaret's life. Although asking Margaret about her love life is a bit like trying to get blood out of a stone, Thomas is one person she's willing to acknowledge. It's easy to see the attraction. The poet Elizabeth Riddell described the thick-haired Thomas as having a long handsome face that was sometimes lively and sometimes saturnine.[8] He was a man addicted to bow ties and timeless suits. Riddell knew Thomas from his time as a journalist; she'd had a desk next to him at the *Australian* newspaper, where he was arts editor and features writer in the late 1960s and early '70s. According to her, Thomas was equally at home at a gallery opening, a pub bar or a newsroom. Though words were his forte, he would have preferred to have been an artist, because painting was a 'more joyous' profession, as he once told art writer Sandra McGrath.[9]

From 1952 to 1956, Thomas was director of the Art Gallery of Western Australia, then in 1961 he succeeded Robert Haines as director of the Queensland Art Gallery, a position he held until 1967. At both the Western Australia and Queensland galleries he was a keen promoter of the work of Aboriginal artists.

But most important of all, Thomas was regarded by almost all artists as a kindred spirit:

Soon after I stopped drinking, we started having a torrid affair in Sydney. He was the most wonderful lover. I think he was slightly drunk all the time but he enriched my life. He just loved art, life and love, and was good mates with everybody. He'd been married in Perth and had children, and he did get married again in Brisbane, but some people never like to be owned. The same is true of me – I've never liked to be owned.

I was always hoping that I might be able to help him to stop drinking. But the very week he came up to Brisbane I was painting at Pam Bell's and missed out on seeing him. It was the end of our affair because he met someone else. I thought, Well, that's over – and just as well, because it might have changed my life. I don't know if I could have been involved with someone who drank like he did then. We stayed good friends afterwards because that was the sort of person Laurie was. Later, when he was being considered for the position as director of the Queensland Art Gallery, I was asked about his drinking habits. I bit my lip and answered, Oh, he drinks, but no more than anybody else. I always felt a bit guilty about that. But I wasn't going to jeopardise his chances of getting the job.

I had a little dalliance with Hal Missingham, too. I always think if people talk a lot about their sex life then there's something wrong with it. If they don't say anything, then it's all right. I'm certainly not going to make a list of men I've had affairs with, but I will mention those two.

Apart from new encounters, romantic and otherwise, Margaret's old friends from Paris were also returning to Australia to pep up her life. In May 1960 David Strachan finally arrived back, having spent much of the previous five years living in London, where he had been deeply involved in Jungian analysis, as well as studying at the C.G. Jung Institute in Zurich. When his ship stopped at Brisbane en route to Sydney, Strachan came ashore with a Vespa, on which he and Margaret scooted happily about. Strachan then went on to Sydney and began teaching at East Sydney Technical College.

At the end of July, Moya Dyring had another show at the Johnstone Gallery and stayed in Brisbane for a month.[10] She and Margaret went on a trip to Tweed Heads to paint the prawn fleet. Dyring also helped out in the antique shop and, to Margaret's relief (since it would otherwise have fallen on her shoulders), found time to paint over one hundred decorations for Ken Olley's

'By Golly it's Olley's' honey stall at the Brisbane Royal Show in the Exhibition Ground.

The next event was Margaret's own show at the Johnstone Gallery. Though she had earlier confided to Friend in her Christmas letter that she was hoping to have a show there in April 1960, it was not until October that she did so. It was her first one-person show in Brisbane in just over four years and the first time she'd exhibited at the Johnstones' new gallery at Cintra Road, Bowen Hills.

As early as 1954, the Johnstones had opened a salon for viewing paintings at their home in Cintra Road to run in conjunction with the Brisbane Arcade gallery. By the end of 1957, Brian Johnstone had been diagnosed and hospitalised with tuberculosis, an illness not helped by working in the dank basement gallery. On top of that, the Brisbane Arcade space had become too cramped for showing the larger canvasses of modern artists. So in December 1957, after a farewell exhibition for artist Jon Molvig (who'd been living in Brisbane since 1954 but was now moving to Melbourne), the gallery in the Brisbane Arcade closed.

It was almost a year before the Johnstones reopened at Bowen Hills. Marjorie had inherited the property where they lived and it included two workman's cottages (one of which they already lived in). The Johnstones now converted these into a series of linked galleries. When you read through the list of artists who showed at Bowen Hills for the next twelve odd years, it's like reading a *Who's Who* of Australian art, at least of the eastern coast. The gallery's Sunday morning private viewings soon became an eagerly awaited ritual for Brisbane art lovers. Writers, architects, musicians and theatre people were often in attendance, as well as artists and collectors. Not only that, but the Johnstones also encouraged the Twelfth Night Theatre to stage productions in the gallery's gardens, so it became even more of a cultural meeting place.

The galleries themselves were surrounded by tropical gardens in which sculpture was often displayed, adding to the ambiance. At the art events, on sunny Sundays those who drank were supplied with copious glasses of wine and left to wander in the dappled light and shade of the garden, which meant that the gallery buildings were never too crammed and pictures could be shown to their best advantage:[11]

It was the best gallery in Australia. I don't think there's been anything else like it. Brian was a battler, I must say. In the Brisbane Arcade, sometimes the only thing he would have sold all day were a few postcards to school children. But then those children became his best clients years later, so those postcards were very worthwhile. The artists and buyers that came to the Sunday morning openings were like a close-knit family. It was a great period in painting. Brian had early Ray Crooke and Bob Dickerson exhibitions; Lawrence Daws was another of his artists; he showed Charles Blackman's 'Alice in Wonderland' paintings; Donald exhibited with him, and I also set Tas up to show there.[12]

Brian had the Cintra Road galleries organised in a very clever military-like fashion. He had a gallery where the current show was on; the residue of the show before would be in another room, so if you'd missed it you could go and catch up with it; and there was a stockroom as well. But people weren't allowed to roam around willy-nilly. He really concentrated on the current show – you had to ask to see anything else. Everyone was sent a little notice at the beginning of the year saying what shows were going to be on, and you were asked to tick which ones you were interested in. If you'd ticked a show, you were sent an invitation to a preview. The galleries also had views out onto the garden to freshen up your eyesight – that was another great plus.

It was actually at the Johnstone Gallery that Margaret was introduced to Ray Crooke. Crooke's first solo exhibition there in

September 1960 was his biggest to date and from then on he would become one of gallery's most popular, fashionable and successful artists. In the next ten years or so, it would become almost a prerequisite for Brisbane middle-class art-loving homes to have a Ray Crooke painting of the tropical north and its people on the wall.[13] It's easy to see why – his works, particularly those that show the interiors of native dwellings, also have a coolness about them that's a welcome contrast to the heat of Brisbane. When you look at his paintings you actually feel that you've stepped inside their dim, sun-sheltered world. Since their initial meeting at Johnstone Gallery, Crooke and his wife June have remained firm friends with Margaret:

Ray was an artist who was always moving his studio from location to location, which fascinated me. They'd been up at Thursday Island, then in Melbourne. Soon after this they went to live at Yorkies Knob, near Cairns, where I stayed with them a bit later on. After that they came down to Sydney. Eventually they went north again. No matter how he tries to get away, the north keeps claiming Ray, as it usually does with people. I've managed to escape – but only just.

Just before her show opened in October 1960, Margaret (who, for once, was ready for it ahead of time) and Pam Bell flew to Sydney for the gala event of the Australian art world that year – Tas Drysdale's retrospective exhibition at the Art Gallery of New South Wales. Drysdale was now nearly fifty and internationally recognised. The retrospective was a big occasion.

'Tas was very proud – and almost bursting with emotion,' Margaret wrote later to Friend.[14] Friend, being in Sri Lanka, was virtually the only close friend missing. As Drysdale sat on the official dais like a terrified dummy, he had a sneaking feeling in his heart, so he confessed to Friend by letter, that Friend would somehow appear with a grin on his face, as he had so often in the Rose Bay days.[15] Drysdale's parents gave a party after the gallery ceremonies at the newly opened Chevron Hilton Hotel in Macleay Street, which was *the* sophisticated venue of the day – nothing could have been more modern or more of the moment – and home of the fabulous Silver Spade night spot. Later on, Bonny and Tas threw another party at their flat in Challis Avenue, Potts Point.

Margaret's Johnstone Gallery show was a quieter affair but still significant. She was back on track again, with twenty-four new oils, most of them now flower studies or still lifes, with just a few landscapes, including one called *Boonah Landscape*, and an almost equivalent number of drawings.[16] Several of the drawings were of Coochin Coochin and there were others done at the Tweed with Moya Dyring. 'Miss Olley has shown herself an artist to be reckoned with in any assessment of serious Australian art,' Frederic Rogers summed up in his appreciative review in the *Sunday Mail*.[17] Rogers liked her still lifes best and praised particularly her 'delineation of antiques – there is real vigour in her glassware – and strangely enough, of fish.' They were garfish this time. There were also two platters of unidentified fish, which appeared in other works, and a painting titled *Fish with Check Cloth*.

While her show was still on, Margaret dashed off a letter of congratulations to Donald Friend about an exhibition of aluminium sculptures he'd just had at the German Cultural Institute in Colombo (co-sponsored, not surprisingly, by the famous multinational aluminium supplier Alcan). 'You've done it again, Congratulations Congratulations: I'm so thrilled and excited, I could give you a hug,' Margaret began, 'if only I could see those wonderful aluminium sculptures.'[18]

Apart from the generosity of the compliments that she showered upon Friend, what is notable – and startling – about Margaret's letter is the poignancy with which she describes her own struggle over the last year: 'It wasn't easy to close the cellar door shut – but working for this exhibition, for me, has been like mounting a steep flight of steps – step by step – to sanity, clarity and freedom – and faith in myself – proving that I can draw and paint. Lord Donald, you'll never know the depths of despair I'd reached.'[19] That last sentence starkly harks back to the image of her leaning despairingly in the night against the pole at the tram stop, surrounded by the bloodhouses of South Brisbane and wondering if she could bear living until she was old enough to die. It's a cutting reminder of just how painful this period of her life really was – something she'd barely admit to now.

The letter then reverts to her normal cheerful self. Interestingly, by this stage Margaret had been converted to television and tells Friend how well a TV story that Brian Johnstone had done on her show went, despite being only in black and white. The segment, billed as 'Brian Johnstone discusses Margaret Olley's paintings', went to air on 13 October 1960 in the ABC's daily half-hour magazine-style program *Woman's World*. If Mrs Oll and Aunt Mary hadn't succumbed to the lure of the television by now, one imagines this would have sent them scurrying in search of a set.

In April 1961, the Queensland Art Gallery staged its own Drysdale retrospective which ran until June. In May of this year, the cottage at Hill End finally passed out of Friend's hands via Bonny Drysdale to Donald Murray.[20] Although Friend had agreed to this in 1959, as a means of repaying the money the Drysdales had lent him for his fare to Sri Lanka, the transfer of the deeds did not go through until 1961. Murray, who'd finally found employment in Sydney with Yates Seeds, stayed at the cottage intermittently until he retired in the late 1960s and thereafter moved permanently to Hill End, living on at the cottage until shortly before his death in 1988. Following his cremation, Murray's ashes were scattered in the rose garden at the cottage and are now marked by a plaque.

The Flood Tide

Margaret was continuing to find sobriety rewarding. In August 1961 she had a successful show at the Macquarie Galleries in Sydney. James Gleeson wrote in the *Sun* that it was the dozen or more still lifes in the exhibition that offered her 'the greatest scope for the singing harmonies of colour she loves and understands so well'.[21] The desire Margaret had brought back from France to infuse her work with colour was clearly now fulfilled. While her themes were conventional, their appeal was intensely sensual, Gleeson continued. They were 'songs in colour' he added – reiterating his earlier metaphor – 'gay, light-hearted and rejoicing in the richness of living'.

In a few short sentences Gleeson articulated exactly Margaret's intentions about her art and also encapsulated her new resolutions about life. Gleeson was not just a critic, but also a painter of acute sensitivities himself, now recognised as Australia's first surrealist. So it's not surprising he was intuitively in tune with a fellow artist. Gleeson would continue to extend the comparisons between music and Margaret's art and write even more eloquently about it in future years.

Back in Brisbane after the opening of her show at the Macquarie Galleries, Margaret finally met Vivien Leigh, who had so captivated Sydney's artistic world over ten years earlier. Leigh was now nearly fifty and divorced from Laurence Olivier. She had been diagnosed as manic depressive and, having undergone shock treatments the year before, had returned to Australia in June on another tour with the Old Vic company.

When Leigh arrived at Brisbane airport at the end of August she was wearing a pale blue linen suit and wide-brimmed hat. She was photographed by the *Courier Mail* like royalty, nursing a large bouquet she'd been presented with, a cigarette elegantly held in her hand behind the flowers. After the first flurry of attention had subsided, she and her companion John Merivale visited the Johnstone Gallery and socialised with the Johnstones. Leigh was also entertained by Ron Sabien – and it was Sabien who took Margaret, this time minus red long johns, to see Leigh on stage at Her Majesty's Theatre:

When we went backstage she invited us to join her and John Merivale for a supper at the Bellevue Hotel. The Bellevue was the wonderful old hotel that occupied a corner near the Botanic Gardens. All the stars used to stay there. It had wide verandas on two sides with iron lace round them and a very gracious dining room. It was the Bellevue which, despite everyone's protests, was pulled down overnight when Sir Joh Bjelke-Petersen was premier. Our supper with Vivien Leigh was a very special evening. She was absolutely exquisite and so pleased that we'd joined her. We hardly ever see people, she said. Everyone either thinks we're too busy to go out or they're too intimidated to ask us. I've never forgotten that.

Leigh's remark also served to reinforce Margaret's often repeated premise that one of life's secrets is, as she says, never to be afraid to ask, provided you don't mind being refused.

◆

By the beginning of 1962, Fred Jessup arrived back for an extended stay in Sydney, where he joined David Strachan in teaching at East Sydney Tech. Donald Friend had also arrived in Sydney on New Year's Eve, 1961. Friend had appeared just in time for a party given by Lynne Drysdale (who was newly married to her first husband, Bill McLaughlin) at which a number of old friends, including David Strachan, Fred Jessup, Justin O'Brien, Jeffrey Smart and Donald Murray were present and at their best.[22]

In 1961, Friend began to feel he was stuck in Sri Lanka's environment of decaying beauty and the peace that he'd initially enjoyed there had vanished.[23] As he became more and more depressed by Sri Lanka's tropical languor he felt an increasingly desperate need for the intellectual life he'd previously enjoyed in Sydney. Also his painting was slowing down, or so he complained in his diary.

He resolved to go on a pilgrimage to Sydney in search of a flat in King Cross, where he might recommence his life. But having stayed a few days in early January with the Drysdales at Challis Avenue, he flew to Perth for his exhibition of gold-leaf 'ikons' at the Skinner Galleries. The show was opened in sweltering heat, made even hotter with television lights, by none other than Vivien Leigh 'who was brief and gracious and had them all fascinated'.[24]

In April, as well as trying to buy a house in Darlinghurst, he met for the first time the art critic Robert Hughes, at this time very young, *very* lively and 'fizzing with ideas' as Friend put it.[25] By the end of July 1962, having shipped off his furniture to Sydney, Friend had finally left Sri Lanka for good. A month later he moved into a tiny house he'd bought in Hampden Street, Paddington, and the artists' enclave of Paddington was underway.[26]

Meanwhile, David Strachan bought a Paddington terrace in Paddington Street. In between teaching and painting, Jessup helped Strachan strip skirting boards and Margaret, if in Sydney, was often a house guest. This was really the beginning of Margaret's long connection to Paddington – a suburb many people tend to assume she's spent her entire life in, so familiar a figure is she, pushing her walking frame around the streets, pausing to investigate a throw-out, picking the odd agapanthus or two from a nature-strip garden or briskly making her way to a gallery.

Fred Jessup had a lot of contact with Margaret in 1962. Together they went on painting excursions in Queensland and northern New South Wales. During these trips Jessup made sketches that he developed into the oil painting *Tarring Nets, Tweed Head*, now owned by the Art Gallery of New South Wales, which he believed to be his best work of that year.[27] Jessup also had an exhibition at the Johnstone Gallery in September, which would have taken him to Brisbane. His time spent as a house guest at Farndon coincided with another important event in Margaret's life:

Once I was out of the clinic and started getting interested in life again, I used to watch people coming into the shop with their dogs. Inevitably it wasn't long before I felt I wanted a dog myself. We used to have fox terriers when we lived on the Tweed River and then cocker spaniels, but I couldn't make up my mind what breed I wanted now. One day somebody arrived with a whole carload of pug dogs. They had little faces like pansies and I thought, That's the dog for me. I arranged to get a pup from the next litter and so Bonnie Sue, as the breeder had named her, entered my life. The problem was she turned out to be the runt of the litter and needed an awful lot of attention. Fred came to the rescue again by taking Bonnie Sue to bed with him and acting as a mother, which stopped her crying.

Jessup's comforting paid off. Bonnie Sue flourished and soon became a subject for Margaret's work. Portraits of her appeared regularly in exhibitions over the next few years and one still hangs in Margaret's front sitting room in Paddington.

However, it was Margaret's series of portraits of Aboriginal women that provided a new departure in her painting this year. Many, such as *Zillah*, are reclining nudes. They lie on brightly patterned lengths of material supplied by Ron Sabien, with just a suggestion of still life behind them. Others show clothed figures with more obvious arrangements of flowers. In *Susan with Flowers*, Susan, wearing a red, pink and blue striped dress, stands pensively by an exuberant bunch of red hibiscus and gloriosa lilies intermixed with pink oleanders. In another haunting work, bought by Margaret's friends Shirley and Ron Wright, a model in a white dress, possibly Dina, sits lost in thought beside a pale bunch of Eucharist lilies from Farndon's front garden.

The nudes, which were described as Gauguin-like by the press at the time, are not provocative. Viewing them is like being admitted to the studio under Farndon. They are women languorously resting from tropical heat and the outside world in a coolly luscious retreat. While it's been said, by Gertrude Langer for one, that they contain no social comment or context – unlike, for instance, Drysdale's paintings of Aboriginal people – their expression, particularly in the eyes of clothed models such as Susan and Dina, is telling.[28] It's not exactly trapped, more wistfully withdrawn into another place of the heart.

The impetus for the studies came from two nudes painted towards the end of 1961 of Odette McLeod, who was the young wife of Adelaide antique dealer Bruce McLeod. Her mother was a French Creole from Tobago and her father from Canton, China. Odette and McLeod had met in Trinidad when he was on a trip overseas, and were now spending a year in Brisbane before returning to Trinidad, where McLeod would have an antique business for the next thirty-odd years. During his year in Brisbane, McLeod made several purchases at Olley's Antiques and started chatting to Margaret. Subsequently he designed the window of the shop for her and helped to organise the interior. Margaret then asked McLeod and Odette to lunch:

She had lovely apricot honeyed skin. When they came for lunch I immediately said I'd love to paint her. That led to me asking if I could paint a nude. I was really very thrilled when she agreed. At another lunch, after I'd finished the painting, I could see Odette was very upset. I asked Bruce what I'd done wrong. He told me that Odette was pregnant and I'd forgotten to paint the wedding ring on her finger. So I quickly put one on.

Odette, in fact, was not nude when she posed on a length of peacock-coloured Thai silk in the leafy latticed underworld of Farndon, but had panties on, which Margaret painted out. McLeod remembers Margaret telling him and Odette beforehand how she'd been inspired by Modigliani's nudes, and there is a similarity between *Odette* and the lush female studies that the Italian painter and sculptor produced in Paris in the early 1900s.

The colours in *Odette* are rich and jewel-like. Round Odette's neck is a jade pendant that picks up the green of the silk underneath her and on one wrist she wears an open-ended gold bracelet she designed herself. Her thick black hair rests against plumped-up chartreuse yellow cushions on a length of magenta and white striped material. As she's lying on her side, unless you look carefully her pregnancy is not that obvious. Although Margaret would have liked to have painted Odette more, she could only pose twice, because a few weeks after their baby daughter Tanya was born, she and McLeod returned to Trinidad. Before they went Margaret did a drawing of the baby, which is now a treasured belonging of the grown-up Tanya. McLeod recalls that as Margaret presented them with the drawing she said that she never usually gave paintings away, but in their case – perhaps out of gratitude for the inspiration Odette had provided – she'd make an exception.

'You become so bold and desperate when you want to do something,' Margaret told oral historian Hazel de Berg a few years later, in reference to plucking up courage to ask Odette to pose.[29] 'It's the same with anything you really want,' she continued to de Berg, 'even if it's a flower in somebody's garden. You wouldn't normally get it, but because you want to paint it you sort of go in, even go in the dead of night . . .'

Margaret's models for the studies of Aboriginal women came from OPAL (One People's Australia League) House, a hostel in Russell Street, South Brisbane. The hostel, which was close to where Margaret used to change trams at South Brisbane on her way to work, provided boarding-house accommodation for Aboriginal women and its co-founder, Mrs Joyce Wilding, arranged for the women to pose for Margaret.

Glenn Cooke, a curator at the Queensland Art Gallery, has written that Margaret was breaking new ground with these studies, in that the reclining nude is more traditionally the domain of male Western artists. Further, he argues that it was also unique for what he calls 'a settler society' female artist to paint such studies of indigenous women.[30] Christine France has pointed out in her book on Margaret that, while the paintings are essentially concerned with light and form, because there is no emphasis on a racial context, they also inadvertently reflect Australia's assimilation policy of 1963.[31] To Margaret herself, the paintings were a much simpler matter.

She found the Aboriginal women – some of whom were of mixed race, including of Islander and Chinese descent, and whose skin was often plum-coloured – far more 'sympathetic' to paint than professional models or the ubiquitous bouffant-haired women, all desperately trying to look alike, of 1960s Brisbane. Although the women were extremely shy, they usually relaxed once she'd tuned her studio transistor to the hit parade they preferred to the classical music she normally painted to.

Not everyone at Farndon was impressed by Margaret's new paintings:

I'd often bring up works in progress from the studio to have a look at them in different surroundings and light. When I was doing the Aboriginal nudes, Aunt Mary used to take one look and snort, Thank God for clothes. If Aunt Mary ever actually liked what I was doing, I used to have to wonder what was the matter with it.

Aunt Mary wasn't the only one to object to the new nudes, however.

Margaret's Cilento's grandmother, Nanny McGlew, was by now living in a flat under the Cilentos' house in Annerley. The other grandmother, Sir Raphael's mother, was also living with them and the two old ladies didn't really get on. My mother, to give the Cilentos a break, used to ask Nanny McGlew to stay a few nights with us. She was given the spare bedroom where everyone stayed. It was quite a small bedroom, more like a passageway, with just enough wall space to hang one of the nudes. Oh Grace, Nanny McGlew said to my mother as soon as she was shown in. Could I please have a towel? I can't sleep looking at that. So the nude had to be covered up with a big towel for Nanny McGlew.

1962 was also the year Margaret began her relationship with the legendary hermit painter Ian Fairweather, who was by this time over seventy and increasingly frail. Fairweather had intensely blue eyes and retained the polite English manners that had been instilled in him during his childhood. 'Tall, thin, battered and bearded' was how Donald Friend described him when Margaret introduced them the following year.[32] Photographs of Fairweather at work in his Polynesian-style hut, with its Tantric Buddhist invocation in Chinese calligraphy above the door, show him with a pipe in one hand and a house painter's brush in the other, with a large assortment of open, dribbled-down paint tins nearby.

Despite his reclusiveness, Fairweather had received a small amount of international recognition as an artist and was something of a beacon to a whole range of Australia painters by this time. Traces of his influence can be found in the output of many artists, including the early works of luminary John Olsen and, later, even Brett Whiteley was indebted to him for inspiration. In 1962 Fairweather, despite his advancing years and lack of physical robustness, was at the height of his powers as a painter, producing works mainly influenced by Cubism, Aboriginal art and his long-standing love of Chinese culture. 'Controlled and yet

The Flood Tide

intensely felt,' writer Murray Bail has described them.[33] 'Poised between abstraction and figuration,' Doug Hall, the director of the Queensland Art Gallery, wrote of Fairweather's painting style, in a foreword to the catalogue for the gallery's exhibition of his work in 1994.[34] Mystic, might be another word.

Fairweather, who was born in Scotland, had had a life of roving. Soon after the start of the First World War, he was captured by German soldiers in France and then spent about three years in various prisoner-of-war camps. In between attempts to escape, he was permitted to read about Chinese and Japanese art and study Japanese language. It was during this period that both his dread of confinement and his love of the Oriental began – two factors that would dominate the rest of his life.

He first came to Australia in 1934 and came into contact with the Melbourne art identities George Bell and William 'Jock' Frater. Following this he took off on more wanderings, spending many months in Peking, painting in poverty and living away from Westerners. In 1936 he had his first one-person show, at the Redfern Gallery in London.

Back in Australia in 1938, he was 'flabbergasted' to find a perfect studio in a vacant cinema theatre at the beach at Sandgate, near Brisbane.[35] However, after a disaster in which the paint he used – dry colour mixed with water – began to crack and fall off his works, he retreated to Malaytown, Cairns – the same refuge Donald Friend had discovered a few years earlier. At Malaytown, Fairweather lived and worked on a boat on Alligator Creek, frightening Islander children with his crankiness to the point that they called him a bogey man.[36]

Fairweather's wandering in and out of Australia continued over the next few years. In 1947 more disaster struck when one hundred and thirty of his paintings that had been sent from Melbourne to the Redfern Gallery failed to arrive. When these works finally reappeared – their packaging apparently having been opened en route – they were damaged beyond repair. Fairweather, who suspected foul play of some sort, was deeply disturbed by this incident, to the point of paranoia.

At the end of 1952, he undertook a hazardous journey from Darwin to Timor on a homemade ten-foot triangular raft made of waterlogged planks of timber and three old aircraft tanks from a dump. This trip may well have been intended as the first stage of a journey to London, but after sixteen days at sea Fairweather collapsed half-dead on a beach on the Indonesian island of Roti.[37] Having refused an Australian government offer to negotiate for his return to Australia, he was then deported – as a British citizen – to Singapore. He finally arrived in London in September 1952, where he saw for himself that his works were, indeed, ruined.

On returning to Australia in 1953, Fairweather built his first hut in the bush calm of Bribie Island, about sixty-five kilometres north of Brisbane. The island remained his primary home for the next twenty-odd years. It was here, in the 1960s, that he produced his most significant paintings. Often, as in works such as *Shalimar*, *Monastery* and *House by the Sea*, these were recollections of his life in China thirty years earlier.

Margaret was first taken to Bribie Island to meet Fairweather by Laurie Thomas:

Laurie was a bit nervous about seeing Fairweather. I think he'd earlier taken some works of Fairweather to the Redfern Gallery in London and then something had happened to them, or he hadn't followed up on them. So he asked me to come along. Laurie was also a great friend of [artist] Lina Bryans and had some fascinating stories of when Fairweather had rented a room from her in Melbourne in 1945. Lina Bryans was apparently thrilled to have him in residence. She kept popping out to see how he was doing in the studio: Now, Mr Fairweather, is there anything else I can get for you? she'd ask. She did it so many times Fairweather became completely fed up. Yes, he replied. I'd like a hammer and some nails. She bustled off and brought him back the hammer and the nails. Fairweather promptly proceeded to hammer the door shut so he couldn't be interrupted anymore. He himself used to go in and out through the window.

Bribie Island is about an hour's drive north of Brisbane and separated from the mainland by the jade waters of Pumicestone Passage, inhabited by dolphins, dugongs and turtles. Once there, you look back at the line of sometimes olive, sometimes purple rocky peaks of the volcanic Glass House Mountains so revered by the Gubbi Gubbi Aboriginal people. The low-lying island itself, with its white beaches and coves of mangroves, must have been a real beachcomber's paradise when Fairweather first lived there. Even when Margaret started visiting him, the bridge to the mainland hadn't yet been built (although it was started soon afterwards), there were only a few beach houses and, apart from the company of swamp wallabies, echidnas and frilled lizards, Fairweather led an isolated existence:

I'm a great admirer of his work, especially his Chinese period. He used to say the Glass House Mountains reminded him of when he lived in Shanghai and the lovely mountains there. My visits over were quite formally arranged. I used write to him and wait for a reply before going over. I addressed him as Mr Fairweather and he always called me Miss Olley. He was living in a glade of casuarinas, way off the road. Unless they knew where to go, people never found him. It was a good spot. Casuarinas give a lovely filtered light, the hanging needles on the branches hum when the wind blows through them and the fallen needles are soft for sleeping on.
  At that time I think he only had the one open hut; it was made out of bits of old timber and the roof was thatched with reeds and bark. His bed was a little palliasse on a frame up off the ground, rather Indian-looking. He was mainly painting in gouache on paper.

I'm allergic to oil paint, he used to say. Then, about the second or third time I went over, he announced he'd found a marvellous paint in one of the local shops called kalsomine [a commonly used interior house paint in the 1950s]. I'd hate to think what that did to him or his paintings.

He was very hard to give anything to. I tried once to give him a Chinese set of black ink and brushes, but he just wouldn't accept it. But he quite enjoyed taking me and whoever I'd brought over – we used to catch the car ferry across – on picnics to his favourite haunts. Sometimes we'd collect driftwood with him. Usually, I think, he slept during the day then moved around and painted at night. Pam Bell often came over with me. I also took Donald to meet him.[38]

Fairweather's castaway living undoubtedly appealed to Margaret and revived memories of her own beach–bush childhood. She would also have felt simpatico with him as an artist, although the friendship was certainly not based on her worship of Fairweather's genius. It soon became, more than anything, a demonstration of a side of Margaret of which the public is not so aware but of which close friends repeatedly talk: the warm, ever-generous Margaret who would do anything for a friend:

After a while I became his representative. Lucy Swanton from the Macquarie Galleries used to stay with me and visit him on Bribie. I think she suggested that I do it. He'd never had any water at the hut and as he became older he felt that he'd like to be able to have a bath. You know, Miss Olley, I used to live quite well when I was in Shanghai, he'd say. So I had to go to the Caboolture Shire and ask them to put water on. They attached the pipe for him to have his shower to a tree, because there wasn't a real building to put it on. Fairweather was still hankering for a bath. I just said, Oh, I think a shower would be safer.

He used to redo the thatched roofs of the huts with more rushes every so often. One year they started leaking because the possums had got to them. When I went over to see him just after the schools had gone back in late January or early February, he'd been to the tip, collected all the old lino that the campers had put on the sand around their tents during the holidays, and draped it over the thatching to make it waterproof. It looked dreadful. He had the shiny surface to the inside and the back to the outside. But after a while the backing aged and it looked a bit like straw, anyway.

Later on, when he was ailing, I lobbied so he could have a shed built where he could paint out of the weather. I could go on and on about poor Fairweather. I remember visiting him in hospital when his pet goanna had bitten his ear. Then there was another time he had a big injury on his skull because, walking down to the shops, he passed under a magpies' nest and they'd dived down and pecked his skull.

In July 1962 the Drysdales, who were among Margaret's closest friends, suffered a terrible family tragedy when their son Tim committed suicide. The family was left reeling from the blow. Tim suffered from manic depression and Tas and Bonny had already been enormously worried by his behaviour over the previous few years; Bonny even came to dread the phone ringing in case it brought more bad new of him. Tim's death now propelled both his parents into a period of acute anguish from which Bonny would never recover, and which would lead to the almost complete unravelling of Tas at a period when he might have been basking in his most public success. And in the aftermath of this, Margaret herself would soon be playing a role.

At the time Tim died, Margaret's professional good fortune accelerated. It was announced in July in Perth with great fanfare that her portrait of Pam Bell had won the Helena Rubenstein

Far from a Still Life

Australia-wide portrait competition, which carried a prize of three hundred guineas. Her winning spree of nine painting prizes in three years was underway. Not only was the cash, as always, welcome but at last the tables had turned – now she was the artist who'd painted a prize-winning portrait, rather than forever the subject of a prize-winning portrait.

Unfortunately, the portrait of Bell no longer exists so it can only be judged from reproductions. In it Bell wore a double strand of pearls, a very '60s cream suit with big buttons and an indistinct pattern of squares, and bore a slight resemblance to Princess Alexandra of Kent. She had a notebook and pencil in her hands, and the abstracted, faintly worried expression of an author on her face. When *Vogue Australia* ran a short piece in 1962 about the artist and the sitter (under a similar one with Dobell), Margaret stressed that, above all, it was the face of a subject that had attracted her.[39]

Bell, in turn, described how there was no real posing for the portrait. She'd just sat in an armchair in the studio under Farndon and continued with some writing; wearing an old pair of men's woollen socks to keep out the cold and to protect her nylons from Bonnie Sue, the pug. She'd had to hold her head still for some of the vital painting, Bell added, and Margaret had sometimes asked her to check in the mirror to see if she thought her nose was long enough or her forehead high enough in the painting. The answer to these questions would have had to have been yes, judging by a newspaper photograph of Margaret and Bell standing on either side of the portrait and looking pleased, at the official handover of the cheque in the department store Finney's auditorium in Brisbane in early August.

On 1 September 1962, Margaret collected her second prize, in the representational oil section of the sixth annual Redcliffe Art Contest, with a figure study called *Barbara*. Then the following month it was time for her next show at the Johnstone Gallery.

The Flood Tide

Even before October there was a buzz about the exhibition. The invitation was striking: a wide card with a black and white drawing of Odette McLeod on the front. Inside there was a short but glowing tribute by Brian Johnstone acknowledging Margaret's years of dedication, hard work and unfailing courage that resulted in her emergence now as a painter 'of major importance in Australian art'. Tas Drysdale (presumably as a member of the Commonwealth Art Advisory Board to which he'd been appointed that year) had already purchased the nude *Odette* for the Commonwealth Government.

There were eleven drawings, including a Paddington street scene and Tweed Heads fishing-scapes. Nine of the oils were nudes of Aboriginal women from Joyce Wilding's hostel. The prize-winning portrait of Pam Bell, marked 'Not for sale', was hanging, and Bonnie Sue was represented as *Pug Dog*. In the past (and again in the future) critics might not have all been in agreement about Margaret's work – but not this time. It had taken over twenty years, but now, at the age of almost forty, Margaret produced the show that took everyone's breath away.

'I'll never forget the opening on the Sunday morning,' Ron Sabien remembers.[40] 'For me that show was the big moment in Oll's life. That was when she came back out of the shadows. It was springtime and the gallery swam with flower paintings. Seeing the whole exhibition together for the first time, it had such colour. The paintings of the girls were beautiful too. I hadn't seen any of those until they were completed. People snapped them up the second they were on the walls. I could tell Oll was nervous as a kitten. But people everywhere were congratulating her and loving her. I thought, dear me, if she's made it after all this. It really was most moving. I just walked into the garden for a while and cried.'

Mrs Oll must have been beside herself and Aunt Mary as well, even if she preferred to avert her eyes from the nudes. Whether

Nanny McGlew attended isn't known. There was actually little chance of avoiding the nudes – being the biggest works, they were very prominently positioned. Except for some life drawings by John Molvig in the 1950s, there had not been an exhibition of nudes at the Johnstone Gallery, but they seem to have created very few raised eyebrows and little apparent racial discord.[41] Although there was one incident – a grim reminder of realities then – that onlookers have later sworn took place, when the strident tones of a woman who thought her son was about to buy a nude suddenly rang out above the excited din to the effect that she wasn't having 'a black gin' hanging in the living room.[42]

Red spots flew thick and fast. 'Margaret Olley top woman painter', the *Courier Mail* headed a news report the Monday after the opening. Thirty-eight paintings had sold for three thousand pounds in total, doubling the record set by Australian women painters, the item trumpeted, as if it was the art Olympics.[43] The Art Gallery of New South Wales had already purchased the nude *Vera* for their collection before the opening. Only the Queensland Art Gallery refused to buy a nude or any other work.

Brian Johnstone was quoted as saying that in the twelve years of running his gallery, he had never seen such an outpouring of truly magnificent paintings. 'No other Australian artist has such a command of colour,' he added, and reiterated: 'Miss Olley's paintings have reached maturity and excellence. They are bursting with colour and vitality.' It was just under ten years ago that Margaret had stepped off the *Strathmore* and tentatively told reporters in Sydney: 'I shall have to absorb that feeling for colour into my work by degrees.' Now, in her new sobriety, it seemed that everyone was intoxicated by her paintings and their colour.

'Margaret Olley is one of those artists who refuse to set their eyes on the dark side of life,' Gertrude Langer wrote in the *Courier Mail*, amid the alarming news of the Cuban Missile Crisis.[44] 'Miss Olley has never been better,' Langer added later in

The Flood Tide

the review, undoubtedly causing Mrs Oll and Aunt Mary to lift their willow-patterned teacups as they perused the morning papers. 'The colours are kept fresh and translucent as Miss Olley works, with gained concentration, yet without loss of freshness, on the constant adjustments required by composition, the happy results are numerous.' To Langer's eyes, *Odette* was 'the choicest' of the nudes.

But it was the elderly pathologist and art critic Dr J.V. Duhig, writing in the *Bulletin* with a review titled 'The Flood Tide', who lavished the most praise on the exhibition.[45] 'The huge blaze of colour throughout makes an almost stunning impact; it is all a joyous bravura,' he began. Before tackling the oils, Duhig was extremely complimentary about the 'superb' drawings, saying that Donald Friend was the only other artist who could compete with Margaret's virtuosity in that medium. Then he really excelled himself: 'The oils, flower still-life studies and nine nudes are literally colossal in power, skill and colour. They gaily refute the current idea that great art, the best in the country according to some commentators, is done exclusively in mud colour and battleship grey.' And in conclusion: 'Margaret Olley has reached the flood tide of her art,' he extolled, continuing his own flood tide of accolades, 'and has stepped up to the top rank of our artists.'

As if that wasn't enough, on the same page the *Bulletin* also carried a review by John Henshaw of an exhibition at the Dominion Art Galleries in Sydney by Margaret Olley, Fred Jessup and David Strachan, which was also very flattering of Margaret's work. Henshaw summed up the work of the three old friends by saying their exhibition reaffirmed that there was still a place for paintings with form, alongside more disintegrated art. He described Strachan, whose paintings were all of Europe and included one of Paul Haefliger's house in Majorca, as 'a sophisticated primitive', which concurs with Margaret's own assessment of Strachan. He also said Strachan's work had obvious affinities with the famous painter of Montmartre street scenes, Utrillo, which seems unfairly to deny Strachan's uniqueness of style. (James Gleeson, writing in the *Sun* about the same show, expressed perhaps more accurately what Strachan was about with the emotive comment: 'His works look like painted memories.'[46])

Henshaw thought the still-life component of Jessup's works succeeded best in 'its assurance of subtle harmonious colour, texture and form'. To him, even in Jessup's recent Tweed Heads paintings, the boats, nets and fish – which he counted as still life – were as much the subject as the fishermen, water or sky. Margaret's forms he found 'denser, more plastic in a sculptural sense than Jessup's', and also drew particular attention to her painting skill in the work titled *Fish* (Margaret obviously did have a way with piscine subjects). What's interesting about Henshaw's review is that while everyone else tended to be overwhelmed by the sheer joyousness of Margaret's colour, Henshaw pointed out how this was sustained by a strong sense of form. The years of modelling classes at Brisbane Central Technical College – though she might prefer to forget them – and the example of Maria Corrie probably did play their part in her current success.

To Ron Sabien, it is the summery *Eucharist Lilies* that he bought from Margaret as soon as he saw it in her studio, which typifies both the emotion of the 1962 exhibition and the gorgeousness of her flower painting all through this period.[47] Reproductions of this work can't really do justice to its delicious invitation to summer ease of living. When the painting – marked 'Not for sale' – was exhibited at Margaret's 1963 show at the Macquarie Galleries, James Gleeson wrote of it: '*Eucharist Lilies* is a cool ensemble of silvery, fluting whites, limpid greens and blues that occasionally show the warmer aspect of their character by way of relief.'[48]

By this time Margaret had devised two different ways of painting, so she told Hazel de Berg in an interview recorded in

The Flood Tide

1963.[49] In one she worked directly from a model or still-life arrangement in the studio under Farndon (the back room of the antique shop never really became her principal place of work) and finished a painting off quickly. The other method consisted of working on a painting for a day then setting it aside for several weeks. This process was then repeated over a month or six weeks, with Margaret often 'taking something out and repainting'. The second method is the way she works almost all the time now, judging by the stacks of seemingly finished works in Paddington you're constantly in danger of kicking, one of which will suddenly be fished out when a new bunch of ranunculi arrives from the florist or the white azalea comes into flower in her own garden. A few judicious strokes and dabs are added to the painting before it disappears again like shifting sand into the ranks of Olleydom endlessly waiting to be released into galleries.

In the same interview with de Berg, Margaret also said she only ever made 'little thumbnail notes', rather than a detailed 'completed sketch', before starting a work, for fear of killing the painting before it was even begun. This enabled her to 'put everything into a painting'. Later in the interview she added: 'I never like to work directly onto a white ground. I might spend weeks building up a surface. As a matter of fact, anybody coming in could take it for an abstract painting but this is really the structure of a work.'[50]

The interview also shed light on another aspect of Margaret's approach to work. 'Painting to me is like drawing,' she offered in explanation to de Berg, 'you draw with your brush or palette knife, so whether one is using a paintbrush or watercolour or pen, it is all creative, and I never mind which medium I'm using.' Margaret's last observation was a sort of half-truth, because drawing in itself, when she couldn't paint, was not sustaining enough for her. But it does explain why she continued to exhibit in various mediums once her muse was restored.

Far from a Still Life

But while things were hunky-dory at Farndon, outside Australia the art world was changing. The year of Margaret's flood tide in painting coincided with the first exhibition of Andy Warhol's controversial Pop Art stencilled pictures of Campbell's soup cans and Coca-Cola bottles. Australian artists caught up with his new Pop Art vision a few months later, via overseas art magazines. Margaret barely blinked at whatever she was painting; although Donald Friend was soon grumbling about being left behind by new movements. Ask Margaret now what she thought of the explosions of art that followed Warhol's soup cans – and which would before too long proliferate in Australian galleries – and she looks almost blank, before answering with a slight curl of the lip:

I just ignored the rotten things. They had nothing to do with me. If I went into a show which had been influenced by them, I'd think: I prefer Morandi, thank you. There's a great spiritual quality to Morandi, I've loved his work ever since I was an art student. To me he continues the tradition of Italian artists like Giotto and Piero della Francesca, who did the wonderful frescos in the church at Arezzo. There's a stillness and reverence about his works – every Morandi is like a little prayer. As for abstraction, look at Braque and Picasso, there was nothing new about that.

Christine France, who's travelled with Margaret several times, has a story of visiting an art gallery with her at Winterthur, Switzerland, that illustrates perfectly Margaret's attitude to art she dislikes. At the gallery there was a joint exhibition of Morandi and Giacometti that Margaret found enchanting. When they passed through a section containing modern art not to her taste, she announced to France: 'Quick, put your hands over your eyes; don't look or you'll pollute your brain.'[51]

During this period of the early 1960s, Ron Sabien frequently kept Margaret company at night in the Farndon studio.[52] 'I'd sand frames while she painted,' Sabien remembers, his voice filled with affection and nostalgia. 'Oll was always very economical with the frames. She had frames there that had been put away for years. We'd pull one out, if there was a bit of paint on it I'd work away until it was nice and smooth. Sometimes she might rub a bit of colour into a frame, but not very often. She was never one for a lot of gilt frames, that came later when life was more prosperous. But it was lovely; we used to talk, talk, talk for hours.

'Somebody once asked me what on earth was Margaret doing, painting at night,' Sabien continues. 'You'll never stop Olley working, I answered, day, night or the early hours of the morning. The flowers she was painting would gradually die but she'd keep them sitting there and still be working on them. She might have three or four paintings going at once, touching up things and so on.'

Margaret had good reason to be busily painting. She had a show coming up at the Bonython Art Gallery in Adelaide in April 1963, to be followed in May by a joint exhibition with Moya Dyring at the Skinner Galleries in Perth, with another show at the Macquarie Galleries in Sydney scheduled for October.

As well as her exhibition in Perth (for which Moya Dyring returned to Australia), in May Margaret collected her third major prize in less than a year: the Finney's Centenary Art Prize, of which Laurie Thomas was the judge, for *Susan with Flowers*. The exhibition of entries was held on the fifth floor of Finney's department store in Queen Street, Brisbane, and was opened by the English poet, art critic, essayist and pacifist Sir Herbert Read, who also presented Margaret with her three-hundred-guinea cheque. 'I'm still not satisfied with what I'm doing,' Margaret was quoted by the *Courier Mail* as saying afterwards. 'I feel I'm just beginning to paint.'[53] But, frustratingly, she did not elaborate further on how she regarded her painter's progress at this point.

Far from a Still Life

At the end of July, Moya Dyring was in Brisbane for a solo show at the Johnstone Gallery. Dyring, who seemed preoccupied with her health, was now boiling up vegetable skins and drinking the liquid they'd been in, as well as taking a strange brew recommended by a French doctor, rather than dancing away the night and quaffing red wine from a penis-like serpent's head. However, nothing had yet been medically diagnosed.

At the same time, Margaret won her fourth prize, two hundred and fifty pounds this time, in the rural traditional oil painting section of the Royal Show art competition, with a largish painting of three men packing bananas in a shed, with tropical landscape glimpsed through the open door and window.[54] The work's intriguing in that it's much more actively about life than her usual figure studies done in her studio under Farndon. However, Margaret says that, in fact, it was also painted at Farndon and the bananas were cut from the garden there. The men, according to her, were actually Aborigines whom she'd organised to pose through her contacts with the OPAL House hostel when Fred Jessup or Donald Friend had wanted a male model.

Early in August 1963, Donald Friend flew up to Brisbane for his new exhibition at the Johnstone Gallery, which followed on from Dyring's. He was picked up at the airport by Brian Johnstone (with his neurotic dachshund, Lindy), who drove him straight to the gallery to see how his show was looking. The paintings had been primarily done in the second half of 1962, while Friend was visiting Sidney Baillieu Myer's newly acquired colonial house 'Yulgilbar Castle' on a cattle property on the Clarence River near Grafton.[55] As Friend was feeling surprised at how good his pictures looked on the gallery walls, Margaret, Pam Bell and Moya Dyring turned up. After much chatter, the three women took Friend off to Farndon, where he was to be a house guest along with Dyring.

'Olley was in high fettle,' Friend reported later in his diary about the day. Mrs Olley as usual had baked him a chocolate cake and, since Dyring had the spare bedroom, he was relegated to Margaret's studio, where he slept 'amidst a maze of stuffed birds, canvasses, driftwood, vases of dead flowers and still-life fruit and all the rest of that strange collection that serves her as a sort of dictionary from which she extracts the phrases of her painting.'[56]

It was on this visit that Margaret introduced Friend to Ian Fairweather, who had written to her in his usual polite way saying that he would like to meet Friend. The day after the big preview, Ken Olley drove them both to Bribie Island. Having found the wallaby track that wound among bracken to Fairweather's two huts, they ate a picnic in the warm sun on sand dunes overlooking the sea. Friend, who thereafter would correspond with Fairweather until his death, was instantly charmed by Fairweather's old-fashioned courtesy and conversation filled with tales not of art but of travelling. Fairweather, in turn, declared that if Friend did go up and live in a hut on Thursday Island, as he was currently contemplating, then he would join him.

Friend's description of Fairweather's living quarters is so evocative of the hermit it's impossible to resist quoting it: 'The huts he has built have a strange beauty of the same order as his paintings: they are very dark inside, and cluttered with books, rustic benches, favourite twisted pieces of driftwood and oddly-shaped *objets trouvés*, and many sheets of paper, covered with Chinese calligraphy. Four or five paintings, unfinished, glimmered on the end wall: they are on cheap cardboard, and the paints he uses of cheap powder colours which easily crack and peel off, to the despair of art collectors.'[57] Friend also noted that the kerosene lamps by which Fairweather used to paint at night were hung dangerously close to the thatched roofs of the huts.

Some of their conversation was about Fairweather's famous raft trip from Darwin to Timor, during which, because of the violent rocking of the craft, he'd had to lie half-submerged on his back for days, tormented by the sun's glare. 'Next time,' he told Margaret and Friend, 'I must remember to take a pair of sunglasses.'[58]

At the end of August 1963, Margaret won the seventh annual Redcliffe Art Contest's Peninsula Prize (for a representational oil) with a painting called *Guitar Player*; then in October she was in Sydney for her exhibition at the Macquarie Galleries. As Friend reported in his diary, lots of old friends gathered for the opening and the paintings sold moderately well.[59] Friend also rather dourly remarked that the critics were 'luke-warm' about the show, because, so he believed, they were now so deeply committed to abstract art that figurative painters like himself and Margaret had to labour under a cloud of disapproval. They were now 'rebels against the decrees of tastemakers', he concluded dramatically.[60]

However, despite Friend's tirade – which may well have been more about dissatisfaction with his own output than with critics – James Gleeson gave Margaret his best review yet in the *Sun*.[61]

'Aglow with sumptuous colour', Gleeson wrote in the opening sentence of his review of Margaret's 1963 exhibition, before in the next sentence again making a musical comparison to her painting: 'She is never wild or fierce like a Fauve; her discords are always discreet and to the point; her harmonies are as full, rich and romantic as a score by Tchaikovsky; and she has a sensuous feeling for the surface of things that gives her paintings an enticing freshness.' Gleeson then went on to discuss this remarkable feeling for surfaces so apparent in Margaret's work: 'she distinguishes the exact differences between the waxen sheen of a magnolia, the more leathery texture of a Solandra, the shimmer of silk, the transparent brittleness of glass or the brown, light-reflecting skin of Aboriginal girls.'

Although there were some fine examples of Margaret's figure painting in the show, Gleeson felt that Donald Friend's greater skill in anatomical draftsmanship and Ray Crooke's feeling for tonal relationships ultimately made them better painters of indigenous people. But as a flower-painter, he concluded, she occupies a niche that is quite her own. In another article in the *Sun* a couple of days later, Gleeson once more described her approach to painting as 'symphonic'.[62]

During the following month, November 1963, tragedy again enveloped the Drysdale family when Bonny, unwell with a cancer she didn't know about and devastated by Tim's death, committed suicide by taking an overdose of tablets.

A television profile of Drysdale was made by the ABC in 1967, written and narrated by George Johnston, who is best known for his semi-autobiographical trilogy of novels, including *My Brother Jack*. In the documentary, Johnston would refer to Drysdale in the period after Tim and Bonny died as being on a razor's edge of despair and self-doubt as he struggled to reach the light. Johnston would also add that some of his most moving canvasses were painted in this period.

'I do hope Tas when you return you will waste no time and start painting,' Margaret wrote to Drysdale at the beginning of December, in response to a letter from him saying he was headed north to the peace of the family sugar plantation at Birralee, inland from the coast, halfway between Mackay and Townsville. 'You are terribly fortunate to have this great gift and I feel you are just arriving at the important age, when Artists paint their best and I have great faith in you, and what you will do,' she continued. 'Tragedy is great sorrow indeed which must be overcome and not given into – and time is a great healer, but I do think that putting everything you have into the work you like doing, which is painting, is the best of all.'[63]

Far from a Still Life

What has not been known before is that during this agonised period Drysdale was deeply succoured by Margaret. While he was housed and looked after by his daughter Lynne and her husband Bill McLaughlin in Sydney, and supported by Maisie Purves-Smith, the widow of his close friend, artist Peter Purves-Smith (who in less than a year would become his second wife), Drysdale also turned to Margaret. He was in his early fifties by now, a large man who looked like he should be on a tractor or driving a Land Rover along dirt tracks rather than sitting on gallery daises. He had a sensual mouth and – in spite of the glasses with the one clouded lens protecting his damaged eye – he was very good-looking:

I was Tas's girlfriend in Brisbane and Maisie was the girlfriend in Melbourne. It started when he was living with Lynne; the bottom just fell out of his world when Bonny died. He was lost without her. Tas and I had always seen one another when he came up to Brisbane and been fond of each other. There was a dam at Hill End where we once went swimming when I was staying with Donald. We must have gone out to draw on a hot day, then stripped off and plunged in. Tas told me afterwards that he'd watched me with desire.

It was nothing like my relationship with Donald. I mean, let's face it, Tas was down to earth and very much a man. I did it out of friendship and compassion. He was feeling so vulnerable after Bonny died I couldn't resist him. I've never regretted it. It was an affair that filled a need of the moment. I can't really tell you exactly how long it went on. I think Maisie knew. I used to be a bit uncomfortable about that but my feeling is that she did know. It was Brian Johnstone who put an end to it. Brian gave me a big talking to and that was that. These things come and go. I wasn't heartbroken. I always had Sam as my great love, anyway.

Drysdale's daughter Lynne Clarke feels that 'Margaret would have been a huge comfort to him. He came and stayed with me and Bill in our big house. He had the studio upstairs but he never did any work; he was hopeless, he just couldn't settle at anything. Why I feel he didn't marry Margaret and instead married Maisie, was that when they were very young, he and Bon, Maisie and Peter Purves-Smith, the four of them were terribly close – he and Peter studied in Paris together – so Maisie went back a long, long way.

'Margaret had her own life and to get married to Tas would have meant becoming Lady Drysdale [Drysdale was knighted in 1969] and I don't think that was really Margaret's thing. She wants to work. Tas liked having someone to look after him. Margaret's an independent woman. So in a way, if Brian Johnstone broke it up, it was good for her.'

If the relationship had continued as a love affair, the collision of two major creative spirits might have brought additional pitfalls. Judging by the excessive drinking in the 1967 film, not continuing their relationship might have been another act of self-protection from her own weaknesses on Margaret's part. Finally, it also seems clear that while saving herself for Sam, consciously or unconsciously Margaret cannily chose to have affairs where there was no real risk of the domestic ensnarement that might have hindered her painting:

As I've already said, I never liked the state of being owned. I've always felt like a free spirit. I also used to observe how people became like each other and like their animals as they got older; not only did they look the same, they hardly spoke to one another because they had nothing to say. I thought it was deadly. I had no desire to be tied down and spend my entire life with someone out of habit. I've also watched people, especially women, who had great potential, being absolutely sacrificed in marriage.

Nor have I ever had an urge to have children. Some women get so clucky that they have to have a baby. They treat it like a doll, instead of a lifelong commitment they'll still be worrying about when they're grandmothers. I've seen all this and thought I really don't want to have any of it. To be quite honest, in a very selfish way I'm far too interested in my work.

If the affair with Drysdale was short-lived, Margaret had plenty to distract her in 1964. She was about to make another decisive move:

The sell-out of paintings of the Johnstone Gallery enabled me to buy my first roof. Having always lived at my mother's, I just felt I needed a house of my own, and not in Brisbane. I found a house in Sydney with a separate loft that had been a furniture upholsterer's in Paddington Street, Paddington, just behind Lucio's [Restaurant] now. I went along to see the bank manager – this was when pounds were pounds – to borrow what I needed. Never be frightened of a bank, he said. We're really just pawnbrokers except we don't hang out our three golden balls. From then on, I've never been intimidated by banks. I turned the house into two flats and kept a loft for myself to stay in when I was in Sydney.

◆

In the middle of April 1964, Margaret was in Newcastle for the opening of her first show at the von Bertouch Galleries. This began an obsession that outlasted any of her love affairs of these years. To put it simply: she fell in love with Newcastle. The director of the Newcastle Region Art Gallery at the time, Gil Docking, was married to an artist Margaret knew from her exhibitions at the Johnstone Gallery, Shay Docking. It was Gil Docking who suggested that Margaret have an exhibition with Anne von Bertouch, whose galleries in a terrace house at 50 Laman Street, Newcastle, had opened the year before.

The Flood Tide

Margaret had fallen for Newcastle even before she arrived in the city itself:

I'd never been to the gallery or Newcastle until that opening. I'd passed by Newcastle often enough. With all the smoke billowing out of it I'd just thought what a dreadful place. But this time was different. I loved the train trip up. The heavy old trains were delightful, not like the sardine-tin trains now. The girls in green, with aprons and caps, came along and took your lunch order. You could have sandwiches or a chicken salad on a folding table in your seat, it was such a restful way to travel. Also I love anything to do with the Hawkesbury River. The light on the waterways is so paintable. Whatever time of day, it's different but always equally appealing. Coming into Newcastle itself I was enchanted by all the boats and the funicular ferries on the Hunter River. It reminded me of Townsville where I first went to boarding school.

Anne [von Bertouch], being such an enthusiastic person, insisted on showing me round Newcastle as well. I loved it even more on closer inspection. Why don't you come back? she said then. I'll book you into a hotel and you can do some drawings of Newcastle. So I did, but not until more than a year later and that's when my love affair with Newcastle really got underway. On my first visit Anne had also, as a surprise, prevailed upon Bill Dobell to open my show. He gave the shortest speech because he was so shy. But it was lovely of him to do it.

At the opening, Dobell – who now possessed more jowls than when he'd painted her portrait, and no longer had a moustache – wore a bow tie, a checked jacket with contrasting lapels and a white handkerchief showing in the pocket, and thick black Clark Kent glasses. Margaret sported a beret-like millinery creation tipped to one side and her expression in the photograph that appeared in the *Sunday Telegraph* afterwards was not all that different from the famous portrait, only this time there was slightly more of a smile.[64]

'Margaret was one of my victims – now it's up to me to be her victim,' Dobell prefaced his short speech. By then Dobell had been long forgiven for his portrait of Joshua Smith and was living quietly at Wangi Wangi with his sister Alice and a loving, non-critical cocker spaniel called Suzie. He was introduced at the opening by Professor Brin Newton-John (father of Olivia Newton-John) 'as our living legend in art'.[65]

Two months later, in June 1964, Margaret had her sixth prize coup of this decade when she won the hundred-guinea Johnsonian Club art award. Margaret's winning entry was a portrait of her friend Hazel Ruddle. According to Margaret, the painting had been inspired by Ruddle's brightly coloured muu-muu – the long, loose brightly coloured Hawaiian-style dresses Australian women went mad about in the 1960s. Ruddle's muu-muu had gone round and round in Margaret's head until she'd expelled it in oil paint, she told a reporter from the *Courier Mail* at the Club's headquarters in Adelaide Street.

At the end of October 1964, there was another solo exhibition of Margaret's work at the Johnstone Gallery. Gertrude Langer began: 'There is something very satisfying about witnessing the full achievement of an Artist's possibilities.' Further on, emphasised like her first sentence in darker print, Langer wrote: 'There was ease and fluency, freshness and vitality before in Olley's painting, but not as much wisdom. Now, wisdom enhances the other qualities.'[66]

Future reviews would be more mixed – some would be raves, others less enthusiastic. Reviewers Frederic Rogers and Gertrude Langer in Brisbane would remain faithfully affirmative in their praise; newer reviewers in Sydney and elsewhere would come to greet Margaret's exhibitions affectionately, like an old friend over the years; still others, from time to time, would deliver hints of rebuke about her work not being up to standard, or not breaking any new ground. But, regardless of what they might write, Margaret's oeuvre was now firmly established on the Australian art scene.

What was staggering about the 1964 Brisbane show was its size. It was a huge exhibition. Sixty-eight oils were on the gallery walls at Cintra Road. Most were of flowers or still lifes (although a few Sydney Paddington street scenes were included and Bonnie Sue made another appearance) and sixty-seven paintings sold – the thirtieth work, *Bush Lemons*, belonged to Ray and June Crooke and was not for sale. The show netted a total of five thousand pounds. Now Margaret was producing so many paintings, it is no wonder that Mrs Oll had a new refrain. 'You're not using those old vases again' was the admonishment she gave her daughter in front of friends like Shirley Wright. 'Use something different, dear,' she'd urge, to Margaret's amused exasperation.[67]

'I can feel for flowers as I can for people,' Margaret said about the paintings to a reporter during her 1964 show at the Johnstone Gallery, between long draws on a cigarette.[68] 'Painting flowers is almost like painting a portrait. I couldn't care less about them as botanical specimens – in fact, I don't know the names of many of the flowers I paint,' she added. It should be pointed out here that Margaret, these days, is very good with the names of plants – or at least with the common names of plants. But her comment is interesting, because it helps to explain why she now seems to have entirely stopped painting portraits of the human kind. 'You don't need to make appointments with them or talk to them,' she later said, in 1995, in reference to the advantages of flower and still-life subjects.[69]

At the end of 1964, another momentous event occurred in Margaret's life. On one of her trips to Sydney, she first spied her present abode in Duxford Street, Paddington. In what would become an increasing real-estate habit of hers, she immediately swooped upon it:

It had a separate ramshackle wooden building at the back, falling into the laneway, which had once been a hat factory and still had a whole shelf of wooden hat moulds inside. I was told that originally this section had been a shed belonging to the man who'd built the row of terrace houses in front. When we had to dig up the garden for some repairs I found some old horseshoes there, which I presumed dated back to when the builder had had materials delivered by horse and cart and the garden had been his yard.

I bought it because I thought it would be a better place for working than my other house in Paddington Street. Every house I've bought I've always imagined I was going to live there, even when it hasn't turned out that way. The bank manager told me I'd have to sell the Paddington Street house if I wanted to purchase this one. Yes, I responded dutifully. Of course I had no intention of doing so. You're having a long time of not being able to sell it, he remarked after a while. I know, there don't seem to be any buyers, I answered.

I'd already let the loft in Paddington Street by then. I'd been so busy painting in Brisbane that I really wasn't spending much time there — and anyway, I could always stay with David Strachan, whose house was in the same street. I wasn't very experienced in working with tradesmen or organising renovations in those days. Although I'd done what I thought was sufficient work to the loft quite soon after the tenants had moved into it, I received a telephone call one night in Brisbane to say the tin roof had just blown off in a storm. You live and learn, is all I can say.

In her newly acquired Duxford Street premises, Margaret kept a couple of tiny rooms as a flat for herself in the section between the front terrace house and the Hat Factory and rented out the rest. The small flat became her base in Sydney, while Brisbane still remained officially 'home'. As for the Duxford Street property's garden back then, Margaret recalls that there was just 'one privet bush and the stump of a palm tree that had been cut down years before'.

The Flood Tide

It's hard to imagine the Hat Factory without a garden these days. Everywhere you look there are nasturtiums, marigolds, stripy ribbon grass, impatiens, clivias and soft pink geraniums growing on top of one another. A camellia bush, citrus and a rambling old-fashioned rose covered in white flowers with yellow stamens compete for space, and in amongst them all are numerous potted cymbidiums and bromeliads. On windy days it's full of the rustling of assorted palms and an elongated grandiflora magnolia mixed with the bell-like sound of wind chimes. Once, when the house was suffering an infestation of bush rats, two barn owls took up residence in the garden and Margaret would see them asleep in the front palm tree during the day. After they'd eaten all the bush rats, the owls moved on.

In the middle of the garden is a fountain made of faded green concrete. A plump Cupid, surrounded by dark green stems of water iris, holds a shell aloft in one hand while his other rests on a tortoise, and an open-mouthed frog spurts water up from his knee. On the wall of the house are two sculptures in relief of angels blowing trumpets and towards the garden's end are two seated stone horses; while another tiered fountain is tucked away against the outside fence. In all, certainly a bit more than a single privet.

❖

Ian Fairweather's hermitic existence on Bribie Island was becoming increasingly less so as the 1960s progressed. The new bridge to the mainland marked the beginning of an influx of tourists eager to view not only the island's natural beauty but also, eventually, Fairweather himself. In 1963, Fairweather had completed a project dear to his heart: a translation of *The Drunken Buddha*, a well-known Chinese novel based on the exploits of a thirteenth-century Buddhist saint called Tao-chi from the province of Chekiang, who confounded his fellow monks by combining drunken and irreverent behaviour with unusual piety. In 1965, Fairweather's translation of *The Drunken Buddha* was handsomely published by the University of Queensland Press, with twelve typical Fairweather paintings as illustrations. There was also a touring retrospective exhibition of his work, which opened at the Queensland Art Gallery the same year. Both of these events meant more attention and visitors for Fairweather:

He'd found a wonderful tree with a curl in it that was almost a circle, so then he paid for the branch to be chopped off and dragged into position with a bulldozer. He referred to it as his Chinese moon gate. If somebody puts up an entrance like that, it means they're expecting people to walk through. So I think he was getting used to the attention. Pam Bell and I went over round about the time The Drunken Buddha *was published. He was so excited. That was the time he painted Pam and me in the bush. It wasn't a literal portrait, just his observation of us having a picnic there.*

Like other Fairweather works, the painting of Margaret and Bell – *MO, PB and the Ti Tree* – was probably painted at night. But Fairweather did also have a camera that he used to take snaps – possibly as aide-memoires – and there is one taken on the day of their visit that shows Bell in a flowerpot sun hat and Margaret with a thick plait of dark hair coming over one shoulder. Both these images emerge quite clearly from the painting's abstract shapes and the work becomes an evocative image of women and bush blending, which might also reflect something of the ease Fairweather felt in Margaret's company.

In 1965 Margaret collected her last three prizes for the 1960s when she won the Redcliffe Art Contest again, the Bendigo Art Prize, Victoria, and the Toowoomba Art Society Competition, Queensland. Then in November 1965 she finally managed to take up Anne von Bertouch's invitation to paint Newcastle.

However, once she'd arrived she more than made up for lost time by working from six in the morning until six at night, ignoring the inevitable remark from passers-by: 'You have an interesting hobby there.' She did drawings and watercolours of the wharves and the harbour; views from the Obelisk overlooking the city, which she liked to call 'her studio' and loved because of its quiet and aloneness; as well as studies of buildings such as the Longworth Institute, which she'd seen when she first stepped off the train, the Customs House and Court Chambers:

Newcastle produced a lot of painters. Besides Dobell, John Olsen came from there, Billy Rose, Jon Molvig. It's a very painterly city. The sea breeze blows all the smoke out west. I just loved it. I loved the railway line, the shunting yards and the old tug boats. I almost wore my shoes out walking all over Newcastle with a drawing book that time. It was summer, there was a terrible plague of flies and Newcastle's very hilly. But I just kept walking. I'd sit on someone's doorstep, do a drawing and then move on. I especially fell in love with Church Street, which is up high overlooking the harbour and the boats.

Sometimes I'd get up before dawn and trudge up to the Obelisk with painting equipment. I'd set myself up and be painting as the sun rose. I remember once I did it in winter and almost got frostbite it was so cold. Another time, I was up there in the late afternoon, not at the Obelisk itself but on the same hill, happy as Larry, painting away using a round piece of metal there to prop up my painting board, when all at once there was a rumbling sound that grew and grew until suddenly a huge amount of water came gushing out. There was a reservoir underneath the soil; they must have topped up the water, which had now forced its way out and was running down the hill.

After this first stay, Margaret often called in at Newcastle after she'd been staying in Sydney. She'd hop off the train at

Newcastle, go and see Anne von Bertouch, catch up with what was happening at the galleries, then catch the next train up to Brisbane. As a consequence, over the years Margaret and von Bertouch's friendship also developed:

Anne had the art of being able to place things: she'd put objects together and they'd look just right. She and her husband lived above the gallery. The walls of the kitchen where she had friends to dinner had been painted white, but instead of re-doing it in another colour, she dipped a brush in black paint and dragged it across the walls giving them a texture – she just had that knack. When I first met her she was very striking, she always wore dramatic clothes and jewellery that had been made by artists exhibiting at the gallery.

Although the Regional Art Gallery existed, Newcastle was devoid of any real art community. Anne was great at gathering people together. She encouraged them to come along to the gallery. Often people are afraid to go through a gallery door; they think they'll be made to buy a painting. Anne offered them a cup of tea or coffee and something to eat; produced art books for them to peruse. Having been a teacher, she was able to help people actually look at paintings. She really gave an artistic fillip to Newcastle.

Margaret's own infatuation with Newcastle resulted in *The Newcastle Watercolours* – twenty-three paintings of the city and waterfront – that, along with eight flower and still-life paintings, opened as the von Bertouch Galleries' 'Third Anniversary Exhibition' on 11 February 1966. The catalogue featured on the front page Margaret's *Sunday Newcastle*, showing the clock tower and the railway tracks running along the harbour's edge. Inside the catalogue, as a sign of the move to decimal currency, prices were given in guineas in one column and dollars in another.

The Flood Tide

In July 1966, Donald Friend was once more 'chez Olley' for another exhibition at the 'beautiful' Johnstone Gallery.[70] Though he thought the paintings were 'well hung', looked 'most impressive' and the opening was 'ordered and elegant', he was disappointed there had only been about ten sales – for which he blamed the current drought in Queensland and a fall in sugar prices. Sales aside, as usual Margaret's company inspired him to work (and also this time provided him with some passing titillation of a different sort): 'Margaret and I go out with sketchbooks drawing the scenery along the banks of the river. It delights one to see in Brisbane how many odd old wooden cottages and curious rickety two-storey boarding-houses still go on giving character to the city, jumbled in amongst the brick and cement boxes of later builders. Margaret stays working longer than I do – I wander off and explore parks, or walk for miles in the suburbs that draggle out over the hills as far as one can go, and find a place to read (or go and decipher the peculiarly different and exciting graffiti scrawled on walls that evokes ideas of a very different and somehow more virile erotic life than exists in the South).'[71] Friend confessed in his diary that it was also the need to escape the non-stop chatter of Mrs Olley and Aunt Mary that sent him out of the house with alacrity. Though they were both dear old ladies, he continued, it was not just their incessant talk that exhausted him, but also their millions of trivial questions: 'Now Donald, will you look after yourself? – are you making tea or is it coffee? Tea? – but don't you always take coffee?' and so on.[72]

Apart from that, Margaret had given a pleasant dinner at which the guests included Charles Blackman and his wife Barbara, whom Friend enjoyed talking to. As well, Margaret had received a letter from Fairweather inviting them to Bribie Island. At the core of the letter was the revelation that he'd had a robbery and six of his paintings were missing, which the police were investigating and had asked him to keep quiet about.[73]

Far from a Still Life

A couple of days later Pam Bell drove Margaret and Friend to see Fairweather, whose missing paintings, the *Courier Mail* announced that morning, had now been recovered and an arrest made. Fairweather looked well in his craggy way and the four of them lunched on a deserted white beach, watched a porpoise, and in all spent a pleasant day wandering about in the open.[74] At the end of the day Margaret spiked her leg on a stump but refused to do anything about it until they were back at Farndon, whereupon she went off to a doctor. The cut turned out to be quite bad and Margaret returned with orders to stay in bed for a week. But what worried her, she said, was the fact that the old doctor couldn't see to thread the needle for her stitches.[75] However, his stitches apparently did the job and she recovered without mishap.

Towards the end of 1966, Margaret had another large show at the Johnstone Gallery: sixty oils and ten drawings. Her friend Mimi Falkiner had her heart set on buying one of Margaret's 'yellow' paintings, 'solandras or lemons', and so rang Brian Johnstone before the show opened.[76] Johnstone invited her to come over to the gallery and look at the paintings in the basement before they were hung. When she did so, a painting of red and green pomegranates 'just glowed' at her. 'I immediately rang my husband Bill and said come and have a look,' Falkiner continues. 'I just couldn't resist it.' The fecund ruby warmth of *Pomegranates*, lighting up the dark Johnstone Gallery basement, is an unforgettable image of Margaret's painting prowess of this period.

◆

New Year 1967 began with a sickening jolt. Unbelievably, on the other side of world, in the early wintry hours of the morning of 4 January, Moya Dyring, the woman who symbolised the joie de vivre of Paris of which Margaret had been instantly enamoured, died in a London hospital. Dyring, who distrusted French doctors, had been feeling unwell for a few years but thought the discomfort stemmed from arthritis in her hip. Eventually, in 1966, she was persuaded by a niece to see a specialist in London. In London, Theo Schlicht was also alarmed by her condition. Schlicht and his wife Katie, whose seemingly unconventional marriage had continued to survive, were by now both close friends of Dyring, who was often their house guest in London.

The diagnosis of kidney cancer shocked Dyring, but she agreed to have a kidney removed, presuming she'd then be able to get on with life as before. She was not told of a secondary cancer and that the operation was only to improve her condition temporarily. Although she did return to Paris briefly, by the end of 1966 Dyring was back in hospital in London with cancer in both lungs, still unaware that she was dying. Schlicht and his wife remained a constant support and her old friend Mary Alice Evatt travelled over from Australia.

The night before she died, Dyring fell asleep listening to Bach on a record player that had been brought into her hospital room, with Theo and Katie Schlicht by her side. In the morning she was gone.[77]

I wish I had seen her. But she was one of these people you think are invincible, it didn't cross my mind that she could actually be dying. Looking back at it, I suppose the brews she was taking the last time she came out to Australia were a sign that something was wrong. David Strachan kept on telling me that she was very ill. I never believed him. I just didn't want to know about it.

≈ 13 ≈

In Search of the Sex House

In Chiang Mai it dawned on me how fabulous the Buddhist religion was in Thailand. Everyone had to spend some time in a monastery. You'd see them first thing in the morning out in the streets in their robes with a begging bowl and people would be giving them their food. I thought what a wonderful way of educating people and controlling the work force: to have everyone regularly go into a retreat.

THE YEAR 1967 BEGAN WITH THE SORROW OF MOYA DYRING'S DEATH. It also initiated Margaret's travelling phase of the late 1960s. Once again, she was 'forever on the move'. In the space of fifteen months leading up to October 1968 she made three trips to New Guinea and on all of them painted furiously. Perhaps the death of Moya Dyring urged her on; perhaps a sense of mortality and the fleetingness of life assailed her; or perhaps, as Margaret would have it, her own natural impulsiveness and insatiable curiosity were responsible. Obviously, she now also felt strong enough to do without the weekly Alcoholics Anonymous sessions that had been her quiet support of the last few years.

It's impossible to work out the precise date or exact itinerary of Margaret's three New Guinea trips. But on the first one, which would seem to have occurred some time between June or July and September 1967, she stayed principally at her old friend Geoff Elworthy's town house in Port Moresby.[1] Elworthy had a strong interest in horticulture and the garden of his Moresby house was full of orchids he was cultivating from around the world, which in itself must have been fascinating for Margaret. But her painting seems to have been done mostly away from the house. The fish markets at nearby Koki provided plenty of tempting subjects. The markets, which also sold smoked tree kangaroo and a variety of fruit, were filled with colourful hustle and bustle and mingled odours, including the sweet smell of powdered lime being mixed with pepper chewed with betel nut. Segeri, the plateau region in the mountains just outside Moresby, also yielded subjects, such as boys catching dragonflies or making music.

Some of these Moresby paintings were then included in a solo exhibition Margaret had at the Darlinghurst Galleries in Sydney, which opened on 19 September 1967. Her next trip to New Guinea, going by the dates on paintings, took place in 1968, probably early 1968. It was now that the adventures really began:

I'd seen reproductions in books of the wonderful collection of Sepik artefacts in German and Swiss museums, and was really keen to go there. So Geoff arranged a trip for us up the Sepik River. You don't go up a fast-flowing river like the Sepik, I said when he told me, surely you must come down it. He was most annoyed that I'd objected to his plans; but nevertheless he reorganised them through a local friend of his called John Pasquarelli. The artist Douglas Annand, whom I'd known since we worked on Hassan *with Sam, was already going up to New Guinea, so I asked him to come along as well. I thought it would be good if there were two artists rather than just me. I wanted a balance.*

Douglas Annand, twenty years older than Margaret, was an outstanding early Australian graphic designer; as well as a watercolourist, textile designer, muralist and sculptor. In the 1930s he became one of Australia's most celebrated advertising designers; he won the Sydney Harbour Bridge poster competition and also designed the brochure and ceiling mural for the Australian Pavilion at the Paris Exposition. Then, in 1939, he was appointed the design director of the Australian Pavilion at the World Fair in New York, which brought much recognition for both him and modern Australian design.

John Pasquarelli, their unofficial guide on the Sepik, was a man with a colourful past, to say the least. A physically big man, who in those days had thick black hair, his boisterous behaviour and right-wing politics are recorded in various contradictory stories. More recently, Pasquarelli was, for a short time, Pauline Hanson's 'media and political adviser', as he describes it.[2]

Pasquarelli's father Joe was a doctor who worked in a field hospital on the Kokoda Trail in New Guinea during the war, a circumstance which accounts in part for Pasquarelli's own attraction to the country. Having studied law at Melbourne University, Pasquarelli ditched it to travel to Coober Pedy to look for opals, before going to New Guinea, where he worked as a cadet patrol officer in 1960. He then became a crocodile shooter and traded in crocodile skins and artefacts along the Sepik and May Rivers. In 1964, aged twenty-seven, he was elected to the first Papua New Guinea House of Assembly.

Pasquarelli, who's long been a keen collector of 'Oceanic art',[3] remembers lunching with Elworthy during the Assembly's sitting and Elworthy saying: 'My friend Margaret Olley wants to see the Sepik.'[4] On the expedition itself, Margaret and Elworthy made their way alone from Moresby to where their journey down the river was to begin. During this stage of the trip Elworthy – through his horticultural connections – organised for Margaret to be presented with a purple and yellow flower propagated by bats when their plane touched down at Madang. Elworthy described the bloom as a flower Picasso would have thought up – which is a rather appealing image. He and Margaret then flew on to Maprik where they were joined by Annand. From there they drove by truck to Pagwi on the Sepik River to meet up with John Pasquarelli:

Pasquarelli was standing there looking immaculate in white socks and white shirt, with a red-and-white spotted bandanna around his throat. He also had a white bull terrier with teeth like a shark's. If the dog goes to bite you, he said, don't pull your arm away, because if you do he'll rip the flesh. You were meant to have the presence of mind to push your arm towards the dog instead. From Pagwi we went on by jet boat to Ambunti, where Pasquarelli had a store and where he gave me his bed for the night. When I retired, I found a gun under the pillow, which I just ignored.

Pasquarelli's trade store at Ambunti was right on the river. Attached to the store was a large fibro shack, the walls of which were covered with Sepik murals by local artists to hide the hideousness of the bare fibro. This shack was where the party stayed. Margaret wasted no time in getting to work on documenting local life. The subjects she painted at Ambunti included medical out-patients and prisoners erecting a fence. Before the trip down the Sepik began they made an expedition further upstream:

Pasquarelli took us in his jet boat to the village of Yambon, where Douglas Newton the photographer and his wife were doing some research for the Metropolitan Museum of Art in New York; they had been collecting little clay figures which came from the Washkuk Hills area. Newton and his wife also gave us a number of travel tips, including how to get to a village which was famous for nose-flutes. Newton told us we wouldn't be able to go inside the Haus Tambaran [Spirit House], but we could listen outside. I found it a wonderful surprise to hear music in such a remoteness.

After leaving Newton and his wife, the journey began down the brown stretches of the Middle Sepik, all the way from Pagwi to Angoram. 'Of course there were eyes watching you everywhere,' Margaret later told a reporter.[5] 'I had so much stuff with me for painting that spare clothes were almost an afterthought,' she continued. In the 1960s, this area was relatively free of tourists and the party of Margaret and her three oddly assorted male companions does rather conjure up images of *The African Queen*, even if Margaret was far from a missionary spinster — neither prissy nor at all proper:

We set off downstream in Pasquarelli's double canoe, which consisted of two canoes with a platform across and a little room with mosquito-proof windows. The canoe had definitely seen better days. The mosquito netting was damaged and there seemed to be more mosquitos congregating inside the little room where my bed was than outside. As a result I was covered with mosquito bites. Douglas Annand gave me a tube of soothing cream to rub on. When I looked at the label the next morning it was for haemorrhoids. God, what am I anointing myself with? I thought.

There was no toot aboard. If you wanted to go to the lavatory you went over the side of the canoe; or waited until we'd pull in to shore late at night and made your way up the bank a bit. It was just before wet season and the mosquitos were rife. As soon as you bared your bottom the mosquitos dive-bombed it. Consequently, I didn't want to *let anything go and there was a lot of daily conversation about constipation. In the end we bought some green beans which did the trick.*

From Pagwi, the party went on down through the Middle Sepik area to see the famous large Haus Tambaran at Kanganaman. (In September 1967, Pasquarelli moved a private member's bill to ensure this sacred building was declared National Cultural Property.) Margaret was rather unexpectedly struck by its construction:

I couldn't get over how similar it was to the Opera House, the shells of which were just being completed then, except that Haus Tambaran was entered from the front not the back. This one at Kanganaman had a frigate bird capping a pole made from a tree trunk that went up to the top of the roof. At the bottom of the tree there was a carved figure of a woman with her legs apart – her legs being made from the tree roots. The entrance was just a tiny hole and when I looked through there seemed to be yams in baskets hanging from the rafters that looked like huge enormous penises.

Apart from some pen and wash sketches of the Haus Tambaran at Kanganaman, a quick oil of flute players and sketches of scenes like women bathing and children fishing, there was not much time for work on the double canoe trip – particularly since part of Margaret's Sepik experience was devoted to collecting artefacts at such a rate that afterwards special crates had to be made at the Angoram saw mill to transport them safely back to Australia. Much to Margaret's horror, when the crates finally arrived back in Brisbane they were unceremoniously thrown off the back of a truck at her doorstep.

It sounds as if extra canoes may very well have been needed to get their shopping spoils to Angoram. While Elworthy sat aloofly reading, Annand and Margaret were in a 'buying frenzy':

Pasquarelli had told us to bring money because there might be a few things we'd like to purchase. Well, of course, we soon ran out of funds. But all of a sudden a mysterious trader appeared who was only too willing to cash our cheques. Then the moment we paid the natives for their artefacts, the trader would sell them canned chicken necks from China to have with their rice or something equally ridiculous.

It was appalling. I have to say some of the white people in New Guinea made me ashamed of the colour of my skin – but that's how the economy operated. The natives would be buying tin dishes because I'd just purchased all their beautiful wooden bowls. I later gave them to the Museum of Mankind in London, but now wish I'd donated them to a collection here.

After Kanganaman, once it was established that the double canoe could get through the waters filled with floating grass, the group visited Chambri Lakes. Crossing Chambri Lakes must have been a bewitching experience. The vast expanse of blue water has a background of purple mountains, not unlike those in Queensland north of Cairns. In between the verdant green of the floating grass there are massed waterlily leaves and resting flocks of white water birds, which intermittently rise up to fill the air with a rhythmic flapping of wings. By the water's edge children would have frolicked on tree limbs, their laughter carrying across the water to mingle with bird calls. At sunset, sky and water melt into a red-gold flow that lingers until dark.

At the village of Aibom, Margaret was again buying, pottery this time. Aibom's famous pottery includes storage pots decorated with distinctive bird and animal faces, and is made from clay collected by the women from pits at the base of the Aibom Mountain:

We actually saw them green firing the fire baskets that they used for cooking inside their stilt houses on the water, and also a batch of those big pots that are used for storing sago when they had just been raked out of the coals. They were putting a solution of sago juice in them and rolling it round inside to seal them while they were still hot. Then the women painted the pots, each one with their own designs. At Aibom, I was also particularly intrigued with the round shape of the houses, which had thatched roofs with a pole poking out the middle. Attached to the pole were pottery finials that looked like gargoyles. I bought one of those. But not off someone's house – I hadn't stooped that low – one that was made to sell.

However, at one place I was forced to buy a crocodile-head prow that somebody had cut off their canoe (they wouldn't take no for an answer), which I found upsetting. One other thing I bought from the canoe, which I had hanging in the hall at Brisbane and absolutely loved, was a big painting of the birth of a child.

Margaret and the group also called in at the village of Tambanum which, according to Pasquarelli, had the finest domestic houses on the Sepik. At Angoram, the canoe trip of a week or so finally came to an end. They went ashore at Pasquarelli's house, which was at the bottom of what was known, by him at least, as Tobacco Road, after Erskine Caldwell's gritty novel of that name (written in the 1930s about the injustices of the American deep South). Here Margaret's three companions departed and she was left to paint in peace in accommodation she rented from a patrol officer.

It was at Angoram that most of Margaret's paintings of the Sepik were probably done, with subjects that ranged from the weaving of fish traps to crocodile hunters. Nature, however, finally put an abrupt halt to art:

Suddenly the rains started. They're closing the airstrip, I was told. There's only one more mission plane flying out and it's leaving this afternoon. When I climbed into the tiny plane the pilot said, Shut the door behind you. I was completely terrified. I clung on to the door handle for grim death as we were taking off. We seemed to be flying very low over the sago palms. Oh well, I thought, if we come down it wouldn't be far to fall into one of the sago palms. But then the clouds parted slightly, the pilot shot through a tiny hole and away we went.

Margaret's third trip to New Guinea, which also took place in 1968, was centred around the Highlands provinces, where it was the people much more than artefacts that made an indelible impression on her:

When I reached Mt Hagen, I looked out the window through the mist and thought, My goodness, I'm in Assyria. The people there were completely different to the coastal people I'd seen before. The Western Highlands people were tall, bearded, with big hair-dos and wore belts woven with designs of which the yellow part came from orchid fibre. At the back they wore green tutus made out of leafy twigs that the Europeans called 'arse grass'. When they sat down, the men folded up their legs and used it like a mat. They made new ones every day so they were always fresh and clean. The women looked Middle Eastern as well. The missionary people had given them pieces of dark blue and maroon cloth, which they draped themselves in like Bedouins.

At Mt Hagen Margaret stayed with a relative of the artist Paul Jones, who was growing white daisies in order to manufacture pyrethrum. She was given her own separate accommodation across the garden from the main house, which was very comfortable. One hot night after dinner, as she was lying on her back reading, Margaret suddenly couldn't stop shaking. 'I had no idea what was the matter with me. I thought I was getting Parkinson's disease,' she recalls. 'The next day I found there'd been an earthquake.'

On this trip Margaret discovered a new and fascinating facet of New Guinean culture:

In Search of the Sex House

Whenever I heard there was going to be a 'Sing-Sing', or a ceremony, I'd grab my sketchbooks and camera and get a ride out on a truck. At one particular payback over pigs, the only other European present was a patrol officer, whom I barely glanced at. There were thousands of people gathered on a series of hill crests. They weren't even aware of us, it was almost as if they were in a trance. The noise and the thumping of the ground I'll never forget, also the costumes. I was enchanted by the old women who had long necklaces going down to their feet made out of little sticks of bamboo. I was told that every piece of bamboo represented a pig; the necklaces were like their bank books.

I did try to make drawings, and every now and again I'd take a photograph, but mainly I was observing. It was so exciting. What struck me about the Highlands was how developed the culture was. Before I arrived, I'd had visions of headlines about the Leahy brothers discovering a lost world. But these people had a highly worked-out society that included land rights to the gardens.

From Mt Hagen, Margaret travelled to Goroka, where she'd been lent a house to attend more Sing-Sings. In the Wagi Valley between Mt Hagen and Goroka, she even managed to catch the men decorating their faces — some of which were covered in 'pure chrome yellow' — before all the stamping and dancing took place.[6] Next she travelled to Tari:

I had to get special permission to go there. It was arranged that I would be put up with an Australian man — not an experience I enjoyed. He had a pet parrot that sat on his shoulders. After his meal, he turned his teeth to the parrot and the parrot picked the remnants of the food out. I was given a native interpreter and spent entire days out painting. Not only was I fascinated by the [Huli] people at Tari and the wigs they wore, I also wanted to get away from my host. The Tari [Huli] wig-wearers seemed more Indonesian in appearance to

Far from a Still Life

me, they didn't have moustaches or beards like the Highland people. They wore small wigs made of human hair decorated with patterns of flowers that looked like bachelor buttons or everlasting daisies. The women reminded me of little brown hens. Early on I was upset by the sight of a man who appeared to have something unusual the matter with his foot. He turned out to be the first of many lepers I saw there.

Margaret did so much work in Tari that she ran out of bits of masonite to paint on and had to persuade the local school to sell her a blackboard, which she proceeded to cut up with the trusty folding saw. Her eventual return to Port Moresby was broken by a stopover at Wau with her cousin Lionel Crawford, who'd helped with the dairy in the early days at Tully. Just before she left for Moresby, Margaret had an unnerving experience:

Lionel had booked me into a motel near the Botanical Gardens, while he'd stayed with friends. Get up early in the morning and go for a walk in them, he said as he took off. I'd been looking forward to going to the Gardens because Geoff Elworthy had been singing their praises, so I thought I'd take advantage of the late afternoon light and go straight away. At the end of the street I was halted in my tracks. I was suddenly gripped by the most terrible fear. I knew it was ridiculous. I'd just been around all sorts of isolated places in New Guinea by myself and never had any trouble. But my legs wouldn't move. Shamefacedly, like a dog with its tail between its legs, I had to turn around and go back to the motel. When Lionel picked me up the next morning, he told me somebody had been murdered there the week before at that exact time of day.

Three major shows resulted from Margaret's trips to New Guinea. The first, called 'Leaves from a New Guinea Sketch Book and Other Paintings', was held at the Johnstone Gallery in

In Search of the Sex House

October 1968. 'I think you'd need to spend a long time in the Highlands to be able to capture the peculiarities of light there. It changes so quickly you can hardly get it down in time,' Margaret told a reporter after the opening, in explanation of why there were so many portraits and only a few landscapes among her seventy-three oils and tempera, plus seventeen pen and wash drawings.[7] A second exhibition was held at the von Bertouch Galleries in May 1969 and the third at the Macquarie Galleries in Canberra in December 1969. As well as these three exhibitions, in 1970 the Horticultural Society of Papua, of which Geoff Elworthy was president, also had a show of her New Guinea paintings at Elworthy's house in Moresby. But after that, there would be no more painting in New Guinea:

I just realised that New Guinea really had nothing to do with me. Painting for those shows was quite a struggle; there was nothing familiar about the subject to fall back on. I've never been back, despite my promise to Jeanette Leahy (whom I had visited with Lionel Crawford on my way back from the Highlands). I think I must have been all New Guinea-ed out by then.

However, despite being 'New Guinea-ed out' and feeling that from now on her travelling might be more looking at art galleries than roughing it painting, Margaret undertook one more expedition that combined both work and adventure in the 1960s. In the middle of 1969, she set off on a pilgrimage to Angkor Wat in Cambodia to visit its ancient temple, which was first Hindu then Buddhist – a gallery in situ, so to speak. The pilgrimage was to begin with a visit to her cousin Edgar Knight (whose mother was Margaret's Aunt Madge, the baby of the Temperley girls) and his wife Wilma in Kuala Lumpur, where she also hoped to explore the possibility of selling a few paintings she'd brought with her. At the end of it all she planned a sojourn with Donald Friend, who

397

was newly residing in Bali. But first there was the sea voyage to Malaysia:

I booked myself on a cargo boat that ran from Tasmania to Penang and took passengers, first and steerage class. I didn't have any money so I went steerage. I embarked at Brisbane. Joyce Vaughan, a friend from the Johnstone Gallery who sometimes used to take me sketching in her car, was on board with her husband George, who was a pilot employed to guide the ship through the Barrier Reef and the Torres Strait, so the journey was very pleasant. I did drawings of the coast going up and when we came to the Torres Strait the water was a glorious milky emerald green – like Ray Crooke used to paint – that I loved.

Just before the ship docked at Jakarta, Margaret had a vivid dream:

I was on a train that abruptly stopped at a siding. It was right out in the middle of the bush. No station, just a little waiting shed. I stepped off the train, started gathering flowers as I'm always prone to do, and wandered further and further away from the siding. When I finally returned to the little shed, the only trace of the train was a puff of smoke disappearing down the track. I thought nothing more about it. At Jakarta I was met by a friend of mine, Helen Jarvis, who was working there, and went off with her without telling anyone.

I had a wonderful time, visiting the museums and the markets; eating saté at roadside stalls, checking out the local theatre at night, which was very bloodthirsty – women being thrown to tigers, blood dripping from swords, monkeys jumping out of bushes. Helen would ring the boat every day to check to see when it was sailing. Suddenly the news came through that it was due to leave. When we arrived at the wharf, I looked around the corner of a shed only to see the boat had gone. It was steaming away, exactly as the train had in my dream.

Helen and I were hurled onto a tug boat which set off in pursuit of my ship. I, of course, was laden down with string baskets full of exotic fruit, pottery and other things I'd bought in the markets. When we caught up with the boat, I had to climb a rope ladder with all my string bags dangling round me. I looked up and thought, one rung after the other. Oh, you are dreadful, Joyce scolded the moment I made it to the deck, what have you been doing, we've all been so worried about you? I was quite startled to be roused on so fiercely. Because I hadn't taken my passport, they'd been imagining the worst: I'd gone overboard, was lost or abducted.

The next stop was Singapore for three days, where Margaret was 'nearly killed with kindness' by Chinese friends.[8] Then it was on to Penang, which she found disappointing and 'the people surly'.[9] After Penang she travelled back to Port Swettenham, Malaysia, to be greeted by the Knights. A photo in their family album shows Margaret wearing a greenish cotton dress and a straw hat; in one hand she has a plastic airline bag of the style ubiquitous in the 1960s and in the other what could be a thin wooden painting box.

It was now close to the end of June. The four-day race riots that had broken out on 13 May 1969 meant that there was no going out to the theatre at night, or anywhere else for that matter, in Kuala Lumpur. The riots had brought to a head the complicated racial tensions underlying Malaysia's multi-racial society: the Malays were the majority race, Islam the national religion and Malay the national language. But the Chinese population firmly dominated business and trade, and most Malays were economically disadvantaged.

The riots immediately followed the May 1969 General Elections, sparked when the inhabitants of a Chinese area were attacked and their houses set fire to. Reports of how many were killed in the four days of rioting varied, but police put the figure at one hundred and seventy-eight.

'Curfew is still on and trouble flares up from time to time,' Margaret wrote in a letter to Donald Friend, filling him in on her travel plans, 'the people seem nervous and shut up shops early. Only evidence of the riots are the burnt out Chinese shops and schools and houses and lots of policemen armed with guns, otherwise you would think things are normal.'[10] Closer to home, however, there was unexpected trouble. Edgar Knight went into hospital for what was thought would be a routine operation on his leg but turned out to be far more serious. Not only did this mean Wilma was unable to join Margaret on most of her local excursions, but it also put an end to the idea of Wilma accompanying her to Cambodia.

Meanwhile, Margaret, having resigned herself to the fact that there did not seem to be much of an art market for her paintings in Kuala Lumpur, explored on her own with Wilma's driver Ahmad:

I was mad about the English version of Indian architecture that Kuala Lumpur was full of then – buildings such as the railway station, which was very grand, with lots of arches, turrets and domes – so I drew all those. The old Mosque, surrounded by a moat, also appealed to me and there were fabulous museums – but if only they'd dusted them; the displays were so crammed and the exhibits so dirty, you had to look hard to make anything out. I saw a big travelling Rodin sculpture exhibition which was very worthwhile, and I spent quite a bit of time at the markets, where they seemed to sell everything under the sun, including what I'd always thought was a green weed. Whether they used it for medicinal or cooking purposes I couldn't discover.

Wilma and I managed a few side trips. One was to Malacca, the old run-down Chinese area, where there were wonderful antique shops and I bought a blue and white teapot with a brass handle, which I left with Wilma to bring down to Sydney for me. And *another time we drove up to Fraser's Hill, where all the English ladies used to go and cool off in the mountains.*

From Kuala Lumpur, Margaret made a day-and-a-half-long train journey right up the Malay Peninsula to Bangkok:

I was travelling very light. You never need much in the tropics, just a couple of dresses and some underwear. I had the folding saw with me as usual, a couple of sketchbooks and not much else – yet – so it made sense to take the train. It was a fantastic way to see the landscape. The train was very hot, no air-conditioning, so everybody had the windows open to let fresh air blow in. But in the middle of the night somebody got into the carriage with a dreaded durian. I'd never smelt such a suffocating, vile stench. I'd been told that if you can bear it for three minutes your senses get used to the smell. Unfortunately mine never did.

I arrived in Bangkok, booked myself into a hotel near the railway station and dutifully went on a couple of regimented tours with a guide hustling us along like sheep. But the whole place was so full of American servicemen on leave from Vietnam that I made tracks again as soon as I could. From Bangkok I took another train to Chiang Mai. It was a very long journey to Chiang Mai, we seemed to pass endless elephants logging. At Chiang Mai itself I found a place to stay near the market, where all the activity was centred, and wandered about with the sketchbook, which is always a good way to see things closely. There were no Europeans about at all.

Then I was told about a temple just outside of town that I should see. I took myself off to it and started drawing, but there was a service going on – not for the American GIs, but for Thai soldiers going off to the war. Although I tried not to look, I still felt as though I was intruding.

On the way back to Bangkok, Margaret stepped off the train to explore the ruins of Ayutthaya, which was Thailand's capital from the fourteenth to the eighteenth century. Having discovered some shops round the approach to a temple selling irresistible little bronzes, she loaded herself up with those and pressed on to the airport. Next, rather than flying directly to Siem Reap, Cambodia, on her pre-paid ticket, she decided to break the journey at Phnom Penh and take in a few museums, to get her in the mood for Angkor Wat. The most extraordinary part of the whole trip now began. It's worth bearing in mind that Margaret had just turned forty-six by this stage:

I found it impossible to catch a flight on to Siem Reap from Phnom Penh, nor could I find any buses. So I decided to go up to Angkor Wat by multiple-hire Peugeot taxis. The French had left a fleet of old-fashioned Peugeot cars behind them, which were now used as taxis. Because I was big and the Cambodians are small, I took up two places and had to pay double. I'd hold up two fingers to show them I wanted two seats. You had to wait until the taxis were filled up with passengers and their baskets before they would set off. Despite the delays and the crowdedness, it was a wonderful way to see Cambodia.

Siem Reap, as Margaret remembers, was like a little village. Although the hotel where she was staying offered tours of the ruins, she decided to organise her own transport out:

Because I wanted to spend a long time drawing, I found the cheapest thing was to do a deal with one of the bicycle boys. The bicycles had a billycart behind with a seat for you to sit on. By now I, too, had taken to travelling with flat-bottomed straw baskets like everyone else. I'd pack something to eat, a bottle of water and a clock in one of those straw baskets and they'd pedal me off.

I'd select the various places I wanted to go to. Then I'd point to the time I wanted to be picked up and wouldn't pay until I was delivered back to the hotel. At the ruins I'd just be settling down to quietly draw when a bus-load of tourists would descend. *Hurry, hurry, this is the best place, take a photograph*, a guide would announce. Click, click, click the cameras went. Then equally quickly the tour would depart and I'd be left alone again. Quite often, after they'd gone, the only person I'd see all day would be an attendant silently moving through an area; or I'd look up and there would be a bat flying out of an empty building. Occasionally I'd hear haunting music being played on a little stringed instrument that looked as if it was made of an armadillo's back, but which I now realise was most likely from an animal called a pangolin.

During her stay in Siem Reap, an event of a vastly different magnitude took place. On the hotel radio Margaret heard the incongruous announcement that America's Apollo 11 had landed on the moon on 21 July and Neil Armstrong, clad in a bulky white suit, had set foot on the dust of the far-off Sea of Tranquillity:

There were a lot of foreign archaeologists staying at the hotel making a great fuss about it. I went out into the street, looked up at the moon and felt vaguely disappointed because I couldn't see anything moving. My mind went back to when we were living in Brisbane as children and used to go to the 'Flash Gordon' serials in the local tin picture theatre with the canvas seats at Annerley. All I could visualise was a man like Flash Gordon wrapped up in alfoil, as I'd seen in the Annerley picture theatre.

I'd been roaming round admiring these marvellous temples and sophisticated waterways of a lost civilisation, while just off the road nearby people were living in squalor in humpies in the bush; the contrast was extraordinary. That was strange enough. Then to hear that the Americans had landed on the moon ... The whole thing was quite bizarre.

Far from a Still Life

Her first trip up the Malay Peninsula inspired Margaret to repeat the experience of train travel. Rather than flying out from Phnom Penh, as planned and paid for, she decided to make her way across to the Thai border, cross over and then catch a train down to Bangkok. She spent the remainder of her Cambodian currency – probably on bicycle driver hire – keeping just enough in reserve to cover the cost of a multiple-hire Peugeot taxi to the border:

The taxi dropped me about five miles from the border. Thank goodness this was before the Pol Pot massacres. Once you're in a country, you're so preoccupied with what you're looking at that you don't even think what else might be happening. I never for a moment stopped to consider if what I was planning was safe or not. After I was dropped off by the taxi, I had to buy a seat in a coffin-like box pulled by a motorbike. The road to the border had the most excruciating potholes. It was raining and I only had a piece of plastic to tie over myself. The ride, in all, was the most uncomfortable of my life.

When she arrived at the border Margaret felt the guards were looking at her oddly, but she insisted they stamp her passport out:

I knew what I was doing: I had my travel itinerary and budget worked out. By now it was the middle of the day and the rain had been replaced by that terrible tropical heat you don't think you can survive. To get into Thailand, I had to walk across a bridge carrying my bag with all the bronzes plus my baskets. Once I'd made it over the bridge, the Thai guard refused to let me in. It passed through my head that this is the time where you cry, bare your breasts. But I'm not up to that. No matter how I entreated, the guard refused to budge. It was so hot I thought I was going to collapse with heat stroke and die. The only option was to pick up my chattels and walk back across the bridge.

In Search of the Sex House

Of course, when I crossed back the head Cambodian was waiting for me. You have a serious problem, Mademoiselle, he said. Not only has your Cambodian visa expired and you've been stamped out of the country, you haven't got a re-entry visa for Thailand. That's what the problem had been at the border; if I'd had a re-entry visa for Thailand I could have crossed over. You must go tout de suite to Phnom Penh and fly straight out of the country, the Cambodian honcho continued, otherwise you go to the police.

Margaret had no Cambodian cash to pay for the ride back to a Peugeot taxi that could take her to Phnom Penh so she could fly out of the country as instructed. All she could do was climb back into the coffin-box cart and, surrounded by a curious crowd of onlookers, sit waving American dollars. Finally the dollars vanished and she was bounced back over the potholes to the taxi drop-off point. The subsequent taxi trip to Phnom Penh was also eventful:

The taxi was continually stopped either by the police or the army. They made everybody except me get out and then searched them as the driver gave money. The very last time this happened was just outside Phnom Penh. The woman sitting beside me pushed a bundle at me, which I sat on while yet more money was paid over. When we finally started up again I gave the bundle back and she proceeded to show me what was inside – broderie anglaise. She was smuggling the lace that people put on their petticoats. At Phnom Penh, my triangular journeying across Cambodia completed, I changed some money at the hotel and departed 'tout de suite'.

From Kuala Lumpur I flew to Singapore, then on to Jakarta, where I changed to Garuda for the flight to Bali, which in itself was quite an experience. Everyone on the plane was smoking kretek cigarettes and they crackled. I loved the smell of them. I was hooked on kreteks for quite a while afterwards. I was sitting next to a woman

Far from a Still Life

who had a basket full of shrunken heads she'd collected in Borneo to sell in a shop in Sydney and who kept telling me excitedly how she was going to visit Donald Friend in Bali.

Since diverting himself with erotic graffiti on Brisbane walls in order to escape the solicitations of Mrs Oll and Aunt Mary, Donald Friend had himself been on the move. At the end of 1966, desperate for change in order to recover from yet another failed love affair and stagnating as far as work was concerned, he planned a trip to Europe with Mitty Lee-Brown and her husband Bill Gordon that was to include time with Justin O'Brien on the Aegean island of Lesbos, off Greece.[11] The escape was to begin with a stopover in Bali. Accordingly, Friend flew out of Sydney the day before Christmas Eve and spent the next two months at the Tandjung Sari bungalows at Sanur in Bali.

Bali at this time was refreshingly empty of tourist shops, resorts and even travellers, except for the dedicated. The sea was blue, the rice paddies overwhelmingly green and a gamelan orchestra was tucked around every corner to thrill the senses nightly. In the mornings, Friend awoke early to the cackle of ducks and geese, the soft chatter of Balinese and the sound of a flute being played as calm tides lapped quietly on the beach.[12] Sanur offered Friend the seaside that had long soothed his soul, a culture he found enchanting, plus very attractive young men to wait on him, and he was instantly seduced. Almost straight away he began negotiations to buy land there on which to build a house.

Although he also went ahead with his European holiday, halfway through 1967 Friend was back in Bali and had settled on another block of land in Sanur. The following year, on 1 May – an auspicious date chosen by a local astronomer – 'Tuan' (a shortened version of Tuan Raksasa, meaning Lord Devil), as Friend was called by the Balinese, moved into what he himself described as more a 'landscape' in tune with the whole local life, than a mere house.[13]

In Search of the Sex House

Bali would be Friend's home for the next twelve years, during which time Attilio Guarracino – their father–son relationship now firmly and affectionately established – would act as his agent, bringing supplies and medicines when needed, and also handling many of his professional affairs in Australia. As for Friend, although the good looks of his youth were disappearing and his sarongs might have holes burnt from kreteks, he was living in a paradise. And the 'landscape' he created over the years enticed a stream of visitors, ranging from Mick Jagger to Gore Vidal and the Duke of Edinburgh, as well as familiar faces such as Lucy Swanton, Marion Hall Best and Mitty Lee-Brown.

※

Margaret's own arrival in Bali on 1 August 1969 coincided with a visit to the island by President Suharto, accompanied by other government ministers and an entourage of three hundred (according to Friend) for the opening of the international airport Ngurah Rai at Tuban.[14] Many, probably Friend included, feared the new airport and the jetloads of tourists soon to follow might prove a 'death blow' to the Balinese way of life. Meanwhile, crowds thronged the streets to welcome the president and Margaret, unruffled by the hubbub, made her way to Sanur.

'Margaret as of old times is an easy guest,' Friend wrote three days later.[15] Margaret herself was charmed both by Friend's house (except for the one small detail below) and the Balinese existence it afforded him:

When I arrived I was shown into the little garden house. It was when I went to wash myself that I noticed his frowsy towels and he then explained how with the sea breeze and the moist air nothing ever dried. His house was delightful. The uprights were made from coconut-palm wood, which is one of the strongest building materials, and the roof was thatched with alang-alang – cogon grass – and bamboo. It was exquisitely furnished with objects and antiques he'd collected. There was no electricity, just lamps. He had a team of outside boys to work in the garden and the boys who worked in the house; every so often he'd change them about so they learnt different skills. He had masters coming in to teach them all musical instruments like the gamelan, so there was always music.

He had the boys posing for him upstairs in the studio and he'd also draw them when they were playing their instruments, so there were models laid on, for both of us. But I wasn't drawing all the time – I did go out exploring, especially at night. Oh, Oll, Donald would say, there's a Wayang Kulit – shadow puppet – performance going on in a little village close by tonight. Have a practice at riding pillion on the head houseboy's bike, then he'll take you through the paddy fields tonight. I won't go because I've seen it all before.

So I'd have a rest, then the head houseboy would wake me and after an early dinner off we'd go on the motorbike. Nothing ever started early because all the performers would have been working all day in the rice fields. I loved the bamboo gamelans that were played as an accompaniment to everything – they're so decorative – and I also loved the nature of the performances: food was being sold all the time, people just went to sleep in the parts they didn't like and then they woke up in the parts they liked.

'Margaret Olley infects me with a compulsion to paint,' Friend entered in his diary on Margaret's fifth day in Bali. 'So the both of us have been daubing away without let-up ever since she came,' he continued.[16] Not only was Margaret inspiring to Friend, she also assisted in other matters. She lent one of Friend's visitors, architect Roy Grounds, her folding saw so he could make Friend a bamboo model of a spiral staircase – something Friend's Balinese builders were unfamiliar with – and a little later proved her worth in another way. Returning at night from a Topeng performance (the masked dance-theatre in which often a solo male will tell an entire story by assuming different masks), Margaret passed a fire that had broken out at the Tandjung Sari bungalows. Friend described her as quite at home with bushfires, which was another exaggeration on his part, but she was undoubtedly practical and immediately instructed the bewildered Balinese standing around to soak bags in water to smother the sparks and stop the flames from spreading.[17]

Another day Margaret and Friend went off to Klungkung to look for antiques, only to find that prices had trebled, Friend grumbled in his diary.[18] To add to his annoyance, Bali, according to him, was now crammed with loud-mouthed, vulgar, bad-mannered, camera-clicking tourists due to the arrival of the first Qantas jet two days earlier.[19] However, despite the tourists and the price hikes, he still managed to buy up porcelain, painted cloths, carvings and a pair of fine doors to add to the many antiques he already possessed:

The Balinese knew Donald collected, so often there'd be a little tap at a door. I'm too busy, Oll. You go and see what they want to sell, he'd say. So I ended up buying lots of what he called 'Kitchen Ming': the distinctive greyish bowls with blue markings that originally came from kilns in China.

In contrast to his crossness at the influx of tourists, Friend continued to find Margaret 'the most encouraging person to have as a guest'.[20] She painted nearly all the time and, as he wrote in his diary, spurred him on to great activities by her example. Although, it must be said, despite various references to his own lethargy, especially when faced with painting commitments and entertaining guests other than Margaret, Friend's days were already quite full in a hedonistic way:

Donald had a very set routine. He'd get up early in the morning and instruct the gardeners in their tasks. Then he'd fix breakfast, do his diaries and paint through until lunchtime. He didn't have to do any shopping for food or cooking. Tati, the wife of Wija Wawo-Runtu, the proprietor of the Tandjung Sari, did all that for him.

At one of the enormous lunches, Donald announced that a durian was on the menu. Donald loved durians. Hold your nose when it comes in and just eat it, Oll, he commanded. As far as I'm concerned, durian smells like rotten onions and potatoes. But I did have a few mouthfuls and all afternoon it kept repeating on me: little disgusting burps of durian. When I complained to Donald the next day he said, Well, that's a plus!

After lunch he'd vanish for a siesta. Then he'd get up and perhaps do a bit more before it was the hour for his drinks party [consisting usually of potent Gin-djeruks served up by obliging houseboys]. People staying further along the beach who had heard about Donald Friend might appear. Sometimes they courteously sent a note, other times they just turned up unannounced. All this was grist for his mill, as far as the diary was concerned. When the drinks were over Donald would often disappear again, having had no evening meal. But occasionally he'd accompany me to the Tandjung Sari. It really was a beautiful hotel. They had the most wonderful musical evenings. You'd walk along the sand to have dinner, there'd be a bamboo gamelan orchestra playing, which I loved so much, and Legong dancers. It was truly magical. Then we'd walk back home along the beach.

In the middle of August, Attilio Guarracino joined Margaret as a house guest. Attilio was returning to Australia after a trip home to Ischia.[21] He arrived bearing bottles of whisky, paintbrushes, shirts for the children and a host of other presents, as well as scandalising gossip about the liberties Swedish women took with young men in their country, which he'd also visited on his trip to

Europe – not to mention the nude sex scenes in Swedish cinemas. At night, with Friend occupied with his own nocturnal activities, whatever they may have been, Margaret and Attilio often ate together:

Attilio and I would have meals by candlelight which had been sent over from Tati's kitchen: dishes in coconut milk, lots of duck and also lovely beef burgers and salad. Then, a couple of months after I came back to Sydney, Attilio telephoned. How have you been, Margaret? he asked. Oh, I'm all right, I answered. I'm not, he said. I've got a bloody tapeworm after staying with Donald. The meat must have been undercooked, but we couldn't see it because of the candlelight.

Margaret next embarked alone on an excursion to the old Dutch port of Singaradja, which also, according to Friend, produced 'the richest most custardly delicious odorous durians in the island'.[22] With her usual 'admirable and stubborn energy' Margaret boarded a dilapidated bus in Denpasar:[23]

We went past the lakes where all the pagodas are and then we climbed up and up to a place called Gitgit, from where you can look out on the green terraced hills and rice paddies that go right down to the sea. So pictorial. I'll never forget that view. From there we wound our way round to Singaradja, where the beaches had purple-black sand. Donald had told me to stay at a hotel out of town [possibly what was once the Dutch governor's palace], the sole transport to and from which was a cart drawn by a horse about the size of a large dog. Donald was always full of instructions about the dos and don'ts of how to behave in Bali, such as never pat a child on the head because it's bad luck. I was not to feel sorry for these horses, he'd admonished in advance, they were not stunted, they were the original horses from which our big horses have come.

When I reached the hotel it was deserted; there were lots of servants but no guests. I was the only one staying there and I was given a vast bedroom. As I was brushing my hair in front of the mirror, I saw the reflection of a ghostly figure gliding past. It was probably just a servant slowly going by, but I thought, I'm getting out of here. So I gathered up my possessions, rode straight back to Singaradja in the horse and cart, took a small room in a Chinese hotel, which was full of life, and immediately felt much happier. The next day I sat for ages drawing on the beach as cattle were being driven onto flat-bottomed barges offshore.

Margaret arrived back from Singaradja at the beginning of September, understandably looking 'pretty worn-out', as Friend commented.[24] Soon afterwards she left for Java, on the last leg of her travels, to see the famous cupolas of the giant Buddhist temple Borobudur and the thousand-year-old spires of the Hindu Prambanan Temple. Not only was she in search of the spiritual, however, she also had other more earthly matters in mind:

Donald and Wija used to go off on expeditions to Java hunting for the small Majapahit terracotta figures [used as house ornaments by the less wealthy in the Kingdom of Majapahit, according to Friend] that people used to dig out of the fields.[25] *They'd discovered a brothel, which actually had a sign outside in English saying 'Sex House', where they made several purchases, including an antique carving of a hare that was the brothel doorstop.*[26] *Donald and Wija were always giggling about the Sex House, as well as gloating over their Majapahit figures.*
Although Wija had said it had now closed down, I was determined to see if I could find the Sex House for myself.[27] *As soon as I'd checked into a cheap hotel at Jogjkarta, which boasted a can of water and the thinnest of towels for showering, I took the bus over to Solo, which was supposed to have a wonderful flea market. So there I was,*

wandering round Solo asking people, Do you speak English? Yes? Could you please tell me where the Sex House is, or the flea market? Eventually a woman whose husband spoke English came to my assistance. Her husband didn't know anything about the Sex House, but he did take me along to a shop that sold wonderful old Dutch gilded furniture. All I could afford and carry, along with the bronzes, was a lovely little Bristol glass man in a striped jacket rowing a boat, which I still have on my mantelpiece in the front room.

In Jakarta, just before flying back to Australia, Margaret did find an antique shop that had the little Majapahit figures she was after. She spent the last of her money on a box of them and so returned to Sydney with some souvenirs, at least, of her search for the Sex House.

14

Living in a Basket

*People used to ask me where I lived. I live in a basket, was all
I could think to answer. I was on an eternal run between
Brisbane, Newcastle and Sydney with studios, paints and clothes
in three places. As in Thailand and Cambodia, I moved around
with a big, flat-bottomed basket – very strong, very capacious –
that would carry anything, including baked dinners.*

FOR MARGARET, THE NEXT TEN YEARS WERE A TIME OF SADNESS, unexpected happiness and of property-owning. As she herself says, by now she was settling into 'long-distance running' with her work. The same cannot be said for her life. Her major struggle, against alcohol, had been won, so long as she was vigilant and kept to the AA prayer. But she was still not entirely out of the woods as far as personal matters went. However, despite a few cruel jabs, the 1970s were a peaceful, if energetic interlude, compared to more tumultuous decades she'd experienced before and others that would follow.

Living in a Basket

Margaret flew back from Jakarta towards the end of September 1969. A letter dated 29 September 1969, written by Russell Drysdale to Donald Friend in Bali, mentions that he and his wife Maisie had met up with 'Meg Olley' in Sydney 'the other day', that she was full of news about Friend and showed them the marvellous little pottery figures she'd brought back.[1] As well as news of Friend, Margaret's head was filled with recently acquired Asian sensibilities, but it wasn't long before the contrasting materialism of Sydney was brought home to her:

I thought the world had gone mad. Everyone was obsessed with the stock market. Even the newspaper boys at Circular Quay were talking about Poseidon shares and whether they'd gone up or down. I stayed with David Strachan in Paddington before I went back up to Brisbane. David was terse. He bought every newspaper with a report of the stock market; listened to the stock exchange on the radio; rang up all the time to glean more information. I'd been in Cambodia surrounded by people who were so poor and then with Donald in Bali, where the Balinese had absolutely nothing but lived in a beautiful way. It seemed absolute craziness. At this point my relationship with David cooled. David was a very complex man. I don't know what exactly caused the cooling off, if it was my fault or not, but our friendship was never the same.

Perhaps it was simply that David Strachan, his friend Lindsay Stewart and Margaret's friends Van Hodgkinson (who'd earlier been married to artist Frank Hodgkinson) and her sister Olwen, had formed a partnership called Ollivada (made up of the first two letters of each of their first names) with which they bought shares and did up properties together, and Margaret felt excluded.[2] Maybe a deeper rivalry of artistic talents was at play, or something entirely different may have been troubling Strachan about his relationship with Margaret. Whatever the cause, it's hardly likely to come to light now:

415

Far from a Still Life

Van [Hodgkinson] said, Oh, I'll tell you one day. But she never did. So to this day I don't know what caused the rift. Anyway, I decided to catch an earlier train home to Brisbane. On the way up I stopped off at Newcastle to see how my exhibition of New Guinean paintings had gone. It was the end of the day when I arrived. Where's the closest estate agent? I said to Anne, on the spur of the moment. I just suddenly thought I'd love to buy a house in Newcastle.

The second agent I dropped in on took me to see a real 'Miss Haversham' house, which I'd actually used as a drawing subject, in a row of terraces in Church Street. The house had been shut up for years. The pigeons had come in and roosted on the lavatory; there was a terrible mess of their poo. Bougainvillea had pushed through the windows and was twining through the house. Talk about being a romantic – I couldn't wait to buy it. No money, of course. Then it turned out that there was also a piece of land for sale at the back of the house, which made it even better. However, because of Newcastle's old land titles it took forever for the sale to go through; there was a complication to do with the deeds to the block of land and also a problem about a neighbour's strawberry patch, which was encroaching on the block.

Meanwhile, the first agent whom I'd seen wrote to me in Brisbane to say there were a couple of two-storeyed wooden houses – very cheap – for sale in a lane off Church Street called Lee Terrace. Without even seeing them, I plunged in and bought the two – numbers three and four. I lived in one as I was doing it up and let the other. From then on, I repeated this pattern. I would always live in a house, do it up and then let it. I realised for the first time in my life how I could make myself financially independent of painting and, also, I rather liked all the physical work. I'd buy the houses because they had wonderful views that I wanted to paint. Views were the main incentive. That they provided me with a number of studios was an added bonus.

Living in a Basket

So began a period of house buying and renovating in Newcastle that went on for about ten years. By the time Margaret had finished in Newcastle, any residue of guilt about wasted time must have been well and truly exorcised in the exercise:

After the two wooden houses were finished, I started on the big house in Church Street. I used to do almost all the work, except for the plumbing and the electrical wiring. The Church Street house had three storeys and the stone basement had been painted in kalsomine. I used to go down there and work away with a chisel, chipping it back to the stone. I kept gallons of methylated spirits, wire wool and gloves beside the doorways and, for a break from chipping, I would strip a bit of skirting. I also scraped all the varnish off the banisters. Doing up the houses was like a game. When I'd had enough of it, I'd go back to Brisbane, start painting again and forget about them.

Margaret used to let her houses out furnished: part of the fun of buying a house, according to her, was being able to choose the furniture for it. Although she'd given up the antique shop by now, it was still in her system, she says, and she haunted second-hand shops run by the Salvation Army in Newcastle, in search of bargain cedar chests of drawers and other pieces. She also made cushions and curtains for the houses, and even hung prints on the walls. It was all part of the game. But she also found the actual doing-up curiously fulfilling:

Because I didn't have very much money to spend, as soon as I'd bought a house I'd think, Now, what's the most offensive thing? – and start removing it. Always, when I was repainting, if I liked the colour in one room I'd leave it untouched, so I retained a little bit of the old along with the new. I had to borrow from the bank for all of them. I used to remember how my father had lost the court case and all his money in Brisbane. If the worst comes to the worst I'll lose the lot, I'd remind myself. Once I'd accepted that I was fearless.

Margaret's method of dealing with bank managers also showed a degree of inventiveness:

I had the theory that every house should have a different bank account, so the books could be kept separate, which meant I was always talking to different bank managers. In those days they used to jot your details down in a notebook. Miss Olley, what is your income going to be this year, they'd inevitably ask. I'd hold out my right hand and answer, I really don't know. It's like asking this hand what it's going to paint. It sufficiently mystified them to quash any further questions. I used this ploy on several occasions to good effect to secure a loan.

Margaret still talks about Newcastle with such passion that you want to jump on a train straight away and cross the Hawkesbury with its ever-changing light to experience the city:

I loved Newcastle on foggy days. Living up in Church Street, I'd walk along and it was like looking into a Hieronymous Bosch painting. You'd see the silhouette of a ship and because of the fog it'd be floating in the air with all the buildings round it. Now it's become boutique around the waterfront, but back then it was a working port. I had an outside toilet in my basement flat and if I went out for a pee at night, the whole sky would be lit up with the bright lights of the dock working. And it hummed; not an aggressive noise, but a sort of powerful hum, a pulse.

Margaret spent so much time in Newcastle that it led naturally to a closer friendship with Anne von Bertouch. In April 1969 von Bertouch had been involved in a car accident in which she had nearly died. Shortly afterwards, she bought four adjoining terrace houses in Laman Street, near her present gallery, that had been allowed to fall into a state of bad disrepair because the previous owner had been planning to demolish them. Von Bertouch, who'd fairly recently separated from her husband, then directed a large amount of her energies into restoring the derelict premises, partly as a means of recuperating from the mental shock of the accident. Her new galleries, in two of these houses, did not open until November 1974, but no doubt the renovation of the premises became a shared interest between her and Margaret.

The Newcastle art collector and philanthropist William Bowmore was another person Margaret grew to know during these years. Bowmore, born Milhelm Yared, was the son of successful Lebanese migrants. Early on he showed considerable talent as a pianist, and after winning a Queensland eisteddfod at the age of fourteen, he began studying piano and cello seriously, eventually enrolling at the Conservatorium of Music in Sydney. In the 1930s he moved to Newcastle; then, after serving with the RAAF during the war, he changed his name by deed poll to Bowmore. As well as being involved with property development in Newcastle, he also taught cello and became a patron of the Newcastle Conservatorium. By the 1960s, he'd begun collecting art and in the 1970s he was Margaret's neighbour in Church Street:

I could never afford to have the phone on. At the end of the day, still in my work clothes, I'd walk down Church Street to a public phone box, which I loved because (again) it had a view of Newcastle, to ring up my mother and workmen about various jobs that needed doing on the houses. One day Bill, who lived opposite the phone box, popped his head out the door and said, Come and have a look, I'm just undoing the Blake. But the first thing I saw when I went into his house was a Roman sculpture of Athena being born from the head of a gorgon. It had the most beautiful folds in the marble drapes of her gown that I could have looked at all day.

Far from a Still Life

> *The [William] Blake turned out to be a small watercolour illustration of the biblical story of Felix and Drusilla, which was enthralling to see. From that day on Bill always asked me in to use his phone and inspect his latest purchases. There were more Blakes and sculpture that included a wonderful collection of Rodin. Knowing Bill and watching his collection grow added to my love of being in Newcastle. It was exciting to think of him at the end of the street collecting art – when I was only collecting mortgages. And later, when he became a benefactor, he was another person who inspired me to begin donating to galleries.*

◆

In the middle of 1970 the art world was shattered by the deaths of two outstanding artists, following closely upon each other. On 13 May Sir William Dobell, who had been knighted four years earlier, died at Wangi Wangi, south of Newcastle. Two days later the art world grieved again when John Molvig, an artist closely associated with the early days of Brisbane's Johnstone Gallery, also passed away. But this was not all. In August, Ian Fairweather was taken to the Royal Hospital in Brisbane suffering from dehydration. Although this was soon remedied, it marked the beginning of the deterioration of both his painting and his life. (Fairweather died of a heart attack at the Royal Hospital nearly four years later, in May 1974.) Then, towards the end of 1970, two more deaths occurred that cut Margaret and her contemporaries especially deeply.

On 23 November, gentle, helpful, generous (as Donald Friend described him) David Strachan and his friend Lindsay Stewart were killed in a car accident at Yass.[3] Strachan and Stewart had been to Strachan's home town of Creswick for the official presentation of a large Creswick landscape by Strachan to the local shire office, as a memorial to his father. Thus at the occasion of making final peace with the father who had not wanted him to be an artist, Strachan's own life was rudely snatched:

I was working on a house in Newcastle and because I didn't have a phone on, it was Anne von Bertouch who came up to tell me about the tragic accident. Although I wasn't as close to Anne as to some of my other friends, her being the bearer of the bad news bound us together. Sharing grief like that does bond you. Lindsay was also a great friend: we'd go off to the cinema in Rose Bay together if I was staying with David in Sydney or have a meal. So it was a terrible double blow. The additional sadness about David's death for me was I never found out what, if anything, I did to him that came between us.

Donald Friend received the news of Strachan's death in Bali. 'We all grew fonder of him the longer we knew him, but I think (as we too) the years made him lonelier and lonelier despite the affection of friends,' Friend concluded his diary entry – foretelling his own last years, as well.[4]

In *Art and Australia,* artist William Salmon, another friend of Strachan's, wrote an obituary that paid special tribute to Strachan's Australian landscape paintings: 'To most of us the landscape is still strange. He appreciated its wry scragginess not as a voyager looking at the exotic, but as a child at home, curious yet loving. To him it is his own.'[5] Paul Haefliger, writing in the same magazine, wound up his praises of Strachan's art – 'where lovers, fruit, flowers, spirits of the night were as much a part of the scene as the more sober landscapes of his later years' – with: 'He had no theory to guide him, only intuition; but when the image – so subtly regarded – partook of the poetic spirit, he knew that it had fulfilled itself and a kind of magic was born.'[6]

The 'trouble with losing friends,' Margaret herself summed up simply to Friend in a letter at the end of the year, is that 'though they are always with you – they leave such unbridgeable gaps.'[7]

In the same letter to Friend, Margaret outlined some changes she was about to make in her own life as an aftermath of the wretched accident: she planned to be out of Australia for most of the second half of 1971, and would probably leave after she'd had an exhibition with Anne von Bertouch in June. She also said that although she was sending the letter to Bali, she hoped that Friend was away somewhere dry and that she often thought of the happy times she'd had in Bali with him.

The trip overseas would not be the only change in Margaret's life. She now sold her house in Paddington Street. It was just too sad to keep it, she felt, after the deaths of Strachan and Stewart. She then promptly bought two more houses, one after another (one also impressively large), near Christ Church Anglican Cathedral in Church Street, Newcastle. In April 1971, when she was working on one of these houses, von Bertouch again brought Margaret bad news: at eighty-three and a half, darling Aunt Mary was dead. Despite this, the exhibition Margaret had mentioned in her letter to Friend still opened at the von Bertouch Newcastle Galleries on 25 June 1971. This was something of a miracle, considering the upheavals of the preceding months. The thirty oils were almost all paintings of Newcastle, with subjects such as *Evening from the Obelisk*, *Evening Docks* and *Industrial Skyline*, but there was also a new theme developing in her work.

Not only had her return from Bali prompted the business of buying houses, on coming back Margaret was also filled with a desire to paint Australian wildflowers. This new urge soon resulted in works like the studies *Hawkesbury Wildflowers* and *Banksia*, which were included in the Newcastle show.

Margaret says that her painting of wildflowers, which had more to do with her appreciation of their forms than of their nativeness, may have stemmed from a visit she and David Strachan had made together to Russell Drysdale's new home at Bouddi, near Gosford, about halfway to Newcastle. She and

Strachan both picked big bunches of wildflowers on the day, which lasted for ages, Margaret remembers. Thereafter, if anyone drove her up to Newcastle, she would ask them to stop the car near Mount White so she could collect more. Interestingly, Christine France has pointed out how *Banksia*, which concentrates on the vermilion-veined, dark green leaves in a clear glass vase even more than the green and orange-coloured flower cones, shows 'the same sense of discovery one gets walking through the Australian bush': at first sight it's all one colour but on closer inspection a far greater variety is revealed.[8]

From the 1970s on, wildflowers would occur in Margaret's paintings nearly as often as exotics, and in Paddington these days her dining room table is as likely to be filled with red gum blossom as with blue delphinium petals or rose-pink hollyhocks from a friend's cottage garden in the Southern Highlands.

Rather strangely, since it would put her right where she'd spent her happiest times with Moya Dyring and Strachan, and would inevitably be painful, Margaret chose to revisit Paris in 1971. Perhaps she thought it might be a way of bridging the unbridgeable gap between her and the dead. Whatever the reason, she applied for and was given the Moya Dyring Studio at the Cité Internationale des Arts for three months. The idea of a studio to honour the memory of Dyring had been initiated by Strachan in 1968 and endowed, due to the generosity of friends, the following year.

But Paris wasn't to be Margaret's only destination. Never one to avoid a challenge, she planned to hop from one exotic location to the next en route to France, an approach that would become typical of the travelling she would undertake again and again over the next three decades. To detail all her journeying during these years would fill a volume in itself.

Far from a Still Life

The year 1971 began with a visit to Donald Friend in Bali.[9] After that, Margaret travelled to Hong Kong, where she stayed with Mitty Lee-Brown. From there she travelled to Katmandu, then on to India, to the holy city of Benares on the Ganges, New Delhi and Kajara – for a quick look at erotic temple sculptures. Next she visited Teheran and Isfahan in Iran, and the ancient Persian capital of Persepolis; after which she made her way across Turkey and ended up in Greece in Athens. She then caught up with Van Hodgkinson in London before settling into the studio in Paris. However, not only was Paris sadly empty of her old friends, Margaret also found the new studio with its white walls and minimal furnishings disturbingly bare:

There was not even a drawing pin to be had. Not even a drawing pin. The cleaners had come in and taken everything away. I couldn't stand it. Straight out, I pulled some ivy off a wall and stuck it in a bottle; put some posters up; pulled out the Indian bedspread and kilims that I'd bought along the way and instantly felt more at home.

The presence of Donald Friend in Paris must also have helped to restore Margaret's sense of the familiar. Friend, who arrived in October at about the same time Margaret did, was in Paris for an exhibition of his work at the Galerie Drouant in November 1971. If he wasn't out of Paris on excursions to Brittany, Normandy and London, Friend spent mornings drawing the Seine and the houses near the Port Marie from the windows of Margaret's studio.[10]

Margaret and Friend also did a little exploring of Paris together, but this was hampered by the fact that Friend, having once been jammed in the automatic closing doors of the Metro, refused to avail himself of its services anymore. Accordingly, one day they set out on foot and walked quite a distance to a Francis Bacon exhibition. When they arrived, Friend felt like lunch but the only café nearby was rejected by him because it smelt of pommes frites.

Living in a Basket

Friend's rule of thumb was that if a café smelt of pommes frites it was to be avoided. So back they walked to Friend's hotel for lunch and never saw the Bacon exhibition. On another outing, besides sniffing out a lunching spot, they made rubbings of a stone wall, one of which Friend later turned into a portrait of Margaret.

When her time at the Moya Dyring Studio was up, Margaret embarked on more tripping about:

I'd bought a round-the-world ticket and I had intended coming back via America and Mexico. It was Mexico that I particularly wanted to see. But then my old friend from London, Sydney Cooper, asked me to spend Christmas with him at Marrakesh in Morocco, so I changed my ticket and visited him. Sydney's financial circumstances were a little reduced by then and he used to take people on trips across the Atlas Mountains to make a little extra money.

After Christmas I also crossed the Atlas Mountains and went on to Zagora and Fez, after which I crossed over to Spain and checked out the Prado Museum in Madrid. Next I retraced my steps so I could visit Isfahan and Teheran in the winter season. Then I came back to Australia because I wanted to see my mother, who by this time was getting on in life. I just felt I should check up on her, but she seemed fine.

On returning to Australia, Margaret again placed herself in an environment that could only evoke memories of David Strachan. There is a contradiction about Margaret's actions here. She had earlier sold her house in Paddington Street because she did not want to live so near Strachan's former residence after the tragedy of his death. But now Margaret approached Strachan's sister, Veronica Rowan, to see if the Strachan family would allow her to paint in his house. One can only surmise that Margaret's spell in Paris had partly bridged the gap that Strachan's death had brought about, and that for her, rather than being confronting, inhabiting the spaces left empty by his death was actually healing. Certainly, working in Strachan's house did not bring Margaret unhappiness. On the contrary, it was there that her real power as a painter of atmospheric interiors emerged.

Already in 1970, Margaret had painted a series of Farndon Interiors in Brisbane. The studies of the living room (*Interior IV* and *Interior VIII*) show comfortable armchairs upholstered in a limey green, a bookcase and a wooden stand displaying pottery from Chambri Lakes in New Guinea. There's also a coffee table with a vase of banksias and wattle, and another little table with an Asian-looking statue. Pot plants are plentiful and the windows are filled with the garden's greenery. The Farndon interiors afford fascinating glimpses of the Olley domicile and, like life there, are reassuringly cheerful – you just know Mrs Oll is going to bustle in any minute and offer you tea in a blue and white cup.

The paintings that came from her time in David Strachan's house, such as *Late Afternoon* and *Afternoon Interior*, are far more intense. Life has been interrupted and an eerie yearning for the return of what's been lost pervades them, whether it be by an open French door; a partially drunk, stoppered bottle beside wine glasses; or just the spill of pale light over accumulated loved objects. Christine France, in her book about Margaret's work, has written of Strachan's study of Jung and his belief in the evening as being the time most pregnant with creativity, and says that this is what Margaret has captured in paint.[11]

Margaret herself is more prosaic both about renting the house and painting there:

I asked to use it for practical reasons. I didn't have any money: I was buying property, so I was up to pussy's bow in mortgages. All of my present house was let except for the little flat in the middle, which was hardly big enough to paint in. But I must say, I've always had a sentimental attachment to that flat, which is why I doggedly keep it intact and have rarely allowed anyone to stay there. In those days it was painted blue, not yellow the way it is now.

Because Brian Johnstone called the exhibition of paintings I did there 'Homage', people think that it was a memorial to David, that I was painting my grief, but I wasn't. David's house was convenient. I knew the light. I'd painted there before when I'd stayed with him. It just physically suited me to use it as a studio. I painted there for several years. I did interiors and still life. An interior is like painting a portrait, so in that sense the paintings are a reflection of David. I've always been intrigued by interiors. You gain a lot of information from a room. I've also always liked artists who painted interiors: Sickert, Bonnard, Vuillard, Matisse. An interior will result in a portrait of the person who lives there, but it's also to do with approaching the room as if it was a person whose portrait you're painting.

Ronnie [Veronica Rowan] was living in Canberra, she only came to Sydney occasionally. When she did I'd tidy everything up, put all the unfinished and finished paintings neatly together inside, and put the old ones that I was going to scrape down on the balcony upstairs, where I thought they'd be quite safe. But they were stolen, which later caused all sort of problems because a few started turning up with David's signature on them.

Since the late 1980s, several paintings have been put in for auction bearing Strachan's signature which Margaret, her agent Philip Bacon and other art experts (as well as Veronica Rowan when she was alive) have identified as being, in fact, her unfinished work – taken from Strachan's balcony in the 1970s. One theory as to why Strachan's signature was forged on them is that because Strachan's work then sold for higher prices than Margaret's, whoever stole the paintings may have thought they'd be worth more signed that way. By now, the fake signature is well documented and Margaret, who has always offered to re-sign works correctly, keeps a vigilant eye on auctions to ensure that any forged signatures, or confusion between her and Strachan's paintings from that time, are identified. As she says emphatically, 'You know your own work anywhere. You recognise what you've painted, the same way you would your handwriting.'

※

In the early 1970s, Margaret's property interests in Newcastle continued to expand at an astonishing rate. Soon two more houses were added to those she had bought near the Cathedral. One could say she was now buying up houses as in the past she had gathered flowers. In her purchases, she was also displaying uncanny real-estate acumen. But, one has to remember, regarding the considerable bunch of properties she was rapidly acquiring, for artists financial independence can often be crucial to creativity – unless they're prepared to live like Fairweather – and does not come easily from painting sales. Income from exhibitions has to be spread out over a year or more; materials have to be bought, frames paid for and galleries also take a commission.

Margaret's painting prices were still modest at this stage. As a woman artist who had chosen not to have a husband or a partner, the opportunity for her to secure an income separate from art would have been even more tempting, if not essential. Besides, real estate was in her blood: it was in Grace Olley's footsteps that Margaret was following. Though Grace had inherited her money rather than made it, she did manage to retain the way of life she enjoyed through clever property buying. The first big house near the Cathedral that Margaret acquired after Strachan's death was easily large enough to accommodate visitors and, not surprisingly, Mrs Oll soon decided to inspect her daughter's purchases:

I'd been working like a dog at night, trying to finish off the house, and her train was due in very early in the morning. Of course the inevitable happened: I overslept. Then I had to find a taxi to get over to Broadmeadow to collect her, which wasn't the easiest at that hour. I finally arrived to find her asleep in the waiting room with a big Christmas pudding that she'd made me beside her. While she was staying with me, the plumber I had working on the house took us to see a house that had belonged to his father. It turned out to be a very grand place that had been divided into flats, and my mother encouraged me to buy that as well. If you'd just stop smoking, she used to lecture me, you could afford to have a row of terrace houses. Well, I did end up with the row of nine terrace houses, but I'm still smoking.

Far more important than any house she might spot, as Margaret entered her fifties Sam Hughes, at long last, came back into her life, as if to make up for her recent losses:

Sam and I used to exchange Christmas cards and correspond. He'd been living in London and various places, including the Greek island of Mykonos, and I'd hoped he might come and stay with me when I had the studio in Paris. But he was too busy and it wasn't to be. Then he arrived back in Sydney on a brief visit and stayed with a friend at Rose Bay. I was painting at David Strachan's when he got in touch with me, so I asked him to lunch there. I'd cleaned up, put the paintings away and started getting lunch ready. I was so excited and distracted by the thought of seeing him again that as I was mixing up the salad dressing I put a slosh of what turned out to be turps in with the oil.

Despite the long hiatus in their relationship, Margaret and Hughes still got on as well as ever, though obviously there must have been a change, if not a reversal, in their roles. Hughes could hardly be opening doors for Margaret now – except, of course, a very large one to personal felicities. In 1973, Margaret again painted David Strachan's upstairs room with the half-open French door, in *Early Morning Interior,* only this time the whole room is flooded with the warm first light of day that makes the fresh orange now spread across the table glow with a joy exceeding even the dawn. The resumption of a relationship with Hughes – even if only in its incipient rekindling when this work was painted – may well have been responsible.

It would seem that Hughes stayed in Australia until early 1974 on this visit. Margaret and he next caught up later in 1974, when Margaret was in Europe. Typically, the reunion was not without a round-about preamble of travelling. Margaret first flew to London to do the rounds of the art galleries and to buy two shirts Hughes wanted from a shop behind Fortnum and Mason in Piccadilly. She then flew off to visit Fred Jessup in the south of France at Espondeilhan, a town in a wine-growing area halfway between the mountains of Languedoc and the Mediterranean beaches. Despite living close to the border, Jessup had never been to Spain, so Margaret suggested they make a little journey to Madrid together:

At Barcelona, the train we were catching to Madrid was late and we had a long wait in the underground station. To fill in the time I was smoking, which involved a good deal of opening and shutting my handbag to get out the cigarettes. I must have been watched, because when the train finally came, as soon I'd heaved myself up onto it and sat down, I knew something was missing. I didn't even have to open my bag, I could tell by the feel of it: traveller's cheques, money, passport – gone.

Fred insisted I couldn't go on without a passport, but the train had already taken off. We had to get off at the first stop and take a taxi back to Barcelona. When we went to the railway station to make a search, it had been fogged with a terrible smelly chemical to drive out the homeless people. It was all very creepy and unhealthy.

Margaret and Jessup then reported the theft to the Barcelona police, who told them to forget about looking for her passport and to proceed to Madrid. Fortunately Margaret had a contact in Madrid and she was issued with a new passport quite swiftly. After this she and Jessup finished their tour of Spain and, somewhat exhausted, Margaret finally arrived in Geneva, where Hughes was then living:

He was staying in a hotel and had a job looking after an old English professor. The professor was so grumpy and rude to Sam I was incensed. I had to say something. I saw Sam was trapped as I had been all those years before with Miss Campbell in Cassis. You have to leave here, I said to him. Come back to Australia and you can stay with me.

So Hughes, having agreed to this, remained in Geneva to find a replacement carer for the old professor and wind up his life in Europe, and Margaret returned to Australia via a 'fantastic, huge' exhibition of the Spanish painter Joan Miró in Paris. Margaret's friend Van Hodgkinson and her daughter Kate were staying with Margaret in Newcastle when Margaret read out the astrology column as she always did. 'There was a reference to someone from the past coming back,' Kate remembers.[12] '"That'll be Sam," Margaret said straight away. I didn't even know who she was talking about. But Mum did. And within a month or two he was there. Margaret and Sam were both so excited to be together. It was a fabulous relationship.'

To begin with, Hughes again stayed with his friend at Rose Bay. Then Margaret asked him to accompany her to Newcastle, and there what had been postponed for decades had its proper start:

I thought long and hard about having Sam come and live with me. It was a big commitment. But after Newcastle, he moved into the little middle flat in Duxford Street [Paddington] with me. Sam, whom I always called Mr Sam, really was the main person for me. He was absolutely perfect because he came and went all the time. He would disappear off overseas to Mykonos or wherever for months, and then I'd join him because there was an exhibition I wanted to see. I never really knew why he went away so much and I never asked. It was ideal as far as I was concerned. I could never have dreamt of having somebody underfoot around me. Somebody underfoot is an abomination.

The two words that friends of Margaret have used most frequently about her and Hughes are 'happy' and 'fun'. 'He was lovely,' Kate Hodgkinson says, 'an absolute gentleman. Very vivacious, very animated. Quite theatrical, he could have been an actor. He wasn't about that much, as I remember, but when he was, he was just a wonderful presence.'

As well as cohabiting in the blue middle flat, Margaret and Mr Sam were still very much living in baskets, or rather probably a well-worn suitcase on his part:

We were travelling between Sydney, Newcastle and Brisbane; we also stayed at Noosa in a holiday house belonging to my friends Ron and Shirley Wright. Sam particularly loved Newcastle. I'd be busy working on the house or painting. He'd be out and about, shopping or going for a swim – he was very keen on the surf in those days. He never did any renovating on the houses, that wasn't his style. But in the late evening we'd go for long walks together right out along the breakwater wall to where the boats come in.

I only have one complaint about Sam. When we were living at Duxford Street and I was painting at David Strachan's, while I was out Sam used to grill himself sardines. I could smell them as I walked home up the lane. It took me a long time to decide whether I wanted to eat fish or not, let alone put up with the leftover smell of somebody else cooking them.

Living in a Basket

By the time Hughes and Margaret became a couple Hughes must have been close to seventy, while Margaret was a spritely fifty. Hughes does not seem to have worked at all after he was free of the professor in Geneva, although to boost his income he did once do a little artistic wheeling and dealing:

When Sam and John Richards had the shop at Edgecliff, one of them came across a painting in an auction of David holding Goliath's head, which was supposed to be a copy of a work by the Italian artist Bernardo Strozzi.[13] *The original had been in the Rotterdam Museum up until the war. The copy wasn't even in a frame and Sam tacked it over a door in the shop. After John Richards' father died, John asked Sam if he could give it to the Art Gallery of New South Wales in memory of his father. So the Strozzi copy went off to the gallery.*

Then when Sam arrived back here and saw the painting cleaned up and hanging, he began investigating. He discovered that the gallery trustees had never actually accepted it as a gift. He also began to suspect that it might be a real Strozzi and not a copy. Apparently the knees and elbows were always very strongly painted in a Strozzi, so a lot of examining of those went on. I don't quite know the ins and outs of it. But the painting was finally handed back to Sam who took it to London to be authenticated.[14]

In London the next year, he put the painting into another auction where it was again sold as a copy.[15] *I've always felt so guilty about it. We could have had that wonderful painting hanging in the gallery here. So when I give something to the gallery, it's always a bit in memory of what Sam took away.*

The actual whereabouts of the painting today seem to be unknown, as is the final word on its authenticity. But a letter received by the Art Gallery of New South Wales from an art expert in Holland indicates that it might indeed be more valuable than was first suggested.[16]

Far from a Still Life

At about the same time that Sam Hughes came back into her life, Margaret's association with the gallery owner Philip Bacon began. Fortuitously, this coincided with the closing of the Johnstone Gallery, which had shut up shop at the end of 1972, not long after Margaret's 'Homage' exhibition. The second last show there was called 'A Time Remembered' and featured works by such artists as Charles Blackman, Arthur Boyd, Ray Crooke, Bob Dickerson, Russell Drysdale, Sidney Nolan and Lloyd Rees, all major names who had helped to make the gallery so special through their exhibitions there.

Philip Bacon's first encounter with Margaret in the early 1970s was one he'll never forget. He was in his early twenties, still at university part-time and not even working at a gallery. After the success of her exhibitions in the 1960s, Margaret was already a bit of a legendary figure. Bacon and Margaret had in common the fact that Bacon had also taken art lessons from Caroline Barker which, as he's quick to point out, in his case only served to prove that he was not destined to be an artist. 'We'd corresponded and I really wanted to meet her,' he says of Margaret. 'It was a summer's day and when I made my way to what was then the blue flat, Margaret was sitting on the doorstep drying her hair in the sun. I'd never seen such long hair, it was streaming down as she combed it through. It was a very Mary Magdalene experience; you could have dried the feet of Christ with that hair, it was terrific.'

Philip Bacon's experience of Margaret is not likely to be experienced by anyone now. These days Margaret takes herself off to the hairdressers to have her hair washed. Occasionally, though, when she's tidying herself up for visitors or getting ready to go out, she'll suddenly remove a few pins and a startling thick fall of hair, with barely a grey thread, will drop to below her shoulders.

Bacon opened his original Brisbane Gallery in 1974 and in September 1975 Margaret had her first show with him. He now

Living in a Basket

possesses the largest and most prestigious gallery in Brisbane. According to Bacon, it was the support of Margaret and a few other artists, such as Lawrence Daws, Charles Blackman and Bob Dickerson, that gave him the courage to leave the Grand Central Gallery in Brisbane, where he was by then working, and set up on his own in 1974.[17] Bacon goes on to add that Margaret also talked other artists into exhibiting with him when they rang her up on the quiet to ask: What about this young bloke from Brisbane?

The premises of Bacon's new gallery had previously been used as a tile warehouse. The space had a low ceiling (which Bacon later raised in a major renovation), a chocolate brown carpet and white walls. 'Margaret had arrived for her exhibition, the paintings had come and I think I'd started to hang them,' he recalls. 'She walked in and said: "Well, this won't do. I hate white walls. I'm not showing here. The pictures look terrible. The walls should be a flesh-coloured pink." "Well, white is what they are," I replied. "You'll have to paint them," she answered. "I can't afford to get painters in," I responded. "Well, we'll do it," she said.

'So, up the ladder the two of us went,' Bacon continues. 'Margaret's a very quick, but not an entirely accurate painter – the paint would only go a certain way up into the corners. She also loaned me furniture to have in the gallery, which then stayed on for years. But the show was a huge success. It was the first sell-out exhibition I'd ever had – absolutely everything sold.'

Not only was the Johnstone Gallery now closed, but at this time Margaret's working relationship with Anne von Bertouch became strained, so the new link with Bacon was doubly timely. Margaret might order Bacon to repaint his gallery without compunction, but an incident occurred in which von Bertouch was involved (not directly to do with her gallery but connected with it) that reveals just how much shyness remained a deeply embedded part of Margaret's personality:

Far from a Still Life

Anne used to take up causes. It was part of her charm. There was a case where she wanted to save a park and she chained herself to a tree. Because she was so involved with everything, she was always having dinners that she wanted me to come to. I didn't mind that. But then she asked me if I'd do a TV interview. I was reluctant, but she persuaded me, saying it would be so helpful for the gallery.

I thought I'd just go into a little box and be interviewed, but when I walked through the studio door I was confronted by a huge audience. I wished the ground would open up and swallow me. It was one of these shows where the studio people put up signs: one saying 'Applaud', then one with 'Silence'. They could control the audience but not me. I went blank. I could not say a word. It was the most awful ordeal. After that experience it's only very recently that I've plucked up the nerve to speak in public – and I've been very proud of myself that I've managed it. Paintings should talk for themselves, I always said in the past.

Margaret and von Bertouch did not ever personally fall out, but there was a parting of the ways in 1976 as far as exhibiting went:

She was in her new gallery by then – she'd turned two of the terrace houses into a showing space and used the third for storage. The galleries had a brick floor and what you might call a 'rusticated look'. There was also a banana tree and various vines growing through them which made it quite busy. I actually preferred the old gallery. But the exhibitions were still terrific; she had particularly good pottery shows and her 'Collector's Choice' was a like a yearly festival with people queuing up and fighting to get in, as they did at the old Macquarie Galleries' 'Show of Sixes'.

She'd also put in red glass windows, like you'd find in a church. When the sun shone through them it cast a red light over everything. So for my last exhibition I asked her if I could paste some brown paper over the windows, which she agreed to. But also, unbeknownst

Living in a Basket

to me, she'd arranged that I share the show with a man who did sculpture with lights in it. I don't mind sharing a show with somebody, so long as each artist has their own area. But on this occasion Anne put his sculptures in between my paintings.

A crowd of friends came up and stayed with me for the opening. A great deal of celebrating went on and the show did well, but I never had another exhibition with Anne after that. I still sent work up to her mixed shows, but that was the end of my having solo shows there.

Other changes were taking place, too. Margaret and Hughes moved out of the little middle flat in Duxford Street into the larger area of the Hat Factory that ran off at right angles from it. Although this building had been a separate structure from the main terrace house when Margaret first bought the property, by this stage all three areas – terrace, factory and flat – were linked. Margaret and Sam's new bedroom, atop an almost perpendicular set of stairs, had a view across the Paddington rooftops that included the Harbour Bridge. The bedroom walls were covered with a voluptuous Persian-looking design of flowers and butterflies on a blue background, which later appeared in several of Margaret's self-portraits, including *Dressing Table*.

Downstairs, paintings went up on the walls and the Hat Factory soon filled with what Donald Friend would describe as 'strange charmingly confused clutter'.[18] The clutter was made up of the 'treasured loot from her travels' and consisted of 'kelim rag-covered sofas, pearl-shell inlaid tabors, carved chests, Melanesian idols, innumerable pots and vases of flowers, old brocades, statues of Buddha, crucifixes'. The jumble, in all, gave the effect 'of a sort of antipodean Old Curiosity Shop', according to Friend.

More living space not only meant more clutter, but also more entertaining, and over the next few years the Hat Factory became the repeated scene of convivial dinner parties. In fact, Margaret's role as a Sydney hostess probably dates from this period, when her guests included friends from the past like Frankie Mitchell, newer ones such as Van Hodgkinson, and also friends of Hughes like theatre-loving lawyer Sir David Griffin, who'd been Lord Mayor of Sydney a few years earlier. Hughes's role was to buy the wine. He'd inevitably stroll in like a character from a Noel Coward play, clutching a paper bag, the bottom of which would be about to give way, with three or four bottles inside, having managed to resist the urge for his favourite retsina:[19]

We used to have a few fights in the kitchen, actually. Sam wanted everything to be spiced up. I used to tell him that you must have mashed potatoes or rice, something bland, to balance it. Then there was the dishwasher, which I've long since dispensed with. Sam used to love loading it up, then he'd turn it on while we were eating. I hated the noise of it. He always used to say to me, You don't keep house, you play cubby houses. He was quite right. I've never liked housework. I get by doing little chores when I feel like them, in between painting. Who wants to chase dust all their life? You can spend your whole lifetime cleaning the house. I like watching the patina grow. If the house looks dirty, buy another bunch of flowers, is my advice.

Often with dinner parties I thought it was better to have two or three at a time. It actually took less effort than having them on separate occasions. Having people for a meal is just a nice thing to do. As far as cooking itself, I had a long apprenticeship watching my mother. Over the years, you come to instinctively know what flavours go together. I'd have ten people here for dinner, maybe twice a week, and think nothing of it. I'd go down to the butcher and get a couple of shoulders of lamb, exactly as my mother used to. For pudding, in between courses I'd make a bread-and-butter pudding or baked custard, and serve it while it was still hot. But those days have gone, I'm afraid.

Living in a Basket

As well as entertaining and traipsing between Sydney, Brisbane and Newcastle, Margaret also found time to squeeze in another jaunt overseas. In 1976, she and her friend Van Hodgkinson joined Hughes in London. From there Margaret and Hodgkinson went on a journey that included Amsterdam, Bruges and Brussels, as well as an excursion through France and Italy. The highlight of their trip was a Paris exhibition of the famous eighteenth-century French still life painter Chardin.[20]

The next change in Margaret's life elicited mixed emotions in her. Mrs Oll, now in her late eighties, left Farndon – which Margaret, through all these years, still regarded as 'home' – and came to Sydney. The move meant Margaret could see more of her mother in Sydney, but also interrupted her painting time (Margaret had four solo exhibitions in the two-year period between 1976 and 1977). Initially Mrs Oll stayed with Margaret's sister Elaine and her family at Mosman. But Elaine was still nursing and Mrs Oll apparently felt isolated. And then there were her health problems:

I watched my mother shrink. Now I'm watching myself shrink; I'm becoming my mother. She was also suffering from carpal tunnel syndrome in both hands and decided to have them operated on at the same time. She should never have done it, because while she was convalescing she was completely helpless. The operation was done at the Mater Hospital at Crows Nest, which meant more rushing around. Then my sister heard about the Scottish Hospital in Paddington, which is close to me, and we thought that would be the best place for her to be permanently, because although she was mentally still alert, she was physically frail.

Once she was established there, she suggested I bring the big Spanish mahogany dining room table and chairs down from Farndon and use them myself. I decided I would, because she used to come and have lunch or dinner with me and I thought sitting at it would make her feel at home. If I was having people for lunch my mother would keep me company in the kitchen while I peeled the vegetables. It helped her feel as if she was participating, that she was back at home cooking, which was really what she'd loved doing most in her life.

And so the large table that is now almost the centre of Margaret's life came to the Hat Factory. Not only did the table serve to put Mrs Oll at ease, it has also facilitated innumerable dinner parties for Margaret over the years. These days it's covered with an Indian tablecloth and laden with bunches of flowers, from exotic gingers to gardenias, in various states of life and decay. In amongst the assorted blooms there's a bright orange wooden carp; a cake stand filled with artificial cactus; and a mountain of paperwork from which vital documents can rise to the surface and then disappear for weeks, if not forever. Any spare space is taken up with the Kama Sutra placemats on which food is served to guests, who struggle to catch a glimpse of each other through the table's melange of flowers and *objets*.

In March 1978 Margaret, and possibly Hughes too, decamped to London for ten days. After this Margaret and Hughes spent three months together in France, which included a month-long stay at the Moya Dyring Studio in Paris. 'Overheated so windows open to let in freezing air,' Margaret jotted in a postcard to Maisie and Tas Drysdale, which was signed, with much love to them both, 'Sam and Olley'.[21]

In the same card, she wrote that Paris was 'wet & cold, but also beautiful' and that the view from the studio was 'fantastic'. She reported that she had been trying to do some painting, but the 'light changing every 5 minutes drives one to distraction'. There were 'lots of exhibitions' to see, including Rubens at the Grand Palais and the Louvre; and a big Russian ballet exhibition of Diaghilev's sets and costumes. Included in this exhibition was the front curtain for Diaghilev's ballet, *Le Train Bleu* (the name given to the train that took Paris society to the Riviera each year for the summer), which was an enlargement of a painting by Picasso. Picasso was so delighted with the reproduction of his two large women, each with a breast exposed, running along a beach, against a sky the colour of a blue Gitane French cigarette packet, that he inscribed a dedication to Diaghilev in one corner. Seeing this curtain made 'one realise just how painters at this time were inspired by the excitement generated by Diaghilev', Margaret concluded.[22]

Margaret and Hughes also took the train to Strasbourg for a 'magnificent Bonnard exhibition', whose brightly dappled canvasses once again confirmed him as a painter of the light of life, in Margaret's view. Then in May the couple embarked on a remarkable car tour of France. From time to time in Australia, Margaret had been chauffeured to Newcastle by artist and architect Rollin Schlicht, a son of Theo and Katie Schlicht. At the time, Rollin was concentrating solely on painting and so accepted with alacrity Margaret's offer to pay his air fare to Europe if, in return, he drove her and Hughes around France.[23]

Their trip had two objectives. The first was to pay a call to Fred Jessup at Espondeilhan. Jessup had planned to visit Margaret and Sam in Paris in April, but his dog had been sick and the garden needed attention.[24] They also wanted to see Bertha Wright in the south-west of France. Their second objective was to visit as many French provincial galleries as possible.

Schlicht arrived in Paris when Margaret and Hughes were at the end of their studio stay, and soon afterwards the three headed south in a rented Renault. Quite apart from anything else, according to Schlicht the journey was made memorable because it coincided with a massive manhunt by French police for the notorious criminal Jacques Mesrine. With a litany of offences to his credit, such as burglaries, bank and jewellery shop robberies, kidnapping and arms smuggling, Mesrine also reputedly claimed to have committed thirty-nine murders. The previous year he'd escaped from prison and had been on the run ever since.

Unfortunately, Schlicht – who was going through a long-haired stage – apparently bore some resemblance to Mesrine, or one of the disguises that he'd adopted. 'There were road blocks everywhere, with armed French police,' Schlicht remembers. 'Sam and Margaret would be in the back, holding hands or chatting away, when we'd be stopped by these gendarmes. As we only had school-boy and school-girl French between us, trying to answer their interrogation was not the easiest – particularly as, because of their brusqueness, I tended to be taciturn and not that cooperative.'

However, the party survived the French police. (Mesrine was not so lucky: in November, a truckload of police on the outskirts of Paris sent a volley of shots through the front windscreen of his car, putting an instant end to the criminal's career.) Margaret and Sam's visit to Jessup passed pleasantly, as expected. The trio then travelled on to Bertha Wright, who was by now quite an old lady, but still retained a hint of flirtatiousness, so Schlicht recalls. Wright had moved from Cassis by this time and was ensconced with her daughter and son-in-law in the romantic, medieval Château de Charry, near the town of Montcuq. The château, which was once also a fort, is notable for its circular towers. When Margaret and her company arrived, the château was surrounded by fields of strongly smelling lavender and peacocks were wandering around its white walls. Also resident within the château grounds and likely to be encountered on strolls in the garden was another member of the Bloomsbury set: the now very ancient writer, David 'Bunny' Garnett.

Along the way to and from these two ports of call, there were spring picnics of bread and the soft cheeses Margaret loved, wine for those who drank, and endless stops at famous churches and museums. At Angoulême there was the church that reminded

Living in a Basket

Margaret of the sparkling white Basilique du Sacré Cœur in Paris. In Autun Cathedral they wondered at the work of the Romanesque sculptor Gislebertus, while at the Cathédrale Sainte-Marie at Auch, they inspected the remarkable carved choir stalls with over fifteen hundred individual biblical scenes and mythological animals. They visited the Musée Goya at Castres, not only to see the collection of Goyas, but also a painting by Velasquez that Margaret had heard about; at Albi, the birthplace of nineteenth-century painter and poster-maker Toulouse-Lautrec, they went through the Toulouse-Lautrec Museum. In Arles they saw the impressive collection of Picasso drawings in the Musée Réattu.

It was quite a tour. When Margaret and Hughes returned to the airy wallpapered boudoir of the Hat Factory in Paddington, Margaret began working frantically towards an exhibition at Sydney's Holdsworth Galleries in October 1978. According to an interview she did with Lenore Nicklin at the time of the show, she rose early and painted away her days at David Strachan's house, drinking cups of black coffee, peeling oranges, downing vitamin B and smoking green Capstan cigarettes.[25] The green Capstans had the added benefit of little cardboard lids, which Margaret was able to use for thumbnail work sketches. Sometimes round five in the afternoon, Mr Sam would receive an urgent summons to inspect her works in progress.

As life sped on and Margaret completed still lifes and flower painting after flower painting, all seemed to be well.

The following year brought breaks away from Sydney with her old friend Frankie Mitchell who, as well as clothing fashionable women from his boutique over the years, had always maintained his connections with the art world. According to Margaret, whenever he had any extra money Mitchell would buy paintings, not as an investment but because he really loved them. If he didn't have enough money to buy them outright, he'd make a layby and pay them off. Margaret and many others adored Mitchell both for his generosity and his wit, which was as sharp as ever:

Frankie Mitchell bought a house down at Milton on the south coast, and we had wonderful weekends there. It was a lovely wooden house with a veranda, which he had made very comfortable. Pam Bell came down with me once. That's where Blackberries *was painted, which Van bought. They were tangling over the fence at the back of the cottage, so Frankie, who was painting as well then, and I set to. I also loved painting landscapes of the headland nearby at Mollymook. It reminded me of the south of France – places like St Tropez.*

For most of 1979 Margaret was painting away for another exhibition. In October that year, her third show with Philip Bacon opened in Brisbane, in his gallery decorated with a profusion of fruit and flowers for the occasion. The event went off smoothly, except for a power failure, which plunged the space into darkness just as the opening crowd was arriving.[26] Among Margaret's friends who attended the opening night were Lady Cilento, Ron and Shirley Wright, and Pam Bell. Sam Hughes had even flown back to Australia especially from a trip to London in order to be there. The only slight sadness was that Mrs Oll, being confined in Sydney, couldn't be present.

Nineteen eighty was again a year of trips. Margaret joined Hughes in London and from there they travelled together to Europe. What Hughes did on his forays to London is a bit of a mystery even to Margaret, but he did have a wide circle of friends there to catch up with and would often use the city as a base from which to visit Mykonos. This time Hughes and Margaret both went from London to Paris to see a small Monet exhibition, before visiting Margaret's old friend from her student days, Ronald Millen, in Florence. Millen told them about an exhibition of twenty-six paintings by Balthus in the Venice Biennale:

I've always admired Balthus. I thought at that time he was the greatest living painter. I especially like his earlier works, those studies of the girls showing the strangeness of disturbed puberty. His paintings have a very quiet quality. Like Morandi's, his style is a continuation of Piero della Francesca.

No one was supposed to see the show before Mr Balthus arrived, but somehow we sneaked in and when he appeared we had to fold ourselves back into a corner. He was using a crutch because he'd hurt his ankle, and his Japanese wife was with him. As he went round the paintings he was talking very angrily in English and shaking his fist at them. Eventually I had a little conversation with him and found out what was wrong. I use a lot of impasto in my paintings, he said, and they've put varnish on them. Of course you can't varnish impasto, because the varnish fills up all the crevices deliberately made with the brush marks.

After a journey along the Adriatic coast to Athens, Margaret and Hughes visited Hughes's favourite haunt of Mykonos:[27]

I went to Mykonos quite frequently with Sam. It was idyllic – marvellous, simple architecture, white houses with blue trim, windmills and glorious sunshine. Sam and I also once went to the island of Cos to stay with Mitty Lee-Brown. We ran into Mitty in Rome, and she and her present partner, Les, were about to drive a car through Yugoslavia before coming on to Cos. She gave us instructions on how to get to the house and we went on ahead.

Cos was heavenly because you looked over to the Turkish coast. We were right up in the hills. Mitty had bought a number of little Greek houses and was joining them together; she and Les were a long time coming, so Sam and I had the place to ourselves. We kept wandering over the hills and finding an even better house in amongst the olive trees with fabulous views that we thought we'd like to buy. I think they belonged to Greeks who emigrated. By this time their only inhabitants were white ants and goats. We had the most wonderful romantic time, but I've never been back there. Buying a house there was just a wild pipe dream.

Apart from tripping about with Hughes (they also had a second short holiday in Bali with Nigel Hawkins from the *Hassan* days and his wife Norma[28]), 1980 was the year in which Margaret started selling some of her twenty properties in Newcastle. The initial fun of doing up the houses had now worn a bit thin and patching up the damage done by tenants was not nearly so diverting:

Some of them were big and full of flats. I used to dread Christmas, when all the students used to vacate, because I'd have to rush about trying to tee up workmen to do maintenance. I was also having quite a lot of trouble with tenants. They were irresponsible. I couldn't believe the damage they did to one of the houses in Lee Terrace. They must have been mad or high on something. There were holes punched in the wall, floorboards ripped up and the electrical wires had been cut. It had become a sort of nightmare. Then also, all of a sudden, property-market-wise friends started saying, Get out of mortgages, because interest rates were going to rise. So I began downscaling the properties.

It would take a few years, but by 1989 the official interest rate would have risen as high as 22 per cent. So Margaret's decision to begin divesting herself of property at this juncture was not only a choice to make painting her priority, but also an extremely shrewd financial move on her part. However, there would soon be a catastrophic shake-up in the busy, burbling pattern of her life.

The View from David's Kitchen, 1962

Eucharist Lilies, 1963

Daphne, 1964

Pomegranates,
1966

Children Playing, Angoram, 1968

Tribal Chieftain, 1968

Interior IV, 1970

Interior VIII, 1970

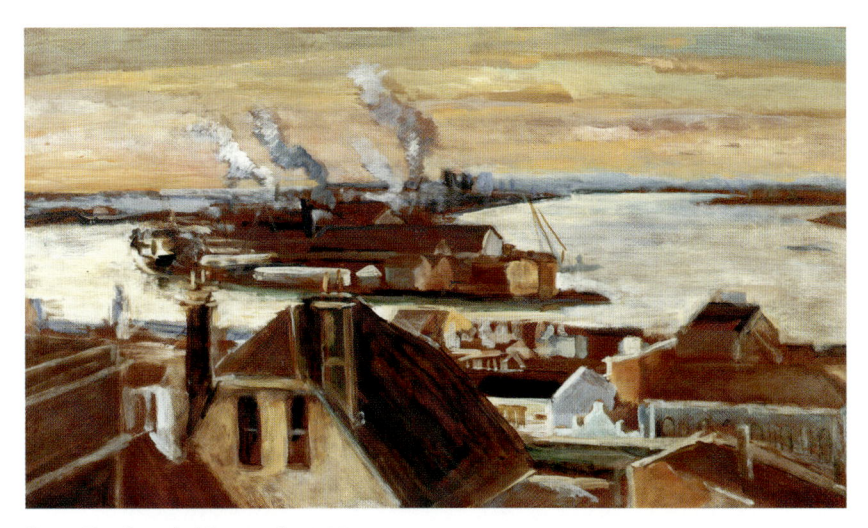

State Dockyard, Newcastle, 1974

Self-Portrait with Everlastings, 1974

Blackberries, 1979

Clivias, 1984

Cherries and Roses, 1985

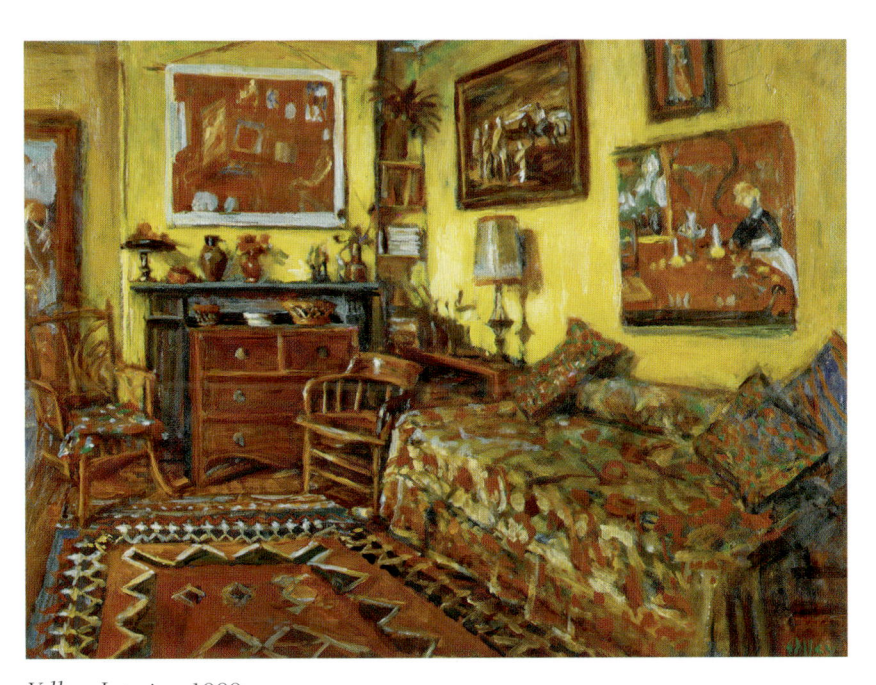

Yellow Interior, 1989

Yellow Room with Lupins, 1994

Elizabeth Bay Summer, 2000

15

Once More, Then No More

I could have burst into tears when my mother told me she couldn't bear her own company. In other words, she never found inner contentment. It's not a matter of being pleased with yourself, it's to do with self-reliance. It's tragic to come to the end of your life and not have found real contentment.

TROUBLES AND SORROWS DESCENDED ON MARGARET LIKE A BIBLICAL plague towards the end of 1980 and into the next few years. Some of their after-effects would linger for twenty-odd years and eventually plunge her into a black despair that, as with her drinking, only a huge effort of will would overcome.

When Grace Olley moved permanently into the Scottish Hospital, the inevitable question was raised of what to do about Farndon:

My Aunt Madge set up a family meeting at the Hat Factory. My brother came down from Brisbane and my sister also attended. Sam was here in the house with me. I had never really considered selling Farndon as an option. I couldn't see the hurry. My mother was still alive. The place was full of my paintings and other belongings. I was the one who used to go up and stay with my mother; who'd coloured my mother's life. I couldn't imagine selling it. But, as I remember it, the meeting became quite heated. I was quite upset by the discussion and after the meeting was over an unpleasant feeling stayed with me.

Perhaps the meeting was an omen, because suddenly in November, in a single stomach-turning day, Farndon, crammed with the treasures of several generations, was no more:[1]

Sam and I had just come back from Newcastle when the phone rang. It was a friend of my mother's, a bank manager's wife, who had the keys to Farndon and kept an eye on things. She said the house was on fire and the front room had just fallen into the street in flames.

There was nothing I could do. Nothing. I was in total shock. The next morning I caught the earliest plane up to Brisbane. The Johnstones picked me up at the airport and took me to their home for a cup of coffee. All I wanted to do was get to the scene of the fire. When I arrived, there was still a fire truck at the end of the street. I couldn't face talking to the firemen. I just walked straight into what remained of the house. The back steps were still intact. The hoses had been trained on that area because they didn't know if there was anyone in the flat downstairs or not.

I could walk right through the kitchen and into part of the living room. After that you just looked out into space. The front of the house, as my mother's friend said, had just dropped away, because it had only been held up by wooden stilts. It was the most surreal experience to be standing there looking into nothingness, into the empty space where the living room ought to be. My bedroom, which was in the corner of what used to be a veranda, was also gone.

Once More, Then No More

What individuals lose in any conflagration is frightening. It's not just the deprivation of personal effects; the vanishing of emotional souvenirs is also devastating. But the list of what went in the Farndon fire is even more horrific, because of the losses of Margaret's paintings. Favourite works hanging on walls were gone forever, as well as an incalculable number of artworks that she stored there:

All my early paintings were off stretchers under mats with newspaper between them in my mother's bedroom, which we thought was the best way to keep them. The fire got the lot. There were also works stacked up downstairs in the studio; they were all gone, too.

Margaret did salvage a very few items from the doused and blackened mess:

I couldn't believe how all the pottery and vases on the shelves upstairs seemed to have disappeared without a trace. I don't see how they could have been so totally destroyed in the fire and I've since suspected that it might have been a case of firemen's perks. But the little china cupboard in the kitchen was still standing and had china in it. So I prised that open, took out as many of the blue and white willow pattern plates as I could and left them in piles downstairs. A South American puppet that I'd brought home from the antique shop and which hung outside the kitchen door had also survived.

After I finished upstairs, I sifted through everything down below. A chest of drawers from my bedroom had dropped through the floor and landed more or less in one piece. Going through it I came across a pair of very fine stockings in a box, untouched, which Kieser Bell had given me and I'd never used because I always wore pantyhose. Also, amazingly, downstairs I found a Christmas card Sam had sent me from Europe years before. The fragments you do save from a fire bring such memories.

Far from a Still Life

The cat-shaped card had a yellow tabby cat on the front; inside was written: 'Good wishes for 1962, from Sam.' There's something terribly sad about the ordinariness of such mementos; one expects grander memorabilia to have survived.

While Margaret rarely talks about the fire, her losses resulting from it crop up again and again in conversation now. For many years it was a subject she simply wouldn't discuss. Not even sympathetic friends dared to bring it up. Probably it was off-limits even to Hughes, though his presence at the Hat Factory must have undoubtedly been a support in the days, weeks and months that followed.

After her first rushed trip, Margaret also refused to go back to the house. Only on a fairly recent visit to Brisbane in the last five years or so, when she was staying with Philip Bacon who lives nearby, did she drive past and see – somewhat to her surprise – that though most everything else has now gone, the paperbark trees that Joe Olley planted round the house long ago are still growing:

Losing things in fires is so final. For years afterwards if I couldn't find anything I used to say it was in Brisbane. It was almost as if I was denying the fire had happened. I just didn't want to think about it. It was quite a while before I accepted that Sydney now really was my home.

I'll never know how it started. It was simply the most terrible occurrence. My mother didn't know about it. I went through all her mail to make sure she never knew – it would have killed her if she'd found out. In her mind the house still existed and she could walk through it as she wished. If that had been taken away she would have been bereft.

Some of the things of invaluable significance Margaret lost in the fire include:

Once More, Then No More

The camisole top cut off the undergarment Mrs Dingle gave her in Tully.
Grace Olley's treadle sewing machine.
The Aboriginal shield her father found at Tully.
Her school hatband from Somerville House.
Her first painting done at Somerville House, of blue flowers with yellow berries.
Her painting of the Somerville House library exterior.
Her painting of the little pocket of palms – Burning Palms – done at Era.
Gouaches from the garden at Careel House, Whale Beach.
Paintings of North Sydney done from the flat at McMahons Point.
The French postcards she collected in the 1940s.
The pot of gold paint she used to paint the set for *Hassan*.
The duchess dress Fred Jessup made her that she's wearing in the Dobell portrait.
The poster on the back of a Mondrian print that David Strachan made for her Paris show.
Sketches from her hotel room in the Place Dauphine, Paris.
The *Ophelia* painting she entered in the Travelling Scholarship in 1948.
The nude of Annie Ross also entered in the Travelling Scholarship.
The best still life she painted while minding the Plates' house at Woronora.
The long red woollen men's underpants that she wore under her taffeta dress to see Laurence Olivier and Vivien Leigh.
Her folding saw.
The best painting of Bonnie Sue the pug.
Letters from Ian Fairweather.
A signed copy of Fairweather's book, *The Drunken Buddha*.
Her prize-winning portrait of Pam Bell.
The collection of artefacts from the Sepik River.

The painting of giving birth bought over the side of the double canoe on the Sepik.

A bridal headdress covered with cowry shells from Papua New Guinea.

Postcards collected on her trip through France with Sam Hughes and Rollin Schlicht.

Items that were salvaged included the willow pattern china; a book Grace Olley had lent Shirley Wright; the pair of unworn stockings; a Christmas card from Sam Hughes; and a burnt roll of film, possibly the television coverage of Margaret's 1960 exhibition in Brisbane. Some time afterwards, a painting of fish by Margaret, which had hung in the Farndon kitchen, was also returned to her, having been mysteriously rescued from the fire by someone she didn't know.

◆

The beginning of the 1980s brought other blows. Donald Friend's health had deteriorated. Having been diagnosed with emphysema, along with malaria and gout in 1979, Friend then decided to leave Bali in order to be looked after by Attilio Guarracino and his wife Ailsa in their modest red-brick house in the Melbourne suburb of Hawthorn. And so Tuan's reign in Bali, with all its accompanying joys and indulgences, ended.

Sickness also claimed another stalwart of Margaret's early painting years in Sydney. In June 1980, Russell Drysdale had suffered a stroke and, not unexpectedly, he died in Westmead hospital a year later, in June 1981. Friend penned a regretful poem as an epitaph that celebrated the laughter and the silences of the kindly man and bon vivant now gone; and honoured his vision, which had captured the solitary bone-dry heart of inland Australia and its inhabitants.[2] At the Hat Factory Margaret, too, mourned. The world of her youth was falling apart as surely as the flames had destroyed her home.

It was probably in early 1981 that Sam Hughes underwent an operation for cancer. The operation was successful and they, or certainly Margaret, thought Hughes's future health was assured. So, in brave defiance of his colostomy bag, Hughes and Margaret journeyed with their friend, artist Paul Jones, to Thailand, India, the Maldives and Sri Lanka, where they visited Mitty Lee-Brown. Margaret now admits the colostomy bag proved to be an utter nightmare on the trip, especially when combined with the spicy Indian food.

In September, Margaret had another show with Philip Bacon in Brisbane. Two weeks later she gave a small dinner party at the Hat Factory. Among those at the dining room table was Donald Friend, who had now removed himself from Melbourne and was set up in a flat at Bondi Junction. The meal was simple and delicious. The talk, according to Friend, was animated and amusing – despite recent sorrows – with copious references to old friendships.[3] The last evocative fragment of Friend's diary entry gives away the real mood of the night. It had turned stormy and, as he describes, 'the sound of the wind outside, the rain pattering on the roof, branches from the tiny tangled garden tapping on the window-panes gave additional comfort – we were like friendly creatures sheltering in a cosy burrow from a storm.'

Shortly after this night, Margaret was again travelling. It's almost as if she was on the run from the reality of what had happened with friends outside her cosy burrow. The trip began an era of her regular travelling with the lively Myvanwy 'Van' Hodgkinson (to whom Margaret had been introduced by Elaine Haxton back in the 1950s while staying with Haxton at Pittwater). Margaret and Hodgkinson had already made one trip together back in 1976, and from now on the two of them were 'on the go' every second year. They rushed round the world on complicated pre-planned routes that always included visits to art galleries for special exhibitions they were dying to view, Margaret especially. From this time on, too, Hodgkinson would keep dated photo albums of their trips and abbreviated diary notes of galleries they viewed, shops they visited (Hodgkinson could never resist a new pair of earrings) and meals they ate – a wonderful, if somewhat dauntingly large, recording of their crammed journeying.

Hodgkinson was three years older than Margaret. Slim-figured and youthfully energetic, she frequently rinsed her short silver-blonde hair blue and upon occasion sported blue eye shadow to match. Her limitless passion for travel included the plotting of itineraries and devising accommodation deals. 'Mum enjoyed planning the trips as much as doing them,' her daughter, Kate Hodgkinson, remembers. 'She'd loved travelling ever since she was a child. Geography, the world and its people were her fascinations. She wanted to go everywhere and see as much as possible.

'She was always a great friend and supporter of Margaret,' Hodgkinson says of her mother's friendship with Margaret. 'Very often, when Margaret was getting an exhibition ready, she'd ask Mum to come round and look at it. Mum was always very reticent as far as detailed criticism went, but she'd say which paintings she liked. She had a wonderful eye. Although she never painted herself, she saw. She would see things that the rest of us would completely miss; she was wonderful at picking out colours and shapes and textures. Mum also loved doing up houses and she had property in Newcastle, so there was that connection as well.'

On this 1981 trip Margaret went first, on her own, to stay with Anne Wienholt in San Francisco, where she saw a huge Morandi exhibition. Then she went on to Boston, Vermont, Cape Cod, Washington, New York and Philadelphia with Hodgkinson and mutual friends, architects Jim Brownlow and Doug Small:

Once More, Then No More

We saw the coloured leaves in Vermont, which surprised me because they were so different from foliage here or even in Europe. But, of course, I was more interested in the galleries. There was a Bonnard exhibition in a private gallery in Washington that I couldn't wait to see. You can look at reproductions, but it's not the same as seeing the real paintings. I like going back to re-see artists' works because in twenty years your taste changes.

I did a lot more drawings when I travelled by myself. Somehow, when you're with somebody, you just keep going and with Van it was always non-stop. But it was never travel just for the sake of travel, it's always been because certain exhibitions were on. If I heard of a show and didn't have the money for the fare overseas, I'd borrow it.

I really didn't see very much of American culture. Everything did seem very big, even the Golden Gate Bridge in San Francisco, which we kept crossing when I stayed with Anne, seemed enormous. Generally, I like Americans. Although years later, on another trip, I had to make a series of plane hops across America and we stopped in Las Vegas, which I found scary. The place was full of weird, stressed-out people with broken marriages who'd been overplaying at the casinos. But I've never travelled around trying to discover what the American way of life was like. I was too busy going from gallery to gallery.

The speed of Van and Margaret's journeying also ensured that there was little time for brooding – it could have been easy for Margaret to slip into morbidity, you'd imagine, given all that had happened in the past months. Following America, she flew to London to meet up with Sam Hughes and to catch up with old friend Annie Ross (now Hughes-Stanton). Hughes's health still seemed all right and, after Margaret left, he continued his tour, travelling to his favourite destination of Mykonos. In retrospect, perhaps he'd gone there to tidy up his affairs.

Far from a Still Life

The year 1982 brought sorrow upon sorrow to Margaret's life. Grace Olley, whom Margaret had watched over the last years shrink even further to become the faintest wisp, now finally faded completely. Though her death on 13 July 1982, at the age of nearly ninety-two, was far from unexpected, for Margaret to lose the mother who'd above all others and for so long supported her was devastating:

My sister and I were visiting her on alternate days. Then my brother came down from Brisbane and saw her. One night shortly afterwards she died in her sleep. They rang me as soon as it happened and I went straight round and sat with her. It was the first time I'd actually seen a dead person. She looked so peaceful, the age seemed to have fallen off her, and I understood straight away why people say 'at rest at last'. I was also overwhelmed by the sense that she would no longer be there. I remembered all the things I hadn't finished saying to her, all the questions I'd meant to ask her and now never could. I've never been one to cry easily – my tears usually come when I'm frustrated, trying to thread a needle or something like that. So I sat there by myself, not crying, just with an awful pain of loss in my heart.

But Margaret had a show coming up at the Holdsworth Galleries in October. As she'd once advised Tas Drysdale, now also so lamentably absent, putting everything into painting was the best healer of tragedy. So she struggled on.

When Donald Friend saw the works before this 1982 exhibition opened, he observed in his diary that they were strong in tone and rich in colour, and proved Margaret was a real painter. But he added a little sting in the tail: he feared they did not provide 'extensions of consciousness' or 'explorations of other visions beyond reality'. Yet, as he went on to say, still there was present in them 'the warm colouring of her own affectionate constant yet feminine unpretending self'.[4] Even if it doesn't do full justice to her paintings, this is an apt description of Margaret.

However, reviewer Susanna Short in the *Sydney Morning Herald* praised 'the sheer excellence' of the twenty-five 'full-bodied still lives' in which flowers were 'arranged in vases or long-necked bottles on dressers and kitchen tables, laden with fruit or draped with kelims'. Margaret, Short said, had imparted to domestic clutter 'the timeless qualities of grandeur, sobriety and finality'. She also pointed out how in the work *Dressing Table* (which she described as a cross between still life and portrait) 'the objects represented – perfumes, precious objects, full blooms, exotic statues, and the artist's own aging visage – call the spectator's attention to the transitoriness of life'.[5]

The exhibition at the Holdsworth Galleries went on display on 2 October, with the formal opening three days later, at which all but three works sold.[6] When a handsome journalist, whom Friend described as dark and glossy as a crow, asked Margaret for an interview, she answered, with a touch of her less warm side that can occasionally prevail: 'I'm talking to Mr Friend just now. And anyway the pictures need no explaining – they represent flowers in vases and fruit: that's all there is to them.'[7]

The exhibition closed on 20 October. A few days later, on 3 November 1982, Margaret suffered another devastating loss:

Sam's death was completely unexpected to me. He seemed fine. But he was very lax about going for check-ups for his cancer. Suddenly it came back. He was so secretive about it. A friend of his who was a nurse used to talk about his medical condition to him. I was no help at all. I knew he was sick, but my mind wouldn't accept how ill he was. We'd been at an opening and when we came home there was something really wrong with Sam. After that he went into Sydney Hospital at the top of Martin Place. I used to visit him twice a day;

after lunch and then again in the evening. I still hadn't grasped the gravity of the situation. It was all a bit unreal.

One afternoon, as I went through the wards, the Melbourne Cup was running and there was quite a jolly atmosphere. An old friend of Sam's was with him – Ulrich Sieveking. 'Uli' had worked with us on Hassan *and owned a house at Bungan Beach, where Sam and I had stayed in those days. They were talking, so I thought I'd let them be – too many visitors can be tiring – and come back as usual in the evening.*

When I came back that night, Sam was in trouble. They brought in a machine and told me to wait out in the waiting room while they did some procedure. I could hear Sam screaming. When I went back in, I just sat by the bed holding his hand. They must have given him morphine, because he wasn't really conscious. In the wee hours of the morning he went. I'd never been with somebody as they died before. You can feel when they've gone. You just know it.

For Margaret and Sam there were so many years apart; then such a brief happiness together – not quite ten interrupted years.

Margaret left the sleeping, darkened hospital, lit by occasional pools of light from nurses' stations, not only grief-stricken but, more immediately, fighting the added feeling of disorientation that descends when a loved one dies at an unnatural hour. Amid the still, quiet bric-a-brac of the Hat Factory, she faced the awfulness of the enforced wait for daylight: the slow hours, with sleep the most alien of states, until the ordinary rhythms of life began anew and arrangements could be made:

All the time I just kept going backwards and forwards to the lavatory. Then, for something to do, I stood on the scales. I'd lost half a stone, just peeing. I think it was the shock.

Apart from memories, Margaret has very few actual souvenirs of Hughes:

Once More, Then No More

Sam first became very sick in Mykonos. When he returned here he spent days up in the bedroom going through his things. He tore up all his papers and photographs. He'd come down the stairs with plastic bags full of torn paper to put out with the rubbish. It was as if he wanted to leave no evidence of his life after he died. I often wonder what happened to all the catalogues he designed for Zwemmer's, if he burnt them then, too. I was so busy working for the show I had no idea what he was doing.

There really was nothing of him left. He'd destroyed everything. But then Nigel [Hawkins] gave me a great gift – the Ivon Hitchens painting Sam had hanging in Elizabeth Bay. Sam had taken the painting to London and left it with Nigel to look after. Nigel and Norma later moved to Toronto and the Hitchens went with them. It was lovely when Nigel presented me with it, because it brought Sam in. I've enjoyed it so much. Eventually it will be given to the Art Gallery of New South Wales as a memorial of Sam; no one is ever the owner of paintings, we're all just custodians.

Today Margaret often prefaces remarks with 'as Sam used to say'. Though it's now more than twenty years since his death, there's a sense at the Hat Factory that he might just be occupied elsewhere in the endless linked rooms of the rest of the house:

Actually, I can still see him sitting down over there, reading. But I have to say, he's very lazy about filling up the salt and pepper cruets! I've often had dreams about Sam. Not so much recently, but in the past I'd dream that he hadn't gone, he was simply living with somebody else. It was a way of throwing my anxieties about his death out of my brain, I suppose.

Once again, Margaret was sustained by painting and her friends. By now she also had an inner strength, concealed under the layers of her paint-spattered work clothes and her eclectic going-out finery. Donald Friend summed up how she coped with her latest tribulations when he wrote of her in his diary: 'capable, matter-of-fact, hard working; a woman who has suffered and not whined – generous, a giver. Her tolerance and wry humour, her rare capacity for love and friendship envelops us.'[8]

There was another aid that helped her through this terrible time, as well:

I was having acupuncture for arthritis in the shoulders from a Chinese man in Campbell Street, near where I used to have lunch in the Chinese restaurants with Sid Nolan when we were working together at the Tivoli Theatre. I think it was the acupuncturist who kept me sane. After he finished taking the needles out I'd sleep for an hour in his room. The treatments obviously released a great deal of tension. I used to wonder how much longer I'd have to continue with it. But one day when I arrived, the acupuncturist just said, Once more, then no more.

With the acupuncturist's pronouncement establishing her fitness, Margaret continued with her life as best she could. In February 1983, she was again playing hostess, this time with a dinner for Jean Bellette, who was in Sydney from Majorca, to welcome her back to Australia. (It was also a night of condolence, since Paul Haefliger had died the year before and part of the reason for Bellette's visit was to organise a posthumous exhibition of his work at the Holdsworth Galleries.) Bellette these days hid enigmatically behind dark glasses, according to Margaret (as relayed by Donald Friend). 'I think it's something to do with the brandy bottle,' Margaret observed about the dark glasses.[9]

The dinner itself was held on a hot, humid night. Among the guests crammed around Margaret's 'long hospitable table' were Justin O'Brien, Frankie Mitchell, Van Hodgkinson and her sister, Olwen Tudor Jones, and Paul Jones. Afterwards Friend wrote that Bellette's beauty as a young woman still clung to her excellent cheekbones and, though 'haggard now and a bit pickled', her 'old mischievous spirit' was still evident. He concluded his remarks about Bellette by noting that she behaved with 'a pathetic bravado', which seems a sad reflection on a woman who had been so respected as a teacher, as well as for her own fine art.[10]

Margaret made two trips overseas in 1983. The first was an exotic journey with Paul Jones and Geoff Kitto, a tribal rug expert, to the Philippines and Burma. 'I don't want to see another pagoda so long as I live' was Margaret's sole comment to Friend afterwards.[11] However, her appetite for travelling was undiminished and around the middle of the year she set off again, with Van Hodgkinson this time, for London, Majorca, Barcelona, Paris (for an exhibition of early Cézanne), Bruges and parts of Greece:

In Majorca, Van showed me Deya, where she lived for three years. Deya was beautiful. It's near a little bay and the ocean, which you can see from the village, is very blue. I was always going to go back and paint it, but sadly I never have. We met Robert Graves, whom I cannot recall at all, and his wife Beryl, who made a bit more of an impression on me. What I do remember is the gnats. We stayed in a small hotel and they must have shut up the room, because it was full of gnats. I ended up covered in bites, which were extremely painful.

Jean Bellette was still away, but we visited Biniaraix and checked out her studio, which looked as if she hadn't done any work there for ages. Then from Majorca we crossed over to Spain and travelled to Barcelona; from Barcelona I went on alone by train to see Fred Jessup in the south of France, and Van flew off elsewhere. When I arrived, Fred took one look at me and said, Oh, God, have you gone back on the drink? He thought I'd lapsed because my face was so blown up. But it was only the gnat bites.

After her visit to Fred Jessup, Margaret and Hodgkinson caught up in Paris. Then they spent time in Bruges and finally joined Van's sister, Olwen Tudor Jones, on an archaeological dig at Toroni, on the coast of northern Greece:

Olwen worked at Sydney University, and every year she'd go over to Greece and dig. To help her out this time, we did our bit scrubbing shards. Those ones had been dug up, but you could walk along the beach and find fragments of pottery thousands of years old – from a cargo on a boat – that had been tossed up by the ocean. It seemed madness to be washing the shards when they were everywhere on the beach.

The following year, in February 1984, a depressed Donald Friend noted in his diary that it might be the last volume he'd bother to write. The pages only revealed 'a sick old man whose talents decay with his body', he wrote, and 'whose reactions to daily existence are boredom and self-disgust'. For most people, he felt 'weary indifference or outright dislike'; his 'loving warmth' was reserved for very few, this bitter entry concludes. One of those very few was undoubtedly Margaret.[12]

In March, Friend's small studio apartment in Bondi Junction became an unbearable irritation to his psyche, despite its snatches of harbour and rooftop views:

Oh, Oll, he said, I can't bear it any longer. Do you think you could find me a place? What he meant was, could he live in one of the flats at the house here. Oh, no, I thought, I can't have Donald too close. He would have been underfoot the whole time. I also knew that if we'd lived under the same roof, it would only have been a matter of time before we fell out. I'd have ended up saying something that offended him and that would have been the end of our friendship.

I went up to the estate agents who handled my flats and they showed me a little two-storeyed house just off Underwood Street. It had a small garden and was the closest thing in Sydney to Hill End. I rang Donald and said, You've got to come immediately, it's just you. He took it straight away. We immediately went up to St Vincent de Paul in Oxford Street and bought him some cane furniture and various bits and pieces. I lent him tapa cloths and other things to decorate it, so he was well set up. He did some of his best work in that house. Gisella Scheinberg put on a little retrospective for his seventieth birthday at the Holdsworth Galleries the next year and the watercolours he'd done there carried strongly right across the room.

There were still some bright moments for Friend. He would wander down and have lunch or dinner with Margaret. But not only were his observations of others, and himself, turning sourer in his diaries, he was becoming more irascible in real life. 'Oh, shut up, do you want me to finish this story or don't you?' Margaret remembers him snapping if anyone dared to interrupt when he was in full flight. But Friend's urge to talk endlessly also had a funny side:

He would hold court in a pub near Juniper Hall in Oxford Street. The staff used to give him free beers because he kept the whole bar amused with his tales. You'd run into friends of his in Oxford Street. I can't stop now, they'd say. I want to hear the end of that story from Donald in the pub.

◈

Friend was not the only one to move house at this time. Margaret was finding the crowded interior of the Hat Factory too empty of Sam Hughes to continue living there – or perhaps too full would be more correct. Hughes may have wished to leave no traces of himself after death, but he was achingly present when Margaret passed through the little middle flat. She could also feel his presence in the Hat Factory itself, frequently busying himself in the kitchen or, disconcertingly, settled on a sofa if she showed a guest into the living room.

Not only was Hughes, or his memory, there to haunt her, but Mrs Oll had a bit to say from the other side of the grave on the subject of finding a proper place to live:

After Sam died, I went to see a clairvoyant. It shows how uncertain I was about my life then. The clairvoyant foresaw that I'd move. My mother had always nagged me about the Hat Factory. You must get out of that shed, she'd say. Even though she was now dead, I could still hear her, Get out of that shed. I had thought that Sam and I might live in another house I owned by then in Stewart Street, Paddington. But Sam didn't like it and the house stayed rented out until I sold it. I'd also bought a little house at Werri Beach next to Gerringong – rolling green hills going right down to the beach – but Sam wasn't keen on that either. So, in the end, we just stayed where we were.

Now, however, my Aunt Madge offered to drive me to vote in a local election one Saturday morning. Instead of driving straight out down Duxford Street, she went the long way round into Gurner Street, where there was a 'For Sale' sign on a three-storeyed house that I'd always admired. I was about to go away again, so I only had the weekend to decide if I was going to buy it before the auction. Come the Monday, I'd made up my mind. I had to scurry round madly organising my finances before I left the country. A bit later on, I also acquired a vacant allotment next to it, which people used like a camping ground – parking their Kombi vans overnight there – but which I planned to turn into a garden.

After setting in motion the purchase of the Gurner Street house in Paddington, Margaret was off overseas again, this time to

Once More, Then No More

Chicago and New York. Here she teamed up with Frankie Mitchell, who, having retired from the couturier business, was enjoying an extended holiday in New York. The holiday had, in fact, been assisted by Margaret. Christine France remembers Mitchell remarking in the course of a social occasion in Sydney that if he had a thousand dollars he'd go to New York.[13] Margaret responded: 'Well, here you are.' Margaret, who also lent him money to buy a flat in Kings Cross, now merely remarks of her generosity: 'He was an old friend and he just loved being in New York.' Later on, for Mitchell's seventieth birthday, Margaret and a number of female friends clubbed together to buy him another ticket there. After her own trip to New York, where the highlight of the visit was a Balthus retrospective at the Metropolitan Museum of Fine Art, Margaret flew on to Paris for another retrospective – Bonnard, this time.

The following year, in 1985, Margaret moved basketload after basketload of cherished possessions – in a wheelbarrow, according to some accounts – on a much shorter journey, from the Hat Factory in Duxford Street down the road to her new abode in Gurner Street.

It was a wonderful house for entertaining: perfect for giving lunches and dinners. It also had lots of bedrooms for people who were visiting from overseas. My studio – the largest I'd ever had – was on the top floor looking out to the harbour. But unfortunately, as I soon realised, the studio had windows on all sides and, really, too much light came in. But the rest of the house, as I said, was great.

Ironically, after Margaret's efforts this year, not so much to forget the past but to give her life a cleaner canvas, 1985 ended in a journey that almost cost her that life. She and Van Hodgkinson had decided that their next excursion would be primarily a trip to Egypt. To prepare themselves properly, the two did a six-month course in Egyptology at Sydney University:

Far from a Still Life

I fell madly in love with the dung beetle. It's the Royal Scarab of Egypt. There was one story about the dung beetle I found particularly enchanting. The Egyptians couldn't understand how the sun set on the western bank of the Nile, then rose the next morning on the other side of the river. They were aware of the dung beetle's habit of burying round balls, so they decided that one of the creatures had worked energetically through the night and brought the sun up. That's why they venerated the dung beetle.

Originally, Margaret had intended to visit Turkey before she and Van Hodgkinson went to Egypt. But as she was organising her travel plans, the police had called on her in Gurner Street to break the news that her friend Geoff Kitto, whom she'd intended meeting in Istanbul, had been killed in a car accident on a bridge across the Bosporus. Margaret says that though she was shocked by the news, Kitto threw himself into life at such a pace that somehow she'd never expected him to make old bones. But his death did mean that Turkey was not a place she now wished to visit. Hodgkinson then suggested that instead she join her and Olwen Tudor Jones on a tour of the Greek islands.

So in October 1985 they flew from Perth, where Margaret was having a show at the Greenhill Galleries, to South Africa, then on to Zimbabwe and the Victoria Falls, before travelling to Greece. After a stay in Athens, Margaret, Hodgkinson and Tudor Jones began their exploration of the Greek islands. First they visited Lindos, at Rhodes, with its famous fort and village of quaint cobbled streets. Then, in late October, they went to Crete, where it was raining heavily and Margaret slept on wet sheets at their hotel. Margaret's night spent on wet sheets resulted in what she thought was terrible flu:

Waiting to get the plane back to Athens, Van and Olwen were standing in one queue and I was in another. I was suddenly so thirsty. I must have looked dreadful, because Olwen came over to see what was wrong. I'm dying for a soda water, I answered, my head's splitting, I hope I make it back to Athens. By that stage I'd also started feeling very hot and as if I might faint. I did make it back to Athens, but when I reached the hotel, there I stayed. I'd never been so sick.

I remember screaming out one night to Van and Olwen, I'd like to go to hospital, I think I've got a tumour on the brain. That's what it felt like. I couldn't eat, couldn't smoke, could only drink soda water. The doctor kept coming. You're very sick, you must fly home, he'd say. Van and Olwen were picking up all the things he injected me with, in case I died, so they'd know what I'd had. I thought I heard them talking about how to make arrangements to get the body back to Sydney. On top of that, the pair of them were scheming about smuggling a friend out of Turkey. I'd come to and hear broken bits of conversation about passports and crossing borders.

The worried Hodgkinson and Tudor Jones, who themselves both had bad colds and were existing on Veganin and Redoxon (dissolving vitamin C tablets), then organised to take Margaret to a chiropractor in a desperate last-ditch attempt to improve her condition:

My head was thumping the whole time. Van and Olwen decided I must have ricked my neck, and that was what was giving me the violent headaches. They thought a chiropractor might be able to fix my neck. But there was a taxi strike on the day we went and we had to make an agonising journey by bus – several buses – right across Athens to reach the man's rooms.

When we arrived the chiropractor, who, it turned out, was also an iridologist, looked into my eyes. You've got a troubled brain, he said. I know, I responded. Then he manipulated my neck. After which we jolted our way back across Athens again. When I was finally home in

Sydney, my own doctor said it was a wonder I didn't die from all the cortisone the Athens doctor was pumping into me, together with the iridologist's neck manipulation. I've also found out since that what I'd probably had was viral meningitis. Meningitis is the swelling of the fluid sack that goes over your brain and down your spinal cord, hence the headaches.

By early November, Margaret began to rally. To her own and her friends' relief, her headaches, along with the constant coughing, eased. The despondency that had accompanied her illness lifted, and she started eating rice puddings and chicken. After Athens, she and Hodgkinson had planned a quick side trip to southern Italy before going on to Egypt. Italy was now cancelled and Margaret fixed on Egypt as a means of recovery:

Egypt, I'd think as I lay in bed. Egypt. I have to make it to Egypt. After a few days, when Van and Olwen had gone out, with enormous effort I forced myself out of bed, got dressed and slowly went out into the street. The first time I walked as far as a nearby shop, where I bought some aspirin, then I crawled home and went back to bed. I didn't tell the other two, but each day I'd go a little further. I was absolutely determined that I'd continue on to Egypt.

By the end of the second week in November, Margaret felt up to travelling – gingerly – again. Olwen Tudor Jones remained in Athens, while Margaret and Hodgkinson flew to Alexandria and then caught a train across Egypt to Cairo. The whole tour had been meticulously booked in advance by Hodgkinson before they'd left Sydney, which had its advantages and disadvantages. On the one hand, it had spurred Margaret on to recovery; on the other, it allowed no time for resting if she relapsed, which fortunately she didn't. In Cairo they had reservations at the famous Mena House Hotel in Giza, which had originally been a lodge used by Egyptian royalty on hunting expeditions and visits to the pyramids. With the opening of the Suez Canal, the lodge was extended into a proper palace, before becoming a hotel:

It still had a very Egyptian feel about it. We ate there the first night and the meat was so tough I decided it was camel. From then on I only had boiled vegetables, which was probably very good for me. We'd insisted on a room overlooking the pyramids. When I woke up and looked through the mosquito netting on the window the morning after we arrived, it was raining. My first view of the pyramids was in the rain!

Of all the galleries and all the art Margaret has seen in them, it's the pyramids that evoke the most powerful passion in her:

I can only describe the pyramids as awesome. To approach the pyramids from a long way away is such a moving experience. As you come closer, they get bigger and bigger. In spite of all the photographs, nothing prepares you for the simplicity of them. The simplest things are always the most moving. I've been three times to the pyramids in my later years and I've never failed to be moved. To think that when I first went overseas on the boat, we had chances to get off and inspect the pyramids and I didn't do it. The young are very careless of opportunity.

After experiencing the pyramids Margaret and Hodgkinson continued their exploration of Egypt by venturing into the huge Cairo Museum of Egyptian antiquities where, as she says, the contents of just one dusty showcase could make up a whole exhibition. But her favourite exhibit there, which she's now seen several times, is the treasures from Tutankhamun's tomb. 'I am fascinated by the past and all the Egyptian culture,' she sums up. From Cairo, with Margaret still taking everything very slowly, she and Hodgkinson went by train to Luxor. Here they actually went inside Tutankhamun's tomb and Margaret was astonished by how small it was, especially knowing how much had come out of it. After this they did a boat trip on the Nile. By now Margaret had recovered sufficiently to, as she puts it, 'stupidly start smoking again'.

Although it may have seemed that everything was well, it wasn't. The meningitis would ultimately have a drastic and permanent effect on Margaret's life in several ways. Not only would it interfere with her balance and hence her walking, it had another consequence:

When I came back from the trip, I'd seen a doctor to discuss the practicalities of having a brain shunt. I have leaked proteins in my spinal column and it's possible to drain those off with a shunt. During the conversation the doctor warned that a shunt could also result in a situation similar to Alzheimer's disease, which is the last thing I'd want to risk happening. As I was leaving, I made some remark to the effect that it was enough to make you depressed. One minute, the doctor said, I'll give you a script . . .

But for the time being, back in Sydney it was Donald Friend's health that was the source of concern. He was suffering from diabetes now, as well as emphysema. On New Year's Eve 1986 he attended a lunch given by art benefactor James Fairfax in honour of a white-haired Harry Tatlock Miller. Margaret, 'in a smart straw hat', as Friend noted, was another guest enjoying the view from the balcony of yachts whipping across the harbour, with their sails 'arching like hundreds of new moons'. Though he was feeling ill and exhausted, as he did every day, Friend wrote in his diary that he relished the afternoon's conversation and its wit. But in the same entry he also wrote: 'To breathe is like physical work.'[14]

Margaret and Lynne Clarke, who'd been like Friend's daughter since he'd first known the Drysdale family, were consistently among those who loyally brightened his days – or attempted to – this year. Margaret would drop in with flowers or duck soup she'd made. Friend was still working. At the beginning of the year he'd begun a series of etchings. By May 1987, his diabetic treatment was converted to insulin injections, which he grumpily conceded to attempt. Then disaster struck. After completing nine etchings (with two more incomplete), Friend somehow injured the fingers of his left drawing hand. 'O God my left hand. My life,' his diary entry for 24 May abruptly concludes.[15]

'What shall I *do* – what *can* I do?' the entry of the next day begins.[16] Worse was to come. In September, Friend suffered the first of several strokes, which paralysed his left hand and leg. He was cared for during the subsequent months – when he was excruciatingly dependent on others and 'could not even piss without assistance' – by his gardener Al Irby, who'd become a close friend.[17] Finally, at the end of the year, he moved out of the Hill End-like house with its steep, dangerous stairs that Margaret had found for him and into a cottage in Holdsworth Street, Woollahra, more suitable for an invalid. For his friends, watching his decline was not easy:

Mitty Lee-Brown came out from Sri Lanka and found him unconscious – this was before the strokes. When he came out of hospital that time he said, I've planned my life very badly. In other words, he should have stayed in Bali, where he could have been surrounded by those boys who really loved him and for whom he did worthwhile things, like teaching them music. I think it would have been kinder if he'd gone then. He was supposed to give himself insulin injections, but he was a very bad patient. He hated being ill; hated it. He couldn't bear illness. I can understand that. When the quality of life goes, I don't want to hang about.

Towards the end I'd take him soup. But I couldn't bear what he became. He was mean and miserable, a bitter person. I almost had to force myself to go, because he'd be so disagreeable. He quarrelled with Attilio – he was rude to Attilio's wife, Ailsa, and Attilio wouldn't stand for it. Gisella Scheinberg from the Holdsworth Galleries used to go and see him every morning, and he was appalling to her. It wasn't like the Donald of the years before. I prefer to think of him the way he used to be.

As for Margaret herself, when she wasn't delivering soup or swamping the Spanish mahogany table with roasts or curry for guests, she was painting as busily as ever. Not only did her trips to exhibitions overseas inform the way she herself painted, but also actual souvenirs of her travels were now included in her works. The most obvious example of this is her *Homage to Manet*.

In this painting, the conventional still life – the white china dish of cherries next to an old-fashioned blue and white jug of plumbago – might seem almost incidental. Above it, Margaret has reproduced the whole of Manet's famous work *The Balcony*, itself a tribute to Goya's *Majas on a Balcony*. These images take up one side of the painting, then on the other side Margaret presents us with a detail from Manet's work. It's the detail – an enlargement of the figure of Berthe Morisot – that's the most intriguing aspect of *Homage to Manet*: leading you into the shadowy recess of Manet's background, to who knows where. The painting as a whole becomes a tantalising exploration of where reality begins and ends, as well as a tribute to other artists; and, of course, the fruit and flowers of the still life are crucial in beginning that journey.

After two years' recuperation from her last ill-fated trip, Margaret was unable to resist the double temptation of an exhibition of van Gogh's last paintings from Saint Rémy and Auvers-sur-Oise and one of Matisse's Nice paintings, which was being shown in New York and Washington. Having shouted Van Hodgkinson a ticket as a bribe to accompany her, at the end of

1987 the two flew off to a freezing northern winter and another reviver of art.

The van Gogh exhibition was made up of works from the year he retreated to the asylum at Saint-Rémy, where he painted the famous *Starry Night*, as well as his tormented-looking *Self-portrait* of 1889; and then his last few months at Auvers-sur-Oise, before he finally shot himself in the wheat fields. His paintings once again confirmed for Margaret the close relationship between his work and music. As she says over and over, 'every stroke of the brush is like a note of music'. She also left this exhibition vastly impressed by van Gogh's 'vibrancy and draftsmanship'.

Matisse's Nice paintings were for Margaret simply 'magical':

Matisse didn't use a lot of paint in them, but they're so beautiful and lyrical. A lot of people used to dismiss these Nice works because the paint was very thin, but now they're being re-evaluated. It was a marvellous show. I kept going back for another look in Washington.

The following year, 1988, brought more change to Margaret's life. She was beginning to find going up and down the cedar staircase to the three floors of the Gurner Street house increasingly difficult. It was time for another of her snap decisions:

I'd always planned to make a garden on the vacant allotment that I'd bought next door. But one day I was shaking a rug over one of the side verandas and I suddenly thought, Do I really want to waste time growing runner beans and pumpkins when I could be painting? So I sold Gurner Street and came back to the Hat Factory – or 'the shed', as my mother called it. The carriers said it was the longest move they'd ever done, because they couldn't get away with dumping pieces of furniture anywhere. I'd worked out exactly where I wanted everything to go.

Afterwards I had a dinner party (I always like to have a dinner party when I move in somewhere, just to make sure everything is in place) and it was almost as if I'd never left. The Hat Factory has stayed virtually the same ever since, except that I no longer sleep upstairs and main room of the middle flat has been painted yellow. It was just as well I did come back, as my walking became progressively worse and worse after that because of my balance, or lack of balance, resulting from the meningitis. It was almost as though I wasn't quite sure where I was walking. I had a stick for years and now I've ended up with the frame.

Her difficulties with walking did not interfere with Margaret's soup-bearing visits to the declining Donald Friend, whose exit from this world was proving to be heartbreakingly protracted. After the series of strokes he'd suffered in 1987, he forced himself to paint and draw with his right hand – which, according to Margaret, he always could do but without finesse – and continued working thus. His final diary entry was made on 19 December 1988. In it he wrote, with a touch of defiant egomania, that if he were God, he'd rearrange things so that healthy laughter and wit did not rely for mirth on the spectacle of aged genius fallen in the mire. 'Goodbye world of lovely colours and amiable nudes,' he then continued touchingly. 'Aloha death, long dull dreamless nights. Ah, mortality I knew you were hiding behind that grey curtain. My soul is transparent, heliotrope pink but not nearly as invisible.'[18]

It was actually another eight months before mortality finally came out from behind its grey curtain to claim him:

Donald was a very complex person. He'd convinced himself he was so evil he was really frightened to die. He had two female nurses at the end, and one day when I thought he was unconscious, I suggested to them that he should see a priest. A priest can help people let go of life. Often people are too frightened to die, they hang on. *The priests know how to make you feel comfortable. The next morning I rang up to ask how he was. I thought he might have gone in the night. But he hadn't. The nurse told me he had woken up and asked for a priest. The priest has been, she added, and he's in such a bright state, he's just had a cup of tea. So I went round and he was almost elated, he'd been relieved of that fear of dying.*

I don't know why he thought he was so evil. His family name was Moses. He came from a very traditional Jewish background on his father's side; perhaps it was to do with that. Whatever it was, I don't think he really felt comfortable with himself. His mother was always a great supporter and encourager of him. Again, I don't know what happened, but I remember him suddenly saying to me, I'm never going to see her again. And he never did. When he was dying and his sister Gwen – who was absolutely marvellous to him – went to visit him, he thought Gwen was his mother. Now there's guilt coming to the surface.

Friend finally died in his sleep at the cottage in Holdsworth Street on 16 August 1989. So ended for him and Margaret a friendship that was nearly a love story and one almost consummated as such. But as an artist whom Friend idolised briefly in his youth, Norman Lindsay, once said of himself and the writer Miles Franklin, though admittedly their encounters were much more fleeting: the best love affairs are those we never had.[19] Margaret, of course, might deny any notion of this, dismissing it as fanciful. Nevertheless, she and Friend were two people who had an accord that went far beyond oil paint, turps and watercolour.

For Margaret, Friend's death brought most of all a sense of relief that he was now released from the physical degradations of the past few years and also from the ugliness that had beset his personality and behaviour. Time has now passed and erased much of her recollection of those. As with Lynne Clarke and Attilio Guarracino's feelings for Friend, Margaret's overriding emotion for him now is one of extraordinary affection.

Far from a Still Life

In her mind Friend is fixed tramping the paddocks at Hill End in search of subjects to paint and mushrooms, tending the fire in the cottage at night, or determinedly reading the paper in the morning, ignoring her youthful chatter. There is also the magic of their camping holiday to north Queensland, the camaraderie as they painted frantically through the night on the Lennons mural, Friend nonchalantly swapping brushes from one hand to the other. Finally, there is the vision of him immersed in the delights – with a touch of decadence – of Balinese life. These images are the stuff of which Margaret's memories of and attachment to Friend are made.

The death of Donald Friend in 1989 marked the end of Margaret's troubled years. The 1980s were by no means constantly unhappy for her, but they did contain a sequence of events that could only be accompanied by deep sadness, and this honed her survival mechanisms. When those close to Margaret die, she doesn't really regard them as gone; their presence still palpably informs her life. Nor does she allow herself to give in to sorrow – although she can't stop its manifestation in her dreams – or surrender to life's grim realities. Rather, the loss of friends seems almost to be a call for her, a challenge even, to go on living and painting.

In the 1990s, Margaret began to receive considerable public recognition, which resulted in her being declared an Australian National Treasure in 1997, as well as a Life Governor of the Art Gallery of New South Wales, and today sees the accolade of 'icon' almost universally bestowed upon her, together with countless mentions in the social pages. The acclamation began in 1990 with a retrospective exhibition of Margaret's work at the S.H. Ervin Gallery of the National Trust in Sydney, which coincided with the publication of *Margaret Olley*, Christine France's book about her art.

Writing of the 1990 exhibition in the *Sydney Morning Herald*, art critic John McDonald stressed that in Margaret's still lifes 'the evocation of atmosphere is intrinsic to the arrangement and choice of objects, the play of light and care given to the moulding of individual shapes.' McDonald's use of the word 'moulding' is again a reminder of how all those early modelling classes did help to shape the many years of painting that have followed. He concluded his review by saying that although Margaret's approach to painting might be strictly formal, it 'conveys considerable breadth of feeling'.[20] In 2005, one feels like extending his observation to say that Margaret's paintings impart a lifetime of feeling.

1990 also saw the real beginning of what could be called Margaret's second career, or calling: that of Margaret Olley, benefactor. Travelling to galleries overseas had inspired her in another way, apart from influencing her painting. Seeing what valuable collections had been bestowed on these foreign galleries by individual benefactors helped to initiate a whole new phase of Margaret's life:

I'd slowly de-escalated the house buying and extricated myself from mortgages in the 1980s. But then I realised I'd moved into another ball game and the money was all going in taxes. So I thought, Well, if I can set up something whereby I can buy with my tax money things that I like and donate them, why not do it? So in 1988 I bought a sculpture by Anne Wienholt and gave it to the Art Gallery of New South Wales. That was how my donating to galleries began.

Although I'd had the earlier examples of Howard Hinton, Lucy Swanton and Major Rubin, who gave so much to the Queensland Art Gallery, I must stress that above all it was witnessing how Edmund Capon was energising the Art Gallery of New South Wales that was pivotal in making me decide to go ahead with the Trust. I was so inspired by seeing how exciting Edmund had made the gallery. When I was an art student the Gallery was such a stagnant place, people only came once a year, to see the Archibald Prize.

On 2 May 1990 the Margaret Hannah Olley Art Trust was formally established. Since then, Margaret has become one of Australia's most generous benefactors. Howard Hinton, were he alive, might well be writing a polite little note of praise to his goddaughter's old flatmate.

Via the Trust and personally, Margaret has contributed over one hundred works to the Art Gallery of New South Wales alone; as well as a substantial number of works to the Queensland Art Gallery and the Newcastle, Bathurst, Maitland and New England regional galleries. 'She is one of the most significant benefactors to the art gallery and I'll give you two reasons for that,' says Edmund Capon, who has been director of the Art Gallery of New South Wales since 1978.[21] 'One is the obvious scale and variety of what she's given; but I think the other, which is just as important, is the spirit in which it's done. She is idiosyncratic in the sense that she has her own views, her own likes and dislikes. But she is really passionate about the pictures she loves and I think that passion translates into her benefaction. Benefaction is a passion for her.'

The bequests to the Art Gallery of New South Wales include paintings by Johnstone Gallery exhibitors Donald Friend, Lawrence Daws, Arthur Boyd and David Strachan; works by overseas artists she deeply admires such as Walter Sickert, Edgar Degas, Giorgio Morandi, Pierre Bonnard, Lucien Freud, Alberto Giacometti and Duncan Grant; and a large collection of Indian sculpture. She's also donated a number of her own works, some of which she has actually bought back when the original owners have died or downsized their collections at auction. These paintings include *Portrait in the Mirror* from her very first one-person show; *Late Afternoon,* her pining in paint for the spirit of David Strachan; and *Still Life with Kettle,* which Donald Friend bought for himself in the 1950s.

She is unequivocally enthusiastic about the reciprocal benefits of giving:

I grew up in a family that gave. It's a lovely feeling to give something, it's like receiving; giving and receiving are intertwined. We should all give, give, give. The public can donate funds to the Trust – which they don't do nearly enough – and I put virtually everything I earn from my paintings into it. Finally, though, I must just reiterate that without the impetus of Edmund's work at the gallery, I really might not have done any of this.

In March 1991, Jean Bellette died in a clinic on Majorca and yet another important figure from Margaret's early years was gone. While Bellette was not one of Margaret's truly close friends, she did have an extraordinary impact on her as a teacher. (It's interesting to note that recently there has been a revival of interest in Bellette's classicist paintings – which writer Bernard Smith once described as 'torn out of the heart'[22] – with the 2004–05 touring retrospective of her work curated by Christine France.)

In 1991 Margaret was also awarded an honorary Doctorate of Letters by Macquarie University and was appointed Officer of the Order of Australia (AO). 'I just accept everything graciously,' she says of such honours. 'I have no idea what it's all about. They make no difference to my life. I accept them graciously and get on with my painting.'

On a less public note, Margaret travelled with Van Hodgkinson to Korea, a country to which she had always wanted to go.

Far from a Still Life

They also visited Kyoto in Japan, and both returned to Australia with their suitcases bursting with second-hand kimonos. The photos in Hodgkinson's album show Margaret with the stick – the first outward sign of the balance problems resulting from her meningitis – but otherwise undaunted by age. The following year, in 1992, she made two more trips overseas. The first was to New York with jeweller Tony White for a Matisse retrospective and the second was to Europe with Van Hodgkinson. Hodgkinson's notes for their itinerary encompassed many of the great cities of Europe: Vienna, Berlin, Paris, Stuttgart, Heidelberg, Munich, Prague, Dresden, London, Glasgow and Edinburgh.

The tour was particularly special because Justin O'Brien, another Merioola boarder from long ago, joined them in Germany. O'Brien for many years had lived in Rome, but in 1989 he stayed several months in Sydney to undergo radiotherapy for cancer. During this time his friendship with Margaret was renewed in a way that made it dearer than ever before. O'Brien had long been an admirer of Margaret's artistic dwelling – 'Everywhere you look,' he said, 'there's another still life just waiting to be painted.'[23] So, during the months of his therapy, he'd go to St Vincent's Hospital in Darlinghurst, have his treatment, then walk on to Margaret's place and draw for the day. She'd work at the front of the house and O'Brien would work in the Hat Factory itself; they'd meet for lunch then go back to work. It was then that O'Brien made his famous remark: 'God gave Olley an extra battery.'[24]

Their trip through Europe in 1992 was one of laughter, eating, opera and, of course, art. In Stuttgart, Margaret, Hodgkinson and O'Brien stayed with a mutual friend, Eugen Lude. When Lude visited Australia in 2003 he recalled how O'Brien brought out Margaret's 'young side' and 'naughtiness'. As Lude remembered, Margaret's youth was remarkable: 'In our flat in the morning Margaret just had a towel around her or barely even a towel, and to me she looked like this young woman artist being just twenty-five years old', which is a rather enchanting image of the artist at almost seventy years old.[25]

It was also Lude who organised one of Margaret's fondest travel memories:

First we visited the mad Bavarian King Ludwig II's over-the-top fairytale castle, which was built in the second half of the nineteenth century and is filled with murals depicting Wagner's operas. Eugen kept telling us to hurry up, because we had an appointment to meet a cart. I thought he meant a hay cart. But there in this little village, drawn by two black horses, was the Bavarian State Carriage. We proceeded to drive through the landscape in this carriage to the Wieskirche, which is a little church with a ravishing interior, with the most heavenly painted ceiling. If there'd been music playing, I think I would have died.

Sadly the memories of this trip have become bitter-sweet to Margaret, for Eugen Lude died at the beginning of 2005, and it was to be Justin O'Brien's last tour of Europe before he died in 1996.

◆

In November 1994 Margaret's first solo exhibition in London opened at Browse & Darby, a gallery in Cork Street that shows contemporary artists and deals in the works of great figures such as Bonnard, Degas and Rodin. At last Margaret's paintings had joined the realm of galleries that had exhibited the work of artists she'd long admired, some of whom, like Bonnard, had been strongly connected to her own vision:

It is very interesting to see how your paintings look, not just in a gallery, but in another country. I have seen mixed exhibitions overseas where the works of Australian artists haven't travelled well, so it is always a relief and a surprise to find that your work does look all right in another country.

The exhibition was opened by the eminent writer John Julius Norwich, the author of many travel and art books. 'Olley chooses to celebrate the possible richness of life, rather than to concentrate on its traumas,' wrote Giles Auty in *The Spectator* of her exhibition.[26] 'Olley's interiors and still lifes pulsate with pleasurable feeling,' he continued in the same vein. 'Hers is the most affirmative vision of life I have seen in a long while.' What is revealing about Auty's comments is that the paintings that inspired them came so soon after a painful period in Margaret's life that could quite reasonably have resulted in a darker, more pessimistic outpouring of art.

Christine France remarks that it's only been through attending Margaret's London exhibitions, peopled with admirers, that she's realised just how wide the artist's network of friends is.[27] The throng has always included expatriate artist Jeffery Smart from Italy; ex-gallery director Robert Haines from France; local London-based writer, literary agent and now film producer Robin Dalton (whom Wolfgang Cardamatis introduced to Margaret on her first trip overseas, way back in the early 1950s); Margaret's fellow art student Jocelyn Rickards (before her recent years of illness prior to her death) and her husband, film director Clive Donner; as well as Barry Humphries and writer Clive James. And, of course, occasions such as these are the way friends best celebrate the achievements of a loved one.

Van Hodgkinson was in London with Margaret for the opening of her show. The two friends continued on to Paris together, where Margaret bought a Degas drawing in black chalk, *After the Bath*, for the Art Gallery of New South Wales. After one more tour together the following year, Margaret and Hodgkinson's whirling round the world to exotic locations and galleries ceased. By this stage, Hodgkinson had about had her fill of travelling and her health over the next few years was to decline. Despite the end of this shared travelling phase, the two remained close friends. Their long phone conversations were an indispensable part of Margaret's day and Hodgkinson continued to be in attendance at the Hat Factory's dining table.

For Margaret, there was more and more recognition. In 1995, as well as having a solo show at the Australian Galleries in Sydney, she exhibited in 'Eight Australian Artists' at Browse & Darby in London. Among the eight besides Margaret, who was the only woman included, were Laurence Daws, Jeffrey Smart, Tim Storrier and Bryan Westwood.

Margaret was now also, once again, becoming a subject for the work of other artists, including both Westwood and Smart, with the latter's *Margaret Olley in the Louvre Museum* (1994–95). Although, as Margaret points out, Smart's work, in which there's more Louvre wall than Margaret Olley, is not really a portrait of her, as such. Rather, it's 'more an idea of a painting' that Smart wanted to realise. It should be pointed out that while people tend to think that Margaret and Smart have always been friends, especially because of their mutual connection with Donald Friend, in fact it's really been only in the last twenty-five years or so that they've become close.

In 1996 a retrospective exhibition of Margaret's work was held at the Art Gallery of New South Wales. In honour of the great occasion, Clive James wrote a lengthy poem titled *To Margaret Olley*. In the poem, James put his finger on one of the keys to appreciating Margaret's work. Not only are Bonnard, Degas, Derain, Matisse, Renoir, Manet, Monet, Vuillard and Cézanne evident in her painting, he observes in the second stanza, but she has drawn on them all 'for something beyond themselves'. James also pays tribute to the intensely personal nature of her work – 'of colour arranged like sound' – and to the unique domestic environment 'of that magic Paddington house'.

Edmund Capon, writing in the foreword to the catalogue, called Margaret a painter of tenacity and distinction who was not one to be diverted by any fleeting fashion.[28] He also placed her in a tradition stretching from Vermeer, of whose work Margaret is deeply admiring, in the seventeenth century to her old favourite, Morandi in the twentieth century. It is a tradition, according to Capon, 'which finds inspiration, beauty and a rich spirit of humanity in the most familiar of subject matter'. Jeffrey Smart, in his catalogue tribute, described Margaret as 'a life-enhancing force'; while Barry Humphries concluded his essay, 'What a fortunate man I am to know Margaret Olley!'[29]

In the late 1990s, despite the passing of more friends, including Elaine Haxton, Margaret was garlanded with fresh public and artistic success. In 1997, there were the honours mentioned earlier. Two years later, another Olley exhibition was held in London, this time at the Nevill Keating Pictures Gallery. Again, a throng of overseas friends were in happy attendance to celebrate the event at the opening celebrations, and Barry Humphries opened the exhibition by reading out a special Olley poem *he'd* written, to Margaret's delight. This same year Margaret was also awarded an Honorary Doctorate of Letters by the University of Queensland.

At the beginning of 2000, Margaret and Barry Humphries had an exhibition of their favourite paintings at the National Trust's S.H. Ervin Gallery. By now Humphries (not only a close friend but also a long-time AA attendee) was often a lunch guest at the 'rich labyrinth' of Duxford Street, as he has described her house.[30] All the paintings Margaret chose for this special exhibition were by artists whom she'd personally known or who had in some way touched her life. Among her 'favourites' was the much-travelled Ivon Hitchens flower piece of poppies and other field flowers that was so closely associated with Sam Hughes. Humphries' choices, coincidentally, included *The Pont Neuf Under Snows* by Albert Marquet, whose studio was opposite Margaret's room in the little Place Dauphine hotel in which she stayed during her early days in Paris.

In 2000, Margaret also collected another Honorary Doctorate, this time from the University of Sydney. Then, in May 2001, the Art Gallery of New South Wales named The Margaret Olley Twentieth-Century European Galleries, in recognition of her bequests. The galleries are situated in the 1988 Bicentennial wing of the gallery and, at the time of writing, mainly British abstracts and French landscape paintings are on view there.

But, just when it might seem that the rest of her life would continue to be a smooth-flowing further accumulation of Olley laurels, things changed. At the beginning of October 2001, an event took place that might be considered the precursor of trouble to come. As Margaret was in the throes of working on an exhibition for Philip Bacon, her zest-filled, travel- and life-loving, blue-rinsed friend Van Hodgkinson died – and for Hodgkinson's many friends, Margaret included, a light went out in the world. The loss was further compounded by the deaths of Van's sister, Olwen Tudor Jones, and her former husband, Frank Hodgkinson, within the same ten-day period.

'My mother was devoted to her sister and, in her strange way, still very connected with my dad, although they had been divorced for thirty-five years,' Kate Hodgkinson says.[31] 'I don't think she would have wanted to be alive without them. She'd travelled everywhere she wanted, except Montevideo in Uruguay, which was something she and I promised each other and didn't happen. She said, "I've had the most fabulous life, done wonderful things and I'm really rather interested in what happens next." Although she didn't really believe anything did happen, she wanted to find out.'

Far from a Still Life

Characteristically, there was no public outpouring of grief from Margaret. Instead, she threw herself into finishing off the paintings for her Brisbane exhibition at the end of November. However, this time her survival mechanisms did not prove to be as effective as they'd been in the past. Although her Brisbane show went off well, Van Hodgkinson's death must surely have added to Margaret's burden of loss, even if she was not aware of it at the time – a burden that was soon to exact a heavy toll on her.

≼ 16 ≽

Celebrating Life

I'm a young person trapped in an old person's body, and sometimes the old person wins. In spite of everything, I'm up at seven. I usually start painting at eight. Sometimes I might go for a walk after breakfast, but usually I'm straight into the brushes and turps and I'm happy as a sand boy.

As Christmas 2001 approached, rather than happily gearing up for festivities, Margaret was spiralling into what she now refers to as the 'black hole'. Though these days she can joke that she's like a cat because of the number of narrow escapes she's had in her life, when it happened, her plummet into biological depression at the age of seventy-eight was simply a 'hell':

I think it must have been coming on for a while. I was really pushing myself for Philip's show in Brisbane. I was putting everything into it. I kept thinking this might be the last painting I do. I always firmly believe you've only ever got one day – my AA philosophy has told me

Far from a Still Life

that. Still, in retrospect, I was struggling more than usual with that show.

I had the show in Brisbane. There was a new 'Favourites' exhibition with Jeffrey Smart and me that was due to open at the National Trust Gallery in the New Year. Christmas mail was coming in. I had the overseas letters to do. I was trying to get hold of the prime minister about an art-related matter that seemed vitally important at the time. Some paintings had gone missing from the house, which was upsetting me. The bushfires were on. On Christmas Day I was at a small lunch with friends and when we looked out at the harbour, it was strangely divided into two triangles. One part was filled with sunlight, the other thick with smoke from the bushfires.

The smell of the bushfires permeated the air for days. It was still very hot but I wouldn't put the air-conditioner on because I thought the exhaust would burn some orchids that were near it. Then I was having some people to lunch. Barry Humphries, Bruce Beresford, the film director, and his wife Virginia Duigan, the writer, and the Capons were coming. I'd done the shopping. I had all the food at the ready. But then I just felt I couldn't do it. I was even more bewildered by the fact that I couldn't.

Margaret's 'black hole' was not merely a matter of her feeling a bit down; it had nothing to do with end-of-the-year exhaustion. She'd fallen into the black disaster of biological depression, where colours are sapped from the world and even getting out of bed can seem too colossal an effort to contemplate. Worst of all for Margaret, forty-two-odd years after her battle with alcohol that had once threatened her painting, she was suddenly deprived of the solace of work – the unfailing constant in her life since then. This depression seemed to Margaret a far more debilitating crisis than her earlier experience of alcoholism. In comparison, she would call her drinking days 'a dark period'. At least then she'd been able to go through the motions of painting, but now she was almost wholly bereft, and much older:

I couldn't paint. I had no energy. My weight went down to almost seven stone, I was like walking tissue paper. My hair was thinner. I thought I was dying. Not only did I think I was dying, I wanted to kill myself. I even worked out how to do it – I won't say what I'd devised – but then I thought I'd probably botch it and everything would be even worse.

I was returning books to the people who'd given them to me because I thought I was about to die, and giving away my clothes for the same reason. All my clothes were held together with big safety pins because of the weight I'd lost. I gave away what was left of a drawerful of materials that I had kept since I had the antique shop in Brisbane back in the 1960s.

I said to my doctor I must be lacking iron, I thought that could be why I had no energy. He had my blood tested and it came back showing I had no iron. So then I had to go and have other tests to see if I had cancer, which I didn't. There was a huge downpour of rain, water came six feet into the dining room, carpets had to be dragged out. Someone broke into the house. Old friends, like Georgie Swift [who for many years was a journalist and publicist and more recently has often travelled with Margaret], were bringing me liver and spinach, which was what I survived on. The anti-depression pills I was on had been upped. My doctor thought there was nothing more he could do for me.

Depleted as she was, the tough, self-reliant part of Margaret kept searching for a way out of the blackness. She rang friends; she asked about more doctors. Then Nettie Joseph (the wife of Peter Joseph, who chairs the board of the Black Dog Institute) suggested that Margaret see Professor Gordon Parker, the Executive Director of the Black Dog Institute. Formally launched in February 2002, the institute offers expertise in mood disorders, such as depression. Margaret's consultation with Parker, a passionate believer in the de-demonising of depression, provided what would prove to be the solutions she'd been seeking:

Philip Bacon was here and asked if he could stay when Professor Parker came to see me, which I thought was a good idea – four ears are always better than two. Philip also said to get out all the medicine I'd been taking, which was another good move. First there were the anti-depressants I'd been on ever since the meningitis in Greece. And also I'd been dosing up on St John's wort.

To begin with, Professor Parker ran through all the standard questions, like who's the prime minister of Australia, to see what my mental capacity was. But then, of course, because I'd just been introduced to him I forgot Professor Parker's name. Next he looked at the pills. Apparently St John's wort can produce side-effects when taken with certain anti-depressants, so he took me off that straight away. He also changed the anti-depressants. In retrospect now, I'd say I was overmedicated. Professor Parker explained as well that when you're biologically depressed your body is chemically out of balance, which made a lot of sense to me. It's similar to the way I'm allergic to alcohol. I've got an intolerance there, so I mustn't touch it.

Depression was a deep hole to claw out of and Margaret's recovery was gradual:

You don't improve overnight. But I was painting again before six months were up. Hannah Dupree, Van's grand-daughter, who was studying art, lived here for quite a while and would go for walks with me and help me with little chores. Nettie Joseph, who'd first suggested I see Professor Parker, also came over and went through my clothes, which were all hanging off me. She very quietly suggested that she take jackets and skirts over to her dressmaker and have them altered: shortened and the sleeves taken up. I hate sleeves that go down to the wrist and get in the way. It revived my interest in what I wore and it was a lot better than thinking I should give all my clothes away because I was going to die.

But the days took forever to pass. I still didn't want to go out.

Celebrating Life

Then my accountant, Tom Lowenstein, rang and said, Come on, we're just having a quick dinner down at Double Bay, I'll call for you in half an hour. I was about to reply, I can't, I can't. Then I thought, Well, why not? And that, of course, is what you must do. You must make yourself go out a little bit at a time. Now I feel better and better each day. I'm on a quest to keep myself healthy and alert so I can do what I want to do with ease.

However, not only was Margaret painting again in six months, by the following year, 2003, her recovery was so complete she was willing to contemplate undertaking two more major exhibitions, one in London, which took place in March 2005, and another in Sydney, scheduled for the end of 2005. For her London exhibition at the Nevill Keating Tollemache Gallery, Margaret, then aged eighty-one, renewed her passport, which had lapsed whilst she was in the 'black hole', and once more flew off from Australia to be in attendance. There, in final vindication of her metier, Olley still lifes and interiors were exhibited with the works of an artist who'd so frequently inspired her over the years – Edouard Vuillard. Of this triumphant event (triumphant in many senses), Margaret admits modestly that she was 'pleasantly surprised' by how well her paintings combined with the Vuillards.

Coming back from her 'black hole' has affected Margaret in several ways. It's made her a generous supporter and advocate of the Black Dog Institute, and acutely sympathetic to anyone suffering from depression, especially anyone older like herself. She believes that people often jump to the wrong conclusion that nothing can be done for older people who are experiencing depression. It's a view she abhors. Her own return to normalcy has given an added poignancy to her joy, both in her paintings and in her life. Now the two are more than ever celebratory.

There is another factor contributing to Margaret's current well-being – the 'amino acids' she now takes: an extraordinary collection of powders she dutifully mixes up, and downs in thick, mud-like drinks at regular intervals during the course of each day:

Iridology is a very old form of medicine. In Greece, when no one knew what was the matter with me, the iridologist could, at least, see from my eyes that my brain was troubled. Not long after I'd started coming out of the black hole, somebody directed me to an iridologist in Manly. I've been on amino acids ever since and it's amazing what a difference it makes. Not only do I feel better, my hair's thicker and my balance seems to have improved around the house. I'd already had a cataract removed from one eye and was supposed to have the other one done. But, brilliantly, ever since I've been taking the amino acids, the cataract has been shrinking.

I've changed my diet since then too. Early in 2005 I gave up the cup of weak black coffee I always used to have in the mornings. For breakfast I now have a vegetable juice: ginger, celery, carrot, beetroot and a green pear or a Granny Smith apple. Then some pumpernickel with butter and banana. For years I had wheatmeal biscuits with the bananas, but now I'm off flour – too many chemicals in the making of it – and onto the pumpernickel. Although I have to confess I do still have a bit of pasta.

There's an extraordinary feeling of peace about the Hat Factory these days, post-'black hole'. French doors, open summer and winter (except for the hottest and coldest days that require the air-conditioning to be put on), lead into the overgrown greenness that seems in part a recreation of the rainforest of Margaret's Tully childhood. Despite her constant smoking, there's never an odour of tobacco, nor, for that matter, of oil paint – perhaps because of the open doors.

To sit at the Farndon dining table facing these doors has several advantages. You are safely away from Margaret's walking track to the kitchen and not in danger of brushing up against works often in progress there. In addition, you have an angst-dissolving vista of her garden, framed by arching branches of creamy yellow hibiscus flowers on which birds love to hang upside down. Beyond the hibiscus water drips quietly over the tiers of the newly restored fountain and all has a soothing, slightly dream-like quality.

Whether it be the skinks that dart across the top of the French doors, or even the cockroaches that boldly nibble away at the artificial fruit and vegetables in the middle of the night – they've shown a distinct preference for a stand of fake aubergines – an at-oneness with nature presides over Margaret's domain:

Little lizards come in from the garden and wander through the house all the time. They know me and if they see me coming they'll stand still till I pass. I get very upset if I find the odd one marooned in a bottle or vase. When they fall into the bath and can't get out, I leave them there for a few days to eat whatever it is they're after, then we have a mutual arrangement that I scoop them up and put them back in the garden.

A classic and inimitable image of Margaret's life at the Hat Factory was created the day she had a new wardrobe built closer to her sleeping area. She and Poppy, her cleaner, had decided to air all her clothes before the transfer to their new home took place, by hanging them on coat hangers on tree branches. The whole garden was alive with Olley outfits gently bobbing in the breeze. Margaret's ironing habits are also rather charmingly unique: she puts the folded garments under her as she sits on her favourite saddle stool, painting.

Inside the house Margaret doesn't use her walking frame, she merely catches hold of furniture to steady herself, which is not a difficult feat, as the Hat Factory is fuller now than ever before of what Donald Friend once described as her 'envisionment of jumble enchantment', leaving only a very narrow track of free space winding through it.[1] Despite her lack of balance, Margaret is still surprisingly agile. She can bend herself double with ease to sift through the mounds of letters and papers that have been deposited on the floor because there's no more room for them on the dining room table.

She has now moved from the bedroom upstairs. In a house full of room upon room, memory upon memory, painting upon painting, Margaret sleeps in a tiny narrow bed she laughingly refers to as 'a two foot six little coffin', with a small old television set within viewing distance, in what could only be called a nook. It's as if sleep, though she makes sure she has an adequate amount of it, is the least of her preoccupations:

As my mother was always saying, You never know who's going on the journey first. She was always urging me to get on with life, while I felt I should be the dutiful daughter and stay with her. Now I feel it really is a case of, as Frankie Mitchell used to say, Hurry, hurry, last days. I really have to hurry and get on with things. Yesterday's gone. Who knows about tomorrow? Today is what's important. Now is the moment, seize it.

All my life, I've had nothing to do with anybody who was idle. I've always been in love with people who were doing things. These days I'm in love with Richard Tognetti, the Artistic Director of the Australian Chamber Orchestra – I'm in love with what he does.

There's nothing else I myself want to do now except paint. If I had my life over again, I might do something differently: I might choose not to go overseas as early as I did. But you are who you are. I'm extremely fortunate I was directed into an occupation that's become a compulsion. We are all prisoners of our upbringing. Some people thrash around in that cage all their lives; only when you find the door and get out do you learn to fly.

Celebrating Life

Since 1970 the painting of interiors has remained a more-or-less constant preoccupation of Margaret's, and from the late 1980s, when her balance first really became impaired, she has turned more and more to painting the rooms of her own house.

The 'Yellow Room', where the couches are covered in Indian bedspreads and Matisse's naked pink women dance against a blue background in a print above the fireplace, has been an ongoing subject. Likewise her own kitchen sink is frequently a still-life setting, a still life with a degree of artistic licence as far as tidiness goes. Its function as a subject for art does also occasionally hinder the process of washing up. Friends of Margaret have a long-standing joke about never looking at the under-side of plates. Often in the kitchen, as well, a still life – such as a profusion of pears next to a glass jar holding a bunch of clivias – will be set up where normally you might prepare food. In the paintings that result from these kitchen arrangements, an electric jug or a blender can look as magical as more purely decorative items, as still life and domestic interior blend intimately to portray a world that is entirely Olley.

Margaret also still paints borrowed interiors. In 2001 she embarked on the now famous studies of the Woollahra home of friend and gallery owner Brian Moore, some of which works included his dog, Nippy. Since Moore's death in 2003 the paintings have, of course, acquired a deeper emotional quality, but they do not possess the haunting quality of the 'Homage' interiors done at David Strachan's. The sessions at Moore's house were organised in a quite business-like fashion and, although she and Moore were close, Margaret insists that the paintings were not, as has been suggested, inspired by deep affection. It was simply that the interiors presented a tempting subject for her:

I loved the orderliness of his house. In the mornings Brian would leave out a clean ashtray; he'd offer me a glass of soda water or cup of coffee, and say, See you later. I'd let myself out with a key he'd given me when I was finished. I think I gave Brian a painting in return. The second time I actually paid him rent because he needed the money.

'Paintings should talk for themselves' has long been a credo of Margaret's. One clue she does give to her work, however, is that a painting must have 'humanity'. So almost always we find traces of living life in her still lifes and interiors: a half-peeled orange with a knife beside it, a partially drunk cup of tea, a half-empty carafe. Despite a distinct reluctance to discuss her paintings further, Margaret, who has a disdain of easels and always just works on a board propped up in front of her, is a little more forthcoming about how she paints:

The beginning is always the most exciting part for me and, of course, it's never really finished in my eyes. I've worked in the same way for years now. To start with, I do a little rough sketch on the back of an envelope or anything that comes to hand. Then I draw it in chalks on the board – my sister Elaine's daughter Sally [Wilkinson] saws up the boards for me – before working with acrylics. Having an additional layer of paint gives it a bit more weight. After that I paint over the acrylics with oil paint. I always like to know where the centre of the board is – don't ask me why – and I put a little mark there.

Margaret can also sometimes be seen busily checking a near-complete painting with a ruler because, as she's quick to point out, 'horizontals and perpendiculars' govern most of the structures of our lives. And there is one other very important tool or ingredient in how she works:

I always paint with music. The radio is the first thing turned on in the mornings. Music transports me, takes me to another plane. I couldn't live without it. I don't have a tape recorder or records; I just have my el cheapo radios all through the house turned to classical FM radio. I get so irritated if they play someone like John Cage. It's torture to me, I have to leave the room. But classical music I love. If I'm painting, sometimes I won't hear the end of a piece of music because the music has helped transport me into what I'm painting and then I've become totally involved with that – which is why, as far as I'm concerned, music and painting go together.

When I'm working, I like wearing old familiar things that I'm not even aware of, so I completely lose myself. Colour is just part of one's psyche. I have an almost instinctive response to colour. I don't believe in theories about colour; it's all in the application. I don't mix colour up like a chemist's prescription. We used to have a joke at art school about, When in doubt, paint umber. Donald always used to say, For Sydney shows there must be umber and for Brisbane lots of colour. I tend to just squeeze the colours out on my palette in some sort of order for whatever I'm doing. But then what colours I pick up depends on what feels right at that moment: it might be more pink and a little bit of green, or green with a touch of pink.

Flesh pink, despite the terrible name, is a colour that has a good body to it. It's a lovely paint to use with green. People are terrified of painting green but I use green all the time; sometimes on its own, sometimes I'll put blue or red in with it. Chrome green is a basic green I particularly love, but I use them all.

Margaret often refers to 'the bones' of things in conversation. It's a phrase that comes from Justin O'Brien, by which is meant the structure of anything. 'The bones' explain the numerous vases of flowers that are past their use-by date on display in the Hat Factory. 'They're dead but still evocative of what they were,' Margaret says. The kerb of the lane outside the Hat Factory is also frequently littered with 'the bones', thrown out after a reluctant purge. A bunch of flowers that has been on the dining room table for weeks, or months, will suddenly be deemed past it, or to be suffering too much from petal 'dandruff', and so chucked out to make way for new, more fleshed-out flowers.

Philip Bacon is both a close friend and confrère of Margaret's. They're frequently on the phone and his trips to Sydney for business discussions at the Hat Factory, which inevitably result in a few paint smears across his neat trousers or jacket sleeve, often include a night at the opera or some other social outing with Margaret. Bacon is one of the very few people whose presence does not put her off painting.

'So much of what I think about her painting is linked with what I think about her as a person. I find it hard to differentiate them,' he says.[2] 'Everything in this house is a still life. It's extraordinary to me how, with that whole panorama around her, she can still concentrate on what she's working on and not be distracted. I know just from the way people approach her paintings that they're life enriching. People collect her pictures because they love them; it's nothing to do with investment. They're everyday, in the sense that they are the way every day should be. That's why they're so celebratory, as she is too.

'The drawing is very good in them,' Bacon continues. 'The placement of objects, and the control of light and colour, is amazing, also her attention to detail. A picture might be finished, signed and in its frame, and she'll say: "I think that stem there should be shorter." It'll only be a fraction out, but she'll have noticed and a bit of paint is added. Put that across a whole large canvas or board and you begin to understand how complicated the process is. A lot of her decisions might seem offhand with that "Let's have a go" attitude she seems to bring to everything, but in fact they're very, very considered.'

Barry Humphries says of Margaret's paintings: 'There's nothing precious about them. If you walk through a museum where there are a lot of still lifes, they tend to blur into each other. But each of

Celebrating Life

Margaret's pictures has a very strong, theatrical character to it. Something is happening; there's an assertive flower of some kind and a cast of inanimate objects. They also give huge pleasure, which is what Matisse said a picture should above all do. Margaret does really belong to that French tradition, though somehow her pictures are rather Australian as well.'[3]

―◆―

While her own paintings reach higher and higher prices, Margaret is still endlessly giving. She's constantly planning how to raise funds for her Trust, as well as providing the actual wherewithal for more additions to our galleries. One of her more impressive efforts occurred in 2003:

Edmund rang me to say that there were some Cézanne sketchbooks coming up for sale in London and the gallery was thinking of buying a leaf from one. You don't want one —they're only small, I said. You should buy three. Go for three. If you go for three, I went on, I'll put in a quarter of a million. Then I had to find out where I could get the quarter of a million from. But I did it – and the gallery ended up with six Cézanne drawings on three leaves from a sketchbook.

Margaret has been known to refuse to chip in for certain of Capon's purchases. The Art Gallery of New South Wales's recently acquired Cy Twombly (who she calls 'Sly Trembly') work was not one she wished to contribute to.[4] But mostly her financial support to the gallery is a harmonious process that distinctly brightens her days, as well as enriching the general public enormously. And these days Margaret's petite layered figure scooting – because it's on wheels, her walking frame does move very fast – around new paintings displayed, or manoeuvring the frame equally deftly outside for a quick cigarette, is almost as familiar at Art Gallery of New South Wales functions as Dobell's image of her in the 'duchess' dress.

Although now in her eighty-third year, Margaret's role as a Sydney hostess seems undiminished by age or the 'black hole'. At the Hat Factory, there are the almost daily simple lunches, grilled fish, potatoes and salad, or smoked pork neck with leeks in cream sauce, followed by a tart from the pâtisserie down the road. She invites various old friends, like Anne Wienholt and Margaret Cilento, should they be in Sydney, and newer acquaintances. Guests are served their meal on a nice line of Woolworths willow-pattern china, along with plates, scratchy with age, from the original blue and white Farndon set. Those who drink are always offered wine.

Though these days it scares 'the living daylights' out of her and she claims to be doing it less and less, she also still throws the odd grand luncheon for visiting celebrities, such as British actress Maggie Smith (who opened Margaret's most recent London exhibition); Viscount John Julius Norwich; talk-show host Michael Parkinson; Neil McGregor, formerly the director of the National Gallery in London (now director of the British Museum); artist Jeffrey Smart – 'Lord Smart', as she affectionately calls him – when he's out from Italy; Barry Humphries with wife, actress and writer Lizzie Spender, if they're in town; and likewise Clive James.

Other guests, a mixture of old friends and more known names, who are also dear to Margaret include: Lady Pagan; artist Tim Storrier and his wife, Janet; Georgie and Snow Swift; active arts lover Leo Schofield; Edmund and Joanna Capon; Barry Pearce, from the Art Gallery of New South Wales; Richard Tognetti and his wine-maker wife, Susie Roberts; the Federal Minister for the Arts, Rod Kemp, whom she's always keen to lobby; Donald McDonald, chairman of the ABC, and his wife, Janet; art benefactor Peter Weiss and his wife, Doris; Richard and Sandie Walker; Christine France and her husband, Steven; music publicist Philippa Drynan;

Celebrating Life

Richard Alston, now Australia's High Commissioner in London; Cressida Campbell, a younger Sydney artist who can also imbue familiar domestic still-life subjects with a quietly sublime quality (and who actually did a body of work in the Hat Factory in 1993) and her husband, film writer Peter Crayford. And so the list goes on . . .

The dining table on these occasions will be cleared of mounting correspondence and decorated with green umbrella plant stalks or little bunches of coloured impatiens from the garden outside. But for the rest of the house, the rule is always: 'You clean up after people, you don't clean up before.'

Margaret still socialises at a staggering pace. She's out most evenings, in fact, not only at gallery openings – she likes to keep an eye on younger artists in smaller spaces, besides attending the Art Gallery spectaculars – but she also squeezes in performances of the Australian Chamber Orchestra and operas between numerous charity dinners to which her presence adds cachet. Recently she was a guest at Kirribilli House, where she sat next to Prime Minister John Howard and at judicious intervals chewed his ear about all her favourite causes, such as replacing cotton growing in Australia with the ancient, sturdy crop of hemp. Just occasionally, she likes to indulge in an early night in her tiny bed to recuperate from it all, then it's on to the next round of engagements.

You do meet people, those who don't know Margaret, who declare she's difficult or even cantankerous; but old friends speak only of her endless generosity and willingness to judge people as she finds them. She's also funny, self-deprecating and blunt. Occasionally, probably without realising it, she is imperious. And she worries ceaselessly about friends' welfare and is always available to help those who might have a problem, especially if it's to do with drinking and, now, depression. But above all, Margaret is warm. As Fred Jessup repeats down the phone from the south of

France, in a voice filled with emotion: 'She's the most important person in my life and I love her dearly.'[5]

Barry Pearce, the Head Curator of Australian Art at the Art Gallery of New South Wales, put together the gallery's 1996 retrospective of Margaret's work and the book that accompanied it. Pearce has also travelled overseas with Margaret four times, beginning with a journey to look at a Vermeer retrospective at The Hague in 1996. On the first three of these trips, they had two or three other companions. For the last, it was just him and Margaret. He's also often been with Margaret to exhibitions and art auctions in Sydney, in search of an unexpected treasure to purchase and, upon request, driven her to Manly to collect fresh stocks of amino acids from the iridologist.

Their most recent overseas excursion was to London for the opening of Margaret's 2005 exhibition. Margaret's favourite memory of the trip, as she reports with bursts of laughter, was when Pearce started calling her walking frame 'Moses', because of the way the crowds parted before it. Their return journey included stopovers at Edinburgh, Paris and Cairo, where once again Margaret was overwhelmed by the sight of the pyramids. 'The grandeur, the spiritual ambition, the enormity of time,' she remarked to Pearce as they stood in front of one. 'How lucky to be here to actually witness it!'[6]

Fittingly, of all the photos of Margaret, it's the one called *Perseverance*, taken by Christine France, of Margaret and her walking frame in front of the sharp triangular shape of a pyramid, on a day so hot that Margaret thought she'd die of heat stroke, that captures most wonderfully her indomitable spirit.

Pearce's observations of his recent travelling with Margaret show that Grace Olley's injunction, 'You never know who's going on the journey first', does ring loudly in her daughter's ears. 'With each of the four trips, there was a definite sentiment in her that this might be the last,' Pearce says. 'She was milking the memories, moving with haste, with almost a tinge of anxiety, to fit in as much as possible because she may not be back.'

Pearce has another insight to offer as to what, at least in part, Margaret's travelling over the last thirty-four years has been about: 'I always felt on these trips Margaret was checking out her sibling spirits, in a kind of measuring exercise of where she stood in terms of her own work, especially against those with whom she shared an interest in subject matter and painterly values, such as Vermeer, Chardin, Cézanne, Bonnard, Vuillard, Morandi. Even when we once looked at the vast David depiction of the coronation of Napoleon in the Louvre, not a painting I particularly wanted to spend a long time looking at, she drew my attention to the bottom of the composition and a beautifully rendered pair of shoes, or slippers, on one of the figures, as if that was an essential point of simpatico. A perfect example of the painter's eye noticing something the rest of us would pass over.

'There was no arrogance in this, or even sense of being equal – she is too self-doubting about painting for that, in spite of her persistence, and too shy, if you can believe it. But she was happy to look at the work of the artists she most admires and feel, yes, we are interested fundamentally in the same thing, we are all part of the same clan. It's about reassurance I suppose. She would be chuffed to be included in their pantheon and okay about sitting at the doorstep, or being made to stand outside the window, perhaps. Some artists may reject the past to feel the excitement of moving forward unencumbered, but at the end of the day they all secretly want to know how they might be judged against the overall scheme of what has gone before. Margaret more than most.'

It's sixty-five years since Margaret, fresh out of Somerville House, started studying art. So, how does she now regard herself as an artist?

I've never considered myself a 'woman' painter. I'm a painter. I sign my works 'Olley', that's the end of it. I'm not bothered by what critics say. I think it made Donald insecure, but why do you have to have it in the papers? If you're happy with your work, it's of no consequence. Although we're obviously influenced all the time, you must be true to yourself, whether it's fashionable or not. I don't paint for money. I never know how much anything is, anyway. I paint for the love of it.

Last year, I felt that the show I had earlier this year [2005] would be my last in London and my upcoming exhibition [which will also include Vuillards] possibly the last in Sydney. I set myself the goals of having these shows because of 'hurry, hurry, last days'; whether anything would sell or not was secondary. Now I'm feeling much stronger, especially since I'm off the coffee and on to the juices. I hope to have an exhibition in Brisbane, and who knows what after that. I've recently done a series of paintings of the harbour from a friend's place at Elizabeth Bay and really enjoyed it. As I've said endlessly before, I've always loved water and boats as a subject.

When she was asked in 2004 to write a piece for an anthology entitled *I Believe This*, Margaret chose to head her statement 'The Colour Green'. In it, like an ardent greenie, she stressed the need to protect the colour green by stopping deforestation and cleaning up clogged waterways. She's always fearlessly quick to buttonhole politicians at social occasions and you sometimes get the feeling that if it was up to her, she'd have the country, if not the world, fixed up in a jiffy. Despite her conservationist stance, she's often regarded as politically conservative and right wing. But she herself is adamant that eighty-two years of life have taught her to be far more fluid than that:

I can swing from one extreme to the other in my political views. Some people think I'm to the right of Genghis Khan. I'm not really, it depends on what's happening around us. I'm almost a communist in regard to the right of everybody to fresh water. We'd all be dead without it and very soon many people will be, unless steps are taken to rectify the situation. Why is money being wasted on sending probes to search for water on Mars when people on earth don't even have water to drink? I'm also appalled that we can be so affected by tragedies of nature, like the tsunami of 2004, and yet we will not face up to the reality of man's inhumanity to man, as in the Sudan.

In answer to the question, Does she believe in God? Margaret's views are encompassing:

I believe there's one great force, be it Buddhist, Hindu or Islamic, it doesn't matter. I remember somebody at an AA meeting saying, Well, if you have any trouble with God as a concept, think of whatever makes the sun get up in the morning. There is a greater force and this is very humbling. Life is not about conquering nature or what we can achieve. We must accept the days as they come; celebrate each day and try to make a difference. Be kind to people, even if it means speaking out.

Donald Friend referred to his soul as being heliotrope pink. When asked what colour her soul might be, Margaret's answer was unhesitating: 'Green.'

Margaret is now arguably Australia's most loved living artist. She has painted great works of art, among them *Portrait in the Mirror*, *Late Afternoon* and *Still Life with Kettle*, not to mention *Pomegranates*, *Eucharist Lilies* and *Homage to Manet*. And there are vast numbers of other highly pleasurable Olleys. And without doubt, she'll be remembered for her 'passionate benefaction', to borrow Edmund Capon's apt phrase.

But this book is not about ascertaining Margaret's place in history or the honour rolls of art academia. Rather, it is about celebrating a life that has been far from still and yet at the same time remarkable in its singular devotion to painting.

Painting has been the love affair of Margaret's life. It's outlasted her lovers and has taken her on an extraordinary journey: from the greenness of her childhood in Tully to almost every country of the world, as well as to about every major art gallery there is. Through painting, Margaret has survived personal crises that would have wrecked lesser spirits. Even now, as mortality's grey curtain (to quote from Donald Friend once more) sweeps up so many of those dearest to her, she defiantly paints on. And, if sometimes loneliness or doubt assails her in that little narrow bed in the hours past midnight, she does not give in to them. The next morning, she is always up and at the brushes, turps and squeezed-out oil paint again.

Here we might conclude this celebration of an un-still life and leave Margaret Hannah Olley, painter and benefactor, in front of an arrangement of potted cyclamen or the flower of her fancy, to daubs of chrome green with a little flesh pink, and dreams of a world that is green, green, green, in which perhaps blue Tully butterflies also flutter – until that time, of course, that she hastily dons her glad rags for whatever social engagement might be next in the offing.

Selected Solo Exhibitions

1948
June — Macquarie Galleries, Sydney
October — Moreton Galleries, Brisbane
1950
July — Moreton Galleries, Brisbane
1951
March — Marodian Gallery, Brisbane
1952
June — Johnstone Gallery, Brisbane
1953
June — Macquarie Galleries, Sydney
1955
April — Macquarie Galleries, Sydney
July — Johnstone Gallery, Brisbane
1956
June — Johnstone Gallery, Brisbane
October — Macquarie Galleries, Sydney
1960
October — Johnstone Gallery, Brisbane
1961
August — Macquarie Galleries, Sydney
1962
October — Johnstone Gallery, Brisbane
1963
April — Bonython Gallery, Adelaide
October — Macquarie Galleries, Sydney
1964
March — Australian Galleries, Melbourne

Far from a Still Life

April	von Bertouch Galleries, Newcastle
October	Johnstone Gallery, Brisbane

1965

September	Darlinghurst Galleries, Sydney

1966

February	'The Third Anniversary Exhibition', von Bertouch Galleries, Newcastle
November	Johnstone Gallery, Brisbane

1967

April	Macquarie Galleries, Canberra
September	Darlinghurst Galleries, Sydney

1968

October	'Leaves from a New Guinea Sketch Book and Other Paintings', Johnstone Gallery, Brisbane

1969

May	von Bertouch Galleries, Newcastle
December	Macquarie Galleries, Canberra

1970

June	'New Guinea Paintings', Port Moresby, New Guinea
October	Johnstone Gallery, Brisbane

1971

June	'Newcastle Paintings', von Bertouch Galleries, Newcastle

1972

October	'Homage', Johnstone Gallery, Brisbane
November	Barry Stern Gallery, Sydney

1973

April	Macquarie Galleries, Canberra
October	Holdsworth Galleries, Sydney

1974

April	von Bertouch Galleries, Newcastle
November	Skinner Galleries, Perth

1975

April	Anna Simons Gallery, Canberra
September	Philip Bacon Galleries, Brisbane

Selected Solo Exhibitions

1976
May   von Bertouch Galleries, Newcastle
September   Holdsworth Galleries, Sydney
1977
September   Philip Bacon Galleries, Brisbane
November   Anna Simons Gallery, Canberra
1978
October   Holdsworth Galleries, Sydney
1979
October   Philip Bacon Galleries, Brisbane
1980
March   'Sixth Anniversary Exhibition', Solander Gallery, Canberra
October   Holdsworth Galleries, Sydney
1981
September   Philip Bacon Galleries, Brisbane
1982
April   Solander Gallery, Canberra
October   Holdsworth Galleries, Sydney
1984
October   Philip Bacon Galleries, Brisbane
1985
October   Greenhill Galleries, Perth
1989
September   Philip Bacon Galleries, Brisbane
1990
February   Greenhill Galleries, Adelaide
August   'The Art of Margaret Olley', National Trust S.H. Ervin Gallery, Sydney
September   Brisbane City Hall Art Gallery and Museum
October   Lismore Regional Art Gallery
               Australian Galleries, Melbourne
1991
October   Australian Galleries, Sydney

1993
September Philip Bacon Galleries, Brisbane
1994
November Browse & Darby, London
1995
October Australian Galleries, Sydney
1996
September Philip Bacon Galleries, Brisbane
October Major retrospective at the Art Gallery of New South Wales, Sydney
1997
January Retrospective tour, Brisbane City Hall Art Gallery and Museum
April Retrospective tour, Newcastle Region Art Gallery
October Australian Galleries, Sydney
1998
October Philip Bacon Galleries, Brisbane
1999
June Nevill Keating Pictures Gallery, London
2000
October Brian Moore Fine Art and Philip Bacon Galleries at Sotheby's Gallery, Sydney
2001
November Philip Bacon Galleries, Brisbane
2002
August Savill Galleries, Melbourne
2003
March 'Celebrating Life', Queensland Art Gallery
2005
March Nevill Keating Tollemache Gallery, London
October Philip Bacon Galleries at Sotheby's Gallery, Sydney
November National Trust S.H. Ervin Gallery, Sydney; Newcastle Region Art Gallery

List of Illustrations

Colour Plates
William Dobell
Margaret Olley, 1948
Oil on hardboard, 114.3 × 85.7 cm
Purchased 1949
Collection: Art Gallery of New South Wales
© Sir William Dobell Art Foundation, licensed by Viscopy
   Australia

Russell Drysdale
Portrait of Margaret Olley, 1948
Oil on canvas, 61.5 × 51.1 cm
National Gallery of Australia, Canberra

Era Landscape, c. 1946
Oil on canvas, 60.5 × 76.5 cm
Collection: the artist

New England Landscape, 1947
Oil on canvas, 72 × 98 cm
Mosman Art Prize Collection, Sydney
Mosman Art Gallery, Mosman Council

St Paul's Terrace, Brisbane, 1946
Oil on cardboard, 35.5 × 43.8 cm
Private collection

North Sydney, 1947
Oil on canvas, 55.5 × 77.5 cm
Private collection

Pink Paper and Kippers, 1947
Oil on canvas, 68 × 94 cm
Private collection

Still Life in Green, 1947
Oil on cardboard, 63 × 72 cm
Jean Cameron Gordon Bequest Fund in memory of her mother
    Mary Gordon, 2001
Collection: Art Gallery of New South Wales, Sydney

Hill End Ruins, 1948
Oil on canvas, 76 × 101.4 cm
Purchased, 1948
National Art Gallery of Victoria, Melbourne

The Cotswolds, c. 1950
Collection: the artist

Chateau Fontcreuais, Cassis, 1951
Watercolour, gouache, brush and ink on smooth wove paper,
396 × 52.8 cm
Purchased 1951
Queensland Art Gallery, Brisbane

Gondolas, Venice, 1951
Collection: the artist

Concarneau, Britanny, 1952
Gouache, pen and watercolour on paper, 40.7 × 52 cm
Private collection

List of Illustrations

Still Life with Kettle, 1955
Oil on hardboard, 68 × 90 cm
Margaret Hannah Olley Art Trust 2001
Collection: Art Gallery of New South Wales

Susan with Flowers, 1962
Oil on canvas, 127.4 × 102.3 cm
Gift of the Finney Islaes and Co Ltd, 1964
Queensland Art Gallery, Brisbane

The View from David's Kitchen, 1962
Oil on hardboard, 75 × 100 cm
Collection: Mr and Mrs Ken Shave, Sydney

Eucharist Lilies, 1963
Oil on hardboard, 72.5 × 98.5 cm
Collection: The artist

Daphne, 1964
Oil on board, 121 × 75 cm
Private collection, Brisbane

Pomegranates, 1966
Oil on hardboard, 75 × 100 cm
Collection: Mrs Mimi Falkiner, Brisbane

Children Playing, Angoram, 1968
Indian ink, watercolour, gouache on paper, 24.9 × 39.5 cm
National Gallery of Australia, Canberra

Tribal Chieftain, 1968
Oil on board, 38 × 50 cm
Collection: Philip Bacon Galleries, Brisbane

Interior IV, 1970
Oil on canvas on hardboard, 121 × 90 cm
Gift of the Margaret Hannah Olley Trust, 2002
Queensland Art Gallery, Brisbane

Interior VIII, 1970
Oil on canvas on hardboard, 75 × 100 cm
Private collection

State Dockyard, Newcastle, 1974
Oil on board, 51.5 × 91.6 cm
Presented in 1986 by Lady Drysdale
Newcastle Region Art Gallery, Newcastle

Self-Portrait with Everlastings, 1974
Oil on hardboard, 74.5 × 59.6 cm
Collection: Anne von Bertouch Bequest
Newcastle Region Art Gallery, Newcastle

Blackberries, 1979
Oil on hardboard, 60 × 75 cm
Collection: Miles Dupree, Catherine Hill Bay

Clivias, 1984
Oil on board, 76.2 × 101.5 cm
Private collection, Sydney

Cherries and Roses, 1985
Oil on hardboard, 68.5 × 91.5 cm
Collection: the artist

Yellow Interior, 1989
Oil on hardboard, 61 × 76 cm
Collection: Philip Bacon Galleries, Brisbane

List of Illustrations

Yellow Room with Lupins, 1994
Oil on hardboard, 60 × 90 cm
Private collection

Elizabeth Bay Summer, 2000
Oil on hardboard, 68.5 × 91.5 cm
Private collection

Black and White Plates
Thomas Temperley, 1908
Photograph courtesy Margaret Olley

Joseph Daniel Olley and his wife Grace, 1921
Photograph courtesy Margaret Olley

Margaret, c. 1924
Photograph courtesy Margaret Olley

Joe Olley with Margaret, Elaine and Ken, 1920s
Photograph courtesy Margaret Olley

Margaret, Ken and Elaine in Murwillumbah, c. 1931
Photograph courtesy Margaret Olley

Grace Olley rowing Margaret, Elaine and Ken to school, c. 1932
Photograph courtesy Margaret Olley

Margaret on Magnetic Island
Photograph courtesy Margaret Olley

Margaret Cilento and Margaret Olley, Sydney, 1940s
Photograph courtesy Margaret Cilento

Far from a Still Life

Margaret Cilento, Marseilles, 1949
Photograph courtesy Margaret Cilento

Donald Friend and Russell Drysdale, 1942
Photograph Russell Drysdale
Collection: Art Gallery of New South Wales Archive

William Dobell, 1944
Collection: Art Gallery of New South Wales Archive

Merioola Group, 1946
Photograph Alec Murray
Collection: Art Gallery of New South Wales Archive

Sir Francis Rose, 1939
Photograph Cecil Beaton
Courtesy Cecil Beaton Studio Archive, Sotheby's, London

Frankie Mitchell, *c.* 1950
Courtesy Powerhouse Museum, Sydney

A painting trip with Moya Dyring, France, early 1950s
Photograph courtesy Margaret Olley

Fred Jessup, David Strachan and Moya Dyring, Paris, early 1950s
Photograph courtesy Margaret Olley

Sam Hughes, 1930s
Photograph courtesy Margaret Olley

Margaret at Elaine's wedding, 1952
Photograph courtesy Margaret Olley

List of Illustrations

Brian and Marjorie Johnstone with Margaret, 1950s
Photograph courtesy Johnstone Gallery Archive,
State Library of Queensland

Geoff Elworthy
Photograph courtesy Liz Abel

Margaret and Elaine Haxton, Sydney, 1960s
Photograph Annette Dupree

Laurie Thomas, Sir Herbert Read and Margaret with
    Susan with Flowers, 1962
Photograph courtesy *Courier-Mail*, Brisbane

Grace Olley, c. 1970
Photograph courtesy Margaret Olley

Margaret and Justin O'Brien
Photograph courtesy Margaret Olley

Margaret with Philip Bacon, receiving her Honorary Doctorate
    from the University of Queensland, 1999
Photograph courtesy Margaret Olley

Margaret and Barry Humphries, 1996
Photograph Lewis Morley

Margaret and Edmund Capon, 1996
Photograph courtesy Margaret Olley

Margaret Whitlam, Sir Roden Cutler, Peter Sculthorpe,
    Margaret, Thomas Keneally and Barry Humphries
Photograph courtesy Margaret Olley

Far from a Still Life

Neil McGregor, Margaret and Edmund Capon, 1998
Photograph courtesy Margaret Olley

Margaret at the Pyramids, 2000
Photograph Christine France

Acknowledgements

This book grew out of a series of tape recordings I first made with Margaret Olley and many of her friends between September 2003 and June 2004.

After our second session, at which Margaret banished me to the garden for trying to interview her while she was painting, on most of these occasions, somewhat to my embarrassment, she cooked lunch for me and whoever else was present, while recollecting with verve the details of her un-still life. So, not only was I inundated with revelations while learning to savour the particular appeal of Margaret's paintings and her house, I was also very well fed.

Earlier in 2003, before I became involved with the project, Margaret had already recorded a number of conversations with friends. Following our first series of conversations, I had innumerable catch-up sessions with Margaret from July 2004 to August 2005, which meant the final amount of material available for the book was dauntingly large. Now, at its completion, I would particularly like to thank Margaret for her boundless cheerfulness, patience and enthusiasm during this whole period; even at the very last, when she herself was busy working on paintings for her Sydney exhibition of 2005.

Another person to whom I wish to pay tribute is the late Donald Friend, for his genius in writing down such a plethora of information from decades of his own and other people's lives, including Margaret's. Thanks are due to the National Gallery, Canberra and the estate of Donald Friend for their kind permission in allowing me to access and quote from Donald's unpublished diaries.

I would like to acknowledge Christine France's study of Margaret Olley's art, which was an invaluable aid in the writing of this book, and to thank France for being so readily being available for consultation. I also wish to particularly thank Daniela Torsh and Eric Riddler for their excellent additional research; Maureen Brooks, the publications editor at the National Library of Australia for her frequent assistance in matters relating to *The Diaries of Donald Friend*, Volumes 2 and 3, as well as the unpublished diaries; Steven Miller, archivist at the Art Gallery of New South Wales, and staff of the Research Library and Archive at the Art Gallery of New South Wales: without access to material held in the Library this book would not have happened.

I am also hugely indebted to Jane Gleeson-White and Catherine Hill of Random House for editing the book; also Pippa Masson of Curtis Brown for her support during its progress; and Carol Davidson of Random House, whose suggestion it first was that I write Margaret's biography.

The following is a list of those who generously gave their time in providing interviews for this book and for so doing deserve special thanks: Liz and Sheila Abel; Murray Abel; Jessie Andrews; Philip Bacon; William Bowmore; Don Burrows; Edmund Capon; Margaret Cilento; Lynne Clarke; Ray and June Crooke; John Duffecy; Mimi Falkiner; Christine France; James Gleeson; the late Sir David Griffin; Attilio Guarracino; Nigel and Norma Hawkins; Kate Hodgkinson; Barry Humphries; Fred Jessup; Wilma Knight; Jeanette Leahy; Mitty Lee-Brown; the late Eugen Lude; Bruce McLeod; Jinx Nolan; John Pasquarelli; Barry Pearce; Jocelyn Plate; Agnes Richardson; Ronald Sabien; William Salmon; Rollin Schlicht; James Somerville; the late Colin Temperley; Douglas Temperley; Bob Turner; the late Joyce Vaughan; Luke Whittington; Anne Wienholt; Elaine and Richard Wilkinson; Sally Wilkinson; Ron and Shirley Wright.

There were also a number of other people who were particu-

Acknowledgements

larly helpful to me: Glenn R. Cooke, research curator at the Queensland Heritage Art Gallery; Carolyn Georgeson; Paul Hetherington, director of the Publications and Events Branch at the National Library of Australia; Caroline Lurie; Sandra McDonald; Professor Gordon Parker of the Black Dog Institute; Cameron Sparks (for essential archival assistance relating to East Sydney Technical College); Douglas Temperley (in helping to sort out the Olley–Temperley family history in Tully); Maggy Todd; Alex Torrens, curator at the Bathurst Regional Art Gallery; Gavin Wilson.

Also: Chris Bastock of the Hyman Kreitman Research Centre for the Tate Library and Archive in London; Patsy Bell; Tim Bell; Kate Bottger, archivist and alumni officer at Somerville House; Julie Brackenreg at the Artarmon Galleries; Sue Brandt at ABC TV; Brooke Brunckhorst; Alison Clark at the S.H. Ervin Gallery; Gael Davies; Jackie Dunn at Artbank; Elizabeth Emanuel; Diana Garder; Janette Garrard at the John Oxley Library, State Library of Queensland; John Herbert Gill; Amber Gooley at Lismore Regional Gallery; Leanne Handreck, rights and permissions coordinator at the National Gallery of Australia, Canberra; Gregory Herringshaw at the Cooper-Hewitt National Design Museum, New York; Mark Hertzberg; Lou Klepac of the Beagle Press; Les McLaren; Mary Mahoney at the Cathedral School, Townsville; Megan Martin at the Historic Houses Trust of New South Wales; Susanne Moir; Ria Murch; Ruth O'Dwyer; Des Partridge at the *Courier Mail*; Antony Penrose; Colin Pfeffer; Elizabeth Pridmore at the Queensland National Trust; Doug Robertson, for sharing a filmed interview with Margaret; Lorraine Ryle at the Cairns Historical Society; Gillian Simpson, librarian at the Australian National Maritime Museum; staff of the Mitchell Library, State Library of New South Wales; Annie Stiven; Jennifer Temperley; Guy Tranter at the ABC Document Archives; Debra Turnbull; Jacklyn Young at the Queensland Art Gallery; Helen Yoxall at the Powerhouse Museum Archives.

Notes

Chapter 1: Green, Green, Green
1. *Art in Australia*, 23 February 1940, 'Australian Painters Look to Europe', William Dobell. Dobell was teaching at East Sydney Technical College at the time the article was written
2. *Truth*, 28 March 1915
3. Wright, *Memories of a Bushwhacker*, p. 99. Wright's second wife was Thomas Temperley's daughter Dora
4. Temperley, *Some Notes on Thomas Temperley and His Family*, p. 4
5. London *Standard*, 8 June 1909, 'Colonial Editors as Orators', John Foster Fraser
6. *Art in Australia*, 1 August 1923
7. Hudson, *By the Banyan: Tully Sugar, the first 75 years*, p. 43
8. France, *Margaret Olley*, p. 13
9. Ibid

Chapter 2: Living on a River
1. Interview with Elaine Wilkinson, September 2003

Chapter 3: Forever on the Move
1. From written notes provided by Douglas Temperley, 2004
2. Interview with Margaret Cilento, 2004
3. Possibly *The rehearsal*, 1873–74, or another in this series
4. *Le Cheval Blanc*, 1895
5. Interview with Agnes Richardson, 2004
6. *Maria Kuhn*, Pamela King, p. 1, unpublished information provided by Queensland Art Gallery archives
7. Ibid, and additional information supplied by the Queensland Art Gallery on Maria Kuhn

8 *Queensland National Art Gallery Bulletin*, vol. 1, no. 4, 1958
9 *Courier Mail*, 17 January 1941
10 *Courier Mail*, 20 January 1942
11 *The Diaries of Donald Friend*, Vol. 2, 27 June 1944, p. 118
12 *Courier Mail*, 9 January 1943

Chapter 4: Life Begins
1 Although it seems to be virtually impossible to extract any archival information from East Sydney Technical College itself, using the exam results published in the *Courier Mail* and in consultation with Cameron Sparks (who was for a period an official archivist for East Sydney Technical College), it is possible to say conclusively that Margaret arrived in Sydney in 1943
2 *The Art of Australia*, pp. 136–67
3 Ibid, p. 170. It took decades for this tag to be discarded and for those in the art world to decide it did the painters a major injustice
4 Name has been changed
5 *Present-Day Art in Australia* 2, p. 60
6 Description of the painting studio was supplied in interview with Cameron Sparks, 2005, who attended East Sydney Tech a couple of years after Margaret
7 Barnard and Ure Smith, *The Sydney Book*, p. 13
8 Ibid
9 *The Student*, 1941, and reproduced in colour in *Art in Australia*, series 4, no. 1, March–April 1941
10 Not her real name
11 Robinson, *The Drift of Things*, p. 216
12 Ibid, p. 215
13 Ibid
14 Accounts of Mitchell's war service vary, but it seems that he joined the air force hoping to be a pilot, but failed his exams and subsequently became an air gunner, or was relegated to the ground in air stations. He then had a nervous collapse and was posted to 'signals' in Brisbane. It was presumably after this, and before the St Louis Vanities tour, that he first met Margaret Olley

Notes

15 Names have been changed
16 Interview with Margaret Cilento, 2004
17 Ibid. Howard Hinton was also Lady Cilento's godfather: *Lady Cilento, My Life*, p. 167

Chapter 5: Doors Open
1 Adams, *Portrait of an Artist*, p. 93
2 *The Diaries of Donald Friend*, Vol. 2, p. 9
3 Ibid, p. 3
4 Ibid
5 Ibid, p. 30
6 Interview with Anne Wienholt and Margaret Olley, 2003
7 *The Diaries of Donald Friend*, Vol. 2, p. 480
8 Ibid, p. 345
9 Ibid, p. 361
10 Ibid, p. 521
11 Jocelyn Zander, phone interview, March 2005
12 'Autobiography', John Reed, *Overland*, no. 101, 1985
13 For information on Clarice Zander I am indebted to *The Heart Garden*
14 This section incorporates details supplied by Jenny Temperley, wife of Gil Temperley (now deceased)
15 Robinson, *The Drift of Things*, pp. 163–4
16 Interview with Jimmy Somerville, 2003
17 *Sydney Morning Herald*, 15 June 1944
18 'Australia', *Brisbane Roundabout*, November 1944
19 Letter to Christine France from Cameron Sparks
20 Murray, *Alec Murray's Album*, p. 64.
21 *Jean Bellette Retrospective*, National Trust of Australia, 2004; *Jean Bellette*, p. 12
22 Robinson, *The Drift of Things*, p. 228
23 *Art in Australia*, 23 February 1940, p. 25
24 Interview with Margaret Olley by Christine France at Laguna, 8 December 2003, included in France's *Jean Bellette*
25 Essay by John McDonald, in Klepac, *David Strachan*, p. 31
26 Ibid

27 Catalogue of the ninth annual exhibition of the Society, 1947 (no author given)
28 *Sun*, 12 November 1946
29 Tilly Devine (1900–70) was a famous Sydney madam from the 1920s to the '50s
30 Eakin, *Aunts up the Cross*, pp. 101–2
31 *The Diaries of Donald Friend*, Vol. 2, p. 312
32 Ibid
33 Rickards, *The Painted Banquet*, p. 20
34 Phelan, *Writing Round the Edge*, pp. 223–5
35 Klepac, *Russell Drysdale*, p. 118
36 Friend, *My Brother Donald*, p. 6
37 *The Diaries of Donald Friend*, Vol. 2, p. 316
38 Ibid
39 Ibid
40 Ibid

Chapter 6: Keeping the Rent Paid
1 'Against the Odds, Margaret Cilento and Margo Lewers', Alison Clark, thesis submitted for BA Hons degree, Department of Art History and Theory, University of Sydney, 2001, p. 18
2 *The Diaries of Donald Friend*, Vol. 2, pp. xv–xvi
3 Ibid, p. 386
4 Ibid, p. 358
5 Ibid, p. 563
6 Phone interview with John Duffecy, February 2005
7 Information on 151 Dowling Street comes from articles in *Pix*, 14 January 1950, and 'A Fabulous House', Julie Norman, in *Woman*, 5 December 1949
8 This spelling of Morriss is taken from an article in *Woman*, Julie Norman, 5 December 1949, although in Donald Friend's *Diaries* her surname is spelt Morris.
9 From the foreword by Sydney Ure Smith in the catalogue of the Society of Artists' 1946 Annual Exhibition
10 *The Diaries of Donald Friend*, Vol. 2, p. 430

Notes

11 *Sun*, 12 November 1946
12 Ibid
13 *Sydney Morning Herald*, 12 November 1946
14 *The Encyclopaedia of Australian Art*, p. 486
15 The program for *Hassan* lists James Cook and Adrian Feint in the credits for designing and painting of scenery
16 Interview with Nigel Hawkins, 2004
17 2004 ABC *Boyer Lectures*, Peter Conrad; Lecture 3: 'Down Under', 28 November 2004
18 *Sydney Morning Herald*, 8 October 1947
19 *Sun*, 9 October 1947
20 'Talkabout', Billy King, *Sunday Telegraph*, 16 November 1947

Chapter 7: 1948
1 *The Diaries of Donald Friend*, Vol. 2, p. 588. The published diaries give the street as Coast Crescent, but since the letter was handwritten one wonders if this was originally East Crescent, which was Olley's street address at McMahons Point
2 Ibid, pp. 530–31
3 Ibid, p. 539
4 Ibid, p. 580
5 Ibid, p. 587
6 Ibid
7 Ibid
8 Rickards, *The Painted Banquet*, p. 2
9 *Sun*, June 1948
10 *The Diaries of Donald Friend*, Vol. 2, p. 589
11 Ibid, p. 591
12 The Beyers and Holtermann Specimen, reputedly the largest single mass of gold, quartz, slate and iron pyrites in the world, was mined on 19 October 1872 in the Star of Hope shaft, Hill End
13 *The Diaries of Donald Friend*, Vol. 2, p. 593
14 Ibid, p. 598
15 Ibid
16 Ibid, p. 602

17 Ibid
18 France, *Margaret Olley*, p. 22
19 Ibid, p. 23
20 *Sun*, 30 June 1948
21 *Sydney Morning Herald*, 30 June 1948
22 *The Diaries of Donald Friend*, Vol. 2, p. 579
23 Ibid, p. 587 (quoted from a letter by Donald Murray to Friend)
24 Ibid, p. 608
25 Ure Smith, *Present-Day Art in Australia*, p. 86; Tatlock Miller, *The Art of the Theatre: Loudon Sainthill*
26 Tatlock Miller (ed.), *Loudon Sainthill*, p. 57
27 Burke, *The Heart Garden*, p. 191
28 Ibid, p. 276
29 For this section introducing Sidney Nolan, I am indebted to Janine Burke and *The Heart Garden*.
30 The program credits for these two plays have the scenery for *Pericles* painted by both Jean Bellette and Margaret, but in fact Bellette was not involved with the actual painting. There is also a scenery painting credit given to Margaret for *Orphée*, but she was not involved with the painting for this.
31 *The Diaries of Donald Friend*, Vol. 2, p. 616
32 Ibid
33 Ibid, pp. 619–20
34 Ibid, p. 621
35 Ibid, p. 627
36 Ibid
37 Adams, *Portrait of an Artist*, p. 237
38 *The Diaries of Donald Friend*, Vol. 2, p. 635
39 *Telegraph*, 22 January 1949
40 *Sun*, 22 January 1949
41 *Truth*, 23 January 1949
42 Beginning with the *Sun*, 22 January 1949; the other comments in this paragraph come from the same *Sun* article headed 'Dobell Finds His Mona Lisa'
43 Ibid

Notes

Chapter 8: Culture Shock

1. Adams, *Portrait of an Artist*, p. 239
2. *The Diaries of Donald Friend*, Vol. 2, p. 639
3. Phone interview with Mitty Lee-Brown in Sri Lanka, July 2004
4. Ibid
5. Rickards arrived at Victoria Station in London, on 2 January 1949, according to her autobiography *The Painted Banquet*, p. 3
6. While previous accounts of Margaret's arrival in London have had her living at the 'House of the Sons of God' with Harry Tatlock Miller and Loudon Sainthill, in fact these two were not yet in London at this time
7. *Daily Mirror*, 7 March 1949
8. *Sun*, 23 March 1949
9. *The Diaries of Donald Friend*, Vol. 2, p. 645
10. Letter from David Strachan to his family, 25 April 1949, Klepac, *David Strachan*, p. 56
11. Letter from David Strachan to his parents, 29 April 1949 (papers of David Edgar Strachan, Archive of the Art Gallery of New South Wales, MS 1973.1)
12. Burke, *The Heart Garden*, pp. 279–94
13. Musée Marmottan Monet in Paris, which houses a collection of Claude Monet's and other Impressionist paintings
14. Eakin, *Aunts up the Cross*, pp. 101–2
15. Burke, *The Heart Garden*, p. 97
16. Ibid
17. Ibid, p. 177
18. Atyeo was, by this stage, managing a coffee plantation in nearby Dominica. In trying to sort out these romantic machinations I am indebted to *The Heart Garden*, Janine Burke
19. *Art and Australia*, no. 4, March 1967, p. 266
20. *The Australian Dictionary of Biography*, vol. 14:1949–80, p. 68 states that Dyring was given the lease in 1948. Gay Cuthbert, in her thesis 'Changing the Landscape: The Life and Art of Moya Dyring', indicates that the date might have been a little later than this and has photos of the studio being renovated in 1950. However,

by September 1950, Alannah Coleman reported to the Reeds that Dyring was well set up there, as Cuthbert quotes on p. 42 of her thesis

21 *The Letters of Virginia Woolf*, Vol. 3, letter to Roger Fry, 16 September 1925, p. 209
22 Ibid
23 Bertha Wright, while married to Alec (Alexander) Penrose, also had an affair with the art critic Clive Bell, according to Antony's Penrose's memoir *Roland Penrose*, p. 30
24 In previous works the château's name has been spelt Fontcreuais, although in two catalogues of the time, which contain a work by that title, it is spelt correctly: Château de Fontcreuse. This spelling was also embossed on Colonel Teed's notepaper and is used by the château today. Teed has been spelt Tied in other works on Margaret Olley; the papers of Angelica Garnett (née Bell) in King's College Library, Cambridge, use the correct spelling
25 *The Letters of Virginia Woolf*, Vol. 3, letter to Vita Sackville-West, 5 April 1927, p. 359
26 Ibid
27 Ibid, letter to Quentin Bell, 15 April 1927, p. 480

Chapter 9: In and Out of Paris

1 From the unpublished diaries of Donald Friend, NLA MS5959, item 34, 19 November 1949
2 Ibid
3 I have been unable to pinpoint a time reference for this particular trip
4 *The Diaries of Donald Friend*, Vol. 3, p. 59
5 Ibid, p. 67
6 The unpublished diaries of Donald Friend, NLA MS5959, item 35, 27 April 1950
7 *The Diaries of Donald Friend*, Vol. 3, p. 667. (Guarracino was and is simply known as Attilio to his friends.)
8 Ibid, p. 87
9 The unpublished diaries of Donald Friend, NLA MS5959, item 35, 7 July 1950

Notes

10 Phone interview with Fred Jessup, 2004
11 *Courier Mail*, 4 July 1950
12 Letter to John and Sunday Reed, 22 August 1950, Reed Estate, as quoted in Cuthbert's 'Changing the Landscape', p. 41
13 This account of Moya Dyring's apartment is from an article that appeared in the *Sydney Morning Herald*, 9 June 1955
14 Gay Cuthbert has Dyring's relationship with Theo Schlicht underway by 1955; and in a letter Cuthbert quotes, written to the Reeds on 5 August 1951 (the Reed Estate), Dyring refers to how her relationship with him had grown over the previous two years, p. 44
15 There are three mentioned in the diaries, see *The Diaries of Donald Friend*, Vol. 3, pp. 90–1; and the unpublished diaries of Donald Friend, NLA MS5959, item 35, 17 August 1950
16 *The Diaries of Donald Friend*, Vol. 3, p. 91
17 Interview with Attilio Guarracino, 2004
18 Tatlock Miller, *Loudon Sainthill*, p. 58
19 This account is based on Rickards' *The Painted Banquet*, pp 20–1
20 *People*, 30 January 1952
21 *The Diaries of Donald Friend*, Vol. 3, p. 94
22 Cuthbert, 'Changing the Landscape', from an interview with Veronica Rowan, March 2000, p. 42
23 'Margaret Olley Steals the Show' by Elizabeth Young, *Courier Mail*, 8 December 1950
24 The papers of Angelica Garnett, King's College Library, Cambridge; reference AG/1/57, autographed letter from Colonel A.S.H. Teed to Vanessa Bell, dated 27 February 1951
25 Ibid, in an autographed letter from Jean Campbell to Vanessa Bell, 14 January 1952
26 Ibid
27 Margaret had two shows in Australia in 1951: one in March at the Marodian Gallery, Brisbane, of watercolours, a few oils and two pastels; and a drawing exhibition in November at the Macquarie Galleries, Sydney, which was shown together with an exhibition of English lithographs by artists including Vanessa Bell and Duncan

Grant. In both these exhibitions was a work by Margaret depicting the Château de Fontcreuse, spelt the correct way

28 *Courier Mail*, 2 March 1951
29 *Sydney Morning Herald*, 7 November 1951
30 *The Letters of Virginia Woolf, Vol. 3*, ed. letter to Quentin Bell, 15 April 1928, pp. 481–2
31 From letters in the papers of Angelica Garnett, it is clear that Colonel Teed was alive at the start of 1951 and writing to Vanessa Bell. By January 1952 it is equally clear in a letter from Jean Campbell to Vanessa Bell that Colonel Teed had been dead for a little while
32 Ibid
33 There is an account of this painting in Rose's *Saying Life*, p. 151
34 Ibid, p. 55
35 Ibid, p. 69
36 Ibid, p. 157
37 Ibid
38 Stein, *Everybody's Autobiography*, p. 57
39 It has been difficult to work out when this trip to Venice occurred. A newspaper article in the *Sunday Herald* of 1 March 1953 mentions that Margaret had been on a sketching trip to Italy with Moya Dyring the summer before. But, according to Gay Cuthbert's research, Margaret and Dyring spent six weeks travelling through Italy camping at the end of 1951, which would have allowed certainly enough time to do the trip and then get the work via airmail to Australia for her show in mid June. Cuthbert does not mention Sir Francis Rose being included in the trip but I feel there is no time after this when a trip with the three of them present could have taken place
40 Postcard from Margaret and Moya Dyring to David Strachan, 4 October 1951, the papers of David Strachan, Archives of the Art Gallery of New South Wales, MS 1973.1
41 Letter to Grace Olley, quoted in an unidentified clipping from the Johnstone Gallery cutting file
42 *A Brief History of the Gallery*, Johnstone Archive, State Library of Queensland
43 *Courier Mail*, 17 June 1952

Notes

44 *The Unexpurgated Beaton Diaries*, p. 154
45 Phone interview with Fred Jessup, 2004
46 *The Diaries of Donald Friend*, Vol. 3, 1 March 1955
47 Ibid, p. 153
48 *Australian Women's Weekly*, 5 November 1952
49 *The Diaries of Donald Friend*, Vol. 3, p. 153
50 Rickards, *The Painted Banquet*, p. 40
51 Ibid, p. 41
52 *The Diaries of Donald Friend*, Vol. 3, p. 155
53 The unpublished diaries of Donald Friend, NLA MS5959, item 35, 4 November 1952
54 *The Diaries of Donald Friend*, Vol. 3, p. 228
55 Ibid
56 *The Diaries of Donald Friend*, Vol. 2, p. 554
57 *The Diaries of Donald Friend*, Vol. 3, p. 228
58 Ibid
59 Ibid

Chapter 10: Back in Brisbane

1 *Sun*, 12 March 1953
2 *Sunday Herald*, 1 March 1953
3 This last sentence is taken from 'The Colourful World of Margaret Olley', *Australian Women's Weekly*, 23 November 1966
4 *Sunday Herald*, 1 March 1953
5 Phone interview with Ron Sabien, 2004
6 Ibid
7 *Sydney Morning Herald*, 5 February 1953
8 Former judge of appeal of New South Wales, the Hon. R.P. Meagher QC LLD
9 Account from the *Sydney Morning Herald*, 5 February 1953
10 *The Diaries of Donald Friend*, Vol. 3, p. 520
11 *Pix*, 18 April 1953
12 *The Diaries of Donald Friend*, Vol. 3, p. 238
13 Ibid, p. 239
14 The *Sunday Mail* ran an article titled 'Drinkers see "the good old

days'" on 20 December 1953, which said that Margaret had finished work on this mural the week before

15 *The Diaries of Donald Friend*, Vol. 3, p. 253
16 The unpublished diaries of Donald Friend, NLA MS5959, item 36, 10 March 1954. Since the territory's name was not changed to Papua New Guinea until 1972, I have decided to use its contemporaneous name
17 The unpublished diaries of Donald Friend, NLA MS5959, item 36, 10 March 1954
18 *The Diaries of Donald Friend*, Vol. 3, p. 258
19 Ibid, p. 261
20 The placement of this incident has been extremely difficult. Although it does seem unusual that Friend has no made no mention of her visit in his diaries, Margaret is adamant that it occurred before her trip to New Guinea (and definitely before the letter she would write to Friend in February 1955) and that Friend had been plotting it ever since his announcement to Clarice Zander in London. It could not have taken place before Christmas of 1953, as Donald Murray was in residence at the cottage; Guarracino's residence afterwards seems to have been a bit more floating. Whatever the precise chronology, I have no doubt that this and several linked events took place within the timeframe of early 1954 to mid 1955
21 *The Diaries of Donald Friend*, Vol. 3, p. 261
22 Ibid, p. 262
23 Ibid
24 Ibid
25 Ibid
26 Ibid, pp. 261, 264
27 Ibid, p. 264
28 The unpublished diaries of Donald Friend, NLA MS5959, item 36, 29 June 1954
29 *The Diaries of Donald Friend*, Vol. 3, p. 265; *Courier Mail*, 'Day to Day', Keith Dunstan, July 1954
30 *The Diaries of Donald Friend*, Vol. 3, p. 265
31 Ibid, pp. 265, 268

Notes

32 Ibid, p. 269
33 The unpublished diaries of Donald Friend, NLA MS5959, item 36, 16 August 1954
34 *The Diaries of Donald Friend*, Vol. 3, p. 271
35 Ibid, pp. 273–4
36 Ibid, p. 274
37 Interview with Sheila Abel, May 2004
38 Phone interview with Murray Abel, May 2004
39 *The Diaries of Donald Friend*, Vol. 3, p. 287
40 Ibid, p. 297
41 Ibid

Chapter 11: Blame it on the Peacock Feathers
1 *Mirror*, 19 April 1955
2 Spelling as per catalogue
3 *Bulletin*, 27 April 1955
4 *The Diaries of Donald Friend*, Vol. 3, p. 302
5 Ibid
6 Ibid, p. 316
7 Ibid, p. 320
8 Ibid
9 The unpublished diaries of Donald Friend, NLA MS5959, item 37, 20 September 1955
10 Letter dated 14 November (1955) from the unpublished diaries of Donald Friend, NLA MS5959, item 37
11 The unpublished diaries of Donald Friend, NLA MS5959, item 37, 8 February 1956
12 *The Diaries of Donald Friend*, Vol. 3, p. 335
13 Ibid, pp. 335–6
14 *Courier Mail*, 13 June 1956
15 *The Diaries of Donald Friend*, Vol. 3, p. 344
16 The unpublished diaries of Donald Friend, NLA MS5959, item 37, 10 October 1956
17 *Sydney Morning Herald*, 17 October 1956
18 *Sun*, 17 October 1956

19 *Daily Telegraph*, 17 October 1956
20 According to the Lismore Regional Gallery Permanent Collection files, it was painted in 1954. (A work with the same title was also included in Margaret's 1955 show at the Macquarie Galleries.)
21 This is according to an unidentified clipping in the Individual Artists' Files, Art Gallery of New South Wales Research Library Archive. I have been unable to obtain a program of this production
22 Phone interview with Fred Jessup in France, 2004

Chapter 12: The Flood Tide
1 The unpublished diaries of Donald Friend, NLA MS5959, item 39, letter by Margaret Olley, 17 December, 1959
2 'Biographical note' supplied by Barry Humphries for Philip Bacon Galleries, 2002
3 Interview with Barry Humphries and Margaret Olley, 2004
4 *The Diaries of Donald Friend*, Vol. 3, p. 479
5 The unpublished diaries of Donald Friend, NLA MS 5959, item 39, entry for 19 November 1959
6 This letter is gratefully mentioned in Margaret's letter to him, so while the text is not available, it seems safe to presume it was supportive
7 The unpublished diaries of Donald Friend, NLA MS5959, item 39, letter by Margaret Olley, 17 December, 1959
8 'Laurie Thomas: An Appreciation', Elizabeth Riddell, *Art and Australia*, October–December 1974
9 Ibid
10 The diaries of Donald Friend from a letter from Margaret to Friend, inserted after his entry for 30 October 1960. This part of the letter is edited out of Volume 3 and is in NLA MS5959, item 39
11 *The Diaries of Donald Friend*, Vol. 3, p. 634
12 Drysdale was among the artists who exhibited with the Johnstone Gallery's opening exhibition of paintings in February 1952. Except for being included in a show of prints, Drysdale did not show there again until his solo show in 1967
13 From the Artists Fact Sheet, the Johnstone Gallery Archive

Notes

14 From *The Diaries of Donald Friend*, Vol. 3, letter pasted in after entry for 30 October 1960, p. 504

15 From a letter by Drysdale to Donald Friend as quoted in Klepac, *Russell Drysdale*; and *The Diaries of Donald Friend*, Vol. 3, letters pasted in after entry for 30 October 1960, p. 505

16 Although the much reproduced work of this name appears to be dated 1962, not 1960, since it stayed in Margaret's possession I wonder whether it could in fact be this same work. Perhaps the date was added later by her or the '2' in the date is actually a 0, especially given there was no work of this title included in her 1962 show. On the other hand, there may simply have been two paintings with this same title

17 *Sunday Mail*, 7 October 1960

18 *The Diaries of Donald Friend*, Vol. 3, letter pasted in with entry for 30 October 1960, p. 501

19 In the original letter, there is no comma after Lord. While Margaret does sometimes refer to artist Jeffrey Smart affectionately as Lord Smart, I feel this not what she intended here and that it should read: 'Lord, Donald . . .' *The Diaries of Donald Friend*, Vol. 3, letter pasted in after entry for 30 October 1960, p. 504

20 According to a letter in the National Library from Solicitors Spicer, Sagar & Broune written in 1964, citing a deed between Friend, Bonny Drysdale and Murray dated 17 May 1961

21 *Sun*, 23 August 1961

22 *The Diaries of Donald Friend*, Vol. 3, p. 525

23 Ibid, pp. 454, 479

24 Ibid, p. 526

25 Ibid, p. 531

26 Ibid, p. 542

27 From notes by Steven Miller for the papers of Frederick Jessup, MS2002.8, Art Gallery of New South Wales Archive

28 *Courier Mail*, 24 October 1962, Gertrude Langer's review of Margaret's 1962 show at the Johnstone Gallery

29 Hazel de Berg Collection, oral history section, National Library of Australia (Oral DeB 101), recording made with Margaret Olley, 8 October 1963

30 From a draft supplied by Glenn Cooke which was finally published as 'Margaret Olley and the Social Context of *Susan with Flowers*', Glenn Cooke, *Australia and New Zealand Journal of Art*, Vol.1, no. 2, 2000
31 France, *Margaret Olley*, p. 42
32 *The Diaries of Donald Friend*, Vol. 3, p. 550
33 Bail, *Ian Fairweather*, p. 218
34 *Fairweather*, Queensland Art Gallery, p. 6
35 Ian Fairweather's letter to William Frater, September 1938, quoted in Wilson, *Escape Artists*, p. 33
36 Ibid, interview between Lala Nicol and Gavin Wilson, p. 35
37 *Fairweather*, Queensland Art Gallery, p. 25
38 Klepac, *Russell Drysdale*, p. 32. Drysdale was another artist that Margaret took to Bribie Island, and on that occasion she was bearing a basket that included paperback novels, which Fairweather apparently liked to read. Klepac dates this incident, as per a letter written by Drysdale to Murray Bail in 1979, as taking place in the late the 1950s, however all Fairweather's correspondence to Margaret held in the Art Gallery of New South Wales Archive, MS1993, is dated 1962–68 and I am confident that Margaret's real relationship with Fairweather did not begin until that decade
39 'Focus on Art', *Vogue Australia*, Clipping from Individual Artists' Files, Art Gallery of New South Wales Research Library Archive 1962.
40 Phone interview with Ron Sabien, 2004
41 Cooke, 'Margaret Olley and the Social Context of *Susan with Flowers*'
42 Ibid
43 *Courier Mail*, 22 October 1962
44 Ibid, 24 October 1962
45 *Bulletin*, 3 November 1962
46 *Sun*, 25 October 1962
47 It seems that Margaret might have titled several paintings *Eucharist Lilies*. While this is not surprising, given Eucharist lilies grew wild in the Farndon garden and artists often do several studies of the same subject, it does make identifying them a little complicated. Ron Sabien's particular *Eucharist Lilies* is now part of Margaret's own

Notes

collection. Sabien's purchase, reproduced in Christine France's books about Margaret, is clearly dated 1963. There was also a painting of this name exhibited in the 1962 Johnstone Gallery show (which we would have to assume was not the one Sabien purchased). Another painting of the same name was included in Margaret's April 1963 show at the Bonython Gallery in Adelaide. A *Eucharist Lilies* then appeared in an exhibition at the Macquarie Galleries, marked 'Not for sale', which we can assume was Ron Sabien's painting

48 *Sun*, 6 October 1963
49 Hazel de Berg Collection, oral history section, National Library of Australia (Oral DeB 101), recording made with Margaret Olley, 8 October 1963
50 A slight cut has been made in the original text of the interview here for reason of readability with the approval of Margaret (14 August 2005)
51 Interview with Christine France and Margaret Olley, 2004
52 Phone interview with Ron Sabien, 2004
53 *Courier Mail*, 22 May 1963
54 A newspaper clipping (possible from the *Age*) gave the title as *Three Negroes Lifting Bunches of Bananas*. Margaret says she would never have called it this and the models were definitely Aborigines. In the Royal Show's catalogue the work appears untitled
55 These works by Friend were commissioned by Sidney Baillieu Myer, then director of the Myer Emporium, and a keen supporter of the Johnstone Gallery
56 *The Diaries of Donald Friend*, Vol. 3, p. 550
57 Ibid, pp. 550–1
58 Ibid, p. 551
59 Ibid, p. 552
60 Ibid
61 *Sun*, 2 October 1963
62 *Sun Herald*, 6 October 1963
63 Letter from Margaret Olley to Russell Drysdale, 5 December 1963, State Library of New South Wales, ML MSS 4191/5, item 8/203
64 *Sunday Telegraph*, 19 April 1964
65 *Newcastle Sun*, 20 April 1964

66 *Courier Mail*, 28 October 1964
67 Interview with Shirley Wright, Brisbane, 2004
68 'The Women in the Yellow Hat', Suzanne Chapple, *Australian*, 10 November 1964
69 Janet Hawley, 'Good Weekend', *Sydney Morning Herald*, 25 March 1995
70 *The Diaries of Donald Friend*, Vol. 3, p. 634
71 Ibid
72 Ibid, and continued in NLA MS5959, item 41, entry for 26 July 1966
73 *The Diaries of Donald Friend*, Vol. 3, p. 634
74 Ibid, pp. 634–5
75 Ibid, plus section from NLA MS5959, item 41, entry for 29 July 1966
76 Interview with Mimi Falkiner, Brisbane, 2004
77 For the detail of Moya Dyring's death I am indebted to 'Changing the Landscape', Gay Cuthbert, and an interview with Rollin Schlicht and Margaret Olley, Sydney, 2004

Chapter 13: In Search of the Sex House

1 Several works by Margaret of subjects close to Port Moresby were included in a show at the Darlinghurst Galleries in Sydney in September 1967. There were works titled *Man from Mount Hagen* and *Woman from Wav* in this exhibition, but it would seem that rather than actually visiting the Highlands or Wav on this trip, Margaret may have seen these subjects elsewhere
2 Phone interview with John Pasquarelli, 2005
3 Ibid
4 Interview with Margaret Olley and John Pasquarelli, 2003
5 From an unidentified clipping of an item that appeared after the opening of her show 'Leaves from a New Guinea Sketchbook and Other Paintings' at the Johnstone Gallery, Brisbane, 1968, Individual Artists' Files, Art Gallery of New South Wales Research Library and Archive
6 From an unidentified clipping from a newspaper article at the time of Margaret's exhibition from the archives of the Art Gallery of New South Wales

Notes

7 Unidentified clipping in the Individual Artists' Files (Margaret Olley) Art Gallery of New South Wales Research Library and Archive
8 From a letter pasted in the unpublished diaries of Donald Friend, National Gallery of Australia, Canberra, entry for 6 July 1969
9 Ibid
10 Ibid. In Margaret's original letter there is a full stop after 'lots of police' then a new sentence starts with 'Armed'. However in the interest of readability, this has been changed to one sentence in this text
11 *The Diaries of Donald Friend*, Vol. 3, p. 640
12 Friend, *Donald Friend in Bali*, p. 11
13 Ibid, p. 41
14 The unpublished diaries of Donald Friend, National Gallery of Australia, Canberra, entry for 1 August 1969
15 Ibid, entry for 3 August 1969
16 Ibid, entry for 5 August 1969
17 Ibid, entry for 7 August 1969
18 Ibid, entry for 10 August 1969
19 Ibid
20 Ibid, entry for 14 August 1969
21 Ibid, entry for 17 August 1969
22 Friend, *Donald Friend in Bali*, p. 25
23 Unpublished diaries of Donald Friend, National Gallery of Australia, Canberra, entry for 4 September 1969
24 Ibid
25 Friend, *Donald Friend in Bali*, p. 67
26 Ibid
27 In his diary entry of 17 August 1969, Friend says that Wija Runta, who had just returned from an antique hunt in Java, had found that the Sex House was now taken down, its light-hearted whores gone and its antiques sold off to other dealers.

Chapter 14: Living in a Basket
1 Letter pasted in the unpublished diaries of Donald Friend held at the National Gallery of Australia, Canberra after entry for 27 September 1969

2. Phone interview with Kate Hodgkinson, 2004
3. The unpublished diaries of Donald Friend, NLA MS5959, item 42, entry for 5 December 1970
4. Ibid
5. *Art and Australia 4*, Vol. 8, 1971, p. 331
6. Ibid
7. Unpublished diaries of Donald Friend, NLA MS5959, letter from Margaret Olley, dated 27 December, pasted in with entry for 22 January 1971
8. France, *Margaret Olley*, p. 53
9. Pearce, *Margaret Olley*, biographical notes supplied by Christine France, p. 27
10. Unpublished diaries of Donald Friend, NLA MS5959, item 42, 17 December 1971
11. France, *Margaret Olley*, p. 65
12. Phone interview with Kate Hodgkinson, 2004
13. According to Steven Miller, archivist at the Art Gallery of New South Wales, the work was submitted to the gallery in 1952 with a label of 'Aldenhovens Art Gallery, Sydney (74 Hunter Street)' on the back
14. On 12 February 1974, according to Art Gallery of New South Wales records, which also show Hughes's address as being 6 rue de Malagnou, Geneva
15. It would appear that the painting was actually put into auctions in London twice in 1975
16. According to information provided by Steven Miller, archivist at the Art Gallery of New South Wales, July 2005
17. Interview with Philip Bacon and Margaret Olley, 2003
18. The unpublished diaries of Donald Friend, NLA MS5959, item 45, 27 September 1981
19. As recounted in an interview with Sir David Griffin, 2003
20. Pearce, *Margaret Olley*, biographical notes suppled by Christine France, p. 27
21. From a postcard from Margaret to Maisie and Tas Drysdale, State Library of New South Wales, ML MSS 4191/3, item 5/2769

Notes

22 Ibid
23 Interview with Rollin Schlicht and Margaret Olley, 2004
24 From a postcard from Margaret to Maisie and Tas Drysdale, State Library of New South Wales, ML MSS 4191/3, item 5/2769
25 'Margaret Olley: Anything But a Still Life', Lenore Nicklin, *Sydney Morning Herald*, 4 November 1978
26 *Sunday Sun*, 21 October 1979
27 Pearce, *Margaret Olley*, biographical notes supplied by Christine France, p. 28
28 Ibid. In the unpublished diaries of Donald Friend, NLA MS5959, item 45, entry for 22 April 1982, Friend mentions having dinner with Margaret, who had just returned from Bali bringing presents with her for him. So Margaret may, in fact, have made two trips to Bali at this period of her life.

Chapter 15: Once More, Then No More

1 Dating the Farndon fire is not straightforward. Those most affected, including Margaret herself, find the timing difficult to pinpoint. After discussion with Margaret and her sister Elaine, who consulted Ken Olley and other family members, it seems likely the fire happened sometime about a week prior to 17 November 1980 (this date coincides with a family birthday party where the news of the fire was broken to them). This date has also been confirmed by Douglas Temperley and his wife
2 The unpublished diaries of Donald Friend, NLA MS5959, item 46, entry for 22 October 1986. In this entry Friend rediscovers what he wrote at the time of Drysdale's death
3 Ibid, item 45, entry for 27 September 1981
4 Ibid, item 46, entry for 14 September 1982
5 'Vegetables Have Never Looked Better', Susanna Short, *Sydney Morning Herald*, 7 October 1982
6 The unpublished diaries of Donald Friend, NLA MS5959, item 46, entry for 7 October 1982
7 Ibid
8 Ibid, entry for 15 February 1983

9 Ibid, entry for 3 February 1983
10 Ibid, entry for 8 February 1983
11 Ibid, entry for 2 April 1983
12 Ibid, entry for 12 February 1984
13 Interview with Christine France and Margaret Olley, 2004
14 The unpublished diaries of Donald Friend, MS5959, item 46, entry for 1 January 1987
15 Ibid, item 47, entry for 24 May 1987
16 Ibid, entry for 25 May 1987
17 Ibid, entry for 1 November 1987
18 Ibid, entry for 19 December 1988
19 Lindsay, *Bohemian of the Bulletin*, p. 145
20 'Overdue Tribute to an Icon of Integrity', John McDonald, *Sydney Morning Herald*, 25 August 1990
21 Interview with Edmund Capon, 2005
22 *The Age*, Melbourne, 19 August 1964
23 France, *Justin O'Brien*, p. 36
24 France, *Margaret Olley*, p. 128
25 Interview with Eugen Lude by Margaret Olley, 2003
26 *The Spectator*, 3 December 1994
27 France, *Margaret Olley*, p. 126
28 Pearce, *Margaret Olley*, p. 7
29 Ibid, pp. 8, 11
30 Ibid, p. 8
31 Phone interview with Kate Hodgkinson, 2004

Chapter 16: Celebrating Life
1 *The Diaries of Donald Friend*, Vol. 3, p. 548
2 Interview with Philip Bacon and Margaret Olley, 2003
3 Interview with Barry Humphries and Margaret Olley, 2004
4 *Sydney Morning Herald*, 'Cézanne gift leaves lasting impression', Steve Meacham, 22–23 November 2003
5 Phone interview with Fred Jessup, 2004
6 Interview with Barry Pearce, 2005

Bibliography

Russell W. Abel, *Charles W. Abel of Kwato: Forty Years in Dark Papua*, Fleming H. Revell Co., New York, 1934

Brian Adams, *Portrait of an Artist: a Biography of William Dobell*, Hutchinson Australia, Sydney, 1983

The Australian Dictionary of Biography, Melbourne University Press, Melbourne, 1996

Murray Bail, *Ian Fairweather*, Bay Books, Sydney, 1981

Marjorie Barnard and Sydney Ure Smith (drawings), *The Sydney Book*, Ure Smith Pty Ltd, Sydney, 1947

Cecil Beaton, *The Unexpurgated Beaton Diaries*, Hugo Vickers (intro.), Orion Books, London, 2002

Frederick Brown, *An Impersonation of Angels: a Biography of Jean Cocteau*, Longman, London, 1968

Janine Burke, *The Heart Garden*, Random House Australia, Sydney, 2004

Eileen Chanin and Steven Miller, *Degenerates and Perverts: the 1939 Herald Exhibition of French and British Contemporary Art*, Miegunyah Press, Melbourne, 2005

Eileen Chanin and Steven Miller, *The Art and Life of Weaver Hawkins*, Craftsman House, Sydney, 1995

Ian Chilvers, Harold Osborne and Dennis Farr, *The Oxford Dictionary of Art*, Oxford University Press, Oxford, 1988

Lady Phyllis Cilento, *Lady Cilento: My Life*, Methuen Haynes, Sydney, 1987

Paul Coombes, *Elaine Haxton: a Biography*, Communication Programs, Sydney, 1990

William Dobell: the Painter's Progress, Art Gallery of New South Wales, Sydney, 1997

Elaine Dundy, *Finch, Bloody Finch*, Michael Joseph, London, 1980

Robin Eakin, *Aunts Up the Cross*, Anthony Blond, London, 1965

Ian Fairweather, *The Drunken Buddha*, University of Queensland Press, Brisbane, 1965

Fairweather, Art and Australia Books in association with the Queensland Art Gallery, Brisbane, 1994

Trader Faulkener, *Peter Finch: a Biography*, Angus & Robertson, London, 1979

James Elroy Flecker, *Hassan: the Story of Hassan of Bagdad*, William Heinemann, London, 1922

Christine France, *Jean Bellette: Early Life and Times*, National Trust of Australia, Sydney, 2004

Christine France, *Justin O'Brien: Image and Icon*, Craftsman House, Sydney, 1987

Christine France, *Margaret Olley*, Craftsman House, Sydney, 2002

The Diaries of Donald Friend, Vol. 1, Anne Gray (ed.), National Library of Australia, Canberra, 2001

The Diaries of Donald Friend, Vol. 2, Paul Hetherington (ed.), National Library of Australia, Canberra, 2003

The Diaries of Donald Friend, Vol. 3, Paul Hetherington (ed.), National Library of Australia, Canberra, 2005

Donald Friend, *Donald Friend in Bali*, William Collins & Son, London, 1972

Gwen Friend, *My Brother Donald: a Memoir of Australian Artist Donald Friend*, Angus & Robertson, Sydney, 1994

Joëlle Gardes, *Virginia Woolf à Cassis*, Imprimerie Espace Graphic, Nice, 2002

John Herbert Gill, *Detecting Gertrude Stein*, Democritus Books, New York, 2003

Bibliography

James Gleeson, *William Dobell*, Thames & Hudson, London, 1964

Noeline Hall, *A Legacy of Honour: the Centenary History of Somerville House*, Boolarong Press, Brisbane, 1999

Howard Hinton, *Patron of Art*, Angus & Robertson, Sydney, 1951

Alan Hudson, *By the Banyan: Tully Sugar, the first 75 years*, Christopher Beck Books, Brisbane, 2000

C.A. Hughes and B.D. Graham, *A Handbook of Australian Government and Politics 1890–1964*, Australian National University Press, Canberra, 1968

C.A. Hughes and B.D. Graham, *Voting for the New South Wales Legislative Assembly 1890–1964*, Australian National University Press, Canberra, 1975

Robert Hughes, *The Art of Australia*, Penguin Books Australia, Melbourne, 1966

Barry Humphries, *More Please: an Autobiography*, Viking Penguin, London, 1992

Jacqueline E. Kearney, *A History of St Anne's, North Queensland 1917–1978*, McGilvray & Co. Ltd, Townsville, 1992 (2nd edn)

Lou Klepac, *Russell Drysdale*, Bay Books, Sydney, 1983

Lou Klepac, *The Genius of Donald Friend: Drawings from the Diaries 1942–1989*, National Library of Australia, Canberra, 2000

Lou Klepac, *David Strachan*, Beagle Press, Sydney, 1993

Norman Lindsay, *Bohemian of the Bulletin*, Angus & Robertson, Sydney, 1965

Alan McCulloch (rev. Susan McCulloch), *Encyclopaedia of Australian Art*, Allen & Unwin, Sydney, 1994

Ross McMullin, *Will Dyson*, Angus & Robertson, Sydney, 1984

Jean McNaught, *An Index to the Northern Star: Vol. 1*, Richmond–Tweed Regional Library, Richmond, 1999

Roddy Meagher and Simon Fieldhouse, *Portraits on Yellow Paper*, Central Queensland University Press, Rockhampton, 2004

Harry Tatlock Miller (ed.), *Loudon Sainthill*, Hutchinson, London, 1973

Alec Murray (Harry Tatlock Miller, intro.), *Alec Murray's Album: Personalities of Australia*, Ure Smith Productions, Sydney, 1949

Nigel Nicolson and Joanne Trautmann (eds), *The Letters of Virginia Woolf 1923–1928*, Vol. 3, Harcourt Publishers, London, 1989

William J. Olley, *Rose Hill on the Richmond*, privately published, 1988

Philip Parsons (ed.), *Companion to Theatre in Australia*, Currency Press, Sydney, 1995

Barry Pearce, *Margaret Olley*, Art Gallery of New South Wales, Sydney, 1996

Barry Pearce, *Donald Friend*, Art Gallery of New South Wales, Sydney, 1990

Antony Penrose, *Roland Penrose: the Friendly Surrealist*, Prestel-Verlag, Munich, 1988

Nancy Phelan, *Writing Round the Edge: a Selective Memoir*, University of Queensland Press, Brisbane, 2003

Jocelyn Rickards, *The Painted Banquet: My Life and Loves*, Weidenfeld & Nicolson, London, 1987

Roland Robinson, *The Drift of Things*, Macmillan Australia, Sydney, 1973

Sir Francis Rose, *Saying Life: the Memoirs of Sir Francis Rose*, Cassell, London, 1961

T.G. Rosenthal, *Sidney Nolan*, Thames & Hudson, London, 2002

Maurice Ryan, *Old Time Nimbin*, Nimbin Chamber of Commerce, Nimbin, 1999

Colin Simpson, *Adam in Plumes*, Angus & Robertson, Sydney, 1949

Sue Smith, *North of Capricorn: the Art of Ray Crooke*, Perc Tucker Regional Gallery, Townsville, 1997

Jeffrey Smart, *Not Quite Straight: a Memoir*, Random House, Sydney 1996

Bibliography

Bernard Smith with Terry Smith, *Australian Painting 1788–1990*, Oxford University Press, Melbourne, 1962

Gertrude Stein, *Everybody's Autobiography*, Vintage Books, London, 1973

Alan T. Temperley, *Some Notes on Thomas Temperley and His Family*, privately compiled, 1998

Sydney Ure Smith (ed.), *Present-Day Art in Australia 2*, Ure Smith Pty Ltd, Sydney, 1945

R.B. Walker, *The Newspaper Press in New South Wales, 1803–1920*, Sydney University Press, Sydney, 1976

Nicholas Watkins, *Bonnard*, Phaidon, London, 1994

Gavin Wilson, *Escape Artists: Modernists in the Tropics*, Cairns Regional Gallery, Cairns, 1998

Gavin Wilson, *The Artists of Hill End*, Beagle Press & Art Gallery of New South Wales, Sydney, 1995

Phillip A. Wright, *Memories of a Bushwacker*, University of New England, Armidale, 1971

Articles, Archives, Catalogues and Recordings

Delys Anthony, 'The Early History of Twelfth Night Theatre 1936–1946', thesis, University of Queensland, Brisbane, 1990

Art in Australia, eds Sydney Ure Smith and Leon Gellert, no. 5, 1 August 1923

Art in Australia, eds Sydney Ure Smith and Leon Gellert, no. 4, 1 May 1923

Australasian Art Obituaries Index, National Gallery of Australia Research Library A–Z

Blake Prize Exhibition catalogues, Finney's Gallery, Brisbane, 1951–55

Gil Brealey (director), *Profile of Russell Drysdale*, written and narrated by George Johnson, ABC, 1967

Scott Carlin (curator), *King's Cross: Bohemian Sydney*, Exhibition Guide, Sydney, 2003

Alison Clark, 'Against the Odds: Margaret Cilento and Margo Lewers', BA (Hons) thesis, University of Sydney, 2001

Jean Cocteau, *Orphée* and William Shakespeare, *Pericles*, Sydney University Dramatic Society, Conservatorium of Music, 1948. Performance programs collection, Mitchell Library, State Library of New South Wales

Glenn Cooke, 'The Social Context of *Susan with Flowers*', *AAANZ Journal*, 2000

Gay Cuthbert, 'Changing the Landscape: the Life and Art of Moya Dyring', thesis, University of Melbourne Library, Melbourne, 2002

William Dobell, 'Australian Painters Look to Europe', *Art in Australia*, 23 February 1940

Russell Drysdale papers, 1912–81, State Library of New South Wales, call nos. MSS 4191/5 and MSS 4191/3

Ian Fairweather letters 1958–1974, Research Library and Archive, Art Gallery of New South Wales, call no. MS1993.2

James Elroy Flecker, *Hassan* (play) presented by Sydney University Dramatic Society, Conservatorium of Music, Sydney, 1947. Performance programs collection, Mitchell Library, State Library of New South Wales

Christine France, *Merioola and After*, S.H. Ervin Gallery, Sydney 1986

Angelica Garnett (née Bell), papers held at King's College, Cambridge, England

Individual Artists' Files relating to Elaine Haxton, Margaret Olley, Loudon Sainthill and David Strachan, as well as Royal Queensland Art Society catalogues 1942–45, held at the Research Library and Archive, Art Gallery of New South Wales, Sydney

Frederick Jessup, papers held at Research Library and Archive, Art Gallery of New South Wales, Sydney, call no. MS 2002.8

Johnstone Gallery Archives, James Hardie Library of Australian Fine Arts, University of Queensland

Bibliography

Ross Johnston, 'The Johnstone Gallery and Art in Queensland, 1940s–70s', *Art and Australia*, no. 4, vol. 15, Johnstone Gallery archive, State Library of Queensland, Brisbane

George W. Lambert, 'The European Art Exhibition', *Art in Australia*, eds Sydney Ure Smith and Leon Gellert, no. 5, 1 August 1923

Therese Kenyon (curator), *The Studio Tradition: National Art School 1883–2001*, Manly Art Gallery and Museum, Sydney, 2001

Pam King, 'Maria Kuhn', article held at the Research Library, Queensland Art Gallery, Brisbane

Kirsova Ballet, Australian Performing Arts (PROMPT) Collection, National Library of Australia, Canberra

Daphne Mayo, 'The Queensland Art Fund', *Queensland National Art Gallery Bulletin*, vol. 1, no. 4, 1958

Bettina MacAuley, *Songs of Colour: the Art of Vida Lahey*, Queensland Art Gallery, Brisbane, 1989

Judith McKay, *Daphne Mayo: a Tribute to her Work for Art in Queensland*, Friends of Daphne Mayo, Queensland, 1983

Frank Mitchell papers, Powerhouse Museum, Sydney

Jane Oehr and Ian Stocks (directors and producer), *Tamu the Guest*, ABC, 1972

Margaret Olley recording, oral history section, Hazel de Berg Collection, National Library of Australia, 8 October 1963

Carolyn Parfitt, *My Country Childhood: Margaret Olley*, Country Style, Sydney, May 2001

'Origins', Cairns & District Family History Society Inc., Cairns, April 1999

Elizabeth Riddell, 'Laurie Thomas – an appreciation', *Art and Australia*, December 1974

William Salmon and Paul Haefliger, 'David Strachan obituary', *Art and Australia*, no. 4, vol. 8

David Edgar Strachan papers, Research Library and Archive, Art Gallery of New South Wales, Sydney, call no. MS 1973.1

David Strachan, 'A Tribute to Moya Dyring', *Art and Australia*, vol. 4, no. 4

Sydney Ure Smith, 'The Revival of the Woodcut', *Art in Australia*, no. 5, 1 August 1923

David Wetherell, *Charles Abel and the Kwato Mission of Papua New Guinea: 1891–1975*, Oxford University Press, Melbourne, 1996

Index

Abel, Beatrice 303
Abel, Cecil 303, 306
Abel, Charles 302–3
Abel, Liz 303
Abel, Murray 303, 305
Abel, Russell 303
Abel, Sheila 303–6
Aboriginal models 350–4, 361, 368
alcoholism 146, 182, 197, 237, 240, 249, 268, 276, 285, 296, 298, 310, 313, 315, 320, 322–9, 333–4, 336–7, 346, 414, 488
Ali, Omar 235
Allen, Arthur Wigram 114, 118
Alston, Richard 501
America 454–5, 464–5
Angkor Wat, Cambodia 397, 402
Annand, Douglas 167, 169, 387–91
Antill, John 165, 166
Arabian Coffee Shop, Sydney 91–2
Archibald Prize 478
    Dobell's Joshua Smith viii, 110, 111, 154, 199, 209
    Dobell's Margaret Olley viii, 199, 201–4, 207–12, 276
Arles, France 234–5
Art Gallery (formerly National Art Gallery) of New South Wales 67, 68, 127, 131, 169, 202, 211, 349, 500
    Australian Women's Weekly Portrait Prize 314–15
    Capon as director 477, 478, 479
    Dobell's portrait of Margaret 202, 211, 500
    Drysdale's show 1960 344
    'French Painting Today' exhibition 1953 271, 282
    Herald exhibition 1939 67, 68, 272
    Life Governor 476, 484
    Margaret Olley Twentieth-Century European Galleries 485
    Margaret visiting 202, 272
    Margaret's donations to 477, 478, 482
    Margaret's paintings at 314, 362
    Missingham as director 131
    Olley retrospective 1996 483
    Strozzi copy 433
Art in Australia 17
Ashbolt, Allan 150
Ashton, Howard 272
Atyeo, Sam viii, 82, 218, 219, 220, 254
Australian Chamber Orchestra 494, 501
Australian Galleries, Sydney 483
Australian National Treasure 476
Australian Women's Weekly Portrait Prize 314–15, 316, 320
Auty, Giles 482

Baboulene, Eugène 220
Bacon, Philip vii, 61, 427, 434–5, 453, 485, 490, 498
    Brisbane Gallery *see* Philip Bacon Galleries
Bali 4, 398, 405–13, 415, 424, 446, 452, 476
Balthus exhibitions 445, 465
Bangkok, Thailand 401
Bannon, Charles 288
Banyan Creek, Queensland 19–22, 27, 34, 53
Barker, Caroline vii, 60–4, 68–70, 78, 130, 434
Bass, Tommy 141
Beaton, Cecil 260
Bell, George 17, 83, 137, 220, 335, 355
Bell, Kieser 339, 449
Bell, Pam vii, 291, 339, 340, 344, 368, 444

553

Bribie Island 358, 359, 384
   Fairweather's painting of Margaret
      and 380
   Margaret's portrait of 359–60, 451
Bell, Vanessa 222, 224, 245, 247, 248
Bellette, Jean vii, ix, 82, 131–4, 136,
    193, 280
   death 479
   dinner for 460–1
   East Sydney Tech 131, 136
   Hill End 197, 318
   marriage to Paul Haefliger 132
   Sydney Group 174
   Westminster School 132, 143
Bellew, Peter 135
Bendigo Art Prize 380
Bennie, Peter 327, 337
Benthall, Michael 264
Beresford, Bruce 488
Bergner, Josl 82
Best, Jeanette 28
Best, Stanley 28
Black Dog Institute 489, 491
Black, Dorrit 81
Blackman, Barbara 383
Blackman, Charles 343, 383, 434, 435
Blake Prize 282–3, 285, 287, 288, 311,
    318
Blake, William 419, 420
Bloomsbury set 222, 224, 248, 442
Bone, Henry 61
Bonnard, Pierre 66, 67, 271, 276, 277,
    427, 478, 465, 481, 483, 503
Bonnie Sue, the pug 350, 360, 361, 377,
    451
Bonython Art Gallery, Adelaide 367
Bowden, Diana and Max 299
Bowmore, William 419–20
Boyd, Arthur 82, 159, 258, 277, 434,
    478
Boyd, Penleigh 17
Brack, John 277
Braque, Georges 252, 271
Bribie Island, Queensland 358, 359,
    369, 379, 383
Brisbane
   Farndon *see* Farndon
   Margaret at school 54–79
   Margaret's return to 272–309
Brisbane Central Technical College
    69–73, 76–8, 364
Brittany, France 261–2
Brown, Colin 154, 171
Brown, Sophia 12
Brownlow, Jim 454
Browse & Darby gallery, London
   'Eight Australian Artists' show 1995
    483
   Margaret's show 1994 481
Bryans, Lina 356
Buchanan, Dorothy 154–7, 162, 163,
    166, 312
'Buggery Barn', Sydney 126–8
Bunny, Rupert 221, 247
Burdett, Basil 66, 272
Burke, Janine 191, 192, 218

Cambodia 397, 402–5, 415
Campbell, Cressida 501
Campbell, Jean 225, 245, 248, 249, 431
Campbell, Robert 281
Capon, Edmund 477, 478, 479, 484,
    498, 500, 505
Capon, Joanna 500
Cardamatis, Dr Raoul 137
Cardamatis, Wolfgang vii, 118, 135,
    137–8, 145, 216–17, 260
   Arles trip 234–5
   London 242, 482
   Paris 216–17, 232–4
   rooming with David Strachan 135
   Spain trip 233
Carr, Muriel 14
Cassis, France 221–5, 229, 231, 234,
    239, 242–3, 244–9, 334
Cézanne, Paul 66, 162, 186, 187, 213,
    215, 219, 335, 483, 498, 503
Chagall, Marc 254, 271
Chambri Lakes, New Guinea 392
Chapman, Gordon 169
'The Charm School' 82, 83
Château de Fontcreuse, Cassis 224–5,
    244–9, 268
Chiang Mai, Thailand 401
Churcher, Betty 61
Churchland, Lindsay 141, 173

Index

Cilento, Diane 63, 77
Cilento, Margaret vii, 56–7, 61–4, 77,
    127, 130, 146–8, 174, 267, 284, 500
    Caroline Barker's art classes 61–3
    Cassis 223, 225, 229, 234
    Diane 77
    East Sydney Tech 146
    Era 123, 126
    flatting with Margaret 100–9
    Florence trip 226–9
    New York 147–8
    Somerville House 56–7, 61–4, 100
    Under 30 Group 128, 129
    Wattle League Scholarship 147
Cilento, Lady Phyllis 64, 100, 121, 327, 444
Cilento, Sir Raphael 64
Cilento, Ruth 100
Cintra Road Gallery *see* Johnstone Gallery
Citizens Military Force 74
Clarke, Lynne *see* Drysdale, Lynne
Cocteau, Jean 193, 250, 251, 252
Coleman, Alannah 157, 194
Collin, Darya 180
Collins, Alwyn 21, 28
Collins, Molly 28
Constable, William 150, 151
Contemporary Art Society 135, 145, 159, 162, 165, 166
    8th Annual Interstate Exhibition 1946 159
    9th Annual Interstate Exhibition 1947 169
    State Exhibition 1946 160
Cook, James 321
Cook, Jimmy 164
Cooke, Glenn 353
Cooper, Sydney 242, 265, 425
Corrie, Maria 70, 76–8, 87, 130, 364
Cos, Greece 445
Cossington Smith, Grace 81, 143, 158, 159
Cramer, Eileen 'The Lion Tamer' 94, 95, 113
Crawford, Lionel 27, 28, 396, 397
Crawford, Thora 42
Crayford, Peter 501

Crooke, June 344, 377
Crooke, Ray 343–4, 371, 377, 398, 434
Cross, Margaret Louisa 8, 9, 12
Cross, Reverend John 8
Crowley, Grace 81, 158, 159

Dadswell, Lyndon 90, 96, 141, 148
Dalí, Salvador 66, 250
Dalton, Robin 137, 482
Darlinghurst Galleries, Sydney 387
Dattilo-Rubbo, Antonio 137, 143
David Jones Gallery, Sydney 67, 145, 158, 171
Daws, Lawrence 277, 343, 435, 478, 483
de Berg, Hazel 352, 364, 365
de Maistre, Roy 17, 81, 143
Degas, Edgar 216, 478, 481, 482, 483
the Depression 38–40, 158
Deshaies, Arthur 128
Deya, Majorca 461
Diaghilev exhibition, Paris 440–1
Diamond Cut Diamond 150–1
Dickerson, Bob 343, 434, 435
Dingle, Elsie 28, 451
Dingle, Percy 28
d'Ivangine, Nicolas 216
Dobell, Alice 376
Dobell, William viii, ix, xiii, 6, 82–4, 110–12, 133, 159, 286
    Archibald Prize viii, 110, 111, 201–4, 276
    death 420
    East Sydney Tech 92, 100, 111
    Haefliger's support for 132
    Joshua Smith portrait viii, 110–12, 154, 376
    Kwato Island 303
    London 143
    Margaret's first meeting 92
    Newcastle roots 381
    nudes of Margaret 191
    opening Margaret's Newcastle show 375, 376
    portrait of Margaret viii, 190–1, 198, 199, 201–4, 276, 311, 317, 335, 500
    Under 30 Group influenced by 129

unique style 82–3
Vogue story 360
Walter Magnus portrait 118
Wynne Prize 202
Docking, Gil 374
Docking, Shay 374
Dominion Art Galleries, Sydney 363
Donner, Clive 482
Drynan, Philippa 500
Drysdale, Elizabeth 'Bonny' viii, 83, 142, 143–5, 180–3, 204, 214, 231, 287, 345, 346, 359, 371, 372
Drysdale, Lynne (later Clarke) viii, 83, 142–4, 183, 318, 348, 372–3, 470, 475
Drysdale, Russell 'Tas' viii, 83, 84, 142–5, 159, 171, 173, 180–3, 204, 214, 231, 288, 293, 415, 440, 456
  Aboriginal people, paintings of 350–1
  Bonny's death 371, 372
  Bouddi 422
  Darling Point house 287
  death 452
  exhibition 1949 213–14
  exhibition 1960 344–5
  Friend's friendship with 83, 143–5, 159, 173, 181, 288, 452
  Haefliger's support for 132
  Hill End 318
  Johnstone Gallery 343, 434
  Margaret influenced by 196
  Margaret's affair with 371–3
  Margaret's first solo show 184, 185, 187
  marriage to Maisie 372, 373
  Oliviers' visit 188
  portrait of Margaret viii, 182–3, 198, 214
  retrospective 1961 346
  Rose Bay house 182–4
  Tim's death 359
  TV story 1967 371
  Under 30 Group influenced by 129
  unique style 83
Drysdale, Tim viii, 83, 142, 143, 318, 359, 371
Duffecy, John 123, 155, 156
Duffecy, Lyndsay 123, 155, 156

Duhig, Dr J.V. 363
Duigan, Virginia 488
Duncan, Isadora 251, 252
Duncan, Raymond 252
Dundas, Douglas 82, 88, 94, 96, 112, 133
Dupain, Max 166
Dupree, Hannah 490
Duxford Street house, Sydney 377–9, 431
Dyring, Moya viii, 217–21, 231, 238, 263, 312, 341, 345
  Brisbane 283–4, 320, 341, 368
  Cassis 242, 243, 249
  death 384–5, 423
  Italy trip 253
  Johnstone Gallery shows 283, 320, 341, 368
  Marodian Gallery 257
  Paris 217–21, 231, 238–9, 249, 267, 423
  Skinner Gallery show 367
  travelling in France 261, 263
Dyson, Will 120

East Crescent Street flat, Sydney 100–9, 148, 162, 199
East Sydney Technical College x, xi, 78, 80–109, 131, 141, 148, 155
  Dobell as teacher 92, 100, 111
  Haxton at 180
  Jessup as teacher 348
  Margaret's friends at 91–109, 113, 141
  Margaret's results 101, 146
  models 94–7
  Strachan as teacher 348
  student exhibition 1945 146
  teachers 88–90, 131
Edgworth Somers, Chica *see* Lowe, Chica
Education Department Gallery, Sydney 129, 157, 159
Edwards, Mary 112, 154
Egypt 465–6, 468–70
Elizabeth Bay House, Sydney 118
Elworthy, Geoff 287, 300–2, 308, 317, 336, 387–91, 396

Index

Epstein, Jacob 121
Era, New South Wales 122–6, 152, 155, 186
Evatt, Herbert 'Doc' 219
Evatt, Mary Alice 219, 313, 385

Fairfax, James 470
Fairweather, Ian viii, 354–9, 369, 379–80, 428
   Bribie Island 358–9, 369, 379, 383
   death 420
   The Drunken Buddha 379–80, 451
   Friend meeting 369
   painting of Margaret and Pam Bell 380
   raft trip from Darwin 356, 369
   theft of paintings 383, 384
Falkiner, Mimi 384
Famula, Julia 298
Farndon, Brisbane 68, 74, 75, 272–4, 278–9, 285, 297, 314–15, 321, 334, 336, 339, 350, 353, 367–8, 426, 439
   fire 447–52
Felgate, Rhoda 282, 322
Fewings, Miss Eliza 58
Finch, Peter 150, 151, 152
Findlay, Elsie 166
Finney's Centenary Art Prize 367
Fizelle, Rah 81, 135, 165
Flecker's *Hassan* 161, 164–7
Florence, Italy 226–9, 235–6
Flower, Cedric 126–9, 148, 181, 247
Flower, Pat 247
Foot, Brigadier Richard 'Dickie' 180, 181, 317, 325–6
Fraenkel, Stella 166, 194
Francart, Yvonne 91, 129, 150
France, Christine 33, 132, 133, 186, 353, 423, 426, 465, 477, 479, 482, 500, 502
Franklin, Miles 475
Frater, William 'Jock' 355
Freud, Lucien 478
Friend, Donald viii, ix, xi, 77, 83, 84, 96, 98, 112, 138, 139, 142–5, 160, 170, 181–9, 254, 263, 277, 278, 280, 285, 336, 349
   aluminium sculptures 345
   Apocalypse mural 195, 197, 210

Bali 4, 398, 406–13, 421, 424, 452, 471, 476
Bellette, view of 460–1
Blake Prize 311
Bribie Island 369, 384
Brisbane 291, 314, 315, 383
death 474–5
donation of paintings 478
drawing of Margaret 182
drawing skill 363, 370
Drysdales, friendship with 83, 143–5, 181–3, 288, 452
Fairweather, meeting 369
family 142
first solo show 143
Flotta Laura Travelling Art Prize 263
Guarracino, Attilio relationship with ix, 235, 240, 407, 452, 475
Haefliger's support for 132
hand injury 471
Hill End viii, 170–9, 194–7, 204, 208, 285, 287, 289, 306, 307, 318–19, 476
illness 452, 462, 470, 471
Italy 214, 234, 235, 263
Johnstone Gallery shows 315, 343, 368, 383
Lennons Hotel mural 291–2, 295–6, 315, 476
London 143, 236, 239–42, 264, 265, 267, 268, 269
Margaret's first meeting 142
Margaret's first solo show 184, 185, 187
Margaret's relationship with 170, 260, 261, 287–91, 307–9, 316, 319–20, 372
Marodian Gallery 257
marriage to Margaret, contemplating 269–70, 285, 287–91, 307–9, 319
Melbourne 452
Merioola viii, 114, 151, 153, 171, 176
north Queensland, 1955 exhibition 315
north Queensland with Margaret 292–9

Oliviers' visit 188
Paddington 462–3
Paris 424
Perth 349
Peter Finch, relationship with 150–1
portrait of Margaret 197, 198
Sri Lanka 320, 336, 344, 345, 346, 348–9
strokes 471, 474
view of Margaret's work 311–12
Westminster School 143
Friend, Gwendolyn 142, 475
Friend, Lesley 142

Garnett, David 'Bunny' 442
Gauguin, Paul 66, 261
George Bell School, Melbourne 135, 137
Germany 480–1
Giacometti, Alberto 478
Gibbs, Cyril 69
Gleeson, James 105, 347, 364, 370, 371
Godson, John Barclay 89–90
Goodwin, Aberdeen 235–6
Gordon, Bill 406
Grano, Paul 237, 238
Grant, Duncan 222, 224, 247, 248, 478
Graves, Beryl 461
Graves, Robert 461
Gray, Bob 123, 124
Greece 445–6, 466
Greenhill Galleries, Perth 466
Griffin, Sir David 438
Grosvenor Gallery, Sydney 157
Grounds, Roy 408
Gruner, Elioth 71
Guarracino, Ailsa 452, 472
Guarracino, Attilio ix, 235, 236, 472
    Bali 407, 410, 411
    Hill End 287, 289
    London 240–2
    Melbourne 452
    relationship with Friend ix, 235, 240, 407, 452, 475
    Sydney 285

Haefliger, Paul vii, ix, 82, 129, 132–4, 160, 168, 363
    artwork for *Orphée* 194

death 460
Herald art critic 132, 321
Hill End 197, 318
Margaret's first show 187
marriage to Jean Bellette 132
Strachan obituary 421
view of Margaret's work 168–9, 187, 247, 321
Haines, Robert 280, 281, 286, 291, 295, 314, 340, 482
Hale, Hugh 243, 258, 278
Hall Best, Marion 171, 227, 407
Harker, Miss Constance 58
Hartung, Hans 272
Hassan 161, 164–7, 194, 458
Hat Factory, Sydney 378–9, 437, 440, 443, 447, 450, 453, 458, 463–4, 473–4, 480, 492–3
Haus Tambaran, New Guinea 391
Hawkins, Nigel 165, 167, 446, 459
Hawkins, Norma 165, 446, 459
Hawkins, Weaver 165, 166
Haxton, Elaine ix, 82, 112, 118, 165, 180–1, 183, 317, 325–6, 453
    career as artist 180
    Claremont restaurant mural 118
    confronting Margaret's alcoholism 325–6
    death 484
    East Sydney Tech 180
    Marodian Gallery 257
Hayter's Atelier 17 147
Helena Rubenstein portrait competition 359–60
Helpman, Robert 264
Henshaw, John 363, 364
Herald exhibition 1939 66–8, 132, 272
Herman, Sali 202, 317
Heysen, Hans 17
Heysen, Nora 71
Hilder, Mary 12
Hill End, New South Wales viii, 170–9, 194–7, 204, 208, 285, 287, 289, 318, 346, 372, 476
Hinton, Howard 108, 109, 159, 477, 478
Hitchens, Ivon 18, 119, 323, 459, 484
Hodgkinson, Frank ix, 415, 485
Hodgkinson, Kate 431, 432, 454, 485

Index

Hodgkinson, Myvanwy 'Van' ix, 415, 416, 424, 431, 438, 439, 444, 453–5, 460–1, 490
　death 485–6
　travels with Margaret 453–5, 461, 465–73, 479–83
Hoff, Raynor 90
Holdsworth Galleries, Sydney
　Friend retrospective 463
　Margaret's show 1978 443
　Margaret's show 1982 456–7
　posthumous Haefliger show 460
Hopwood, Alan 156
Horseshoe Creek, New South Wales 15, 16, 18
'House of the Sons of God', London 240–1
Howard, John 501
Howland, Bob 156
Hughes, Robert 82, 349
Hughes, Sam ix, xi, 115–22, 148, 154, 159, 160, 192–3, 198–200, 204, 209, 272, 312, 429
　cancer 453, 457
　Careel House 155
　Contemporary Art Society shows 159, 160
　death 457–9, 464
　Era 123
　France 440–3, 444
　Geneva 431
　Greece 445–6
　Hassan 164–7, 387, 458
　Hat Factory 437, 450, 458, 463–4
　interior decorating business 157
　living with Margaret 431–3, 437
　London 322, 444
　Margaret's love for 115–16, 152, 199–200, 373, 429, 431–3
　Mykonos 445, 455, 459
　Nepean River camping trip 155–6, 174
　Paddington 431–3, 437
　party for Nolans 192–3
　Zwemmer Gallery ix, 116, 119, 121, 159, 198, 459
Hughes-Stanton, Blair 138
Humphries, Barry 335, 482, 484, 488, 498, 500

Huxley, Elspeth 325

Indonesia 398, 405–13
Irby, Al 471
Italy 226–9, 235–6, 253–4

Jagger, Mick 407
James, Clive 482, 483, 500
Japan 480
Jarrett, Miss Marjorie 58–61
Jarvis, Helen 398
Jessup, Fred ix, 141, 144, 173, 174, 183, 185, 190, 214, 231, 226, 260
　Cassis 223, 225, 229
　confronting Margaret's alcoholism 326–7, 333, 336
　Dominion Art Galleries 363
　dresses for Margaret 183–4, 190, 451
　East Sydney Tech 348
　Espondeilhan 430, 441, 461
　Hassan 165
　Margaret's first show 185, 187
　monotypes 255
　Paris 214, 216, 221, 232, 238, 267
　relationship with Margaret 260–1, 349, 501–2
　Spain trip 430–1
John, Augustus 120
Johnson, Robert 71
Johnsonian Club art award 376
Johnston, George 371
Johnstone, Brian 243, 246, 257, 258, 275, 277, 278, 281, 314, 327, 335, 342, 343, 346, 361, 368, 373, 384
Johnstone Gallery, Brisbane
　'A Time Remembered' show 434
　Blackman 434
　Boyd 434
　Brisbane Arcade 257, 277, 278, 280, 282, 283, 291, 300, 334
　Cintra Road 342, 343, 347, 376
　closing 434
　Crooke 343–4, 434
　Dickerson 434
　Drysdale 343, 434
　Dyring 283, 320, 341, 368
　Friend 315, 343, 368, 383

559

Haxton 325
Jessup 326, 350
Margaret's show 1955 314
Margaret's show 1956 319
Margaret's show 1960 342, 345, 346
Margaret's show 1962 361–3
Margaret's show 1964 376–7
Margaret's show 1966 384
Margaret's show 1968 396–7
Margaret's show 1972 434
Molvig 342, 362, 420
Nolan 434
Rees 434
Strachan 291
Jones, Marion 62
Jones, Pat 242
Jones, Paul 123, 155–7, 209, 210, 394, 453, 460, 461
Joseph, Nettie 489, 490
Joyce, Ena 91, 146
Julian Ashton Art School, Sydney 90, 111, 132, 143

Kaiser, Peter 140–1, 187, 197, 214, 242, 269
Kaufman, Edgar 138
Kay, Sydney John 149–52
Kemp, Rod 500
Kershaw, Alister 255
Kirsova, Hélène 135, 137
Kitto, Geoff 461, 466
Klippel, Bob 141, 217
Kmit, Michael 283
Knight, Edgar 397, 399, 400
Knight, Wilma 397, 399, 400
Korea 479
Kuala Lumpur 397–401
Kwato Island, New Guinea 302–5

Lahey, Vida 62, 70–2, 78
Lambert, George 17, 18, 111
Langer, Gertrude 280, 319, 321, 334, 351, 362, 376
Langer, Karl 280
Leahy, Dan 28
Leahy, Jeanette 397
Leahy, Jim 28
Leahy, Mick 28

Leahy, Paddy 28
Lee-Brown, Mitty ix, x, 91, 152, 153, 201, 214, 406, 471
  Bali 407
  Cassis 221, 224
  Cos 445
  East Sydney Tech, 91
  Hong Kong 424
  London 236, 267
  Merioola 152, 153
  Paris 214, 216, 220
  Sri Lanka 453
  voyage to London 201, 208–11
Leigh, Vivien 150, 152, 187–8, 347–8, 451
Lennons Hotel mural, Brisbane 291–2, 295–6, 315, 476
Liliom 116
Lindsay, Lionel 17, 67, 112, 197
Lindsay, Norman 17, 142, 475
Lismore Art Prize 322
Lister, Mrs 177, 318
Lloyd Jones, Charles 66
Lloyd Wright, Frank 184
London 198, 211–14, 239–42, 264–9, 444, 482
  Margaret's show 1994 481–2
  Margaret's show 2005 491, 502
London, Jack 127
Long, Sydney 142
Longstaff, Sir John 118
Lowe, Bernard 115
Lowe, Chica 113, 114, 115
Lowenstein, Tom 491
Lude, Eugen 480, 481
Lymburner, Francis 71, 127, 128, 129, 175

McCubbin, Frederick 61
McCubbin, Sheila 62
McDonald, Donald and Janet 500
McDonald, John 135, 477
MacDonald, John Stuart 66, 81, 120, 211
Mace, Mavis and Robert 127
McGlew, Alice 'Nanny' 108, 354, 362
McGlew, Charles 108
McGrath, Sandra 340

Index

McGregor, Neil 500
Mackerras, Charles 129
McLaughlin, Bill 348, 372
McLeod, Bruce 351–2
McLeod, Odette 351–2, 361
McLeod, Tanya 352
McMahons Point flat, Sydney 100–9, 148, 162, 199
Macquarie Galleries, Sydney 157, 158, 173, 184, 198, 213, 279, 283
   Friend's portrait of Margaret 198
   Margaret's first solo show 184
   Margaret's show 1953 283
   Margaret's show 1955 311
   Margaret's show 1956 321
   Margaret's show 1961 347
   Margaret's show 1963 364, 370
   Margaret's show 1969 397
   'Show of Sixes' 279–80, 436
   Strachan exhibition 288
Magnetic Island, Queensland 293–5
Magnus, Walter 118
Majorca 461
Makaroff, Dmitri 165, 323
Malaysia 397–401
Manet, Edouard 216, 472, 483
Mant, Marjorie 258
Margaret Hannah Olley Art Trust vii, 478
Margaret Hannah Olley Twentieth-Century European Galleries, Art Gallery of New South Wales 485
Marodian Gallery, Brisbane 257–8, 277
   1950 exhibition 243–4
   Margaret's solo show 1951 245–7
Marquet, Albert 231, 485
Marten, Conrad 291
Matisse, Henri 66, 154, 222, 252, 254, 271, 427, 472, 473, 480, 483, 495, 498
Mayo, Daphne 70–2
Meagher, Roddy 279, 280
Medworth, Frank 88–9, 94
Melbourne 207, 452, 453
   artists of 1930s and '40s 82, 191
Meninsky, Bernard 132, 143
Mercury Mobile Players 152
Mercury Theatre Company 150

Merioola, Sydney viii, x, xi, 113–15, 120, 139–40, 151–4, 171, 241
Merivale, John 347, 348
Mesrine, Jacques 441–2
Millen, Ronald 93, 96, 129, 134, 445
Miller, Godfrey 163
Miller, Harry Tatlock x, xi, 114, 115, 139–40, 153, 154, 161, 168, 186–9, 203, 210, 213, 470
   London 241, 264
   Margaret's first show 186, 187
   Merioola 114, 115, 139–40, 153, 154
   Oliviers' escort 188
   on Dobell's portrait 203
   on Drysdale's work 213
   on Friend's work 210
   on Margaret's work 168–9, 174, 186–7
Miró, Joan 271, 431
Missingham, Hal 123, 131, 160, 211, 271, 341
Mitchell, Frankie x, 96–9, 157, 312, 313, 438, 443–4, 460, 465, 494
Molnár, Ferenc 116
Molvig, John 277, 342, 362, 381, 420
Moncrieff, Gladys 130
Monet, Claude 216, 483
monotypes 255, 257, 265
   Crucifix, Dieppe 258
   Dieppe Harbour 258
   Gondolas, Venice 258, plate
   Rainy Day, Venice 258
   Venetian Houses 258
Moore, Brian 495, 496
Moore, Henry 116, 174
Morandi, Giorgio 366, 478, 484, 503
Moreton Galleries, Brisbane 196, 237, 277
   exhibition 1950 237
Morihien, Paul 265
Morriss, Ina 157
Mosman Art Prize 168
Mulley, Mary 13
Mulley, Robert 13
murals
   Lennons Hotel 291–2, 295–6, 315, 476

561

New South Wales Leagues' Club 286–7, 322
Queensland Art Gallery 281
Murch, Arthur 71, 82, 165
Murdoch, Sir Keith 66
Murray, Alec 131, 152, 188, 211, 241
Murray, Donald viii, 170–3, 195–6, 285, 287, 346, 348
Murray, Jacques 255
Myer, Sidney Baillieu 368
Mykonos, Greece 445, 455, 459

Namatjira, Albert 247
National Art Gallery of New South Wales *see* Art Gallery of New South Wales
National Trust S.H. Ervin Gallery 477, 484, 488
Nazare 256–7
Nepean River camping trip 155–6, 174
Nevill Keating Pictures, London 484, 491
New Guinea 28, 287, 299–306, 386–96
    Margaret's paintings from 311, 314, 396–7
    Mt Hagen 394–5
    Sepik River trip 387–94, 452
New South Wales Leagues' Club mural 286–7, 322
New York 147–8, 465, 480
Newcastle 374–5, 380–2, 416
    Margaret's properties 416–18, 446
Newcastle Region Art Gallery 374, 478
Newman, Keith 83
Newton, Douglas 389, 390
Newton-John, Brin 376
Nicklin, Lenore 443
Nolan, Cynthia (née Reed) 192, 193, 286
Nolan, Jinx 192, 286
Nolan, Sidney xi, 82, 159, 160, 175, 191–4, 277, 286
    artwork for *Orphée* 193–4
    impact of paintings on Margaret 159, 160
    Johnstone Gallery 434
    Ned Kelly series 82
    relationship with Reeds 191–2, 218

Sydney group 175
north Queensland 292–9
Norton, Rosaleen 'Roie' 94, 127
Norwich, John Julius 482, 500
Notanda Gallery, Sydney 161, 162, 186
Nutting, Miss 59, 60

O'Brien, Justin x, xv, 82, 129, 140, 174, 175, 348, 406, 460, 497
    cancer 480
    death 481
    Florence 227–8
    Hat Factory 480
    Merioola 140
    Sydney Group 175
    Under 30 Group 129
Old Vienna Coffee Inn, Brisbane 278
Olivier, Laurence 150, 152, 187–8, 347, 451
Olley, Alf 47, 48
Olley, Alfred 12, 13, 14
Olley, Elaine (later Wilkinson) 19–24, 29, 35–7, 40–2, 51, 52, 66, 72, 79, 262, 266, 274, 439, 447, 456, 496
Olley, Grace 4, 6, 9, 15–16
    carpal tunnel syndrome 439
    death 456
    family background 6–12
    family holidays 46–52, 75
    farewelling Margaret 1949 200
    Farndon 68–79, 272–3, 277–9, 285, 314, 334, 383, 426, 439, 447
    gallstones 296–7
    Joe's death 266, 275, 279
    Margaret's childhood 16–56, 66–79, 99, 106
    Margaret's relationship with 275
    Margaret's shows 243, 361
    marriage to Joe 16
    Olley's Antiques 325, 337–8
    property buying 428
    Scottish Hospital 447
    support for Margaret 275, 319, 346, 456
    Sydney 288, 439–40, 444
Olley, Hannah 14
Olley, Helen Rose 284, 314
Olley, Jacob 12, 14

Index

Olley, Joseph 'Joe' 4, 6, 14–16
   death 266–7, 275, 310, 323
   family background 12–16
   farewelling Margaret 1949 200
   Margaret's childhood 16–54, 65–79, 99
   marriage to Grace 16
   trees planted by 273, 450
   World War I 15
Olley, Ken 21–4, 35, 37, 40–2, 51, 52, 66, 72, 266, 274, 284, 314, 317, 324, 338, 341, 447, 456
Olley, Laurel 284, 314
Olley, Margaret
   AA meetings 327–9, 387, 414, 505
   Aboriginal women, paintings of 350–4
   abortion 308, 309
   alcoholism 146, 182, 197, 237, 240, 249, 268, 276, 285, 296, 298, 310, 313, 315, 320, 322–9, 333–4, 336–7, 346, 414, 488
   art classes at school 60–3
   Art Trust 478
   Australian National Treasure 476
   birth 16–18
   Brisbane Tech 69–73, 76–8
   broken ankle 319, 320
   broken nose 313–14
   childhood 3–6, 16–79
   critics' views of work 129, 130, 161, 168–9, 174, 186–7, 196, 244, 247, 345, 347, 361–3, 370, 376, 457, 477, 482
   depression 487–92
   donations to galleries 477–9
   East Sydney Tech 78, 80–109, 131, 146, 148
   family background 6–16
   family holidays 46–52, 75
   father's death 266–7, 275, 310, 323
   first house purchase 374
   first picture sale 129
   first solo show 184–8
   flatting with Margaret Cilento 100–9
   honorary doctorates 479, 484, 485
   influences 66, 162, 483
   marriage, contemplating 289–91, 307–9, 319, 373
   meningitis 468, 470, 480
   methods of painting 364–5
   monotypes 255, 257–8, 265
   murals by *see* murals
   new art movements, view of 366
   Order of Australia 479
   painting in Strachan's house 425–7, 430, 432, 443, 495
   paintings by *see* paintings
   physical culture 106
   portraits of *see* portraits of Margaret
   pregnancy 308, 309, 336
   prizes won by *see* prizes
   property buying 374, 377, 416–18, 422, 428, 446
   relationships with men 260–1, 335, 340–1, 373
   role models 44, 121
   schooling 30–3, 40–1, 56–65
   sculpture 76–7, 90
   second solo show 196–7
   sitting for Dobell 190–1
   Somerville House 56–65, 68, 100, 451
   twenty-first birthday 130
   theatre set painting 148–9, 167, 193, 282, 322
   TV story 1960 346
   Under 30 Group 128–30, 145
   Vogue story 360
   voyage to London 201, 208–11
   walking frame 502
   wallpaper designs 259
Olley, Rose 47
Olley, William 12, 13
Olley's Antiques 324–6, 334, 337, 341, 351
Ollivada 415
Olsen, John 354, 381
OPAL House, Brisbane 352–3, 361, 368
Orban, Desiderius 154, 155, 175, 203
Orphée 193–4, 250

Paddington, Sydney
   Duxford St house 377–9, 431, 484
   Gurner St house 464, 465, 473

Hat Factory 378–9, 437, 440, 443, 447, 450, 453, 458, 463–4, 473–4, 480, 492–3
Paddington St house 374, 378, 422, 425
paintings
  Aboriginal women 350–4, 361
  Afternoon 160
  Afternoon Interior 426
  Ann 320
  Banksia 422, 423
  Barbara 360
  Blackberries 444, plate
  Boonah Landscape 345
  Bourton on the Water 244
  Bowl of Fruit and Flowers 196
  Boys in a Grandstand 129
  Breakfast Creek, Brisbane 160
  Bush Lemons 377
  Cane Farmer's House 311
  Chateau Fontcreuse, Cassis 246, 247, plate
  Crucifixion 282
  Dieppe 244
  Dressing Table 457
  Early Morning, Lavender Bay 160
  Era Landscape 160, 185, plate
  Eucharist Lilies 364, 505, plate
  Evening Betrothal 160
  Evening Docks 422
  Evening from the Obelisk 422
  Farndon Interiors 426, plate
  Fish 364
  Grey Day 174
  Guitar Player 370
  Hawkesbury Wildflowers 422
  Hazel Ruddle portrait 376
  Helen Rose and Laurel Olley portrait 314
  Hill End Ruins 129, plate
  Homage to Manet 472, 505
  Honey Boy 129
  Industrial Skyline 422
  Interior IV 426, plate
  Interior VIII 426, plate
  Jardin de Luxembourg 247
  Kilmorey Terrace 129
  L'Arc de Triomphe du Carrousel 246
  Late Afternoon 426, 505
  Late Afternoon, Berrie's Bay 159, 161
  Lilies and Grapes 322
  Little Middle Street 129
  Moreton Bay Lobsters 311
  New England Country 168
  New England Landscape 168, plate
  The Newcastle Watercolours 382
  Notre Dame 279, 280
  Nottinghill Gate 244
  Odette 351–2, 361
  Ophelia 174, 185, 196, 197, 451
  Palais de Justice – Place Dauphin, Paris 246
  Pam Bell portrait 359–60, 361
  The Pink Church, Choiselle 237
  The Pink House 129
  Pink Paper and Kippers 169, 185, 186, 187, plate
  Plums and Prawns 185
  Pomegranates 384, 505
  Pont des Arts, Paris 246
  Pont Neuf, Paris 246
  Portrait in the Mirror 186, 196, 479, 505
  Pug Dog 361
  Quay Building 159
  The Red House 129
  St Paul's Terrace, Brisbane 129, 160, plate
  Sister and Brother 130
  Still Life 196
  Still Life in Green 162, 185, plate
  Still Life with Kettle 311, 312, 479, 505, plate
  Still Life with Pink Fish 185
  Still Life with Post Cards 174
  Sunday, Newcastle 382
  Susan with Flowers 350, 367, plate
  Tourettes-Sur-Louys 244
  Trafalgar Square 244
  Venus and Cupid Reclining 159, 161
  Venus with Rose 196
  Vera 362
  Zillah 350
Papua New Guinea *see* New Guinea
Paris 214–21, 232–4, 238–9, 249–56, 334, 423–5, 440–3, 461–2

Index

Margaret's exhibition 265–6
Parker, Professor Gordon 489, 490
Parkinson, Michael 500
Pasquarelli, John 387–93
Paterson, Elizabeth 192
Pearce, Barry 500, 502, 503
Peisley, Errol 105
Penang, Malaysia 399
Pensione Morandi, Florence, 227, 228
Perceval, John 82
Pericles 193–4
Perry, Adelaide 62
Philip Bacon Galleries, Brisbane vii, 434–5
   Margaret's show 1975 434
   Margaret's show 1979 444
   Margaret's show 1981 453
Picabia, Francis 251
Picasso, Pablo 66, 67, 116, 154, 215, 219, 226, 236, 249, 250, 252, 271, 281, 282, 441
the Pink Elephant, Brisbane 97, 98
Pitt, Dulcie 98, 173, 187
Plate, Carl xi, 161–2, 163, 186
Poiret, Paul 189
portraits of Margaret
   Dobell viii, 190–1, 198, 199, 201–4, 207–12, 276, 311, 317, 335, 500, plate
   Drysdale viii, 182–3, 198, 214, plate
   Friend 197, 198
   Smart 483
Portugal 256–7
Preston, Margaret 17, 81, 121
Price, Ray 127, 128
prizes
   Bendigo Art Prize 380
   Finney's Centenary Art Prize 367
   Helena Rubenstein portrait competition 359–60
   Johnsonian Club art award 376
   Lismore Art Prize 322
   Mosman Art Prize 168
   Redcliffe Art Contest 360, 370, 380
   Royal Show art competition 368
   Toowoomba Art Society Competition 380
Proctor, Thea 160

Pugh, Clifton 277
Pullen, Roland 'Roly' 153
Purves-Smith, Maisie (later Drysdale) 372, 373, 415, 440
Purves-Smith, Peter 372, 373

Queensland Art Fund 71
Queensland Art Gallery 67, 71, 280, 281, 286, 314, 340, 362, 477
   Drysdale retrospective 1961 346
   Fairweather retrospective 1965 380
   French Painting Today exhibition 1953 281, 282
   Jubilee Art Train exhibition 246
   Margaret's donations to 478
   Margaret's mural 281
Queensland Art Library 71

Read, Sir Herbert 367
Redcliffe Art Contest 360, 370, 380
Redfern Gallery, London 236, 264, 265, 288, 289, 355
Reed, Cynthia 192, 193
Reed, John 82, 120, 191, 192, 215, 216, 218, 284
Reed, Sunday 82, 191, 192, 215, 216, 218, 284
Reed, Sweeney 215
Rees, Lloyd 107, 168, 434
Richards, John 117–19, 122, 123, 129, 155–7, 165–7, 322, 433
Richardson, Agnes 62, 63, 64
Richmond, Oliffe 174
Richmond River Times 9, 10, 11, 15
Rickards, Jocelyn 'Yossie' x, 91, 129, 146, 152, 153, 173, 187, 188
   East Sydney Tech, 91, 146
   London 211, 241, 264, 265, 482
   Margaret's first show 187
   Merioola 152, 153
   Oliviers' visit 188
   Under 30 Group 129
Riddell, Elizabeth 340
Roberts, Susie 500
Roberts, Tom 108, 247
Robinson, Roland 'Rollo' 95, 96, 123, 124, 132
Roehm, Ernst 260

Rogers, Frederic 345, 376
Romano's, Sydney 180, 185
Rose, Bill 381
Rose, Sir Francis 249–56, 259–60, 263, 267, 328
Rose, Lady Frederica 252, 259
Ross, Annie 138, 139, 174, 197, 199, 234, 235, 240, 451, 455
Rowan, Marian Ellis 303
Rowan, Veronica 'Ronnie' 242, 243, 425, 427
Royal Queensland Art Society
   Exhibition 1944 130
   54th Annual Exhibition 77
Royal Show art competition 368
Rubin, Major 281, 477
Ruddle, Hazel 376
Russell, Elsa 169
Russo, Peter 209

Sabien, Ron 277–8, 334, 348, 350, 361, 364, 367
Sackville-West, Vita 225
St Anne's, Townsville 30–3, 56
St Louis Vanities 97
Sailor family 143, 297, 299
Sainthill, Loudon x, xi, 114, 115, 139–40, 153, 154, 168–9, 179, 187, 189
   exhibition 1948 189
   Hassan 164
   London 241, 264–5
   Margaret's first show 187
   Merioola 114, 115, 139–40, 153, 154
   theatre/ballet designs 189, 264–5
Salmon, William 421
Scheinberg, Gisella 463, 472
Schlicht, Katie 323, 385, 441
Schlicht, Rollin 441, 442, 452
Schlicht, Theo 239, 261, 323, 324, 385, 441
Schofield, Leo 500
schools
   Annerley 55
   Ascot 56
   Brisbane Tech 69–73, 76–8
   Hendra 55

   Murwillumbah 40–1
   St Anne's, Townsville 30–3, 56
   Somerville House 56–65, 68, 100, 451
sculptures 77
Sepik River trip 387–94, 452
Sex House, Java 412, 413
Ship and Mermaid Inn, Sydney 126
Short, Susanna 457
Sickert, Walter 120, 478
Sieveking, Ulrich 458
Simes, Hannah Sophia 14
Simes, John 14
Skinner Galleries, Perth
   Friend's 'ikon' exhibition 349
   joint exhibition with Dyring 367
Small, Doug 454
Smart, Jeffrey 234, 235, 240, 348, 482, 483, 484, 488, 500
Smith, Joshua 112
   Dobell's portrait of viii, 110–12, 154, 199, 209, 376
Smith, Maggie 500
Smith, Treania 158
Society of Artists annual show 160
Sofala, New South Wales 171, 172, 195
Somerville House, Brisbane 56–65, 68, 72, 74, 100, 451
Somerville, Jimmy 127, 128
Spain 233, 430–1, 461
Spender, Lizzie 500
Sri Lanka 320, 336, 344, 345, 346, 348–9, 453
Stein, Gertrude 154, 250, 251, 252, 254
Stephen, John 180, 185, 187, 188, 314
Stephens, William 57
Stewart, Lindsay 415, 420, 421
Stewart, Warren 92
Storrier, Janet 500
Storrier, Tim 483, 500
Strachan, David xi, 82, 134–7, 145, 174, 184, 186, 260, 385
   Brisbane 291, 297
   Cassis 222, 242, 243, 249
   Civil Construction Corps 136
   death 420–1, 423, 425
   Dominion Art Galleries 363
   donation of paintings by 478

Index

East Sydney Tech 348
etchings 255
first solo exhibition 136
Hassan 165
influence on Margaret 186
Margaret painting in house 425–7, 430, 432, 443, 495
Marodian Gallery 257
Paris 214–15, 217, 221, 233–4, 236, 238, 255–6, 265, 267, 423
return to Australia 341
rift with Margaret 415–16
Sick Girls paintings 136, 137, 145
Sydney 288–9, 349, 378, 415
Sydney Group 174
travelling in France 261
visiting Drysdale 422–3
Streeton, Arthur 108
Swanton, Lucy 109, 158, 181, 191, 198, 358, 407, 477
Sweetapple, Dora 227, 321
Swift, Georgie 489, 500
Swift, Snow 500
Sydney artists of 1940s 82
Sydney Group 174
Sydney University Dramatic Society (SUDS) 166, 193

Takashige, Masato 118
Tatlock Miller, Harry *see* Miller, Harry Tatlock
Taylor, James 28
Tchinarova, Tamara 150
Teed, Colonel 224–5, 244–5
Temperley, Ann 122
Temperley, Colin 122
Temperley, Dorothy 30
Temperley, Douglas 5, 11, 19, 23, 29, 30
Temperley, Erasmus 6, 11, 18–20, 23, 27, 29, 53, 66, 68, 73
Temperley, Gertrude 22, 23, 66, 68, 73
Temperley, Gil 122, 123
Temperley, Grace *see* Olley, Grace
Temperley, Madge 10, 211, 213, 397, 447
Temperley, Mary 10, 19, 44, 55, 65, 67, 68, 75, 99, 121, 211, 272, 274, 314, 324, 336–9, 346, 353, 361, 383, 422

Temperley, Thomas (Grandpa) 6–12, 15, 19, 26, 43, 48
Temperley, Tom (cousin) 122, 123
Temperley, Tom (uncle) 36, 43, 44, 49
Temperley, Will 19, 122, 123
Thailand 401–2, 453
theatre sets 148–9, 167, 193, 282, 322
Thomas, Laurie 340–1, 356, 367
Thomson, Ann 61
Thornhill, Dorothy 88, 96
Thornton, Wallace 118, 174
Tognetti, Richard 494, 500
Toklas, Alice B. 251, 252, 254
Toowoomba Art Society Competition 380
Travelling Scholarship 111, 113, 136, 174, 451
  Dobell 111
  Friend 263
  Margaret missing out 174, 198
Tucker, Albert 82, 159
Tuckson, Tony 141
Tudor Jones, Olwen 415, 460, 462, 466–8, 485
Tully, Queensland 3–7, 18–33, 53, 65, 298
Twelfth Night Theatre, Sydney 282, 322, 342
Twombly, Cy 499
Tygalgah, Queensland 35–53

Under 30 Group 128–30, 145
Ure Smith, Sydney 17, 82

Vagarini, Cesare 169
van Gogh, Vincent 220, 321, 335, 472, 473
Vassilieff, Danila 82
Vaughan, George 398
Vaughan, Joyce 398
Vidal, Gore 407
Villiers, Irene 165, 166
Vogue Australia 360
von Bertouch, Anne xi, 374, 375, 380, 382, 416, 418–22, 435–7
von Bertouch Galleries, Newcastle 374, 382
  Margaret's show 1964 374
  Margaret's show 1969 397

Margaret's show 1971 422
Third Anniversary Exhibition 382
Vuillard, Edouard 66, 427, 483, 491, 503

Wakelin, Roland 17, 81, 107, 143, 158
Walker, Frederick 302, 303
Walker, Richard and Sandie 500
Wallace Collection, London 212
Warhol, Andy 366
Wawo-Runta, Tati 410, 411
Wawo-Runta, Wija 410, 412
Weiss, Peter and Doris 500
Welcome Hôtel, Villefranche 250
Westwood, Brian 483
White, Tony 480
Whiteley, Brett 354
Wienholt, Anne xi, 113–16, 118, 123, 128, 129, 174, 454, 477, 500
Wilding, Joyce 353, 361
Wilkinson, Kenneth 88
Wilkinson, Richard 263, 274
Wilkinson, Sally 496
Wilson, Eric 100
Wilson, Gavin 298
Wolinski, Joseph 112
Wollner, Igor 278
Wollner, Magda 278
Wood, Christopher 'Kit' 135, 250, 251

Wood, Noel 256
Wood, Rex 256
Woolf, Virginia 222, 225
World War I 14, 20, 163
World War II 6, 67, 72–5, 81, 84, 139
Woronora, New South Wales 162–3, 174
Wright, Bertha 224, 441, 442
Wright, David 49
Wright, Dora 48, 49, 168
Wright, Judith 48, 49
Wright, Philip 48
Wright, Pollyanne 49, 311
Wright, Ron 350, 432, 444
Wright, Shirley 350, 377, 432, 444, 452

Young, Elizabeth 244, 246
Young, John 158

Zander, Charles 120
Zander, Clarice xi, 115, 120, 121, 128, 174, 192, 220, 242
   London 220, 242, 265, 267–9, 285, 289
Zander, Jocelyn xi, 116, 120, 121, 128, 129, 161–2
Zwemmer Gallery, London ix, 116, 119, 121, 159, 198, 459